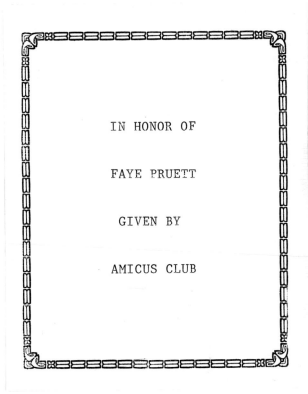

IN HONOR OF

FAYE PRUETT

GIVEN BY

AMICUS CLUB

CONTEMPORARY FOREIGN
LANGUAGE WRITERS

EDITED BY
James Vinson and Daniel Kirkpatrick

ST MARTIN'S PRESS
NEW YORK

© St. Martin's Press 1984

All rights reserved. For information, write:
St. Martin's Press, Inc., 175 Fifth Avenue, New York, N.Y. 10010
Printed in the United States of America
First published in the United States of America in 1984

Library of Congress Catalog Card Number 83-40550

ISBN 0-312-16663-X

CONTENTS

EDITOR'S NOTE

The selection of writers included in this book is based on the recommendations of the advisers listed on page ix.

The entry for each writer consists of a biography, a complete list of separately published books, a selected list of published bibliographies and critical studies on the writer, and a signed critical essay.

In the biographies, details of education, military service, and marriage(s) are generally given before the usual chronological summary of the life of the writer; awards and honours are given last.

The Publications section is meant to include all book publications, including translations into English, though as a rule broadsheets, single sermons and lectures, minor pamphlets, exhibition catalogues, etc., are omitted. Under the heading Collections, we have listed the most recent collections of the complete works; on-going editions are indicated by a dash after the date of publication; often a general selection from the writer's works is included.

Titles are given in modern spelling; often the titles are "short." The date given is that of the first book publication, which often followed the first periodical or anthology publication by some time. No attempt has been made to indicate which works were published anonymously or pseudonymously, or which works of fiction were published in more than one volume. Reprints of books (including facsimile editions) and revivals of plays are not listed unless a revision of title is involved.

In the essays, short references to critical remarks refer to items cited in the Publications section or in the Critical Studies section. Introductions, memoirs, editorial matter, etc., in works cited in the Publications section are not repeated in the Critical Studies.

We would like to thank the advisers and contributors for their patience and help.

ADVISERS

A. James Arnold
Thomas G. Bergin
Gordon Brotherston
Ruby Cohn
Wallace Fowlie
Michael Freeman
Janet Garton
Igor Hájek

Peter Hutchinson
Harry Levin
Earl Miner
Christopher R. Pike
Dušan Puvačić
Olga Ragusa
James Russell Stamm
Daniel Weissbort

CONTRIBUTORS

M. Ian Adams
Hans Christian Andersen
A. James Arnold
Gabrielle Barfoot
Roderick Beaton
Lucille Frackman Becker
David J. Bond
Sandra María Boschetto
Denis Brass
Peter Broome
Glenn S. Burne
Sue-Ellen Case
Mary Ann Caws
Suzanne Cowan
David Coward
Sally McMullen (Croft)
Santiago Daydi-Tolson
Thomas J. Donahue
Herman Ermolaev
John Fletcher
Wallace Fowlie
Marketa Goetz-Stankiewicz
George Gömöri
Peter Graves
Edith Grossman
David T. Haberly
Igor Hájek
Talat S. Halman
E.C. Hawkesworth
Robert M. Henkels, Jr.
Richard G. Hodgson
William M. Hutchins
Peter Hutchinson
Neil Jackson

Regina Janes
W. Glyn Jones
Louis Kibler
Robert Kirsner
George L. Kline
Charles Klopp
Emanuele Licastro
Gregory L. Lucente
Keith McMahon
Valerie Minogue
Michael Mitchell
Augustus Pallotta
Janet Pérez
Donald Peter Alexander Pirie
Valentina Polukhina
Robert Porter
Dušan Puvačić
Judy Rawson
J.H. Reid
Michael Robinson
Hugh Rorrison
Frank Rosengarten
John Rothfork
Christine A. Rydel
Barbara Saunders
Barry P. Scherr
Grace Schulman
Kessel Schwartz
Irene Scobbie
G. Singh
C.N. Smith
Raymond D. Souza
James Russell Stamm
Mary E. Stewart

Arrigo V. Subiotto
Yasunari Takahashi
Philip Thody
Hugo J. Verani
Maïr Verthuy
Paul Vincent
Jennifer Waelti-Walters

Anthony Waine
George Walsh
George E. Wellwarth
David Welsh
Kenneth S. Whitton
Hisaaki Yamanouchi
Florence L. Yudin

CONTEMPORARY
FOREIGN LANGUAGE
WRITERS

Abe Kobo
Bella Akhmadulina
Rafael Alberti
Vincente Aleixandre
Jorge Amado
Yehuda Amichai
Jean Anouilh
Fernando Arrabal

Giorgio Bassani
Simone de Beauvoir
Juan Benet
Thomas Bernhard
Marie-Claire Blais
Heinrich Böll
Yves Bonnefoy
Jorge Luis Borges
Joseph Brodsky
Antonio Buero Vallejo
Michel Butor

Guillermo Cabrera Infante
Italo Calvino
Elias Canetti
Ernesto Cardenal
T. Carmi
Carlo Cassola
Camilo José Cela
Aimé Césaire
René Char
Ch'ien Chung-shu
Hugo Claus
Julio Cortázar
Dobrica Ćosić

Eduardo De Filippo
Miguel Delibes
José Donoso
Marguerite Duras
Friedrich Dürrenmatt

Odysseus Elytis
Hans Magnus Enzensberger
Luciano Erba
Evgeny Evtushenko

Dario Fo
Gilberto Freyre
Max Frisch
Carlos Fuentes

Gabriel García Márquez
Jean Genet
Natalia Ginzburg
José María Gironella

Natalya Gorbanevskaya
Juan Goytisolo
Julien Gracq
Günter Grass
Julien Green
Jorge Guillén

Peter Hacks
Peter Handke
Václav Havel
Anne Hébert
William Heinesen
Zbigniew Herbert
Willem Frederik Hermans
Stefan Heym
Rolf Hochhuth
Fritz Hochwälder
Miroslav Holub
Bohumil Hrabal

Eugène Ionesco

Philippe Jaccottet
Tove Jansson
Uwe Johnson

Yashar Kemal
Danilo Kiš
Tadeusz Konwicki
Franz Xaver Kroetz
Milan Kundera
Günter Kunert

André Langevin
Halldór Laxness
J.-M.G. Le Clézio
Stanislaw Lem
Ivar Lo-Johansson
Lucebert
Artur Lundkvist
Mario Luzi

Naguib Mahfouz
Françoise Mallet-Joris
Ana María Matute
Claude Mauriac
João Cabral de Melo Neto
Henri Michaux
Czeslaw Milosz
Elsa Morante
Alberto Moravia
Slawomir Mrozek
Harry Mulisch
Heiner Müller

Oe Kenzaburo
Juan Carlos Onetti

Nicanor Parra
Octavio Paz
André Pieyre de Mandiargues
Robert Pinget
Francis Ponge
Vasko Popa
Vasco Pratolini
Michele Prisco

Valentin Rasputin
Gerard Reve
Klaus Rifbjerg
Yannis Ritsos
Alain Robbe-Grillet
Tadeusz Rózewicz
José Ruibal
Juan Rulfo

Armand Salacrou
Nathalie Sarraute
Alfonso Sastre
Leonardo Sciascia
Léopold Senghor

Mikhail Sholokhov
Georges Simenon
Claude Simon
Josef Skvorecký
Mario Soldati
Alexander Solzhenitsyn
Villy Sørensen

Jean Tardieu
Tawfiq al-Hakim
Miguel Torga
Michel Tournier
Tomas Tranströmer

Mario Vargas Llosa
Vladimir Voinovich
Paolo Volponi
Andrei Voznesensky

Martin Walser
Sándor Weöres
Christa Wolf
Jan Wolkers

Yoshioka Minoru
Marguerite Yourcenar

ABE Kobo. Japanese. Born in Tokyo, 7 March 1924. Educated at schools in Mukden, Manchuria; Seijo High School, Tokyo, 1940, then ill with tuberculosis; Tokyo University, 1943-48, M.D. 1948. Married Machi Yamada in 1947; one daughter. Writer; since 1973, Director, Kobo Theatre Workshop, Tokyo. Recipient: Post-War Literature Prize, 1950; Akutagawa Prize, 1951; Kishida Prize, 1958; Yomiuri Prize, 1962; Cannes Film Festival Prize, 1964; Tanizaki Prize, 1967; Foreign Book Prize (France), 1968. Address: 1-22-10 Wakaba-cho, Chofu City, Tokyo, Japan.

PUBLICATIONS

Fiction

Owarishi michino shirubeni [The Road Sign at the End of the Road]. Tokyo, Shinzenbi, 1948.

Kiga domei [Hunger Union]. Tokyo, Kodan, 1954.

Kemonotachi wa kokyo o mezasu [The Animals Go Homeward]. Tokyo, Kodan, 1957.

Daiyon Kampyoki. Tokyo, Kodan, 1959; as *Inter Ice Age Four*, New York, Knopf, 1970; London, Cape, 1971.

Ishi no me [Eyes of Stone]. Tokyo, Shincho, 1960.

Suna no onna. Tokyo, Shincho, 1962; as *The Woman in the Dunes*, New York, Knopf, 1964; London, Secker and Warburg, 1965.

Suichu toshi [The City in Water]. Tokyo, Togen, 1964.

Tanin no kao. Tokyo, Kodan, 1964; as *The Face of Another*, New York, Knopf, 1966; London, Weidenfeld and Nicolson, 1969.

Omaenimo tsumi ga aru [You Are Guilty Too]. Tokyo, Gakusyukenkyu, 1965.

Enomoto Buyo. Tokyo, Tyuokaron, 1965.

Moetsukita chizu. Tokyo, Shincho, 1967; as *The Ruined Map*, New York, Knopf, 1969; London, Cape, 1971.

Yume no tobo [Runaway in the Dream]. Tokyo, Tokuma, 1968.

Hakootoko. Tokyo, Shincho, 1973; as *The Box Man*, New York, Knopf, 1975.

Warau Tsuki [The Laughing Moon]. Tokyo, Shincho, 1975.

Mikkai. Tokyo, Shincho, 1977; as *Secret Rendezvous*, New York, Knopf, 1979; London, Secker and Warburg, 1980.

Kozo wa Shinda [The Little Elephant Is Dead]. 1979.

Plays

Seifuku [The Uniform]. Tokyo, Aoki-syoten, 1955.

Yurei wa kokoniiru [Here Is a Ghost]. Tokyo, Shincho, 1959.

Woman of the Dunes (screenplay), with Hiroshi Teshigahara. New York, Phaedra, 1966.

Tomodachi, Enemoto Takeako. Tokyo, Kawade, 1967; as *Friends* (produced London, 1975), New York, Grove Press, 1969.

Bo ni natta otoko. Tokyo, Shincho, 1969; as *The Man Who Turned into a Stick: Three Related Plays*, Tokyo, University of Tokyo Press, 1975.

Gikyoku zenshu [Collected Plays]. Tokyo, Shincho, 1970.

Mihitsu no koi [Willful Negligence]. Tokyo, Shincho, 1971.

Ai no megane wa irogarasu [Love's Spectacles Are Colored Glass]. Tokyo, Shincho, 1973.

Midoriiro no stocking [Green Stocking]. Tokyo, Shincho, 1974.

Ue [Cry of the Fierce Animals]. Tokyo, Shincho, 1975.

Screenplay: *Suna no onna* (*Woman of the Dunes*), with Hiroshi Teshigahara, 1964.

Verse

Mumei shishu [Poems by an Unknown].   Privately printed, 1948.

Other

Akai mayu [Red Cocoon].   1950.
Uchinaro henkyo [Inner Border].   Tokyo, Tyuokoron, 1971.
Zensakuhin [Collected Works].   Tokyo, Shincho, 15 vols., 1972-73.
Han gekiteki ningen [Anti-Dramatic Man].   Tokyo, Shincho, 1973.
Hasso no shuhen [Circumference of Inspiration].   Tokyo, Shincho, 1974.

*

Critical Study: *The Search for Authenticity in Modern Japanese Literature* by Hisaaki Yamanouchi, Cambridge, Cambridge University Press, 1978.

*   *   *

In Japan Abe Kobo became publicly recognized as an important writer with the award of the Akutagawa Prize to his "The Wall" in 1951. Abroad he has enjoyed a reputation comparable to that of pre-war writers such as Tanizaki and Kawabata and post-war writers such as Mishima. He differs, however, from these three writers in deliberately working outside the heritage of traditional Japanese literature.

A piece of work written at the beginning of a writer's career often foreshadows his later works. This is true of *Owarishi michino shirubeni*. The protagonist is uprooted from his native country, confined, and deprived of freedom in the alienating, desert-like environment of Manchuria, where he has lost his personal and national identity. This work shares its theme of alienation and lost identity with *Kemonotachi wa kokyo o mezasu*, another novel set in Manchuria. A variation of this central theme is that of metamorphosis in such stories as "Dendrocacalia," "Red Cocoon," and "Stick," which some people might call Kafkaesque.

The protagonist of *The Woman in the Dunes*, captured and confined in the waste and sterile dunes, is deprived of freedom and of his identity, which he initially wants to restore. Eventually, showing no interest in escaping even when a ladder is available, he seems aware of the futility of his wish to regain the previous mode of his life. However, his liaison with the woman in the dunes results only in extra-uterine pregnancy; and the implication of water accumulated by capillary action remains equivocal.

In *The Face of Another* Abe pursues his preoccupation with alienation and lost identity by creating a character who has suffered facial burns that have left keloid scars (somewhat like those caused by the atomic bombs), and, as a result, has been estranged from his wife. He is initially subject to an illusory assumption that one's face is the mark of one's identity and that it should be a medium with which to establish a rapport with other people, including his wife. He thus produces a mask to conceal his scarred face. Contrary to his expectation, however, he comes to realize that wearing a mask does not serve to restore his lost identity but can be a means of impersonally fulfilling an erotic impulse or committing a crime. With the use of a mask notions such as strangers, family, nation, rights, and duties all disappear. His attempt to re-establish a rapport with his wife under the guise of the mask proves virtually to be a kind of rape and only deepens his alienation from her.

Alienation and lost identity pervade practically all Abe's works, including plays, either original or adapted from his own stories. Abe's objective, however, is not simply to depict these themes but also to bring home the falsity of the common assumptions about personal identity.

In this respect he dissociates himself from the preoccupations with the "self" in modern Japanese literature, especially in the so-called "I-novels." His recurrent themes are most appropriately presented against the desolate background of Manchuria and post-war Japan, and later against that of urban, industrial society heading towards immense economic growth. Abe's works, whether in the original or in translation, attain universality by virtue of their highly logical and lucid style.

—Hisaaki Yamanouchi

AKHMADULINA, Bella (Akhatovna). Russian.   Born in Moscow, 10 April 1937. Attended Gorky Institute of World Literature, Moscow. Married 1) Evgeny Evtushenko, *q.v.*, in 1954 (divorced); 2) the writer Yuri Navigin. Delegate, All-Russian Congress of Writers, 1965. Address: c/o USSR Union of Writers, Ulitsa Vorovskogo 20, Moscow 69, USSR.

PUBLICATIONS

Verse

> *Struna* [String].   Moscow, Pisatel', 1962.
> *Oznob* [A Chill] (includes prose).   Frankfurt, Posev, 1968; as *Fever and Other New Poems*, translated by Geoffrey Dutton, Melbourne, Sun, 1968; New York, Morrow, 1969; London, Owen, 1970.
> *Uroki muzyki* [Music Lessons].   Moscow, Pisatel', 1969.
> *Stikhi* [Poems].   Moscow, Khudozhestrennaya Literatura, 1975.
> *Metel'*.   Moscow, Pisatel', 1977.
> *Three Russian Poets* (with Margarite Aliger and Yunna Moritz), translated by Elaine Feinstein.   Manchester, Carcanet Press, 1979.
> *Three Russian Women Poets* (with Akhmatova and Tsvetayeva), translated by Mary Maddock.   Trumansburg, New York, Crossing Press, 1983.

Play

> Screenplays: *Clear Ponds*, 1965.

Other

> *Svecha*.   Moscow, Sovetskaia Rossiia, 1977.
> *Sny o Gruzii*.   Tbilisi, Merani, 1977.

*

AKHMADULINA

Bibliography: by Christine A. Rydel, in *Russian Literature Triquarterly 1*,1971.

*   *   *

The subjectivity with which Bella Akhmadulina pursues her art imbues her writing with a highly personal, lyrical tone. Even her attempts at prose and her translations from Georgian poetry contain favorite images and characteristic word-play. The poems of her first collection, *String*, look at various objects in the world through a whimsical perspective; they describe quotidian sights and scenes with a magical wonder that transforms a construction site into a ballet and streetlights into kindly old Slavs.

Akhmadulina steps into her longer poems and participates in the fantastic adventures she recounts. In *"An Adventure in an Antique Store"* she meets the ancient owner who takes her back to the age of Pushkin's Ethiopian ancestor Gannibal, while she observes the actions of her own Italian and Tatar precursors in *"My Genealogy."* In *"Chill"* she describes a malady which causes her to shake so violently that she alienates her neighbors by causing the furnishings of their apartments to rattle loudly enough to prevent their children from sleeping. But her best and most popular poem is "A Fairytale about the Rain." This long verse narrative contains all of her favorite symbols and combines them in a highly structured work which tells of the joy and pain of poetic inspiration.

"Fairytale" describes the process of creation that Rain (inspiration) activates within her. Akhmadulina explains how uncomfortable the Rain makes her and how its constant presence alienates her from other people. She feels that it is improper to be "soaked to the skin" while everyone else suffers from drought; to ease her mind she sends Rain away. She next enters a house where various guests ask her about her "gift"; only then does she realize how desperately she loves the Rain and calls it back. But when Rain comes into the house the guests destroy it, mop it up with rags and pour it down the commode. Left without the Rain Bella runs into the street, avows her love for it, and demonstrates this love by kissing a small puddle of water on the dry asphalt. This puddle is all that is left of the Rain and "Plunged into fear, the weather bureau/ Never again predicted precipitation."

Unfortunately Akhmadulina also suffered a period of drought in which she produced almost no new poetry. The poetry she did write after "Fairytale" contains the themes of sickness, insomnia, and suffering over her inability to write in contrast to her early themes of poetry, inspiration and love. Instead of the recurring symbols of flowers, children, puppies, snowmen, and rain, her poems of this period are full of images of shadows, darkness, muteness, and unfriendly houses. However, in the mid-1970's her poems again began to appear regularly in the press and in a number of collections. In these poems some of her old images re-appear, but new ones are gradually emerging.

In her recent poems Akhmadulina returns to the themes of writing, her love of foreign lands—especially Georgia—evocation of the past through visions of the poets Pushkin, Lermontov, Akhmatova, and Tsvetayeva, and affection for her friends. She now finds consolation in the freshness of Russian forests and walking in the snow: she feels joy in her surroundings: the cities of Moscow, Leningrad, and Tbilisi: the rural scenes of Peredelkino, Georgia, and the lands surrounding Russia's rivers. Her poetry is now more nostalgic; it is richer and deeper than it has ever been and certainly reflects her growing maturity as a poet.

An emerging complexity of style parallels Akhmadulina's more profound reflection on life. In her early poems she relied mainly on short iambic lines (tetrameters and pentameters) with great variation in rhythm through use of participles and polysyllabic words. She now experiments more with ternary meters and longer iambic lines. In all of her poetry the rhymes are linguistically complex with emphasis on near-rhymes, consonant reversals, compound, deep, and internal rhymes. The texture of her language is even richer now than it was in her early years. Each poem contains complicated tropes and figures of speech, especially puns and varieties of semantic and syntactic parallelisms.

The new reflective quality of Akhmadulina's poems combined with her extensive experimentation with form does not in any way destroy the vivacity and spontaneity of expression which distinguished her early poems. The young girl who wrote about motorcycles and soda water still exists within a more meditative woman: occasionally she still interjects a playful view. But Bella Akhmadulina is no longer merely a talented, young Russian writer; she now combines skill and vision with her talent to take her place among the finest poets writing today.

—Christine A. Rydel

ALBERTI (Merello), Rafael. Spanish. Born in Puerto de Santa María, 16 December 1902. Educated at Colegio de San Luis Gonzaga, Puerto de Santa María, to age 15; studied painting in Madrid, 1917; joined Residencia de Estudiantes, Madrid. Married María Teresa León c. 1930; one daughter. Ill with tuberculosis as a young man; writer in Madrid: founded *Octubre* magazine, 1934, and involved in communist politics; lived in Paris, 1939-40, Buenos Aires, 1940-64, and in Rome since 1964, though he served as a communist in the Spanish Cortes in 1977. Also a painter. Recipient: National Prize (Spain), 1924; Lenin Prize, 1965; Etna-Taormina Prize, 1975. Address: c/o Aguilar, Juan Bravo 38, Madrid 6, Spain.

PUBLICATIONS

Verse

Marinero en tierra. Madrid, Biblioteca Nueva, 1925.
La amante: Canciones. Malaga, 1926.
El alba del alhelí. Santander, Ediciones para Amigos de J.M. de Cossío, 1927.
Sobre los ángeles. Madrid, CIAP, 1929; as *Concerning the Angels*, translated by Geoffrey Connell, London, Rapp and Carroll, 1967.
Cal y canto. Madrid, Revista de Occidente, 1929.
Consignas. Madrid, Octubre, 1933.
Un fantasma recorre Europa. Madrid, La Tentativa Poética, 1933; as *A Spectre Is Haunting Europe: Poems of Revolutionary Spain*, edited by Angel Flores, New York, Critics Group, 1936.
Poesía 1924-1930. Madrid, Cruz y Raya, 1934.
Verte y no verte. Madrid, Aguirre, 1935.
13 bandas y 48 estrellas. Madrid, 1936.
Poesía 1924-1937. Madrid, Signo, 1938.
Poesía 1924-1938. Buenos Aires, Losada, 1940.
Entre el clavel y la espada 1939-1940. Buenos Aires, Losada, 1941.
Pleamar 1942-1944. Buenos Aires, Losada, 1944.
Selected Poems, translated by Lloyd Mallan. New York, New Directions, 1944.
A la pintura: Cantata de la línea y del color. Buenos Aires, Lopez, 1945; revised edition, Buenos Aires, Losada, 1948, 1953; Madrid, Aguilar, 1968; as *A la pintura*, translated by Ben Belitt, West Islip, New York, Universal Art Editions, 1972.
Antologia poética 1924-1944. Buenos Aires, Losada, 1945; revised edition, 1959.
Poesía 1924-1944. Buenos Aires, Losada, 1946.
El ceñidor de Venus desceñido. Buenos Aires, Botella al Mar, 1948.

Coplas de Juan Panadero (Libro I).   Montevideo, Pueblos Unidos, 1949.
Buenos Aires en tinta china, edited by Attilio Rossi.   Buenos Aires, Losada, 1951.
Retornos de lo vivo lejano 1948-1952.   Buenos Aires, Losada, 1952; revised edition, Barcelona, Libres de Sinera, 1972.
Ora marítima.   Buenos Aires, Losada, 1953.
Baladas y canciones del Paraná.   Buenos Aires, Losada, 1954.
Diez liricografías.   Buenos Aires, Bonino, 1954.
María Carmen Portela.   Buenos Aires, Losada, 1956.
Sonríe China, with María Teresa León, illustrated by Alberti.   Buenos Aires, Muchnok, 1958.
Cal y canto, Sobre los ángeles, Sermones y moradas.   Buenos Aires, Losada, 1959.
El otoño, otra vez.   Lima, 1960.
Los viejos olivos.   Caracas, Dirección de Cultura y Bella Artes, 1960.
Poesías completas.   Buenos Aires, Losada, 1961; and later editions.
Poemas escénicos.   Buenos Aires, Losada, 1962.
Diez sonetos romanos.   Buenos Aires, Bonino, 1964.
Abierto a todas horas 1960-1963.   Madrid, Aquado, 1964.
El poeta en la calle: Poesía civil 1931-1965.   Paris, Globe, 1966.
Selected Poems, edited and translated by Ben Belitt.   Berkeley, University of California Press, 1966.
Poemas de amor.   Madrid, Alfaguara, 1967.
Roma, peligro para caminantes 1964-1967.   Mexico City, Mortiz, 1968.
Libro del mar, edited by Aitana Alberti.   Barcelona, Lumen, 1968.
Poesía anteriores a Marinero en tierra 1920-1923.   N.p., V.A., 1969.
Los 8 nombres de Picasso, y No digo más que lo que no digo 1966-1970.   Barcelona, Kairós, 1970.
Canciones del alto valle del Aniene, y otros versos y prosas 1967-1972.   Buenos Aires, Losada, 1972.
Poesía.   Madrid, Aguilar, 1972.
The Owl's Insomnia, edited and translated by Mark Strand.   New York, Atheneum, 1973.
Poemas del destierro y de la espera, edited by J. Corredor-Matheos.   Madrid, Espasa Calpe, 1976.
Poesía.   Havana, Arte y Literatura, 1976.
Coplas de Juan Panadero 1949-1977, seguida de Vida bilingüe de un refugiado español en Francia 1939-1940.   Madrid, Mayoría, 1977.
Poesía 1924-1977.   Madrid, Aguilar, 1977.
El matador: Poemas escénicos 1961-1965.   Barcelona, Seix Barral, 1979.
Fustigada luz (1972-78).   Barcelona, Seix Barral, 1980.
Canto de siempre.   Madrid, Espasa Calpe, 1980.
101 sonetos (1924-75).   Barcelona, Seix Barral, 1980.
The Other Shore: 100 Poems, edited by Kosrof Chantikian, translated by José A. Elgorriaga and Paul Martin.   San Francisco, Kosmos, 1981.
Versos sueltos de cada día (1979-82).   Barcelona, Seix Barral, 1982.

Plays

El hombre deshabitado (produced Madrid, 1931).   Madrid, Gama, 1930.
Fermín Galán (produced Madrid, 1931).   Madrid, Chulilla y Angel, 1931.
La pájara pinta (produced Madrid, 1931?).   Included in *Lope de Vega y la poesia contemporanea,* 1964.
Bazar de la providencia (includes *Farsa de los Reyes Magos*).   Madrid, Octubre, 1934.
De un momento a otro: Poesía y historia.   Madrid, Europa-America, 1937.
Numancia, from the play by Cervantes (produced Madrid, 1937).   Madrid, Signo, 1937.

El ladron de niños, from a play by Jules Supervielle (produced Montevideo, 1943).
El adefesio. Buenos Aires, Losada, 1944.
Teatro (includes *El hombre deshabitado*, *El trébol florido*, *La gallarda*). Buenos Aires,
Losada, 1950; augmented edition (includes *El adefesio*), 1959.
Noche de guerra en el Museo del Prado. Buenos Aires, Losada, 1956.
Las picardías de Scapin, from the play by Molière (produced Buenos Aires, 1958).
Teatro 2 (includes *Lizana andaluza*, *De un momento a otro*, *Noche de guerra en el Museo
del Prado*). Buenos Aires, Losada, 1964.
Farsa del licenciado Pathelin, from a French work (produced Buenos Aires, 1970).
Buenos Aires, Centro Editor de América Latina, 1970.

Screenplay: *La dama duende*, with María Teresa León, 1944.

Fiction

Imagen primera de.... Buenos Aires, Losada, 1945.
Relatos y prosa. Barcelona, Bruguera, 1980.
Prosas. Madrid, Alianza, 1980.

Other

La poesía popular en la lirica española contemporánea. N.p., Gronan, 1933.
Nuestra diaria palabra. Madrid, Héroe, 1936.
El poeta en la España de 1931. Buenos Aires, Patronato Hispano-Argentino de Cultura,
1942.
La arboleda perdida y otras prosas. Mexico City, Seneca, 1942; revised edition, Buenos
Aires, Fabril, 1959; as *The Lost Grove: Autobiography of a Spanish Poet in Exile*,
Berkeley, University of California Press, 1976.
Vida bilingüe de un refugiado español en Francia. Buenos Aires, Bajel, 1942.
Eh, los toros!, illustrated by Luis Seoane. Buenos Aires, Emecé, 1942.
Suma taurina: Verso, prosa, teatro, illustrated by the author, edited by Rafael Montesi-
nos. Barcelona, RM, 1963.
Lope de Vega y la poesía contemporánea (includes the play *La pájara pinta*). Paris,
Centre de Recherches de l'Institut d'Études Hispaniques, 1964.
Prosas encontradas 1924-1942, edited by Robert Marrast. Madrid, Ayuso, 1970.
A Year of Picasso's Paintings. New York, Abrams, 1971.
Obras completas. Madrid, Aguilar, 1972; and later editions.
Picasso, el rayo que no cesa. Parets del Vallés, Polígrafa, 1975.
Maravillas con variaciones acrósticas en el jardín de Miró. Parets del Vallés, Polígrafa,
1975.
Aire, que me lleva el aire (juvenile). Barcelona, Labor, 1981.
X a X: Correspondencia en verso, with José Bergamín. Torremolinos, Litoral, 1982.

Editor, *Églogas y fábulas castellanas*. Buenos Aires, Mirto, 2 vols., 1944.
Editor, *Romancero general de la guerra española*. Buenos Aires, Patronato Hispano-
Argentino de Cultura, 1944.
Editor, with Guillermo de Torre, *Antología poética 1918-1936*, by García Lorca. Bu-
enos Aires, Losada, 1957.
Editor and Translator, *Doinas y baladas populares rumanas*. Buenos Aires, Losada,
1964.
Editor, *Poesías*, by Lope de Vega. Buenos Aires, Losada, 1965.
Editor, *Antología poética: Antonio Machado, Juan Ramón Jiménez, Federico García
Lorca*. Barcelona, Nauta, 1970.

Translator, *Visages*, by Gloria Alcorta. Buenos Aires, Botella al Mar, 1951.

*

Critical Studies: *Alberti's Sobre los ángeles: Four Major Themes* by C.B. Morris, Hull, University of Hull, 1966; *El mundo poético de Alberti* by Solita Salinas de Marichal, Madrid, Gredos, 1968; *Alberti* edited by Manuel Durán, Madrid, Taurus, 1975; *The Theatre of Alberti* by Louise B. Popkin, London, Tamesis, 1975; *The Poetry of Alberti: A Visual Approach* by Robert C. Manteiga, London, Tamesis, 1978; "Alberti Issue" of *Malahat Review*, July 1978; *El teatro de Alberti* by Gregorio Torres Nebrera, Madrid, Sociedad General Española de Libreria, 1982.

*   *   *

Rafael Alberti, a member of the Generation of 1927, has written thousands of poems from the early 1920's into the 1980's. A master of poetic technique and with an almost unlimited range, he fuses the cultured with the popular in graceful poems of great verbal beauty and striking visual imagery, especially involving descriptions of the sea. Often an intellectual poet, Alberti has nonetheless treated the quotidian, the comic, the pageantry of bullfighting, the form and technique of painting and the arts, experiences in China, and, less successfully, social protest.

In *Marinero en tierra* (Sailor on Land), his first prize-winning volume of poetry, he combines joy and nostalgia and the popular ballad tradition with an elaborate metaphorical technique, evoking with longing and musical, colorful lines the sea of his dreams, of youthful innocence and freedom. In another early colorful collection, *El alba del alhelí* (Gillyflower Dawn), Alberti mixes merriment and mystery in poems about the Andalusian countryside. *Cal y canto* (Quicklime and Song) contains many dehumanized, baroque poems, but beyond the hermetic form and formal beauty we discover an anguished poet unable to find love, to comprehend both the tangible *cal* and the poetic *canto*, or to create order out of chaos. Alberti's dislocated and destructive symbology in this volume prepared the way for *Concerning the Angels*, his acknowledged masterpiece.

Concerning the Angels treats of a personal and universal spiritual crisis. The poet, having lost Paradise, love, and religious faith, confronts potential death. Angry and frustrated at his loss of innocence and facing the emptiness of life, he sinks into an anguished and despairing spiritual abyss. The angels, representing human drives and affects and both the positive and negative of human potential, sometimes obfuscate and impede, but one leads him from darkness and despair. The poet, recovering from chaotic time and space, achieves a kind of reintegration of faith and redemption in a dehumanized world of disintegrating values. Surrealistic and almost mystical, this collection contains at times incoherent and almost irrational imagery to convey an apocalyptic vision of existential mortality.

Exiled in 1939, Alberti sought peace in America, but he was unable to forget his native land. *Entre el clavel y la espada* (Between the Carnation and the Sword) reveals that the Civil War for him is still an unbearable memory, and his obsession with Spain as a lost Paradise prevents his enjoyment of a new land. In several other collections of American poetry, not as profound as his early works, Alberti continues to remember the sea of Cadiz and the Civil War. The best of these collections, *Retornos de lo vivo lejano* (Recurrences of Painful Recall), stresses memories of childhood, friends, and fellow poets. As the soul of other landscapes passes before his eyes, Alberti exudes sadness, resignation, and melancholy, for the past continues to exist in an eternal present of poetic fantasy, a memory which sustains him in his present life.

Each year a new volume of original poetry, a thematic anthology, or a new version of his selected poems appears. Typical of such poetry, *Canciones del alto valle del Aniene* (Songs of the Deep Valley of Aniene) contains poetry written in Italy between 1967 and 1971 about friends and the anguish and solitude of the world.

—Kessel Schwartz

ALEIXANDRE (Merlo), Vicente. Spanish. Born in Seville, 26 April 1898. Educated at the University of Madrid, licence in law and diploma in business administration, both 1919. Taught at Central School of Commerce, Madrid, 1919-22, and Residencia de Estudiantes, 1921; worked for Andalusian Railroads, 1921-25; staff member, *La Semana Financiera* magazine; since 1925, full-time writer. Recipient: National Prize, 1933; Critics Prize (Spain), 1963, 1969, 1975; Nobel Prize for Literature, 1977. Member, Spanish Academy, 1949, Hispanic Society of America, and Monde Latin Academy, Paris. Corresponding Member, Arts Academy, Malaga, and Sciences and Arts Academy, Puerto Rico; Honorary Fellow, Professors of Spanish Association (USA). Grand Cross of Order of Carlos III, 1977. Address: Vicente Aleixandre 3, Madrid 3, Spain.

Publications

Verse

Ámbito. Málaga, Litoral, 1928.
Espadas como labios. Madrid, Calpe, 1932.
Pasión de la tierra. Mexico City, Fábula, 1935; revised edition, Madrid, Adonais, 1946.
La destrucción o el amor. Madrid, Signo, 1935.
Historia del corazón. Madrid, Calpe, 1940.
Poemas paradisíacos. Madrid, 1942.
Sombra del paraíso. Madrid, Adan, 1944.
Mundo a solas 1934-1936. Madrid, Clan, 1950.
Nacimiento último. Madrid, Insula, 1953.
Mis poemas mejores. Madrid, Gredos, 1956; revised edition, 1976.
Poesías completas. Madrid, Aguilar, 1960.
Poemas amorosos. Buenos Aires, Losada, 1960.
Antigua casa madrileña. Santander, Bedia, 1961.
En un vasto dominio. Madrid, Revista de Occidente, 1962.
Presencias. Barcelona, Seix Barral, 1965.
Retratos con nombre. Barcelona, El Barda, 1965.
Dos vidas. Málaga, El Guadalhorce, 1967.
Poemas de la consumación. Barcelona, Plaza & Janés, 1968.
Poems. Athens, Ohio University Department of English, 1969.
Poesía superrealista. Barcelona, Seix Barral, 1971.
Sonido de la guerra. Valencia, Fomento de Cultura, 1972.
Diálogos del conocimiento. Barcelona, Plaza & Janés, 1974.
Selected Poems, with Luis Cernuda. Providence, Rhode Island, Copper Beech Press, 1974.
Antología total, edited by Pere Gimferrer. Barcelona, Seix Barral, 1975.
The Cave of Night. Atascadero, California, Solo Press, 1976.
Twenty Poems, translated by Robert Bly. Madison, Minnesota, Seventies Press, 1977.
A Longing for the Light: Selected Poems, edited by Lewis Hyde. New York, Harper, 1979.
A Bird of Paper, translated by Willis Barnstone and David Garrison. Athens, Ohio University Press, 1982.

Other

En la vida del poeta: El amor y la poesía. Madrid, Real Academia Española, 1950.
El niño ciego de Vázquez Díaz. Madrid, Ateneo, 1954.

ALEIXANDRE

Algunos caracteres de la nueva poesía española. Madrid, Gongora, 1955.
Los encuentros. Madrid, Guadarrama, 1958.
Obras completas. Madrid, Aguilar, 1968; revised edition, 2 vols., 1977-78.

*

Critical Studies: *La poesía de Aleixandre* by Carlos Bousoño, Madrid, 1950, revised edition, 1968, 1977; *Aleixandre* by Kessel Schwartz, New York, Twayne, 1970; *Aleixandre: A Critical Appraisal* edited by Santiago Daydi-Tolson, Ypsilanti, Michigan, Bilingual Press, 1981.

*   *   *

A member of the "Generation of 27," a group of Spanish poets which includes such world renowned writers as Federico García Lorca and Jorge Guillén, Vicente Aleixandre represents for literature what Salvador Dali, Luis Buñuel, and Joan Miró, also his contemporaries, represent for the visual arts. But although Aleixandre deservedly belongs among the best European Surrealist artists and writers—a fact that has been acknowledged by the Nobel Prize—his works are little known by the general public. No other Spanish poet presents such difficulties to the reader as he does. His poems, particularly those written before the Civil War, are the startling result of a Surrealist view of the world expressed in Surrealistic literary techniques. Interest in the subconscious and in the interpretation of reality in terms of the irrational, the use of oneiric and visionary images, and the practice of automatic writing have always been important aspects in Aleixandre's poems and define his very personal and sometimes hermetic style.

His first book, *Ámbito,* a manifest imitation of Juan Ramón Jiménez, a leading figure in Spanish poetry before the Civil War, already shows Aleixandre's preference for the obscure subconscious processes of the mind, and for a cosmic view of man in communion with all of creation. His first truly Surrealist work, *Pasión de la tierra,* a series of prose poems dealing with the experience of death and the love of existence, appeared in Mexico and was little known in Spain at the time of its publication. Only his third and fourth books, *Espadas como labios* and *La destrucción o el amor,* were to become recognized in the highly demanding Spanish poetic circles of the pre-Civil War period as the works of a novel and original poet.

After the war Aleixandre became more aware of historical circumstances, and soon was accepted as a leader by the younger poets. One of his most inspired books, *Sombra del paraíso,* was published in this period; in it the interpretation of man's existence in terms of cosmic communion is enriched by the growing importance given to more concrete human experiences. The community of men appears to take central interest for the poet during the three decades following the end of the war. This new attitude is summarized in Aleixandre's conviction that poetry is above all a form of human communication, and that the poet should talk for all men. These ideas, which supported to a certain extent the movement for social poetry in Franco's Spain, inspired *Historia del corazón* and *En un vasto dominio.*

In later years, after a period of great literary activity which included writing some brief theoretical articles and a few prose texts, Aleixandre returned to a more intimate poetry, this time centered mostly on a philosophical, even metaphysical, inquiry into the nature of reality and of human knowledge. *Poemas de la consumación* and *Diálogos del conocimiento* are a clear indication of Aleixandre's mastery of the lyric genre as a means to attain and to communicate an understanding of man and reality impossible to obtain and to express in any other way. It is obvious, then, that Vicente Aleixandre represents in Spain the modern tradition of European poetic writing.

—Santiago Daydi-Tolson

AMADO, Jorge. Brazilian. Born in Ilhéus, Bahia, 10 August 1912. Educated at Federal University, Rio de Janeiro, J.D. 1935. Married Zelia Gattai in 1945; one son and one daughter. Imprisoned for political reasons, 1935; exiled 1937, 1941-43, 1948-52. Communist deputy of Brazilian parliament, 1946-47. Editor, *Para Todos*, Rio de Janeiro, 1956-59. Recipient: Stalin Peace Prize, 1951; Gulbenkian Prize, 1971; Italian-Latin American Institute Prize, 1976. Member, Brazilian Academy of Letters. Address: Rua Alagoinhas 33, Rio Vernelho, Salvador, Bahia, Brazil.

PUBLICATIONS

Fiction

A país do carnaval. Rio de Janeiro, Schmidt, 1932.
Cacáu. Rio de Janeiro, Olympio, 1934.
Jubiabá. Rio de Janeiro, Olympio, 1935.
Mar morto. Rio de Janeiro, Olympio, 1936.
Capitães de Areia. Rio de Janeiro, Olympio, 1937.
A B C de Castro Alves. São Paulo, Martins, 1941.
Vida de Luis Carlos Prestes, o cavaleiro da esperança. São Paulo, Martins, 1942.
Terras do sem fim. São Paulo, Martins, 1942; as *The Violent Land*, New York, Knopf, 1945; revised edition, 1965.
São Jorge dos Ilhéus. São Paulo, Martins, 1944.
Seara vermelha. São Paulo, Martins, 1946.
O amor de Castro Alves. Rio de Janeiro, Povo, 1947; as *O amor do soldado*, São Paulo, Martins, 1958.
Os subterrâneos da liberdade: Os asperos tempos, Agonia da noite, A luz no tunel. São Paulo, Martins, 3 vols., 1954.
Gabriela, cravo e canela. São Paulo, Martins, 1958; as *Gabriela, Clove and Cinnamon*, New York, Knopf, 1962; London, Chatto and Windus, 1963.
Os velhos marinheiros. São Paulo, Martins, 1961; as *Home Is the Sailor*, New York, Knopf, and London, Chatto and Windus, 1964.
A morte e a morte de Quincas Berro Dágua. Rio de Janeiro, Sociedade dos Cem Bibliófilos do Brasil, 1962; as *The Two Deaths of Quincas Wateryell*, New York, Knopf, 1965.
Os pastores da noite. São Paulo, Martins, 1964; as *Shepherds of the Night*, New York, Knopf, 1966.
Dona Flor e seus dois maridos: História moral e de amor. São Paulo, Martins, 1966; as *Dona Flor and Her Two Husbands: A Moral and Amorous Tale*, New York, Knopf, 1969; London, Weidenfeld and Nicolson, 1970.
Tenda dos milagres. São Paulo, Martins, 1969; as *Tent of Miracles*, New York, Knopf, 1971.
Tereza Batista, cansada de guerra. São Paulo, Martins, 1972; as *Tereza Batista, Home from the Wars*, New York, Knopf, 1975; London, Souvenir Press, 1982.
O gato malhado e a andorinha sinha. Rio de Janeiro, Record, 1976; as *The Swallow and the Tom Cat: A Grown-Up Love Story*, New York, Delacorte Press, 1982.
Tieta do Agreste. Rio de Janeiro, Record, 1977; translated as *Tieta the Goat Girl*, New York, Knopf, 1979; London, Souvenir Press, 1981.

Other

Bahia de todos os santos. São Paulo, Martins, 1945.
Homens e coisas do partido comunista. Rio de Janeiro, Horizonte, 1946.

O mundo da paz: União Soviética e democracias populares.   Rio de Janeiro, Vitoria, 1952.
Trinta anos de literatura (selection).   São Paulo, Martins, 1961.
O poeta ze trinidade.   Rio de Janeiro, Ozon, 1965.
Bahia boa terra Bahia.   Rio de Janeiro, Image, 1967.
O compadre de Ogun.   Rio de Janeiro, Sociedade dos Cem Bibliófilos do Brasil, 1969.
Bahia (Portuguese/English text).   São Paulo, Brunner, 1971.
Quarenta anos de literature (selection).   São Paulo, Martins, 1972.
Porto Seguro recriado por Sergio Telles, with Luis Viana Filho and Jeanine Warnod.   Rio de Janeiro, Bolsa de Arte, 1976.

*

Critical Studies: *Brazil's New Novel: Four Northeastern Masters* by Fred P. Ellison, Berkeley, University of California Press, 1954; *Perfil sociológico da literatura brasileira: O sertão-Jorge Amado* by Giorgio Marotti, Porto, Paisagem, 1975; *Amado: Política e literatura: Um estudo sobre a trajetória intelectual de Amado* by Alfredo Wagner Berno de Almeida, Rio de Janeiro, Campus, 1979.

*   *   *

Jorge Amado's writing career has lasted over 50 years. From his beginnings as a regional writer associated with the Northeast of Brazil, writing novels with strong social and political themes, he has become a writer whose books transcend any restrictive value the word "regional" might imply. Along with the ever-increasing authority of his work has come an opening out of his style: as the *Times Literary Supplement* critic of *Gabriella, Clove and Cinnamon* put it, compared to the black and white novels of his earlier career, *Gabriella* "is like a burst of Technicolor illumined by geniality."

Genial is hardly the word to apply to his early works. His first novel, *A país do carnaval*, is a typical young man's political novel, a picture of the young intelligentsia searching for social and political answers in the exuberant, confusing period immediately following the Revolution of 1930, with the dominant figure a young radical communist. The next few novels almost set out a program for the young radical to follow: exploitation of black and mulatto workers in Bahia (*Cacáu*), poor fishermen of the coast (*Mar morto*), dockers, prostitutes, and waifs (*Suór*), the Bahia slums (*Capitães de Areia*), even the prospect of a black radical emerging from the poverty and restraints of his world, resisting both the capitalist exploiters and the African tradition of the witch doctor (*Jubiabá*). Fred P. Ellison calls *Suór* a "propagandist's notebook"—and Amado mentions his deliberate search for material in the preface to *Capitães de Areia*; for many this implies imposition of theoretical doctrine onto a fictional world, harmful to both.

The culmination of this period of his work was *The Violent Land*, relatively unburdened with a political scenario, and obviously close to the background of his own life (Amado's father was a frontier landowner). This is the story of the conflict between Colonel Horácio and the Badáro family for a large tract of uncleared land to be used for cultivating cacao, the important crop that was ousting coffee in the Bahia region of Brazil in the early years of the 20th century. Amado's use of the image of the cacao pod (rich and golden, but also exuding a slime that hardens into a crust that can't be washed off) is worked into the narrative with a perception that goes beyond making a mere dialectical point about capitalism. (In fact, his next novel, *São Jorge dos Ilhéus*, makes a more obvious capitalist point—about the way the bankers attempted to get control of the large plantations during the economic crisis after World War I.) If the influence of Zola had been condemned by critics of his early novels, Carlos Fuentes suggested that, in *The Violent Land*, Balzac rather than Zola was the underlying influence, and called it "the novel of a master craftsman."

The later novels have become generally less explicitly political still. Behind all of them lie the violent background of the wars for possession of the rich frontier lands, the corrupt officials who falsified records of ownership, and the emergence of strong families who controlled entire sections of the district, but now the simpler human implications, described with zest and humor, are the major concern. *Gabriella, Clove and Cinnamon*, for instance, is a book that sums up many of the themes of Amado in a charming though always thoughtful way. Set in 1925, at a time when "civilization" is coming to Ilhéus, the novel contains half a dozen plots, cunningly running together at the same time, but Amado, through a masterful use of short sketches, like a mosaic of both present and past, is able to weld them into a unified whole. He centers his attention on one social aspect of the period: the tradition that the husband of an adulterous wife could kill both the wife and her lover with impunity. Using this as the central motif (and it applies in this hot-blooded land to many of the book's relationships), Amado shows the gradual loss of power of the colonels (as the cacao landowners are almost always called) in the political life of the area, the cultural and economic assimilation of new ideas from the larger world outside Ilhéus, and, amusingly, the breakdown of the right of the wronged husband to kill. Through the book runs, like the sinuous thread of a symbol, the figure of Gabriella, the completely natural woman, with no ulterior motives, no taint of "civilization" about her, a token of simplicity and truth.

Amado has obviously not lost his social awareness or his compassion, but he is now willing to make his points through irony and charm, and to express them in a delightful poetic, individual style.

—George Walsh

AMICHAI, Yehuda. Israeli.   Born in Würzburg, Germany, in 1924; emigrated to Palestine in 1936: naturalized Israeli citizen.   Educated at Bet Sefer Maaleh, Jerusalem; Hebrew University, Jerusalem. Served with the Jewish Brigade in the British Army during World War II, and as an infantryman in the War of Independence: Sergeant-Major in reserve. Married 1) Tamar Horn, one son; 2) Chana Sokolov, one son and one daughter. Former teacher of Hebrew literature and the Bible in secondary schools, Jerusalem; visiting poet, University of California, Berkeley, 1971, 1976; Dorot Visiting Fellowship, New York University, 1983-84. Recipient: Shlonsky Prize; Acum Prize (twice); Bialik Prize; Israel Prize. Address: 26 Malki Street, Yemin Moshe, Jerusalem, Israel.

Publications

Verse

> *Akhshav uba-yamin na aherim* [Now and in Other Days].   Tel Aviv, 1955.
> *Be-merhak shete tikrot* [Two Hopes Away].   Tel Aviv, 1958.
> *Ba-ginah ha-tsiburit* [In the Park].   Jerusalem, 1959.
> *Shirim 1948-1962* [Poetry].   Jerusalem, 1962-63.
> *Selected Poems*, translated by Assia Gutmann.   London, Cape Goliard Press, 1968; as
>   *Poems*, New York, Harper, 1969.
> *'Akshav ba-ra'nsh* [Now in the Turmoil].   1968.
> *Selected Poems*, translated by Ted Hughes.   London, Penguin, 1971.

Ve-lo 'al menat lizkor [And Not in Order to Remember].   1971.
Songs of Jerusalem and Myself, translated by Harold Schimmel.   New York, Harper, 1973.
Me-ahore kol zeh mistater osher gadol [Behind All This Hides Great Happiness].   1974.
Amen, translated by the author and Ted Hughes.   New York, Harper, and London, Oxford University Press, 1978.
On New Year's Day, Next to a House Being Built.   Bedford, Sceptre Press, 1979.
Time, translated by the author and Ted Hughes.   New York, Harper, and London, Oxford University Press, 1979.
Love Poems.   New York, Harper, 1981.
Great Tranquillity: Questions and Answers, translated by Glenda Abramson and Tudor Parfitt.   New York, Harper, 1983.

Plays

Masa' le-Ninveh [Journey to Nineveh] (produced Tel Aviv, 1964).   Jerusalem, 1962.
Pa 'amonim ve-rakavot (radio play).   1968; as *Bells and Trains*, in *Midstream*, October 1966.

Fiction

Be-ruah ha-nora'ah ha-zot.   Tel Aviv, Merhavya, 1961.
Lo me-'akhshav, lo mi-kan.   Tel Aviv, 1963; as *Not of This Time, Not of This Place*, New York, Harper, 1968.
Mi yitneni malon [Hotel in the Wilderness].   1971.
The World Is a Room: Short Stories.   Philadelphia, Jewish Publication Society, 1984.

Other

Mah she-karah le-Roni bi-Nyu-York.   1968.

Editor, with Allen Mandelbaum, *The Syrian-African Rift and Other Poems*, by Avoth Yeshurun.   Philadelphia, Jewish Publication Society, 1980.
Editor, with Allen Mandelbaum, *Points of Departure*, by Dan Pagis.   Philadelphia, Jewish Publication Society, 1982.

Translator of works by Rolf Hochhuth, Else Lasker-Schüler, and Yitzhak Pugatz.

*

Critical Studies: *Escape into Siege* by Leon Yudkin, London, Routledge, 1974.

*   *   *

Yehuda Amichai has a rare ability for transforming personal situations into universal ones, thereby conveying the largeness of individual passions. He speaks with harshness, insight, and wisdom, qualities that are often deflected by irony, understatement, and humor.

Amichai and his family emigrated from Germany to Palestine in 1936 when he was twelve. He served in the Jewish Brigade of the British Army in World War II and as an infantryman in Israel's war of independence. In his poetry, he writes of Israel, of this time, this valley, this burning country, in ways that belong to people of other nations, as well. Paradoxically, his own particularity assures universality.

Many of his poems are set in Jerusalem, a hard city in which the landscape and the loved one are defined each by the other: "And like the contours of the Judean hills,/we shall never find peace" ("In the Middle of This Century"). He writes with urgency of the present moment, often setting it against a background of biblical places and religious legends; his juxtaposition of the immediate and the eternal is especially witty, as when a lover exclaims joyfully, "All one hundred and fifty psalms/cry out at once" ("Six Songs for Tamar").

In his love poems, Amichai speaks of war, at times equating the struggle between a man and a woman, and at other times contrasting war with love's peace. In "A Wedding Song," he writes: "Your parents supplied the woman and my parents the man./God supplied the war and the ceasefire." And in another poem, he writes:

> I remember that the city was divided
> Not only between Jews and Arabs,
> But between me and you,
> When we were there together.
>
> We made ourselves a womb of dangers
> We built ourselves a house of deadening wars
> Like men of the far north
> Who build themselves a safe warm house
> Of deadening ice.

To love, in Amichai's world, is, sadly, to imagine permanence in a world of change. The theme recalls Shakespeare's mutability: love, rooted in time, is destroyed by time; our vision of permanence is a reaction against the knowledge that we will die. In Amichai's poems, time's shifting sands are more volatile because they are the sands of Israel, and his notion of change involves also a divided country in a troubled world. In nearly every poem, there is a heightened awareness of the external world, a clarity generated by passion. He writes of the present moment, intensified by the transitory quality of friendship and love, and made more poignant by constant reminders of ancient tradition and eternal values.

Another theme that emerges in Amichai's poetry is the distrust of language for its unfulfilled promise to master our temporal condition. It is a familiar theme in poetry, but especially in the Hebrew of Amichai, for he invents an idiom by using the language of industry, commerce, and colloquial speech, gaining ironic and even violent effects from their juxtaposition, in the manner of the English metaphysical poets. In addition, his daring images of transcience ("Again love has ended, like a successful citrus season") are abundant and exact.

Amichai writes of national tragedy, as in "Since Then," with its haunting refrain, "For I fell in the soft, pale sands/Of Ashdod in the War of Independence." Or, "What's Jewish Time? God's experimental places/Where he tests new ideas and new weaponry," he writes in "For Ever and Ever, Sweet Distortions." He does so in ways that evoke the world's disorder. Or, he writes of the pain of loss (in "Two Fragments of the Population Explosion"):

> How poor in years and even days
> Are those about to part but how rich
> They are in minutes and seconds.

And yet his poems, though tragic, are tempered with outrageous irony. Often they exhibit the sanguine good humor of a man who has known suffering and cherishes every moment of life in his time, in his place:

> Even though I know I'll die
> And even though I know the Messiah won't come,
> I feel good.

—Grace Schulman

ANOUILH, Jean (Marie Lucien Pierre). French. Born in Cérisole, Bordeaux, 23 June
1910. Educated at École Colbert, Bordeaux; Collège Chaptal; studied law at the Sorbonne,
Paris, 1931-33. Military service during the 1930's. Married 1) Monelle Valentin, one daughter;
2) Nicole Lançon in 1953, two daughters and one son. Publicity and gag writer for films, and
advertising copywriter for Publicité Damour, Paris, 2 years; secretary, Louis Jouvet's Comédie
des Champs-Elysées, Paris, 1931-32; assistant to the director Georges Pitoeff; then full-time
writer; also a film director. Recipient: Grand Prize of French Cinema, 1949; Tony Award
(USA), 1955; New York Drama Critics Circle Award, 1957; Cino del Duca prize, 1970; French
Drama Critics award, 1970; Paris Critics Prize, 1971. Address: c/o Éditions de la Table Ronde,
40 rue du Bac, 75007 Paris; or, 7 rue Saint-James, 92200 Neuilly-sur-Seine, France.

PUBLICATIONS

Plays

L'Hermine (produced Paris, 1932). Paris, Fayard, 1934; as The Ermine (produced
  Nottingham, 1955), in Plays of the Year 13, London, Elek, 1956; in Five Plays, 1958.
Mandarine (produced Paris, 1933).
Y'avait un prisonnier (produced Paris, 1935). Published in La Petite Illustration, 18
  May 1935.
Le Voyageur sans bagage (produced Paris, 1937). Included in Pièces noires, 1942; as
  Traveller Without Luggage (produced London, 1959; New York, 1964), London,
  Methuen, 1959; in Seven Plays, 1967.
La Sauvage (produced Paris, 1938). Paris, Fayard, 1938; as The Restless Heart (pro-
  duced London, 1957), London, Methuen, 1957; in Five Plays, 1958.
Le Bal des voleurs (produced Paris, 1938). Paris, Fayard, 1938; as Thieves Carnival
  (produced London, 1952; New York, 1955), London, Methuen, and New York, French,
  1952.
Léocadia (produced Paris, 1940). Included in Pièces roses, 1942; as Time Remembered
  (produced London, 1954; New York, 1957), London, Methuen, 1955; New York,
  Coward McCann, 1958.
Marie-Jeanne; ou, La Fille du peuple, from a play by Dennery and Mallian (produced
  Paris, 1940).
Le Rendez-vous de Senlis (produced Paris, 1941). Included in Pièces roses, 1942; as
  Dinner with the Family (produced London, 1957; New York, 1961), London, Methuen,
  1958.
Eurydice (produced Paris, 1942). Included in Pièces noires, 1942; as Point of Departure
  (as Eurydice, produced Hollywood, 1948; as Point of Departure, produced London,
  1950), London, French, 1951; as Legend of Lovers (produced New York, 1951), New
  York, Coward McCann, 1952.
Pièces roses (includes Le Bal des voleurs, Le Rendez-vous de Senlis, Léocadia). Paris,
  Balzac, 1942; augmented edition (includes Humulus le Muet), Paris, Table Ronde,
  1958.
Pièces noires (includes L'Hermine, La Sauvage, Le Voyageur sans bagage, Eurydice).
  Paris, Balzac, 1942.
Antigone, from the play by Sophocles (produced Paris, 1944). Paris, Table Ronde,
  1946; translated as Antigone (produced New York, 1946; London, 1949), New York,
  Random House, 1946; London, Methuen, 1957.
Roméo et Jeannette (produced Paris, 1946). Included in Nouvelles pièces noires, 1946;
  as Romeo and Jeannette (as Fading Mansions, produced London, 1949; as Jeannette,
  produced New York, 1960), in Five Plays, 1958.
Nouvelles pièces noires (includes Jézabel, Antigone, Roméo et Jeannette, Médée). Paris, Table Ronde, 1946.

Médée (produced Paris, 1953). Included in *Nouvelles pièces noires*, 1946; as *Medea* (produced London, 1956; New York, 1972), in *Plays of the Year 15*, London, Elek, 1956; in *Seven Plays*, 1967.

L'Invitation au château (produced Paris, 1947). Paris, Table Ronde, 1948; as *Ring round the moon* (produced London and New York, 1950), London, Methuen, and New York, Oxford University Press, 1950.

Ardèle; ou, La Marguerite, with *Episode de la vie d'un auteur* (produced Paris, 1948). Paris, Table Ronde, 1949; as *Ardele* (as *Cry of the Peacock*, produced New York, 1950; as *Ardele*, produced London, 1951), London, Methuen, 1951; in *Five Plays*, 1958.

Humulus le Muet, with Jean Aurenche (produced Paris, 1948). Grenoble, Editions Françaises Nouvelles, n.d.; as *Humulus the Great* (produced New York, 1976).

La Répétition; ou, L'Amour puni (produced Paris, 1950). Geneva, La Palatine, 1950; as *The Rehearsal* (produced Edinburgh, 1957; London, 1961; New York, 1963), in *Five Plays*, 1958; published separately, London, Methuen, 1961.

Monsieur Vincent (screenplay), with Jean Bernard Luc. Munich, Bayerisch Schülbuch-Verlag, 1951.

Colombe (produced Paris, 1951). Included in *Pièces brillantes*, 1951; as *Colombe* (produced London, 1951; New York, 1954), London, Methuen, 1952; New York, Coward McCann, 1954; revised version, music by T.M. Damaye (produced Paris, 1961).

Pièces brillantes (includes *L'Invitation au château*, *Colombe*, *La Répétition*, *Cécile*). Paris, Table Ronde, 1951.

Cécile; ou, L'École des pères (produced Paris, 1954). Included in *Pièces brillantes*, 1951; as *Cecile; or, The School for Fathers*, in *Seven Plays*, 1967.

La Valse des toréadors (produced Paris, 1952). Paris, Table Ronde, 1952; as *Waltz of the Toreadors* (produced London, 1956; New York, 1957), London, Elek, 1956; New York, Coward McCann, 1957.

Trois comédies (includes adaptations of *As You Like It*, *A Winter's Tale*, and *Twelfth Night* by Shakespeare). Paris, Table Ronde, 1952.

La Nuit des rois, from the play *Twelfth Night* by Shakespeare (produced Paris, 1961). Included in *Trois comédies*, 1952.

Le Loup (ballet scenario), with Georges Neveux. Paris, Ricordi, 1953.

L'Alouette (produced Paris, 1953). Paris, Table Ronde, 1953; as *The Lark* (produced London and New York, 1955), London, Methuen, 1955; New York, Oxford University Press, 1956.

Ornifle; ou, Le Courant d'air (produced Paris, 1955). Paris, Table Ronde, 1956; translated as *Ornifle*, New York, Hill and Wang, 1970; London, Davis Poynter, 1971; as *It's Later Than You Think*, Chicago, Dramatic Publishing Company, 1970.

Il est important d'être aimé, with Claude Vincent, from the play *The Importance of Being Earnest* (produced Paris, 1964). Published in *L'Avant-scène 101*, 1955.

Pauvre Bitos; ou, Le Diner de têtes (produced Paris, 1956). Included in *Pièces grinçantes*, 1956; as *Poor Bitos* (produced London, 1963; New York, 1964), New York, Coward McCann, and London, Methuen, 1964.

Pièces grinçantes (includes *Ardèle*, *La Valse des toréadors*, *Ornifle*, *Pauvre Bitos*). Paris, Table Ronde, 1956.

Five Plays. New York, Hill and Wang, 1958.

L'Hurluberlu; ou, Le Réactionnaire amoreux (produced Paris, 1959). Paris, Table Ronde, 1959; as *The Fighting Cock* (produced New York, 1959; Chichester and London, 1966), New York, Coward McCann, 1960; London, Methuen, 1967.

Becket; ou, L'Honneur de Dieu (produced Paris, 1959). Paris, Table Ronde, 1959; as *Becket; or, The Honor of God* (produced New York, 1960; London, 1961), New York, Coward McCann, 1960; London, Methuen, 1961.

Madame de... (in English; produced London, 1959). London, French, 1959.

La Petite Molière, with Roland Laudenback (produced Paris, 1959). Published in *L'Avant-scène*, 15 December 1959.

Le Songe du critique (produced Paris, 1960). Published in *L'Avant-scène 143*, 1959.

Pièces costumées (includes *L'Alouette, Becket, La Foire d'empoigne*). Paris, Table Ronde, 1960.

La Foire d'empoigne (produced Paris, 1962). Included in *Pièces costumées*, 1960; as *Catch as Catch Can*, in *Seven Plays*, 1967.

Tartuffe, from the play by Molière (produced Paris, 1960). Published in *L'Avant-scène*, 15 May 1961.

La Grotte (produced Paris, 1961). Paris, Table Ronde, 1961; as *The Cavern* (produced London, 1965; Cincinnati, 1967; New York, 1968), New York, Hill and Wang, 1966.

Victor; ou, Les Enfants au pouvoir, from the play by Roger Vitrac (produced Paris, 1962). Published in *L'Avant-scène*, 15 November 1962.

L'Amant complaisant, with Nicole Anouilh, from the play *The Complaisant Lover* by Graham Greene (produced Paris, 1962). Paris, Laffont, 1962.

L'Orchestre (produced Paris, 1962). Paris, Table Ronde, 1970; as *The Orchestra* (produced Buffalo, New York, 1969), in *Seven Plays*, 1967; published separately, London, French, 1975.

Richard III, from the play by Shakespeare (produced Paris, 1964). Paris, Livre de Poche, n.d.

L'Ordalie; ou, La Petite Catherine de Heilbronn, from a story by Heinrich von Kleist (produced Paris, 1966). Published in *L'Avant-scène*, 15 January 1967.

Seven Plays. New York, Hill and Wang, 1967.

Le Boulanger, la boulangère, et le petit mitron (produced Paris, 1968). Paris, Table Ronde, 1969; as *The Baker, The Baker's Wife, and the Baker's Boy* (produced Newcastle upon Tyne, 1972).

Théâtre complet. Paris, Table Ronde, 9 vols., 1968.

Cher Antoine; ou, L'Amour raté (produced Paris, 1969). Paris, Table Ronde, 1969; as *Dear Antoine; or, The Love That Failed* (produced Chichester, 1971; Cambridge, Massachusetts, 1973), London, Methuen, and New York, Hill and Wang, 1971.

Le Théâtre; ou, La Vie comme elle est (produced Paris, 1970(?)).

Ne réveillez pas Madame (produced Paris, 1970). Paris, Table Ronde, 1970.

Les Poissons rouges; ou, Mon Père, ce héros (produced Paris, 1970). Paris, Table Ronde, 1970.

Nouvelles pièces grinçantes (includes *L'Hurluberlu; La Grotte; L'Orchestre; Le Boulanger, la boulangère, et le petit mitron; Les Poissons rouges*). Paris, Table Ronde, 1970.

Tu étais si gentil quand tu étais petit (produced Paris, 1971). Paris, Table Ronde, 1972; as *You Were So Sweet* (produced London, 1974).

Le Directeur de l'Opéra (produced Paris, 1973). Paris, Table Ronde, 1972; as *The Director of the Opera* (produced Chichester, 1973), London, Eyre Methuen, 1973.

Pièces baroques (includes *Cher Antoine, Ne réveillez pas Madame, Le Directeur de l'Opéra*). Paris, Table Ronde, 1974.

L'Arrestation (produced Paris, 1975). Paris, Table Ronde, 1975; as *The Arrest* (produced Bristol, 1974), New York, French, 1978.

Le Scénario (produced Paris, 1976). Paris, Table Ronde, 1976; as *The Scenario* (produced Billingham, County Durham, 1976).

Chers Zoizeaux (produced Paris, 1976). Paris, Table Ronde, 1977.

Pièces secrètes (includes *Tu étais si gentil quand tu étais petit, L'Arrestation, Le Scénario*). Paris, Table Ronde, 1977.

Vive Henri IV. Paris, Table Ronde, 1977.

La Culotte (produced Paris, 1978). Paris, Table Ronde, 1978.

La Belle Vie, suivi de Episode de la vie d'un auteur. Paris, Table Ronde, 1980.

Le Nombril. Paris, Table Ronde, 1981.

Screenplays: *Les Dégourdis de la onzième*, with Jean Aurenche, 1936; *Vous n'avez rien à declarer*, with Jean Aurenche, 1937; *Les Otages*, with Jean Aurenche, 1939; *Cavalcade d'amour*, 1939; *Le Voyageur sans bagage* (Identity Unknown), with Jean Aurenche, 1944; *Monsieur Vincent*, with Jean Bernard Luc, 1947; *Anna Karenina*, with Julien Duvivier and Guy Morgan, 1948; *Pattes blanches*, with Jean Bernard Luc, 1949; *Caroline chérie*, 1951; *Deux sous de violettes*, with Monelle Valentin, 1951; *Le Rideau rouge*, 1952; *Le Chevalier de la nuit*, 1953; *La Mort de belle* (*The Passion of Slow Fire*), 1961; *La Ronde* (*Circle of Love*), 1964; *A Time for Loving*, 1971.

Television Plays: *Le Jeune Homme et le lion*, 1976; *La Belle Vie*, 1979.

Ballet Scenarios: *Les Demoiselles de la nuit*, 1948; *Le Loup*, with Georges Neveux, 1953.

Other

Michel-Marie Poulain, with Pierre Imbourg and André Warnod. Paris, Braun, 1953.
Fables. Paris, Table Ronde, 1962.

*

Bibliography: *Anouilh: An Annotated Bibliography* by Kathleen White, Metuchen, New Jersey, Scarecrow Press, 1973.

Critical Studies: *Anouilh* by Marguerite Archer, New York, Columbia University Press, 1951; *Anouilh, Poet of Pierrot and Pantaloon* by Edward O. Marsh, London, W.H. Allen, and New York, British Book Centre, 1953; *The World of Anouilh* by Leonard C. Pronko, Berkeley, University of California Press, 1961; *Anouilh: A Study in Theatrics* by John Harvey, New Haven, Connecticut, Yale University Press, 1964; *Anouilh* by Philip Thody, Edinburgh, Oliver and Boyd, 1968; *Anouilh* by Alba della Fazia, New York, Twayne, 1969; *Anouilh* by Lewis W. Falb, New York, Ungar, 1977; *The Theatre of Anouilh* by H.G. McIntyre, London, Harrap, and New York, Barnes and Noble, 1981; *Anouilh: Antigone* by W.D. Howarth, London, Arnold, 1983.

*　　*　　*

Jean Anouilh's long career as a highly successful playwright began with naturalistic drama with *Traveller Without Luggage*, continued in a more fanciful vein with *Thieves' Carnival*, and reached its first peak with *Antigone*. Like Jean Giraudoux in *La Guerre de Troie n'aura pas lieu*, or Jean-Paul Sartre with *The Flies*, Anouilh used Greek myth to give allegorical expression to contemporary political and philosophical concerns, and the confrontation between the idealistic Antigone and the world-weary, realistic Creon was widely interpreted as reflecting the debates between resistance and collaboration in German-occupied France. The play also seemed to critics and audiences at the time to express both the pessimism and the yearning for unattainable absolutes which characterised mid-20th-century existentialism, and the romantic melancholy of *Eurydice* echoed the same feeling of total despair which understandably afflicted audiences during and immediately after the Second World War. Like his many other plays, however, these explorations of some of Anouilh's own obsessions also owed their success to his very real professionalism as a man of the theatre, and he is unique among French writers of the 1940's and 1950's in having concerned himself solely with the drama and eschewed both the novel and the philosophical essay as potential vehicles for his views. A number of his plays, *The Rehearsal*, or *Colombe*, like the much later *Dear Antoine* and *The Director of the Opera*, take place within the world of the theatre, and exploit the popular device of the play within a play. In commercial terms, Anouilh's career was at its height in the late 1940's and early 1950's, when he had four or five plays running simultaneously in Paris and London, but from an intellectual and literary point of view he did not seriously renew himself until the historical *Pièces Costumées* of *The Lark* and *Becket; or, The Honour of God*, and, more especially, his one conscious and deliberate incursion into contemporary French politics with *Poor Bitos*. Anouilh also differed from the majority of mid-20th-century French writers in being conservative rather than revolutionary in his political views, and his analysis and denunciation of political extremes in *Poor Bitos*, and in *The Fighting Cock* and *Catch as Catch Can*, produced some of his most satisfying work.

He had a great admiration for Molière, and brilliantly transferred the famous scene of the Sonnet from *Le Misanthrope* into a satire of *avant-garde* drama in *The Fighting Cock*. But the mockery remained good-humoured, and Anouilh did in fact come out publicly in support of Ionesco's early plays at a time when they were still highly controversial. His later plays seemed to the admirers of his early work to be somewhat mannered and self-indulgent, and it is probable that he will be best remembered both for his historical plays, especially his version of the Joan of Arc legend in *The Lark*, and for his lighter fantasies such as *Ring round the Moon*. He was very much a man of the theatre, taking a continued, professional interest in the production of all his plays, and insisting on the duty of the playwright to entertain his public in order to "stop them thinking about death." Quite how this was supposed to happen when the action of many of his plays ended with the death of the principal character was never made wholly clear, but Anouilh was more interested in the effectiveness of dramatic paradoxes than in normal logic. He was, essentially, an actor's playwright, one whose dialogues never needed the slightest change in order to be spoken effectively on stage, and he also took the professional's view that a good performance in the theatre required the audience to have rehearsed its part conscientiously as well.

—Philip Thody

ARRABAL (Terán), Fernando. Born in Melilla, Spanish Morocco, 11 August 1932. Educated at a school in Getafe; a military academy; Escuela Teórico-Práctica de la Industria del Papel, Valencia; studied law at the University of Madrid. Married Luce Moreau in 1958; one daughter and one son. Writer, and theatre and film director; moved to France in 1955; jailed for several months in 1967 during a trip to Spain; taught at the University of California, Santa Cruz, 1971. Editor, *Le Théâtre*, 1968. Recipient: Ford grant, for travel to the USA, 1959; Lugné-Poë theatre prize, 1966; Society of Authors prize, 1966; Grand Prix du Théâtre, 1967; Nadal Prize, 1983. Address: 22 rue Jouffroy, 75017 Paris, France.

PUBLICATIONS

Plays

Théâtre I (includes *Oraison, Les Deux Bourreaux, Fando et Lis, Le Cimetière des voitures*). Paris, Julliard, 1958.
Oraison, in *Théâtre I*. 1958; as *Orison* (produced London, 1961; Lock Haven, Pennsylvania, 1967; New York, 1968), in *Four Plays*, 1962.

Les Deux Bourreaux, in *Théâtre I*. 1958; as *The Two Executioners* (produced London, 1966; New York, 1967), with *The Automobile Graveyard*, 1960; in *Four Plays*, 1962.
Fando et Lis (produced Paris, 1961). Included in *Théâtre I*, 1958; as *Fando and Lis* (produced London, 1961; New York, 1967), in *Four Plays*, 1962.
Le Cimetière des voitures (produced Dijon, 1966; Paris, 1967). Included in *Théâtre I*, 1958; as *The Automobile Graveyard* (produced New York, 1961), with *The Two Executioners*, 1960; as *The Car Cemetery* (produced London, 1969), in *Four Plays*, 1962.
Le Tricycle (produced Madrid, 1958). Included in *Théâtre II*, 1961; as *The Tricycle* (produced New York, 1970), in *Plays*, 1967; in *Guernica and Other Plays*, 1969.
Pique-nique en campagne (produced 1959). Included in *Théâtre II*, 1961; as *Picnic on the Battlefield* (produced London, 1964; New York, 1967), in *Plays*, 1967; in *Guernica and Other Plays*, 1969.
The Automobile Graveyard, and The Two Executioners. New York, Grove Press, 1960.
Dieu tenté par les mathématiques (as *Theatrical Orchestrations*, produced Paris, 1960). Included in *Théâtre VIII*, 1970.
Théâtre II (includes *Guernica*, *Le Labyrinthe*, *Le Tricycle*, *Pique-nique en campagne*, *La Bicyclette du condamné*). Paris, Julliard, 1961.
Guernica, in *Théâtre II*. 1961; translated as *Guernica* (produced New York, 1969), in *Plays*, 1967; in *Guernica and Other Plays*, 1969.
Le Labyrinthe (produced Paris, 1967). Included in *Théâtre II*, 1961; as *The Labyrinth* (produced London and Waltham, Massachusetts, 1968), in *Plays*, 1967; in *Guernica and Other Plays*, 1969.
La Bicyclette du condamné, in *Théâtre II*. 1961; as *The Condemned Man's Bicycle* (produced London, 1968), in *Plays*, 1967.
Four Plays (includes *Orison*, *The Two Executioners*, *Fando and Lis*, *The Car Cemetery*). London, Calder, 1962.
La Communion solennelle (produced Paris, 1964). Included in *Théâtre V*, 1967; as *The Solemn Communion* (produced Lock Haven, Pennsylvania, 1967; London, 1970), in *The Architect and the Emperor of Assyria*, 1970.
Le Couronnement (produced Paris, 1965). Included in *Théâtre III*, 1965; revised version, as *Le Lai de Barabbas*, in *Théâtre IV*, 1969.
Théâtre III: Théâtre panique (includes *Le Couronnement*, *Le Grand Cérémonial*, *Concert dans un oeuf*, *Cérémonie pour un noir assassiné*). Paris, Julliard, 1965.
Cérémonie pour un noir assassiné, in *Théâtre III*. 1965; as *Ceremony for a Murdered Black* (produced New York, 1972; London, 1973).
Strip-tease de la jalousie (produced Paris, 1965). Included in *Théâtre V*, 1967; as *Striptease of Jealousy*, in *Drama Review*, Fall 1968.
La Princesse (produced Paris, 1966).
Les Amours impossibles (produced Paris, 1966). Included in *Théâtre V*, 1967; as *Impossible Loves* (produced London, 1971), in *Drama Review*, Fall 1968.
Plays (includes *Guernica*, *The Labyrinth*, *The Tricycle*, *Picnic on the Battlefield*, *The Condemned Man's Bicycle*). London, Calder and Boyars, 1967.
L'Architecte et l'empereur d'Assyrie (produced Paris, 1967). Included in *Théâtre V*, 1967; as *The Architect and the Emperor of Assyria* (produced London, 1967; San Francisco, 1968), New York, Grove Press, 1969; London, Calder and Boyars, 1970.
Théâtre V (includes *Théâtre panique—La Communion solennelle*, *Les Amours impossibles*, *Une Chèvre sur un nuage*, *La Jeunesse illustrée*, *Dieu est-il devenu fou?*, *Strip-tease de la jalousie*, *Les Quatres Cubes*—and *L'Architecte et l'empereur d'Assyrie*). Paris, Bourgois, 1967.
Théâtre IV (includes *La Lai de Barabbas*, *Concert dans un oeuf*). Paris, Bourgois, 1969.
Revolution-Imagination (produced Brussels, 1969).
Le Jardin des délices (produced Paris, 1969). Included in *Théâtre VI*, 1969; as *Garden of Delights*, New York, Grove Press, 1974.

Théâtre VI (includes *Le Jardin des délices, Bestialité érotique, Une Tortue nommée Dostoievsky*). Paris, Bourgois, 1969.

Et ils passerent des menottes aux fleurs (produced Paris, 1969). Included in *Théâtre VII*, 1969; as *And They Put Handcuffs on the Flowers* (produced New York, 1971; London, 1973), New York, Grove Press, 1973.

L'Aurore rouge et noire (produced Brussels, 1969). Included in *Théâtre VII*, 1969; as *Dawn: Red and Black* (produced New York, 1971); section entitled *Groupuscule of My Heart* published in *Drama Review*, Summer 1969.

Théâtre VII: Théâtre de guerilla (includes *Et ils passerent des menottes aux fleurs, L'Aurore rouge et noire*). Paris, Bourgois, 1969.

Théâtre 1969 (includes *La Contestation* and *Le Grand Guignol*). Paris, Bourgois, 2 vols., 1969.

Guernica and Other Plays (includes *The Labyrinth, The Tricycle, Picnic on the Battlefield*). New York, Grove Press, 1969.

Théâtre VIII: Deux opéras paniques (includes *Ars Amandi, Dieu tenté par les mathématiques*). Paris, Bourgois, 1970.

Ars Amandi, in *Théâtre VIII*. 1970; translated as *Ars Amandi*, London, Calder, 1983.

Théâtre 1970: Théâtre en marge. Paris, Bourgois, 1970.

The Architect and the Emperor of Assyria, The Grand Ceremonial, The Solemn Communion. London, Calder and Boyars, 1970.

Viva la muerte (screenplay), with *Baal Babylone*. Paris, Bourgois, 1971.

Théâtre 1971: Les Monstres. Paris, Bourgois, 1971.

Théâtre IX (includes *Le Ciel et la merde, La Grande Revue du XXe siècle*). Paris, Bourgois, 1972.

Bella Ciao: La Guerre de mille ans (produced Paris, 1972). Paris, Bourgois, 1972.

La Marche royale (produced Paris, 1973). Included in *Théâtre XI*, 1976.

Sur la fil; ou, La Ballade du train fantôme (produced Paris, 1974). Paris, Bourgois, 1974.

Théâtre X (includes *La Guerre du mille ans; Sur le fil, ou, La Ballade du train fantôme; Jeunes barbares d'aujourd'hui*). Paris, Bourgois, 1975.

La Gloire en images, music by Graziano Mandozzi (produced Paris, 1976). Included in *Théâtre XI*, 1976.

Théâtre XI: La Tour de Babel (includes *La Marche royale, Une Orange sur le Mont de Vénus, La Gloire en images*). Paris, Bourgois, 1976.

Le Ciel et la merde II (produced Paris, 1976). Included in *Théâtre XIII*, 1981.

Vole-moi un petit milliard (produced Paris, 1977). Included in *Théâtre XII*, 1978.

Théâtre XII: Théâtre bouffe (includes *Vole-moi un petit milliard; La Pastaga des loufs, ou, Ouverture orang-outan; Punk et punk et Colégram*). Paris, Bourgois, 1978.

Le Roi de Sodome (produced Paris, 1979). Included in *Théâtre XIII*, 1981.

Baal Babylone, from his own novel (produced Paris, 1980).

Théâtre XIII (includes *Mon doux royaume saccagé, Le Roi de Sodome, Le Ciel et la merde II*). Paris, Bourgois, 1981.

L'Extravagante Réussite de Jésus-Christ, Karl Marx, et William Shakespeare, in *Théâtre XIV*. 1982; as *The Extravagant Triumph of Jesus Christ, Karl Marx, and William Shakespeare* (produced New York, 1981).

Théâtre XIV (includes *L'Extravagante Réussite de Jésus-Christ, Karl Marx, et William Shakespeare; Lève-toi et rêve*). Paris, Bourgois, 1982.

Screenplays: *Viva la muerte*, 1971; *The Tricycle*; *J'irai comme un cheval fou*, 1973; *Guernica*, 1975; *Odyssey of the Pacific*, 1982.

Fiction

> *Baal Babylone.* Paris, Julliard, 1959; translated as *Baal Babylon*, New York, Grove Press, 1961.
> *L'Enterrement de la sardine.* Paris, Julliard, 1961; as *The Burial of the Sardine*, London, Calder and Boyars, 1965; New York, Riverrun Press, 1980.
> *Arrabal celebrando la ceremonia de la confusion.* Madrid, Alfaguara, 1966; as *Fêtes et rites de la confusion*, Paris, Le Terrain Vague, 1967.
> *La torre herida por el rayo.* Barcelona, Destino, 1983; as *La Tour prends garde*, Paris, Grasset, 1983.

Verse

> *La Pierre de la folie.* Paris, Julliard, 1963.
> *Le New York d'Arrabal.* Paris, Balland, 1973.

Other

> *Lettre au General Franco.* Paris, Bourgois, 1972.
> *Sur Fischer: Initiation aux échecs.* Monaco, Editions du Rocher, 1973.
> *Carta a los militantes comunistas españoles.* Barcelona, Actuales, 1978.
> *Les Échecs féeriques et libertaires: Chronique de l'express.* Monaco, Editions du Rocher, 1980.
> *Lettre à Fidel Castro.* Paris, Bourgois, 1984.

*

Bibliography: *Bibliographie d'Arrabal* by Joan P. Berenguer, Grenoble, Presses Universitaires de Grenoble, 1978.

Critical Studies: *Arrabal* by Bernard Gille, Paris, Seghers, 1970; *Arrabal* by Peter L. Podol, Boston, Twayne, 1978; *The Theatre of Arrabal: A Garden of Earthly Delights* by Thomas John Donahue, New York, New York University Press, 1980; *The Festive Play of Arrabal* by Luis Oscar Arata, Lexington, University Press of Kentucky, 1982.

*   *   *

Once considered an offshoot of the theater of the absurd of the 1950's the theater of Fernando Arrabal now occupies a niche of its own. In his earliest plays Arrabal creates a type of character whose beguiling innocence places the world of war, torture, love, and murder in a surreal setting. In *Fando and Lis*, the child-like characters wander about looking for Tar, a lost paradise. The paralysed Lis is carried in a child's wagon by her lover, Fando. Fando and Lis engage in sado-masochistic games that seem at first innocent but that eventually lead to Lis's violent death. *Automobile Graveyard*, Arrabal's first full-length play, is a naive representation of Christ's Passion and death. Emmanou (for Emmanuel), pursued by the police for murder, plays his trumpet nightly for a group of poor wretches who live in an automobile graveyard. He is betrayed with a kiss by a friend and is stretched out on a bicycle frame in a modern crucifixion. In this play Arrabal exploits the basic themes of his canon: the master-slave relationship, sado-masochism, moral ambiguity, and erotic love. Adding to the theatricality of the work, his adult-children speak a colorful, surreal poetry.

Of his Panic Theater Arrabal says: "I dream of a theater in which humor and poetry, panic and love are united...like the humanoid dreams that haunt the nights of an IBM machine." In the masterful *The Architect and the Emperor of Assyria*, the sole survivor of an airplane accident encounters a savage on a deserted island. The self-styled Emperor of Assyria teaches the savage the sum of his knowledge while the "architect" maintains his intimate rapport with nature that permits him to control the sun and the moon. Playing a series of roles, the two recreate scenes from the Emperor's past in the civilized world. When the Emperor finally confesses to the murder of his mother, he is tried by the architect-judge, condemned to die, and executed by a hammer-blow to the head. Upon the Emperor's request, the architect eats his flesh and is thereby transformed into the Emperor. With a terrible crash and the entrance of another representative of civilization the action ends as it began. The sheer theatricality of the piece, the multiple transformations of the characters, the ritual of confession and expiation, and the cannibalistic communion represent a critique of our civilization and a surreal celebration of man's imaginative genius.

In his Guerilla Theater, Arrabal mixes "panic" and politics. In *And They Put Handcuffs on the Flowers*, Arrabal shows us some of the horrors of life in a Spanish prison. Using the techniques he had perfected in the Panic Theater, Arrabal creates stunning theatrical images that reflect the shattering of the lives of young men whose only error was to crave freedom. The seemingly disparate sequences take form around the last days of Tosan, a political prisoner who is condemned to die. Despite his wife's desperate efforts to save him, Tosan is garrotted. The play ends with a ritual washing of the characters in his blood and urine. Tosan, like many of Arrabal's heroes, becomes a Christ-figure, not just a mere victim of ideology.

During the 1970's, Arrabal's blend of art and polemics served him with uneven results. In a satiric stance, he acerbically attacks all the ills of contemporary society: from the influence of the press, sports, and television in the musical revue *Bella Ciao* to the "panicky" themes of oppression with a dash of Lewis Carroll in *Jeunes barbares d'aujourd'hui*. In contrast *Sur la fil* provides a haunting and nostalgic view of an exiled Spaniard and *La Tour de Babel* deals with Spain's present order and past glory. In the three plays placed under the title *Théâtre bouffe*, Arrabal uses the traditional techniques of fast-moving plot, mistaken identity and stereotypical but comic characters to create some surreal effects while treating topics such as women's liberation, DNA research, and Eurocommunism. More recently, *Inquisition* and *The Extravagant Triumph of Jesus Christ, Karl Marx, and William Shakespeare* present a potpourri of provocative ideas and occasional glimpses of Arrabal's frightening theatricality.

Relying primarily on a rich repertoire of personal dreams and fantasies, Arrabal creates explosive theatrical images that breathe new life into the theater, but his excessive playfulness and diffuse structure sometimes mitigate his statements on issues such as human freedom, sexuality, and nuclear warfare.

—Thomas J. Donahue

<hr>

BASSANI, Giorgio. Italian. Born in Bologna, 4 April 1916. Educated at the University of Bologna. Married Valeria Sinigallia in 1943; one son and one daughter. Lived in Ferrara until 1943; after World War II worked as scriptwriter and film dubbing editor; Editor, Feltrinelli publishers, Milan, 1958-64; Instructor in history of the theatre, Accademia Nazionale d'Arte Drammatica, Rome, 1957-68; Vice President, Radio Televisione Italiana, Rome, 1964-65. Editor, *Botteghe Oscure*, Rome, 1948-60; Co-Editor *Paragone*, Milan, 1953-55. President, Italia Nostra, from 1966. Recipient: Veillon Prize, 1956; Strega Prize, 1956; Viareggio Prize, 1962; Campiello Prize, 1969; Sachs Prize, 1969. Address: c/o Mondadori, CP 1772, 20100 Milan, Italy.

Fiction

Una città di pianura (as Giacomo Marchi).   Milan, Lucini, 1940.
La passeggiata prima di cena.   Florence, Sansoni, 1953.
Gli ultimi anni di Clelia Trotti.   Pisa, Nistri Lischi, 1955.
Cinque storie ferraresi.   Turin, Einaudi, 1956; as *A Prospect of Ferrara*, London, Faber,
    1962; as *Five Stories of Ferrara*, New York, Harcourt Brace, 1971.
Gli occhiali d'oro.   Turin, Einaudi, 1958; as *The Gold-Rimmed Spectacles*, New York,
    Atheneum, and London, Faber, 1960.
Una notte del '43.   Turin, Einaudi, 1960.
Il giardino dei Finzi-Contini.   Turin, Einaudi, 1962; as *The Garden of the Finzi-Continis*,
    New York, Atheneum, and London, Faber, 1965.
Dietro la porta.   Turin, Einaudi, 1964; as *Behind the Door*, New York, Harcourt Brace,
    1972; London, Weidenfeld and Nicolson, 1973.
Due novelle.   Venice, Stamperia di Venezia, 1965.
L'airone.   Milan, Mondadori, 1968; as *The Heron*, New York, Harcourt Brace, and
    London, Weidenfeld and Nicolson, 1970.
L'odore del fieno.   Milan, Mondadori, 1972; as *The Smell of Hay* (with *The Gold-
    Rimmed Spectacles*), New York, Harcourt Brace, and London, Weidenfeld and Nic-
    olson, 1975.
Il romanzo di Ferrara (collection).   Milan, Mondadori, 1974; revised edition, 1980.

Play

Screenplay: *The Stranger's Hands*, with Guy Elmes and Graham Greene, 1954.

Verse

Storie dei poveri amanti e altri versi.   Rome, Astrolabio, 1946.
Te lucis ante.   Rome, Ubaldini, 1947.
Un'altra libertà.   Milan, Mondadori, 1951.
L'alba ai vetri: Poesie 1942-1950.   Turin, Einaudi, 1963.
Epitaffio.   Milan, Mondadori, 1974.
In gran segreto.   Milan, Mondadori, 1978.

Other

Le parole preparate e altri scritti di letteratura.   Turin, Einaudi, 1966.
Aldila dal cuore.   Verona, Mondadori, 1984.

*

Critical Study: *Prisoners of Hope: The Silver Age of Italian Jews 1924-1974* by H. Stuart
Hughes, Cambridge, Massachusetts, Harvard University Press, 1983.

*   *   *

Although he has also written poetry and essays and held important editorial posts, Giorgio
Bassani is best known both in Italy and abroad (where he has been widely translated) for his
narrative fiction. The stories collected in 1956 as *Five Stories of Ferrara* are his earliest writing

of this sort. Most of them were composed in the decade immediately following WW II, but all of them have been thoroughly, even obsessively, reworked for republication since. The focus in each of these stories is on the relationship of a central character with some larger social entity—the family, the Ferrarese Jewish community (whose unofficial modern chronicler Bassani has in many ways become), or Ferrara itself, especially during the Fascist era. This partly imaginary, partly historical city in the Po valley during the 1920's and 1930's is the setting for virtually all of Bassani's fiction. It is also, in some ways, the most important character in the ongoing "novel" or "romance" of Ferrara Bassani has been slowly and meticulously creating throughout his career. Recent collections of these short stories bear the subtitle, "inside the walls," a reference not only to their physical setting, but also to the social and psychological barriers which separate Bassani's characters from one another as well as protect them from a world usually, but not always, beyond their ken. Although most of the action in these stories occurs before WW II, the narrator who recounts them does so from a perspective after the War, Civil War, and Holocaust. This retrospective view makes possible their characteristically elegiac tone which is designed to awaken pity rather than condemnation of the often petty cruelties and banal disappointments of a time "before" which has now disappeared forever.

This same spatial-historical setting and temporal perspective are present also in *The Gold-Rimmed Spectacles*, a longer "Ferrarese story" in which Bassani introduces for the first time the unnamed but clearly autobiographical narrator whose fall from innocence into a world of infectious but enigmatic Evil will be traced in two other novels of the early '60's—*The Garden of the Finzi-Continis* and *Behind the Door*. In all three of these novels the adolescent protagonist is struggling to establish his identity in a world outside the protective circle of his family. Here he encounters increasingly complex social configurations of inclusion and exclusion which have the power not only to wound emotionally, but also to destroy physically, as in the case of both the homosexual Doctor Fadigati and the 183 Ferrarese Jews deported to Buchenwald from Ferrara. In *The Garden of the Finzi-Continis*, set at the time of the anti-Semitic proclamations, the narrator makes the not uncommon but nonetheless extremely painful error of mistaking expressions of fraternal solidarity for signs of the unqualified love he is desperately seeking—a personal tragedy which is given special poignancy by the ominous political storm clouds gathering on the horizon. The *cupio dissolvi* which hangs over these pages becomes even more explicit in *The Heron*, the only one of Bassani's works set entirely in the postwar period, and a chronicle of the last day in the life of a survivor of the war and Holocaust who is nonetheless unable to cope with the anguish of his existential condition and so commits suicide.

Bleak as these themes of loneliness, exclusion, and death may seem, the elegance and moral seriousness of Bassani's writings give the actions they recount considerable dignity in a memorialization meant to redeem these characters and their tragic vicissitudes from the indifference of time and history.

—Charles Klopp

BEAUVOIR, Simone (Lucie Ernestine Marie) de. French. Born in Paris, 9 January 1908. Educated at Institut Normal Catholique Adeline-Désir, Paris, 1913-25; Institut Sainte-Marie, Neuilly-sur-Seine; École Normale Supérieure, Paris, agrégation in philosophy 1929. Began lifelong relationship with the writer Jean-Paul Sartre, 1929. Part-time teacher, Lycée

Victor Duruy, Paris, 1929-31; philosophy teacher, Lycée Montgrand, Marseilles, 1931-32, Lycée Jeanne d'Arc, Rouen, 1932-36, Lycée Molière, Paris, 1936-39, and Lycée Camille-Sée and Lycée Henri IV, both Paris, 1939-43. Founding Editor, with Sartre, *Les Temps Modernes*, Paris, from 1945. Member of the Consultative Committee, Bibliothèque Nationale, 1969; President, Choisir, 1972. Since 1974, President, Ligue des Droits des Femmes. Recipient: Goncourt Prize, 1954; Jerusalem Prize, 1975; Austrian State Prize for European Literature, 1978. LL.D.: Cambridge University. Address: 11 bis rue Schoelcher, 75014 Paris, France.

PUBLICATIONS

Fiction

L'Invitée. Paris, Gallimard, 1943; as *She Came to Stay*, London, Secker and Warburg, 1949; Cleveland, World, 1954.

Le Sang des autres. Paris, Gallimard, 1945; edited by John F. Davis, London, Methuen, 1973; as *The Blood of Others*, London, Secker and Warburg, and New York, Knopf, 1948.

Tous les hommes sont mortels. Paris, Gallimard, 1946; as *All Men Are Mortal*, Cleveland, World, 1956.

Les Mandarins. Paris, Gallimard, 1954; as *The Mandarins*, Cleveland, World, 1956; London, Collins, 1957.

Les Belles Images. Paris, Gallimard, 1966; translated as *Les Belles Images*, New York, Putnam, 1968; London, Collins, 1969.

La Femme rompue (includes *L'Âge de discrétion* and *Monologue*). Paris, Gallimard, 1968; as *The Woman Destroyed* (includes *The Age of Discretion* and *The Monologue*), London, Collins, and New York, Putnam, 1969.

Quand prime le spirituel. Paris, Gallimard, 1979; as *When Things of the Spirit Come First: Five Early Tales*, London, Deutsch-Weidenfeld and Nicolson, 1981; New York, Pantheon, 1982.

Play

Les Bouches inutiles (produced Paris, 1945). Paris, Gallimard, 1945.

Other

Pyrrhus et Cinéas. Paris, Gallimard, 1944.

Pour une morale de l'ambiguïté. Paris, Gallimard, 1947; as *The Ethics of Ambiguity*, New York, Philosophical Library, 1948.

L'Amérique au jour le jour. Paris, Morihien, 1948; as *America Day by Day*, London, Duckworth, 1952; New York, Grove Press, 1953.

L'Existentialisme et la sagesse des nations. Paris, Nagel, 1948.

Le Deuxième Sexe: Les Faits et les mythes and *L'Expérience vécue.* Paris, Gallimard, 2 vols., 1949; as *The Second Sex*, London, Cape, and New York, Knopf, 1953; vol. 1 as *A History of Sex*, London, New English Library, 1961, and as *Nature of the Second Sex*, 1963.

Must We Burn de Sade? London, Nevill, 1953; in *The Marquis de Sade*, edited by Paul Dinnage, New York, Grove Press, 1953.

Privilèges (includes *Faut-il brûler Sade?*). Paris, Gallimard, 1955.

La Longue Marche: Essai sur la Chine. Paris, Gallimard, 1957; as *The Long March*, London, Deutsch-Weidenfeld and Nicolson, and Cleveland, World, 1958.

Mémoires d'une jeune fille rangée. Paris, Gallimard, 1958; as *Memoirs of a Dutiful Daughter*, London, Deutsch-Weidenfeld and Nicolson, and Cleveland, World, 1959.
Brigitte Bardot and the Lolita Syndrome. London, Deutsch-Weidenfeld and Nicolson, and New York, Reynal, 1960.
La Force de l'âge. Paris, Gallimard, 1960; as *The Prime of Life*, London, Deutsch-Weidenfeld and Nicolson, and Cleveland, World, 1962.
Djamila Boupacha, with Gisèle Halimi. Paris, Gallimard, 1962; translated as *Djamila Boupacha*, London, Deutsch-Weidenfeld and Nicolson, and New York, Macmillan, 1962.
La Force des choses. Paris, Gallimard, 1963; as *Force of Circumstance*, London, Deutsch-Weidenfeld and Nicolson, and New York, Putnam, 1965.
Une Mort très douce. Paris, Gallimard, 1964; as *A Very Easy Death*, London, Deutsch-Weidenfeld and Nicolson, and New York, Putnam, 1966.
La Vieillesse. Paris, Gallimard, 1970; as *Old Age*, London, Deutsch-Weidenfeld and Nicolson, 1972; as *The Coming of Age*, New York, Putnam, 1972.
Toute compte fait. Paris, Gallimard, 1972; as *All Said and Done*, London, Deutsch-Weidenfeld and Nicolson, and New York, Putnam, 1974.
La Cérémonie des adieux. Paris, Gallimard, 1981.

*

Bibliography: *Les Écrits de Simone de Beauvoir* by Claude Francis and Fernande Gontier, Paris, Gallimard, 1980.

Critical Studies: *de Beauvoir: Encounters with Death* by Elaine Marks, New Brunswick, New Jersey, Rutgers University Press, 1973; *de Beauvoir* by Robert D. Cottrell, New York, Ungar, 1975; *de Beauvoir on Women* by Jean Leighton, Rutherford, New Jersey, Fairleigh Dickinson University Press, 1976; *Hearts and Minds: The Common Journey of de Beauvoir and Jean-Paul Sartre* by Axel Madsen, New York, Morrow, 1977; *de Beauvoir* by Konrad Bieber, Boston, Twayne, 1979; *de Beauvoir and the Limits of Commitment* by Anne Whitmarsh, Cambridge, University Press, 1981.

*   *   *

The name of Simone de Beauvoir is inevitably linked with that of Jean-Paul Sartre, and this for two reasons. From the mid-1930's until his death in 1979, she was his mistress, constant companion, and closest personal friend, so that her five-volume autobiography (see below) is the fullest account ever likely to be published of what he was like as a man. Her ideas, especially on woman's liberation as expressed in *The Second Sex*, reflect Sartre's vision of human beings as essentially free but nevertheless forced into certain social roles by the opinion which other people have of them. Thus de Beauvoir insisted that "You're not born a woman, you become one," and argued that the so-called biologically imprinted "natural feminine characteristics" were solely the result of centuries of women being required by the physically dominant male sex to play the kind of part which men found useful. Like Simone de Beauvoir's other semi-sociological, philosophical essays, *The Coming of Age*, *The Second Sex* is a long book, but one which became a best-seller in several countries and can be seen as the starting point for the Women's Movement in American and British society from the 1960's onwards. Again like Sartre, de Beauvoir was strongly left-wing in her political views, siding with the Soviet Union during the Cold War of the 1940's and 1950's (American soldiers in France as a result of the NATO alliance reminded her, she said, of the German troops who occupied France between 1940 and 1944), supporting the Arab *Front de Libération Nationale* during the Algerian war of 1954-1962, writing a most enthusiastic book about the Communist revolution in China, *The Long March*, and making well-publicised visits to Cuba and other newly liberated countries which adopted a strong anti-colonialist stance.

Although from a purely literary point of view her novels and plays never achieved the same standard as those of Sartre, her semi-autobiographical novel *The Mandarins*, won the Prix Goncourt and gives an intriguing account of the political and sexual behaviour of French left-wing intellectuals in the 1940's and early 1950's. Her two most readable books are a collection of short stories illustrating the unhappiness which women bring upon themselves by accepting the secondary, passive role which men force upon them—*The Woman Destroyed*—and a most moving description in *A Very Easy Death* of how her mother was made to suffer when she was biologically ready to die but was kept alive by the medical profession. In thus addressing herself constantly to the social and political issues of the day, Simone de Beauvoir was also putting into practice Sartre's firmly held view that writers should take sides, and her defence of a woman's right to an abortion can also be seen as an illustration of how existentialist ethics work in a specific instance. Once society leaves women free to decide whether to interrupt a pregnancy or not—and the legalisation of abortion in France in 1974 followed a vigorous campaign by Simone de Beauvoir and her supporters—then her decision brings into being a set of moral values for which she alone is responsible. If she decides to have the child, she asserts the absolute primacy of the right of biological life to continue. If she decides to interrupt the pregnancy, she is saying that her health and happiness, or those of her husband and their children, or the demands of her career, or the danger of world over-population, are more important. But she, and she alone, can decide, and Simone de Beauvoir unhesitatingly endorsed Sartre's view that there is no God whose teachings or commandments can serve as a guide to human beings as to how they ought to behave.

Like other French women intellectuals—Madame de Stael, George Sand—Simone de Beauvoir often strikes the prejudiced male observer as writing books that are rather too long, as lacking both humour and charity, in being endowed with a self-confidence and a seriousness of purpose that are ultimately self-defeating in persuading people to accept her views. There is also a frequently observed paradox in the fact that the most famous apostle for women's independence should have derived her views from a man, though it should be observed that Sartre himself had the highest regard for her intellect and discussed all his own books with her before they were published. The possibility cannot therefore be excluded that she influenced him, and the sales of her books also support the view that as many if not more people were directly influenced by her writings as by his. The more conventional supporters of traditional values cannot but regret the decision, discussed in detail in her autobiography, not to have children because they would distract her from her career as a writer. For it would indeed have been intriguing to see whether her and Sartre's daughters and sons reacted against their parent's views by becoming, respectively, Catholic nuns or successful businessmen, or whether they followed their parents' example by becoming members of an extreme, left-wing, revolutionary political party. Like Sartre, she also considered it to be more important to influence people's conduct than to create perfectly finished works of art, and in so far as there are, nowadays, more women than ever prepared to assert themselves as women and proclaim their values against those of the male world, this aim has undoubtedly been achieved. In reply to the argument that this could well have happened anyway as a result of the general development of society, Simone de Beauvoir would undoubtedly reveal how close the similarities are between Existentialism and Protestantism by saying that it is always the duty of the individual to assert the values in which she or he believes, whether these values are destined to triumph or to disappear.

—Philip Thody

BENET, Juan. Spanish. Born in Madrid, 7 October 1927. Educated as civil engineer, degree 1954. Married Nuria Jordane (died, 1974); three sons and one daughter. Sub-Director, CMZ, Madrid, since 1956, as dam and tunnel builder. Tinker Larocque Professor, Columbia University, New York, 1982. Recipient: Biblioteca Breve prize, 1969. Address: Pisuerga 7, Madrid 2, Spain.

PUBLICATIONS

Fiction

Nunca llegarás a nada. Madrid, Tebas, 1961.
Volverás a Región. Barcelona, Destino, 1968; as *Return to Region*, New York, Columbia University Press, 1984.
Una meditación. Barcelona, Seix Barral, 1969.
Un viaje de invierno. Barcelona, La Gaya Ciencia, 1972.
Cinco narraciones y dos fábulas. Barcelona, La Gaya Ciencia, 1972.
Sub-rosa. Barcelona, La Gaya Ciencia, 1973.
La otra casa de Mazón. Barcelona, Seix Barral, 1973.
En el estado. Madrid, Alfaguara, 1977.
Cuentos completos. Madrid, Alianza, 1977.
Saúl ante Samuel. Barcelona, La Gaya Ciencia, 1980.
El aire de un crimen. Barcelona, Planeta, 1980.
Trece fábulas y media. Madrid, Alfaguara, 1981.
Una tumba y otros cuentos. Madrid, Taurus, 1982.
Herrumbrosas lanzas. Madrid, Alfaguara, 1983.

Plays

Teatro (includes *Anastas; o, El origen de la constitución* and *Agonía confutans, un caso de consciencia*). Madrid, Siglo Veintiuno, 1970.

Other

La inspiración y el estilo. Madrid, Revista de Occidente, 1966.
Puerta de tierra. Barcelona, Seix Barral, 1970.
El ángel del señor abandona a Tobías. Barcelona, La Gaya Ciencia, 1976.
En ciernes. Madrid, Taurus, 1976.
Que fue la guerra civil. Barcelona, La Gaya Ciencia, 1976.
Del pozo y del Numa. Barcelona, La Gaya Ciencia, 1978.
La moviola de Eurípides. Madrid, Taurus, 1982.

*

Critical Studies: *The Novelistic World of Benet* by David K. Herzberger, Bloomington, Indiana, American Hispanist, 1976; *Critical Approaches to the Writings of Benet* edited by Robert Manteiga, David K. Herzberger, and Malcolm A. Compitello, Hanover, New Hampshire, University Press of New England, 1983.

*   *   *

A civil engineer with special hydrographic interests, Juan Benet came to literature late and primarily for aesthetic satisfaction. Principally a novelist and essayist, he has written short stories and attempted theater, but is emphatically not a "professional writer." Rejecting reigning Spanish literary fashions, he has read widely from European and American authors, with Joyce, Faulkner, Nietzsche, Henry James, and Kafka being important in his development. Literary friends during formative years included Luis Martín Santos and Rafael Sánchez Ferlosio.

Benet's fiction and essays reflect his vision of literature as intellectualized, non-mimetic, and playful. Intellectuality imbues his cultivation of the novel as a mental discipline, requiring arduous exercise of the reader, not as critic or interpreter, but merely to grasp the content of his elliptical, allusive, and deliberately self-contradictory texts. Although Benet specifically rejects the "open novel," readers are disconcerted by the extraordinary linguistic difficulty of *Volverás a Región*, *Una meditación*, and *Un viaje de invierno*, the carefully elaborated rhetoric of ambiguity in the short stories and later novels, from *La otra casa de Mazón* to culmination in *En el estado*. The obscure, abnormal, and mysterious abound in his works, replete with inexplicable phenomena, oneiric and telluric forces, and happenings beyond the bounds of human comprehension.

Benet frequently employs technical and scientific vocabulary, neologisms, foreign words, archaisms, and hermetic or esoteric expressions, together with enormously long, complex, convoluted sentences. Baroque or latinized syntax, numerous asides and parenthetical digressions, language as an end in itself (independent of communication or message), emphasis on stylistic density, formal and structural experimentation, use of mythical or allegorical figures, and play upon Castilian's inherent morphological ambivalences all contribute to distancing his fiction from the sometimes pedestrian Neo-Realism prevalent in Spain during the 1950's and 1960's. This movement's sociopolitical *engagement*, regionalism or provincialism, narrowly nationalistic concerns, moralizing or criticism, and colloquial or quotidian language are eschewed. Didacticism is avoided, as are "typically Spanish" settings, themes, and characters. He invents patronymics, toponymy, the geography and chronicles of Spain's mythical double, "Región," reductively mirroring national history, legends, and heroes without duplicating them, within a minutely detailed microcosm stripped of traditional grandeur, shorn of false virtue, and trivialized to the point of absurdity.

Although Benet has briefly essayed such forms as the detective novel (*El aire de un crimen*) and seldom long abandons irony and incisive humor, he most characteristically portrays a universe governed by chance and populated by the most vulnerable and defenseless of beings, eccentric, retarded, or deranged characters or monotonously pedestrian personalities, in atmospheres ranging from the most mundane and insignificant to ambients of mystery, foreboding, magic, unknown dangers, decadence, putrefaction, and controlled terror. He exploits fears born of mortal limitations (physical, rational, temporal), the insufficiency of science, philosophy, and human knowledge to deal with even the known, much less the unknown and supernatural. Totally independent of Spanish literary tradition, movements, and values, his is a work of exceptional unity and obscurity, whose dominant motifs are ruin, decay, abandonment, fratricide, solitude, darkness, mutilation, desolation, despair, and death, pointing indirectly toward Spain's Civil War (1936-39) as a paralyzing, insuperable tragedy which has indelibly scarred the land and the survivors.

—Janet Pérez

BERNHARD, Thomas. Austrian. Born near Maastricht, Netherlands, of Austrian parents, 11 September 1931. Educated at schools in Salzburg; studied music in Vienna and Salzburg. Commercial apprenticeship, then patient in a tuberculosis sanatorium; worked as a court reporter, critic, and librarian. Recipient: Bremen Prize, 1965; Austrian State Prize, 1967; Wildgans Prize, 1968; Büchner Prize, 1970; Grillparzer Prize, 1971; Séguier Prize, 1974. Address: A-4694 Ohlsdorf (Oberösterreich), Austria.

PUBLICATIONS

Fiction

Frost. Frankfurt, Insel, 1963.
Amras. Frankfurt, Suhrkamp, 1964.
Vestörung. Frankfurt, Insel, 1967; as *Gargoyles*, New York, Knopf, 1970.
Prosa. Frankfurt, Suhrkamp, 1967.
Ungenach. Frankfurt, Suhrkamp, 1968.
Watten: Ein Nachlass. Frankfurt, Suhrkamp, 1969.
Ereignisse. Berlin, Literarisches Colloquium, 1969.
An der Baumgrenze. Salzburg, Residenz, 1969.
Das Kalkwerk. Frankfurt, Suhrkamp, 1970; as *The Lime Works*, New York, Random House, 1970.
Gehen. Frankfurt, Suhrkamp, 1971.
Midland in Stilfs: Drei Erzählungen. Frankfurt, Suhrkamp, 1971.
Der Kulterer. Salzburg, Residenz, 1974.
Korrektur. Frankfurt, Suhrkamp, 1975; as *Correction*, New York, Knopf, 1979.
Der Wetterfleck. Stuttgart, Reclam, 1976.
Der Stimmenimitator. Frankfurt, Suhrkamp, 1978.
Ja. Frankfurt, Suhrkamp, 1978.
Die Erzählungen, edited by Ulrich Greiner. Frankfurt, Suhrkamp, 1979.
Die Billigesser. Frankfurt, Suhrkamp, 1980.
Beton. Frankfurt, Suhrkamp, 1982.
Die Untergeher. Frankfurt, Suhrkamp, 1983.

Plays

Die Rosen der Einöde: Fünf Sätze für Ballet, Stimmen und Orchester. Frankfurt, Fischer, 1959.
Ein Fest für Boris (produced Hamburg, 1970). Frankfurt, Suhrkamp, 1970.
Der Berg, in *Literatur und Kritik 5*, June 1970.
Der Italiener (screenplay). Salzburg, Residenz, 1971.
Der Ignorant und der Wahnsinnige (produced Salzburg, 1972). Frankfurt, Suhrkamp, 1972.
Die Jagdgesellschaft (produced Vienna, 1974). Frankfurt, Suhrkamp, 1974.
Die Macht der Gewohnheit (produced Salzburg, 1974). Frankfurt, Suhrkamp, 1974; as *The Force of Habit* (produced London, 1976), London, Heinemann, 1976.
Die Salzburger Stücke (includes *Der Ignorant und der Wahnsinnige* and *Die Macht der Gewohnheit*). Frankfurt, Suhrkamp, 1975.
Der Präsident (produced Vienna, 1975). Frankfurt, Suhrkamp, 1975; as *The President*, with *Eve of Retirement*, New York, Performing Arts Journal, 1982.
Minetti: Ein Porträt des Künstlers als alter Mann (produced Stuttgart, 1976). Frankfurt, Suhrkamp, 1977.
Die Berühmten (produced Vienna, 1976). Frankfurt, Suhrkamp, 1976.

Immanuel Kant (produced Stuttgart, 1978). Frankfurt, Suhrkamp, 1978.
Der Weltverbesserer (produced Bochum, 1980). Frankfurt, Suhrkamp, 1979.
Vor dem Ruhestand (produced Bochum, 1980). Frankfurt, Suhrkamp, 1979; as *Eve of Retirement* (produced Minneapolis, 1982); with *The President*, New York, Performing Arts Journal, 1982.
Über allen Gipfeln ist Ruh: Ein deutscher Dichtertag um 1980. Frankfurt, Suhrkamp, 1981.
Am Ziel. Frankfurt, Suhrkamp, 1981.

Verse

Auf der Erde und in der Hölle. Salzburg, Müller, 1957.
Unter dem Eisen des Mondes. Cologne, Kiepenheuer & Witsch, 1958.
In hora mortis. Salzburg, Müller, 1958.
Ave Vergil. Frankfurt, Suhrkamp, 1981.

Other (autobiographical writings)

Die Ursache: Eine Andeutung. Salzburg, Residenz, 1975.
Der Keller: Eine Entziehung. Salzburg, Residenz, 1976.
Der Atem: Eine Entscheidung. Salzburg, Residenz, 1978.
Die Kälte: Eine Isolation. Salzburg, Residenz, 1981.
Ein Kind. Salzburg, Residenz, 1982.
Wittgensteins Neffe: Eine Freundschaft. Frankfurt, Suhrkamp, 1983.

*

Bibliography: *Bernhard Werkgeschichte* by Jens Dittmar, Frankfurt, Suhrkamp, 1981.

Critical Studies: *Über Bernhard* edited by Anneliese Botond, Frankfurt, Suhrkamp, 1970; *Bernhard* edited by Heinz Ludwig Arnold, Munich, Boorberg, 1974; *Bernhard* by Bernard Sorg, Munich, Beck, 1977; "The Plays of Bernhard: A Report" by Alfred Barthoder, in *Modern Austrian Literature 11*, 1978; "Bernhard's Austria: Neurosis, Symbol, or Expedient?" by A.P. Dierick, in *Modern Austrian Literature 12*, 1979; *New German Dramatists* by Denis Calandra, London, Macmillan, 1983.

*   *   *

Thomas Bernhard's work has captured a mood in contemporary Austrian society, and yet the image the media have created of this writer has not always been appealing. His novels, such as *Frost* and *The Lime Works*, concentrate on themes of individual loneliness, the ugliness and cruelty of nature, the absence of communication, death, illness, pain, metaphysical crisis, madness, suicide, and despair. Bernhard is also strongly critical of Austrian social and political institutions, both past and present. He sees society as structured to sublimate fear into coherent philosophical ideologies in order to maintain a falsely optimistic view of progress. His intense preoccupation with man's fallibility is deeply rooted in his own experience. Profoundly disadvantaged by the years of Nazism and frequent illness, Bernhard now lives alone in a small Austrian village. This has given the media cause to highlight his apparent misanthropy and misogyny. His autobiographical writings (*Die Ursache, Der Keller, Der Atem, Die Kälte, Ein Kind*, and *Wittgensteins Neffe*) have in recent years underlined the source of many of his pessimistic attitudes, but have also stressed his personal determination and integrity.

Bernhard's style is closely linked to his themes. His sentences are long, complex, and repetitive. The absence of paragraphs and the abundance of relative and adjectival clauses create an impression of claustrophobia and hopelessness as well as a sense of urgency. The reader's patience is severely tested by such a style. His search for clarity and direction is constantly frustrated, emphasizing the limits of human understanding and individual isolation. The reader is also drawn into accepting the paradox of Bernhard's "absurd" view of the world—"telling the truth" involves uncovering the hypocrisy behind which people shelter in order to maintain the "accepted" truth (the lie). We all participate in this hypocrisy even if we recognize its hollowness because the lie is *necessary*. The reader is invited to distinguish between the necessary lie (that there is a purpose) and self-deception (failure to recognize the paradox).

Bernhard embraces views which may seem extreme, but he completely lacks self-pity and bases his criticism on an intellectual and emotional curiosity which commands respect. Although he shares man's (especially the writer's) striving for perfection, he realizes that life refuses to be shaped artistically into perfected patterns (as shown in *The Lime Works*). Such awareness makes him capable of self-irony and humour. This is particularly obvious in the plays (e.g., *The President*) where it is clear that Bernhard sees the theatre as a stage for demonstrating existence as a game, not as a forum for enlightenment. Both comedy and tragedy are part of this game and constantly remind the audience of the inevitable pointlessness of human endeavour.

Music is seen as a redeeming feature of a society which otherwise crushes the individual creative spirit. Whether we accept Bernhard's view of Austrian society depends to a large extent on our personal readiness to examine his points in depth. If we are reluctant to look below the surface, Bernhard's work is the more poignant since he seeks constantly to discredit superficiality and narrowmindedness.

—Barbara Saunders

BLAIS, Marie-Claire. Canadian. Born in Quebec, 5 October 1939. Educated at Pensionnat St. Roch and Laval University, both Quebec. Lived in the United States 1963-74; now lives in Quebec. Recipient: Canada Council Fellowship, 1960; French Language prize, 1961; Guggenheim grant, 1963, 1965; France-Quebec Prize, 1966; Médicis Prize (France), 1966; Governor-General's Award, 1969, 1979; Belgium-Canada Prize, 1976; Athanase David prize, 1982; French Academy prize, 1983. Honorary doctorate: York University, Toronto, 1975; honorary professor: University of Calgary, 1978. Companion, Order of Canada, 1975. Agent: Louise Myette, 3507 Aylmer Street, Montreal, Quebec H2X 2B9, Canada.

PUBLICATIONS

Fiction

La Belle Bête. Quebec, Institut Littéraire, 1959; as *Mad Shadows*, Toronto, McClelland and Stewart, and London, Cape, 1960; Boston, Little Brown, 1961.
Tête blanche. Quebec, Institut Littéraire, 1960; translated as *Tête blanche*, Toronto, McClelland and Stewart, and Boston, Little Brown, 1961; London, Cape, 1962.

Le Jour est noir.   Montreal, Jour, 1962; in *The Day Is Dark, and Three Travelers*, 1967.
Une Saison dans la vie d'Emmanuel.   Montreal, Jour, 1965; as *A Season in the Life of Emmanuel*, New York, Farrar Straus, 1966; London, Cape, 1967.
Les Voyageurs sacrés.   Montreal, HMH, 1966; in *The Day Is Dark, and Three Travelers*, 1967.
L'Insoumise.   Montreal, Jour, 1966; as *The Fugitive*, Ottawa, Oberon Press, 1978.
The Day Is Dark, and Three Travelers.   New York, Farrar Straus, 1967.
David Sterne.   Montreal, Jour, 1967; translated as *David Sterne*, Toronto, McClelland and Stewart, 1973.
Manuscrits de Pauline Archange:
  1. *Manuscrits de Pauline Archange.*   Montreal, Jour, 1968.
  2. *Vivre! Vivre!*   Montreal, Jour, 1969.
  3. *The Manuscripts of Pauline Archange* (includes translations of *Manuscrits de Pauline Archange* and *Vivre! Vivre!*).   New York, Farrar Straus, 1970.
  4. *Les Apparences.*   Montreal, Jour, 1970; as *Durer's Angel*, Vancouver, Talonbooks, 1976.
Le Loup.   Montreal, Jour, 1972; as *The Wolf*, Toronto, McClelland and Stewart, 1974.
Un Joualonais, sa joualonie.   Montreal, Jour, 1973; as *À coeur joual*, Paris, Laffont, 1974; as *St. Lawrence Blues*, New York, Farrar Straus, 1974; London, Harrap, 1975.
Une Liaison parisienne.   Montreal, Stanké, 1975; as *A Literary Affair*, Toronto, McClelland and Stewart, 1979.
Les Nuits de l'Underground.   Montreal, Stanké, 1978; as *Nights in the Underground*, Toronto, General Publishing, 1982.
La Sourd dans la ville.   Montreal, Stanké, 1979; as *Deaf to the City*, Toronto, Dennys, 1981.
Visions d'Anna.   Montreal, Stanké, 1982; as *Anna's World*, Toronto, Dennys, 1984.
Printemps 1981.   Montreal, Primeur, 1984.

Plays

La Roulotte aux poupées (produced Montreal, 1962); as *The Puppet Caravan* (televised, 1967).
Eleonor (produced Quebec, 1962).
L'Exécution (produced Montreal, 1967).   Montreal, Jour, 1968; as *The Execution*, Vancouver, Talonbooks, 1976.
Fièvre et autres textes dramatiques: Théâtre radiophonique (includes *L'Envahisseur, Le Disparu, Deux Destins, Un Couple*).   Montreal, Jour, 1974.
La Nef des sorcières (Marcelle).   Montreal, Quinze, 1976.
L'Ocean, suivi de Murmures (broadcast, 1976).   Montreal, Quinze, 1977.

Radio Plays: *L'Ocean, suivi de Murmures*, 1976.

Verse

Pays voilés.   Quebec, Garneau, 1963.
Existences.   Quebec, Garneau, 1964.

*

Critical Studies: *Blais* by Philip Stratford, Toronto, Forum House, 1971; *Le Monde perturbé des jeunes dans l'oeuvre de Blais* by Thérèse Fabi, Montreal, Agence d'Arc, 1973; *Blais: Le Noir et le tendre* by Vincent Nadeau, Montreal, Presses de l'Université de Montreal, 1974.

*   *   *

Marie-Claire Blais has attracted national and international attention since the appearance of her first novel *Mad Shadows*, published when she was barely twenty years old. Since then, she has continued to publish, mainly novels, at almost yearly intervals.

From the beginning, she has revealed her preoccupation with the lives of those who live on the fringes of, or in opposition to, an oppressive, stifling society, variously—or jointly—symbolised by the Church, parents, school and other social institutions, marriage, etc. In almost all cases the young are victims of their elders, although, in her recent writings, the horrors of solitary old age are also depicted.

Some are outcasts, rejected by society for nonconformity to a prevailing norm. For Isabelle in *Mad Shadows*, it is her ugliness that sets her apart. Elsewhere it is sexual preference or the mere fact of youth. Others choose to reject what they see as mediocrity and freely assume marginal lives. In both *David Sterne*, and her play *The Execution*, for instance, the central characters, in a gesture reminiscent of Leopold and Loeb, perform gratuitous murders.

All her writing before 1977 reveals a bleak, despairing universe in which individual suffering is the mirror of larger horrors stalking the world, like racism or war. Hope is limited. Perhaps the ordered perfection of mathematics can offer temporary release (*David Sterne*) or, for the privileged few, the act of writing itself, which offers escape into the future (see, in particular, the first volume of her Pauline Archange triptych, *The Manuscripts of Pauline Archange*).

With the publication of *Nights in the Underground* in 1978, however, it is possible to discern a shift in her writing that becomes even more apparent in *Anna's World*. If the world has not improved, the feminism she has gradually adopted allows her both to posit a variety of warm, loving relationships between women and to offer positive, nurturing values in opposition to the legalised violence of army and state that she now sees to be inherent in a society organised on a patriarchal basis.

Blais has chosen to give her writing a universal dimension. Only rarely does she evoke a specific neighbourhood or city, and the few country or cityscapes she offers are symbolic rather than real, frequently shrouded in mist or snow. Even her preoccupation with the literary use of *joual* (a popular form of French spoken in the Montreal area) stems less from a wish to localize her text than from the desire both to explore the social dimension of language and to revitalize written French.

One of the most important characteristics of her work is this constant experimentation with form, which involves the visual dimension of the printed page as much as other more properly linguistic or stylistic effects. Her concern is certainly aesthetic; it is also part and parcel of her general questioning of accepted norms.

—Maïr Verthuy

BÖLL, Heinrich (Theodor). German. Born in Cologne, 21 December 1917. Educated at gymnasium, Cologne; University of Cologne. Served in the German army, 1939-45; prisoner of war, 1945. Married Annemarie Cech in 1942; three sons. Joiner in his father's shop, then apprentice in the book trade before the war; full-time writer since 1947: Co-Editor, *Labyrinth*, 1960-61, and *L*, since 1976. Recipient: German industry grant; Gruppe 47 prize, 1951; Schickele Prize, 1952; Critics Prize (Germany), 1953; Tribune de Paris prize, 1953; Foreign Book Prize (France), 1955; Heydt Prize, 1958; Bavarian Academy of Fine Arts award, 1958; Nordrhein-Westfalen Prize, 1959; Veillon prize, 1960; Cologne Prize, 1961; Elba Prize, 1965; Büchner

Prize, 1967; Nobel Prize for Literature, 1972. Honorary degrees: Aston University, Birmingham, 1973; Brunel University, Uxbridge, Middlesex, 1973; Trinity College, Dublin, 1973. Address: 5165 Hürtgenwald-Grosshau, an der Nülheck 19, 5 Cologne 1, Germany.

PUBLICATIONS

Fiction

Der Zug war pünktlich.   Opladen, Middelhauve, 1949; as *The Train Was on Time*, New York, Criterion, 1956; London, Secker and Warburg, 1973.

Wanderer, kommst du nach Spa....   Opladen, Middelhauve, 1950; as *Traveller, If You Come to Spa*, London, Arco, 1956.

Die schwarzen Schafe.   Opladen, Middelhauve, 1951.

Wo warst du, Adam?   Opladen, Middelhauve, 1951; as *Adam, Where Art Thou?*, New York, Criterion, 1955; as *And Where Were You Adam?*, London, Secker and Warburg, 1974.

Nicht nur zur Weihnachtszeit.   Frankfurt, Frankfurter Verlagsanstalt, 1952.

Und sagte kein einziges Wort.   Cologne, Kiepenheuer & Witsch, 1953; as *Acquainted with the Night*, New York, Criterion, 1954; as *And Never Said a Word*, London, Secker and Warburg, 1978.

Haus ohne Hüter.   Cologne, Kiepenheuer & Witsch, 1954; as *Tomorrow and Yesterday*, New York, Criterion, 1957; as *The Unguarded House*, London, Arco, 1957.

Das Brot der frühen Jahre.   Cologne, Kiepenheuer & Witsch, 1955; as *The Bread of Our Early Years*, London, Arco, 1957; as *The Bread of Those Early Years*, New York, McGraw Hill, 1976.

So ward Abend und Morgen.   Zurich, Der Arche, 1955.

Unberechenbare Gäste: Heitere Erzählungen.   Zurich, Der Arche, 1956.

Im Tal der donnernden Hufe.   Frankfurt, Insel, 1957.

Doktor Murkes gesammeltes Schweigen und andere Satiren.   Cologne, Kiepenheuer & Witsch, 1958.

Der Mann mit den Messern.   Stuttgart, Reclam, 1958.

Die Waage der Baleks und andere Erzählungen.   Lübeck, Matthiessen, 1958.

Der Bahnhof von Zimpren.   Munich, List, 1959.

Billard um Halbzehn.   Cologne, Kiepenheuer & Witsch, 1959; as *Billiards at Half Past Nine*, London, Weidenfeld and Nicolson, 1961; New York, McGraw Hill, 1962.

Als der Krieg ausbrach, Als der Krieg zu Ende war.   Frankfurt, Insel, 1962.

Ansichten eines Clowns.   Cologne, Kiepenheuer & Witsch, 1963; as *The Clown*, New York, McGraw Hill, 1965; London, Calder and Boyars, 1972.

Entfernung von der Truppe.   Cologne, Kiepenheuer & Witsch, 1964.

Absent Without Leave (2 novellas).   New York, McGraw Hill, 1965.

Ende einer Dienstfahrt.   Cologne, Kiepenheuer & Witsch, 1966; as *End of a Mission*, New York, McGraw Hill, 1967; London, Weidenfeld and Nicolson, 1968.

Eighteen Stories.   New York, McGraw Hill, 1966.

Absent Without Leave and Other Stories.   London, Weidenfeld and Nicolson, 1967.

Geschichten aus zwölf Jahren.   Frankfurt, Suhrkamp, 1969.

Children Are Civilians Too.   New York, McGraw Hill, 1970; London, Secker and Warburg, 1973.

Gruppenbild mit Dame.   Cologne, Kiepenheuer & Witsch, 1971; as *Group Portrait with Lady*, New York, McGraw Hill, and London, Secker and Warburg, 1973.

Der Mann mit den Messern: Erzählungen (selection).   Stuttgart, Reclam, 1972.

Die verlorene Ehre der Katharina Blum.   Cologne, Kiepenheuer & Witsch, 1974; as *The Lost Honor of Katharina Blum*, New York, McGraw Hill, and London, Secker and

Warburg, 1975.
Berichte zur Gesinnungslage der Nation. Cologne, Kiepenheuer & Witsch, 1975.
Fürsorgliche Belagerung. Cologne, Kiepenheuer & Witsch, 1979; as *The Safety Net*, New York, Knopf, and London, Secker and Warburg, 1982.
Du fährst zu oft nach Heidelberg. Bornheim-Merten, Lamuv, 1979.
Gesammelte Erzählungen. Cologne, Kiepenheuer & Witsch, 2 vols., 1981.

Plays

Die Brücke von Berczaba (broadcast, 1952). Published in *Zauberei auf dem Sender und andere Hörspiele*, Frankfurt, Kramer, 1962.
Der Heilige und der Räuber (broadcast, 1953). Published in *Hörspielbuch des Nordwestdeutschen und Süddeutschen Rundfunks 4*, Frankfurt, Europäischer Verlag, 1953; as *Mönch und Räuber*, in *Erzählungen, Hörspiele, Aufsätze*, 1961.
Zum Tee bei Dr. Borsig (broadcast, 1955). Included in *Erzählungen, Hörspiele, Aufsätze*, 1961.
Eine Stunde Aufenthalt (broadcast, 1957). Included in *Erzählungen, Hörspiele, Aufsätze*, 1961.
Die Spurlosen (broadcast, 1957). Hamburg, Hans Bredow-Institut, 1957.
Bilanz (broadcast, 1957). Stuttgart, Reclam, 1961.
Klopfzeichen (broadcast, 1960). With *Bilanz*, 1961.
Ein Schluck Erde (produced Dusseldorf, 1961). Cologne, Kiepenheuer & Witsch, 1962.
Zum Tee bei Dr. Borsig (includes *Mönch und Räuber, Eine Stunde Aufenthalt, Bilanz, Die Spurlosen, Klopfzeichen, Sprechanlage, Konzert für vier Stimmen*). Munich, Deutscher Taschenbuch Verlag, 1964.
Hausfriedensbruch (broadcast, 1969). Cologne, Kiepenheuer & Witsch, 1969.
Aussatz (produced Aachen, 1970). With *Hausfriedensbruch*, 1969.

Radio Plays: *Die Brücke von Berczaba*, 1952; *Ein Tag wie sonst*, 1953; *Der Heilige und der Räuber*, 1953; *Zum Tee bei Dr. Borsig*, 1955; *Anita und das Existenzminimum*, 1955, revised version, as *Ich habe nichts gegen Tiere*, 1958; *Die Spurlosen*, 1957; *Bilanz*, 1957; *Eine Stunde Aufenthalt*, 1957; *Die Stunde der Wahrheit*, 1958; *Klopfzeichen*, 1960; *Hausfriedensbruch*, 1969.

Verse

Gedichte. Berlin, Literarisches Colloquium, 1972.

Other

Irisches Tagebuch. Cologne, Kiepenheuer & Witsch, 1957; as *Irish Journal*, New York, McGraw Hill, 1967; London, Secker and Warburg, 1983.
Im Ruhrgebiet, photographs by Karl Hargesheimer. Cologne, Kiepenheuer & Witsch, 1958.
Unter Krahnenbäumen, photographs by Karl Hargesheimer. Cologne, Greven, 1958.
Menschen am Rhein, photographs by Karl Hargesheimer. Cologne, Kiepenheuer & Witsch, 1960.
Brief an einen jungen Katholiken. Cologne, Kiepenheuer & Witsch, 1961.
Erzählungen, Hörspiele, Aufsätze. Cologne, Kiepenheuer & Witsch, 1961.
Assisi. Munich, Knorr & Hirth, 1962.

Hierzulande. Munich, Deutscher Taschenbuch Verlag, 1963.
Frankfurter Vorlesungen. Cologne, Kiepenheuer & Witsch, 1966.
Aufsätze, Kritiken, Reden 1952-1967. Cologne, Kiepenheuer & Witsch, 1967.
Leben im Zustand des Frevels. Berlin, Berliner Handpresse, 1969.
Neue politische und literarische Schriften. Cologne, Kiepenheuer & Witsch, 1973.
Nobel Prize for Literature (lecture). Bonn, Inter Nationes, 1973.
Politische Meditationen zu Glück und Vergeblichkeit, with Dorothee Sölle. Neuwied, Luchterhand, 1973.
Drei Tage in März, with Christian Linder. Cologne, Kiepenheuer & Witsch, 1975.
Der Lorbeer ist immer noch bitter: Literarische Schriften. Munich, Deutscher Taschenbuch Verlag, 1976.
Briefe zur Verteidigung der Republik, with Freimut Duve and Klaus Staeck. Reinbeck, Rowohlt, 1977.
Einmischung erwünscht: Schriften zur Zeit. Cologne, Kiepenheuer & Witsch, 1977.
Werke, edited by Bernd Balzer. Cologne, Kiepenheuer & Witsch-Middelhauve, 10 vols., 1977-78.
Missing Persons and Other Essays. New York, McGraw Hill, and London, Secker and Warburg, 1977.
Querschnitte: Aus Interviews, Aufsätzen, und Reden, edited by Viktor Böll and Renate Matthaei. Cologne, Kiepenheuer & Witsch, 1977.
Gefahren von falschen Brüdern: Politische Schriften. Munich, Deutscher Taschenbuch Verlag, 1980.
Warum haben wir aufeinander geschossen?, with Lew Kopelew. Bornheim-Merten, Lamuv, 1981.
Was soll aus dem jungen bloss werden? Bornheim-Merten, Lamuv, 1981.
Vermintes Gelände. Cologne, Kiepenheuer & Witsch, 1982.

Editor, with Erich Kock, *Unfertig ist der Mensch.* Munich, Mensch und Arbeit, 1967.

Translator, with Annemarie Böll:

Kein Name bei den Leuten [No Name in the Street], by Kay Cicellis. Cologne, Kiepenheuer & Witsch, 1953.
Ein unordentlicher Mensch, by Adriaan Morriën. Munich, Biederstein, 1955.
Tod einer Stadt [Death of a Town], by Kay Cicellis. Cologne, Kiepenheuer & Witsch, 1956.
Weihnachtsabend in San Cristobal [The Saintmaker's Christmas Eve], by Paul Horgan. Olten, Walter, 1956.
Zur Ruhe kam der Baum des Menschen nie [The Tree of Man], by Patrick White. Cologne, Kiepenheuer & Witsch, 1957.
Der Teufel in der Wüste [The Devil in the Desert], by Paul Horgan. Olten, Walter, 1958.
Die Geisel [The Hostage], by Brendan Behan. Cologne, Kiepenheuer & Witsch, 1958.
Der Mann von Morgen früh [The Quare Fellow], by Brendan Behan. Cologne, Kiepenheuer & Witsch, 1958.
Ein Wahrer Held [The Playboy of the Western World], by J.M. Synge. Cologne, Kiepenheuer & Witsch, 1960.
Die Boot fahren nicht mehr aus [The Islandman], by Tomás O'Crohan. Olten, Walter, 1960.
Eine Rose zur Weihnachtszeit [One Red Rose for Christmas], by Paul Horgan. Olten, Walter, 1960.
Der Gehilfe [The Assistant], by Bernard Malamud. Cologne, Kiepenheuer & Witsch, 1960.
Kurz vor dem Krieg gegen die Eskimos, by J.D. Salinger. Cologne, Kiepenheuer & Witsch, 1961.
Das Zauberfass [The Magic Barrel], by Bernard Malamud. Cologne, Kiepenheuer &

Witsch, 1962.

Der Fänger im Roggen [The Catcher in the Rye], by J.D. Salinger. Cologne, Kiepenheuer & Witsch, 1962.

Ein Gutshaus in Irland [The Big House], by Brendan Behan, in *Stücke*. Neuwied, Luchterhand, 1962.

Franny und Zooey, by J.D. Salinger. Cologne, Kiepenheuer & Witsch, 1963.

Die Insel der Pferde [The Island of Horses], by Eilís Dillon. Freiburg, Herder, 1964.

Hebt den Dachbalken hoch, Zimmerleute; Seymour wird vorgestellt [Raise High the Roof Beam, Carpenters; Seymour: An Introduction], by J.D. Salinger. Cologne, Kiepenheuer & Witsch, 1965.

Caesar und Cleopatra, by G.B. Shaw. Frankfurt, Suhrkamp, 1965.

Der Spanner [The Scarperer], by Brendan Behan. Cologne, Kiepenheuer & Witsch, 1966.

Die Insel des grossen John [The Coriander], by Eilís Dillon. Freiburg, Herder, 1966.

Das harte Leben [The Hard Life], by Flann O'Brien. Hamburg, Nannen, 1966.

Neun Erzählungen [Nine Stories], by J.D. Salinger. Cologne, Kiepenheuer & Witsch, 1966.

Die schwarzen Füchse [A Family of Foxes], by Eilís Dillon. Freiburg, Herder, 1967.

Die Irrfahrt der Santa Maria [The Cruise of the Santa Maria], by Eilís Dillon. Freiburg, Herder, 1968.

Die Springflut [The Sea Wall], by Eilís Dillon. Freiburg, Herder, 1969.

Seehunde SOS [The Seals], by Eilís Dillon. Freiburg, Herder, 1970.

Erwachen in Mississippi [Coming of Age in Mississippi], by Anne Moody. Frankfurt, Fischer, 1970.

Candida, Der Kaiser von Amerika, Mensch und Übermensch [Candida, The King of America, Man and Superman], by G.B. Shaw. Frankfurt, Suhrkamp, 1970.

Handbuch des Revolutionärs, by G.B. Shaw. Frankfurt, Suhrkamp, 1972.

*

Bibliography: *Der Schriftsteller Böll: Ein biographisch-bibliographischer Abriss* edited by Werner Lengning, Munich, DTV, 5th edition, 1977; *Böll in America 1954-1970* by Ray Lewis White, Heidelberg, Olms, 1979.

Critical Studies: *Böll, Teller of Tales: A Study of His Works and Characters* by Wilhelm Johannes Schwartz, New York, Ungar, 1969; *A Student's Guide to Böll* by Enid Macpherson, London, Heinemann, 1972; *Böll: Withdrawal and Re-Emergence* by J.H. Reid, London, Wolff, 1973; *The Major Works of Böll: A Critical Commentary* by Erhard Friedrichsmeyer, New York, Monarch Press, 1974; *The Writer and Society: Studies in the Fiction of Günter Grass and Böll* by Charlotte W. Ghurye, Bern, Lang, 1976; *The Imagery in Böll's Novels* by Thor Prodaniuk, Bonn, Bouvier, 1979; *Böll* by Robert C. Conard, Boston, Twayne, 1981.

*   *   *

More consistently than any of his contemporaries Heinrich Böll has documented the development of the Federal Republic since its inception. In doing so he has achieved the remarkable feat of becoming a best-selling author who is under constant attack from the popular press. His works are invariably provocative and the subject of critical disagreement in both academic and non-academic circles. Abroad he has a solid reputation as "the good German" who has unambiguously condemned fascism and the less appealing features of the land of the Economic Miracle. Sales of his books in Eastern Europe are considerable and in the Soviet Union he is one of the best-known Western writers.

Old enough to have consciously experienced the rise of Hitler and to have taken part in his war from beginning to end, fortunate enough to have been brought up in a family and among friends who detested National Socialism, he has remained faithful to the insight expressed in one of his earliest stories, "that the war would never be over, never, as long as somewhere a wound it had inflicted was still bleeding" ("The Message"). His early works, notably the novel *Adam Where Art Thou?* and the short story *Traveller, If You Come to Spa*, present war as a "disease," something unheroic and repulsive, where the individual is alone and frightened. But already by 1950 Böll was criticising his contemporaries for their failure to tend the wounds of the past, their facile and superficial embracing of democracy as one might change from one train to another ("Business Is Business"), their restoration of pre-war values and customs as if these had not been contaminated by the Nazis ("Christmas Every Day"). The *summa* of this aspect of Böll's writings came with *Billiards at Half Past Nine* and its grandiose central symbol of St. Anthony's Abbey, designed by one Fähmel in the self-confident years of Emperor William II, destroyed by his son in the closing months of the Second World War, and in process of being restored by the third generation of the same family in 1958. In this novel, as in *Acquainted with the Night* and *The Clown*, Böll reserves much of his scorn for the Roman Catholic Church, which he regards as having betrayed its mission by signing the concordat with Hitler in 1933 and allying itself with capital since the war.

The 1960's saw the increasing politicisation of German writers, and Böll was no exception. If his early works could be criticised for their pessimism, the implication that resistance was futile, his later ones explore the possibility of action. The title-figure of *The Clown* experiences the dilemma of the committed artist: his satirical sketches are accepted and applauded only as long as he observes the proprieties; in order to have a more immediate impact he takes to the streets. *Group Portrait with Lady*, Böll's most ambitious and possibly most satisfying novel, a panorama of 20th-century German society, includes two parallel and successful acts of resistance, the one the saving of a Russian prisoner-of-war during the Third Reich, the other the frustration of an attempt by contemporary business to destroy a haven for the disadvantaged of West German society. The hysteria whipped up by the right-wing press over urban terrorism is the subject of *The Lost Honour of Katharina Blum*, in which the shooting of an obnoxious journalist is shown to be merely the obverse of the violence latent in the press itself. More recently, however, Böll has returned to a more pessimistic stance: in *The Safety Net* he apparently retracts his invitation to active resistance; protest has led to unacceptable acts of terror, the state has become all-powerful, a retreat into privacy seems the only way out.

Implicit in all Böll's works is the theme of the individual under threat from impersonal forces of all kinds: the war machine, the Church establishment, post-war bureaucracy and big business. His standpoint is that of a left-wing humanism tinged with a strong element of non-conformist, anti-clerical Catholicism. Over the past quarter of a century he has been publicly involved in all the important issues of the day, protesting against the invasion of Czechoslovakia in 1968 and the destabilisation of Chile in 1973, against the government's emergency legislation in 1968 and the planned deployment of Pershing missiles in 1983. His particular literary strength lies in satire, the medium most suited to his conception of a literature which must in content be socially committed and in technique "exaggerate" ("Second Wuppertal Speech," 1960), test the limits to artistic freedom by "going too far" ("The Freedom of Art," 1966); it also relates to his notable sense of humour allied to his eye for the significant, absurd detail. Thus his most memorable writings include those on the broadcaster who collects "silences," the family which celebrates Christmas all the year round, and the man who is employed to defeat the packaging industry by *unpacking* goods for the customer.

Böll is essentially a writer of prose fiction—his few excursions into other genres have been failures. He has experimented in a moderate way with narrative techniques. In the 1950's his favourite form was the short story, that genre peculiarly suited to existentialist statement. His novels of these years are marked by a pre-occupation with the phenomenon of time and make extensive play with fluctuating narrative perspectives. *Billiards at Half Past Nine* comes closest to the *nouveau roman* of the day. In the more politically charged atmosphere of the 1960's and later, his writing became deliberately more casual and direct, although the ironic play with the convention of a first-person biographer-narrator in *Group Portrait with Lady* betrays a continued concern for questions of form. It is interesting therefore that *The Safety Net* reverts to the peculiar narrative economy of the earlier works with its condensation of narrated time and its use of multiple limited points of view.

—J.H. Reid

BONNEFOY, Yves. French. Born in Tours, 24 June 1923. Educated at the University of Poitiers; University of Paris, degree in philosophy. Married Lucille Vine in 1968; one daughter. Has taught literature at many universities, including Brandeis University, Waltham, Massachusetts, 1962-64, Centre Universitaire, Vincennes, 1969-70, Johns Hopkins University, Baltimore, Princeton University, New Jersey, Yale University, New Haven, Connecticut, University of Geneva, University of Nice, 1973-76, University of Provence, Aix, 1979-81, and Collège de France, Paris, since 1981. Co-Founder, *L'Éphémère*, Paris, 1967. Recipient: *L'Express* prize, for essays, 1959; Cecil Hemley prize, 1967; Critics Prize (France), 1971; Fémina-Vacaresco Prize, 1977; Montaigne Prize (Hamburg), 1978. Address: 63 Rue Lepic, 75018 Paris, France.

PUBLICATIONS

Verse

> *Du mouvement et de l'immobilité de Douve.* Paris, Mercure, 1953; as *On the Motion and Immobility of Douve*, translated by Galway Kinnell, Athens, Ohio University Press, 1968.
> *Hier régnant désert.* Paris, Mercure, 1958.
> *Anti-Platon.* Paris, Maeght, 1962.
> *Pierre écrite.* Paris, Mercure, 1965; as *Pierre écrite/Words in Stone*, translated by Susanna Lang, Amherst, University of Massachusetts Press, 1976.
> *Selected Poems*, translated by Anthony Rudolf. London, Cape, 1968; New York, Grossman, 1969.
> *Dans le leurre du seuil.* Paris, Mercure, 1975.
> *Poèmes.* Paris, Mercure, 1978.

Other

> *Traité du pianiste.* Paris, Révolution la Nuit, 1946.
> *Peintures murales de la France gothique.* Paris, Hartmann, 1954.
> *L'Improbable.* Paris, Mercure, 1959.
> *La Seconde simplicité.* Paris, Mercure, 1961.
> *Rimbaud par lui-même.* Paris, Seuil, 1961; as *Rimbaud*, New York, Harper, 1973.
> *Miró.* Paris, Bibliothèque des Arts, 1964; translated as *Miró*, New York, Viking Press, 1967.
> *Un Rêve fait à Mantoue.* Paris, Mercure, 1967.
> *La Poésie française et le principe d'identité.* Paris, Maeght, 1967.
> *Rome 1630: L'Horizon du premier baroque.* Paris, Flammarion, 1970.

L'Arrière-pays. Geneva, Skira, 1972.
Garache, with Jacques Thuillier. Paris, Maeght, 1975.
L'Ordalie, illustrated by Claude Garache. Paris, Maeght, 1975.
Terre seconde. Ratilly, Association des Amis de Ratilly, 1976.
Rue traversière. Paris, Mercure, 1977.
La Nuage rouge: Essais sur la poétique. Paris, Mercure, 1977.
Entretiens sur la poésie. Neuchâtel, À la Baconnière, 1981.

Translator, *Une chemise de nuit de flanelle.* Paris, Les Pas Perdus, 1951.
Translator, *1 Henri IV, Jules César, Hamlet, Le Conte d'hiver, Vénus et Adonis,* and *Le Viol de Lucrèce,* by Shakespeare. Paris, Club Français du Livre, 1957-60.
Translator, *Jules César, Hamlet, Le Roi Lear, Roméo et Juliette,* and *Macbeth,* by Shakespeare. Paris, Mercure, 1960-83.

*

Critical Studies: *The Inner Theatre of Recent French Poetry,* Princeton, New Jersey, Princeton University Press, 1972, and *Bonnefoy*, Boston, Twayne, 1984, both by Mary Ann Caws; *Bonnefoy*, Paris, Seghers, 1976, and *La Question du moi: Un Aspect de la modernité poétique européenne: T.S. Eliot, Paul Celan, Bonnefoy,* Neuchâtel, À la Baconnière, 1978, both by J.E. Jackson.

*   *   *

One of France's best-loved and most widely translated poets, Bonnefoy writes both poetry and critical prose in a style at once deceptively simple and powerful in its metaphysical reverberation, in its few figures, and against the few elements of its backdrop.

His first well-known volume of poems, *On the Motion and Immobility of Douve,* creates for us a figure at once a woman loved, the moat of defense for a castle, a deepening of the earth, and of poetry itself. In his next volumes, the desert dryness which was reigning only yesterday leaves its needed ardor, and promises, for tomorrow, a future less arid (*Hier régnant désert*). Then, against a landscape of always greater metaphysical depth, a stone is inscribed, written like the pages (*Pierre écrite/Words in Stone*). In his latest volume of poems, the scene is cast in a dry landscape but is moving with the sight of the river, where a child is found and poetry is reborn (*Dans le leurre du seuil*). These volumes are made up of successive and simple poems seeming to join together all the voices essential to Bonnefoy's universe, voices of a phoenix and a maenad, of myth and of a real landscape. The ideas on which Bonnefoy's poetics are based hold in an extremely complex and yet apparently simple equilibrium. Our "excarnation" outside ourselves, when we are extended in the world by our collective passions, is balanced by our "incarnation" as we are one with our senses and our intellect; the passion of our art and writing is set against the "unwriting" characteristic of our present critical moment; our literary and artistic past, as it infuses its traditional values into the present by means of intertextual visual and verbal references, may clash with but be included in the future projection of our path. This delicate balance must influence any critical study of Yves Bonnefoy, as that study itself must respond to the various contrary and yet interrelated impulses.

In a writer whose own critical production is known for its perception and deeply human values, the apparent modes of difference—poems and literary essays, tales and critical commentary on art—have their own coherence and even their forms of repetition, so that the reassembling view of what might have seemed dispersed efforts retells and recalls an integrity we already sensed, underlying all the parts.

In any commentary on Yves Bonnefoy, a strong emphasis should be laid on the idea of place: the place of the essay, of the poem, of the critical vision, and the place of the reader in response to these texts, each related to a time and a space, a now and a here. Each image in the world his texts inhabit has the power to key in the whole, so that one stone, a cloud, or a salamander is able to speak of far more than itself. So too such commentary should, in fact must, reach out past its individual parts to the function and the place of poetry as a whole.

In some remarkable way, Bonnefoy's criticism, both literary and artistic, reflects the simple engagement of the poems and the massive power of a thought fully involved in a morally luminous consideration of what it is to create and to be, here and now on this earth. As we respond to our actual condition, we transcend it, but never for some heaven, only for what humans are able to make with human thought and love and perception. So Bonnefoy suggests we consider the Tombs of Ravenna for their statement about death as a part of life and about the lies of the concept, or the abstract idea, that bloodless refusal of what most counts: being here, using the language we love, seeing the red cloud Mondrian, for example, taught us to see, or hearing the ant scurrying across the leaves, as a haiku might have had us listen to the smallest detail.

As he celebrates the small and the available, as well as what is unseen but sensed, that back country beyond the one in which we live, but which—as we feel it present—gives our time and our space its meaning and its loveliness, Bonnefoy makes of himself one of the great teachers as he is already one of the great poets of our time.

—Mary Ann Caws

BORGES, Jorge Luis. Argentinian. Born in Buenos Aires, 24 August 1899. Educated at Collège de Géneve, Switzerland; Cambridge University. Married. Co-Founding Editor, *Proa*, 1924-26, and *Sur*, 1931; also associated with *Prisma*; Literary adviser, Emecé Editores, Buenos Aires. Municipal librarian, Buenos Aires, 1939-43; Director, National Library, 1955-73; Professor of English Literature, University of Buenos Aires, 1955-70. Norton Professor of Poetry, Harvard University, Cambridge, Massachusetts; Visiting Lecturer, University of Oklahoma, Norman, 1969. President, Argentine Writers Society, 1950-53. Recipient: Buenos Aires Municipal Prize, 1928; Grand Prize (Argentina), 1944; Argentine Writers Society prize, 1945; National Prize for Literature, 1957; International Publishers Prize, 1961; Ingram Merrill Award, 1966; Bienal Foundation Inter-American Prize, 1970; Jerusalem Prize, 1971; Reyes Prize, 1973. D.Litt.: Oxford University, 1971; Ph.D.: University of Jerusalem, 1971. Member, Argentine National Academy; Uruguayan Academy of Letters. Honorary Fellow, Modern Language Association (USA), 1961. Member, Legion of Honor. Honorary K.B.E. (Knight Commander, Order of the British Empire). Address: Maipú 994, Buenos Aires, Argentina.

PUBLICATIONS

Fiction

Historia universal de la infamia. Buenos Aires, Tor, 1935; as *A Universal History of Infamy*, New York, Dutton, 1971; London, Allen Lane, 1973.
El jardín de senderos que se bifurcan. Buenos Aires, Sur, 1942.
Seis problemas para don Isidro Parodi (with Adolfo Bioy Casares, as H. Bustos Domecq). Buenos Aires, Sur, 1942; as *Six Problems for Don Isidro Parodi*, New York, Dutton, and London, Allen Lane, 1981.
Ficciones (1935-1944). Buenos Aires, Sur, 1944; augmented edition, Buenos Aires,

Emecé, 1956; translated as *Ficciones*, New York, Grove Press, 1962; as *Fictions*, London, Calder, 1965.

Dos fantasías memorables, with Adolfo Bioy Casares. Buenos Aires, Oportet y Haereses, 1946.

Un modelo para la muerte, with Adolfo Bioy Casares. Buenos Aires, Oportet y Haereses, 1946.

El Aleph. Buenos Aires, Losada, 1949; as *The Aleph and Other Stories 1933-1969*, New York, Dutton, 1970; London, Pan, 1973.

La muerte y la brújala. Buenos Aires, Emecé, 1951.

Los orilleros; El paraíso de los creyentes, with Adolfo Bioy Casares. Buenos Aires, Losada, 1955.

Crónicas de Bustos Domecq, with Adolfo Bioy Casares. Buenos Aires, Losada, 1967; as *Chronicles of Bustos Domecq*, New York, Dutton, 1979; London, Allen Lane, 1982.

El informe de Brodie. Buenos Aires, Emecé, 1970; as *Dr. Brodie's Report*, New York, Dutton, 1972; London, Allen Lane, 1974.

El congreso. Buenos Aires, El Archibraza, 1970; as *The Congress*, London, Enitharmon Press, 1974.

El libro de arena. Buenos Aires, Emecé, 1975; as *The Book of Sand*, New York, Dutton, 1977; London, Allen Lane, 1979.

Verse

Fervor de Buenos Aires. Buenos Aires, Serrantes, 1923.

Luna de enfrente. Buenos Aires, Proa, 1925.

Cuaderno San Martín. Buenos Aires, Proa, 1929.

Poemas 1922-1943. Buenos Aires, Losada, 1943.

Poemas 1923-1958. Buenos Aires, Emecé, 1958.

El hacedor. Buenos Aires, Emecé, 1960; as *Dreamtigers*, London, Souvenir Press, 1963; Austin, University of Texas Press, 1964.

Obra poética 1923-1964. Buenos Aires, Emecé, 1964.

Para las seis cuerdas. Buenos Aires, Emecé, 1965; revised edition, 1970.

Obra poética 1923-1967. Buenos Aires, Emecé, 1967.

Obra poética. Buenos Aires, Emecé, 5 vols., 1969-72.

Elegio de la sombra. Buenos Aires, Emecé, 1969; as *In Praise of Darkness*, New York, Dutton, 1974; London, Allen Lane, 1975.

El otro, el mismo. Buenos Aires, Emecé, 1969.

El oro de los tigres. Buenos Aires, Emecé, 1972.

Selected Poems 1923-1967, edited by Norman Thomas di Giovanni. New York, Delacorte Press, and London, Allen Lane, 1972.

Obra poética 1923-1976. Buenos Aires, Emecé, 1978.

Other

Inquisiciones. Buenos Aires, Proa, 1925.

El tamaño de mi esperanza. Buenos Aires, Proa, 1926.

El idioma de los Argentinos. Buenos Aires, Gleizer, 1928; augmented edition, as *El lengaje de Buenos Aires*, with José Edmundo Clements, Buenos Aires, Emecé, 1963.

Evaristo Carriego. Buenos Aires, Gleizer, 1930.

Discusión. Buenos Aires, Gleizer, 1932.

Las Kennigar. Buenos Aires, Colombo, 1933.

Historia de la eternidad. Buenos Aires, Viau y Zona, 1936; augmented edition, Buenos Aires, Emecé, 1953.

Nueva refutación del tiempo. Buenos Aires, Oportet y Haereses, 1947.

Aspectos de la literatura gauchesca. Montevideo, Número, 1950.

Antiguas literaturas germánicas, with Delia Ingenieros. Mexico City, Fondo de Cultura Económica, 1951.

Otras inquisiciones 1937-1952. Buenos Aires, Sur, 1952; as *Other Inquisitions 1937-1952,* Austin, University of Texas Press, 1964; London, Souvenir Press, 1973.

El "Martín Fierro," with Margarita Guerrero. Buenos Aires, Columba, 1953.

Obras completas. Buenos Aires, Emecé, 10 vols., 1953-60.

Leopoldo Lugones, with Betina Edelberg. Buenos Aires, Torquel, 1955.

Manual de zoología fantástica, with Margarita Guerrero. Mexico City, Fondo de Cultura Económica, 1957; revised edition, as *El libro de los seres imaginarios,* Buenos Aires, Kier, 1967; as *The Imaginary Zoo,* Berkeley, University of California Press, 1969; revised edition, as *The Book of Imaginary Beings,* New York, Dutton, 1969; London, Cape, 1970.

Labyrinthe. Buenos Aires, Sur, 1960; as *Labyrinths: Selected Stories and Other Writings,* edited by Donald A. Yates and James E. Irby, New York, New Directions, 1962; London, Penguin, 1970.

Antología personal. Buenos Aires, Sur, 1961; as *A Personal Anthology,* edited by Anthony Kerrigan, London, Cape, 1968.

The Spanish Language in South America: A Literary Problem; El Gaucho Martín Fierro (lectures). London, Hispanic and Luso-Brazilian Councils, 1964.

Introducción a la literatura inglesa, with María Esther Vázquez. Buenos Aires, Columba, 1965; as *An Introduction to English Literature,* Lexington, University Press of Kentucky, and London, Robson, 1974.

Literaturas germánicas medievales, with María Esther Vázquez. Buenos Aires, Falbo, 1966.

Introducción a la literatura norteamericana, with Esther Zemborain de Torres. Buenos Aires, Columba, 1967; as *An Introduction to American Literature,* Lexington, University Press of Kentucky, 1971.

Nueva antología personal. Buenos Aires, Emecé, 1968.

Conversations with Borges, by Richard Burgin. New York, Holt Rinehart, 1968.

Borges on Writing, edited by Norman Thomas di Giovanni, Daniel Halpern, and Frank MacShane. New York, Dutton, 1973; London, Allen Lane, 1974.

Obras completas, edited by Carlos V. Frías. Buenos Aires, Emecé, 1974.

Prólogos. Buenos Aires, Torres Agüero, 1975.

Editor, with Pedro Henriques Ureña, *Antología clásica de la literatura argentina.* Buenos Aires, Lapelusz, 1937.

Editor, with Silvana Ocampo and Adolfo Bioy Casares, *Antología de la literatura fantástica.* Buenos Aires, Sudamericana, 1940.

Editor, with Silvana Ocampo and Adolfo Bioy Casares, *Antología poética argentina.* Buenos Aires, Sudamericana, 1941.

Editor, with Adolfo Bioy Casares, *Los mejores cuentos policiales.* Buenos Aires, Emecé, 2 vols., 1943-51.

Editor, with Silvina Bullrich Palenque, *El Campadrito: Su destino, sus barrios, su música.* Buenos Aires, Emecé, 1945.

Editor, with Adolfo Bioy Casares, *Prosa y verso,* by Francisco de Quevedo. Buenos Aires, Emecé, 1948.

Editor, and translator with Adolfo Bioy Casares, *Poesía gauchesca.* Mexico City, Fondo de Cultura Económica, 2 vols., 1955.

Editor, with Adolfo Bioy Casares, *Cuentos breves y extraordinarios.* Buenos Aires, Raigal, 1955; as *Extraordinary Tales,* New York, Herder, 1971; London, Souvenir Press, 1973.

Editor, with Adolfo Bioy Casares, *Libro del cielo y del infierno.* Buenos Aires, Sur,

1960.

Editor, *Paulino Lucero, Aniceto y gallo, Santos Vega*, by Hilario Ascasubi. Buenos Aires, Eudeba, 1960.

Editor, *Macedonia Fernández* (selection). Buenos Aires, Ediciones Culturales Argentinas, 1961.

Editor, *Páginas de historia y de autobiografía*, by Edward Gibbon. Buenos Aires, Eudeba, 1961.

Editor, *Prosa y poesía*, by Almafuerte. Buenos Aires, Eudeba, 1962.

Editor, *Versos*, by Evaristo Carriego. Buenos Aires, Eudeba, 1963.

Translator, *La metamorfosis*, by Kafka. Buenos Aires, Losada, 1938.

Translator, *Bartleby*, by Herman Melville. Buenos Aires, Emecé, 1944.

Translator, *De los héroes; Hombres representativos*, by Carlyle and Emerson. Buenos Aires, Jackson, 1949.

*

Bibliography: *Borges: Bibliografía total 1923-1973* by Horacio Jorge Becco, Buenos Aires, Casa Pardo, 1973.

Critical Studies: *Borges, The Labyrinth Maker* by Ana Marie Barrenchea, New York, New York University Press, 1965; *The Narrow Act: Borges' Art of Illusion* by Ronald J. Christ, New York, New York University Press, 1969; *Borges* by Martin S. Stabb, New York, Twayne, 1970; *Prose for Borges* edited by Charles Newman and Mary Kinzie, Evanston, Illinois, Northwestern University Press, 1974; *Borges: Ficciones* by Donald Leslie Shaw, London, Grant and Cutler, 1976; *Paper Tigers: The Ideal Fictions of Borges* by John Sturrock, Oxford, Clarendon Press, 1977; *Borges: Sources and Illumination* by Giovanni De Garayalde, London, Octagon Press, 1978; *Borges and His Fiction* by Gene H. Bell-Villada, Chapel Hill, University of North Carolina Press, 1981.

* * *

Jorge Luis Borges is the main innovator of Spanish-American fiction, as well as a major poet and essayist. Since sharing the International Publishers Prize with Samuel Beckett in 1961, he has become one of the most influential living authors.

Borges began his literary career as a poet. In *Fervor de Buenos Aires* he rediscovers his native city and founds it again, mythologically. Streets, houses, patios and doorways of the outskirts of the city, the South, ever present in his writing, appear metamorphosed in inner reality. It is the beginning of a timeless and impersonal art (influenced by Ultraism, an avant-garde movement introduced to Argentina by him in 1921), an art that attempts to correlate distant realities through the use of the metaphor. His poetry progressively leaves behind rhetorical devices and evolves toward intimacy and elegiac forms, becomes concerned with human destiny. Borges fascinates with his capacity to transform philosophical reflections, as well as historical and literary erudition, into poetry. Borges also begins writing essays very early in life (*Inquisiciones*); he never abandons poetry and essay writing, but his lasting contribution to world literature is to be found in his short-stories. *Fictions* and *The Aleph* collect his classic tales, the ones that secured his place among the masters of world literature and became the cornerstone of the new Spanish-American narrative. It is in these two books, along with the essays of *Other Inquisitions* and the texts (poetry, fiction, fragments) of *Dreamtigers*, where the synthesis of his literary art can be found. In later books of short-stories, such as *Dr. Brodie's Report*, he turns to simplicity, to straightforward storytelling. *The Book of Sand*, however, his most recent collection of short stories, continues creative lines developed early. The recurrent aesthetic and philosophical concerns of his writing (time, the identity of the self, human destiny, eternity, infinite multiplicity, the double, the mirages of reality) remain the predominant themes, but the rigorous verbal precision of his celebrated stories becomes a freer, simpler and more direct prose.

Borges's narrative develops within a tradition that has been called fantastic literature. Borges himself highlights the four basic procedures of fantastic literature: the work of art within the work of art, the contamination of reality by dream, travels through time, and the use of the double. These procedures, along with his favorite devices and symbols (the labyrinth, mirrors, symmetry, plurality and multiplicity, infinite bifurcations, the cyclical nature of reality), contribute to reveal the essential unreality of all human constructions. His stories problemize man's relation with the world and convey a deep and disquieting uneasiness: "Reality is impenetrable and we will never know what is the universe," we read in *Other Inquisitions*, but man is condemned to search for an occult meaning to the incomprehensible mystery of human identity, to attempt to decipher the "inconceivable universe," although all efforts are provisory and no one ever finds the secret key to the cosmos. Borges's fictions are a lengthy interrogation (philosophical, theological, metaphysical) without a possible answer, a terrifying questioning of the problematic and illusory nature of reality, of the existence itself of the universe. In "Everything and Nothing," Borges summarizes his ideas about the problem of identity, the dissolution of the image of the self: "I, who have been so many men in vain, want to be one man, myself alone. From out of a whirlwind the voice of God replied: I am not, either. I dreamed the world the way you dreamed your work, my Shakespeare: one of the forms of my dream was you, who, like me, are many and one." In "A New Refutation of Time" he writes a paragraph that synthesizes perhaps better than any other one of the key meanings of his work, the anguish caused by the implacable destiny of humanity haunted by the passing of time:

> And yet, and yet.... To deny temporal succession, to deny the self, to deny the astronomical universe, are measures of apparent despair and of secret consolation. Our destiny...is not frightful because it is unreal; it is frightful because it is irreversible and ironbound. Time is the substance of which I am made. Time is a river which sweeps me along, but I am the river; it is a tiger which mangles me, but I am the tiger; it is a fire which consumes me, but I am the fire. The world, unfortunately, is real; I, unfortunately, am Borges.

Borges founds an imaginary universe based on intellectual premises (Idealism is a guiding principle of his writing), discovers in literature a coherent order in contrast with the chaos of the world, but his fictions always end up by being a terrifying duplication of our chaotic universe. Uncapable of comprehending reality, he writes self-reflective, involuted, ironic or *ludic* stories, that become continuous dialogues with nothingness, where reality and dream are indistinguishable. Each of his stories mirrors the human condition, and reflects, according to Juan García Ponce, "the spectral character of a world in which everything is appearance and lacks all transcendent possibility.... The juxtaposition in almost all the stories of real and absolute levels succeeds to contaminate of unreality all the actions, turning them into a reflection of a reflection, into the image of nothingness."

Borges's technical control, the evocative and allusive strength of his prose, the verbal rigor, the subtle conceptual irony, the lucid exercise of intelligence, and the power to create a world of his own, distinguishable from any other, are lasting contributions of his prose. He proposes that literature be, above all, literature, and that fiction accept, in the words of Emir Rodríguez Monegal, "deliberately and explicitly its character of fiction, of verbal artifice."

Borges's writing can be seen, in short, as an elaborate way to justify life through art. His inexhaustible imagination justifies, aesthetically, his reason for being. Borges finds in the creative act and in the invention of ideal worlds a provisory salvation. He creates his own reality in order to erase the inscrutable chaos of the world. "Unreality is the condition of art," he writes in "The Secret Miracle," and in "Examination of the Work of Herbert Quain" he "affirmed that of the many joys that literature can provide, the highest is invention." Borges's skepticism with the elusive and inexplicable universe becomes elaborately constructed fictions, games that mirror life but undermine all facile assumptions.

—Hugo J. Verani

BRODSKY, Joseph (Alexandrovich). American. Born in Leningrad, USSR, 24 May 1940; emigrated to the USA in 1972: naturalized, 1977. Attended schools in Leningrad to age 16. Has one son. Convicted as a social "parasite," and served 20 months of a five-year sentence at hard labor; later exiled by the Soviet government. Poet-in-Residence, University of Michigan, Ann Arbor, in the 1970's; now Adjunct Professor, Columbia University, New York. Recipient: Guggenheim Fellowship; Mondello Prize (Italy), 1979; MacArthur Fellowship. Member, American Academy of Arts and Sciences, and American Academy; Corresponding Member, Bavarian Academy of Sciences. Address: Writing Division, School of the Arts, Columbia University, New York, New York 10027, U.S.A.

PUBLICATIONS

Verse

Stikhotvoreniya i poemy [Longer and Shorter Poems]. Washington D.C., Inter-Language, 1965.
Elegy to John Donne and Other Poems, translated by Nicholas Bethell. London, Longman, 1967.
Ostanovka v pustyne [A Halt in the Wilderness]. New York, Chekhov, 1970.
Poems. Ann Arbor, Michigan, Ardis, 1972.
Selected Poems, translated by George L. Kline. New York, Harper, and London, Penguin, 1973.
Konets prekrasnoy epokhi: Stikhotvoreniya 1964-1971 [The End of a Wonderful Era: Poems]. Ann Arbor, Michigan, Ardis, 1977.
Chast rechi: Stikhotvoreniya 1972-1976 [A Part of Speech: Poems]. Ann Arbor, Michigan, Ardis, 1977.
V Anglii [in England]. Ann Arbor, Michigan, Ardis, 1977.
A Part of Speech. London, Oxford University Press, and New York, Farrar Straus, 1980.
Rimskiye elegii [Roman Elegies]. New York, Russia, 1982.
Verses on the Winter Campaign 1980. London, Anvil Press, 1982.
Novye stansy k Avguste: Stikhi k M.B. 1962-1982 [New Stanzas to Augusta: Poems to M.B.]. Ann Arbor, Michigan, Ardis, 1983.
Uraniia: Novaia kniga stikhov [Urania: A New Book of Poems]. Ann Arbor, Michigan Ardis, 1984.

Other

Less Than One. New York, Farrar Straus, 1984

Editor, with Carl Proffer, *Modern Russian Poets on Poetry: Blok, Mandelstam, Pasternak, Mayakovsky, Gumilev, Tsvetaeva.* Ann Arbor, Michigan, Ardis, 1982.

*

Bibliography: by George L. Kline, in *Ten Bibliographies of Twentieth Century Russian Literature*, Ann Arbor, Michigan, Ardis, 1977.

Critical Studies: "The Poem as Scapegoat" by Richard D. Sylvester, in *Texas Studies in Literature and Language 17*, 1975; "Niotkuda s liubov'iu: Zametki o stikhakh Iosifa Brodskogo" by A. Losev, in *Kontinent 14*, 1977; "Brodskii" by George L. Kline and Richard D. Sylvester, in *Modern Encyclopedia of Russian and Soviet Literature 3*, 1979; "A Struggle

Against Suffocation" by Czeslaw Milosz, in *New York Review*, 14 August 1980; *The Poetic Word and the Sacred Word: Biblical Motifs in the Poetry of Brodsky* by Irene M. Steckler, Bryn Mawr College, unpublished dissertation, 1982.

*   *   *

Joseph Brodsky is a traditionalist and a "classicist" both in his adherence to strict poetic forms and in his attachment to the historical sources of the fundamental values—cultural, moral, religious, mythological—of Western civilization. In his poetry, sources and origins, whether Greek, Christian, or Old Testament, tend to be characterized by wholeness, the presence of love and of miracle, a sense of the sacredness of life. The break with such origins, in the "imperial" stages of Byzantium and Rome, is marked by fragmentation and dividedness: the individual, especially the artist, in opposition to the state, and the corollary themes of betrayal, coercion, and banishment—themes clangorously repeated in our own "imperial" age.

Brodsky has drawn most heavily for his inspirations upon such Russian poets as the 18th-century Gavriil Derzhavin, the 19th-century Yevgeni Baratynsky, and the three 20th-century giants: Osip Mandelstam, Marina Tsvetayeva, and Boris Pasternak. Equally strong has been the influence of the English "metaphysical poets" John Donne and Andrew Marvell, along with that of Robert Frost, Dylan Thomas, T.S. Eliot, and certain 20th-century Polish poets, especially Czeslaw Milosz. Brodsky was personally close to Anna Akhmatova from 1960 until the time of her death (in 1966) and to W.H. Auden from June 1972 until the latter's death (in September 1973). For the young poet the two older poets served not as direct literary models but rather as vivid exemplars of what it means to be a great poet, and a great human being, living with courage and dignity in desperate times.

Brodsky employs the traditional forms of Russian prosody in strikingly untraditional ways, with impressive technical virtuosity. His language is robust and unsentimental, by turns bookish and colloquial. He is a master of poetic ambiguity and an accomplished ironist, although his irony tends to be playful or gentle rather than harsh or bitter. Some of his most powerful poems evoke, in controlled "classical" form, a series of disturbing "existentialist" and even "absurdist" visions of the "horrors and atrocities" of human existence and the "infernal Nothingness" of death. Poetry, for Brodsky, is a revelation of "what time does to the existing individual"—as manifested in loss, separation, deformity, madness, old age, and death. Yet it is poetry which offers a way, in the end perhaps the *only* way, of enduring these horrors. Consciously alluding to the works, and the lives, of his illustrious predecessors in exile—Ovid, Martial, Dante, Mandelstam—Brodsky expresses in haunting images, untinged by self-pity, the searing sense of loss and isolation which comes with banishment from one's native city and native language. Loss of language, for Brodsky, is a form of death-in-life.

As a verse translator, Brodsky has produced brilliant Russian versions of Donne, Marvell, and Milosz. He has written penetrating critical essays on Mandelstam, Tsvetayeva, Akhmatova, Cavafy, Montale, Milosz, and Auden. Although he continues to write poetry predominantly in Russian, he has also written moving elegies—to Auden and to Robert Lowell—directly in English.

—George L. Kline

BUERO VALLEJO, Antonio. Spanish. Born in Guadalajara, 29 September 1916. Educated at the Instituto de Segunda Enseñanza, Guadalajara; studied painting at San Fernando School of Fine Arts, Madrid, 1934-36. Married Victoria Rodríguez in 1959; two sons. Writer. Recipient: Lope de Vega Prize, 1949; National Theatre Prize, 1956, 1957, 1958, 1980; March Foundation Prize, 1956; *El Espectador y la Crítica* prize, 1967, 1970, 1974, 1976, 1977, 1981; Leopoldo Cano Prize, 1968, 1972, 1974, 1975, 1977; Mayte Prize, 1974. Member, Royal Spanish Academy, 1971, and Hispanic Society of America, 1971; Honorary Fellow, Modern Language Association (USA), 1978. Agent: Sociedad General de Autores de España, Fernando VI 4, Madrid 4, Spain. Address: General Díaz Porlier 36, Madrid 1, Spain.

PUBLICATIONS

Plays

Historia de una escalera (produced Madrid, 1949). Barcelona, Janés, 1950.
Las palabras en la arena (produced Madrid, 1949). With *Historia de una escalera*, Madrid, Alfil, 1952.
En la ardiente oscuridad (produced Madrid, 1950). Madrid, Alfil, 1951.
La tejedora de sueños (produced Madrid, 1952). Madrid, Alfil, 1952; as *The Dream Weaver*, in *Masterpieces of the Modern Spanish Theatre*, edited by Robert W. Corrigan, New York, Macmillan, 1967.
La señal que se espera (produced Madrid, 1952). Madrid, Alfil, 1952.
Casi un cuento de hadas: Una glosa de Perrault (produced Madrid, 1953). Madrid, Alfil, 1953.
Madrugada (produced Madrid, 1953). Madrid, Alfil, 1954.
El terror inmóvil. Madrid, Alfil, 1954; complete version, Murcia, Universidad, 1979.
Irene; o, El tesoro (produced Madrid, 1954). Madrid, Alfil, 1955.
Aventura en lo gris. Madrid, Puerta del Sol, 1955; revised version (produced Madrid, 1963), Madrid, Alfil, 1964.
Hoy es fiesta (produced Madrid, 1956). Madrid, Alfil, 1957.
Las cartas boca abajo (produced Madrid, 1957). Madrid, Alfil, 1957.
Un soñador para un pueblo (produced Madrid, 1958). Madrid, Alfil, 1959.
Teatro. Buenos Aires, Losada, 2 vols., 1959-62.
Las Meninas (produced Madrid, 1960). Madrid, Alfil, 1961.
Hamlet, from the play by Shakespeare (produced Madrid, 1961). Madrid, Alfil, 1962.
El concierto de San Ovidio (produced Madrid, 1962). Madrid, Alfil, 1963; as *The Concert at Saint Ovide* (produced London, 1973), in *The Modern Spanish Stage*, edited by Marion Holt, New York, Hill and Wang, 1970.
Madre Coraje y sus hijos, from the play *Mother Courage* by Brecht (produced Madrid, 1966). Madrid, Alfil, 1967.
Teatro selecto, edited by Luce Moreau-Arrabal. Madrid, Escelicer, 1966.
La doble historia del Doctor Valmy (produced Madrid, 1976); as *The Double Case History of Doctor Valmy* (produced Chester, 1968). Both Spanish and English versions published in *Artes Hispánicas I*, no. 2, 1967.
El tragaluz (produced Madrid, 1967). Madrid, Alfil, 1968; as *The Basement Window*, in *Plays of Protest from the Franco Era*, edited by Patricia W. O'Connor, Madrid, S.G.E.L., 1981.
Mito: Libro para una ópera. Madrid, Alfil, 1968.
El sueño de la razón (produced Madrid, 1970). Madrid, Escelicer, 1970.
Llegada de los dioses (produced Madrid, 1972). Published in *Teatro español 1971-72*, Madrid, Aguilar, 1973.
La fundación (produced Madrid, 1974). With *El concierto de San Ovidio*, Madrid, Calpe, 1974.

La detonación (produced Madrid, 1977). Madrid, Calpe, 1979.
Jueces en la noche (produced Madrid, 1979). Madrid, Vox, 1979.
Caimán (produced Madrid, 1981). Madrid, Calpe, 1981.
El pato silvestre, from the play *The Wild Duck* by Ibsen (produced Madrid, 1982).

Other

García Lorca ante el esperpento (address). Madrid, Real Academia Español, 1972.
Tres maestros ante el público (Valle-Inclán, Velázquez, Lorca). Madrid, Alianza, 1972.

*

Bibliography: "Buero Vallejo: A Bibliography (1949-70)" by John Kronik, in *Hispania*, December 1971.

Critical Studies: *The Tragic Stages of Buero Vallejo* by Robert L. Nicholas, Chapel Hill, University of North Carolina Press, 1972; *Buero Vallejo: The First Fifteen Years* by Joelyn Roeple, New York, Eliseo Torres, 1972; *Buero Vallejo* by Martha T. Halsey, New York, Twayne, 1973; *El teatro de Buero Vallejo* by Ricardo Doménech, Madrid, Gredos, 1973; *The Contemporary Spanish Theatre (1949-1972)* by Marion Holt, Boston, Twayne, 1975; *Buero Vallejo: El hombre y su obra* by Carmen Gonzalez-Cobos Dávila, Salamanca, Universidad de Salamanca, 1979; *La trayectoria dramática de Buero Vallejo* by Luis Iglesias Feijoo, Santiago, Universidad de Santiago de Compostela, 1982.

*   *   *

Antonio Buero Vallejo emerged as a major and popular playwright in the difficult years of Spain's post-civil-war poverty and political isolation, a period in which Spanish theatre was nearly extinct as a dynamic cultural activity. The opening of *Historia de una escalera* in the fall of 1949 by the unknown playwright came as an astonishing dramatic surprise and had unusual popular and critical success. The play deals with the realities of poverty, desperation, and the lack of mobility of Madrid's lower classes, ill housed, unemployed, and lacking effective means to remedy the situation. Yet the work is neither dreary nor polemic. Buero had found a dramatic means to represent pathos, subdued fury, and the resources of personal integrity, a means that made for good theatre and was acceptable to the severe censorship of the period. The play was strongly challenging to an audience that had seen nothing like this in almost a generation: "hard" theatre with serious dramatic intent.

This social realism could not serve Buero indefinitely as thematic material in the political climate of Spain in the 1950's. He broadened his thematic range through the use of two types of metaphor. The first, represented in his very successful *En la ardiente oscuridad* and the later *The Concert at Saint Ovide*, deals with the enclosed and limited society of the institutionalized blind. His treatment of the world of those who have irrevocably lost what many would consider the most basic of the senses which defend us against exploitation and personal manipulation projected his vision of a maimed and restricted society in terms not difficult to relate to the context of Spain's authoritarian government. His second metaphor turns to Spain's history. Buero's historical plays deal with crises in the lives of the painters Velázquez and Goya and the statesman Esquilache, the Italian minister of finance in the government of Charles III. These figures represent the spirit of creative art and enlightened humanism opposed to the tyranny and short-sighted policies of absolutism exercised in different periods by the church, by bigots, and by manipulated masses. Velázquez (*Las Meninas*) is threatened by the Inquisition when it is learned that he has painted a nude figure of Venus in defiance of Spanish church policy. Envious courtiers use this peccadillo to attack the easy-going freedom which Velázquez had enjoyed as court painter to the household of Philip IV. Goya (*El sueño de la razón*) is persecuted by the repressive government of Fernando VII, which saw all freedom of expression as a threat to an unpopular government supported by a foreign power. Esquilache (*Un soñador para un pueblo*) is forced to abandon his idealistic plans for a renovation of the cultural and economic conditions of Spain by an uprising of the reactionary masses, incited to violence by vested interests.

A moral consideration underlies all of Buero's plays, but he deals with individualized human problems on a human scale in each, and this is the component of his work that makes it truly vital and impressive theatre. He has used fables and mythological themes as well as socially or politically charged materials. In all of these modes, he pits hope and integrity against formidable odds. The outcome is not, in much of his work, a happy one. Overwhelming odds tend to overwhelm, and Buero does not invent miracles to save the hopeless cases that are frequently the theme of his work. His doctrine, expressed in some two dozen plays, is that human hope and dignity, while often betrayed and constantly under attack by the circumstances of life, triumph by the very fact of existing and exalting the individual, however futile and momentary that triumph may be.

Buero's early training as a painter is always evident in his use of space and color, chiaroscuro, foreground and background. As a subtle master of staging, his theatre invariably stimulates us visually and plays well, although it is often flawed by overstatement and the use of facile, obvious symbols. His dialogue is generally sharp, but sometimes excessive. His work tends to have superb moments immersed in lengthy, sometimes leaden, exposition.

With the death of Franco and the opening of Spanish culture to a much broader range of expression, Buero seems to have found little more to say. His art grew from a need to camouflage his dramatic vision in a "theatre of the possible," and this circumstance was a powerful shaping condition for the development of his art. But theatre itself is the overriding interest of Buero Vallejo, and his best work is dramatic art of very high quality by any standards we might want to apply to the theatre of the period 1950 to 1975.

—James Russell Stamm

BUTOR, Michel (Marie François). French. Born in Mons-en-Baroeul, 14 September 1926. Educated at Lycée Louis-le-Grand, Paris; the Sorbonne, Paris, license 1946 and diploma 1947 in philosophy. Married Marie-Josèphe Mas in 1958; four daughters. Philosophy teacher, Sens, 1950; French teacher, Al Minya, Egypt, 1950-51, University of Manchester, England, 1951-53, in Salonika, 1954-55, and Geneva, 1956-57; Associate Professor, Centre Universitaire, Vincennes, 1969, and University of Nice, 1970-73. Since 1975, Professor, University of Geneva. Visiting Professor of French, Bryn Mawr College, Pennsylvania, and Middlebury College, Vermont, 1960, State University of New York, Buffalo, 1962, Northwestern University, Evanston, Illinois, 1965, University of New Mexico, Albuquerque, 1969-70 and 1973-74. Since 1958, Advisory Editor, Gallimard publishers, Paris. Recipient: Fénéon Prize, 1957; Renaudot Prize, 1957; Grand Prize for Literary Criticism, 1960; Ford Foundation grant, 1964. Chevalier, National Order of Merit. Address: Aux Antipodes, Chemin de Terra Amata, 23 Boulevard Carnot, 06300 Nice, France.

PUBLICATIONS

Fiction

Passage de Milan. Paris, Minuit, 1954.
L'Emploi du temps. Paris, Minuit, 1956; as *Passing Time*, London, Faber, and New York, Simon and Schuster, 1960.
La Modification. Paris, Minuit, 1957; as *Second Thoughts*, London, Faber, 1958; as *A Change of Heart*, New York, Simon and Schuster, 1959.
Degrés. Paris, Gallimard, 1960; as *Degrees*, New York, Simon and Schuster, 1961; London, Methuen, 1962.
Portrait de l'artiste en jeune singe: Capriccio. Paris, Gallimard, 1967.
Intervalle. Paris, Gallimard, 1973.
Matière de rêves:
　1. *Matière de rêves.* Paris, Gallimard, 1975.
　2. *Second sous-sol.* Paris, Gallimard, 1976.
　3. *Troisième dessous.* Paris, Gallimard, 1977.
　4. *Quadruple fond.* Paris, Gallimard, 1977.
La Rêve d'Irénée. Paris, Cercles, 1979.
Vanité: Conversation dans les Alpes-Maritimes. Paris, Balland, 1980.

Plays

Reseau aerien (broadcast, 1962). Paris, Gallimard, 1962.
6 810 000 litres d'eau par seconde: Étude stéréophonique. Paris, Gallimard, 1965; as *Niagara*, Chicago, Regnery, 1969.
Votre Faust... (opera), music by Henri Pousseur. Paris, Centre d'Études et de Recherches Marxistes, 1968.
Elseneur: Suite dramatique. La Chaux-de-Cossonay, Volumen, 1979.

Radio Play: *Reseau aerien*, 1962.

Verse

Cycle sur neuf gouaches d'Alexandre Calder. Paris, La Hune, 1962.
Illustrations 1-4. Paris, Gallimard, 4 vols., 1964-76.
Litanie d'eau. Paris, La Hune, 1964.
Comme Shirley. Paris, La Hune, 1966.
La Banlieue de l'aube à l'aurore: Mouvement brownien. Montpellier, Fata Morgana, 1968.
Tourmente. Montpellier, Fata Morgana, 1968.
Travaux d'approche. Paris, Gallimard, 1972.
Envois. Paris, Gallimard, 1980.

Other

Zanartu. Geneva, Galerie Éditions, 1958.
Le Génie du lieu:
　Le Génie du lieu. Paris, Grasset, 1958.
　Mobile: Étude pour un représentation des États-Unis. Paris, Gallimard, 1962; as *Mobile: Study for a Representation of the United States*, New York, Simon and

Schuster, 1963.
Description de San Marco. Paris, Gallimard, 1963; as *Description of San Marco*, New York, French and European Publications, 1983.
Où. Paris, Gallimard, 1971.
Boomerang. Paris, Gallimard, 1978; translated in part as *Letters from the Antipodes*, Athens, Ohio University Press, 1981.
Répertoire 1-4. Paris, Minuit, 4 vols., 1960-74.
Une histoire extraordinaire: Essai sur un rêve de Baudelaire. Paris, Gallimard, 1961; as *Histoire extraordinaire: Essay on a Dream of Baudelaire's*, London, Cape, 1969.
Les Oeuvres d'art imaginaires chez Proust (lecture). London, Athlone Press, 1964.
Essais sur les modernes. Paris, Gallimard, 1964.
Le Masque, with Harold Rosenberg. Paris, Maeght, 1966.
Essais sur les Essais (on Montaigne). Paris, Gallimard, 1968.
Inventory: Essays, edited by Richard Howard. New York, Simon and Schuster, 1968; London, Cape, 1970.
Essais sur le roman. Paris, Gallimard, 1969.
Les Mots dans la peinture. Geneva, Skira, 1969.
La Rose des vents; 32 rhumbs pour Charles Fourier. Paris, Gallimard, 1970.
Dialogue avec 33 variations de Ludwig van Beethoven sur une valse de Diabelli. Paris, Gallimard, 1971.
Rabelais; ou, C'était pour rire. Paris, Larousse, 1972.
Les Compagnons de Pantagruel (lecture). Oxford, Clarendon Press, 1976.
Dotremont et ses écrivures: Entretiens sur les logogrammes, with Michel Sicard. Paris, Place, 1978.
Matières et talismans (interview), with Michel Sicard. Paris, Place, 1978.

Editor, *Essais*, by Montaigne. Paris, Union Générale de Éditions, 1964.

Translator, with Lucien Goldmann, *Brève Histoire de la littérature allemande*, by Georg Lukács. Paris, Nagel, 1949.
Translator, *La Théorie du champ de la conscience*, by Aaron Gurwitsch. Brussels, Desclée de Brouwer, 1957.
Translator, *Tout est bien qui finit bien*, by Shakespeare. Paris, Formes et Reflets, 1958.

*

Bibliography: *Butor: A Checklist* by Barbara Mason, London, Grant and Cutler, 1979.

Critical Studies: *Butor* by Leon S. Roudiez, New York, Columbia University Press, 1965; *The French New Novel: Claude Simon, Butor, Alain Robbe-Grillet* by John Sturrock, London, Oxford University Press, 1969; *Butor: L'Emploi du temps* by Marion A. Grant, London, Arnold, 1973; *Butor* by Michael Spencer, Boston, Twayne, 1974; *Butor* by Jennifer Waelti-Walters, Victoria, British Columbia, Sono Nis Press, 1977; *The Narrative of Butor: The Writer as Janus* by Dean McWilliams, Athens, Ohio University Press, 1978; *Intentionality and Intersubjectivity: A Phenomenological Study of Butor's La Modification* by Lois Oppenheim, Lexington, Kentucky, French Forum, 1980.

*   *   *

Michel Butor became known in the late 1950's among the writers of the "nouveau roman," the group who were famous for their refusal of traditional concepts of plot, characterization, and use of chronology. Thus began Butor's systematic exploration/description of the networks of relationships that make up our perception of the world: an exploration that has continued until this time, involving him in collaboration with other artists, experiments in structure and typography and a total rejection of any concept of *genre*.

By tradition Michel Butor has been spoken of as novelist, poet, critic, dramatist, and experimental writer, but this is not satisfactory, for in his hands each of these categories spills over into the next. The distinctions they draw are not those which matter in his growing body of work. It would perhaps be better to think of Butor as "Notre Faust," defining Faust as an explorer of the universe and a famous teacher, for his work is voluntarily didactic and operates on all the planes of a good education; it requires the reader to attend to what he is being told, make an active attempt to follow instructions in the manipulation of the material at hand, understand symbolic communication of all kinds, utilize the resources of the outside world in his study and finally take what he has achieved out into his daily life.

The novels, *Passage de Milan, Passing Time, Change of Heart*, and *Degrees*, demonstrate how architecture, myth, literature, geography form the context in which we live and create networks of interconnecting experience in which each person is a single junction or knot. Having adjusted his readers' perception of the world in this way and presented to them the complexities of understanding, Butor proceeds to examine human creativity from as many aspects as he can in series of inter-connected texts. The *Répertoire* series of critical essays and the volumes on Montaigne, Baudelaire, Rabelais, *et al.* provide an analysis of the development of individual creative expression; the *Illustrations* series are personal texts (frequently poems) in response to works by other artists (creativity growing from creative expression); the *Génie du Lieu* series, *Description de San Marco*, and *Intervalle* show the importance of landscape, myth, culture on collective expression of experience—the growth of cities, sacred places and so on—while the *Matière de rêves* series ventures into the psychology of creativity by the way the ironic pseudo-dreams are described.

The immensity of Butor's undertaking and the systematic way in which he works are expressed clearly in the organization of the special Butor issue of the journal *L'Arc* which Butor was invited to edit himself. He divided the volume into five chapters: "Arts and Crafts," "Sites," "Museums," "Spectacles," "Books," and his interests—craftsmanship and technique, collective expression in the past, individual creativity from the past, living collective expression, contemporary works of art—can be studied under those headings, although it very soon becomes evident that the categories are indivisible and that the resonances between them are all important.

In the breadth of his vision Butor defies classification. Sartre was quite right when, in 1960, he said that Butor was the only contemporary writer capable of formulating the problem of totality.

—Jennifer Waelti-Walters

CABRERA INFANTE, Guillermo. British. Born in Gibara, Cuba, 22 April 1929; emigrated to England in 1966: British citizen. Educated at University of Havana, 1949, 1950-54. Married Miriam Gomez in 1961 (second marriage); two daughters. Film critic, journalist, and translator. Recipient: Biblioteca Breve Prize, 1964; Guggenheim Fellowship, 1970; Foreign Book Prize (France), 1971. Address: 53 Gloucester Road, London, S.W. 7, England.

Fiction

Así en la paz como en la guerra: Cuentos. Havana, Revolución, 1960.
Tres tristes tigres. Barcelona, Seix Barral, 1965; as *Three Trapped Tigers*, New York, Harper, 1971; London, Pan, 1980.
Vista del amanecer en el trópico. Barcelona, Seix Barral, 1974; as *A View of Dawn in the Tropics*, New York, Harper, 1978.
La Habana para un infante difunto. Barcelona, Seix Barral, 1979.
Infante's Inferno. New York, Harper, 1984.

Plays

Screenplays (as Guillermo Cain): *Wonderwall*, 1968; *Vanishing Point*, 1970.

Other

Un oficio del siglo veinte (as Guillermo Cain). Havana, Revolución, 1960; revised edition, Barcelona, Seix Barral, 1973.
O. Barcelona, Seix Barral, 1975.
Exorcismos de estilo. Barcelona, Seix Barral, 1976.
Arcadia todas las noches. Barcelona, Seix Barral, 1978.

Editor, *Mensajes de libertad: ¡La España rebelde! Ensayos selectos.* Lima, Movimiento Universitario Revolucionario, 1961.

Translator, *Dubliners*, by James Joyce. Barcelona, Lumen, 1972.

*

Critical Studies: *Major Cuban Novelists: Innovation and Tradition* by Raymond D. Souza, Columbia, University of Missouri Press, 1976; *Cabrera Infante y "Tres tristes tigres"* by Reynaldo L. Jiménez, Miami, Universal, 1977; *Cabrera Infante* by Rosa María Pereda, Madrid, EDAF, 1979; *Discontinuidad y ruptura en Cabrera Infante* by Isabel Alvarez-Borland, n.p., Hispamérica, n.d.; *Cabrera Infante in the Menippean Tradition* by Ardis L. Nelson, Newark, Delaware, Juan de la Cuesta, 1983.

*   *   *

Guillermo Cabrera Infante is a versatile writer whose audacious works have continually surprised his readers. Under his influence even a deceptively innocent book like *Un oficio del Siglo XX* (A Twentieth-century Profession), a collection of film reviews originally published in Cuba between 1954 and 1960, is transformed into something more than criticism as the author, the critic (Cain), and films continually merge and separate in a cultural dialogue of change and identity. *Three Trapped Tigers*, which the publisher labels a novel and Guillermo Cabrera Infante prefers to call a book, is widely recognized for its explosive humor and experimental form. And *A View of Dawn in the Tropics* presents a pessimistic panorama of Cuban history by adeptly using vignettes as the basic structural unit.

His latest work, *Infante's Inferno*, blurs the distinctions between autobiography and fiction. Set in Havana during the 1940's and 1950's, there are numerous direct references to people, places, and events which form important aspects of the author's personal past. His parents and their activities in the Cuban Communist Party, their residence at Zulueta 408 in Havana, and his association with the magazine *Carteles* are examples of an extraordinary number of autobiographical references. Just where the autobiography ends and the fiction begins is difficult to ascertain, and it is doubtful that the author always knows. Cabrera Infante professed to be confused about the matter when the writer of this article broached the subject, perhaps with good reason, since much of the novel concerns a young man's obsession with sexual escapades. *Infante's Inferno* demythologizes the Don Juan legend in Hispanic culture or, at least, every Latin male's aspiration to be a Don Juan. As far as autobiographical elements are concerned, it is best to say that Guillermo Cabrera Infante maintains a dialogue in this work with his own past. That is, rather than simply attempting to recreate the past, he maintains a dialogue with it and the emphasis is on the dynamic quality of the relationship. At times a desire to recapture an element from the past seems to predominate, at others, a device from the past is merely used as a springboard for creative fiction. Memory and the transformation of the past is also a theme in *Three Trapped Tigers* and *View of Dawn in the Tropics*, and at times these concerns are combined with a preoccupation with history.

Three Trapped Tigers, Cabrera Infante's most widely acclaimed and recognized work, contains a section which is entitled "The Death of Trotsky as Described by Various Cuban Writers, Several Years after the Event and Before." This section, which is supposedly a tape recording made by some of the main characters, uses the literary style of several Cuban writers to narrate the assasination of Trotsky in Mexico City in August 1940. "The Death of Trotsky" parodies the literary styles and personalities of several important Cuban literary figures, but it also brings into question the relativity of historical truth. In "The Death of Trotsky" we see the presentation of an historical event according to the stylistic norms of different writers and each is based on its own conceptualization or stylization of reality. This section maintains a dialogue with both the historical and literary past and is indicative of the innovative and experimental nature of Cabrera Infante's works as well as his remarkable ability to manipulate language.

—Raymond D. Souza

CALVINO, Italo. Italian. Born in Santiago de las Vegas, Cuba, 15 October 1923; grew up in San Remo, Italy. Educated at the University of Turin, graduated 1947. Served in the Italian Resistance, 1943-45. Married Chichita Singer in 1964; one daughter. Since 1947, Member of the Editorial Staff, Einaudi, publishers, Turin. Co-Editor, *Il Menabò*, Milan, 1959-67. Recipient: Viareggio Prize, 1957; Bagutta Prize, 1959; Veillon Prize, 1963; Feltrinelli Prize, 1972; Austrian State Prize for European Literature, 1976; Nice Festival Prize, 1982. Honorary Member, American Academy, 1975. Address: Einaudi Editore, Via Gregoriana 38, 00187 Rome, Italy.

PUBLICATIONS

Fiction

Il sentiero dei nidi di ragno. Turin, Einaudi, 1947; as *The Path to the Nest of Spiders*, London, Collins, 1956; Boston, Beacon Press, 1957.
Ultimo viene il corvo. Turin, Einaudi, 1949; as *Adam, One Afternoon, and Other Stories*, London, Collins, 1957.
I nostri antenati. Turin, Einaudi, 1960; as *Our Ancestors*, London, Secker and Warburg, 1980.

Il visconte dimezzato. Turin, Einaudi, 1952; as *The Cloven Viscount* (with *The Non-Existent Knight*), London, Collins, and New York, Random House, 1962.
Il barone rampante. Turin, Einaudi, 1957; as *The Baron in the Trees*, London, Collins, and New York, Random House, 1959.
Il cavaliere inesistente. Turin, Einaudi, 1959; as *The Non-Existent Knight* (with *The Cloven Viscount*), London, Collins, and New York, Random House, 1962.
Fiabe italiane: Raccolte della tradizione popolare durante gli ultimi cento anni e trans-critte in lingua dai vari dialetti. Turin, Einaudi, 1956; as *Italian Fables*, New York, Orion Press, 1959; as *Italian Folk Tales*, London, Dent, 1975; complete translation, as *Italian Folktales*, New York, Harcourt Brace, 1980; London, Penguin, 1982.
I racconti. Turin, Einaudi, 1958.
Marcovaldo; ovvero, Le stagioni in città. Turin, Einaudi, 1963; as *Marcovaldo; or, The Seasons in the City*, London, Secker and Warburg, and New York, Harcourt Brace, 1983.
La giornata d'uno scrutatore. Turin, Einaudi, 1963.
La nuvola di smog e La formica argentina. Turin, Einaudi, 1965.
Le cosmicomiche. Turin, Einaudi, 1965; as *Cosmicomics*, New York, Harcourt Brace, 1968; London, Cape, 1969.
Ti con zero. Turin, Einaudi, 1967; as *T Zero*, New York, Harcourt Brace, 1969; as *Time and the Hunter*, London, Cape, 1970.
Gli amori difficili. Turin, Einaudi, 1970; as *Difficult Loves*, New York, Harcourt Brace, and London, Secker and Warburg, 1984.
The Watcher and Other Stories. New York, Harcourt Brace, 1971.
Le città invisibili. Turin, Einaudi, 1972; as *Invisible Cities*, New York, Harcourt Brace, 1974; London, Secker and Warburg, 1975.
Il castello dei destini incrociati. Turin, Einaudi, 1973; as *The Castle of Crossed Desti-nies*, New York, Harcourt Brace, and London, Secker and Warburg, 1977.
Se una notte d'inverno un viaggiatore. Turin, Einaudi, 1979; as *If on a Winter's Night a Traveller*, London, Secker and Warburg, and New York, Harcourt Brace, 1981.
Palomar. Turin, Einaudi, 1983.

Other

Una pietra sopra: Discorsi di letteratura e società. Turin, Einaudi, 1980.

Editor, *Poesie edite e inedite*, by Cesare Pavese. Turin, Einaudi, 1962.
Editor, *Vittorini: Progettazione e letteratura*. Milan, All'insegno del pesce d'oro, 1968.

*

Critical Studies: *Calvino: A Reappraisal and an Appreciation of the Trilogy* by J.R. Wood-house, Hull, Yorkshire, University of Hull, 1968; *Calvino, Writer and Critic* by JoAnn Cannon, Ravenna, Longo, 1981; "Calvino" by Richard Andrews, in *Writers and Society in Contemporary Italy* edited by Michael Caesar and Peter Hainsworth, Leamington Spa, Warwickshire, Berg, 1984.

*   *   *

Italo Calvino is a storyteller above all things. His first novel, *The Path to the Nest of Spiders*, was born out of his experiences in a communist brigade in the Maritime Alps during the Resistance in 1943-44. It might have been a straight neo-realist work had his hero not been a young boy, modelled to some extent on Hemingway's Nick Adams, with an imagination as vivid as the author's. Pavese spotted Calvino's Ariostesque vein of fantasy and called him "the squirrel of the pen." As if to bear out this description—although Calvino usually tries to give the lie to his critics—he wrote during the Cold War years of the 1950's three fantastic "historical" novels with the overall title of *Our Ancestors*. *The Cloven Viscount* is set against the background of a war against the Turks in the late 17th century. The hero is neatly bisected by a cannonball into a Jekyll and Hyde duo (Calvino is a great admirer of Robert Louis Stevenson). The bad half comes home sowing destruction wherever he goes, to be followed some time later by the good half who revives the victims and binds up the wounds. The protagonist of *The Baron in the Trees* is an 18th-century figure who lives his whole benevolent and enlightened life up in the trees owing to a boyhood rebellion against eating snails prepared diabolically by his sister. And *The Non-Existent Knight* rounds off the trilogy with another twosome: the knight who is all pure reason and identity but nevertheless does not exist inside his suit of armour in Charlemagne's army, and his squire who is all existence but cannot discriminate between himself and the rest of the universe. In the preface to these novels Calvino explained how he came to storytelling through the active practice of the art during the Resistance, when the partisans would retail their latest escapades over the campfire in the evening. He spoke of "suspense" (using the English word) as the salt in narrative and added that he was not particularly interested in psychology or drawing-room scenes but preferred "a certain attack" and settings like railway stations—all of which imply plot and action rather than character study. Nevertheless the theme of each of the three novels is given as "how to affirm oneself as a human being."

At this time Calvino was collecting folk-tales from all over Italy and, from studying Propp's *Morphology of the Folktale*, was becoming particularly interested in the shape and functions of the story. He has said that this study helped him to learn about the economy of the tale. Calvino has always written short stories, many of his longer works being collections of shorter pieces fitting into an overall, often mathematical, pattern. Some of his collections, like *Marcovaldo*, attempt to come closer to everyday reality. Marcovaldo is an ordinary city worker whose foibles and misfortunes lead him into fantastic situations, such as, in a bad fog, boarding an airliner bound for Bombay instead of the local bus. Other collections, like *Cosmicomics* and *Time and the Hunter*, use a scientific background to tackle problems that are philosophical and metaphysical. Calvino's parents were both scientists. This may well explain his confident use of exact technical terms which curiously become part of his fantastic style in giving the peculiar essence of the object or situation described, be it a plant or an animal, a cake shop or a galaxy. It would also explain his approaching the wider implications of scientific problems without the usual timidity of the ordinary humanist. In these two "science fiction" collections Calvino uses a narrator with a name like a chemical formula, Qwfwq. Despite his name and his ubiquity in time and place, Qwfwq has very human characteristics and pumps through his human consciousness and language simple accounts of such events as the first big bang (the original spaghetti party), the first appearance of individuation by colour, a running commentary on the division of the individual cell, and the creation by Qwfwq as mollusc of an attractive spiral shell, despite there being no sighted creature to appreciate it. Calvino's fantasy usually leans towards the humorous precisely in its attempt not to be escapist.

Invisible Cities marks a change in tone but not in theme. Unusually it is without plot, consisting of 55 descriptions given by Marco Polo to Kublai Khan of cities he has visited as ambassador, in order to help Kublai Khan grasp some idea of his vast and changing empire. The power of the mind and of language—which is ultimately a problem of narration—has increasingly become Calvino's central concern. In fact he became involved in the 1960's and 1970's in modern literary criticism in both Italy and France, and particularly in the study of semiotics.

His three most recent books all tackle various aspects of narrative, and could be too cursorily dismissed as writing about writing. *The Castle of Crossed Destinies* concerns the question of plot and the individual. The Tarot cards are used by dumb narrators to set out stories as diverse as *Faust* and *Orlando Furioso*. *If on a Winter's Night a Traveller*, which starts promisingly in a railway station, is about suspense and the author's power over the reader as he manipulates the reader's desire, even sexually interpreted, for an ending. And *Palomar*, with the chief character (and narrator's eye) named after the 200-inch Hale reflecting telescope in California, investigates the shaping point of view of the observer. Though firmly based in a reality that includes shopping for cheese and weeding the lawn, this character is still to be found inquiring, measuring, and balancing the physical against the metaphysical. Calvino wrote for the Communist paper *L'unità* in the 1940's. He left the Communist Party over Hungary in 1957. He inherited Pavese's mantle at Einaudi and like him also worked with Vittorini; together they helped found and edit *Il Menabò di Letteratura* until Vittorini's death in 1966. The concern of this periodical (not surprisingly, given Vittorini's involvement) was to bring literature into closer contact with modern society. Calvino contributed a number of important essays, including "The Sea of Objectivity" and "Defying the Labyrinth," now to be found alongside essays on modern literary theory, such as "Cybernetics and Ghosts" (about storytelling), in *Una pietra sopra.*

—Judy Rawson

CANETTI, Elias. Born in Russe, Bulgaria, 25 July 1905. Educated at schools in England, Austria, Switzerland, and Germany; University of Vienna, Ph.D. 1929. Married Venetia Toubner-Calderon in 1934 (died, 1963). Full-time writer; resident of England since 1938. Recipient: Foreign Book Prize (France), 1949; Vienna Prize, 1966; Critics Prize (Germany), 1967; Great Austrian State Prize, 1967; Bavarian Academy prize, 1969; Büchner Prize, 1972; Sachs Prize, 1975; Keller Prize, 1977; Hebbel Prize, 1980; Nobel Prize for Literature, 1981. Address: c/o John Wolfers, 3 Regent Square, London WC1H 8HZ, England.

PUBLICATIONS

Fiction

Die Blendung. Vienna, Reichner, 1936; translated as *Auto-da-Fé*, London, Cape, 1946; as *The Tower of Babel*, New York, Knopf, 1947.

Plays

Hochzeit (produced Braunschweig, 1965). Berlin, Fischer, 1932.
Komödie der Eitelkeit (produced Braunschweig, 1965). Munich, Weismann, 1950; as *Comedy of Vanities*, with *Life-Terms*, New York, Performing Arts, 1982.
Die Befristeten (produced Vienna, 1967). Included in *Dramen*, 1964; as *Life-Terms* (as *The Numbered*, produced Oxford, 1956), with *Comedy of Vanities*, New York, Performing Arts, 1982.
Dramen. Munich, Hanser, 1964.

Other

Fritz Wotruba. Vienna, Rosenbaum, 1955.

Masse und Macht. Hamburg, Claassen, 1960; as *Crowds and Power*, New York, Viking Press, and London, Gollancz, 1962.
Welt im Kopf (selection), edited by Erich Fried. Graz, Stiasny, 1962.
Aufzeichnungen 1942-1948. Munich, Hanser, 1965.
Die Stimmen von Marrakesch: Aufzeichnungen nach einer Reise. Munich, Hanser, 1967; as *The Voices of Marrakesh*, London, Calder and Boyars, and New York, Continuum, 1978.
Der andere Prozess: Kafkas Briefe an Felice. Munich, Hanser, 1969; as *Kafka's Other Trial: The Letters to Felice*, New York, Schocken, and London, Calder and Boyars, 1974.
Alle vergeudete Verehrung: Aufzeichnungen 1949-1960. Munich, Hanser, 1970.
Die gespaltene Zukunft: Aufsätze und Gespräche. Munich, Hanser, 1972.
Macht und Überleben: Drei Essays. Berlin, Literarisches Colloquium, 1972.
Die Provinz des Menschen: Aufzeichnungen 1942-1972. Munich, Hanser, 1973; as *The Human Province*, New York, Continuum, 1978.
Der Ohrenzeuge: 50 Charaktere. Munich, Hanser, 1974; as *Earwitness: Fifty Characters*, New York, Continuum, 1979.
Das Gewissen der Worte: Essays. Munich, Hanser, 1975; as *The Conscience of Words*, New York, Continuum, 1979.
Der Beruf des Dichters. Munich, Hanser, 1976.
Die gerettete Zunge: Geschichte einer Jugend. Munich, Hanser, 1977; as *The Tongue Set Free*, New York, Seabury Press, 1979.
Die Fackel im Ohr: Lebensgeschichte 1921-1931. Munich, Hanser, 1980; as *The Torch in My Ear*, New York, Farrar Straus, 1982.

*

Critical Studies: "Canetti's Novel *Die Blendung*" by Idris Parry, in *Essays in German Literature* edited by F. Norman, London, University of London Institute of Germanic Studies, 1965; "Canetti," in *Text und Kritik*, October 1970 and November 1973; *Canetti: Stationen zum Werk* by Alfons-M. Bischoff, Bern, Lang, 1973; *Kopf und Welt: Canettis Roman "Die Blendung"* by D.G.J. Roberts, Munich, Hanser, 1975; *Canetti* by Dagmar Barnouw, Stuttgart, Metzler, 1979.

*   *   *

Elias Canetti has never been widely known in Britain, although he came to live here in 1938. Since 1981 when he won the Nobel Prize for Literature, the contemporary relevance of his work has once again attracted attention. A reticent man, Canetti has dedicated his life to the study of a single theme: the behaviour of the individual within the mass and the power struggle associated with this conflict. The single-mindedness and objective distance with which he confronts these issues are clearly a product both of his own personal education and of a specific literary and political climate.

The works for which he is best known are his novel, *Auto-da-Fé*, and a study of the behaviour of the mass, *Crowds and Power*. His autobiographies of recent years, *The Tongue Set Free* and *The Torch in My Ear*, have underlined the origins of and the inspiration for his lifetime's work. His dramas and essays, too, reflect a preoccupation with hallucination, political pressure, linguistic ambiguity, and the destructive power of the masses.

Canetti experienced many changes in environment as a child. Born in Bulgaria in a community of Spanish-speaking Jews, Canetti moved to Manchester, Vienna, Zurich, and Frankfurt in his early years. The variety of linguistic and cultural influences to which he was exposed engendered a detachment from his native country and an objective stance towards certain political developments which appeared common to Europe as a whole. He left Vienna for London in 1938, and his spiritual isolation from the German-speaking world has further reinforced certain strongly held views and the breadth of his historical understanding.

The events of most outstanding significance for Canetti in the formation of his interest in crowd psychology and the hypnotic power of the masses were the awaited arrival of a comet in Rustschuk, the sinking of the Titanic and the patriotic response it caused, the fire at the Law Courts in Vienna in 1927, and an emotional experience in Vienna's Alserstrasse in the winter of 1924-25. All these events emphasized the vulnerability of the individual in crowds and the manipulative power of large groups of all kinds. It is the Alserstrasse experience which convinced Canetti that the masses have their own instinct which is in conflict with the instinct of individual personality, and that one could explain the human race as a history of this conflict. (Indeed, Canetti attempts to do just this in his essays in *Crowds and Power*.)

These powerful emotional experiences are linked in Canetti's mind and in his work by images of great energy, of blood, of a rushing sound, and of fire. Fire is frequently seen as a magnetic driving force and is associated with the uncontrolled rhythm of the masses. These symbols recur in Canetti's work. Sight and blindness, insight and illusion are related themes. In *Auto-da-Fé* (the title is inspired by a painting by Rembrandt called *The Blinding of Samson*), the central character, Kien, who becomes increasingly deluded by his world of books, eventually perishes in a fire with them. Canetti is always at pains to point out the contrasts and similarities between a character's appearance and his external environment, and to highlight his use of language in relation to the self-image he projects. Listening became an important skill for Canetti after attending talks given by Karl Kraus who held Canetti spellbound in Vienna in the 1920's. And yet there is an important difference between Canetti and Kraus. Kraus used witty anecdote to denounce people whose characteristics he despised. Canetti uses visual and auditory imagery to *describe* different kinds of people with equal understanding of all types, e.g., the man of books, the collector, the spendthrift.

Each character has "fixed ideas" which stand out because reality is portrayed as fragmented and communication as very partial. Canetti distances himself as narrator from the suggestiveness of his characters, and yet he has clearly been involved with the experience of each of them. Such distance tends to establish a world of "objective" events outside the subjective viewpoints of the characters. And yet the underlying premise of the works is that the boundaries between fantasy and reality are very fluid, making it difficult for individuals to validate their experience except through communication with others. Attempts at such communication are often portrayed as grotesque, leading only to an intensification of individual isolation.

Despite themes which are characteristic of a period of social and political upheaval, Canetti's style is serene, controlled, and lucid, almost part of another era and tradition. His privileged education and his fair-minded liberal parents clearly established a concept of personal identity free from self-doubt. His style reflects such self-assurance and composure. Its authoritative epic breadth must rank alongside that of figures to whom he pays tribute in his essays, Hermann Broch and Robert Musil. They share with Canetti a confidence in humanist values which may appear anachronistic in comparison with the deep-seated suspicion of younger writers. It is manifest in the autobiographies that Canetti is a self-effacing man without the excessive pride and arrogance which a long rich life may give rise to. The poise and balance of his account, his outstanding memory of events, his detachment and control, together with his commanding use of language, rich in imagery, set him apart from many younger contemporary writers. Nevertheless, his subject matter is complex and his vision powerful—a resistance to illusion, manipulation, and death, a confidence in one's own destiny, and a respect for the experience of others which absolve him from dependence on popular theories and fashionable trends.

—Barbara Saunders

CARDENAL, Ernesto. Nicaraguan. Born in Granada, 20 January 1925. Educated at the University of Mexico, 1944-48; Columbia University, New York, 1948-49. Trappist monk, 1957; ordained Roman Catholic priest, 1965. Minister of Culture for Nicaragua. Address: Ministry of Culture, Aptdo. Postale, 3514 Managua, Nicaragua.

PUBLICATIONS

Verse

La ciudad deshabitada. 1946.
Proclama del conquistador. 1947.
Gethsemani, Ky. Mexico City, Ecuador O, ' O' O" 1960; revised edition, Medellín, Colombia, La Tertulia, 1965.
La hora O. Mexico City, Revista Mexicana de Literatura, 1960.
Epigramas: Poemas. Mexico City, Universidad Nacional Autónoma de México, 1961.
Oración por Marilyn Monroe, y otros poemas. Medellín, Colombia, La Tertulia, 1965; as *Marilyn Monroe and Other Poems*, translated by Robert Pring-Mill, London, Search Press, 1975.
El estrecho dudoso. Madrid, Ediciones Cultura Hispánica, 1966.
Antología. Santiago, Chile, Editora Santiago, 1967.
Poemas. Havana, Casa de las Américas, 1967.
Salmos. Avila, Institución Gran Duque de Alba, 1967; as *Psalms of Struggle and Liberation*, translated by Emile G. McAnany, New York, Herder, 1971; as *Psalms*, translated by Thomas Blackburn, London, Sheed and Ward, and New York, Crossroad, 1981.
Mayapán. Managua, Alemana, 1968.
Poemas reunidos 1949-1969. Valencia, Venezuela, Universidad de Carabobo, 1969.
Homenaje a los indios americanos. León, Universidad Nacional Autónoma de Nicaragua, 1969; as *Homage to the American Indians*, translated by Carlos and Monique Altschul, Baltimore, Johns Hopkins University Press, 1973.
La hora cero y otros poemas. Barcelona, Saturno, 1971; as *Zero Hour and Other Documentary Poems*, New York, New Directions, 1980.
Canto nacional. Buenos Aires, Lohlé, 1973.
Oráculo sobre Managua. Buenos Aires, Lohlé, 1973.
Poesía escogida. Barcelona, Seix Barral, 1975.
Apocalypse and Other Poems. New York, New Directions, 1977.
Tocar el cielo. Salamanca, Loguez, 1981.

Other

Vida en el amor. Buenos Aires, Lohlé, 1970; as *To Live Is to Love*, New York, Herder, 1972; London, Search Press, 1974.
En Cuba. Buenos Aires, Lohlé, 1972; as *In Cuba*, New York, New Directions, 1974.
Cristianismo y revolución, with Fidel Castro. Buenos Aires, Quetzal, 1974.
El evangelio en Solentiname. Salamanca, Sígueme, 1975; as *The Gospel in Solentiname*, Mary Knoll, New York, Orbis, 1976; as *Love in Practice: The Gospel in Solentiname*, London, Search Press, 1977.
La santidad de la revolución. Salamanca, Sígueme, 1976.
Nostalgia del futuro. Salamanca, Loguez, 1982.

Editor, with José Coronel Urtecho, *Antología de la poesía norteamericana.* Madrid, Aguilar, 1963.

Editor, with Jorge Montoya Toro, *Literatura indígena americana: Antología.* Medellín, Colombia, Universidad de Antioquía, 1964.
Editor, *Poesía nicaragüense.* Havana, Casa de las Américas, 1973.
Editor, *Poesía nueva de Nicaragua.* Buenos Aires, Lohlé, 1974.
Editor, *Poesía cubana de la revolución.* Mexico City, Extemporáneos, 1976.

* * *

It is impossible to talk about Ernesto Cardenal's poetic works without considering the subjects of politics and religion. His literary accomplishments are very much dependent on present-day Latin American socio-political and cultural developments. One of the most outspoken representatives of the new church, Cardenal has managed to combine, in one complex and controversial profile, the spiritual strength and leadership of a Catholic priest with the verbal richness of a poet and the activism of a Sandinista revolutionary.

As a youth Cardenal was influenced by the political circumstances in his country and by the literary teachings of Jose Coronel Urtecho, an older poet who introduced in Nicaragua the works of contemporary American poets, in particular those of Ezra Pound, and invented with Cardenal a new poetic school: "Exteriorism." *Epigramas* is a first indication of Cardenal's adoption of a poetic technique learnt from the American master—the imitation, and better yet, the rewriting of previous works. He uses this technique to review the historical accounts of the Latin American conquest, as in *El estrecho dudoso*, to reinterpret the American Indian's myths shattered by the Colonial policies, and to include in his poetry countless documents related to contemporary politics in his country.

In 1957, after a spiritual crisis, he became a Trappist monk. It seems too coincidental that he was received at the monastery by another religious poet of great political influence: Thomas Merton, who was to imprint his mark in the spiritual life and the political views of Cardenal. The poetry written by Cardenal while in the monastery combines profound spiritual, almost mystical experiences with a passionate awarenesss of the world. *Gethsemani Ky.*, a collection of religious poetry, expresses in a very simple and direct language the almost liturgical character of life and nature. *Marilyn Monroe and Other Poems* and *Psalms* express religious concerns in worldly political matters. These poems, imitative of Biblical texts, are conceived as prayers to be said by the congregation during liturgical ceremonies. From this fact Cardenal develops a highly rhetorical poetry directed almost exclusively to communal recitation.

With time the subject matter and style of his works have become more and more involved with the immediate circumstances of Nicaraguan politics, and have evolved in a clear ideological direction in harmony with the developments of theological thought in Post-Conciliar Latin America. For Cardenal poetry is a form of popular teaching and of communal prayer. Inspired by a religious faith in the earthly triumph of Christian values in the form of a perfect society which will be, actually, the Kingdom of God promised by Christian eschatology, Ernesto Cardenal constitutes a good example of both contemporary religious thought and artistic political commitment in Latin America.

—Santiago Daydi-Tolson

CARMI, T. Israeli. Born Charmi Charny in New York City, 31 December 1925; settled in Israel in 1947. Educated at Yeshiva University, New York, B.A. 1946; Columbia University, New York, 1946; the Sorbonne, Paris, 1946-47; Hebrew University, Jerusalem, 1949-51. Served in the Israeli Defense Forces, 1947-49: Captain. Married 1) Shoshana Heiman in 1951, one child; 2) Tamara Rikman, one child. Worked in children's homes in France, 1946; co-editor, *Massa*, Tel Aviv, 1952-54; Editor, *Orot*, Jerusalem, 1955; editor, Sifriyat Hapoalim Publishers, Tel Aviv, 1957-62, and Am Oved Publishers, Tel Aviv, 1963-70; Editor, *Ariel*, 1971-74. Ziskind Visiting Professor, Brandeis University, Waltham, Massachusetts, 1970; Associate Professor, Institute for Arts and Communications, Tel Aviv University, 1973; Visiting Fellow, Oxford Centre for Post-Graduate Hebrew Studies, 1974-76; Visiting Professor, English Department, Stanford University, California, 1979. Since 1978, Visiting Professor of Hebrew Literature, Hebrew Union College, Jewish Institute of Religion, Jerusalem. Recipient: Shlonsky Prize, 1958; National Translation Center commission, 1966, and fellowship, 1968; Littauer Foundation grant, 1969; Matz Foundation grant, 1971; Brenner Prize, 1972; Prime Minister's Award, 1973; Jewish Book Council Kovner Award, 1978; Irving and Bertha Neuman Award, 1982; Kenneth Smilen Award (*Present Tense*), for translation. Address: c/o Hebrew Union College, 13 King David Street, Jerusalem 94101, Israel.

PUBLICATIONS

Verse

Mum Vahalom [Blemish and Dream]. Tel Aviv, Mahbarot Lesifrut, 1951.
Eyn Perahim Shehorim [There Are No Black Flowers]. Tel Aviv, Mahbarot Lesifrut, 1953.
Sheleg Byrushalayim [Snow in Jerusalem]. Tel Aviv, Sifriyat Hapoalim, 1956.
Hayam Ha'aharon [The Last Sea]. Tel Aviv, Mahbarot Lesifrut, 1958.
Nehash Hanehoshet. Jerusalem, Tarshish Books, 1961; as *The Brass Serpent*, translated by Dom Moraes, London, Deutsch, and Athens, Ohio University Press, 1964.
Ha'unicorn Mistakel Banar'ah [The Unicorn Looks in the Mirror]. Jerusalem, Tarshish Books, 1967.
Tevi'ah [The Claim]. Jerusalem, Tarshish Books, 1967.
Davar Aher [Another Version: Selected Poems and Translations 1951-1969]. Tel Aviv, Am Oved, 1970.
Somebody Like You, translated by Stephen Mitchell. London, Deutsch, 1971.
Hitnatslut Hamehaber [Author's Apology]. Tel Aviv, Dvir, 1974.
Selected Poems (with Dan Pagis), translated by Stephen Mitchell. London, Penguin, 1976.
El Erets Aheret [Into Another Land]. Tel Aviv, Dvir, 1977.
Leyad Even Hato'im [At the Stone of Losses]. Tel Aviv, Dvir, 1981.
At the Stone of Losses (selected edition), translated by Grace Schulman. Berkeley, University of California Press, and Manchester, Carcanet Press, 1983.

Plays

The Firstborn, from the play by Christopher Fry. Tel Aviv, Israel Anniversary Committee, 1958.
Herr Puntila und sein Knecht Matti (Hebrew version), from the play by Brecht. Jerusalem, Tarshish Books, 1962.
Pantagleize (Hebrew version), from the play by Michel de Ghelderode. Tel Aviv, Amikam Books, 1963.
A Midsummer Night's Dream (Hebrew version), from the play by Shakespeare. Tel

Aviv, Sifriyat Hapoalim, 1964.

Antigone (Hebrew version), from the Robert Fitzgerald version of the play by Sophocles. Tel Aviv, Dvir, 1969.

Measure for Measure (Hebrew version), from the play by Shakespeare. Tel Aviv, Sifriyat Hapoalim, 1979.

La Folle de Chaillot (Hebrew version), from the play by Jean Giraudoux. Tel Aviv, Dvir, 1979.

Hamlet (Hebrew version), from the play by Shakespeare. Tel Aviv, Dvir, 1981.

Much Ado about Nothing (Hebrew version), from the play by Shakespeare. Tel Aviv, Dvir, 1983.

Also made Hebrew versions of the following works for stage production: *Spoon River Anthology* by Edgar Lee Masters, *Noé* by André Obey, *Rosencrantz and Guildenstern Are Dead* by Tom Stoppard, *The Beaux' Stratagem* by George Farquhar, *The Zoo Story* by Edward Albee, *Look Back in Anger* by John Osborne, *The Hostage* by Brendan Behan, *The Little Foxes* by Lillian Hellman.

Other

Editor, with Stanley Burnshaw and Ezra Spicehandler, *The Modern Hebrew Poem Itself, From the Beginnings to the Present: Sixty-Nine Poems in a New Presentation.* New York, Holt Rinehart, 1965.

Editor and translator, *The Penguin Book of Hebrew Verse.* London, Penguin, and New York, Viking Press, 1981.

Translator, *Selected Poetry* (Hebrew versions), by Nazim Hikmet. Tel Aviv, Sifriyat Hapoalim, 1958.

*   *   *

T. Carmi is a poet whose vision is simultaneously historical and miraculous. He has, like others of his time and place, an acute awareness of human suffering, and he recognizes the absurdity of individual lives in the context of social and political events. At the same time, his focus is intensely personal, and in many ways close to the surrealist mode of pursuing the marvelous in everyday life by discovering and using strange images close to subconscious thought.

Carmi has an international background, and has absorbed French and English literary traditions. Born in New York, having lived in Paris, the poet settled in Israel in 1947, where he expressed formal ideas in language he heard in parks and cafés, from bartenders and taxicab drivers. He was familiar not only with biblical and midrashic tradition, but with the full range of Hebrew poetry. As editor of *The Penguin Book of Hebrew Verse*, Carmi read those texts for years to represent, in the anthology, an uninterrupted tradition in Hebrew poetry from biblical times to the present.

Throughout Carmi's poetry, there is a startling fusion of tradition and modern speech. For example, a recent poem, "At the Stone of Losses," begins:

> I search
> for what I have not lost.
>
> For you, of course.
> I would stop
> if I knew how.

I would stand
at the Stone of Losses
and proclaim,
shouting:

Forgive me.
I've troubled you for nothing.

The poem refers to a real stone of losses (*even hato'im*) in Jerusalem, a kind of "lost-and-found" connected with the return of lost property during the Second Temple period, as mentioned in the Talmud. The language is reminiscent of Pascal's *Pensées* ("Console toi; tu ne me chercherais pas, si tu ne m'avais pas trouvé"), and, incidentally, of a talmudic passage about an old man searching for his youth. At the same time, the language is characterized by a bareness of utterance that is in keeping with the central situation: that of a lost modern man searching for wholeness in the other.

One of the striking characteristics of his poetry is the unexpected transposition of sacred images and religious ideas into erotic experience. In his poetic sequence, "I Say 'Love,' " for example, the opening lines are:

You untie the vows
within me.

You erase my handwriting
from the old drafts.

They are, of course, a portrayal of a modern love scene, and are spoken by a man to his woman. At the same time, they are a transmutation of the Kol Nidre prayer for the Eve of the Day of Atonement ("Let our personal vows, pledges, and oaths, be considered neither vows nor pledges nor oaths...").

Carmi's knowledge of the sacred, and of Hebrew literature and legend, affords images that are used as agents of transmutation, enabling him to focus on a divided world and see the wonder in daily life. Even in his poems of historical awareness, he is concerned with people not as nameless victims, not as ennobled human beings, but as ordinary men and women turning slightly away from the tragedy of public events.

In all of his poems, Carmi envisions two worlds. These may be, for example, the world of the immediate present and the luminous world beyond it, as in an early poem, "Story," whose two worlds are metaphor and experience. It is one of his most compelling techniques, early and late, to present one world as metaphor for the other, with the mysteries of an unfragmented life suggested by the terms of the metaphor.

Seeing a world that is divided by time and by the notions of being and becoming, Carmi focuses his gaze on ordinary things in the struggle to redeem a broken universe. His hallucinatory clarity calls back the surrealists, as do many of his images of flaming visionary change, despite their origin in midrashic sources. "I Say 'Love' " and "Song of Thanks," with their images of sun and fire, exemplify this method. However, while the surrealists unified a divided world, often using fiery images of transformation to illuminate contradictions and make them whole, Carmi's opposites are never reconciled. His poetry is a quest for a day that is alive, that does not end in death.

—Grace Schulman

CASSOLA, Carlo.   Italian.   Born in Rome, 17 March 1917.   Educated at the University of Rome School of Law, degree 1935.   Married Giuseppina Rabage; one daughter.   Secondary school teacher, 1942-61; professor of history and philosophy to 1971.   Recipient: Prato Prize, 1955; Salento Prize, 1958; Marzotto Prize, 1959; Strega Prize, 1960; Naples Prize, 1970; Bancarella Prize, 1976; Bagutta Prize, 1978.   Address: Via Vespucci 5, 57022 Marina di Castagneto Carducci, Italy.

PUBLICATIONS

Fiction

Alla periferia.   Florence, Rivoluzione, 1941.
La visita.   Florence, Parenti, 1942; augmented edition, Turin, Einaudi, 1962.
Fausto e Anna.   Turin, Einaudi, 1952; revised edition, 1958; as *Fausto and Anna*, New York, Pantheon, and London, Collins, 1960.
I vecchi compagni.   Turin, Einaudi, 1953.
Il taglio del bosco.   Milan, Fabbri, 1954.
La casa di via Valadier.   Turin, Einaudi, 1956.
Un matrimonio del dopoguerra.   Turin, Einaudi, 1957.
Il soldato.   Milan, Feltrinelli, 1958.
La ragazza di Bube.   Turin, Einaudi, 1960; as *Bébo's Girl*, New York, Pantheon, and London, Collins, 1962.
Un cuore arido.   Turin, Einaudi, 1961; as *An Arid Heart*, New York, Pantheon, 1964.
Il cacciatore.   Turin, Einaudi, 1964.
Tempi memorabili.   Turin, Einaudi, 1966.
Storia di Ada.   Turin, Einaudi, 1967.
Ferrovia locale.   Turin, Einaudi, 1968.
Una relazione.   Turin, Einaudi, 1969.
Paura e tristezza.   Turin, Einaudi, 1970.
Monte Mario.   Milan, Rizzoli, 1973; as *Portrait of Helena*, London, Chatto and Windus, 1975.
Gisella.   Milan, Rizzoli, 1974.
Troppo tardi.   Milan, Rizzoli, 1975.
L'Antagonista.   Milan, Rizzoli, 1976.
Il gigante cieco.   Milan, Rizzoli, 1976.
Ultima frontiera.   Milan, Rizzoli, 1976.
La disavventura.   Milan, Rizzoli, 1977.
L'uomo e il cane.   Milan, Rizzoli, 1977.
La lezione della storia.   Milan, Rizzoli, 1978.
Un uomo solo.   Milan, Rizzoli, 1978.
Il superstite.   Milan, Rizzoli, 1978.
Il paradiso degli animali.   Milan, Rizzoli, 1979.
La morala del branco.   Milan, Rizzoli, 1980.
Vita d'artista.   Milan, Rizzoli, 1980.

Other

I Minatori della Maremma, with Luciano Bianciardi.   Rome, Laterza, 1956.
Viaggio in Cina.   Milan, Feltrinelli, 1956.
Fogli di diario.   Milan, Rizzoli, 1974.
Conversazione su una cultura compromessa, edited by Antonio Cardella.   Palermo, Il Vespro, 1977.

CASSOLA

Letteratura e disarmo, edited by Domenico Tarizzo.   Milan, Mondadori, 1978.

*

Critical Studies: *Cassola* by R. Macchioni Jodi, Florence, La Nuova Italia, 1967; *Cassola* by Renato Bertacchini, Florence, Le Monnier, 1977.

*   *   *

Although born in Rome in 1917, Carlo Cassola chose Tuscany and the Maremma as the background against which he placed much of his early work, including the autobiographical novel *Fausto and Anna* based on his experiences as a partisan in 1944. This choice of a topographical setting which is neither city nor countryside but a twilight zone between the two—it is significant that one of his early works was in fact called *Alla periferia*—provided Cassola with the possibility of exploiting to the full his predilection for an understated, almost colourless style of writing such as that used by Joyce in *Dubliners,* a book which Cassola admitted profoundly influenced him. More significantly, however, the peripheral setting of much of Cassola's early—and best—work underlines his attitude to life and the transformation of life into art. In other words it gives him the possibility of expressing his fascination with a life lived on the margins of society, a life that does not have any precise or easily defined characteristics or outlines. Hence Cassola's adoption, at the beginning of his career, of the word "sublimare" to describe his poetics which he saw as the translation of the subconscious emotions of the artist into a language that was divested of all overt ideological, ethical, or psychological attributes. This early, understated, style adopted by Cassola reaches its highest point artistically in the short novel *Il taglio del bosco,* written shortly after the death of Cassola's wife.

In the novels published after *Il taglio del bosco,* and in particular in *Fausto and Anna, I vecchi compagni, La casa di via Valadier,* and *Un matrimonio del dopoguerra,* there emerges a rather polemical tone as the author seeks to investigate the disappointed hopes and aspirations of the partisans. His often ambiguous attitude to the achievements of the Resistance movement as expressed through the conversation and through the protagonists' attitudes which characterizes this second phase of Cassola's writing has been criticized by the Italian Left, including such writers as the late Pier Paolo Pasolini and Giorgio Bassani, as for instance when the prize-winning *Bebo's Girl* was published in 1960.

From 1961 onwards (with the publication of *Un cuore arido*) Cassola may be said to have returned, more or less, to his early style in which the rhythm of the narration seems to coincide with the rhythm of life itself—the humble, usually uneventful life of unsophisticated characters who nevertheless impart dignity to that life by virtue of their calm and stoical acceptance of the odds against them, mostly of an economic character. It must be added, however, that it is only in such works as *Ferrovia locale* that Cassola manages to recapture the high artistic tone of his best work. For the most part, unfortunately, in this last phase, the reader is made increasingly uneasy by a sense of aridity in the lives of Cassola's protagonists—a sense of lost opportunities and in the last analysis of an inability to live life in any full or meaningfully human sense of the term.

—Gabrielle Barfoot

CELA (y Trulock), Camilo José. Spanish.   Born in Iria Flavia, La Coruña, Spain, 11 May 1916. Attended the University of Madrid, 1933-36, 1939-43. Served in Franco's forces, 1936-39: Corporal. Married Maria del Rosario Conde Picavea in 1944; one son. Free-lance writer in Madrid until 1954, then in Mallorca; Founder, *Papeles de Son Armadans,* 1956. Recipient: Critics Prize (Spain), 1956. Member, Spanish Academy. Honorary doctorate: Syracuse University; University of Birmingham; John F. Kennedy University, Buenos Aires; Interamericana University, Puerto Rico; University of Palma, Mallorca; University of Santiago de Compostela. Address: La Bonanova, Palma de Mallorca, Spain.

Fiction

La familia de Pascual Duarte. Madrid, Aldecoa, 1942; as *The Family of Pascual Duarte,* London, Eyre and Spottiswoode, 1946; Boston, Little Brown, 1964.
Pabellón de reposo. Madrid, Afrodisio Aguado, 1943; as *Rest Home,* New York, Las Americas, 1961.
Nuevas andanzas y desventuras de Lazarillo de Tormes. Madrid, La Nave, 1944.
Esas nubes que pasan. Madrid, Afrodisio Aguado, 1945.
El bonito crimen del carabinero, y otras invenciones. Barcelona, Janés, 1947.
La colmena. Buenos Aires, Emecé, 1951; as *The Hive,* New York, Farrar Straus, and London, Gollancz, 1953.
El gallego y su cuadrilla, y otros apuntes carpetovetónicos. Madrid, Aguilera, 1951.
Santa Balbina 37, gas en cada piso. Melilla, Mirto y Laurel, 1952.
Timoteo el incomprendido. Madrid, Rollán, 1952.
Café de artistas. Madrid, Tecnos, 1953.
Mrs. Caldwell habla con su hijo. Barcelona, Destino, 1953; as *Mrs. Caldwell Speaks to Her Son,* Ithaca, New York, Cornell University Press, 1968.
Baraja de invenciones. Valencia, Castalia, 1953.
La catira. Barcelona, Noguer, 1955.
El molino de viento, y otras novelas cortas. Barcelona, Noguer, 1956.
Nuevo retablo de don Cristobita: Invenciones, figuraciones, y alucinaciones. Barcelona, Destino, 1957.
Cajón de sastre. Madrid, Cid, 1957.
Historias de España: Los ciegos, Los tontos. Madrid, Arión, 1958; as *A la pata de palo: Historias de España, La familia del héroe, El ciudadano Iscariote Reclús, Viaje a U.S.A.,* Madrid, Alfaguara, 4 vols., 1965-67; as *El tacatá oxidado: Florilegio de carpetovetonismos y otras lindezas,* Barcelona, Noguer, 1973.
Los viejos amigos. Barcelona, Noguer, 2 vols., 1960-61.
Gavilla de fábulas sin amor. Palma de Mallorca, Papeles de Son Armadans, 1962.
Tobogán de hambrientos. Barcelona, Noguer, 1962.
Once cuentos de fútbol. Madrid, Nacional, 1963.
Los compañías convenientes, y otros fingimientos y cegueras. Barcelona, Destino, 1963.
El solitario, Los sueños de Quesada. Palma de Mallorca, Papeles de Son Armadans, 1963.
Garito de hospicianos; o, Guirigay de imposturas y bambollas. Barcelona, Noguer, 1963.
Toreo de salón. Barcelona, Lumen, 1963.
Izas, rabizas, y colipoterras. Barcelona, Lumen, 1964.
Cuentos 1941-1953, Nuevo retablo de don Cristobita. Barcelona, Destino, 1964.
Apuntes carpetovetónicos: Novelas cortas 1949-1956. Barcelona, Destino, 1965.
Nuevas escenas matritenses. Madrid, Alfaguara, 7 vols., 1965-66; as *Fotografías al minuto,* Madrid, Sala, 1972.
San Camilo, 1936: Vísperas, festividad, y octava de San Camilo del ano 1936 en Madrid. Madrid, Alfaguara, 1970.
Oficio de tinieblas 5; o, Novela de tesis escrita para ser cantada por un coro de enfermos. Barcelona, Noguer, 1973.
Cuentos para leer despues del baño. Barcelona, La Gaya Ciencia, 1974.

Mazurca para dos muertos.   Barcelona, Seix Barral, 1983.

Play

Homenaje al Bosco I: El carro de heno, o, El inventor de la guillotina.   Palma de Mallorca, Papeles de Son Armadans, 1969.

Verse

Poemas de una adolescencia cruel.   Barcelona, Zodiaco, 1945; as *Pisando la dudosa luz del día,* 1945.
Maria Sabina.   Palma de Mallorca, Papeles de Son Armadans, 1967.

Other

Mesa revuelta.   Madrid, Sagitario, 1945.
San Juan de la Cruz (as Matilde Verdú).   Madrid, 1948.
Viaje a la Alcarria.   Madrid, Revista de Occidente, 1948; as *Journey to the Alcarria,* Madison, University of Wisconsin Press, 1964.
Ávila.   Barcelona, Noguer, 1952; revised edition, 1968.
Del Miño al Bidasoa: Notas de un vagabundaje.   Barcelona, Noguer, 1952.
Mis páginas preferidas.   Madrid, Gredos, 1956.
Judíos, moros, y cristianos: Notas de un vagabundaje por Ávila, Segovia, y sus tierras.   Barcelona, Destino, 1956.
La rueda de los ocios.   Barcelona, Mateu, 1957.
La obra literaria del pintor Solana.   Palma de Mallorca, Papeles de Son Armadans, 1957.
Recuerdo de don Pío Baroja.   Mexico City, De Andrea, 1958.
La cucaña: Memorias.   Barcelona, Destino, 1959.
Primer viaje andaluz: Notas de un vagabundaje por Jaen, Córdoba, Sevilla, Huelva, y sus tierras.   Barcelona, Noguer, 1959.
Cuatro figuras del '98: Unamuno, Valle-Inclán, Baroja, Azorín, y otros retratos y ensayos españoles.   Barcelona, Aedos, 1961.
Obra completa.   Barcelona, Destino, 14 vols., 1962-83.
Páginas de geografía errabunda.   Madrid, Alfaguara, 1965.
Viaje al Pirineo de Lérida: Notas de un paseo a pie por el Pallars Sobira, el Valle de Aran, y el Condado de Ribagorza.   Madrid, Alfaguara, 1965.
Viajes por España.   Barcelona, Destino, 3 vols., 1965-68.
Madrid.   Madrid, Alfaguara, 1966.
Diccionario Secreto.   Madrid, Alfaguara, 2 vols., 1968-72.
Al servicio de algo.   Madrid, Alfaguara, 1969.
Barcelona, illustrated by Federico Lloveras.   Madrid, Alfaguara, 1970.
La Mancha en el corazón y en los ojos.   Barcelona, Edivsen, 1971.
La bola del mundo: Escenas cotidianas.   Madrid, Sala, 1972.
A vueltas con España.   Madrid, Seminarios y Ediciones, 1973.
Rol de cornudos.   Barcelona, Noguer, 1976.
La Rosa.   Barcelona, Destino, 1979.
Los sueños vanos, los ángeles curiosos.   Barcelona, Argos Vergara, 1980.
Vuelta de hoja.   Barcelona, Destino, 1981.
Los vasos comunicantes.   Barcelona, Bruguera, 1981.
El juego de los tres madroños.   Barcelona, Destino, 1983.

*

Critical Studies: *El sistema estético de Cela* by Olga Ferrer Prjevalinsky, Valencia, Castalia, 1960; *The Novels and Travels of Cela* by Robert Kirsner, Chapel Hill, University of North Carolina Press, 1963; *La novelística de Cela* by Paul Ilie, Madrid, Gredos, 1963; *Forms of the Novel in the Work of Cela* by David W. Foster, Columbia, University of Missouri Press, 1967; *Cela* by D.W. McPheeters, New York, Twayne, 1969.

*   *   *

Camilo José Cela has been the dominant novelist of Spain for over forty years. Since 1942, when his first novel, *The Family of Pascual Duarte*, made its appearance, Cela has prevailed as the foremost figure among prose writers in Spain. Actually, his writings extend beyond fiction; he has also dedicated himself to very valuable but explosive scholarship, such as *Diccionario secreto*, a veritable thesaurus of *forbidden* words and expressions. In erudition as in fiction, Cela is forever the iconoclast who seeks to shock his audiences by awakening them to the horrors of our existence. Small wonder that he is regarded as the father of *Tremendismo*, a literary movement which is identified with unseemly and unforseen outbursts of brutality. Nonetheless, it would be inaccurate to perceive the art of Cela in simplistic terms as a revel of ruthlessness, for the pen of Cela also touches our innermost sympathetic chords. Love and tenderness, incongruously as it might seem, permeate the most obvious acts of cruelty.

To be sure, *The Family of Pascual Duarte* stunned the readers with its seemingly senseless savagery. Pío Baroja, who was at the time the best-known Spanish novelist, admittedly was too frightened to write a prologue for the novel, which was destined to incur the wrath of the Spanish government after the second edition became available. (Apparently, the Franco Censors had not read very well or had not understood the work when it was first printed.) The blood baths that were celebrated in the narrative of family relationships vividly bore on the consanguineous carnage that characterized the Spanish Civil War, 1936-39.

Cela's most accomplished novel, *The Hive*, on the other hand, recreated daily existence in Madrid in the aftermath of the Civil War with gentleness and feeling for every aspect of life, however insignificant, however incongruous. Whatever the occasion, be it in sadness or in joy, the experience of the event stands out as an homage to life. Lest it be misunderstood, *Tremendismo*, a sort of Hispanic Existentialism, constitutes, even when the libation is composed of bitter leaves, a toast to the living. The consciousness of one's existence, for all its incongruity, is the ultimate reality.

Cela's zest for life reveals itself in his person as in his art and erudition. His imposing personality, distinguished by his propensity for candidness, has not always endeared him to colleagues and critics. Although he has been proposed for the Nobel Prize by various institutions and individuals, in the minds of some he remains as a forceful, combative person. Especially in Spain it is not unusual to confuse the writer with his creative achievements. In person as in his literature, Cela has championed unpopular causes. As a member of the prestigious Spanish Royal Academy, or as a former Senator by direct appointment of the King, Cela has been in the midst of bio-political activities. As though he were the protagonist of his literary accomplishments, his sensitivity to suffering and social disservice has made him appear as the feared Conscience of his peers.

Although Cela's output is vast and varied, and he is still actively engaged in writing (at present he is working on a new novel), it can be said that the four works which have commanded the greatest attention are: *The Family of Pascual Duarte*, *Journey to the Alcarria*, *The Hive*, and *San Camilo, 1936*. Any of these would suffice to give the author a lasting place in the annals of Spanish literary history; however, together they embody an outstanding collection which affords its author a unique place in 20th-century literature in Spain, and in the world. With his art, Cela has objectively perpetuated an historical epoch which by its reflection of inhumanity could well serve as a conscience for us all.

—Robert Kirsner

CÉSAIRE, Aimé (Fernand). Born in Basse-Pointe, Martinique, West Indies, 25 June 1913. Educated at Lycée Schoelcher, Fort-de-France, Martinique, 1924-31; Lycée Louis-le-Grand, Paris, 1931-35; École Normale Supérieure, Paris, 1935-39, licencié ès lettres 1936. Married Suzanne Roussy in 1937 (died, 1966); three children. Teacher, Lycée Schoelcher, Fort-de-France, 1939-45. Member of the two French constituent assemblies, 1945-46, and since 1946, Deputy for Martinique in the French National Assembly: member of the Communist bloc, 1946-56, and since 1958, Founding-Member, later President, Parti Progressiste Martiniquais. Since 1945, Mayor of Fort-de-France (councillor for 4th Canton, 1956-70). Founder, with Léopold Senghor and Léon Damas, *L'Etudiant Noir*, Paris, 1934; Editor, *Tropiques*, Fort-de-France, 1941-45. Recipient: Laporte Prize, 1960; Viareggio-Versilia Prize, 1968. Address: Assemblée Nationale, 75007 Paris, France; or, Mairie, 97200 Fort-de-France, Martinique, West Indies.

PUBLICATIONS

Verse

Les Armes miraculeuses. Paris, Gallimard, 1946; revised edition, 1970.
Cahier d'un retour au pays natal. Paris, Bordas, 1947; revised edition, Paris, Présence Africaine, 1956; as *Memorandum on My Martinique*, translated by Ivan Goll and Lionel Abel, New York, Brentano's, 1947; as *Return to My Native Land*, Présence Africaine, 1968; translated by John Berger and Anna Bostock, London, Penguin, 1969; as *Notebook of a Return to the Native Land*, translated by Clayton Eshleman and Annette Smith, New York, Montemora, 1979.
Soleil cou-coupé. Paris, K, 1948; revised version, in *Cadastre*, 1961.
Corps perdu, illustrated by Picasso. Paris, Fragrance, 1950; revised version, in *Cadastre*, 1961.
Ferrements. Paris, Seuil, 1960.
Cadastre. Paris, Seuil, 1961; as *Cadastre*, translated by Emile Snyder and Sanford Upson, New York, Third Press, 1973.
State of the Union, translated by Clayton Eshleman and Denis Kelly. Bloomington, Indiana, Caterpillar, 1966.
Moi, Laminaire. Paris, Seuil, 1982.
Collected Poetry, translated by Clayton Eshleman and Annette Smith. Berkeley, University of California Press, 1983.

Plays

Et les chiens se taisaient. Paris, Présence Africaine, 1956.
La Tragédie du roi Christophe (produced Salzburg, 1964; Paris, 1965). Paris, Présence Africaine, 1963; revised edition, 1970; as *The Tragedy of King Christophe*, New York, Grove Press, 1970.
Une saison au Congo (produced Brussels and Paris, 1967). Paris, Seuil, 1966; as *A Season in the Congo* (produced New York, 1970), New York, Grove Press, 1969.
Une Tempête: Adaptation pour un théâtre negre, adaptation of *The Tempest* by Shakespeare (produced Hammamet, Tunisia, 1969). Paris, Seuil, 1969.

Other

Discours sur le colonialisme. Paris, Réclame, 1950; 5th edition, Paris, Présence Africaine, 1970; as *Discourse on Colonialism*, New York, Monthly Review Press, 1972.

Lettre à Maurice Thorez. Paris, Présence Africaine, 1956; as *Letter to Maurice Thorez,* Présence Africaine, 1957.
Toussaint Louverture: La Révolution française et le probleme colonial. Paris, Club Français du Livre, 1960; revised edition, Paris, Présence Africaine, 1962.
Oeuvres complètes. Fort-de-France, Désormeaux, 3 vols., 1976.

*

Bibliography: *Césaire: Bibliographie* by Frederick I. Case, Toronto, Manna, 1973; "Les Écrits d'Aimé Césaire" by Thomas A. Hale, in *Études Littéraires 14,* October 1978.

Critical Studies: *Césaire: L'Homme et l'oeuvre* by Lilyan Kesteloot and Barthélemy Kotchy, Paris, Présence Africaine, 1973; *Césaire, Black Between Worlds* by Susan Frutkin, Coral Gables, Florida, University of Miami Center for Advanced International Studies, 1973; *Césaire: Un Homme à la recherche d'une patrie* by M. a M. Ngal, Dakar, Senegal, Nouvelles Editions Africaines, 1975; *Modernism and Negritude: The Poetry and Poetics of Césaire* by A. James Arnold, Cambridge, Massachusetts, Harvard University Press, 1981.

*   *   *

Aimé Césaire is the best-known black poet and playwright in the Third World. This reputation is based largely on two plays and one long poem, the *Notebook of a Return to My Native Land,* and on the historical impact of the Negritude movement as a rallying cry for colonized Africans in the 1950's. His writing has developed a broad, quasi-political appeal, on the one hand, while pursuing a much more craftsmanlike goal in poetry and theatre published between 1939 and 1982.

In the mid-1930's a Martinican, Césaire, a Senegalese, L.S. Senghor, and a Guianean, L.-G. Damas, all students in Paris, all subjects of France, resolved to affirm their shared blackness, their Africanness, in their writing. Césaire coined the neologism Negritude and a movement was born that would, some twenty years later, furnish the intellectual focus and much of the momentum for the decolonization of the French colonies in Africa, around 1960. This political context provided the expectations and the cultural norms for readings of the *Notebook* until a critical reassessment of Césaire's poetic accomplishment was begun in the mid-1970's. His *Discourse on Colonialism,* a polemical attack on the racist process of deculturation attendant upon colonialism, contributed to establishing Césaire as one of the most articulate mid-century spokesmen for the liberation of Africa. Sartre's proclaiming him a "Black Orpheus" in 1948 did much to establish Césaire as a political poet.

During the second World War, which Césaire spent entirely in Martinique, he cultivated Surrealist techniques in the poetry he published in the magazine *Tropiques,* of which he was the principal editor. The poems written during that period were published in 1946 as *Les Armes miraculeuses.* André Breton heralded their author as "A Great Negro Poet" in a critical essay that has often been cited. Critical appreciation of this collection has varied in direct relation to the critic's judgement of Surrealism. Not surprisingly, Césaire's most politicized critics seldom mention it. His Surrealist practice as a poet reached its peak in 1948 with the publication of *Soleil cou-coupé,* which contained a high concentration of automatic poetry. When Césaire revised this collection for a re-edition in 1961, he lessened its Surrealist impact considerably and removed many of the automatic poems from the collection. *Ferrements* is a more mature work, but some of the poetry testifies as well to a crisis in Césaire's vision of a unified neo-African civilization. Between 1960 and 1982 Césaire published no further collections of poetry. *Moi, laminaire* is good poetry, but most of its themes and techniques were more fully and convincingly treated in *Ferrements.* It does, however, accentuate the elegiac strain that first appeared in *Ferrements.*

After 1960, Césaire launched a second career as a playwright in conjunction with the French director Jean-Marie Serreau. Together they produced one very significant and theatrically effective play, *The Tragedy of King Christophe,* and a very original adaptation of Shakespeare's *Tempest. A Season in the Congo* has been less well received, in part on political grounds, in part because the author may have been too close to his subject, the political murder of Patrice Lumumba. Ngal, who has written most convincingly on Césaire's theatre, considers these plays, and the earlier *Et les chiens se taisaient*, to be tragedies of decolonization.

—A. James Arnold

CHAR, René (-Émile). French. Born in L'Isle-sur-Sorgue, Vaucluse, 14 June 1907. Educated at Lycée d'Avignon, baccalaureate degree; École-de-Commerce, Marseilles, 1925. Served in the French artillery, Nimes, 1927-28, and Alsace, 1939-40; with the Resistance in France and North Africa: Chevalier, Legion of Honor; Médaille de la Résistance; Croix de Guerre. Married Georgette Goldstein in 1933. Moved to Paris in 1929 and met Aragon, Éluard, and Breton: associated with the surrealists during the second period of the movement, 1930-34. Recipient: Critics Prize (France), 1966. Member, Bavarian Academy; Honorary Member, Modern Language Association (USA). Address: Les Busclats, 84800 L'Isle-sur-Sorgue, Vaucluse, France.

PUBLICATIONS

Verse

> *Les Cioches sur le coeur.* Paris, Le Rouge et le Noir, 1928.
> *Arsenal.* Privately printed, 1929; as *De la main à la main*, 1930.
> *Ralentir travaux*, with André Breton and Paul Éluard. Paris, Editions Surréalistes, 1930.
> *Le Tombeau des secrets.* Nimes, Larguier, 1930.
> *Artine.* Paris, Editions Surréalistes, 1930; augmented edition, as *Artine et autres poèmes*, Paris, Tchou, 1967.
> *L'Action de la justice est éteinte.* Paris, Editions Surréalistes, 1931.
> *Le Marteau sans maître.* Paris, Corti, 1934.
> *Dépendance de l'adieu.* Paris, GLM, 1936.
> *Placard pour un chemin des écoliers.* Paris, GLM, 1937.
> *Dehors la nuit est gouvernée.* Paris, GLM, 1938.
> *Seuls demeurent.* Paris, Gallimard, 1945.
> *Le Poème pulvérisé.* Paris, Fontaine, 1947.
> *Fureur et mystère.* Paris, Gallimard, 1948.
> *Fête des arbres et du chasseur.* Paris, GLM, 1948.
> *Les Matinaux.* Paris, Gallimard, 1950.
> *Art bref, suivi de Premières alluvions.* Paris, GLM, 1950.
> *Quatre fascinants: La Minutieuse.* Paris, SN, 1951.
> *À une sérénité crispée.* Paris, Gallimard, 1951.
> *Poèmes.* Paris, SN, 1951.
> *La Paroi et la prairie.* Paris, GLM, 1952.

Le Rempart de brindilles.   Paris, Broder, 1952.
Lettera amorosa.   Paris, Gallimard, 1953.
Choix de poèmes.   Mendoza, Argentina, Brigadas Liricas, 1953.
A la santé du serpent.   Paris, GLM, 1954.
Le Deuil des nevons.   Brussels, Le Cormier, 1954.
Poèmes des deux années 1953-1954.   Paris, GLM, 1955.
Chanson des étages.   Alès, PAB, 1955.
La Bibliothèque est en feu, etchings by Braque.   Paris, Broder, 1956.
Hypnos Waking, edited by Jackson Mathews.   New York, Random House, 1956.
Pour nous, Rimbaud.   Paris, GLM, 1956.
En trente-trois morceaux.   Paris, GLM, 1956.
Jeanne qu'on brûla verte.   Alès, PAB, 1956.
Les Compagnons dans le jardin.   Paris, Broder, 1956.
La Bibliothèque est en feu et autres poèmes.   Paris, GLM, 1957.
L'Une et l'autre.   Alès, PAB, 1957.
De moment en moment, engravings by Miro.   Alès, PAB, 1957.
Poèmes et prose choisis.   Paris, Gallimard, 1957.
Elisabeth, petite fille.   Alès, PAB, 1958.
Sur la poésie.   Paris, GLM, 1958.
Cinq poésies en hommage à Georges Braque.   Geneva, SN, 1958.
L'Escalier de Flore, engravings by Braque.   Alès, PAB, 1958.
La Faux relevée.   Alès, PAB, 1959.
Nous avons (prose poem), engravings by Miro.   Paris, Broder, 1959.
Pourquoi la journée vole.   Alès, PAB, 1960.
Le Rebanque.   Alès, PAB, 1960.
Anthologie.   Paris, GLM, 1960; revised edition, as *Anthologie 1934-1969,* 1970.
Les Dentelles de Montmirail.   Alès, PAB, 1960.
L'Allégresse.   Alès, PAB, 1960.
Deux poèmes, with Paul Éluard.   Paris, Hugues, 1960.
L'Inclémence lointaine.   Paris, Berès, 1961.
L'Issue.   Alès, PAB, 1961.
La Montée de la nuit.   Alès, PAB, 1961.
La Parole en archipel.   Paris, Gallimard, 1962.
Deux poèmes.   Alès, PAB, 1963.
Poèmes et prose choisis.   Paris, Gallimard, 1963.
Impressions anciennes.   Paris, GLM, 1964.
Commune présence.   Paris, Gallimard, 1964; revised edition, 1978.
L'An 1964.   Alès, PAB, 1964.
L'Âge cassant.   Paris, Corti, 1965.
Flux de l'aimant.   Veilhes, GP, 1965.
La Provence, point Omega.   Privately printed, 1965.
Retour amont.   Paris, GLM, 1966.
Le Terme epars.   Paris, Imprimerie Union, 1966.
Les Transparents.   Alès, PAB, 1967.
Dans la pluie giboyeuse.   Paris, Gallimard, 1968.
Le Chien de coeur.   Paris, GLM, 1969.
L'Effroi la joie.   Paris, Hugues, 1971.
Le Nu perdu.   Paris, Gallimard, 1971.
La Nuit talismanique.   Geneva, Skira, 1972.
Le Monde de l'art n'est pas le monde du pardon.   Paris, Maeght, 1975.
Aromates chasseurs.   Paris, Gallimard, 1975.
Poems, edited by Mary Ann Caws and Jonathan Griffin.   Princeton, New Jersey, Princeton University Press, 1976.
Chants de la Balandrame 1975-1977.   Paris, Gallimard, 1977.

Fenêtres dormantes et porte sur le toit. Paris, Gallimard, 1979.

Plays

Trois coups sous les arbres: Théâtre saisonnier (includes *Sur les hauteurs, L'Abominable Homme des neiges, Claire, Le Soleil des eaux, L'Homme qui marchait dans un rayon de soleil, La Conjuration*). Paris, Gallimard, 1967.

Other

Moulin premier. Paris, GLM, 1936.
Feuillets d'Hypnos (war journal). Paris, Gallimard, 1946; as *Leaves of Hypnos*, New York, Grossman, 1973.
Arrière-histoire de "Poème pulvérisé." Paris, Hugues, 1953.
Recherche de la base et du sommet; Pauvreté et privilège. Paris, Gallimard, 1955.
Sur la poésie. Paris, GLM, 1958.
La Postérité du soleil, with Camus. Geneva, Engelberts, 1965.
L'Endurance de la pensée, with Martin Heidegger. Paris, Plon, 1968.
Sur la poésie 1936-1974. Paris, Mano, 1974.
Oeuvres complètes. Paris, Gallimard, 1983— .
Many catalogs and tracts also published.

Translator, *Le Bleu de l'aile,* by Tiggie Ghika. Paris, Cahiers d'Art, 1948.
Translator, with Tina Jolas, *La Planche de vivre: Poésies.* Paris, Gallimard, 1981.

*

Bibliography: *Bibliographie des oeuvres de Char de 1928 à 1963* by P.A. Benoit, Ribautes-les-Tavernes, Demi-Jour, 1964.

Critical Studies: *The Poetry and Poetics of Char* by Virginia La Charité, Chapel Hill, University of North Carolina Studies in Romance Languages and Literatures, 1968; *Worlds Apart: Structural Parallels in the Poetry of Paul Valéry, Saint-John Perse, Benjamin Péret, and Char* by Elizabeth R. Jackson, The Hague, Mouton, 1976; *The Presence of Char*, Princeton, New Jersey, Princeton University Press, 1976, and *Char*, Boston, Twayne, 1977, both by Mary Ann Caws; *Char: The Myth and the Poem* by James R. Lawler, Princeton, New Jersey, Princeton University Press, 1978; *Lightning: The Poetry of Char* by Nancy Kline Piore, Boston, Northeastern University Press, 1981.

*   *   *

The world of René Char's poetry is rural and Mediterranean. All the familiar elements of his native Provence are in it: crickets and almond trees, olives, grapes, figs, oranges, branches of mimosa. The frequently recurring name of Heraclitus helps to fuse the Greek spirit with the Provençal. The country he describes is sun-flooded, a kingdom of space and dazzling light. Char's love of the land and his solicitude for living growing things are traits of the peasant in him. His manner of considering the objects of his landscape, of undertaking the hardest tasks and facing the gravest risks might be explained by the deep sense of fraternity that characterizes the poet's love of man and of the soil. Like most lovers of the land, he has often shown hostility toward modern mechanization and modern forms of exploitation.

About 1930, Char joined the group of surrealists. Although he soon cut himself off from any strict allegiance to surrealism, he profited from many aspects of the school. From surrealism he learned that revolt against conformity is a natural instinct of the poet, a natural instinct of poetry. Surrealism was a collective experiment that deepened Char's sense of brotherhood.

In the early 1940's, Char participated in the Resistance movement as captain of the maquis in Provence. His partisan poems are the noblest of the war poems and the most likely to endure. The group *Feuillets d'Hypnos*, dedicated to Albert Camus, and included in *Fureur et mystère*, best represent the poetry written in France between 1940 and 1944. In this book Char analyzes the basic mysteriousness of all poetry: "le poème est l'amour réalisé du désir demeuré désir." Heraclitus also was called obscure in his will to effect harmony between opposites. The transformation of time into eternity, associated with the philosopher, has its counterpart in the poet's will to fix in rhythmical language an emotion destined to pass quickly.

The verses of René Char, the aphorisms in his work, and the brief condensed tales that appear in company with the aphorisms, all speak of the nature of poetry. The outside world in which the poet lives is the natural world of constant change, a flowering river of things such as Heraclitus described. But this is the site of risks and provocations. The things he sees there are not poems but they discover their reality in poems. The poetic act is the finding of a form for things that otherwise would never emerge from their silence.

The myth of tragedy is man's principal heritage, but it may accompany a lifetime of revolt against this fate. This revolt is the subject matter of some of the leading prose writers of modern France: Malraux, Saint-Exupéry, Camus. It is also the subject matter of Char's poetry. Man's ever-increasing awareness of his fate is equivalent to what Char calls the continuous presence of risk felt by the poet.

The purity and the conciseness of Char's language make it appear more primitively faithful to his reactions, to his first responses. He has sustained in his style, which is devoid of the usual poetic rhetoric, something of the secret meaning of his reactions. In this will to record and explain his reaction to the world and to human experience, he places himself quite centrally within the tradition of French moralists. With his ever-increasing understanding of life, Char the poet and Char the moralist both denounce the vanity of life. Poetry is both a critique of poetics and a critique of illusions.

The strong stylistic and moralist claims made by this poet designate him as the heir both of symbolism and surrealism. He is surrealist in the way in which he feels an event. He is symbolist in the distance he knows exists between the occurrence of the event and its narration. He actually speaks of the enigmas of poetry as often as Mallarmé did, but he defines the actions of the poet as the results of these enigmas: "Les actions du poète ne sont que la conséquence des énigmes de la poésie" (*À une sérénité crispée*). Mallarmé would call the poet the creator of enigmas. Char would agree with Mallarmé in calling a poem a quintessence, but in the straining of Char's language, in the tension of each aphoristic utterance, he defines the natural movement of poetry as a revolt.

As Char's writing has become more and more visibly affected by the events of his time, he has made the effort in his poetical work more and more consciously to transform what he sees and feels. But his age seen in an image is both transformation and interpretation. It is the understanding of the essence of things, an abstraction which, when successful, is the container of opposites.

Despite the fact that René Char is a difficult poet in almost every sense, he has today reached an eminent degree of fame. The best way to approach Char is a study of those moments in his writings when he is aware of the poet's vocation. They are the moments of natural perception when he greets the world. This poet is essentially an analogist.

The vigor of Char's mind puts him into a separate poetic world. We are moved by the vitality of his thought, but especially by the vitality of his concreteness. The truths of the world as he sees them are constantly demanding his allegiance. He is a poet characterized by the habit of seeing things charged with meaning—an ordered meaning regarding the relationships between nature and men.

The walker, the man who is bound to the earth and who walks on its surface, is granted some knowledge of the secret existence of things, secrets of the wind, of trees, of water. At moments in history when total destruction seems inevitable, man is unable to believe that the world, which has always been redeemed in the past, is facing its death in the very presence of man. In the future, Char may be looked upon as the apocalyptic poet of our day, as the poet the most persistently oppressed by the Apocalypse aspect of the mid-century and the post mid-century.

—Wallace Fowlie

CH'IEN CHUNG-SHU (Qian Zhongshu). Chinese. Born in Wuhsi, Kiangsu province, 10 November 1910. Educated at St. John's University Affiliated High Schools in Soochow and Wuhsi; Tsing-hua University, Peking, graduated 1933; Exeter College, Oxford, 1935-37, B.Litt. 1937; also studied in Paris, 1937-38. Married the writer Yang Chiang in 1935; one daughter. Taught at Kuang-hua University, Shanghai, 1933-35; National Southwest Associated University, Kun-ming; National Teachers College, Lan-t'ien; Aurora Womens' College, Shanghai; Chi-nan University, Shanghai. Since 1949, teacher at Tsing-hua University, Peking. Since 1952, Fellow, Institute of Literature, and since 1982, Vice President, Academy of Social Sciences. Editor, *Philobiblion*, English-language periodical, Nanking, 1946-48. Address: Academy of Social Sciences, Peking, China.

PUBLICATIONS

Fiction

Jen, Shou, Kuei [Men, Beasts, Ghosts]. Shanghai, Enlightenment Press, 1946.
Wei-ch'eng. Shanghai, Aurora Press, 1947; as *Fortress Besieged*, Bloomington, Indiana University Press, 1979.

Other

Hsieh tsai jen-sheng pien-shang [In the Margin of Life]. Shanghai, Enlightenment Press, 1941.
T'an yi lu [On Poetry and Poetics]. Shanghai, Enlightenment Press, 1948.
Sung-shih hsüan-chu [Critical Anthology of Sung Poetry]. Peking, People's Literature Press, 1958; revised edition, 1979.
Kuan-chui Pien [Partial Views: Essays on Letters and Ideas]. Peking, Chunghua Books, 4 vols., 1979-81.
Chiu-wen Ssu-p'ien [Four Old Essays]. Shanghai, Chinese Classics, 1979.
Ye-shi Ji [Some Essays]. Hong Kong, Wide Angle Press, 1984.

*

Critical Studies: *A History of Modern Chinese Fiction* by C.T. Hsia, Bloomington, Indiana University Press, 1968; *Qian Zhongshu* by Theodore Huters, Boston, Twayne, 1982.

*   *   *

Ch'ien Chung-shu is one of the most brilliant and erudite comparers of Chinese and Western cultures in the 20th century. Having early on written what is among China's greatest modern novels, *Fortress Besieged*, he has maintained an honored position in contemporary Chinese letters. However, he has written relatively little fiction (none after 1949) and in the past thirty years has concentrated on scholarship. Since the late 1970's he has met with foreign scholars and friends and has continued to impress people with an astounding depth of memory and perception about Chinese and European culture.

In the 1930's and 1940's he published essays in both English and Chinese, some scholarly and others primarily satirical. His most famous pre-1949 study is *On the Art of Poetry*, an examination of the style and diction of a broad range of traditional Chinese poets. He also wrote short stories in which he reflected his responses to the social and intellectual scene in China leading up to the Japanese invasion. There are humorous caricatures and satirical vignettes, any of which focus on one of his favorite targets, the pseudo-modernized or Westernized intellectual. Some of these stories were anthologized in his 1946 volume, *Men, Beasts, Ghosts*.

His major work of fiction appeared in 1947, *Fortress Besieged*. It is a novel about a student returning from Europe and witnessing, in somewhat picaresque fashion, the panorama of China's pre-war condition. He is isolated by the fact of his heightened but ineffective awareness of the world beyond China and of the hypocrites, imposters, and incompetents that people his native land. In the confrontation between old and new worlds, he repeatedly discovers that whatever is modern and advanced always ends up seeming as equally hollow and ludicrous as the thing it supplants.

One of the novel's outstanding accomplishments is its portrayal of love and marriage. The returned student, Fang Hung-chien, is at loose ends and takes up with whomever accidentally falls in his way. However, at the same time that he is driven to marital attachment, he is himself inherently detached and ultimately finds nothing but misunderstanding and entrapment. The "forteresse assiégiée" is thus Ch'ien Chung-shu's metaphor for marriage: "Those who are outside want to get in, and those who are inside want to get out."

The novel strikes most readers as an exuberant work always worth remembering for this or that brilliantly comic scene. But at times it suffers from an excess of topical satire and a tendency to lampoon; this fault is especially characteristic of his stories. In addition, the novel seems to have a pointedly vague sense of political or ideological identity, a factor that undoubtedly contributed to the extreme criticism he and his works received after the communist revolution. Had Ch'ien continued to write fiction he very possibly would have corrected the first of these defects (the progress from his stories to the novel is already clear). As for the second, to write a novel with such irony as *Fortress Besieged* is impossible in the Peoples' Republic of China. There the emphasis is on broad-ranging social depiction (*Fortress Besieged* concentrates too much on the individual) and a critical stance that avoids clever ambiguity. The ironic viewpoint would be looked upon as a Western phenomenon and as a sign of vacillation and reactionary leanings in general.

Since 1949 Ch'ien has worked as a teacher and scholar in Peking. He has published three works, an *Annotated Selection of Sung Poetry* in 1958; *Chiu-wen Ssu-p'ien* in 1979, a book of four studies; and also in 1979, *Kuan-chui Pien*, a lengthy study of major classical Chinese works such as the *Book of Changes*, the *Classic of Poetry*, and others. He has written this last piece in an elegant, literary style, and has included both philological and cross-cultural comments about what he considers the most important aspect of the Chinese past. Such a style and focus cannot but seem to counter the trends of recent history in China which were to completely deny just this cultural past.

—Keith McMahon

CLAUS, Hugo (Maurice Julien). Belgian. Born in Bruges, 5 April 1929. Educated at schools in Eke, Aalbeke, Kortrijk, Deinze, Ghent. Married Elly Overzier in 1955; one son. Worked as housepainter, agricultural worker, actor, etc., then full-time writer: editor, *Tijd en Mens*, in early 1950's. Recipient: Krijn Prize, 1951; Lugné-Poë Prize (France), 1955; Triennial Belgian State Prize, for drama, 1955, 1967, 1973, and for verse, 1971; Roland Holst Prize, 1965; Huygens Prize, 1979. Address: Kasteelstraat 166, 9000 Gent, Belgium.

PUBLICATIONS

Plays

De getuigen [The Witnesses] (produced Brussels, 1955).
Een Bruid in de morgen (produced Rotterdam, 1955). Antwerp/Amsterdam, Ontwikkeling/Bezige Bij, 1955; as *A Bride in the Morning* (produced New York, 1960).
Het lied van de moordenaar [The Song of the Murderer] (produced Rotterdam, 1957). Antwerp/Amsterdam, Ontwikkeling/Bezige Bij, 1957.
Dantons dood, adaptation of a play by Büchner. Amsterdam, Bezige Bij, 1958.
Suiker [Sugar]. Antwerp/Amsterdam, Ontwikkeling/Bezige Bij, 1958.
Mama, kijk, zonder Handen! [Look, Ma, No Hands] (produced Brussels, 1960). Amsterdam, Bezige Bij, 1959.
Het Mes (scenario). Amsterdam, Bezige Bij, 1961.
De dans van de reiger [The Heron's Dance]. Amsterdam, Bezige Bij, 1962.
Uilenspiegel, adaptation of a work by Charles de Coster (produced Leiden, 1965). Amsterdam, Bezige Bij, 1965.
Thyestes, adaptation of the play by Seneca (produced 1966). Amsterdam/Antwerp, Bezige Bij/Contact, 1966.
Het Goudland [The Gold Country], adaptation of a novel by Henrik Conscience (produced Antwerp, 1966). Amsterdam, Bezige Bij, 1966.
Acht toneelstukken [Eight Stageplays]. Amsterdam, Bezige Bij, 1966.
De dans van de reiger [The Heron's Dance] (screenplay). Amsterdam, Bezige Bij, 1966.
De vijanden [The Enemies] (screenplay). Amsterdam, Bezige Bij, 1967.
Masscheroen (produced Knokke, 1967). Amsterdam, Bezige Bij, 1968.
Wrrraak!, adaptation of the play *The Revenger's Tragedy* by Cyril Tourneur (produced Eindhoven, 1968). Amsterdam, Bezige Bij, 1968.
Morituri (as *Hyperion en het geweld*, produced Brussels, 1968). Amsterdam, Bezige Bij, 1968.
Motet (produced Ghent, 1969).
Reconstructie (libretto), with others (produced Amsterdam, 1969). Amsterdam, Bezige Bij, 1969.
Vrijdag (produced Amsterdam, 1969). Amsterdam, Bezige Bij, 1969; as *Friday*, London, Davis Poynter, 1972.
Tand om tand [A Tooth for a Tooth]. Amsterdam, Bezige Bij, 1970.
Het leven en de werken van Leopold II: 29 taferelen uit de Belgische oudheid [The Life and Works of Leopold II: 29 Scenes from Belgian Antiquity]. Amsterdam, Bezige Bij, 1970.
De Spaanse hoer [The Spanish Whore], adaptation of *La Celestina* by Rojas (produced Eindhoven, 1970). Amsterdam, Bezige Bij, 1970.
Interieur, from his novel *Omtrent Deedee* (produced Amsterdam, 1971). Amsterdam, Bezige Bij, 1971.
Oedipus, adaptation of the play by Seneca. Amsterdam, Bezige Bij, 1971.
De vossejacht, adaptation of the play *Volpone* by Ben Jonson. Amsterdam, Bezige Bij, 1972.
Blauw blauw [Blue Blue], adaptation of the play *Private Lives* by Noël Coward. Am-

sterdam, Bezige Bij, 1973.
Pas de deux. Amsterdam, Bezige Bij, 1973.
Thuis [Home]. Amsterdam, Bezige Bij, 1975.
Orestes, adaptation of the play by Euripides. Amsterdam, Bezige Bij, 1976.
Jessica! Amsterdam, Ziggurat, 1977.
Het huis van Labdakos [The House of Labdakos], adaptation of a scenario by Frans Marijnen. Amsterdam, Bezige Bij, 1977.
Phaedra, adaptation of the play by Seneca. Amsterdam, Bezige Bij, 1980.
Het haar van de hond [The Hair of the Dog]. Amsterdam, Bezige Bij, 1982.

Fiction

De Metsiers. Brussels, Manteau, 1950; as *The Duck Hunt,* New York, Random House, 1965; as *Sister of Earth,* London, Panther, 1966.
De hondsdagen [The Dog Days]. Amsterdam, Bezige Bij, 1952.
Natuurgetrouw: Schetsen, verhalen, fabels... [True to Life: Sketches, Stories, Fables...]. Amsterdam, Bezige Bij, 1954.
De koele minnaar [The Cool Lover]. Amsterdam, Bezige Bij, 1956.
De zwarte keizer [The Black King]. Amsterdam, Bezige Bij, 1958.
Omtrent Deedee [About Deedee]. Amsterdam, Bezige Bij, 1963.
De verwondering [Wonderment]. Amsterdam, Bezige Bij, 1963.
Het jaar van de kreeft [The Year of the Cancer]. Amsterdam, Bezige Bij, 1972.
Schaamte [Shame]. Amsterdam, Bezige Bij, 1972.
Aan de evenaar [At the Equator]. Amsterdam, Rap/Bezige Bij, 1973.
De groene ridder en de paladijnen [The Green Knight and the Paladins]. Amsterdam, Rap, 1973.
Jessica! Amsterdam, Bezige Bij, 1977.
De vluchtende Atalanta [Atalanta in Flight]. Antwerp, Pink Editions, 1977.
Het verlangen [Longing]. Amsterdam, Bezige Bij, 1978.
De verzoeking [The Temptation]. Antwerp, Pink Editions, 1980.
Het verdriet van België [The Sorrow of Belgium]. Amsterdam, Bezige Bij, 1983.

Verse

Kleine reeks [Small Series]. Moeskroen, Aurora, 1947.
Registreren [Registration]. Ostend, Carillon, 1948.
Zonder vorm van proces [Without Trial]. Brussels, Draak, 1950.
De blijde en onvoorziene week [The Happy, Unexpected Week], illustrated by Karel Appel. Paris, Cobra, 1950.
Tancredo infrasonic. The Hague, Stols, 1952.
Een Huis det tussen nacht en morgen staat [A House Between Night and Morning]. Antwerp, De Sikkel, 1953.
Paal en perk [Limits]. The Hague, De Sikkel, 1955.
De Oostakkerse gedichten [Poems from Oostakker]. Amsterdam, Bezige Bij, 1955.
Een geverfde ruiter [A Painted Horseman]. Amsterdam, Bezige Bij, 1961.
Love Song, illustrated by Karel Appel. New York, Abrams, 1963.
Oog om oog [A Tooth for a Tooth], photographs by Sanne Sannes. Amsterdam, Bezige Bij, 1964.
Gedichten [Poems]. Amsterdam, Bezige Bij, 1965.
Relikwie [Relic]. Antwerp, Monas, 1967.
Heer Everzwijn [Lord Boar]. Amsterdam, Bezige Bij, 1970.
Van horen zeggen [On Hearsay]. Amsterdam, Bezige Bij, 1970.
Dag, jij [Hello, Love]. Amsterdam, Bezige Bij, 1971.

Figuratief. Amsterdam, Bezige Bij, 1973.
Het Jansenisme [Jansenism]. Antwerp, Pink Editions, 1977.
De wangebeden [No-Good Prayers]. Amsterdam, Bezige Bij, 1977.
Van de koude grond [Outdoor Grown].Antwerp, Ziggurat, 1978.
Het teken van de hamster [The Sign of the Hamster]. Antwerp, Lotus, 1979.
Gedichten 1969-1978 [Poems]. Amsterdam, Bezige Bij, 1980.
Claustrum: 222 knittelverzen [Claustrum: 222 Doggerel Verses]. Antwerp, Pink Editions, 1980.
Dertien manieren om een fragment van Alechinsky te zien [Thirteen Ways of Looking at a Fragment of Alechinsky's]. Antwerp, Ziggurat, 1980.
Jan de Lichte. Antwerp, Ziggurat, 1981.

(Selections in English), in *Delta*, Spring 1970 and Spring 1971.

Other

Over het werk van Corneille [On the Work of Corneille]. Amsterdam, Martinet en Michels, 1951.
Karel Appel, Schilder. Amsterdam, Strengholt, 1964; as *Karel Appel, Painter*, Strengholt, 1962; London, Thames and Hudson, 1963.
De man van Tollund: Schilderijen 1962-1963 [The Tollund Man: Paintings]. Rotterdam, Galerie Delta, 1963.
Louis Paul Boon. Brussels, Manteau, 1964.
De schilderijen van Roger Raveel [The Paintings of Roger Raveel]. Amsterdam, Galerie Espace, 1965.
Het landschap [The Landscape] (on Maurice Wyckaert). Amsterdam, Galerie M.A.S., 1965.
De avonturen van Belgman I [The Adventures of Belgman I] (strip cartoon), drawings by Hoguké. Antwerp, Standaard, 1967.
Schola Nostra (as Dorothea van Male). Amsterdam, Bezige Bij, 1971.

Translator, *Onder het melkwoud* [Under Milkwood], by Dylan Thomas. Amsterdam, Bezige Bij, 1958.
Translator, *Als een jonge hond* [Portrait of the Artist as a Young Dog], by Dylan Thomas. Rotterdam, Donker, 1958.
Translator, *Het Hooglied* [The Song of Solomon]. Antwerp, Pink Editions, 1982.

*

Critical Studies: *Claus: Experiment en traditie* by Jean Weisgerber, Leiden, Sijthoff, 1970; *Claus* by Bert Kooijman, Bruges, Orion, 1973.

* * *

As poet, novelist, playwright, translator, scriptwriter, theatre director, film-maker and painter, Hugo Claus is one of the most versatile and prolific figures on the contemporary Dutch cultural scene, bringing to each of his manifold activities the same restless energy, inventiveness, and cosmopolitan erudition, together with a shrewd feel for publicity and commercial appeal.

His experimentalist *De Oostakkese gedichten*, with their abundance of primitive, often grotesque nature images, have, like the work of many contemporaries, links with the painting of the Cobra group, but a powerfully individual voice is already unmistakable. No less striking than the linguistic and rhythmical virtuosity of these poems is their urgent physicality: few poets in Dutch can match Claus's evocation, at his best, of an animal eroticism which alternates with bleakness and futility. In subsequent collections the discovery of T.S. Eliot and above all Pound leads Claus to seek a more sophisticated, mythically rooted synthesis of instinct and reason, as in the long, canto-like *Het teken van de hamster*. Much of his later poetry is more outward-looking and explicit in its social criticism and political allegiances, the latter always more instinctively anti-authoritarian and individualist than systematic.

A dense, sometimes cryptic allusiveness also characterises much of Claus's varied output of fiction, and works like the nightmarish collage *De verwondering*, in which a Flemish schoolteacher journeys back through a private inferno to a National Socialist past, have been criticised as well as admired for their baroqueness and (over)arch allegorising. Nevertheless, works as diverse as his Faulkner-inspired debut, *Sister of Earth*, with its alternating narrative, *Schaamte*, an obliquely understated commentary on the moral bankruptcy of modern Western man set in the Caribbean during the filming of Christ's passion, and the more conventional bestseller *Het jaar van de kreeft*, based on a love-affair between the author and a well-known actress, have established Claus as a considerable novelist. Of his more recent work, the novella *De verzoeking*, whose central figure is a decrepit nun, is ultimately more impressive than the magnum opus, *Het verdriet van België*, which contains many effective scenes derived from the author's Catholic boarding-school days in wartime Belgium, but tends to the episodic and lacks the resonance its title leads one to expect.

It is as a playwright that Claus's reputation is, at least at present, securest: his stagecraft and gift for dialogue have produced a dramatic oeuvre unmatched in this century in an area which cannot boast of an abundance of indigenous modern theatre. Highlights of his wide-ranging production, in which the early influences of Artaud and Beckett are apparent without being obtrusive, are the poignant melodrama *Suiker*, set among migrant agricultural workers in France, the tragi-comic family dramas *A Bride in the Morning*, *De dans van de reiger*, and *Friday* (the last successfully performed in London in an adaptation by Christopher Logue), an epic debunking of King Leopold II's colonial exploits in the Congo, and the Senecan adaptations *Thyestes*, *Oedipus*, and *Phaedra*.

Hailed as a prodigy on his first emergence in the 1950's, Claus has been accused of profligacy of talent and on occasion wilful mystification. Yet despite, or perhaps partly by virtue of, the intense Flemishness of his language, imagery, and themes (central among them his love-hate relationship with Belgium, whose provincialism and religious bigotry in particular he mercilessly evokes and castigates), he has received wide public as well as critical acclaim throughout the Low Countries.

Rather than "dig one plot" like some of his (especially Northern) contemporaries, Claus prefers unashamedly to "flit," attaching as much value to the creative process as to the finished artefact. Such adventurousness, with the challenges and risks it implies, may account for Claus's ability repeatedly to surprise, disturb, and, at his best, enthral.

—Paul Vincent

CORTÁZAR, Julio. Born in Brussels, Belgium, 26 August 1914; grew up in Argentina. Educated at teachers college, Buenos Aires, literature degree. Married Aurora Bernardez in 1953. Taught in secondary schools in several small towns and in Mendoza, Argentina, 1935-45; translator for publishers, 1945-51; has lived in Paris since 1951: writer, and free-lance translator for Unesco. Recipient: Grand Aigle d'Or (Nice), 1976. Address: Place Général Beuret, 75015 Paris, France. *Died 12 February 1984.*

CORTÁZAR

PUBLICATIONS

Fiction

Bestiario. Buenos Aires, Sudamericana, 1951.
Final del juego. Mexico City, Los Presentes, 1956.
Las armas secretas. Buenos Aires, Sudamericana, 1959.
Los premios. Buenos Aires, Sudamericana, 1960; as *The Winners*, New York, Pantheon, and London, Souvenir Press, 1965.
Historias de cronopios y de famas. Buenos Aires, Minotauro, 1962; as *Cronopios and Famas*, New York, Pantheon, 1969; London, Boyars, 1978.
Rayuela. Buenos Aires, Sudamericana, 1963; as *Hopscotch*, New York, Pantheon, 1966; London, Collins-Harvill Press, 1967.
Cuentos. Havana, Casa de las Americas, 1964.
Todos los fuegos el fuego. Buenos Aires, Sudamericana, 1966; as *All Fires the Fire and Other Stories*, New York, Pantheon, 1973; London, Boyars, 1979.
End of the Game and Other Stories (selection). New York, Pantheon, 1967; London, Collins-Harvill Press, 1968; as *Blow-Up and Other Stories*, New York, Collier, 1968.
La vuelta al día en ochenta mundos. Mexico, Siglo Veintiuno, 1967.
El perseguidor y otros cuentos. Buenos Aires, Centro Editor de America Latina, 1967.
62: Modelo para armar. Buenos Aires, Sudamericana, 1968; as *62: A Model Kit*, New York, Pantheon, 1972; London, Calder and Boyars, 1976.
Ceremonias (selection). Barcelona, Seix Barral, 1968.
Relatos (selection). Buenos Aires, Sudamericana, 1970.
La isla a mediodia y otros relatos. Estella, Salvat, 1971.
Libro de Manuel. Buenos Aires, Sudamericana, 1973.
La casilla de los Morelli, edited by Julio Ortega. Barcelona, Tusquets, 1973.
Octaedro. Buenos Aires, Sudamericana, 1974.
Vampiros multinacionales. Mexico, Excelsior, 1975.
Los relatos. Madrid, Alianza, 3 vols., 1976.
Territorios. Mexico City, Siglo Veintiuno, 1978.
Un tal Lucas. Buenos Aires, Sudamericana, 1979; as *A Certain Lucas*, New York, Knopf, 1984.
A Change of Light and Other Stories. New York, Knopf, 1980.
Queremos tanto a Glenda. Madrid, Alfaguara, 1981; as *We Love Glenda So Much and Other Tales*, New York, Knopf, 1983.

Play

Los reyes. Buenos Aires, Gulab y Aldabahor, 1949.

Verse

Presencia (as Julio Denis). Buenos Aires, 1938.

Other

Buenos Aires, Buenos Aires (includes English translation). Buenos Aires, Sudamericana, 1968.
Último round. Mexico City, Siglo Veintiuno, 1969.
Literatura en la revolución y revolución en la literatura, with Oscar Collazos and Mario

Vargas Llosa. Mexico City, Siglo Veintiuno, 1970.
Viaje alrededor de una meas. Buenos Aires, Rayuela, 1970.
Pameos y meopas. Barcelona, Llibres de Sinera, 1971.
Prosa del observatorio, with Antonio Galvez. Barcelona, Lumen, 1972.
Paris: The Essence of an Image. New York, Norton, 1981.

Translator, *Obras en prosa*, by Edgar Allan Poe. Madrid, Universidad de Puerto Rico, 1956.

*

Critical Studies: *Cortázar* by Evelyn P. Garfield, New York, Ungar, 1975; *Cortázar: Rayuela* by Robert Brody, London, Grant and Cutler, 1976; *The Final Island: The Fiction of Cortázar* (includes bibliography) edited by Ivar Ivask and Jaime Alazraki, Norman, University of Oklahoma Press, 1978; *The Novels of Cortázar* by Steven Boldy, Cambridge, Cambridge University Press, 1980; *Keats, Poe, and the Shaping of Cortázar's Mythopoesis* by Ana Hernández del Castillo, Amsterdam, Benjamins, 1981.

* * *

Julio Cortázar is one of the most widely recognized Spanish-American writers outside the Spanish-speaking world, due particularly to the critical acclaim of *Hopscotch*, a novel where the most experimental narrative innovations find an original form, and to the filming by Michelangelo Antonioni of one of his best short-stories, "Blow-Up."

Cortázar's narrative is unclassifiable. His fiction breaks away from the habitual categories of narrative and all conventional forms, blurs the uncertain boundaries between reality and the fantastic. The realistic and social milieu of his stories (be it Buenos Aires or Paris) is continuously compromised by elements of the absurd, the mythical, and the oneiric, by surrealist undercurrents where artistic freedom and imaginative possibilities disturb all routine representations of reality. Cortázar searches for an opening toward the other side of reality, toward—in his own words—" a more secret and less communicable order."

Cortázar's experimentation with the techniques of narrative can best be exemplified with *Hopscotch*, his masterpiece. The novel is written in loose fragments—the *collage* is the basic associative procedure—sequences of a totality that the reader is forced to recompose. The search for harmony and authenticity is the guiding motif of the novel; the search for the "key," "the other side," "the center," "the heaven of the hopscotch," "the love-passport," "the wishful Kibutz," illustrate Cortázar's attempts to apprehend an absolute order, a "sacred space" or mandala (a mystical labyrinth used by the Buddhists as a spiritual exercise), where integration and ultimate harmony can be attained. This ontological search for unity is one of the distinctive aspects of Cortázar's narrative. In his fiction it is common to find a character embarked on the search for a secret order, pursuing something undefinable to bring him inner harmony. Some characters intuitively explore the mysteries of the self (Johnny Carter, the jazz musician of "The Pursuer"), others chase truth and self-knowledge (Medrano, in *The Winners*), but most attempt failed intellectual projections into a world of their dreams (Oliveira in *Hopscotch*, Juan in *62: A Model Kit*, Andrés in *Libro de Manuel*). Fascinated by the unreachable absolute, all of Cortázar's major characters seek to jump into authenticity, rebel against a civilization governed by reason.

Hopscotch is a questioning of the art of storytelling, as well as a questioning of reality and all rational knowledge, an attempt to break away from all routine narrative formulas. The disintegration of the traditional novel begins with "The Table of Instructions," where Cortázar suggests at least two ways of reading the novel and the reader is invited to select between expendable and unexpendable chapters. The complex point of view, movable chapters, montage, *dédoublement*, dissociation of personality, simultaneity of creation and theoretical reflection within the novel, and, above all, the destruction of inherited language and syntax, the search for a new syntax to reunite unreconcilable languages, are the predominant features of

Cortázar's writing. The constant questioning of the capability of language to represent reality can best be seen by quoting the opening paragraph of "Blow-Up": "It'll never be known how this has to be told, in the first person or in the second, using the third person plural or continually inventing modes that will serve for nothing. If one might say: I will see the moon rose, or: we hurt me at the back of my eyes, and especially: you the blond woman was the clouds that race before my your his our yours their faces. What the hell."

These two aspects of Cortázar's narrative—innovation of language and form, and the metaphysical search—reveal his talent as a storyteller of universal appeal.

—Hugo J. Verani

ĆOSIĆ, Dobrica. Born in Velika Drenova, Serbia, in 1921. Political commissar for partisans during World War II; after the war held various Communist Party and cultural positions, and was a representative to the Yugoslav Parliament; Member of the Central Committee, League of Communists of Serbia (expelled, 1968); President, Society of Serbian Letters, until 1968. Member, Serbian Academy of Sciences and Arts, 1977. Address: c/o Prosveta, Dobračina 30, 11000 Belgrade, Yugoslavia.

PUBLICATIONS

Fiction

Daleko je sunce. Belgrade, Prosveta, 1951; as *Far Away in the Sun*, Belgrade, Jugoslavija, 1963.
Koreni [Roots]. Belgrade, Prosveta, 1954.
Deobe [Divisions]. Belgrade, Prosveta, 1961.
Bajka [Fairy Tale]. Belgrade, Prosveta, 1966.
Vreme smrti. Belgrade, Prosveta, 4 vols., 1972-79; as *A Time of Death, Reach to Eternity*, and *South to Destiny*, New York, Harcourt Brace, 3 vols., 1978-81; as *This Land, This Time*, Harcourt Brace, 4 vols., 1983.

Other

Akcija [Action]. 1965.
Sabrana dela [Collected Works]. Belgrade, Prosveta, 8 vols., 1966.
Moc i strepnje [Power and Foreboding]. 1972.
Stvarno i moguće [The Real and the Possible]. 1982.

* * *

Dobrica Ćosić is a controversial figure, outspoken and independent-minded, representing an unofficial, intellectual opposition in his native Serbia. He was expelled from the Central Committee of the League of Communists of Yugoslavia in 1968, accused of "nationalism." This is a real and inflammatory issue in the complex fabric of Yugoslavia, but one which may be exploited to isolate a troublesome individual. A collection of the statements and essays for which Ćosić has been attacked was published in 1982, entitled *Stvarno i moguće*. Like all his other controversial works, it rapidly became unobtainable.

Ćosić's fundamentally political orientation is reflected in his fiction. His work represents an examination of the fate of his country and its people, its history, and the forces shaping its destiny. Ćosić sees the upheavals of the 20th century as having driven people to a new concern with history as an all-powerful force governing their lives in the place of a lost God. By offering a poetic transposition of history, Ćosić believes that literature can "revitalize the spiritual life of the people." Most of Ćosić's fiction has been concerned with the recent past of Serbia, as are his essays and the allegory *Bajka* (Fairy Tale, 1966). His first novel, *Far Away in the Sun*, examines the process of decision-making among the Partisans and their relations with the peasant population during the Second World War. An insubstantial work, the novel nevertheless demonstrates Ćosić's readiness to explore sensitive areas. This is still more clearly the case with his second novel about the Second World War, the three-volume study *Deobe*, in which he considers the various reasons which drove the Chetniks (guerrillas loyal to the king) to turn their arms against their fellow-Serbs, the Partisans. *Koreni* focuses on the years of Serbia's emergence from a patriarchal agricultural province of the Ottoman Empire and the beginnings of its development as an independent state.

Ćosić's next work, perhaps his most important to date, was his lengthy study of the First World War in Serbia, published in four volumes as *Vreme Smrti* (*A Time of Death*). The novel takes up the set of characters introduced in *Koreni*, and draws on official documents, diaries, and letters, merging historical and fictitious characters. It covers the whole spectrum of Serbian society, following the decision-making processes of the government and army commanders, portraying the generals, King Peter, Prime Minister Pašić and their closest associates. At the same time, it describes the life of the village and the fate of its population. The novel offers a detailed and moving account of the little kingdom's struggle against the Habsburg forces, its unexpected successes in the first year of the war, the appalling scale of its losses in battle and through disease, the devastation of the army and civilian population in the great retreat through the mountains of Montenegro and Albania in the winter of 1915, and the regrouping of the remains of the army to fight again with the allies. The novel, in a slightly abridged version has been published in English in three volumes (*A Time of Death*, *Reach to Eternity*, *South to Destiny*). The epic scale of the work, inherent in the material can be seen as reflecting the cultural heritage of the South Slavs. The style is discursive and at times overstated but it is a powerful story, movingly told, of wide general interest and appeal.

—E.C. Hawkesworth

DE FILIPPO, Eduardo. Italian. Born in Naples, 24 May 1900. Educated at Istituto Chierchia, Naples, 1911. Served in the Italian Army, 1920-22. Married 1) Dorothy Pennington in 1928 (marriage annulled, 1952); 2) Thea Prandi in 1956 (separated, 1959; died, 1960), two children (one deceased); 3) Isabella Quarantotti in 1977. Child actor with family troupe: debut, 1904; also actor with troupes of Scarpetta, Altieri, Corbinci, Villani, and others; founder, with his brother and sister, Teatro Umoristico, 1931 and toured with it until 1944; formed Il Teatro di Eduardo, 1945; director and owner, Teatro San Ferdinando, Naples, from 1954. Also film and opera director and actor. Recipient: Institute of Italian Drama Prize, 1951, 1968; Simoni Prize, 1969; Feltrinelli Prize, 1972; *Evening Standard* Award (London), 1972; Pirandello Prize,

1975. D.Litt.: University of Birmingham, England, 1977; University of Rome, 1980. Named Senator of the Italian Republic, 1980. Agent (English language): Dr. Jan Van Loewen Ltd., 21 Kingly Street, London W1R 5LB, England. Address: Via Aquileia 16, Rome, Italy.

PUBLICATIONS

Plays

Sik-Sik, L'Artefice magico (produced Naples, 1929). Naples, Tirrena, 1932; as *Sik-Sik, The Masterful Magician*, in *Italian Quarterly 11*, 1967.
Natale in casa Cupiello (produced Naples, 1931; revised version, 1942). Included in *Cantata dei giorni pari*, 1959; as *Ducking Out* (produced London, 1982).
Farmacia di turno (produced Naples, 1931). Included in *Cantata dei giorni pari*, 1959.
Ogni anno punto e da capo (produced Naples, 1931). Turin, Einaudi, 1971.
Quei figuri di trent'anni fa (produced Naples, 1932). Included in *Cantata dei giorni pari*, 1959.
Chi è cchiù felice 'e me!...(produced Naples, 1932). Included in *Cantata dei giorni pari*, 1959.
Gennariniello (produced Naples, 1932). Included in *Cantata dei giorni pari*, 1959.
Ditegli sempre di sì (produced Naples, 1932). Included in *Cantata dei giorni pari*, 1959.
I morti non fanno paura (as *Requie all'anima soia*, produced Naples, 1932; revised version, as *I morti non fanno paura*, produced Rome, 1952). Included in *Cantata dei giorni dispari 2*, 1958.
L'ultimo bottone (produced Naples, 1932).
Cuoco della mala cucina, with Maria Scarpetta (produced Naples, 1932).
Uomo e galantuomo (produced Naples, 1933). Included in *Cantata dei giorni pari*, 1959.
Parlate al portiere, with Maria Scarpetta (produced Naples, 1933).
Scorzetta di limone, from play by Gino Rocca (produced Naples, 1933).
Il dono di Natale (produced Naples, 1934). Included in *Cantata dei giorni pari*, 1959.
Tre mesi dopo (produced Naples, 1934).
Sintetici a qualunque costa (produced Naples, 1934).
Il berretto a Sonagli, from a play by Pirandello (produced Naples, 1936).
Quinto piano, ti saluto! (produced Rome, 1936). Included in *Cantata dei giorni pari*, 1959.
L'Abito nuovo, from story by Pirandello (produced Milan, 1937). Included in *Cantata dei giorni pari*, 1959.
Uno coi capelli bianchi (produced Rome, 1938). Included in *Cantata dei giorni pari*, 1959.
Si salvi chi può, from work by Gino Rocca (produced Naples, 1940).
Non ti pago! (produced Rome, 1940). Florence, Libreria del Teatro, 1943.
La parte di Amleto (produced Milan, 1940). Included in *Cantata dei giorni pari*, 1959.
In licenza, from work by Eduardo Scarpetta (produced Rome, 1941).
La fortuna con l'effe maiuscola, with Armando Curcio (produced Turin, 1942).
Io, l'erede (produced Florence, 1942). Included in *Cantata dei giorni pari*, 1959.
Il diluvio, from play by Ugo Betti (produced Rome, 1943).
Napoli milionaria! (produced Naples, 1945). Turin, Einaudi, 1946.
Occhiali neri (produced Naples, 1945). Included in *Cantata dei giorni dispari 2*, 1958.
Questi fantasmi! (produced Rome, 1946). Included in *Cantata dei giorni dispari 1*, 1951; as *Oh, These Ghosts* (as *Too Many Ghosts*, produced Oxford, 1958), London, Faber, 1963.
Filumena Marturano (produced Naples, 1946). Included in *Cantata dei giorni dispari 1*, 1951; as *The Best House in Naples* (produced New York, 1956), in *Three Plays*, 1976; as

Filumena (produced London, 1977; New York, 1980), London, Heinemann, 1978.

Pericolosamente (produced Turin, 1947).   Included in *Cantata dei giorni pari*, 1959.

Le bugie con le gambe lunghe (produced Rome, 1948).   Included in *Cantata dei giorni dispari 1*, 1951.

Le voci di dentro (produced Naples, 1948).   Included in *Cantata dei giorni dispari 1*, 1951; as *Inner Voices* (produced London, 1983).

La grande magia (produced Naples, 1949).   Included in *Cantata dei giorni dispari 1*, 1951; as *Grand Magic*, in *Three Plays*, 1976.

La paura numero uno (produced Venice, 1950).   Included in *Cantata dei giorni dispari 2*, 1958.

Cantata dei giorni dispari:

1. *Napoli milionaria!*; *Questi fantasmi!*; *Filumena Marturano*; *Le bugie con le gambe lunghe*; *La grande magia*; *Le voci di dentro*.   Turin, Einaudi, 1951; revised edition, 1971.

2. *Non ti pago!*; *Occhiali neri*; *La paura numero uno*; *I morti non fanno paura*; *Amicizia*; *Mia famiglia*; *Bene mio e core mio*; *De Pretore Vincenzo*.   Turin, Einaudi, 1958; revised edition, 1971.

3. *Il figlio di Pulcinella*; *Dolore sotto chiave*; *Sabato, domenica e lunedi*; *Il sindaco del Rione Sanità*; *Tommaso D'Amalfi*; *L'arte della commedia*; *Il cilindro*.   Turin, Einaudi, 1966; revised edition, 1971.

Amicizia (produced Rome, 1952).   Included in *Cantata dei giorni dispari 2*, 1958.

Miseria e nobiltà, from a play by Eduardo Scarpetta (produced Naples, 1953).

Bene mio e core mio (produced Rome, 1955).   Turin, Einaudi, 1956.

Mia famiglia (produced Perugia, 1955).   Turin, Einaudi, 1955.

Il medico dei pazzi, from work by Eduardo Scarpetta (produced Rome, 1957).

De Pretore Vincenzo (produced Rome, 1957).   Turin, Einaudi, 1957.

Tre cazune furtunate, from a play by Eduardo Scarpetta (produced Milan, 1958).

Sabato, domenica e lunedi (produced Rome, 1959).   Turin, Einaudi, 1960; as *Saturday, Sunday, Monday* (produced London, 1973; New York, 1974), London, Heinemann, 1974.

Cantata dei giorni pari (includes *Farmacia di turno*; *Uomo e galantuomo*; *Filosoficamente*; *Sik-Sik*; *Quei figuri di trent'anni fa*; *Chi è cchiù felice 'e me!...*; *Natale in casa Cupiello*; *Gennariniello*; *Il dono di Natale*; *Ditegli sempre di sì*; *Quinto piano, ti saluto!*; *Uno coi capelli bianchi*; *L'Abito nuovo*; *Pericolosamente*; *La parte di Amleto*; *Io, l'erede*).   Turin, Einaudi, 1959.

Il sindaco del Rione Sanità (produced Rome, 1960).   Turin, Einaudi, 1961; as *The Local Authority*, in *Three Plays*, 1976.

Il figlio di Pulcinella (produced Rome, 1962).   Included in *Cantata dei giorni dispari 3*, 1966.

Peppino Girella, with Isabella Quarantotti (televised, 1963).   Rome, Riuniti, 1964.

Dolore sotto chiave (produced Naples, 1964).   Turin, Einaudi, 1965 (with *L'arte della commedia*).

L'arte della commedia (produced Naples, 1965).   Turin, Einaudi, 1965 (with *Dolore sotto chiave*).

Il cilindro (produced Rome, 1966).   Included in *Cantata dei giorni dispari 3*, 1966.

Il contratto (produced Venice, 1967).   Turin, Einaudi, 1967.

Cani e gatti, from work by Eduardo Scarpetta (produced Bari, 1970).

Il monumento (produced Florence, 1970).   Turin, Einaudi, 1971.

'Na santarella, from work by Eduardo Scarpetta (produced Rome, 1972).

I capolavori.   Turin, Einaudi, 2 vols., 1973.

Gli esami non finiscono mai (produced Florence, 1973).   Turin, Einaudi, 1973.

Lu curaggio de nu pumpiere napulitano, from work by Eduardo Scarpetta (produced Florence, 1974).

Three Plays.   London, Hamish Hamilton, 1976.

Screenplays: "Adelina" episode, with Isabella Quarantotti, of *Ieri, oggi e domani* (*Yesterday, Today and Tomorrow*), 1963; *Matrimonió all'italiana* (*Marriage Italian Style*), 1964; *Spara forte, più forte...non capisco* (*Shoot Loud, Louder...I Don't Understand*), with Suso Cecchi D'Amico, 1966.

Television Plays: *Peppino Girella*, with Isabella Quarantotti, 1963; *Li nepute de lu sinneco*, from work by Eduardo Scarpetta, 1975; *'O Tuono 'e marzo*, from work by Vincenzo Scarpetta, 1975; and adaptations of about 20 of his own plays.

Verse

Il paese di Pulcinella. Naples, Casella, 1951.
'O canisto. Naples, Teatro San Ferdinando, 1971.
Le poesie. Turin, Einaudi, 1975.

Other

Editor, *Manzù: Album inedito.* Rome, Franca May, 1977.

*

Critical Studies: *In Search of Theatre* by Eric Bentley, New York, Knopf, 1953, London, Dobson, 1954; *Il teatro di Eduardo*, Rome, Laterza, 1975, and *De Filippo* (in Italian), Rome, Gremese, 1978, both by Fiorenza Di Franco; *De Filippo* by Mario Mignone, Boston, Twayne, 1984.

* * *

The content of any drama by Eduardo De Filippo—even an act or scene—is never distanced or abstracted from daily living. This mirror of reality is also illuminated by a stagecraft for the most part pre-Pirandellian and pre-Absurdist. In fact, the immediacy of representation in the Commedia dell'Arte reverberates anew in De Filippo's theatre. His originality consists in transferring the concreteness of the universal quotidian onto the stage. He succeeds by historicizing his plays not just by situating their plots and characters in near past or present-day Naples—which by itself could be taken as a sign of provincialism and limitation—but by choosing as the archetypal persona *homo neapolitanus* in all his creaturality. De Filippo is not tempted to ennoble his world by forcing facts into themes or by endowing *homo neapolitanus* with openly universal attitudes; he rather dares leave him in the concreteness of his creaturality with all possible apparent incongruities and contradictions. And so it has happened that one of his plays was once censured in Italy by the clerical right and later, for a different scene, by the left.

Besides making De Filippo a direct heir of the Commedia dell'Arte and of certain aspects of Goldoni and Molière, the concreteness of plots and especially the creaturality of his personae lend his plays that special element of the bitter sweetly comic, which superimposes on the pity and terror of life the pity and pleasure and the thrill and terror of daily living. Yet De Filippo's temperament doesn't allow a complete obliteration of the tragic—indeed the creaturality of daily living, itself the basis of the comedic element, is at times thinly distinguished from and at times actually suggests the existential finitude of being human, the basis of tragedy.

The projection of doubled foci (on life and daily living) permits De Filippo to represent human existence more fully; this representation is the reason for the success of his theatre. But what makes it a popular theatre in the same sense that the Commedia dell'Arte is popular is the language which shapes De Filippo's dialogue: the Neapolitan content is reflected in the Neapolitan dialect, but, again, as in matter of content, the author neither attempts a purposeful elevation of the dialect into a more universally comprehensible language nor does he use it in its idiomatic character for exotic or picturesque effects. His is a personal Neapolitan dialect, a poetic language in the sense that only a personal language can be poetic. In fact, his most successful pieces are in dialect, and they are the more popular of his plays both in the original and in translation. The translation is not disfiguring, exactly because of the individuality of the koine. In the last analysis, it is through the lightness, the weight, the harshness, the mellifluity, the pounding, and the rhythm of the range of his language that De Filippo can invent, express, and communicate. His range divides into several modes—farce, irony, satire—and moods—pathos, bathos, sentimentalism, sentimentality. His concerns are many: love, enthusiasm, family, sex, jealousy, hate, war, poverty, humiliation, madness, resignation, and rebellion.

De Filippo's acting is a unique feature of his theatre. His movements and gestures are constrained and conscious, his delivery low-keyed, sonorous, and sustained, with intimate silences which give depth to his Neapolitan characters. The face with which he plays the parts of his characters always projects an uncomfortableness between the surprise of being alive and the surprise of being condemned to be not more alive. His sad comedy rebels against this condemnation.

—Emanuele Licastro

DELIBES (Setien), Miguel. Spanish. Born in Valladolid, 17 October 1920. Educated at Hermanos Doctrina Christiana school; University of Valladolid, doctor of law, 1944; Escuela Altos Estudios Mercantiles; Escuela Periodismo. Served in the Spanish Navy, 1938-39. Married Angeles de Castro in 1946 (died, 1974); seven children. Taught mercantile law at Valladolid; visiting professor, University of Maryland, College Park, 1964. Director, El Norte de Castilla, Valladolid. Recipient: Nadal Prize, 1948; Ministry of Information Cervantes Prize, 1955; Fastenrath Prize, 1959; Critics Prize (Spain), 1963; Asturias Prize, 1982. Member, Real Academia de la Lengua. Agent: Ediciones Destino, Consejo de Ciento 425, Barcelona 9. Address: Dos de Mayo 10, Valladolid, Spain.

PUBLICATIONS

Fiction

La sombra del ciprés es alargada. Barcelona, Destino, 1948.
Aún es de día. Barcelona, Destino, 1949.
El camino. Barcelona, Destino, 1950; as *The Path,* New York, Day, and London, Hamish Hamilton, 1961.
Mi idolatrado hijo Sisí. Barcelona, Destino, 1953.

El loco. Madrid, Prensa Española, 1953.
La partida. Barcelona, Caralt, 1954.
Diario de un cazador. Barcelona, Destino, 1955.
Siestas con viento sur. Barcelona, Destino, 1957.
Diario de un emigrante. Barcelona, Destino, 1958.
La hoja roja. Barcelona, Destino, 1959.
Las ratas. Barcelona, Destino, 1962; as *Smoke on the Ground*, New York, Doubleday, 1972.
Cinco horas con Mario. Barcelona, Destino, 1966.
La mortaja. Madrid, Alianza, 1969.
Parábola del náufrago. Barcelona, Destino, 1969; as *The Hedge*, New York, Columbia University Press, 1983.
El príncipe destronado. Barcelona, Destino, 1973.
Las guerras de nuestros antepasados. Barcelona, Destino, 1975.
El disputado voto del señor Cayo. Barcelona, Destino, 1978.
Los santos inocentes. Barcelona, Planeta, 1981.

Plays

Cinco horas con Mario, from his own novel (produced Madrid, 1980).

Television Plays: *Tierras de Valladolid*, 1966; *La Mortaja*; *Castilla, esta es mi tierra*, 1983.

Other

Un novelista descubre América: Chile en el ojo ajeno. Madrid, Nacional, 1956.
La barbería. Barcelona, Pulga, 1957.
Castilla, photographs by Ramon Masats. Barcelona, Lumen, 1960; as *Viejas historias de Castilla la Vieja*, 1964.
Por esos mundos: Sudamérica con escala en las Canarias. Barcelona, Destino, 1961.
La caza de la perdiz roja, photographs by Oriol Maspons. Barcelona, Lumen, 1963.
Europa: Parada y fonda. Madrid, Cid, 1963.
El libro de la caza menor. Barcelona, Destino, 1964.
Obras completas. Barcelona, Destino, 1964— .
USA y yo. Barcelona, Destino, 1966.
Vivir al día. Barcelona, Destino, 1968.
La primavera de Praga. Madrid, Alianza, 1968.
Con la escopeta al hombre. Barcelona, Destino, 1970.
Un año de mi vida. Barcelona, Destino, 1972.
La caza en España. Madrid, Alianza, 1972.
Castilla en mi obra. Madrid, Editorial Magisterio Español, 1972.
S.O.S.: El sentido del progreso desde mi obra. Barcelona, Destino, 1975.
Aventuras, venturas, y desventuras de un cazador a rabo. Barcelona, Destino, 1977.
Mis amigas las truchas. Barcelona, Destino, 1977.
Castilla, lo castellano, y los castellanos. Barcelona, Planeta, 1979.

*

Critical Studies: *Cinco horas con Delibes, el hombre y el novelista* by Leo Hickey, Madrid, Prensa Española, 1968; *Delibes* by Francisco Umbral, Madrid, Emesa, 1970; *Conversaciones con Delibes* by César Alonso de los Ríos, Madrid, Emesa, 1971; *Delibes* by Janet W. Díaz, New York, Twayne, 1971; *La novelística de Delibes* by Luis López Martínez, Murcia, University of

Murcia, 1973; *La originalidad novelística de Delibes* by Alfonso Rey, Santiago, Editorial Universidad de Santiago, 1975; *Delibes: Desarrollo de un escritor* by Edgar Pauk, Madrid, Gredos, 1975; *Delibes en su guerra constanta* by Esther Bartolomé Pons, Barcelona, Victor Pozaneo, 1979; *La novela experimental de Delibes* by Agnes Gullón, Madrid, Taurus, 1981; *Analisis de la novela "Las guerras de nuestros antepasados"by Delibes* by Carolyn Richmond, Barcelona, Destino, 1982; *Estudios sobre Delibes*, Madrid, Universidad Complutense, 1983.

* * *

Miguel Delibes, one of Spain's best novelists, has also written essays, travel books, and non-fiction. Some of his characters, whose psychological penetration is central to his novels, are innocent and idealistic; others are solitary and alienated; but simple or complicated, they personify the fight for human dignity and freedom.

La sombra del ciprés es alargada, his first and partly autobiographical novel, follows the tenets of traditional Spanish fiction. Delibes's characters seek in vain for the affirmation of love and faith in a world of solitude and death. *The Path*, based on the recollections of an 11-year-old boy just before his trip from country to city, idealizes small village life in contrast with so-called progress. Through picturesque and at times poetic anecdotal incidents, told with great warmth and humor, Delibes stresses the importance of nature in the process of growing up. *Diario de un cazador*, another early work, concerns the passion for the hunt of a non-intellectual but proud beadle. Delibes, masterfully transcribing oral and colloquial language, shows that man, overwhelmed by civilization, must from time to time seek out his primitive roots.

Many consider *Cinco horas con Mario* to be his masterpiece and a sample of Delibes's new sophistication as a novelist. The long interior monologue (a kind of free association conveyed through a chaotic temporal technique) by Carmen before the corpse of her husband becomes a dialogue between the living and the dead. Carmen, who presumably typifies the Spanish middle class and its hypocritical and vulgar viewpoints, is shallow, bigoted, and unforgiving. Delibes contrasts, through appropriate Biblical passages at the beginning of each chapter, Christian charity with her own false values. An attack on Franco Spain, the novel, in spite of its irony, may be read as a defense of individual liberties.

The Hedge, a fantasy of modern man trapped in a dehumanizing Orwellian State, depicts the author's nightmare vision of technology and authoritarianism which turns men into helpless beasts. Delibes, in this, his most experimental novel, employs free association, allegory, and oneiric imagery, together with distorted grammar and punctuation.

Among Delibes's later works, *Las guerras de nuestros antepasados*, told through seven taped conversations between the protagonist, a marginal victim of society, and a psychiatrist, shows how modern Spaniards were prepared by tradition to indulge in violence, an integral part of humanity, which each man carries in his soul.

In Delibes's novels rural Old Castile and nature suffer from the destruction caused by an ever more technological world. Humanity, says Delibes, must learn to accommodate its thirst for liberty with the needs of society, but, in spite of his pessimism, he has not given up hope that man may yet find happiness, even in a grotesque and dehumanized world.

—Kessel Schwartz

DONOSO (Yañez), José. Chilean. Born in Santiago, 5 October 1924. Educated at the Grange School, Santiago; University of Chile Instituto Pedagógio, 1947; Princeton University,

New Jersey (Doherty scholar), A.B. 1951. Married María P. Serrano in 1961; one son. Worked as shepherd in Patagonia; taught English, Catholic University of Chile, 1954, and journalism at University of Chile; staff member, *Revista Ercilla*, Santiago, 1959-64; and at Colorado State University, Fort Collins, 1969. Literary critic, *Siempre* magazine, 1964-66. Recipient: City of Santiago Prize, 1955; Chile-Italy Prize, for journalism, 1960; William Faulkner Foundation Prize, 1962; Critics Prize (Spain), 1979; Guggenheim Fellowship. Agent: Carmen Balcells, Generalisimio 580, Barcelona 11. Address: Calaceite, Teruel, Spain.

PUBLICATIONS

Fiction

Veraneo y otros cuentos. Santiago, 1955.
Coronación. Santiago, Nascimiento, 1957; as *Coronation*, New York, Knopf, and London, Bodley Head, 1965.
El charleston. Santiago, Nascimiento, 1960; as *Charleston and Other Stories*, Boston, Godine, 1977.
Los mejores cuentos. Santiago, Zig-Zag, 1966.
El lugar sin límites. Mexico, Moritz, 1966; as *Hell Hath No Limits*, in *Triple Cross*, New York, Dutton, 1972.
Este domingo. Santiago, Zig-Zag, 1966; as *This Sunday*, New York, Knopf, 1967; London, Bodley Head, 1968.
El obsceno pájaro de la noche. Barcelona, Seix Barrral, 1970; as *The Obscene Bird of Night*, New York, Knopf, 1973; London, Cape, 1974.
Tres novelitas burguesas. Barcelona, Seix Barral, 1973; as *Sacred Families*, New York, Knopf, 1977; London, Gollancz, 1978.
Casa de campo. Barcelona, Seix Barral, 1978; translated as *Casa de campo*, New York, Knopf, 1984; as *A House in the Country*, London, Allen Lane, 1984.
La misteriosa desaparición de la marquesita de Loria. Barcelona, Seix Barral, 1980.
El jardin de la lado. Barcelona, Seix Barral, 1981.

Other

Historia personal del "boom." Barcelona, Anagrama, 1972; as *The Boom in Spanish American Literature: A Personal History*, New York, Columbia University Press, 1977.

Editor, with others, *The Tri-Quarterly Anthology of Contemporary Latin American Literature.* New York, Dutton, 1969.

*

Critical Study: *Donoso: La destrucción de un mundo* edited by Antonio Cornejo Polar, Buenos Aires, Cambeiro, 1975.

*   *   *

José Donoso has been obsessed throughout his writing career with the themes of the family in all its ramifications. His early stories deal with children and adolescents, often at odds with their surroundings; later works center on complications in marital relationships; and his masterpiece, *The Obscene Bird of Night*, takes the family to an expanded arena, where the "household" can encompass a wealth of "familial" relationships.

For Donoso the family includes not only the husband, wife, and children, but also the servants and family friends, all the complex relationships that constitute a small world within which the individual can function—or not. Late works like *Sacred Families* (*Tres novelitas burguesas*), three inter-related novelas, emphasize the falsity of middle-class life. "Chattanooga Choo-Choo" presents two sophisticated Barcelona women, Sylvia and Magdalena, who are willing to play a role for their husbands as long as they can control their husbands' roles as well: with the vanishing cream from her well-stocked dressing table, Sylvia makes Magdalena's husband's sexual organ disappear: his consequent disorientation allows Magdalena to dismantle him, pack him in a small suitcase, and reassemble him at a party to tap dance to the popular 1940's song (a role Sylvia has already had to play). Another couple has assembled a "perfect" apartment in a fashionable district, only to find it slowly disappearing just as they realize their own relationship is false. In "Gaspard de la Nuit" Sylvia's adolescent son refuses to acknowledge her "perfect" (actually completely conventional) values, but obligingly produces a street urchin who is happy to accommodate them. The banality of such lives is cleverly and wittily shown in a lucid style which runs counter to the bizarre events.

Earlier works also center on closed, unsustainable relationships. *Coronation* describes a brittle fantasy household of aged servants and a middle-aged grandson catering to the needs of a 90-year-old matriarch; the intrusion of a real, full-blooded peasant girl breaks the pattern. In *This Sunday* characters on the fringe of an ordinary middle-class couple—the servant girl seduced by the husband, and the convict for whom the do-gooder wife has arranged a parole—destroy the marriage. In other works lonely people escape into fantasy or dependence on children.

The Obscene Bird of Night takes Donoso's obsessive themes onto another level. The epigraph, by Henry James, Sr., touches the central theme of the book: "Every man who has reached even his intellectual teens begins to suspect that life is no farce; that it is not genteel comedy even; that it flowers and fructifies on the contrary out of the profoundest tragic depths of the essential dearth in which its subject's roots are plunged. The natural inheritance of everyone who is capable of spiritual life is an unsubdued forest where the wolf howls and the obscene bird of night chatters." This disturbing book is set in the Casa de Ejercicios Espirituales, an independent retreat house originally set up for the specific purpose of accommodating the heiress of the Azcoitía family in the late 18th century, but now reduced to housing a few old ladies and orphans, three nuns, and the porter, Humberto. What might seem a rather charming, though fading, example of a long Catholic tradition is for Donoso, however, a talisman of the underlying conflict between the masters and the servants—who collect the "privileges of misery" and humiliation just as they collect the small parcels hidden under their beds. The simple setting slowly turns into a nightmare, as we come to realize that the deaf-mute Humberto was once the secretary to Jerónimo Azcoitía, the current head of the family which founded the Casa, is in love with Jerónimo's wife, Inez (also the name of the original heiress—who might have been a witch as well as saint), and has arranged the (seeming) pregnancy of one of the orphan girls toward whom the deranged old women residents of the Casa have adopted a reverential attitude, assuring themselves that she will give birth to a saint who will carry them with him to heaven. The crumbling, partly boarded-up and disused Casa is contrasted with another emblem of the Azcoitía family—the estate at La Rinconada that Jerónimo has established for his deformed child (possibly sired by Humberto): it is a complete "utopian" community, self-contained and self-sufficient, but all the members are deformed freaks and monsters. (Ironically, this section contains the work's most lucid and simple prose.)

The novel is complex and obscure: Humberto, the nominal narrator, assumes many roles, the most terrifying being that of the *imbunche*, the witch victim: all his bodily orifices are sewn up and he is wrapped into a tight bundle. At the end of the novel, the Casa has been sold for demolition, Jerónimo has been killed in a bizarre costume ball at La Rinconada, Inez has been put in a mad house, and Humberto (we think) has been packaged and burned. The imagery of servant and master, masks and clothing, saint and witch, virgin and prostitute, *imbunche* and swaddled child, seclusion and freedom almost beggar interpretation, assuming the frightening proportions of a real nightmare.

—George Walsh

DURAS, Marguerite. French. Born Marguerite Donnadieu in Giadinh, near Saigon, Indochina (now Vietnam), 4 April 1914. Educated at Lycée de Saigon; the Sorbonne, Paris, 1933-34. Has one son. Secretary, Ministry of Colonies, Paris, 1935-41; then free-lance writer; also film writer and director. Recipient: Ibsen prize, 1970. Address: 5 Rue Saint-Benoît, 75006 Paris, France.

<small>PUBLICATIONS</small>

Fiction

Les Impudents.   Paris, Plon, 1943.
La Vie tranquille.   Paris, Gallimard, 1944.
Un Barrage contre le Pacifique.   Paris, Gallimard, 1950; as *The Sea Wall*, New York, Pellegrini and Cudahy, 1952; as *A Sea of Troubles*, London, Methuen, 1953.
Le Marin de Gibraltar.   Paris, Gallimard, 1952; as *The Sailor from Gibraltar*, London, Calder and Boyars, and New York, Grove Press, 1966.
Les Petits Chevaux de Tarquinia.   Paris, Gallimard, 1953; as *The Little Horses of Tarquinia*, London, Calder, 1960.
Des journées entières dans les arbres.   Paris, Gallimard, 1954; edited by George Craig, London, Methuen, 1972; as *Whole Days in the Trees*, New York, Riverrun, 1981; London, Calder, 1983.
Le Square.   Paris, Gallimard, 1955; edited by W.J. Strachan, London, Methuen, 1974; as *The Square*, New York, Grove Press, and London, Calder, 1959.
Moderato cantabile.   Paris, Minuit, 1958; edited by Jean Bessière, Paris, Bordas, 1972; translated as *Moderato Cantabile*, New York, Grove Press, 1960.
Dix heures et demi du soir en été.   Paris, Gallimard, 1960; as *Ten-Thirty on a Summer Night*, London, Calder, 1962; New York, Grove Press, 1963.
L'Après-midi de Monsieur Andesmas.   Paris, Gallimard, 1962; as *The Afternoon of Monsieur Andemas*, with *The Rivers and Forests*, London, Calder, 1964; in *Four Novels*, 1965.
Le Ravissement de Lol V. Stein.   Paris, Gallimard, 1964; as *The Ravishing of Lol Stein*, New York, Grove Press, 1967; as *The Rapture of Lol V. Stein*, London, Hamish Hamilton, 1967.
Four Novels (includes *The Square, Moderato Cantabile, Ten-Thirty on a Summer Night, The Afternoon of Mr. Andesmas*).   New York, Grove Press, 1965.
Le Vice-consul.   Paris, Gallimard, 1966; as *The Vice-Consul*, London, Hamish Hamilton, 1968.
L'Amante anglaise.   Paris, Gallimard, 1967; translated as *L'Amante Anglaise*, New

York, Grove Press, 1968.

Détruire, dit-elle. Paris, Minuit, 1969; as *Destroy, She Said,* New York, Grove Press, 1970.

Abahn Sabana David. Paris, Gallimard, 1970.

L'Amour. Paris, Gallimard, 1971.

Ah! Ernesto, with Bernard Bonhomme. Paris, Ruy-Vidal, 1971.

Plays and Texts for Voices

Le Square, with Claude Martin, from the novel by Duras (produced Paris, 1957; revised version, produced Paris, 1965). Included in *Théâtre 1,* 1965; as *The Square* (produced Bromley, Kent, 1961; London, 1963), in *Three Plays,* 1967.

Hiroshima mon amour (screenplay). Paris, Gallimard, 1960; translated as *Hiroshima Mon Amour,* New York, Grove Press, 1961; with *Une Aussi Longue Absence,* London, Calder and Boyars, 1966.

Les Viaducs de la Seine-et-Oise. Paris, Gallimard, 1960; as *The Viaducts of Seine-et-Oise* (as *The Viaduct,* produced Guildford, Surrey, 1967), in *Three Plays,* 1967.

Une Aussi Longue Absence (screenplay), with Gérard Jarlot. Paris, Gallimard, 1961; translated as *Une Aussi Longue Absence,* with *Hiroshima Mon Amour,* London, Calder and Boyars, 1966.

Les Papiers d'Aspern, with Robert Antelme, adaptation of the play *The Aspern Papers* by Michael Redgrave based on the story by Henry James (produced Paris, 1961).

Miracle en Alabama, with Gérard Jarlot, adaptation of the play *The Miracle Worker* by William Gibson (produced Paris, 1961).

La Bête dans la jungle, with James Lord, adaptation of the story *The Beast in the Jungle* by Henry James (produced Paris, 1962).

Théâtre 1 (includes *Les Eaux et fôrets, Le Square, La Musica*). Paris, Gallimard, 1965.

Les Eaux et fôrets, in *Théâtre 1.* 1965; as *The Rivers and Forests* (produced London, 1976), with *The Afternoon of Monsieur Andesmas,* London, Calder, 1964.

La Musica, in *Théâtre 1.* 1965; as *The Music* (produced Edinburgh and London, 1966; New York, 1967); in *Suzanna Andler, La Musica, and L'Amante Anglaise,* 1975.

Des journées entières dans les arbres (produced Paris, 1965). In *Théâtre 2,* 1968; as *Days in the Trees* (produced London, 1966), in *Three Plays,* 1967.

Three Plays. London, Calder and Boyars, 1967.

Théâtre 2 (includes *Susanna Andler; Yes, peut-être; Le Shaga; Des journées entières dans les arbres; Un Homme est venu me voir*). Paris, Gallimard, 1968.

Le Shaga (also director: produced Paris, 1968). Included in *Théâtre 2,* 1968.

Susanna Andler (produced Paris, 1969). Included in *Théâtre 2,* 1968; as *Suzanna Andler* (produced Cambridge and London, 1973), in *Suzanna Andler, La Musica, and L'Amante Anglaise,* 1975.

L'Amante anglaise, from her own novel (produced Paris, 1969). Paris, Théâtre National Populaire, 1968; as *A Place Without Doors* (produced New Haven, Connecticut, and New York, 1970; as *The Lovers of Viorne,* produced London, 1971); included in *Suzanna Andler, La Musica, and L'Amante Anglaise,* 1975.

Nathalie Granger; La Femme du Gange (screenplays). Paris, Gallimard, 1973.

India Song (in French). Paris, Gallimard, 1973; translated as *India Song,* New York, Grove Press, 1976.

Home (in French), from the play by David Storey. Paris, Gallimard, 1973.

Suzanna Andler, La Musica, and L'Amante Anglaise. London, Calder, 1975.

L'Eden Cinéma (produced Paris, 1977). Paris, Mercure, 1977.

Le Camion (screenplay). Paris, Minuit, 1977.

La Navire Night, Césarée, Les Mains négatives, Aurélia Steiner, Aurélia Steiner, Aurélia Steiner. Paris, Mercure, 1979.

DURAS

Vera Baxter; ou, Les Plages de l'Atlantique (screenplay).   Paris, Albatros, 1980.
L'Homme assis dans le couloir.   Paris, Minuit, 1980.
Agatha.   Paris, Minuit, 1981.
L'Homme Atlantique.   Paris, Minuit, 1982.
Savannah Bay.   Paris, Minuit, 1983.
La Maladie de la mort.   Paris, Minuit, 1983.

Screenplays: *Hiroshima mon amour*, 1959; *Moderato Cantabile*, with Gérard Jarlot and Peter Brook, 1960; *Une Aussi Longue Absence* (*The Long Absence*), with Gérard Jarlot, 1961; *10:30 P.M. Summer*, with Jules Dassin, 1966; *La Musica*, 1966; *Détruire, dit-elle* (*Destroy, She Said*), 1969; *Les Rideaux blancs*, 1966; *Jaune le soleil*, 1971; *Nathalie Granger*, 1972; *La ragazza di Passaggio/La Femme du Gange*, 1973; *Ce que savait Morgan*, with others, 1974; *India Song*, 1975; *Des journées entières dans les arbres*, 1976; *Son Nom de Venises dans Calcutta désert*, 1976; *Baxter—Vera Baxter*, 1977; *Le Camion*, 1977; *La Navire Night*, 1978; *Césarée*; *Les Mains négatives*; *Aurélia Steiner*.

Television Play: *Sans merveille*, with Gérard Jarlot, 1964.

Other

Les Parleuses (interviews), with Xaviere Gauthier.   Paris, Minuit, 1974.
Étude sur l'oeuvre littéraire, théâtrale, et cinématographique de Duras, with Jacques Lacan and Maurice Blanchot.   Paris, Albatros, 1976.
Territoires du féminin, with Marcelle Marini.   Paris, Minuit, 1977.
Les Lieux de Duras (interview), with Michelle Porte.   Paris, Minuit, 1978.
L'Été 80.   Paris, Minuit, 1980.
Les Yeux ouverts (special "Duras Issue").   Paris, Les Cahiers du Cinema 312-313, June 1980.
Outside: Papiers d'un jour.   Paris, Michel, 1981.

*

Critical Studies: *Duras* by Alfred Cismaru, New York, Twayne, 1971; *Duras: Moderato Cantabile* by David Coward, London, Grant and Cutler, 1981; *Alienation and Absence in the Novels of Duras* by Carol J. Murphy, Lexington, Kentucky, French Forum, 1982.

*   *   *

Marguerite Duras has always responded positively to current intellectual trends. Her first novels trailed wisps of existentialism and in the 1950's her writing reflected something of the distaste of the *nouveau roman* for the props of realistic fiction (plot, psychology, etc.). A member of the Communist Party until she was expelled for revisionism in 1950, she has remained on the left, though her mistrust of totalitarianism is as great as her opposition to bourgeois imperialism. Understandably, therefore, she took an anti-colonial line on Algeria and in May 1968 supported the students. During the 1970's, she espoused the feminist cause which she has recently renounced. In 1971, she abandoned the novel for the cinema and, since 1980, the cinema for brief, elusive fictions which continue her preoccupations with individualism and personal freedom.

Like Samuel Beckett, Duras has never written a literary manifesto though she has discussed her work in magazine articles and interviews. Her early novels were relatively traditional, owing much to writers as diverse as Mauriac, Hemingway, and Virginia Woolf, but were remarkable for the use of elliptic dialogue and their insistence on inner states and struggles. By the early 1960's, the dialogue had become almost cinematographic, her plots minimal, and her characters elusive: they are defined against the concerted symbolism of nature and the occurrence of extraneous events which trigger highly personal responses. Between 1952 and 1962, the pattern frequently shows a middle-class wife in her thirties, often with a child, who exists in a state of spiritual *ennui*. Alcohol, violence, or the pressures of a routine life bring her to the point of revolt. She commits an action (adultery, willed or real, is a popular choice) through which she glimpses the intense self-fulfilment which she has been seeking. But the "death" of the self brings only temporary relief. Since it is impossible to exist permanently in a state of total liberation, she sinks into a contemplative trance (called "madness"). This is the sense of the "ravissement" of Lol V. Stein and the "folie" of the Vice-Consul whose predicament inaugurates a cycle of interrelated novels and films (notably, *India Song*) linking colonial oppression with the poverty of our personal lives. For what is true of love—that it is "impossible"—will henceforth also be true of politics. *Détruire, dit-elle* states the necessity for the "impossible revolution," but though political commitment is explored subsequently in feminist, revolutionary, and colonial contexts in the novels, plays, and especially the films of the 1970's, it is to the theme of "impossible love" that Duras has returned in her most recent short fiction which, dense and sensuous, aspires to the condition of poetry. For aesthetically, films and novels are also impossible since all representational art is specific and restricted: Duras's vision of the absolute can only be rendered in abstract terms.

Always a controversial figure, stronger on passion than on feeling, continually experimenting with new forms of expression, Marguerite Duras commands attention by the intensity of her commitment and the evocative power of her incantatory prose style.

—David Coward

DÜRRENMATT, Friedrich. Swiss. Born in Konolfingen bei Bern, Switzerland, 5 January 1921. Educated at Grosshöchstetten school; Freies Gymnasium and Humboldtianum, Bern; University of Zurich, one term; University of Bern. Married Lotti Geissler in 1947; one son and two daughters. Writer: drama critic, *Die Weltwoche*, Zurich, 1951, and co-owner, *Zürcher Sonntags-Journal*, 1969-71; also stage and television director: co-director, Basel Theaters, 1968-69. Recipient: City of Bern Prize, 1954, 1979; Radio Play Prize (Berlin), 1957; Italia Prize, for radio play 1958; Schiller Prize (Mannheim), 1959; New York Drama Critics Circle Award, 1959; Schiller Prize (Switzerland), 1960; Grillparzer Prize, 1968; Kanton of Bern Prize, 1969; Welsh Arts Council International Writers Prize, 1976; Buber-Rosenzweig Medal, 1977; Austrian State Award, 1983. Honorary doctorate: Temple University, Philadelphia, 1969; Hebrew University, Jerusalem, 1977; University of Nice, 1977; University of Neuchatel, 1981. Honorary Fellow, Modern Language Association (USA). Agent: Reiss AG, Bühnenvertrieb, Bruderholzstrasse 39, CH-4053 Basel; or, Diogenes Verlag, Sprecherstrasse 8, CH-8032 Zurich; or, Verlag der Arche, Rosenbuhlstrasse 37, CH-8044 Zurich. Address: Pertuis du Sault 36, 2000 Neuchatel, Switzerland.

PUBLICATIONS

Plays

Es steht geschrieben (produced Zurich, 1947). Basel, Sammlung Klosterberg, 1947; revised version, as *Die Wiedertäfer* (produced Zurich, 1967), Zurich, Der Arche, 1967;

as *The Anabaptists* (produced Cardiff, 1976).

Der Blinde (produced Basel, 1948). Zurich, Der Arche, 1960.

Romulus der Grosse (produced Basel, 1949). Basel, Reiss, 1956; revised version (produced Zurich, 1957), Zurich, Der Arche, 1958; translated as *Romulus* (produced Glasgow, 1961; New York, 1962), New York, Dramatists Play Service, 1962; in *Four Plays*, London, Cape, 1964.

Die Ehe des Herrn Mississippi (produced Munich, 1952). Zurich, Oprecht, 1952; revised version, Zurich, Der Arche, 1957, film version, 1961; as *The Marriage of Mr. Mississippi* (as *Fools Are Passing Through*, produced New York, 1958; as *The Marriage of Mr. Mississippi*, produced London, 1959), New York, Grove Press, 1966.

Ein Engel kommt nach Babylon (produced Munich, 1953). Zurich, Der Arche, 1954; revised version, 1958; as *An Angel Comes to Babylon* (produced Berkeley, California, 1962; Bristol, 1963), published with *Romulus the Great*, New York, Grove Press, 1964.

Der Besuch der alten Dame (produced Zurich, 1956). Zurich, Der Arche, 1956; film version, 1963; as *The Visit* (produced New York, 1958; London, 1960), New York, Random House, 1958; London, Cape, 1962.

Nächtliches Gespräch mit einem verachteten Menschen (radio play). Zurich, Der Arche, 1957; as *Conversation at Night with a Despised Character* (produced Los Angeles, 1981), Chicago, Dramatic Publishing Company, n.d.

Komödien I-III. Zurich, Der Arche, 3 vols., 1957-72.

Das Unternehmen der Wega (radio play). Zurich, Der Arche, 1958.

Frank V, music by Paul Burkhard (produced Zurich, 1959). Zurich, Der Arche, 1960; translated as *Frank V* (produced Cardiff, 1976).

Der Prozess um des Esels Schatten (radio play). Zurich, Der Arche, 1959; as *The Jackass* (produced New York, 1960).

Stranitzky und der Nationalheld (radio play). Zurich, Der Arche, 1959.

Abendstunde im Spätherbst (radio play; also produced Berlin, 1959). Zurich, Der Arche, 1959; as *Episode on an Autumn Evening* (produced New York, 1978; also produced as *One Autumn Evening*, London, 1968), Chicago, Dramatic Publishing Company, n.d.; as *Incident at Twilight*, in *Postwar German Theatre*, edited by Michael Benedikt and George E. Wellwarth, London, Macmillan, 1968.

Der Doppelgänger (radio play). Zurich, Der Arche, 1960.

Herkules und der Stall des Augias (radio play; also produced Zurich, 1963). Zurich, Der Arche, 1960; as *Hercules and the Augean Stables* (produced London, 1966), Chicago, Dramatic Publishing Company, n.d.

Die Panne (radio play). Zurich, Der Arche, 1961; revised version, 1979; as *The Deadly Game* (produced Croydon, Surrey, 1963; New York, 1966; London, 1967), New York, Dramatists Play Service, 1966.

Gesammelte Hörspiele (includes *Abendstunde im Spätherbst*, *Der Doppelgänger*, *Herkules und der Stall des Augias*, *Nächtliches Gespräch mit einem verachteten Menschen*, *Die Panne*, *Der Prozess um des Esels Schatten*, *Stranitzky und der Nationalheld*, *Das Unternehmen der Wega*). Zurich, Der Arche, 1961.

Die Physiker (produced Zurich, 1962). Zurich, Der Arche, 1962; television version, 1963; as *The Physicists* (produced London, 1963; New York, 1964), London, Cape, 1963; New York, Grove Press, 1964.

Der Meteor (produced Zurich, 1966). Zurich, Der Arche, 1966; as *The Meteor* (produced London, 1966; Philadelphia, 1969), London, Cape, 1973; New York, Grove Press, 1974.

König Johann, from the play by Shakespeare (produced Basel, 1968). Zurich, Der Arche, 1968.

Play Strindberg: Totentanz nach August Strindberg (produced Basel, 1969). Zurich, Der Arche, 1969; as *Play Strindberg: The Dance of Death* (produced New York, 1971; Newcastle upon Tyne, 1972), London, Cape, 1972; New York, Grove Press, 1973.

Titus Andronicus, from the play by Shakespeare (produced Dusseldorf, 1970). Zurich,

Der Arche, 1970.

Porträt eines Planeten (produced Dusseldorf, 1970; revised version, produced Zurich, 1971). Zurich, Der Arche, 1971; as *Portrait of a Planet* (produced Falmer, Sussex, 1973).

Urfaust, from the play by Goethe (produced Zurich, 1970). Zurich, Diogenes, 1980.

Der Mitmacher (produced Zurich, 1973). Zurich, Der Arche, 1973; as *The Conformer* (produced Sheffield, 1975).

Die Frist (produced Zurich, 1977). Zurich, Der Arche, 1977.

Achterloo (produced Zurich, 1983). Zurich, Diogenes, 1983.

Screenplays: *Es geschah am hellichten Tag* (*It Happened in Broad Daylight*), 1960.

Fiction

Pilatus. Olten, Vereinigung Oltner Bücherfreunde, 1949.

Der Nihilist. Zurich, Holunderpresse, 1950.

Der Richter und sein Henker. Einsiedeln, Benziger, 1952; as *The Judge and His Hangman*, London, Jenkins, 1954; New York, Harper, 1955.

Die Stadt. Zurich, Der Arche, 1952.

Der Verdacht. Einsiedeln, Benziger, 1953; as *The Quarry*, New York, Grove Press, 1961; London, Cape, 1962.

Grieche sucht Griechin. Zurich, Der Arche, 1955; as *Once a Greek...*, New York, Knopf, 1965; London, Cape, 1966.

Das Versprechen: Requiem auf den Kriminalroman. Zurich, Der Arche, 1958; as *The Pledge*, New York, Knopf, and London, Cape, 1959.

Die Panne: Eine noch mögliche Geschichte. Zurich, Der Arche, 1960; as *Traps*, New York, Knopf, 1960; as *A Dangerous Game*, London, Cape, 1960.

Der Sturz. Zurich, Der Arche, 1971.

Other

Theaterprobleme. Zurich, Der Arche, 1955; as *Problems on the Theatre*, with *The Marriage of Mr. Mississippi*, 1966.

Friedrich Schiller: Rede. Zurich, Der Arche, 1960.

Der Rest ist Dank (addresses), with Werner Weber. Zurich, Der Arche, 1961.

Die Heimat im Plakat: Ein Buch für Schweizer Kinder (drawings). Zurich, Diogenes, 1963.

Theater-Schriften und Reden, edited by Elisabeth Brock-Sulzer. Zurich, Der Arche, 2 vols., 1966-72; translated in part as *Writings on Theatre and Drama*, edited by H.M. Waidson, London, Cape, 1976.

Monstervortrag über Gerechtigkeit und Recht. Zurich, Der Arche, 1968.

Sätze aus Amerika. Zurich, Der Arche, 1970.

Zusammenhänge: Essay über Israel. Zurich, Der Arche, 1976.

Gespräch mit Heinz Ludwig Arnold. Zurich, Der Arche, 1976.

Der Mitmacher: Ein Komplex. Zurich, Der Arche, 1976.

Frankfurter Rede. Zurich, Der Arche, 1977.

Lesebuch. Zurich, Der Arche, 1978.

Bilder und Zeichnungen, edited by Christian Strich. Zurich, Diogenes, 1978.

Albert Einstein: Ein Vortrag. Zurich, Der Arche, 1979.

Werkausgabe. Zurich, Diogenes, 30 vols., 1981.

Stoffe 1-3: Winterkrieg in Tibet, Mondfinsternis, Der Rebell. Zurich, Diogenes, 1981.

Plays and Essays, edited by Volkmar Sander. New York, Continuum, 1982.

*

Critical Studies: *Dürrenmatt* by Murray B. Peppard, New York, Twayne, 1969; *Dürrenmatt* by Armin Arnold, New York, Ungar, 1972; *Dürrenmatt: A Study in Plays, Prose, and Theory* by Timo Tiusanen, Princeton, New Jersey, Princeton University Press, 1977; *Dürrenmatt: A Study of His Plays* by Urs Jenny, London, Eyre Methuen, 1978; *The Theatre of Dürrenmatt: A Study in the Possibility of Freedom* by Kenneth S. Whitton, London, Wolff, 1980.

*   *   *

"He [the author] presents the work *for* interpretation, not the interpretation itself." Since his entry onto the international literary scene in 1947, the Swiss author Friedrich Dürrenmatt has waged a war against critics and academics who persist in finding in his works...what they set out to find! "No one beheads more easily than he who hasn't got a head," was an early savage retort to one such unkind criticism. Dürrenmatt has been fairly well mauled by critics in his day—and no more so than in the last ten years when the comparative failure of his last works (e.g., *Der Mitmacher* and *Die Frist*) has led him to withdraw from the hurly-burly of stage productions to his lovely house in Neuchâtel and concentrate on writing political and philosophical treatises.

The publication (in 30 paperback volumes) of "revised" editions of his works on the occasion of his 60th birthday in 1981, however, reminded some of the younger critics of Dürrenmatt's great days (c.1955-70) when he was (after Brecht and Shakespeare) the most frequently performed dramatist on German-speaking stages, and that his prose works (particularly *The Judge and His Hangman* and *A Dangerous Game*) have been required reading in schools and universities since their publication.

Dürrenmatt, along with his older Swiss colleague Max Frisch, filled the vacuum left by the absent German playwrights immediately after World War II when his particular brand of neo-Expressionist grotesque, witty, yet peculiarly profound "Komödie" mirrored the shifting moral values of the post-war world. Dürrenmatt's works dealt with the post-war unease, political and philosophical, at the development in international and personal relations. The Cold War, the acquisition of great wealth by some at the expense of the poorer countries, the growing bureaucratization of, and intrusion into, our private lives, the breaking-down of societal relationships, particularly of those between husband and wife, were all reflected in his plays, and in his novels and short stories.

After his early plays, *Es steht geschrieben* and *Der Blinde*, up to *An Angel Comes to Babylon* (1953), Dürrenmatt produced what has remained his masterpiece, *The Visit*, in 1956. The theoretical basis to this great international success was to be found in the lecture-essay *Theaterprobleme*, given in several West German cities during 1954 and 1955. Building on the various theories of drama propounded in the past, Dürrenmatt concluded that *our* Age was "too serious for tragedy": "Tragedy assumes the presence of guilt, moderation, trouble, the overview, responsibility..., in the mess that is our century...there are no longer any guilty men, nor are there any to be held responsible any more..."

Thus tragedy, as the Greeks knew it, in a world with a fixed moral order where guilt and retribution, suffering, and redemption can be meted out, is no longer possible in our world of ambiguous moral values—so "only the Komödie can reach us now." But Dürrenmatt's *Komödien* are light-years removed from the frothy social comedies known to the western stage.

Full of paradoxes, savage ironies, grotesque caricatures of human beings set, often, in "impossible" milieux, an anachronistic Babylon, a lunatic asylum, an invented Swiss village ("Güllen" in *The Visit* is the Swiss for "liquid cattle dung"), or in the corpse-filled basement of an apartment block (*Der Mitmacher*), Dürrenmatt's plays present us with provocative views of the 20th century's human condition.

The Visit is the story of the return to her now ailing village of Clare Zachanassian, once driven out because she had been made pregnant by the village shop-keeper Alfred Ill and now the richest woman in the world, bent on obtaining revenge by offering "eine Milliarde" (a billion) if the shop-keeper is murdered. The greed of Güllen's citizenry when they hypocritically promise to stand by their prospective Mayor, Alfred, and at the same time rush to his shop to buy (on credit) all kinds of luxury goods in anticipation of the coming cheque, mirrors the materialism of the 20th century. Both sides of the Iron Curtain have claimed the play as an attack on the other's ideological values; on balance, it has been felt that the attack was more on American capitalism than on Soviet bureaucratization—but both systems came in for a fair share of Dürrenmatt's wicked saitre. (After the publication of his short novel on the Politburo *Der Sturz*, in 1971, which followed his equally satirical depiction of American mores in his *Sätze aus Amerika* (1970), one could hear Dürrenmatt chuckle (as his wont): "A plague o' both your houses"!)

Dürrenmatt's strengths—both as playwright and novelist—lie in his superb sense of stage and dialogue and in his comic touch which does at times desert him and results in the rather obvious and flat "corny joke" (*Kalauer* in German). His best works, however, *The Visit*, *The Physicists*, and *Romulus*, and the short novels *The Judge and His Hangman*, *The Quarry*, and *Once a Greek*, few European writers were able to match for wit and invention.

On his gradual withdrawal from the stage, say, after 1977, Dürrenmatt has concentrated on writing political and philosophical treatises, contributing one of the very few western defences of the Israeli case in the Yom Kippur war (in *Zusammenhänge: Essay über Israel*) which shows Dürrenmatt's polemical style at its best, containing as it does a lecture, a philosophical discourse, a travelogue, and a Swiftian short story; all the volume lacked were illustrations in Dürrenmatt's Hieronymus Bosch manner, some of which have now been published.

Dürrenmatt, a man who has suffered grievously all his life from diabetes, and (in recent years) from a series of heart-attacks, remains a major figure in European letters, an uncompromising and uncomfortable opponent of all those who display pomposity or who seek to impose their will on their weaker brethren. Dürrenmatt, the neutral Swiss, clings, now as always, to the "possibility of Freedom" for all men, and will continue to attack those who deny it to others.

—Kenneth S. Whitton

ELYTIS, Odysseus. Pseudonym for Odysseus Alepoudelis. Greek. Born in Heraklion, Crete, 2 November 1911. Educated at the University of Athens, 1930-33; the Sorbonne, Paris, 1948-52. Served in the First Army Corps, in Albania, 1940-41: Lieutenant. Program director, National Broadcasting Institution, 1945-47, 1953-54; art and literary critic, *Kathimerini* magazine, 1946-48; adviser to Art Theatre, 1955-56, and Greek National Theatre, 1965-68. President of the Governing Board, Greek Ballet, 1956-58, and Greek Broadcasting and Television, 1974; Member of the Administrative Board, Greek National Theatre, 1974-76. Recipient: National Prize in Poetry, 1960; Nobel Prize for Literature, 1979; Royal Society of Literature Benson Medal (UK), 1981. D.Litt.: University of Salonica, 1976; the Sorbonne, 1980; University of London, 1981. Member, Order of the Phoenix, 1965. Address: Skoufa Street 23, Athens, Greece.

PUBLICATIONS

Verse

Prosanatolismoi [Orientations]. Athens, Pirsos, 1939.
O Ilios o protos [Sun the First]. Athens, Glaros, 1943.

To axion esti. Athens, Ikaros 1959; as *The Axion Esti*, translated by Edmund Keeley and G.P. Savidis, Pittsburgh, University of Pittsburgh Press, 1974; London, Anvil Press, 1980.
Exi ke mia typseis ghia ton ourano [Six and One Regrets for the Sky]. Athens, Ikaros, 1960.
To fotodhendro ke i dhekati tetarti omorfia [The Light Tree and the Fourteenth Beauty]. Athens, Ikaros, 1971.
O Ilios o iliatoras [The Sovereign Sun]. Athens, Ikaros, 1971.
Thanatos ke anastasis tou Konstandinou Paleologhou [Death and Resurrection of Constandine Palaiologos]. Athens, Duo d'Art, 1971.
To monogramma [The Monogram]. Athens, Ikaros, 1972.
Ta ro tou erota [The Ro of Eros]. Athens, Asterias, 1972.
Villa Natacha. 1973.
O fillomandis [The Leaf Diviner]. Athens, Asterias, 1973.
Ta eterothali [The Stepchildren]. Athens, Ikaros, 1974.
The Sovereign Sun: Selected Poems, edited by Kimon Friar. Philadelphia, Temple University Press, 1974.
Maria Nefeli. Athens, 1978; as *Maria Nephele*, translated by Athan Anagnostopoulos, Boston, Houghton Mifflin, 1981.
Selected Poems, edited by Edmund Keeley and Philip Sherrard. London, Anvil Press, and New York, Viking Press, 1981.
Tria poiemata me simaia evkairias [Three Poems with Flags of Convenience]. Athens, 1982.

Other

Ho zographos Theophilos [The Painter Theophilos]. Athens, Asterias, 1973.
Anihta hartia [The Open Book]. Athens, Asterias, 1974.
I mayia tou papadhiamandhi [The Magic of Papadiamandis]. Athens, Ermias, 1976.

*

Critical Studies: "Elytis Issue" of *Books Abroad*, Autumn 1975; *Elytis: Analogies of Light* edited by Ivar Ivask, Norman, University of Oklahoma Press, 1980.

*   *   *

The pseudonym "Elytis," chosen by O. Alepoudelis, has been connected with such central themes in his poetry as *Ellás* (Greece), *elpída* (hope), and *eleftheria* (freedom), but has more plausibly been accounted for as combining three elements: the name of the French poet Paul Eluard to whom Elytis acknowledges a debt, the idea of an *élite* to which the poet belongs, and the Greek word *alítis* (vagabond) which is also found in Homer and used to describe Odysseus, disguised, on his return to Ithaca. All of these are key elements in describing the poetic individuality of Odysseus Elytis.

Profoundly influenced by Surrealism, both French and Greek, Elytis began his poetic career in the 1930's. His first volumes of poetry betray the influence of Surrealism most clearly. In them an apparently free association of ideas and images appears to be governed only by an exuberance, a sensuous celebration of beauty, the sun and the Greek landscape, and a love of life, to which all formal constraints are secondary. After his experience of war on the Albanian front in 1940, Elytis went on to weigh these ideas in the balance with the grim experience of violence and the proximity of death, in the "Heroic and elegiac song for the lost sublieutenant of Albania" (1945). A much more successful handling of this juxtaposition, however, is to be found in *To axion esti* (Worth Is), which was 14 years in the writing and appeared in 1959.

This long poem is probably Elytis's finest achievement, in which the creative exuberance of the poet is set against, and at first overwhelmed by, violence and destruction at the hands of his own and his country's enemies, only, in the final part of the poem, to overcome them and turn defeat into victory, by drawing up out of the poet's own creative spirit all the unfettered creative power of Nature that he has absorbed in early life. The poem ends with a hymn of praise to life, in which the forces of death and destruction have been, imaginatively, at least, vanquished by the poet's creative power in alliance with the creative powers of Nature.

Many of Elytis's subsequent poems also deal with the emergence of victory from defeat, life from death, but often in a more introspective manner, which has been characterised by one critic as "interior lyricism," in contrast with the more open, public manner of *To axion esti*. The finest poems of this "interior lyricism" are to be found in *To fotodhendro* and *To monogramma*. Since then Elytis has published another long poem which looks back to the ambitious, complex structure of *To axion esti*, *Maria Nefeli*; his most recent publication is *Tria poiemata me simaia evkairias*.

Unlike the Surrealists in whose company he started out, Elytis has sought to achieve a synthesis between the freedom of association and spontaneity of Surrealism on the one hand, and more traditional demands on the artwork, on the other. In Elytis's poetry spontaneity coexists with an almost mathematical precision and complexity of form, thus dramatising the victory of the creative spirit over rationally derived forms of restraint. As he once put it, Elytis believes in "the creation of new restrictions which the poet sets up so as to overcome them and so to succeed, once again, in creating a stable edifice." For Elytis, poetry is not only the Surrealist exploration of consciousness, but the creation, out of that exploration, of a well-made artefact, the poem.

—Roderick Beaton

ENZENSBERGER, Hans Magnus. German. Born in Kaufbeuren, 11 November 1929. Educated at schools in Nuremberg; universities of Freiburg and Hamburg; University of Erlangen, doctorate in literature 1955. Served in the Volkssturm, 1944-45. Married 1) Dagrun Christensen, one daughter; 2) Maria Makarova (divorced). Program editor, South German Radio, 1955-57, and guest lecturer, Academy of Design, Ulm, 1956-57; editor, Suhrkamp, publishers, Frankfurt, since 1960; Founder, 1965, and publisher since 1970, *Kursbuch*; Founding Editor, *TransAtlantik*, 1980-82; lived in Norway, 1961-65, then in Berlin and, since 1979, Munich. Fellow, Center for Advanced Studies, Wesleyan University, Middletown, Connecticut (resigned, 1968). Recipient: Jacobi prize, 1956; Critics Prize (Germany), 1962, 1979; Büchner Prize, 1963; Etna-Taormina Prize, 1967. Address: c/o Suhrkamp Verlag, Lindenstrasse 29-35, Postfach 4229, 6000 Frankfurt am Main, Germany.

PUBLICATIONS

Verse

Verteidigung der Wölfe. Frankfurt, Suhrkamp, 1957.
Landessprache. Frankfurt, Suhrkamp, 1960.
Gedichte. Frankfurt, Suhrkamp, 1962.

Blindenschrift. Frankfurt, Suhrkamp, 1964.
Poems, translated by Michael Hamburger. Newcastle upon Tyne, Northern House, 1966.
Poems for People Who Don't Read Poems, translated by the author, Michael Hamburger, and Jerome Rothenberg. London, Secker and Warburg, and New York, Atheneum, 1968; as *Selected Poems,* London, Penguin, 1968.
Gedichte 1955-1970. Frankfurt, Suhrkamp, 1971.
Mausoleum: 37 Balladen aus der Geschichte des Fortschritts. Frankfurt, Suhrkamp, 1975; as *Mausoleum,* translated by Joachim Neugroschel, New York, Urizen Press, 1976.
Der Untergang der Titanic. Frankfurt, Suhrkamp, 1978; as *The Sinking of the Titanic,* translated by the author, Boston, Houghton Mifflin, 1980; Manchester, Carcanet Press, 1981.
Die Furie des Verschwindens: Gedichte. Frankfurt, Suhrkamp, 1980.
Die Gedichte. Frankfurt, Suhrkamp, 1983.

Plays

Das Verhör von Habana (produced Essen). Frankfurt, Suhrkamp, 1970; as *The Havana Inquiry,* New York, Holt Rinehart, 1973.
El Cimarron, music by Hans Werner Henze, from a work by Miguel Barnet (produced Aldeburgh, Suffolk, 1970). Mainz, 1971.
La Cubana, music by Hans Werner Henze (produced Munich, 1975).
Der Menschenfeind, from the play *Le Misanthrope* by Molière (produced Berlin, 1979). Frankfurt, Insel, 1979.

Radio Play: *Der tote Mann und der Philosoph,* 1978.

Other

Brentanos Poetik. Munich, Hanser, 1961.
Einzelheiten. Frankfurt, Suhrkamp, 1962.
Einzelheiten II: Poesie und Politik. Frankfurt, Suhrkamp, 1964.
Politik und Verbrechen. Frankfurt, Suhrkamp, 1964; as *Politics and Crime,* edited by Michael Roloff, New York, Seabury Press, 1974.
Deutschland, Deutschland unter anderm: Äusserungen zur Politik. Frankfurt, Suhrkamp, 1967.
Der kurze Sommer der Anarchie. Frankfurt, Suhrkamp, 1972.
The Consciousness Industry, edited by Michael Roloff. New York, Seabury Press, 1973.
Palaver: Politische Überlegungen (1967-1973). Frankfurt, Suhrkamp, 1974.
Raids and Reconstructions: Essays on Politics, Crime, and Culture. London, Pluto Press, 1976.
Critical Essays, edited by Reinhold Grimm. New York, Continuum, 1982.
Politische Brosamen. Frankfurt, Suhrkamp, 1982.

Editor, *Gedichte, Erzählungen, Briefe,* by Clemens Brentano. Frankfurt, Fischer, 1958.
Editor, *Museum der moderne Poesie.* Frankfurt, Suhrkamp, 1960.
Editor, *Vorzeichen: Fünf neue deutsche Autoren.* Frankfurt, Suhrkamp, 1962.
Editor, *Gedichte,* by Andreas Gryphius. Frankfurt, Insel, 1962.
Editor, *Der Hessische Landbote,* by Georg Büchner. Frankfurt, Insel, 1965.
Editor, *Kurzgefasstes Bericht,* by Bartolome de Las Casas. Frankfurt, Insel, 1966; as *The Devastation of the Indies,* New York, Seabury Press, 1974.
Editor, *Freisprüche: Revolutionäre vor Gericht.* Frankfurt, Suhrkamp, 1970.

Editor, *Klassenbuch: Ein Lesebuch zu den Klassenkämpfen in Deutschland 1756-1971.* Neuwied, Luchterhand, 1972.
Editor, *Gespräche mit Marx und Engels.* Frankfurt, Insel, 1973.
Editor, *Allerleirauh: Viele schöne Kinderreime.* Frankfurt, Suhrkamp, 1973.
Editor, *Der Weg ins Freie.* Frankfurt, Suhrkamp, 1975.

Translator, *Die Bettleroper,* by John Gay, in *Dreigroschenbuch.* Frankfurt, Suhrkamp, 1960.
Translator, *Quoat-Quoat,* by Audiberti, in *Theaterstücke 1.* Neuwied, Luchterhand, 1961.
Translator, *Gedichte,* by William Carlos Williams. Frankfurt, Suhrkamp, 1962.
Translator, *Gedichte,* by César Vallejo. Frankfurt, Suhrkamp, 1963.
Translator, *Poesie,* by Franco Fortini. Frankfurt, Suhrkamp, 1963.
Translator, *Das Maschinen: Gedichten,* by Lars Gustafsson. Munich, 1967.
Translator, *Poesie impure: Gedichte,* by Pablo Neruda. Hamburg, Hoffmann & Campe, 1968.
Translator, *Komplettes Nonsens,* by Edward Lear. Frankfurt, Insel, 1977.
Translator, *Der Vampir von St. Petersburg,* by Alexander Suchovo-Kobylin. Frankfurt, Verlag des Autoren, 1978.

*

Critical Studies: *Enzensberger* by Heinz Ludwig Arnold, Munich, Text und Kritik, 1976; *Enzensberger* by Henning Falkenstein, Berlin, Colloquium 1977; *Enzensberger* by Knut Brusewitz, Bonn, Bouvier, 1977; *Über Enzensberger* (includes bibliography) by Reinhold Grimm, Frankfurt, Suhrkamp, 1984.

* * *

Hans Magnus Enzensberger is a legitimate heir to the generation of European and American modernist poets writing between 1910 and 1945. In particular he is indebted to Bertolt Brecht and Gottfried Benn. In his poetry, which he began producing in the mid-1950's, he too eschews rhyme, inclines towards irregular rhythms, employs counterpointing and montage techniques, and appeals more to the intellect through his elliptical, laconic style. Added to these features is his particular penchant for grotesque verbal distortions which render familiar realities in a new and alarming light.

His work has a distinctly cosmopolitan feel and this is even evident in the titles of several poems, such as "Corps diplomatique socialiste," "La forza del destino," "Doomsday," "Countdown," and "Middle Class Blues." This last poem is typical in a number of respects. It criticises the materialism and consumerism of contemporary society, while evoking a sense of spiritual emptiness underneath the façade of satiety. Like many of his poems it is a melancholic lament rather than an aggressive indictment and invalidates the early labelling of Enzensberger as an "angry young man." If "anger" exists in his work, then it is expressed rather as the result of his own frustration as one who seeks self-liberation but finds himself enchained firmly to the middle class.

This frustration boiled over in the mid-1960's when he announced that he was giving up writing poetry in order to make his country "politically literate," but he did ultimately return to his artistic role of poet-mentor to the German nation. The poems from his period of political *engagement,* now published in the sections *Davor* (Before) and *Danach* (After) in the *Collected Poems* (1983) are the least convincing of his output due to their over-intellectualised, narrow focus on radical, left-wing politicking. Here his gift for verbal play and innovation, which truly demasks the way our minds have been infested with the jargon of modern technology, industry, commerce, and the media, is wasted on facile parody.

Enzensberger's involvement in the Berlin student movement and his pilgrimage to Cuba in 1968-69 are put into (self-)critical perspective in his remarkable epic poem *The Sinking of the*

Titanic. Berlin and Cuba, these former idylls of progress, are as quietly shattered by the poet as the ostensibly unsinkable passenger steamer was by an iceberg. Man-made symbols of progress, be they a new ship or a new society, are revealed as ephemeral artefacts threatened by failure almost as soon as they are created. But individuals prefer to remain blind to impending disasters because their basic instinct is to live for the present and believe in survival, irrespective of all the lessons of history and the writing on the wall (cf. his earlier poem "Braille"). The poet's responsibility is therefore to make us face the reality and recognise the technological and political icebergs which can sink our entire planet with the same chilling suddenness as the real one which destroyed the *Titanic.*

—Anthony Waine

ERBA, Luciano. Italian. Born in Milan, 18 September 1922. Educated at Liceo Manzoni, Milan, graduated 1940; Catholic University, Milan, Ph.D. 1947. Member of anti-fascist group in Milan, 1943, then refugee in Switzerland, 1944-45. Married Maria Giuseppina Sain in 1961; three daughters. Lecturer in Italian, Lycée Saint-Louis, Paris, 1948-50; Assistant in French, 1953-54, Lecturer, 1954-57, and Associate Professor, 1957-63, Catholic University, Milan; Visiting Professor, 1963-64, and Associate Professor of Comparative Literature, 1964-65, Rutgers University, New Brunswick, New Jersey; Associate Professor of Comparative Literature, University of Washington, Seattle, 1965-66, University of Bari, 1967-70, University of Trieste, 1970-71, and University of Bologna, 1971-72; Professor of French Literature, University of Trieste, 1972-73, and University of Padua, 1973-82. Since 1982, Professor of French Literature and Comparative Literature, University of Verona. Recipient: Carducci Prize, 1977; Viareggio Prize, 1980. Agent: Mondadori, CP 1772, 20100 Milan. Address: Via Giason del Maino 16, 20146 Milan, Italy.

Verse

Linea K. Modena, Guanda, 1951.
Il bel paese. Milan, Meridiana, 1956.
Il prete di Ratanà. Milan, Scheiwiller, 1959.
Il male minore. Milan, Mondadori, 1960.
Il prato più verde. Milan, Guanda, 1977.
Il nastro di Moebius. Milan, Mondadori, 1980.
(Selection) in English, in *The New Italian Poetry*, edited and translated by Lawrence R. Smith. Berkeley, University of California Press, 1981.
Il cerchio aperto. Milan, Scheiwiller, 1983.

Plays

Radio Play: *Robinson Crusoe*, 1977.

Television Play: *La valle del Po al tempo dei Galli e dei Romani*, 1983-84.

Fiction

Françoise. Brescia, Farfengo, 1982.

Other

Magia e Invenzione: Note e ricerche su Cyrano de Bergerac e altri autori del primo Seicento francese. Milan, Scheiwiller, 1967.
Huysmans e la liturgia, e alcune note di letteratura francese contemporanea. Bari, Adriatica, 1971.
Storia e Antologia della letteratura francese: Il Novecento. Milan, Fabbri, 2 vols., 1972.

Editor, *Lettres*, by Cyrano de Bergerac. Milan, Scheiwiller, 1965.
Editor, *Gli Stati e Imperi della Luna*, by Cyrano de Bergerac. Rome, Theoria, 1982.
Editor, *Viaggio al centro della Terra*, by Jules Verne. Rome, Theoria, 1983.

Translator, *L'altro mondo*, by Cyrano de Bergerac. Florence, Sansoni, 1956.
Translator, *Poesie*, by Blaise Cendrars. Milan, Nuova Accademia, 1961.
Translator, *Vita del testo*, by Francis Ponge. Milan, Mondadori, 1971.
Translator, *Giles Ragazzo-Capra*, by John Barth. Milan, Rizzoli, 1972.
Translator, *Tatto*, by Thom Gunn. Milan, Guanda, 1979.

*

Critical Studies: "La poesia di Erba 'Super flumina'" by Angelo Jacomuzzi, in *Forum Italicum 10*, 1976; by A. Di Benedetto, in *Novecento 9*, Milan, Marzorati, 1980; by G. Stipi, in *Testo 4*, January-June 1983.

*   *   *

In the immediate postwar period, a large circle of younger poets committed to cultural and artistic renewal reacted against hermeticism, the prevailing current in Italian poetry represented by such established figures as Montale and Quasimodo. Luciano Erba and other poets of the so-called fourth generation—Cattafi, Orelli, Spaziani, and Zanzotto, among others—chose a different course. To the quest for social engagement they opposed a disenchanted view of contemporary life; to the perceived need for new modes of experimentation they responded with a continued attachment to the formal means of expression identified with hermetic verse: semantic concentration, understatement, attention to the allusive qualities of the poetic word.

In Luciano Erba the adherence to the basic tenets of hermeticism generates a poetry of simple emotions and the epiphany of seemingly insignificant actions and events associated with the past. *Il male minore*, which includes three books of verse issued between 1951 and 1959, is distinguished by a low-key existential disposition and a deep disillusionment with the present often compensated by a mnemonic return to adolescence and early youth. The indulgence in retrospection stands out consistently as an antidote to alienation. Yet the search for an idyllic past, though contemplated, is not seriously nurtured in Erba's work as it is, for instance, in Pavese's narrative. Memory, while assuring evasive comfort, serves the functional need of counteracting "the senseless passage of time." In other words, memory is denied a cognitive function inasmuch as Erba's existential consciousness is veined with corrosive irony and a sense of ambivalence, if not mistrust, toward rationality and ideology. When poetic diction takes the form of epigram—as in "Nothing is certain" and "Of Life we knew only its tedium"—it crystallizes a vision of our time so lucidly cognizant of the impotence to arrest the tide of materialism that even art is deemed irrelevant. As Erba puts it, "Poetry changes nothing."

Il prato più verde reaffirms the poet's conscious estrangement from the mainstream of life and his position in society as a marginal and disaffected observer. But fresh elements are also in evidence. The texture of the verse alternates between spontaneous expression of remarkable simplicity and complex, syntactic constructs in which the signified becomes intelligible only through a patient decoding process. More importantly, the elegiac tone and resigned pessimism of the earlier period give way to a more assertive existential outlook grounded in metaphysical reflection which, even in its recurring moments of negativism, entertains a glimmer of hope for the fate of mankind.

The poems of *Il prato più verde*, together with a few recent verses that reinforce the foregoing assessment, are included in the volume *Il nastro di Moebius*.

—Augustus Pallotta

EVTUSHENKO, Evgeny (Alexandrovich). Born in Stanzia Zima, Siberia, 18 July 1933. Attended Gorky Institute of World Literature, Moscow, 1951-54. Married 1) Bella Akhmadulina, *q.v.*, in 1954 (divorced); 2) Galina Evtushenko (divorced); 3) Jan Batle in 1978; three sons. Address: c/o USSR Union of Writers, Ulitsa Vorovskogo 20, Moscow, 69, USSR.

PUBLICATIONS

Verse

Razvedchiki gryadushchevo [The Prospectors of the Future]. Moscow, Sovietsky Pisatel', 1952.
Trety sneg [Third Snow]. Moscow, Sovietsky Pisatel', 1955.
Shosse entuziastov [Highway of the Enthusiasts]. Moscow, Moskovsky Rabochy, 1956.
Obeshchaniye [Promise]. Moscow, Sovietsky Pisatel', 1957.
Luk i lira [The Bow and the Lyre]. Tbilisi, Zara Vostoka, 1959.
Stikhi raznykh let [Poems of Several Years]. Moscow, Molodaya Gvardia, 1959.
Red Cats. San Francisco, City Lights, 1961.
Vzmakh ruki [A Wave of the Hand]. Moscow, Molodaya Gvardia, 1962.
(Selection), translated by Peter Levi and Robin Milner-Gulland. London, Penguin, 1962; as *Selected Poems*, New York, Dutton, 1962.
Yabloko [The Apple]. Moscow, Molodaya Gvardia, 1962.
Nezhnost': Novye Stikhi [Tenderness: New Poems]. Moscow, Sovietsky Pisatel', 1962.
Posle Stalina [After Stalin]. Chicago, Russian Language Specialties, 1962.
Nasledniki Stalina [Stalin's Heirs]. London, Flegon Press, 1963.
Selected Poetry. Oxford, Pergamon Press, 1963.
Winter Station, translated by Oliver J. Frederiksen. Munich, Gerber, 1964.
Poetry, edited by George Reavey. New York, October House, 1964; London, Calder and Boyars, 1969.

Bratskaya GES. Chicago, Russian Language Specialties, 1965; as *Bratsk Station*, New York, Praeger, 1966.
Kater svyazi [Torpedo Boat Signalling]. Moscow, Molodaya Gvardia, 1966.
New Works: The Bratsk Station, translated by Tina Tupikina-Glaessner and Geoffrey Dutton. Melbourne, Sun, 1966; as *Bratsk Station and Other New Poems*, New York, Praeger, and London, Hart Davis, 1967.
Poems, translated by Herbert Marshall. New York, Dutton, 1966; Oxford, Pergamon Press, 1967.
Poems Chosen by the Author, translated by Peter Levi and Robin Milner-Gulland. London, Collins, 1966; New York, Hill and Wang, 1967.
The City of Yes and the City of No and Other Poems. Melbourne, Sun, 1966.
New Poems. Melbourne, Sun, 1968.
Idut belye snegi [The White Snows Are Falling]. Moscow, Khudozhestvennaya Literatura, 1969.
Flowers and Bullets, and Freedom to Kill. San Francisco, City Lights, 1970.
Stolen Apples. New York, Doubleday, 1971.
Kazansky universitet [Kazan University]. Tatar, Tatarsk Knizhnoye, 1971; as *Kazan University and Other New Poems*, Melbourne, Sun, 1973.
Doroga nomerodin [Highway Number One]. Moscow, Sovremennik, 1972.
Poyushchaya damba [The Singing Dam]. Moscow, Sovietsky Pisatel', 1972.
Ottsovsky slukh [Father's Hearing]. Moscow, Sovietsky Pisatel', 1975.
Izbrannye proizvedeniya [Selected Works]. Moscow, Khudozhestvennaya Literatura, 2 vols., 1975.
From Desire to Desire. New York, Doubleday, 1976; as *Love Poems*, London, Gollancz, 1977.
V polny rost: Novaya kniga stikhov i poem [At Full Growth: New Book of Verse and Poetry]. Moscow, Sovremennik, 1977.
Utrenny narod: Novaya kniga stikhov. Moscow, Molodaya Gvardia, 1978.
The Face Behind the Face, translated by Arthur Boyars and Simon Franklin. London, Boyars, and New York, Marek, 1979.
Ivan the Terrible and Ivan the Fool, translated by Daniel Weissbort. London, Gollancz, 1979.
Starka vzryvom: Stikhotvoreniya i poemy. Moscow, Moskovsky Rabochy, 1980.
Invisible Threads. London, Secker and Warburg, and New York, Macmillan, 1981.
Dve pary lyzh. Moscow, Sovremennik, 1982.
A Dove in Santiago, translated by D.M. Thomas. London, Secker and Warburg, 1982; New York, Viking Press, 1983.

Plays

Bratskaya GES (produced Moscow, 1968).
Under the Skin of the Statue of Liberty (produced Moscow, 1972).

Screenplay: *Kindergarten*, 1983 (?).

Fiction

Yagodnye mesta [The Berry Places]. Moscow, Sovietsky Pisatel', 1982.

Other

Avtobiografiya. London, Flegon Press, 1963; as *A Precocious Autobiography*, New

117

York, Dutton, 1963.

Yevtushenko's Reader: The Spirit of Elbe, A Precocious Autobiography, Poems. New York, Dutton, 1966.

Talent es't chudo ne sluchainoe [Talent Is a Miracle Coming Not by Chance]. Moscow, Sovietsky Pisatel', 1980.

Tochka opory [Fulcrum]. Moscow, Molodaya Gvardia, 1981.

*   *   *

Evgeny Evtushenko is Russia's most celebrated living poet. He became famous after the publication of his autobiographical long poem "Zima Junction" (1956). This "noisy Siberian François Villon," as he describes himself, was at the centre of the polemics about truth, ethics, and the duty of a poet during Khrushchev's "thaw." Like Mayakovsky, he belongs to the tradition of "civic" poetry. For him "poetry is not a tranquil chapel, poetry is civil war. The poet is a warrior." He writes with a strong rhetorical note about the burning topics of the day. In "Babi Yar" (1961) he evoked the horrors of the massacre in Kiev. The poem lent itself to interpretation as an attack on antisemitism in the Soviet Union. In his *Nasledniki Stalina* (Stalin's Heirs) he demanded that the guards around Stalin's grave be doubled and tripled lest the dictator rise from the dead and bring back the past with him. More recently, however, Evtushenko has tended to criticise his country only indirectly, often by means of historical parallel, as in the poem "The Calicos from Ivanovo" (1976). He peers into the heart of Russia's tumultuous history with clear political resonances: "For Russians to live in Russia is past bearing, but it is more so to live without her." Whether in or out of official favour, he maintains, as he has put it, "a proud and difficult faith in the revolution." His lyrical hero is a committed participant in all that happens both in his own country and in the world at large.

But, as A. Sinyavsky said, "...we are often astonished at his skill in touching the acute and painful questions of our time without stating them profoundly, we are also astonished by his ability to meditate on everything in the world but not to speak to the essence of anything." His greed for new experience often leads to superficiality. He is well aware of this. "We are all suffering from the same disease of soul: superficiality which is worse than dumbness." Having admitted this however he goes on producing superficial work. "Seventy per cent of what I wrote I don't like," he says. His publicly oriented poems often lapse into the commonplace and sentimental: "O my Russian people! You are really international in heart! But the unclean have often loudly taken in vain your most pure name." His lyrical poems are more emotionally credible. He has fully realized what Pasternak called "the idea of a poet's biography as spectacle." With stunning frankness and directness he has introduced into his poetry the details of his private life. His poetics seem to waver between the folk style of Esenin and rather unsuccessful attempts to utilize that of Mayakovsky. There is no lack of vigour and skill in his verse but there is almost an excess of clarity. He repeatedly declares that his essential aim is to communicate with his fellow men, and he tends to simplify his language and imagery. As a result, there is nothing hidden or enigmatic about his poetry. He is still amazingly productive: he writes critical prose for the *Literary Gazette*; satirical verse for *Krokodil*; he has taken part in dramatisations of his verse in the Taganka Theatre; played the leading role in the film *Tsiolkovsky* (1978). In his book *Invisible Threads* he attempts to combine poetry and photography. And he has published a novel *Yagodnye mesta* (Berry Places).

Evtushenko continues to elicit a wide range of value judgments, some of which are too severe—"cynical opportunist," "an ambassador for the Kremlin." A more serious criticism is that in every aspect of his writing—his technique, his cultural accoutrements, and aesthetic outlook—there are the signs of a manifest regression.

—Valentina Polukhina

FILIPPO, Eduardo de. *See* **DE FILIPPO, Eduardo.**

FO, Dario. Italian. Born in San Giano, Lombardy, in 1926. Married the writer Franca Rame in 1957. Wrote for caberets and theatres, including Piccolo Teatro, Milan, and worked for Italian radio and television networks; Founder, with Rame, Compagnia Dario Fo-Franca Rame, 1959; performed comic sketches with Rame on *Canzonissima* television program; founded Nuova Scena, which had connection with Italian communist party; broke with the communist party and founded Il Collettivo Teatrale La Comune, 1970-73. Address: c/o Einaudi, Via Umberto Biancamano, CP 245, 10121 Turin, Italy.

PUBLICATIONS

Plays

Teatro comico (includes *La marcolfa*; *Gli imbianchini non hanno ricordi*; *I tre bravi*; *Non tutti i ladri vengono per nuocere*; *Un morto da vendere*; *I cadaveri si spediscono e le donne si spogliano*; *L'uomo nudo e l'uomo in frak*).   Milan, Garzanti, 1962.
Le commedie:
  1. Struzzi series 54 and 55: *Gli arcangeli non giocano a flipper*; *Aveva due pistole con gli occhi bianchi e neri*; *Chi ruba un piede è fortunato in amore*; *Isabella, tre caravelle, e un cacciaballe*; *Settimo, ruba un po' meno*; *La colpa è sempre del diavolo*.   Turin, Einaudi, 1966.
  2. Struzzi series 78: *Grande pantomima con bandiere e papuzzi piccoli e medi*; *L'operaio conosce 300 parole il padrone 1000 per questo lui è il padrone*; *Legami pure che tanto io spacco tutto lo stesso*.   Turin, Einaudi, 1975.
Morte accidentale di un anarchico.   Verona, Bertani, 1970; as *Accidental Death of an Anarchist* (produced London, 1979), London, Pluto Press, 1980.
Vorrei morire anche stasera se dovesi pensare che non è servito a niente.   Verona, Bertani, 1970.
Compagni senza censura:
  1. *Mistero Buffo*; *L'operaio conosce 300 parole il padrone 1000 per questo lui è il padrone*; *Il Telaio*; *Il funerale del padrone*.   Milan, Marzotta, 1970.
  2. *Morte accidentale di un anarchico*; *Vorrei morire anche stasera se dovesi pensare che non è servito a niente*; *Morte e resurrezione di un pupazzo*; *Tutti uniti! Tutti insieme!*; *Me scusa, quello non è il padrone?*; *Fedayn*.   Milan, Marzotta, 1972.
L'operaio conosce 300 parole il padrone 1000 per questo lui è il padrone, in *Campagni senza censura 1*.   1970; as *The Worker Knows 300 Words, The Boss 1000* (produced Coventry, 1983).
Mistero Buffo, in *Campagni senza censura 1*.   1970; published with *Testi della passione*, Verona, Bertani, 1973; translated as *Mistero Buffo* (produced London, 1983).
Tutti uniti! Tutti insieme!   Verona, Bertani, 1971.
Morte e resurrezione di un pupazzo.   Milan, Sapere, 1971.
Fedayn.   Milan, Sapere, 1972.

119

Pum pum! Chi e? La polizia!   Verona, Bertani, 1972; revised edition, 1974.
Ordine! Per Dio.000.000.000.   Verona, Bertani, 1972.
Ci ragione e canto.   Verona, Bertani, 1972.
Guerra di popolo in Cile.   Verona, Bertani, 1973.
Non si paga, non si paga.   Verona, Bertani, 1974; as *We Can't Pay? We Won't Pay!*
   (produced Los Angeles, 1981; as *Can't Pay, Won't Pay*, produced London, 1981),
   London, Pluto Press, 1978.
Il caso Marini.   Verona, Bertani, 1974.
La Fanfani rapito.   Verona, Bertani, 1975.
La giullarata.   Verona, Bertani, 1975.
La marjuana della mamma è la più bella.   Verona, Bertani, 1976.
La Signora è da buttare.   Turin, Einaudi, 1976.
Tutta casa, letto, e chiesa, with Franca Rame.   Verona, Bertani, 1978.
Storia delle tigre et altre storie.   Milan, La Comune, 1980.
Betty (produced Edinburgh, 1980).
Female Parts: One Woman Plays, with Franca Rame (produced London, 1981).   London, Pluto Press, 1981.
The Fourth Wall (produced London, 1983).
Orgasmo Adulto (8 short plays; produced New York, 1983).
Clacson, trombette e pernacchi, as *About Face*, in *Theater*, Winter 1983.
A Woman Alone, with Franca Rame (produced London, 1984).

Verse

Ballate e canzoni.   Verona, Bertani, 1974; revised edition, Rome, Newton Compton, 1976.

Other

Fo parla di Fo: Intervista e saggio.   Cosenza, Lerici, 1977.

*

Critical Studies: "The Throw-Away Theatre of Fo" by Suzanne Cowan, in *Drama Review*, 1975; *Fo* (in Italian) by Lanfranco Binni, Florence, La Nuova Italia, 1977; *La Storia di Fo* by Chiara Valentini, Milan, Feltrinelli, 1977; *Das politische Theater Fos* by Helga Jungblut, Frankfurt, Lang, 1978; *Il teatro di Fo* by Paolo Puppa, Venice, Marsilio, 1978.

*   *   *

Dario Fo is undoubtedly the most original, prolific, and versatile comic playwright modern Italy has produced. Since World War II he has acquired the status of something like a living cultural monument, although certainly not of the classical style—an artist who has borrowed liberally from the myriad sources of traditional popular comedy, forging them into a unique language and expression which, while absolutely personal, remains at the same time profoundly collective and public in spirit.

Fo's uniqueness lies, first of all, in his artistic eclecticism. Not only does he write his own scripts, but researches and annotates documents from early theater history, designs stage-sets, costumes, posters and handbills, composes incidental music, directs his own and others' works, and—as chief performer in his own plays—dominates the stage with a gigantic, irrepressible comic presence. At the same time, intimately connected with his theatrical work has been his activity as a political-cultural organizer, the driving force behind a nationwide network of grassroots organizations allied to the radical movement for social and political change during the most convulsive period of recent Italian history.

Fo's theater, from his earliest experiences with vaudeville-style variety shows shortly after the Second World War through his latest political farces, has drawn from the rich vein of popular comic sources: medieval jester performances, *commedia dell'arte*, slapstick, French farce, circus, vaudeville, puppet and magic shows, Laurel and Hardy. His first commercial successes were a series of ambitiously staged "social" comedies, all sharing a common theme: ridicule of the dominant classes. The language and subject matter of these comedies grew increasingly explicit and radical; in the late 1960's, along with his wife, the actress Franca Rame, he broke with the commercial stage and formed a theater company affiliated with the Italian Communist Party.

The plays he wrote and directed during the two years of this association, specific in their critical message, were intended as instruments of militant organizing and political debate. While effective, the shows came under criticism from the Party hierarchy for their outspoken indictments of political elitism and compromise—certain aspects of which touched on the Party's legalistic, moderate strategy—and particularly for their bitter satire of Soviet-style bureaucracy. In 1970, Fo dissolved the theater company, broke with the Communist Party cultural association, and established an independent collective allied with the "extra-parliamentary" elements of the Italian revolutionary movement. From that point on his comedies, while scenically simple and limited to the most rudimentary of costumes, props, and technical accessories, have grown increasingly flamboyant in their use of farcical techniques, touching on the grotesque and even surreal.

Although some of Fo's comedies have been performed abroad, and in recent years his work has gained wide popularity outside Italy, it is significant that in his own country it is nearly impossible to imagine "*il teatro di Fo*" without the pervasive physical presence of Fo himself. His comic style, while a catch-all of other approaches and modes, is itself singular; openly imitative, it cannot be imitated. Fo has established no trend, generated no "school." In fact, because of his total dominance of his own dramatic enterprise both as creator and performer, many have objected that Fo's theater contradicts the very social and collective purpose it purports to serve. No doubt there is some truth to this. Nevertheless, his work continues to draw a huge following from all levels and classes of Italian society. It remains a rallying point for the left, and plays an important role "on the cultural front" in the movement for social change in his country. Italy is, after all, a nation imbued with social, economic, political, and historical paradox. In this respect, Fo's work—paradoxically!— may be seen as a thorough embodiment of his national culture.

—Suzanne Cowan

FREYRE, Gilberto (de Mello). Brazilian. Born in Recife, 15 March 1900. Educated at American Colégio Gilreath, Recife, graduated 1917; Baylor University, Waco, Texas, 1918-21, B.A. 1921; Columbia University, New York, 1921-22, M.A. in anthropology. Married Maria Magdalena Guedes Pereira in 1941; one daughter and one son. Private Secretary to Governor of Pernambuco, Recife, 1927-30; Director, *A Província* newspaper, Recife, 1928-30; Professor of Sociology, State School of Recife, 1928, and Faculty of Law, Recife, 1935; Professor of Social Anthropology, University of Rio de Janeiro, 1935-38. Representative to National Assembly, 1946, and to House of Deputies, 1947-50; Brazilian Ambassador to United Nations

General Assembly, 1949. Founder, Joaquim Nabuco Institute, Recife, 1949. Visiting Professor, Stanford University, California, 1931, and Indiana University, Bloomington, 1966. Recipient: Felippe d'Oliveira Award, 1934; Anisfield-Wolf Award, 1957; Machado de Assis Prize, 1963; Aspen Award, 1967; La Madonnina International Literary Prize (Italy), 1969; Jose Vasconcelos Gold Medal (Mexico), 1974. Honorary doctorate: Columbia University, 1954; University of Coimbra, 1962; University of Paris, 1965; University of Sussex, Falmer, 1965; University of Münster, 1965. Member, Academy of Letters of São Paulo, 1961, and Brazilian Academy of Letters, 1962; Royal Anthropological Institute; American Academy of Arts and Sciences. K.B.E. (Knight Commander, Order of the British Empire), 1971. Address: Rua Dois Irmãos 320, Apipucos, 50000 Recife, PE, Brazil.

PUBLICATIONS

Fiction

Dona Sinhá e o Filho Padre. Rio de Janeiro, Olympio, 1964; as *Mother and Son*, New York, Knopf, 1967.
O outro amor do Dr. Paulo. Rio de Janeiro, Olympio, 1977.

Verse

Talvez poesia. Rio de Janeiro, Olympio, 1962.
Gilberto poeta: Algumas confissões. Recife, Ranulpho, 1980.
Poesia reunida. Recife, Pirata, 1980.

Other

Casa-grande & Senzala. Rio de Janeiro, Maia & Schmidt, 1933; revised edition, Rio de Janeiro, Olympio, 2 vols.,1943; as *The Masters and the Slaves: A Study in the Development of Brazilian Civilization*, New York, Knopf, 1946; London, Secker and Warburg, 1947; revised edition, Knopf, 1956, 1964.
Guia Prático, Histórico, e Sentimental de Cidade do Recife. Recife, 1934; revised edition, Rio de Janeiro, Olympio, 1942, 1961, 1968.
Artigos de jornal. Recife, Casa Mozart, 1935.
Sobrados e mucambos. São Paulo, Nacional, 1936; revised edition, Rio de Janeiro, Olympio, 1951, 1961; as *The Mansions and the Shanties: The Making of Modern Brazil*, New York, Knopf, 1963.
Mucambos do Nordeste. Rio de Janeiro, Servico do Patrimônio Histórico e Artístico Nacional, 1937; revised edition, Recife, Instituto Joaquim Nabuco de Pesquisas Sociais.
Nordeste. Rio de Janeiro, Olympio, 1937; revised edition, 1951, 1961.
Olinda: 2° Guia Prático, Histórico, e Sentimental de Cidade Brasileira. Rio de Janeiro, Olympio, 1939; revised edition, 1944, 1960, 1968.
Açúcar. Rio de Janeiro, Olympio, 1939.
Um Engenheiro francês no Brasil. Rio de Janeiro, Olympio, 1940; revised edition, 2 vols., 1960.
O Mundo que o Português criou. Rio de Janeiro, Olympio, 1940.
Região e tradição. Rio de Janeiro, Olympio, 1941.
Uma cultura ameaçada. Rio de Janeiro, Casa do Estudante do Brasil, 1942.
Ingleses. Rio de Janeiro, Olympio, 1942.
Problemas brasileiros de antropologia. Rio de Janeiro, Casa do Estudante do Brasil,

1943; revised edition, Rio de Janeiro, Olympio, 1954.

Na Bahia em 1943. Rio de Janeiro, Artes Gráficas, 1944.

Perfil de Euclydes e outros perfis. Rio de Janeiro, Olympio, 1944.

Sociologia. Rio de Janeiro, Olympio, 2 vols., 1945; revised edition, 1957, 1962.

Brazil: An Introduction (written in English). New York, Knopf, 1945; revised edition, as *New World in the Tropics: The Culture of Modern Brazil,* 1959.

Ingleses no Brasil. Rio de Janeiro, Olympio, 1948.

Quase política. Rio de Janeiro, Olympio, 1950; revised edition, 1966.

Aventura e rotina. Rio de Janeiro, Olympio, 1953.

Um Brasileiro em terras portuguêsas. Rio de Janeiro, Olympio, 1953.

Assombrações do Recife velho. Rio de Janeiro, Condé, 1955; revised edition, Rio de Janeiro, Olympio, 1970.

Integração portuguesa nos trópicos. Lisbon, Ministério do Ultramar, 1958; as *Portuguese Integration in the Tropics,* Lisbon, Silvas, 1961.

A propósito de frades. Salvador, 1959.

A propósito de Morão, Rosa, e Pimenta. Recife, Estadual, 1959.

Ordem e progresso. Rio de Janeiro, Olympio, 2 vols., 1959; as *Order and Progress: Brazil from Monarchy to Republic,* edited and translated by Rod W. Horton, New York, Knopf, 1970.

Brasis, Brasil, e Brasília. Lisbon, 1960; revised edition, Rio de Janeiro, Record, 1968.

O Luso e o trópico. Lisbon, 1961; as *The Portuguese and the Tropics,* Lisbon, Committee for the Commemoration of the Vth Centenary of the Death of Prince Henry the Navigator, 1961.

Vida, forma, e côr. Rio de Janeiro, Olympio, 1962.

Homen, cultura, e trópico. Recife, Imprensa Universitária, 1962.

O escravo nos anúncios de jornais brasileiros do século XIX. Recife, Universidade Federal de Pernambuco, 1963; revised edition, São Paulo, Nacional, 1979.

Retalhos de jornais velhos. Rio de Janeiro, Olympio, 1964.

O Recife, sim! Recife, não! Sao Paulo, Arquimedes, 1967.

Sociologia da medicina. Lisbon, Fundação Gulbenkian, 1967.

Como e porque sou e não sou sociólogo. Brasília, Editôra Universidade de Brasília, 1968.

Contribução para uma sociologia da biografia. Lisbon, Academia Internacional da Cultura Portuguesa, 2 vols., 1968.

Oliveira Lima, Don Quixote gordo. Recife, Universidade Federal de Pernambuco, 1968.

A casa brasileira. Rio de Janeiro, Grifo, 1971.

Nós e a Europa germânica. Rio de Janeiro, Grifo, 1971.

A condição humana e outros temas, edited by Maria Elisa Dias Collier. Rio de Janeiro, Grifo, 1972.

Além do apenas moderno Rio de Janeiro, Olympio, 1973.

The Gilberto Freyre Reader. New York, Knopf, 1974.

A presença do açúcar na formação brasileira. Rio de Janeiro, M.I.C., 1975.

Tempo morto e outros tempos: Trechos de um diário de adolescência e primeira mocidade 1915-1930. Rio de Janeiro, Olympio, 1975.

O brasileiro entre os outros hispanos. Rio de Janeiro, Olympio, 1975.

Alhos & bugalhos. Rio de Janeiro, Nova Fronteira, 1978.

Cartas do próprio punho sobre pessoas e coisas do Brasil e do estrangeiro, edited by Sylvio Rabello. Rio de Janeiro, Conselho Federal de Cultura, 1978.

Prefácios desgarrados, edited by Edson Nery da Fonseca. Rio de Janeiro, Cátedra, 2 vols., 1978.

Heróis e vilões no romance brasileiro. São Paulo, Cultrix, 1979.

Oh de casa! Recife, Instituto Joaquim Nabuco de Pesquisas Sociais, 1979.

Tempo de aprendiz, edited by José Antônio Gonsalves de Mello. São Paulo, Ibrasa,

1979.
Arte, ciencia, e trópico. São Paulo, Martins, 1980.
Pessoas, coisas e animais Rio de Janeiro, Globo, 1981.
Insurgências e ressurgências atuais: Cruzamentos de sins e naos num mundo em transicao.
Rio de Janeiro, Globo, 1983.
Médicos, doentes e contextos sociais. Rio de Janeiro, Globo, 1983.

*

Critical Studies: *Freyre* by Diogo de Melo Menezes, Rio de Janeiro, C.E.B., 1944; *Freyre: Sua ciencia, sua filosofia, sua arte,* Rio de Janeiro, Olympio, 1962.

*   *   *

Gilberto Freyre is the single most influential Brazilian intellectual of this century. His extraordinary reputation is largely based upon his social history of colonial Brazil, *The Masters and the Slaves*, first published in 1933, which Freyre wrote to accomplish three separate and sometimes contradictory goals: to deny the validity of 19th-century "scientific" racism, still almost universally accepted among the Brazilian elite, by endeavoring "to discriminate between the effects of purely genetic relationships and those resulting from social influences, the cultural heritage and the milieu"; to insist that Brazil was a multi-racial nation, and that no Brazilian could claim to have escaped the genetic and cultural influence of the nation's Amerindian and African populations; and to assert that his own ancestors, the plantation aristocrats and slave-owners of the Northeast, had created a remarkably humane social system which encouraged both cultural fusion and sexual miscegenation between blacks and whites.

A few Brazilian intellectuals had presented some of the same ideas earlier, but their works had been ignored. Gilberto Freyre succeeded because his education abroad enabled him to buttress his claims with dozens of references to North American and European theorists almost unknown in Brazil; their prestige, as foreigners, finally put to rest the ghosts of Gobineau, Haeckel, and Le Bon. Secondly, Freyre exemplified his theories with masses of detailed information about every aspect of plantation life. Because he was convinced that sex was the primary vehicle of both physical and cultural change in Brazilian society, moreover, Freyre included a great deal of very racy anecdotal material which helped to popularize his works and his ideas. And all of these theories and details, finally, were superbly presented in complex and powerful prose.

The Masters and the Slaves and Freyre's many subsequent works—including some rather mediocre verse and two semi-autobiographical novels—have sometimes been utilized in ways he did not envision: to defend the continued existence of Portuguese colonialism in Africa, for example, or to insist that contemporary Brazil is a harmonious racial paradise entirely free of any sort of prejudice. It is also clear that Freyre sometimes contradicted himself, and that some of his judgements are the products of privilege and naivety—as in his belief that Africans were perfectly adapted for hard labor in the tropics because they, unlike Europeans, were able to sweat over all their bodies. And one of Freyre's most fundamental ideas, that slavery was generally far more humane in Brazil than elsewhere in the Americas, has been vigorously attacked by a number of Brazilian and foreign scholars.

Nonetheless, there is no doubt that the popularization of Freyre's works has transformed the ways in which educated Brazilians think about their nation and about themselves—freeing them from a self-destructive conviction of racial and cultural inferiority and bringing about a psychological and intellectual liberation which has profoundly influenced contemporary Brazil.

—David T. Haberly

FRISCH, Max (Rudolf). Swiss. Born in Zurich, 15 May 1911. Educated at the University of Zurich, 1931-33; Zurich Institute of Technology, diploma in architecture 1940. Served in the Swiss Army, 1939-45. Married Gertrud Anna Constance von Meyenburg in 1942 (divorced, 1959); two daughters and one son. Free-lance journalist after 1933; architect in Zurich, 1945-54; then full-time writer. Recipient: C.F. Meyer Prize, 1938; Rockefeller grant, 1951; Raabe Prize, 1954; Schleussner Schüller Prize, for radio play, 1955; Büchner Prize, 1958; Zurich Prize, 1958; Veillon Prize, 1958; Nordrhein-Westfalen Prize, 1962; Schiller Prize (Baden-Württemberg), 1965; Jerusalem Prize, 1965; Schiller Prize (Switzerland), 1974; German Book Trade Freedom Prize, 1976. Honorary doctorate: University of Marburg, 1962, Bard College, Annandale-on-Hudson, 1980; City University of New York, 1982. Honorary Member, American Academy, 1974. Address: 6611 Berzona, Switzerland; or c/o Suhrkamp, Lindenstrasse 29-35, Postfach 4229, 6000 Frankfurt am Main, Germany.

PUBLICATIONS

Plays

Nun singen sie wieder: Versuch eines Requiems (produced Zurich, 1945). Basel, Schwabe, 1946.

Santa Cruz (produced Zurich, 1946). Basel, Schwabe, 1947.

Die chinesische Mauer (produced Zurich, 1946). Basel, Schwabe, 1947; revised edition, Frankfurt, Suhrkamp, 1955; as *The Chinese Wall*, New York, Hill and Wang, 1961; in *Four Plays*, London, Methuen, 1969.

Als der Krieg zu Ende war (produced Zurich, 1948). Basel, Schwabe, 1949; as *When the War Was Over* (produced New York, 1980), in *Three Plays*, New York, Hill and Wang, 1967.

Graf Öderland (produced Zurich, 1951). Frankfurt, Suhrkamp, 1951; as *Count Oderland* (produced Edinburgh, 1968; as *A Public Prosecutor Is Sick of It All*, produced Washington, D.C., 1973), in *Three Plays*, London, Methuen, 1962; published separately, New York, Harcourt Brace, 1966.

Don Juan; oder, Die Liebe zur Geometrie (produced Zurich, 1953). Frankfurt, Suhrkamp, 1953; translated as *Don Juan*, in *Three Plays*, New York, Hill and Wang, 1967; in *Four Plays*, London, Methuen, 1969.

Rip van Winkle, from the story by Washington Irving (broadcast, 1953). Frankfurt, Suhrkamp, 1969.

Biedermann und die Brandstifter (broadcast, 1953; produced Zurich, 1958). Frankfurt, Suhrkamp, 1958; as *The Fire Raisers* (produced London, 1961), London, Methuen, 1962; as *The Firebugs* (produced New York, 1963), New York, Hill and Wang, 1963.

Die grosse Wut des Philipp Hotz (produced Zurich, 1958). Frankfurt, Suhrkamp, 1958; as *The Great Fury of Philipp Hotz* (produced London, 1963; produced New York, 1969), in *Three Plays*, New York, Hill and Wang, 1967; in *Four Plays*, London, Methuen, 1969.

Andorra (produced Zurich, 1961). Frankfurt, Suhrkamp, 1962; translated as *Andorra* (produced New York, 1963; London, 1964), in *Three Plays*, London, Methuen, 1962; published separately, New York, Hill and Wang, 1964.

Stücke. Frankfurt, Suhrkamp, 2 vols., 1962.

Zurich Transit (televised, 1966). Frankfurt, Suhrkamp, 1966.

Biografie (produced Zurich, 1968). Frankfurt, Suhrkamp, 1967; as *Biography*, New York, Hill and Wang, 1969; in *Four Plays*, London, Methuen, 1969.

Triptychon. Frankfurt, Suhrkamp, 1978; as *Triptych*, London, Eyre Methuen, and New York, Harcourt Brace, 1981.

Radio Plays: *Rip van Winkle*, 1953; *Biedermann und die Brandstifter*, 1953.

Television Plays: *Zurich Transit*, 1966; *Bluebeard*, 1984.

Fiction

Jürg Reinhart: Eine sommerliche Schicksalsfahrt. Stuttgart, Deutsche Verlagsanstalt, 1934.
Antwort aus der Stille: Eine Erzählung aus den Bergen. Stuttgart, Deutsche Verlagsanstalt, 1937.
J'adore ce qui me brûle; oder, Die Schwierigen. Zurich, Atlantis, 1943.
Bin; oder, Die Reise nach Peking. Zurich, Atlantis, 1945.
Marion und die Marionotten: Ein Fragment. Basel, Gryff-Presse, 1946.
Stiller. Frankfurt, Suhrkamp, 1954; as *I'm Not Stiller*, New York and London, Abelard Schuman, 1958.
Homo Faber. Frankfurt, Suhrkamp, 1957; translated as *Homo Faber*, New York, Abelard Schuman, 1959; London, Eyre and Spottiswoode, 1974.
Mein Name sei Gantenbein. Frankfurt, Suhrkamp, 1964; as *A Wilderness of Mirrors*, London, Methuen, 1965; New York, Random House, 1966; as *Gantenbein*, New York, Harcourt Brace, 1982; London, Methuen, 1983.
Wilhelm Tell für die Schule. Frankfurt, Suhrkamp, 1971.
Montauk. Frankfurt, Suhrkamp, 1975; translated as *Montauk*, New York, Harcourt Brace, 1976.
Der Mensch erscheint im Holozän. Frankfurt, Suhrkamp, 1979; as *Man in the Holocene*, London, Eyre Methuen, and New York, Harcourt Brace, 1980.
Blaubart. Frankfurt, Suhrkamp, 1982; as *Bluebeard*, London, Methuen, and New York, Harcourt Brace, 1983.

Other

Blätter aus dem Brotsack. Frankfurt, Atlantis, 1940.
Tagebuch mit Marion. Frankfurt, Atlantis, 1947; revised edition, as *Tagebuch 1946-1949*, Frankfurt, Suhrkamp, 1950; as *Sketchbook 1946-1949*, New York, Harcourt Brace, 1977.
Achtung: Die Schweiz. Basel, Handschin, 1955.
Ausgewählte Prosa. Frankfurt, Suhrkamp, 1961.
Öffentlichkeit als Partner. Frankfurt, Suhrkamp, 1967.
Tagebuch 1966-1971. Frankfurt, Suhrkamp, 1972; as *Sketchbook 1966-1971*, New York, Harcourt Brace, and London, Eyre Methuen, 1974.
Dienstbüchlein. Frankfurt, Suhrkamp, 1974.
Stich-Worte (selection), edited by Uwe Johnson. Frankfurt, Suhrkamp, 1975.
Gesammelte Werke. Frankfurt, Suhrkamp, 12 vols., 1976.
Kritik, Thesen, Analysen. Bern, Francke, 1977.

*

Critical Studies: *Frisch* by Ulrich Weisstein, New York, Twayne, 1967; *The Novels of Frisch* by Michael Butler, London, Wolff, 1976; *The Dramatic Works of Frisch* by Gertrud Bauer Pickar, Bern, Lang, 1977; *Frisch: His Work and Its Swiss Background* by Malcolm Pender, Stuttgart, Heinz, 1979; *Gombrowicz and Frisch: Aspects of the Literary Diary* by Alex Kurczaba, Bonn, Bouvier, 1980.

*   *   *

Max Frisch has reached a wide public through both narrative and dramatic works. Though many touch upon issues of particular relevance to Swiss society, his central concerns have always been broadly humanitarian. His earliest works already show a preoccupation with the individual's need to discover and realize his own personality, with all the attendant problems of relating to others and their social or emotional claims upon one. This has indeed become the central focus of his work, encompassing a rich variety of emphases, moods, and stylistic approaches. Frisch's earliest works stand in the tradition of the German *Bildungsroman* (novel of development), but in the immediate post-war years he began to experiment much more with genre and form, from *Bin; oder, Die Reise nach Peking*—a whimsical, fairy-tale-like reflection on the unfulfilled longing to escape self—to a drama like *Nun singen sie wieder*, an episodic, almost surrealist portrayal of how crude egotism and humanitarian feeling conflict amid the horrors of war. Other early dramas such as *Santa Cruz* or *Count Oderland* are quasi-mythical presentations of the problem of marrying personal dream to social reality. Frisch's concern to reflect the simultaneous and conflicting levels upon which individuals lead their lives makes these dramas overweighted with incident and symbol; though clearly owing a debt to Brecht's epic theatre, they lack its imaginative coherence. Yet Frisch's later themes have their roots here, and the better controlled *When the War Was Over*, for example, is a striking presentation of "image-making," one of the major leitmotifs of Frisch's later work: the arbitrariness in pure human terms of the labels which society, class, race attach to us, here reflected in a love affair between German and Russian.

It was in the late 1950's and 1960's that Frisch began to produce the works upon which his international reputation is really founded. *The Fire Raisers* and *Andorra* have become modern stage classics: both still rely upon a stylised, episodic structure, but with greater simplicity and power. *The Fire Raisers* is a satirical attack upon complacent middle-class attitudes; behind a mask of kindness towards others lie cowardly conformism and an opportunistic egotistical concern for the "right" image, which produce a situation of grotesque comedy as the attempt to preserve respectability leads straight to destruction. The combination of farce and deeply serious social comment is irresistible.

Much more emotive in its critique of social attitudes is *Andorra*, a play which concerns the destructive nature of "images" created by ignorance, fear, self-interest, or convenience. In the story of Andri, wrongly assumed to be a Jew and treated accordingly, Frisch has given us not just a powerful comment on contemporary history but also a lasting picture of the mental mechanisms by which we refuse others any reality which does not conform to our own needs. The play is an interesting mixture of highly emotive visual symbolism and distancing effects: individual characters periodically reflect on their involvement in Andri's destruction, thus both extracting the main issues and showing most disturbingly how the "images" continue.

It is this ability to encapsulate complex themes in formal structure which makes the novel *I'm Not Stiller* probably Frisch's finest work to date. Sheer entertainment, in the form of playfully maintained doubt over the legal identity of the main character, combines with a probing investigation into the possibility of realizing a "true" self. Taking the problem of "image-making" to its logical conclusion, Frisch abandons the stance of the omniscient narrator and presents the main figure through his own first-person jottings. The result is a fascinating picture of marital, family, and social relationships which are at the same time a subtle reflection of the problematic search for identity: Stiller's self-portrayal is the shifting meeting-ground of the resistant images imposed by others in their need, of the deeply feared and ambiguous images offered by language itself as the necessary medium of self-projection, and—most problematic of all—of those questionable because exclusive images which the self creates even in moments of apparently existential clarity. The complexity of this study is more than a compositional tour de force; it dares the reader, while engaging him, to impose his own easy images.

In subsequent works Frisch presents further inventive variations on the theme of identity. *Homo Faber* concerns the hubris of man in the technological age. Walter Faber has a neat image of existence as calculable, as a series of separate units and moments as manageable as technical data; but it is challenged by the encroachment of time and responsibility, which combine in a tragic encounter with his own unadmitted, guilt-laden past in the guise of his unknown daughter. The language of the novel perfectly reflects Faber's inflexibility, and the complex time-scale of his writings—again in the first person—captures the intricate texture of human experience which he is at pains to deny. Again Frisch refuses to do the reader's thinking for him. *Gantenbein* progresses even further along this path. An unnamed character seeks by endlessly "trying on" different shapes and types of possible identity to encircle the elusive core of selfhood. Here Frisch's comic inventiveness comes again to the fore.

In his later works, both dramatic and narrative, Frisch has tended to use shorter forms, shedding glancing light on the same central themes. The style and structure are more varied than ever. In *Biography*, for example, there is sophisticated, bitter comedy; in *Montauk*, painful personal confession; in *Bluebeard*, scurrilous wit allied with a more profound scepticism on human relations than ever before.

One final aspect of Frisch's oeuvre: his various essays and diaries, which present a rich compilation of reflections on his central themes, of aesthetic considerations, and of cultural and political comment. While without the overt artifice of some literary diaries, these are no simple chronicles: they are one more—and not the least fascinating—venture into the uncharted and turbulent sea of self.

—Mary E. Stewart

FUENTES, Carlos. Mexican. Born in Mexico City, 11 November 1928. Educated at Colegio Frances Morelos, LL.B. 1948; graduate work at National University of Mexico, Mexico City, and Institut des Hautes Études Internationales, Geneva. Married 1) Rita Macedo in 1959 (divorced, 1966), one daughter; 2) Sylvia Lemus in 1973, one son and one daughter. Member, then Secretary, Mexican delegation, International Labor Organization, Geneva, 1950-52; assistant chief of press section, Ministry of Foreign Affairs, Mexico City, 1954; Press Secretary, United Nations Information Center, Mexico City, 1954; Secretary, then Assistant Director of Cultural Department, National University of Mexico, 1955-56; Head of Department of Cultural Relations, Ministry of Foreign Affairs, 1957-59; Mexican Ambassador to France, 1974-77. Lecturer, Columbia University, New York, University of Pennsylvania, Philadelphia, Barnard College, New York, and Cambridge University. Editor, *Revista Mexicana de Literatura*, 1954-58, *El Espectador*, 1959-61, *Siempre*, 1960, and *Politica*, 1960. Recipient: Mexican Writers Center fellowship, 1956; Biblioteca Breve Prize, 1967; Villaurrutia Prize, 1975; Gallegos Prize (Venezuela), 1977. Agent: c/o Editorial Joaquin Mortiz, Tabasco 106, Mexico 7, D.F., Mexico. Address: 42 Cleveland Lane, Princeton, New Jersey 08540, U.S.A.

PUBLICATIONS

Fiction

Los días emmascarados. Mexico City, Los Presentes, 1954.
La región más transparente. Mexico City, Fondo de Cultura Económica, 1958; as *Where the Air Is Clear*, New York, Obolensky, 1960.
Las buenas conciencias. Mexico City, Fondo de Cultura Económica, 1959; as *Good Conscience*, New York, Obolensky, 1961.

La muerte de Artemio Cruz.   Mexico City, Fondo de Cultura Económica, 1962; as *The Death of Artemio Cruz*, New York, Farrar Straus, and London, Collins, 1964.
Aura.   Mexico City, Era, 1962; translated as *Aura*, New York, Farrar Straus, 1965.
Cantar de ciegos.   Mexico City, Mortiz, 1964.
Zona sagrada.   Mexico City, Siglo Veintiuno, 1967; as *Holy Places*, in *Triple Cross*, New York, Dutton, 1972.
Cambio de piel.   Mexico City, Mortiz, 1967; as *A Change of Skin*, New York, Farrar Straus, and London, Cape, 1968.
Cumpleaños.   Mexico City, Mortiz, 1969.
Chac Mool y otros cuentos.   Estella, Salvat, 1973.
Terra nostra.   Barcelona, Seix Barral, 1975; translated as *Terra Nostra*, New York, Farrar Straus, 1976; London, Secker and Warburg, 1977.
La cabeza de la hidra.   Mexico City, Mortiz, 1978; as *The Hydra Head*, New York, Farrar Straus, 1978; London, Secker and Warburg, 1979.
Una familia lejana.   Mexico City, Era, 1980; as *Distant Relations*, New York, Farrar Straus, and London, Secker and Warburg, 1982.
Agua quemada.   Mexico City, Fondo de Cultura Económica, 1981; as *Burnt Water*, New York, Farrar Straus, and London, Secker and Warburg, 1981.

Plays

Todos los gatos son pardos.   Mexico City, Siglo Veintiuno, 1970.
El tuerto es rey.   Mexico City, Mortiz, 1970.
Las reinos originarios (includes *Todos los gatos son pardos* and *El tuerto es rey*).   Barcelona, Seix Barral, 1971.

Screenplays: *Pedro Paramo*, 1966; *Tiempo de morir*, 1966; *Los caifanes*, 1967.

Verse

Poemas de amor: Cuentos del alma.   Madrid, Cruces, 1971.

Other

Paris: La revolución de Mayo.   Mexico City, Era, 1968.
La nueva novela hispanoamericana.   Mexico City, Mortiz, 1969.
El mundo de Jose Luis Cuevas.   Mexico City, Tudor, 1969.
Casa con dos puertas.   Mexico City, Mortiz, 1970.
Tiempo mexicano.   Mexico City, Mortiz, 1971.
Cervantes; o, La crítica de la lectura.   Mexico City, Mortiz, 1976; as *Don Quixote; or, The Critique of Reading*, Austin, University of Texas Institute of Latin American Studies, 1976.

Editor, *Los signos en rotación y otra ensayos*, by Octavio Paz.   Madrid, Alianza, 1971.

*

Critical Studies: *Fuentes* by Daniel de Guzman, New York, Twayne, 1972; *Fuentes: A Critical View* edited by Robert Brody and Charles Rossman, Austin, University of Texas Press, 1982; *Fuentes* by Wendy D. Faris, New York, Ungar, 1983.

*   *   *

Carlos Fuentes is a Mexican novelist in the same way that Tolstoy is Russian and Joyce is Irish: one cannot conceive of these writers' books growing out of any other soil. And it may well be that the thread that can help to lead the reader through the labyrinth of Fuentes's complex themes and experimental style is the manner in which he deals with the question of what it means to be Mexican and, ultimately, with the even more basic question of what it means to be human.

Although Fuentes has written in many genres—drama, film, the essay, and the short story among them—he is best known for his work in the novel, where he has developed an extraordinarily allusive and elusive expressive mode. He is an innovative writer who, like Joyce before him, has drastically expanded and altered the formal, thematic, and referential possibilities of the novel in his search for national and personal definition.

The problem of individual and societal demarcations is a pressing one in those areas of Latin America where Indian cultures were not completely annihilated by the European invasion and conquest. The *mestizo* (a term meaning a person of mixed Indian and European background) is the child of two races; a *mestizo* society like Mexico is the inheritor of two traditions. The overriding question is to whom the *mestizo* owes spiritual allegiance, the (historically speaking) Indian mother or the Hispanic father? Who are the forebears who give solidity and a sense of continuity to an individual life and to a society? How do contemporary Mexicans come to terms with the fact that their origins lie in the meeting of two oppressive barbarisms: the Aztec with its human sacrifices to bloodthirsty gods, and the Spanish with its Inquisition and burning of heretics? Is human society doomed to an eternal power struggle between victim and killer? Are we really and exclusively the creatures of our past? Clearly, the peculiarly Mexican problem is one of many larger questions concerning our relationship to the historical, social, and political forces that surround us, and our befuddled perception of ourselves as temporal beings.

Fuentes approaches the complexity of these issues from two different yet complementary directions, both of which infuse his writing with ambiguity and, often, obscurity. One approach has its origins in the work of Miguel de Cervantes, that imaginative catalyst for the modern novel and much of what we think of as the modern sensibility. Fuentes has formally acknowledged his debt to Cervantes in *Cervantes; o, La crítica de la lectura*, the study he published just prior to his controversial *Terra Nostra*, but he has discussed the importance of Cervantes to his own writing on other occasions as well, for example in an interview with MacAdam and Coleman published in *Book Forum* IV (1979), where Fuentes describes the theoretical significance of the Spanish master:

> *Don Quixote* is the first modern novel because it is the first novel in which there is no absolute truth. It is the anti-medieval novel, the novel where truth is everywhere and nowhere. The book can be read in a thousand ways, and, miracle of miracles and unorthodoxy of unorthodoxy, Don Quixote is a man who goes mad and his madness is then compounded because he then reads about himself. And this is the first hero in literature who ever opens up a book only to find that his adventures are written there.

As a legitimate heir and devoted practitioner of the ambivalence which Cervantes introduced into the writing of fiction, Fuentes consistently and purposefully blurs the distinction between history and fiction as he speculates on the nature of a reality composed of these two aspects of experience. He historicizes fiction, making full use of real persons, places, and events in his writing and, at the same time, documenting the fictional as if it were part of our historic past; he simultaneously fictionalizes history, destroying the already tenuous distinctions between past, present, and future and reordering their elements as if history were a work of art. A relevant example of Fuentes's game with time, history, and fiction is the fact that both Cervantes and Don Quixote are personages in the novel *Terra nostra*, and further, that their identities merge with those of other characters, both literary and historic, as if the differences between the two realms were purely arbitrary.

The confusion of history and fiction, fact and imagination, can play havoc with our perception of reality, our sense of permanence, our certainty of a place in an orderly sequence of events. It is an apparently schizophrenic response to the world. These confusions are compounded by a human past that is unbelievably—almost fictionally—full of atrocity and grotesquerie, foible and horror. Fuentes, in his second approach to his novels' themes, further confounds his readers by introducing the mythic sense into his historical and temporal concerns. Myth must be understood here not as a particular set of stories, legends, and beliefs (although these too play their part in Fuentes's novels) but rather as a kind of cosmic attitude that ritualizes human events, strips them of their historicity, and frees them of their dependence on time. Christ, for example, from the mythic point of view, is born and crucified only once in time.

Fuentes brings the mystery of two mythic traditions, the Indian and the European, to the problem of where one's place is in the stream of historical continuity when historicity itself is suspect. In much of his writing Fuentes suggests that history is an endlessly repeating mythic cycle of eternally present actions and actors. Past and future are thereby negated, and individual character is seen as a constantly changing and interchangeable series of masks or identities, destined—or doomed—to play a foreordained role in a predetermined rite. In other words, Fuentes's fictional characters may seem to live in a specific time and place, but they are also avatars and future creatures repeating endlessly the phantasmagoria of ritual actions that negate history and time itself.

Fuentes's art is one of semblances and resemblances in which things are, at once, not what they seem and more than they seem. In the Fuentesian world of eternal simultaneities, the perfect representation of his vision of mythic fictional history is the fact (not the fiction) that the great cathedral in Mexico City occupies the site of an Aztec pyramid destroyed by the Spaniards. That is, significant events are not linear and sequential in Fuentes's construct. Rather, they occupy vertical space and superimposed time, and if the notion of their cyclical recurrence causes vertigo in the reader, the effect is no more dizzying than that produced by even the most casual reading of history.

—Edith Grossman

GARCÍA MÁRQUEZ, Gabriel. Colombian. Born in Aracataca, 6 March 1928. Educated at a Jesuit school; studied law and journalism at the National University of Colombia, Bogota. Married Mercedes Barcha; two sons. Journalist, 1950-65; then full-time writer. Recipient: Colombian Association of Writers and Artists award, 1954; Esso Literary Prize, 1961; Chianciano Prize (Italy), 1968; Foreign Book Prize (France), 1970; Gallegos Prize (Venezuela), 1972; Neustadt International Prize, 1972; Nobel Prize for Literature, 1982. Honorary doctorate: Columbia University, New York, 1971. Agent: Carmen Balcells, Diagonal 580, Barcelona 11, Spain. Address: P.O. Box 20736, Mexico, D.F., Mexico.

PUBLICATIONS

Fiction

La hojarasca. Bogota, Organizacion Continental de los Festivales del Libro, 1955.

El coronel no tiene quien le escriba.   Mexico City, Era, 1957; as *No One Writes to the Colonel*, London, Cape, 1971.
La mala hora.   Madrid, Luis Pérez, 1962.
Los funerales de la mamá grande.   Xalapa, Universidad Veracruzana, 1962; as *Big Mama's Funeral*, with *No One Writes to the Colonel*, London, Cape, 1971.
Cien años de soledad.   Buenos Aires, Sudamericana, 1967; as *One Hundred Years of Solitude*, New York, Harper, and London, Cape, 1970.
No One Writes to the Colonel and Other Stories.   New York, Harper, 1968.
Relato de un náufrago.   Barcelona, Tusquets, 1970.
Leafstorm and Other Stories.   New York, Harper, and London, Cape, 1972.
La increíble y triste historia de la cándida Eréndira y de su abuela desalmada: Siete cuentos.   Barcelona, Seix Barral, 1972; as *Innocent Erendira and Other Stories*, New York, Harper, 1978; London, Cape, 1979.
El negro qui hizo esperar a los ángeles.   Montevideo, Alfil, 1972.
Ojos de perro azul: Nueve cuentos desconocidos.   Buenos Aires, Equis, 1972.
Todo los cuentos 1947-1972.   Barcelona, Plaza & Janés, 1975.
El otoño del patriarca.   Barcelona, Plaza & Janés, 1975; as *The Autumn of the Patriarch*, New York, Harper, 1976; London, Cape, 1977.
El ultimo viaje del buque fantasma.   Parets del Vallés, Polígrafa, 1976.
Crónica de una muerte anunciada.   Barcelona, Brugüera, 1981; as *Chronicle of a Death Foretold*, London, Cape, 1982; New York, Knopf, 1983.

Other

Cuando era feliz e indocumentado.   Barcelona, Plaza & Janés, 1976.
De viaje por los países socialistas: 90 días en la "Cortina de Hierro."   Cali, Macondo, 1978.
El olor de la quayaba.   Barcelona, Brugüera, 1982; as *The Fragrance of Guava*, London, Verso-New Left, 1983.

*

Bibliography: *García Márquez: An Annotated Bibliography 1947-1979* by Margaret Eustella Fau, Westport, Connecticut, Greenwood Press, 1980.

Critical Studies: *García Márquez: Historia de un deicidio* by Mario Vargas Llosa, Barcelona, Seix Barral, 1971; *García Márquez* by George R. McMurray, New York, Ungar, 1977; *García Márquez: Revolutions in Wonderland* by Regina Janes, Columbia, University of Missouri Press, 1981.

*   *   *

Novelist, polemical journalist, recipient of the Nobel Prize for Literature, Gabriel García Márquez has been among the most influential of 20th-century Latin American writers of prose. Celebrated for his rhetorical exuberance and endless fund of invention, he is equally estimable as a disciplined craftsman and architect of fictive forms. The most immediately striking feature of his mature work is its "magic realism": the practice of rendering possible events as if they were wonders and rendering impossible events as if they were commonplace. In his short stories, one impossible or hyperbolic event may serve as the center, or a possible event may be embroidered with incongruities to make it strange. In the longer fictions and some short stories, the narrative proceeds by a rapid oscillation between possible and impossible events, controlled by an intricate, carefully planned, almost diagrammatic structure that signifies in itself.

Character is rendered externally, by actions, speech, dreams, or symbols; changes in historical time or class standing through physical objects, different styles of architecture, alterations in a house, i.e., sharply focussed, discrete images. Such images, bizarre, beautiful, or incongruous, tessellate the prose surface, and the story is usually told by a single epic voice with a predilection for remembering what has happened before it happens in the narrative, for casting the reader forward until time and the narrative catch up. To elaborate his idiosyncratic, rococo fictive world, García Márquez has abandoned the analytic consciousness assigned to a character or the narrator, associated with the novel since its 18th-century origins, and reinvented the narrative mode of the *Quixote*, with characters witty and simple, literary and realistic, and a "Cervantes" whose narrative judgments are grounded in such 20th-century topics as politics, history, the isolation of individuals, and the problems of community, the resources of writing and the recourse that is writing.

To critics who objected that his fourth novel, *One Hundred Years of Solitude*, evaded the social and political problems treated in his earlier fictions, García Márquez replied that reality includes what men dream and imagine as well as what they pay for tomatoes. Striking a different attitude, he echoed Alejo Carpentier's contention that the reality of Latin America is marvelous and that what the rest of the world call marvels actually happens in Latin America. At another level, he responded by writing a political novel, *The Autumn of the Patriarch*, in the same fantastic mode, though in a different style and with a different shape. The strength of García Márquez's manipulation of the fantastic is its firm root in social and political concerns and in psychological realites. The delight of it is its evocation in the reader of the same imaginative capacity that the narrative itself embodies. Instead of rendering a world the reader recognizes because it is familiar, García Márquez renders a world that seems at first very strange, but which the reader comes to recognize as containing both the familiar limitations of human experience and the somewhat less familiar aspirations of the human imagination beyond "even miracles and magic." The reader's ceaseless shifting from one level of possibility to another, from what happens only in books or in dreams to what occurs every day—war, death, aging, frustrated or fulfilled love—is also a shifting from one interpretive framework to another, from the psychological to the political, to the historical to the literary and back. The effect is dazzling, but there are costs. The power of the method to provoke general implications beyond the reach of the particular case of the realistic novel means a corresponding diminution of the impression of psychological and social density that is the great achievement of the realistic novel. A principal reason for its influence on other writers, however, is that it permits worlds remote from the traditional centers of western culture (like the Atlantic littoral of Colombia) that have usually been treated in fiction either with condescending comedy or gritty realism as poor, bitter, sour, and alien to be imaginatively transformed into worlds of value. The poverty, bitterness, and limitation are still present, but a large part of the world's peoples often rendered as anthropological curiosities, sociological objects, or marginal provincials are redeemed for literature.

García Márquez's first short stories, collected in *Ojos de perro azul*, were vague, Kafkaesque renditions of psychological states from the inside. His first novel, written under Faulkner's influence, attempted to tell the history of a town, Macondo, still internally through such devices as shifting narrative points of view and interior monologues. In *La mala hora* García Márquez, with Hemingway as model, began to externalize his style as he evoked indirectly the repercussions on another town of *la violencia*, a period of civil war between 1948 and 1968 in which some 200,000 Colombians died. The finest of the earlier fictions are the novella *No One Writes to the Colonel* and the short stories of *Big Mama's Funeral*. The context of the novel and some of the stories is again *la violencia*, and the novel develops through the quixotic figure of the colonel the value of symbolic resistance when one lacks power. In both, the use of bizarre and witty detail, particularly to highlight political implications, reflects the influence of Carpentier.

One Hundred Years of Solitude is García Márquez's "total" novel, a work that brings together, among many other things, by name the author, his friends, and relations, by allusion authors he admires from Hemingway to Carpentier, the history of science from the Greeks to the present, Spanish galleons shrouded in orchids, and Colombian politics, including the platforms of the Liberal and Conservative parties, from independence to the present. The novel charts the history of a family, a house, and a town, Macondo, from edenic, mythic beginnings through the descent into history of war, politics, and economic exploitation to annihilation at a moment of apocalyptic revelation. The enormous variety of incident and character in the fiction is controlled by a linear principle of historical progression conveyed by allusion and a cyclic principle of repetition in which there is constant parallelism but only very rarely identity. The novel closes in a brilliant act of self-duplication in which the book read by the reader is discovered to be a book written with the novel and read within the novel. It is all, after all, a book.

The Autumn of the Patriarch, a "total" novel of dictatorship, took up the problem of the dictator as he has flourished in Latin America and throughout human time. The dictator lives between 107 and 232 years, long for an individual, short for a species that includes, allusively, Joab, Stalin, Somoza, and Julius Caesar. Abandoning the conventional markers of paragraphs, periods, and quotation marks, García Márquez wraps him in a tapestry of shifting voices: his own, the common people who find him, his master torturer, his mother, an endless stream of ambassadors, soldiers, suppliants, and conspirators, and an omniscient narrator. (The style and some of the topics can be seen developing in the short stories "The Handsomest Drowned Man in the World," "Blacamán the Good, Vendor of Miracles," "The Last Voyage of the Ghost Ship.") Comical and horrifying, the episodes reveal the patriarch's strengths as well as his monstrosity, mortal and physical. The novel's conclusion promises the end of him, but the duplication of the patriarch's first death in the structure of the novel qualifies optimism without destroying hope.

Chronicle of a Death Foretold reconstructs a single hour, with the present and future interwoven, in which a death by violence, known to be impending, is not prevented. Simpler in style, it is modelled on the classic severities of Greek tragedy, an interest evident in the author's work since his first story, *Leafstorm*.

In addition to his fictions, García Márquez writes much polemical journalism in the service of revolutionary socialism. While the fictions are alive to the ambiguities of political action as the journalism is not, both the fictions and the journalism share certain stylistic features and a decisiveness that permits effective closure, a satisfying finality.

—Regina Janes

GENET, Jean. French. Born in Paris, 19 December 1910; abandoned by his parents, and reared by foster parents in Le Morvan. In reformatory, Mettray, 1926-29, and lived the life of a criminal in several countries until 1942; began writing during term in Fresnes Prison. Address: c/o Gallimard, 5 rue Sébastien-Bottin, 75007 Paris, France.

PUBLICATIONS

Fiction

Notre-Dame des Fleurs. Privately printed, 1944; revised edition, in *Oeuvres complètes*

2, 1951; as *Our Lady of the Flowers*, Paris, Morihien, 1949; as *Gutter in the Sky*, Philadelphia, Levy, 1956; as *Our Lady of the Flowers*, New York, Grove Press, 1963; London, Blond, 1964.

Miracle de la rose. Lyons, L'Arbalète, 1946; revised edition, in *Oeuvres complètes 2*, 1951; as *Miracle of the Rose*, New York, Grove Press, and London, Blond, 1965.

Pompes funèbres. Privately printed, 1947; revised edition, in *Oeuvres complètes 3*, 1953; as *Funeral Rites*, New York, Grove Press, and London, Blond, 1969.

Querelle de Brest. Privately printed, 1947; revised edition, in *Oeuvres complètes 3*, 1953; as *Querelle of Brest*, London, Blond, 1966; New York, Grove Press, 1967.

Plays

Les Bonnes (produced Paris, 1946; revised version, produced Paris, 1954). Sceaux, Pauvert, 1954; as *The Maids* (produced London, 1956; New York, 1963), with *Deathwatch*, New York, Grove Press, 1954; published separately, London, Faber, 1957.

'Adame Miroir (ballet scenario), music by Milhaud. Paris, Hengel, 1948.

Haute surveillance (produced Paris, 1949). Paris, Gallimard, 1949; as *Deathwatch* (produced New York, 1958; London, 1961), with *The Maids*, New York, Grove Press, 1954; published separately, London, Faber, 1961.

Le Balcon (produced Paris, 1956). Décines, L'Arbalète, 1956; revised version, 1956, 1961; as *The Balcony* (produced London, 1957; New York, 1960), London, Faber, 1957; New York, Grove Press, 1958.

Les Nègres (produced Paris, 1959). Décines, L'Arbalète, 1958; as *The Blacks* (produced London and New York, 1961), London, Faber, and New York, Grove Press, 1960.

Les Paravents (produced Berlin, 1961). Décines, L'Arbalète, 1961; as *The Screens* (produced New York, 1971; Bristol, 1973), New York, Grove Press, 1962; London, Faber, 1963.

Screenplays: *Un Chant d'amour*, 1950; *Goubbiah*, 1955; *Mademoiselle*, 1966.

Verse

Chants secrets. Lyons, L'Arbalète, 1947.
La Galère. Paris, J. Loyau, 1947.
Poèmes. Lyons, L'Arbalète, 1948; revised edition, Décines, L'Arbalète, 1966.
Poems. San Francisco, Man-Root, 1980.
Treasures of the Night: Collected Poems, translated by Steven Finch. San Francisco, Gay Sunshine Press, 1981.

Other

Journal du voleur. Paris, Gallimard, 1949; as *The Thief's Journal*, Paris, Olympia Press, 1954; New York, Grove Press, 1964; London, Blond, 1965.

L'Enfant criminel, 'Adame Miroir. Paris, Morihien, 1949.

Oeuvres complètes. Paris, Gallimard, 4 vols., 1951-68.

Lettres à Roger Blin. Paris, Gallimard, 1966; as *Letters to Roger Blin: Reflections on the Theatre*, New York, Grove Press, 1969.

May Day Speech. San Francisco, City Lights, 1970.

Reflections on the Theatre and Other Writings. London, Faber, 1972.

*

Bibliography: *Genet and His Critics: An Annotated Bibliography 1943-1980* by Richard C. Webb, Metuchen, New Jersey, Scarecrow Press, 1982.

Critical Studies: *Saint-Genet, Actor and Martyr* by Jean-Paul Sartre, New York, Braziller, 1963, London, W.H. Allen, 1964; *The Imagination of Genet* by Joseph H. McMahon, New Haven, Connecticut, Yale University Press, 1963; *Genet* by Tom F. Driver, New York, Columbia University Press, 1966; *Genet* by Bettina Knapp, New York, Twayne, 1968; *Genet: A Study of His Novels and Plays* by Philip Thody, London, Hamish Hamilton, 1968, New York, Stein and Day, 1969; *The Visions of Genet* by Richard N. Coe, London, Owen, and New York, Grove Press, 1968, and *The Theatre of Genet: A Casebook* edited by Coe, New York, Grove Press, 1970; *Profane Play, Ritual, and Genet: A Study of His Drama* by Lewis T. Cetta, University, University of Alabama Press, 1974; *Genet: A Collection of Critical Essays* edited by Peter Brooks and Joseph Halpern, Englewood Cliffs, New Jersey, Prentice Hall, 1979; *Genet* by Jeannette Savona, London, Macmillan, 1983.

*   *   *

When Jean-Paul Sartre published his long study *Saint Genet, comédien et martyr*, in 1952, many readers came to Jean Genet through Sartre's evaluation and sympathy. The book proposed that Genet be classified among the greatest French writers of the century. At every step of the way, Genet has known what he was doing. Hence Sartre's term to designate him *comédien* or actor. And Genet never failed to acknowledge the condition imposed upon him by society when he was young; hence the second term in the title of *martyr*.

One day the parallels will be studied that exist between Rimbaud's revolt against his condition in the world, and Genet's submission to his fate. A world only half-seen by Rimbaud in episodes of *Une Saison en enfer* is raucously dramatized in Genet's first novel *Notre-Dame des Fleurs*. Extravagant in every sense, this late adolescent world of Montmartre, engendered by the early adolescent world in the prisons of Mettray and Fontevrault, is the *légende dorée* of Jean Genet, in which existence is a cult, a ceremony of evil where the male is female. Death in violence obsesses the minds of the tough heroes of Genet (*Les durs*: Bulkaen, Pilorge, Harcamone), and martyrdom obsesses the minds of the effeminate (Divine and Notre-Dame des Fleurs). The guillotine is the symbol of the male and of his greatest glory.

The central drama in his books is always the struggle between the man in authority and the young man to whom he is attracted. The psychological varieties of this struggle are many. Each of the novels and each of the plays is a different world in which the same drama unfolds. *Querelle de Brest* is the ship: naval officers and sailors. *Pompes funèbres* is the Occupation: Nazi officers and young Frenchmen of the capital. *Notre-Dame des Fleurs* is Montmartre, with its world of male prostitutes and pimps. *Miracle de la rose* is the prison, with the notorious convicts and slaves.

The play *Deathwatch* is also the prison cell with the intricate hierarchy of criminals where those standing under the death sentence exert the greatest power and prestige over those with lesser sentences. *The Maids* is the household, where in the absence of the mistress one of the maids plays her part. *The Blacks* is the world of colonialism: the conflict between whites and blacks. It is much more than a satire on colonialism. The oppression from which the blacks suffer is so hostile, so incomprehensible, as to be easily the oppression of mankind. The hostility which Genet persistently celebrates throughout all his work, in his opulent language, is the strangely distorted love joining the saint and the criminal, the guard and the prisoner, the policeman and the thief, the master and the slave, the white and the black.

The heroes of *Deathwatch* walk back and forth in their cell and provide thereby a picture of their obsessions from which they cannot escape. Theirs is a self-contained world of damnation. Genet does not move outside of the world of the damned and gives to it the inverted vocation of evil. His subject matter is that which is condemned by society, and to it he gives, as an authentic playwright, an infernal order. The revolt of the maids against the order of the bourgeois world takes place only in their minds. By their repetitive antics they almost reach the state of schizophrenia, but it is clear that they wish to be enslaved, that they have no desire to change their state of subservience. Likewise, the young criminals of *Deathwatch* have no inclination to cease being criminals and hence lose the prestige of evil and martyrdom.

In all of his books Genet is concerned with the type of man who has been given a role outside of society and who accepts it. Sartre can easily discover in the writings of Genet examples of a gratuitous and absurd existence. The maids and the criminals in the two plays have only one recourse. They have to play at being normal, at being integrated characters. But they know that they are counterfeiting society. They know that the actions they invent will not justify their existence. So in reality they are always playing their own alienated selves. We watch simultaneously two actions in Genet's plays: the invented actions of the characters playing at being something they are not, and the fatal drama of alienation.

The concept of sovereignty has always obsessed the imagination of Genet. Sartre believes that he chose evil because that was the realm in which he could hope to reach a status of sovereignty. And Sartre makes clear his conviction that evil is a myth created by the respectable members of society. They tend to call Genet wicked and to use him as a scapegoat who committed the acts which they have been tempted to commit and which they may or may not have committed.

The theme of alienation is prevalent in contemporary literature, but it has never been orchestrated so richly, with such tragic and sensual poignancy, as in Genet's novels and plays. The existences evoked in these works cannot find their realization. These characters fully understand how estranged they are, and they are both obsessed and fascinated by this state. The anomalies Genet sings of, as if they were the noblest themes for a poet, are all present in *The Blacks* and *The Screens*. Simone de Beauvoir is justified in seeing Genet as a descendent of the *poètes maudits*, and in placing him at the end of a lineage of blasphemers: Lautréamont, Nietzsche, Jarry. But Genet is not a philosopher and he is not a blasphemer in the real sense. He is the artist who feels guilty by simply being.

—Wallace Fowlie

GINZBURG, Natalia (née Levi).   Born in Palermo, Sicily, 14 July 1916.   Educated at home and at schools in Turin. Married 1) Leone Ginzburg in 1938 (died, 1944), three children; 2) Gabriele Baldini in 1950 (died, 1969). Forced to live in Abruzzi, 1940-43; worked for Einaudi publishers, Turin, 1944-49; settled in Rome, 1950; lived in London, 1959-62. Recipient: Veillon Prize, 1953; Viareggio Prize, 1957; Chianciano Prize, 1961; Strega Prize, 1963; Marzotto Prize, for play, 1968. Address: Piazza Campo Marzio 3, Rome, Italy.

PUBLICATIONS

Fiction

La strada che va in città (as Alessandra Torimparte).   Turin, Einaudi, 1942; revised edition, 1945; as *The Road to the City*, New York, Doubleday, 1949; London, Hogarth Press, 1952.

È stato così. Turin, Einaudi, 1947; as *The Dry Heart*, in *The Road to the City*, 1949.
Tutti i nostri ieri. Turin, Einaudi, 1952; as *A Light for Fools*, New York, Dutton, 1956;
  as *Dead Yesterdays*, London, Secker and Warburg, 1956.
Valentino (includes *La madre* and *Sagittario*). Turin, Einaudi, 1957.
Le voci della sera. Turin, Einaudi, 1961; as *Voices in the Evening*, New York, Dutton,
  and London, Hogarth Press, 1963.
Lessico famigliare. Turin, Einaudi, 1963; as *Family Sayings*, New York, Dutton, and
  London, Hogarth Press, 1967.
Caro Michele. Milan, Mondadori, 1973; as *No Way*, New York, Harcourt Brace, 1974;
  as *Dear Michael*, London, Owen, 1975.
Famiglia. Turin, Einaudi, 1977.

Plays

Ti ho sposato per allegria (produced Turin, 1966). Included in *Ti ho sposato per allegria
  e altre commedie*, 1967.
Ti ho sposato per allegria e altre commedie (includes *L'inserzione*, *Fragole e panna*, *La
  segretaria*). Turin, Einaudi, 1967.
L'inserzione (produced Rome, 1968). Included in *Ti ho sposato per allegria e altre
  commedie*, 1967; as *The Advertisement* (produced London, 1968; New York, 1974),
  London, Faber, 1969.
Paese di mare e altre commedie (includes *Dialogo*, *La porta sbagliata*, *La parrucca*). Milan, Garzanti, 1973.

Other

Le piccole virtù (essays). Turin, Einaudi, 1962.
Mai devi domandarmi (essays). Milan, Garzanti, 1970; as *Never Must You Ask Me*,
  London, Joseph, 1973.
Vita immaginaria (essays). Milan, Mondadori, 1974.
La famiglia Manzoni. Turin, Einaudi, 1983.

*

Critical Study: *Ginzburg* by Luciana Marchionne Picchione, Florence, La Nuova Italia, 1978.

*   *   *

As a child Natalia Ginzburg was conscious of being set apart. Her father was a non-practicing Jew from Trieste. In Turin, where he was a professor of anatomy, Ginzburg did not attend elementary school but had a governess, even though the family was not rich. Her parents held anti-fascist views and helped the socialist leader Turati to escape. She married Leone Ginzburg, a professor of Russian and editor of *La Cultura*, who was twice imprisoned by the fascists and died in prison in Rome in 1944. Her second husband was a professor of English and director of the Italian Institute in London.

Like many important writers of the 1930's, Ginzburg had her first stories published in *Solaria* and *Letteratura*. Her first short novel, *The Road to the City*, was written in Abruzzi and catches the claustrophobia of a small provincial town. The naive heroine, who buys her freedom with an unwanted pregnancy and an ill-judged marriage, bears the hallmark of Ginzburg's suffering and misguided women. *La madre* examines the situation of a war widow through the critical eyes of her children as she works to keep them at her parents' house and finds release in an unlamented suicide. *A Light for Fools* follows a family through the events of the war. War is also the background for *Voices in the Evening*, in which the heroine/narrator tells the life stories of the five children of a factory owner. She retreats into silence in the all-important final dialogues when it is her turn to live through the mismanagement of her engagement to the youngest son. *Family Sayings* is based on Ginzburg's reminiscences of her own family in Turin. The novels of the 1970's examine the break-up of family ties. However much families may have warped and victimised their members—and particularly their women—through ignorance, selfishness, or carelessness, modern separations and dispersals continue the same process. Men and women in her shrewdly observed world need mothers and fathers, wives, husbands, and children—or they will seek substitutes which will be equally unsuccessful and lead to equally tragic (and comic) situations. Calvino has likened Ginzburg to Jane Austen. Ginzburg herself acknowledges a great admiration for Ivy Compton-Burnett whom she discovered in 1959, as well as a childhood fascination for the 19th-century novelist Marchesa Colombi. Susan Hill, with her studies in grief and inarticulateness, provides a good contemporary comparison.

In her plays Ginzburg has tried to transfer her dialogue of non-communication to the stage. She has also published some poems. Her essays and journalism deal with recognisable human problems like old age, childhood, and housework. Even her literary criticism on Emily Dickinson and Ivy Compton-Burnett becomes imaginative and highly personalised portraiture of two heroic women. It is not surprising to find this same personal technique applied to the family of the famous Italian novelist in her scholarly biography *La famiglia Manzoni*.

—Judy Rawson

GIRONELLA, José María. Spanish. Born in Darnius, Gerona, 31 December 1917. Educated at a seminary, briefly. Married Magda Castañer in 1946. Worked as day laborer and factory apprentice; clerk, Arús Bank, Gerona, 1935-36; served with ski patrol in Huesca in the Nationalist Army; reporter and editor in Gerona, 1940-42; correspondent, *Informazione*, Rome, 1942; traveled extensively in Europe; in clinics in Vienna and Helsinki, 1951-53. Recipient: Nadal Prize, 1947; Ministry of Information Cervantes Prize, 1953; Planeta Prize, 1971. Address: c/o Editorial Planeta, Corcega 273, Barcelona, 8, Spain.

PUBLICATIONS

Fiction

Un hombre. Barcelona, Destino, 1946; as *Where the Soil Was Shallow*, Chicago, Regnery, 1957.
La marea. Barcelona, Planeta, 1949.
Los cipreses creen en Dios. Barcelona, Planeta, 1953; as *The Cypresses Believe in God*, New York, Knopf, 1955.
Un millon de muertos. Barcelona, Planeta, 1961; as *One Million Dead*, New York, Doubleday, 1963.
Mujer, levántate y anda. Barcelona, Planeta, 1962.
Ha estallado la paz. Barcelona, Planeta, 1966; as *Peace after War*, New York, Knopf, 1969.

Condenados a vivir. Barcelona, Planeta, 2 vols, 1971.
Cita en el cementerio. Barcelona, Planeta, 1983.

Verse

Ha llegado el invierno y tú no estas aquí. Barcelona, Entregas de Poesía, 1945.

Other

El novelista ante el mundo. Madrid, Rialp, 1954.
Los fantasmas de mi cerebeo. Barcelona, Planeta, 1958.
Todos somos fugitivos. Barcelona, Planeta, 1961.
On China and Cuba. Notre Dame, Indiana, Fides, 1963.
Personas, ideas, mares. Barcelona, Planeta, 1963.
Phantoms and Fugitives: Journeys to the Improbable (includes translation of *Los fantasmas de mi cerebeo* and *Todos somos fugitivos*). New York, Sheed and Ward, 1964.
El Japón y su duende. Barcelona, Planeta, 1964.
China, lagrima innumerable. Barcelona, Planeta, 1965.
Gritos del mar. Barcelona, Planeta, 1967.
Conversaciones con don Juan de Borbón. Madrid, Aguado, 1968.
En Asia se muere bajo las estrellas. Barcelona, Plaza & Janés, 1968.
Cien españoles y Dios. Barcelona, Nauta, 1969.
Gritos de la tierra. Barcelona, Planeta, 1970.
El Mediterráneo es un hombre disfrazado de mar. Barcelona, Plaza & Janés, 1974.
El escándalo de Tierra Santa. Barcelona, Plaza & Janés, 1977.
Carta a mi padre muerto. Barcelona, Planeta, 1978.
100 españoles y Franco (interviews). Barcelona, Planeta, 1979.
Mundo tierno, mundo cruel. Barcelona, Planeta, 1981.
El escándalo del Islam. Barcelona, Planeta, 1982.

*

Critical Study: *Gironella* by Ronald Schwartz, New York, Twayne, 1972.

*   *   *

The outstanding literary creations of José María Gironella deal with the Spanish Civil War, 1936-1939. The predominant theme of his best received novels, *The Cypresses Believe in God* and *One Million Dead*, focuses on the suffering and eventual disintegration of family life. Gironella, a traditionalist in all respects, intones the lament of a society which has forsaken its sense of order. Vengeful survival becomes a way of life. In his portrayal of war-torn Spain, the author attempts, really tries very hard, to be objective. However, he cannot divest himself of his strong commitment to his orthodox religious background, and consequently to the conservative political position. Unquestionably, his devotion to his personal principles has a marked influence on his characters; although seemingly they confront their tragic circumstances as individuals, in truth they carry with them symbolic identities. That is to say, in the last analysis, they are *types* rather than singular characters. Yet, even as generic projections of an agonizing existence, they achieve a significant measure of artistic reality. Through the description of their lives, the reader is able to identify with the day-to-day struggle for subsistence amid the ravages of a war which tears families asunder, as fanaticism grows in intensity on all sides of the political spectrum.

The warring hostilities depicted in *The Cypresses Believe in God* violently expand in *One Million Dead* which, as the title suggests, dwells on the terrible loss of life. (Even though "one million" is an exaggeration, the number of dead did run into the hundreds of thousands.) Historical events are interwoven with fictional accounts quite skilfully; on the surface both novels would appear to be a reliable recording of dramatic incidents through the personal vicissitudes of the Alvear family, which microcosmically serves as the axis for the national catastrophe. Essentially, the tragedy of Spain is reflected in the misfortunes that befall one family. To be sure, it is a family that predominantly leans toward the cause of Franco.

The third volume of Gironella's trilogy on the Spanish Civil War, *Peace after War*, hardly deserves the same recognition. The first two, voluminous indeed, will give Gironella a respectable place in the annals of Spanish literature. While not achieving, by any means, the stature of a weaver of fictionalized history like Benito Pérez Galdós in the 19th century, Gironella has succeeded in establishing himself as the literary historian of the Spanish Civil War. Other novelists have centered their attention on the consequences of the consanguineous conflict, but Gironella has been the only outstanding writer who has addressed the question in the form of novels.

The other writings of Gironella comprise many themes: religion, death, politics, and a variety of subjects that refer to human problems as they affect daily existence. However, they are by and large essay-type expressions of the author's concern for life and death. In themselves they would not constitute a testimony to a writer who is worthy of being considered as the novelistic chronicler of the three most harrowing years that Spaniards have known. Without a doubt, for those who would want to view the drama of a Spain embarked on self-destruction *The Cypresses Believe in God* and *One Million Dead* are indispensable reading.

—Robert Kirsner

GORBANEVSKAYA, Natalya (Evgen'evna). Russian. Born in Moscow, in 1936. Educated at the University of Moscow, expelled twice; University of Leningrad, external degree, 1964. Two sons. Librarian, All-Union Book Center, 1958-64; acute fear of heights led to a short stay in Kashchenko psychiatric hospital, 1959; translator and editor, State Institute of Experimental Pattern Design and Technical Research, 1964-68; co-founder and editor, samizdat journal *Khronika Tekushchikh Sobytiy*, 1968-75; arrested for civil rights activities, 1969: in prison hospital, 1970-72; has lived in France since 1975: Editor, *Kontinent*. Address: c/o YMCA Press, 11 rue de la Montagne Sainte-Geneviève, 75006 Paris, France.

PUBLICATIONS

Verse

Stikhi [Poems]. Frankfurt, Posev, 1969.
Selected Poems, translated by Daniel Weissbort. Oxford, Carcanet Press, 1972.
Poberezh'e [The Littoral]. Ann Arbor, Michigan, Ardis, 1973.
Tri tetradi stikhotvoreniya [Three Books of Poetry]. Bremen, K Presse, 1975.
Peceletaya snezhnuyu granitsu: Stikhi 1974-1978. Paris, YMCA Press, 1979.

Other

Polden'. Frankfurt, Posev, 1970; as *Red Square at Noon*, London, Deutsch, 1972.

*   *   *

The Russian émigré poet Natalya Gorbanevskaya underwent a cruel literary apprenticeship in the Soviet Union where only a handful of her poems ever officially appeared in print. She published most of her poems in Western journals, an offense which alone would have earned her government censure if her political activities had not already made her a target of official persecution. Active in the dissident movement, she protested against the closed trials of other dissidents, signed letters of protest against incidents of injustice in the Soviet Union, and even demonstrated in Red Square against the Soviet invasion of Czechoslovakia in 1968. She described the events of this demonstration in her book *Red Square at Noon*. Arrested and sent to psychiatric hospitals for observation, she was there diagnosed as a schizophrenic. Gorbanevskaya recounts her sufferings in these hospitals in a series of letters ironically called "Free Health Service." Except in a poem against Soviet treatment of Poles and Czechs and a few works called "prison poems," Gorbanevskaya's poetry is not political; instead it explores the themes of love, poetry, and self-definition in a world full of suffering.

Understandably Gorbanevskaya's poems evoke a sense of despair, disillusionment, confinement, frustration, melancholy, and loneliness. In her poetic world love is rare, and rejection—even by God—is normal. She can find relief and consolation in poetry, but she repeatedly tells of the pain and torture she must undergo to write. Gorbanevskaya counterbalances the bleakness of her vision of life with ornate, luxurious, musical language and a complex symbolic system which generates new images, almost like a chain reaction.

Gorbanevskaya's symbolic system is based on a contrast between images of heat and cold. Within this framework exist sub-systems of image clusters which depend on the primary recurring symbols: burning, flames, and intense heat. However, other motifs cluster around symbolic candles, ashes and soot, and dryness which in turn generates another group of images relating to tears and grass. But grass also takes on its own special meaning which sometimes relates to the basic images of heat and cold. Her symbolic sub-systems often form independent sets.

Images of coldness form the same type of generative system. Gorbanevskaya's primary symbols of chills and snowbanks contain a network of motifs relating to metallically cold settings, wind, and the icy waters of oblivion. Water imagery dominates poems about oblivion and nothingness. Gorbanevskaya usually bemoans a sad and loveless state in settings that are cold and frigid; sometimes, though, she finds passion, love, and affection in settings that are warm or hot. Even though these images may seem conventional, Gorbanevskaya does not use them in a trite manner. Occasionally she even seems to confuse the images, but is always consistent within the context of each poem. For example, in one work she gives her lover a handful of snow but she feels warmth since this shared snow is a sign of affection. Gorbanevskaya sometimes combines images oxymoronically to produce an ambiguous effect: in one poem she sheds dry tears.

Even though Gorbanevskaya expresses her feelings in tactile images, sound play brings real richness to her poetry. Alliteration and assonance appear in each poem, often forming symmetric patterns. She also uses repeated sounds as transitions among stanzas to produce a true welding of sound and sense. Often she repeats entire words or composes paronomasial repetitions. Not surprisingly her favorite trope is anaphora. Gorbanevskaya also pays special attention to rhymes which are highly assonantal and rarely banal. She likes to use various parts of speech in rhymes that are both rich and deep.

Gorbanevskaya also combines sound play with similes and metaphors to strengthen her comparison. In her poetry similes are a rare but varied phenomenon. They are usually not part of her main symbolic system but consistent with it. Sometimes her complex, epic similes generate even more comparisons. Occasionally she uses a simile to introduce a poem, the first stanza of which becomes the tenor of a metaphor realized in the second stanza.

Meter is another important structural device in Gorbanevskaya's poetry. In contrast to most Russian poets, she frequently writes free verse, but many of these free forms are really meters she invents as symmetric patterns of combinations of trochees and iambs. She has written one poem entirely in trochees except for the rhymed words which are all iambs. Almost all meters appear in her poetry from the standard iambic tetrameters and pentameters to trochaic trimeters and even anapaestic hexameters.

Gorbanevskaya is an experimental poet whose formal innovations turn her poems into music. But this is appropriate since she herself tells us in one of her most famous and characteristic works that music is the only consolation in her bleak world.

> There is music, but nothing else—
> neither happiness, nor peace, nor will,
> in all of this dulled, glassy sea of pain
> only music is salvation, so mind it.

> Yes, for an hour or an hour and a half,
> when there is neither a tomorrow, nor a yesterday,
> in the midst of winter, mind the flute
> that sings of golden summer like a woodland oriole.

> But an end comes to this brief oblivion,
> the human nestling grows silent,
> and again we walk into the wilderness, the blizzard, the shadows,
> completely barefoot on the broken glass.

> A star from the skies or a delightful sonnet,
> nothing will fool you anymore,
> and you utter "Peaceful night,"
> but silently you shout out "there is no Peace."

—Christine A. Rydel

GOYTISOLO, Juan. Spanish. Born in Barcelona, 5 January 1931; brother of the writer Luis Goytisolo. Educated at the universities of Madrid and Barcelona to 1953. Member of Turia literary group, with Ana Maria Matute and others, Barcelona, 1951; staff member, Gallimard publishers, Paris, 1958-68; also a journalist in Cuba and Europe; visiting professor at universities in the USA. Recipient: Young Literature Prize, 1953; Indice Prize, 1955. Address: c/o Seix Barral, Apdo de Correos 31, Tambor del Bruch s/n, Sant Joan Despi, Barcelona, Spain.

PUBLICATIONS

Fiction

Juegos de manos. Barcelona, Destino, 1954; as *The Young Assassins,* New York, Knopf, 1959; London, MacGibbon and Kee, 1960.
Duelo en el paraíso. Barcelona, Planeta, 1955; as *Children of Chaos,* London, MacGibbon and Kee, 1958.
El circo. Barcelona, Destino, 1957.

La resaca. Paris, Club de Libro Español, 1958.
Fiestas. Buenos Aires, Emecé, 1958; translated as *Fiestas*, New York, Knopf, 1960; London, MacGibbon and Kee, 1961.
Para vivir aquí. Buenos Aires, Sur, 1960.
La isla. Barcelona, Seix Barral, 1961; as *Island of Women*, New York, Knopf, 1962; as *Sands of Torremolinos*, London, Cape, 1962.
Fin de fiesta: Tentativas de interpretación de una historia amorosa. Barcelona, Seix Barral, 1962; as *The Party's Over: Four Attempts to Define a Love Story*, New York, Grove Press, and London, Weidenfeld and Nicolson, 1966.
Señas de identidad. Mexico City, Mortiz, 1966; as *Marks of Identity*, New York, Grove Press, 1969.
Reivindicación del Conde don Julián. Mexico City, Mortiz, 1970; as *Count Julian*, New York, Viking Press, 1974.
Juan sin tierra. Barcelona, Seix Barral, 1975; as *Juan the Landless*, New York, Viking Press, 1977.
Obras completas (fiction). Madrid, Aguilar, 1977.
Makbara. Barcelona, Seix Barral, 1980; translated as *Makbara*, New York, Seaver, 1981.
Paisajes después de la batalla. Mexico City, Montesinos, 1982.

Other

Problemas de la novela. Barcelona, Seix Barral, 1959.
Campos de Níjar. Barcelona, Seix Barral, 1960.
La chanca. Paris, Librería Española, 1962.
Pueblo en marcha: Instantáneas de un viaje a Cuba. Paris, Librería Española, 1963.
El furgón de cola. Paris, Ruedo Ibérico, 1967.
Disidencias. Barcelona, Seix Barral, 1977.
Libertad, libertad, libertad. Barcelona, Anagrama, 1978.
España y los españoles. Barcelona, Lumen, 1979.
El problema del Sahara. Barcelona, Anagrama, 1979.
Crónicas sarracinas. Madrid, Ruedo Ibérico, 1982.

Editor, *Obra inglesa de José María Blanco White*. Buenos Aires, Formentor, 1972.

*

Critical Studies: *Goytisolo* by Kessel Schwartz, New York, Twayne, 1970; *Goytisolo* edited by Julián Ríos, Madrid, Fundamentos, 1975; *Goytisolo: La destrucción creadora* by Linda Gould Levine, Mexico City, Mortiz, 1976; *Formalist Elements in the Novels of Goytisolo* by Genaro J. Pérez, Madrid, José Porrúa Turanzas, 1979; *La novela de Goytisolo* by Gonzalo Navajas, Madrid, Sociedad General Española de Librería, 1979; *La evolución literaria de Goytisolo* by Hector Romero, Miami, Universal, 1979; *Trilogy of Treason: An Intertextual Study of Goytisolo* by Michael Ugarte, Columbia, University of Missouri Press, 1982.

*   *   *

Juan Goytisolo, who has written short stories, travel books, and several volumes of non-fiction prose, in his early novels concentrates on social realism and a Spain haunted by the Civil War, contrasting the world of reality with one of make-believe and lyric force. Through the eyes of children and adolescents he gives us a pessimistic view of the misery in his native land. *The Young Assassins* brilliantly analyzes a group of disillusioned, frustrated, and guilt-ridden middle-class adolescents who rebel against a stultifying adult world. Their plan to kill a politician fails, and they immolate the sensitive member who was unable to pull the trigger. *Children of Chaos*, set during the Civil War, treats the theme of innocence destroyed in an evil war.

About 1963, disavowing aspects of social realism, Goytisolo adopted many of the formalist and structuralist doctrines, but both his early and later novels involve also criticism of the Catholic Church, capitalism, tourism, and Spanish culture. Throughout he insists on descriptions of bodily secretions and excretions and explicit sexual situations. Most of Goytisolo's protagonists search in vain for a mother figure, and their sense of guilt and frustration gives rise to various oedipal and incestuous fantasies.

In *Marks of Identity* Alvaro Mendiola, through recall, dream, and revery, searches his family past for identity. An outspoken attack on the Franco regime, the novel combines myth with various kinds of stylistic devices to assail a petrified culture and language. In the second volume of the Mendiola trilogy, *Count Julian*, Goytisolo, combining free association with temporal dislocations, presents as an alter-ego the modern reincarnation of Spain's betrayer to the Arabs in the 8th century. With hallucinatory intensity, he attacks Spanish orthodoxy in an effort to demolish his country's hypocritical ideas about spiritual and physical purity together with Spain's sacrosanct literary heroes. In the novel, a corruscating collage of incoherent dissolving dream states, Julian, both victim and executioner, cannot fully destroy the language. *Juan the Landless*, the third volume, intensifies the literary discourse and intertextuality of the first two novels as the narrator discusses the art of writing the very novel being created. The novel parodies a Spain no longer his, and the protagonist, finally managing to disintegrate language itself, achieves the possibility of freedom. A fantastic, hallucinatory, spatial-temporal travelogue, the novel glorifies sodomy, anal aggression, and the defecatory process. In all of these novels Goytisolo engages in linguistic experimentation, employing non-sentences, associative chains, foreign languages, and first, second, and third person discourse.

Makbara, a defense of the pariahs of the world, explores the relations between a fallen angel and a phallic Moor. *Paisajes después de la batalla*, a post-structuralist experiment, plays with the concept of literary text and authorship, here involving Lewis Carroll, Juan Goytisolo, and the reader.

Best known for his eleven novels, Goytisolo ultimately writes about personal conflicts, but in the process, as one of the masters of contemporary fiction, he has created magnificent and unusual works of great imagination.

—Kessel Schwartz

GRACQ, Julien. Pseudonym for Louis Poirier. French. Born in Saint-Florent-le-Vieil, 27 July 1910. Educated at Lycée de Nantes; Lycée Henri IV, Paris; École Normale Supérieure, Paris, agrégation 1934. History teacher at lycées in Quimper, 1937-39, Nantes, 1937-38, and Amiens, 1941-48, and Lycée Claude-Bernard, Paris, 1948-70. Recipient: Goncourt Prize, 1951 (refused). Address: 61 rue de Grenelle, 75007 Paris, France.

PUBLICATIONS

Fiction

Au Château d'Argol. Paris, Corti, 1938; as *The Castle of Argol*, New York, New

Directions, and London, Owen, 1951.
Un Beau Ténébreux.   Paris, Corti, 1945; as *A Dark Stranger*, New York, New Directions, and London, Owen, 1951.
Le Rivage des Syrtes.   Paris, Corti, 1951.
Un Balcon en forêt.   Paris, Corti, 1958; as *Balcony in the Forest*, New York, Braziller, 1959; London, Hutchinson, 1960.
La Presqu'île (stories).   Paris, Corti, 1970.

Play

Le Roi pêcheur.   Paris, Corti, 1948.

Other

Liberté grande.   Paris, Corti, 1946.
André Breton.   Paris, Corti, 1948.
La Littérature à l'estomac.   Paris, Corti, 1950.
La Terre habitable, with Jacques Herold.   Paris, Corti, 1951.
Prose pour l'étrangère.   Paris, Corti, 1952.
Farouche à quatre feuilles, with others.   Paris, Grasset, 1954.
Préférences.   Paris, Corti, 1961.
Lettrines.   Paris, Corti, 2 vols., 1967-74.
Les Eaux étroites.   Paris, Corti, 1976.
En lisent, en écrivant.   Paris, Corti, 1981.

Translator, *Penthésilée*, by Kleist.   Paris, Corti, 1954.

*

Bibliography: *Gracq: Essai de bibliographie 1938-1972* by Peter C. Hoy, London, Grant and Cutler, 1973.

Critical Studies: *Gracq* by J.-L. Leutrat, Paris, Éditions Universitaires, 1966; *Dramaturgie et liturgie dans l'oeuvre de Gracq* by A.-C. Dobbs, Paris, Corti, 1972; *Gracq*, Paris, L'Herne, 1972; *Les Débuts narratifs de Gracq (1938-1945)* by Friedrich Hetzer, Munich, Minerva, 1980; *Gracq et le surréalisme* by Simone Grossman, Paris, Corti, 1980.

*   *   *

By temperament an individualist who chose to go his own way, Julien Gracq pursued his personal vision in a relatively small number of works produced at a slow rate over the years from just before World War II. Though he has been chary of identifying himself with any party, group, or movement, critics are unanimous in recognising in him traits which link him with the second generation of the Surrealists. He was a friend of André Breton, on whom he published an important study in 1948. There is further evidence of Gracq's literary affiliations in some of his minor writings. He contributed a preface to an edition of Lautréamont's *Les Chants de Maldoror*, and accepted Jean-Louis Barrault's challenging invitation to translate *Penthesilea*, the powerful and erotic tragedy by the German Romantic dramatist Heinrich von Kleist. In *Le Roi pêcheur* of 1948, a play whose Arthurianism has distinct Wagnerian overtones, he reworked the Grail theme in characteristically free and individual fashion. Another significant influence on Gracq was the "magic realism" of Ernst Jünger's fiction, especially *Auf den Marmorklippen* (On the Cliffs of Marble).
Gracq has one play to his credit and wrote prose poems and attractive and trenchant criticism

of literature and literary life. But his reputation rests on four novels. Though different in many ways, they share certain distinct similarities. They show small groups of people set apart from the rest of humanity in situations which are mysterious and tense. Placed within an environment that seems to mirror his psychological state, the hero sets out, whether intentionally or not, in search of the meaning of life in ominous circumstances. The theme of the quest is predominant, and the prevailing mood is one of tense anticipation rather than of fulfilment. Forests and restless water are the backcloth to the human emotions as Gracq seeks to convey a poetic intuition of the one-ness of man and the cosmos which transcends rationality. Though sometimes, especially in early works, verging on the Gothic in its symbol-laden descriptions of natural forces, its brooding atmosphere and strange implausibilities, Gracq's fiction recreates myth for the modern reader.

The Castle of Argol, Gracq's first novel, presents the disturbing story of a young man who comes to Brittany and purchases a mysterious chateau in the depths of the forests where he is visited by his friend Herminien and a beautiful woman. Tensions mount, and there is bloodshed, yet behind the fantastic tale lies the major theme of the search for the ideal. *A Dark Stranger* is also set in Brittany, and the hero of the novel whose Romantic associations are clear even from its title is a fated man who can find no satisfactions in life and concludes a suicide pact. In *Le Rivage des Syrtes*, which won Gracq the Goncourt Prize, though he refused to accept it, personal discovery is given an imaginary historical setting. For *Balcony in the Forest* Gracq was able to draw on his personal experiences of serving in the French army in 1940. Yet though there is much reflection of actuality, the hero becomes increasingly detached from mundane detail as the novel explores the development of his inner life as rationality is displaced by reverie that seems to open up more valid perspectives.

—C.N. Smith

GRASS, Günter (Wilhelm). German. Born in Danzig (now Gdańsk, Poland), 16 October 1927. Educated at Volksschule and Gymnasium, Danzig; trained as stone mason and sculptor; attended Academy of Art, Dusseldorf, 1948-49, and State Academy of Fine Arts, Berlin, 1953-55. Served in World War II: prisoner of war. Married 1) Anna Margareta Schwarz in 1954, three sons and one daughter; 2) Ute Grunert in 1979. Worked as farm laborer, miner, apprentice stonecutter, jazz musician; speechwriter for Willy Brandt when Mayor of West Berlin; writer-in-residence, Columbia University New York, 1966; also artist and illustrator; Co-Editor, *L*, since 1976, and the publishing house Verlages L'80, since 1980. Recipient: Gruppe 47 prize, 1958; Bremen Prize, 1959 (withdrawn); Critics Prize (Germany), 1960; Foreign Book Prize (France), 1962; Büchner Prize, 1965; Berlin Academy Fontane Prize, 1968; Heuss Prize, 1969; Mondello Prize (Palermo), 1977; Viareggio-Versilia Prize, 1978; Majkowski Medal, 1978; Vienna Literature Prize, 1980; Feltrinelli Prize, 1982. Honorary doctorate: Kenyon College, Gambier, Ohio, 1965; Harvard University, Cambridge, Massachusetts, 1976. Member, 1963, and since 1983 President, Academy of Art, Berlin; Member, American Academy of Arts and Sciences. Address: Niedstrasse 13, 1000 Berlin 41, Germany.

PUBLICATIONS

Fiction

Die Blechtrommel. Neuwied, Luchterhand, 1959; as *The Tin Drum*, London, Secker

147

and Warburg, and New York, Random House, 1962.

Katz und Maus. Neuwied, Luchterhand, 1961; as *Cat and Mouse*, London, Secker and Warburg, and New York, Harcourt Brace, 1963.

Hundejahre. Neuwied, Luchterhand, 1963; as *Dog Years*, London, Secker and Warburg, and New York, Harcourt Brace, 1965.

Örtlich betäubt. Neuwied, Luchterhand, 1969; as *Local Anaesthetic*, London, Secker and Warburg, 1969; New York, Harcourt Brace, 1970.

Aus dem Tagebuch einer Schnecke. Neuwied, Luchterhand, 1972; as *From the Diary of a Snail*, New York, Harcourt Brace, 1973; London, Secker and Warburg, 1974.

Der Butt. Neuwied, Luchterhand, 1977; as *The Flounder*, London, Secker and Warburg, and New York, Harcourt Brace, 1978.

Das Treffen in Telgte. Neuwied, Luchterhand, 1979; as *The Meeting at Telgte*, London, Secker and Warburg, and New York, Harcourt Brace, 1981.

Kopfgeburten; oder die Deutschen sterben aus. Neuwied, Luchterhand, 1980; as *Headbirths; or, The Germans Are Dying Out*, London, Secker and Warburg, and New York, Harcourt Brace, 1982.

Plays

Noch zehn Minuten bis Buffalo (produced Bochum, 1954). Included in *Theaterspiele*, 1970; as *Only Ten Minutes to Buffalo* (produced Edinburgh, 1969), in *Four Plays*, 1967.

Hochwasser (produced Frankfurt, 1957). Frankfurt, Suhrkamp, 1963; as *Flood*, in *Four Plays*, 1967.

Onkel, Onkel (produced Cologne, 1958). Berlin, Wagenbach, 1965; as *Onkel, Onkel*, in *Four Plays*, 1967.

Die bösen Köche (produced Berlin, 1961). Included in *Theaterspiele*, 1970; as *The Wicked Cooks* (produced New York, 1967; Birmingham, 1979), in *Four Plays*, 1967.

Die Plebejer proben den Aufstand (produced Berlin, 1966). Neuwied, Luchterhand, 1966; as *The Plebeians Rehearse the Uprising* (produced Kingston, Rhode Island, and Oxford, 1968; London, 1970), New York, Harcourt Brace, and London, Secker and Warburg, 1966.

Four Plays (includes *Flood*; *Onkel, Onkel*; *Only Ten Minutes to Buffalo*; *The Wicked Cooks*). New York, Harcourt Brace, 1967; London, Secker and Warburg, 1968.

Davor (produced Berlin, 1969). Included in *Theaterspiele*, 1970; as *Max* (as *Uptight*, produced Austin, Texas, 1970), New York, Harcourt Brace, 1972.

Theaterspiele. Neuwied, Luchterhand, 1970.

Die Blechtrommel als Film, with Volker Schlöndorff. Frankfurt, Zweitausendeins, 1979.

Screenplay: *Katz und Maus*, 1967.

Ballet Scenario: *Stoffreste*, 1957.

Verse

Die Vorzüge der Windhühner. Neuwied, Luchterhand, 1956.

Gleisdreieck. Neuwied, Luchterhand, 1960.

Selected Poems, translated by Michael Hamburger and Christopher Middleton. London, Secker and Warburg, and New York, Harcourt Brace, 1966.

Ausgefragt. Neuwied, Luchterhand, 1967; as *New Poems*, translated by Michael Hamburger, New York, Harcourt Brace, 1968.

Poems, translated by Michael Hamburger and Christopher Middleton. London, Penguin, 1969; as *Selected Poems*, 1980.

Gesammelte Gedichte. Neuwied, Luchterhand, 1971.
Mariazuehren/Inmarypraise. Munich, Bruckmann, 1973.
Liebe geprüft. Bremen, Schünemann, 1974.
In the Egg and Other Poems, translated by Michael Hamburger and Christopher Middleton. London, Secker and Warburg, and New York, Harcourt Brace, 1977.

Other

O Susanna: Ein Jazzbilderbuch: Blues, Balladen, Spirituals, Jazz. Cologne, Kiepenheuer & Witsch, 1959.
Die Ballerina. Berlin, Friedenauer Presse, 1963.
Rede über das Selbstverständliche. Neuwied, Luchterhand, 1965.
Dich singe ich, Demokratie (pamphlets). Neuwied, Luchterhand, 6 vols., 1965.
Briefe über die Grenze; Versuch eines Ost-West Dialogs, with Pavel Kohout. Hamburg, Wegner, 1968.
Über meinen Lehrer Döblin und andere Vorträge. Berlin, Literarisches Colloquium, 1968.
Ausgewählte Texte, Abbildungen, Faksimiles, Bio-Bibliographie, edited by Theodor Wieser. Neuwied, Luchterhand, 1968; as *Porträt und Poesie,* 1968.
Der Fall Axel C. Springer am Beispiel Arnold Zweig. Neuwied. Luchterhand, 1968.
Über das Selbstverständliche: Politische Schriften. Munich, Deutscher Taschenbuch Verlag, 1969; translated in part as *Speak Out! Speeches, Open Letters, Commentaries,* London, Secker and Warburg, and New York, Harcourt Brace, 1969.
Die Schweinekopfsülze. Hamburg, Merlin, 1969.
Dokumente zur politischen Wirkung, edited by Heinz Ludwig Arnold and Franz Josef Görtz. Munich, Boorberg, 1971.
Der Bürger und seine Stimme. Neuwied, Luchterhand, 1974.
Denkzettel: Politische Reden und Aufsätze 1965-76. Neuwied, Luchterhand, 1978.
Aufsätze zur Literatur. Neuwied, Luchterhand, 1980.
Zeichnungen und Texte 1954-1977. Neuwied, Luchterhand, 1982; as *Drawings and Words 1954-1977,* London, Secker and Warburg, and New York, Harcourt Brace, 1983.

Illustrator, *Ein Ort für Zufälle,* by Ingeborg Buchmann. Berlin, Wagenbach, 1965.

*

Bibliography: *Grass: A Bibliography 1955-1975* by P. O'Neill, Toronto, University of Toronto Press, 1976; *Grass in America: The Early Years* edited by Ray Lewis White, Hildesheim, Olms, 1981.

Critical Studies: "Grass" by Arrigo V. Subiotto, in *German Men of Letters 4,* edited by Brian Keith-Smith, London, Wolff, 1966; *Grass: A Critical Essay* by Norris W. Yates, Grand Rapids, Michigan, Eerdmans, 1967; *Grass* by W. Gordon Cunliffe, New York, Twayne, 1969; *Grass* by Kurt Lothar Tank, New York, Ungar, 1969; *A Grass Symposium* edited by A. Leslie Willson, Austin, University of Texas Press, 1971; *Grass* by Irene Leonard, Edinburgh, Oliver and Boyd, 1974; *A Mythic Journey: Grass's Tin Drum* by Edward Diller, Lexington, University Press of Kentucky, 1974; *Grass* by Keith Miles, London, Vision, 1975; *The "Danzig Trilogy" of Grass* by John Reddick, London, Secker and Warburg, 1975; *Grass: The Writer in a Pluralist Society* by Michael Hollington, London, Boyars, 1980.

*   *   *

Günter Grass has shown in his novels that he is one of the most acute observers and critics of

West Germany, after beginning his career in the 1950's with short prose pieces, poems, and plays in the then dominant "poetic" or "absurd" style. He has never wholly abandoned this attitude to reality, and he shares with other German writers—especially the dramatists—a tendency to oscillate between an existential, "absurd," private philosophy and a polemically political sense of responsibility in public affairs. At the beginning of his career he was still undecided on the choice of medium: writing, painting, or sculpture. Despite his subsequent success as a writer, he has continued his graphic practice, often illustrating his own books, for writing and drawing are to him simply different metaphorical modes of expressing reality.

Grass made a dramatic debut on the literary scene with *The Tin Drum*, *Cat and Mouse*, and *Dog Years*, later named the Danzig Trilogy after Grass's native city which, detached and distant like Joyce's Dublin, became the prism through which he conveyed his vision of the world about him. In Danzig, with its mixed German and Polish population, the Second World War began. The city was a paradigmatic setting for the gradual growth of Nazism amid the banality of the petty bourgeoisie, and symbolised the lost homelands from which millions of Germans would be forever exiled after 1945.

The hero of the huge novel *The Tin Drum*, the dwarf Oskar Matzerath, who managed to stop growing at the age of three (with the advent of the Nazis), tells the story from the safety and tranquillity of his bed in a mental asylum, a symbol of refuge and escapist withdrawal from the stresses and confusion of post-war society. Physically and figuratively, his perspective is that from the outside and underside of things. Grass invents for Oskar the appurtenance of the toy in the title with which he "drums up" in a wealth of realistic detail characteristic episodes of his life. He also possesses a glass-shattering scream that enables him to intervene in events around him. Similarly, the vast epic sweep of *Dog Years* is given unity by the allegorical and symbolic implications of the scarecrow factory and the saga of the dynasty of Alsatian dogs.

In this picaresque trilogy Grass, with great zest and wide-ranging scope, imaginatively investigated both recent German history—the monstrous crimes of the Nazis, the acquiescence and cowardice of the ordinary citizen—and contemporary post-war reality—the suppression of responsibility and guilt, economic reconstruction and the return to affluence and complacency, the loss of moral values. Inevitably Grass became identified with the new generation of critical realists, which included Heinrich Böll and Martin Walser, who implacably satirized the faults and errors of their fellow-countrymen and untiringly reminded them of the guilty involvement in Nazi Germany they were eager to forget.

Grass's sense of social justice and his contentious nature took him into the political arena where he threw his authority and weight behind the Social Democratic Party in the general elections of the 1960's. His personal friend Willy Brandt became Chancellor in 1969, and Grass's fiery, hard-hitting campaign speeches, open letters, and commentaries were variously published in *Über das Selbstverständliche* and *Der Bürger und seine Stimme*. The creative work accompanying this intense activity was also coloured by Grass's political commitment; the play *Davor* and the novel *Local Anaesthetic* thematize the dominant preoccupations of intellectual and public life, namely the war in Vietnam and radical student protest in German universities. Though imbued with socialist ideas Grass stopped short of violence and destruction, advocating reform rather than revolution, practical measures for eradicating injustice rather than ideological posturings. As a left-wing intellectual he showed a certain sympathy for the "extra-parliamentary opposition" and condemned as vigorously as anyone the witch-hunt associated with the iniquitous "Berufsverbot" of 1972; but he never let it be forgotten that he believed in the democratic process through the ballot-box. When the party he so vehemently supported, the SPD, came in from the cold and achieved power in 1969, it was to be expected that Grass's own stridency would become muted: the realities of government had a sobering effect on rhetoric.

The anti-ideological scepticism of Grass's political stance is articulated in the novel *From the Diary of a Snail*, which charts the author's reflections on his active participation in the election campaign of 1969 as well as telling the fictional story of the teacher Ott, "nicknamed Doubt," who resisted the Nazis and clandestinely helped the persecuted Jews to the best of his ability. The metaphor of the snail served to epitomize Grass's down-to-earth, realistic sense of political possibility: its qualities of sensitive hesitancy, patient persistence, and almost unnoticed but continuous movement are harnessed by Grass to illustrate the potential of social democracy for evolutionary political progress. It was perhaps a mark of his generation that Grass fell foul of dynamic and impatient younger radical intellectuals in opting for gentle melancholy and sceptical Utopian hope in the form of a "politics of tiny steps."

During the mid-1970's Grass seemed to be out of tune with the more extreme progressive forces in Germany, and his literary talents appeared to lie dormant and inactive. In fact this proved to be the period of gestation of another epic masterpiece. *The Flounder* incorporates so many autobiographical details—Grass's private life was almost public property by this time—that the blurring of the distinction between author and narrator already initiated in *From the Diary of a Snail* is here completed. *The Flounder* is a complementary piece to the Danzig Trilogy; where the latter focusses on the enormities of contemporary events, *The Flounder* embraces in its narrative structure the whole sweep of German social and political history from the Stone and Iron ages through the medieval, reformation, baroque, and Seven Year War periods on to the 19th and 20th centuries. The perennial human endeavour to ascribe progress and meaning to historical process as well as the more topical question of feminism and the secular domination of women by men are central themes given expression by Grass. But he never lets the profounder philosophical musings take control of the narrative. This anti-fairy-tale, with all its indignation, regret, fury and pessimism, is told with a sustained verve and imaginative boundlessness that recalls the appetite for life in all its problematic complexity of the earlier Danzig Trilogy.

In his most recent "fictional" work, *Headbirths; or, The Germans Are Dying Out*, Grass displayed his political persona once more, thematizing the massive and urgent problems facing the industrialised nations: energy crises, the threat of nuclear war, a declining birth-rate, the Third World. Yet, despite all his concern as a citizen with the struggles of the real world, Grass's faith in the significance of literature and the aesthetic dimension still shines through; he maintains that even in the most catastrophic destruction of civilisation "a hand holding a pen would reach up out of the rubble."

—Arrigo V. Subiotto

GREEN, Julien (Hartridge). American. Born Julian Green in Paris, of American parents, 6 September 1900. Educated at Lycée Janson-de-Sailly, Paris; University of Virginia, Charlottesville, 1919-22; studied drawing at La Grande Chaumière, Paris, 1922-23. Served in the American Field Service, 1917, and the Norton-Harjes Service (later the Red Cross), 1917-18; in the French Army, 1918-19; joined the United States Army, 1942; later with the Office of War Information. Free-lance writer from 1924. Taught at the University of Virginia, 1933-34, and at Princeton University, New Jersey, Goucher College, Baltimore, Mills College, Oakland, California, and Jesuit College, Baltimore, 1940-42. Recipient: French Academy Paul Flat prize, 1927, and Grand Prize, 1970; Heinemann Prize, 1928; Harper Prize, 1929, 1942; Monaco Grand Prize, 1951; National Grand Prize for Letters (France), 1966; Ibico Reggino prize, 1968; German Universities prize, 1973; Proust Prize, 1974. Member, Bavarian Academy, Royal Academy of Belgium, 1951, French Academy (first foreign member), 1971, American Academy, 1972. Honorary Member, Phi Beta Kappa, 1948. Address: c/o Editions de Seuil, 27 rue Jacob, 75006 Paris, France.

Fiction

Mont-Cinère. Paris, Plon, 1926; revised edition, 1928, 1984; as *Avarice House*, New York, Harper, 1927; London, Benn, 1928.
Le Voyageur sur la terre (short story). Paris, Gallimard, 1927; as *The Pilgrim on the Earth*, New York, Harper, 1929.
Adrienne Mesurat. Paris, Plon, 1927; as *The Closed Garden*, New York, Harper, and London, Heinemann, 1928.
La Traversée inutile. Paris, Plon, 1927.
Les Clefs de la mort. Paris, Schiffrin, 1928.
Léviathan. Paris, Plon, 1929; as *The Dark Journey*, New York, Harper, and London, Heinemann, 1929.
Le Voyageur sur la terre (collection). Paris, Plon, 1930; as *Christine and Other Stories*, New York, Harper, 1930; London, Heinemann, 1931.
L'Autre sommeil. Paris, Gallimard, 1931.
Épaves. Paris, Plon, 1932; revised edition, 1978; as *The Strange River*, New York, Harper, 1932; London, Heinemann, 1933.
Le Visionnaire. Paris, Plon, 1934; as *The Dreamer*, New York, Harper, and London, Heinemann, 1934.
Minuit. Paris, Plon, 1936; as *Midnight*, New York, Harper, and London, Heinemann, 1936.
Varouna. Paris, Plon, 1940; revised edition, 1979; as *Then Shall the Dust Return*, New York, Harper, 1941.
Si j'étais vous. Paris, Plon, 1947; revised edition, 1970; as *If I Were You*, New York, Harper, 1949; London, Eyre and Spottiswoode, 1950.
Moïra. Paris, Plon, 1950; translated as *Moïra*, New York, Macmillan, and London, Heinemann, 1951.
Le Malfaiteur. Paris, Plon, 1955; revised edition, 1974; as *The Transgressor*, New York, Pantheon, 1957; London, Heinemann, 1958.
Chaque homme dans sa nuit. Paris, Plon, 1960; as *Each in His Darkness*, New York, Pantheon, and London, Heinemann, 1961.
L'Autre. Paris, Plon, 1971; as *The Other One*, New York, Harcourt Brace, and London, Collins, 1973.
L'Apprenti psychiâtre (translation by Eric Jourdan of *The Apprentice Psychiatrist*, originally published in *Quarterly Review*, University of Virginia, 1920). Paris, Livre de Poche, 1976.
Le Mauvais Lieu. Paris, Plon, 1977.
Histoires de vertige. Paris, Seuil, 1984.

Plays

Sud (produced Paris, 1953; opera version, music by Kenton Coe, produced Paris, 1973). Paris, Plon, 1953; as *South* (produced London, 1955), in *Plays of the Year 12*, London, Elek, 1955.
L'Ennemi (produced Paris, 1954). Paris, Plon, 1954.
Je est un autre (broadcast, 1954). Included in *Oeuvres complètes*, 1973-77.
L'Ombre (produced Paris, 1956). Paris, Plon, 1956.
Léviathan (screenplay), in *Les Cahiers du cinéma*. 1962.
Inigo, La Dame de Pique, La Mort d'Ivan Ilytch (screenplays), in *Oeuvres complètes*. 1973-77.

Screenplays: *Inigo*, 1947; *Léviathan*, 1962; *La Dame de Pique*, 1965; *La Mort d'Ivan Ilytch*, 1965.

Radio Play: *Je est un autre*, 1954.

Other

Pamphlet contre les Catholiques de France (as Théophile Delaporte).   Paris, Revue des Pamphletaires, 1924.

Suite anglaise.   Paris, Cahiers de Paris, 1927; revised edition, Paris, Plon, 1972.

Un Puritain Homme de lettres: Nathaniel Hawthorne.   Toulouse, Cahiers Libres, 1928.

Journal:
1. *Les Années faciles 1928-1934*.   Paris, Plon, 1938; revised edition, as *Les Années faciles 1926-1934*, 1970.
2. *Derniers Beaux Jours 1935-1939*.   Paris, Plon, 1939; vols. 1 and 2 as *Personal Record 1928-1939*, New York, Harper, 1939; London, Hamish Hamilton, 1940.
3. *Devant la porte sombre 1940-1943*.   Paris, Plon, 1946.
4. *L'Oeil de l'ouragan 1943-45*.   Paris, Plon, 1949.
5. *Le Revenant 1946-1950*.   Paris, Plon, 1951.
6. *Le Miroir intérieur 1950-1954*.   Paris, Plon, 1955.
7. *Le Bel Aujourd'hui 1955-58*.   Paris, Plon, 1958; vols, 1-7 as *Journal: 1928-1958*, 1961; abridged translation as *Diary 1928-1957*, edited by Kurt Wolff, New York, Harcourt Brace, and London, Collins, 1964.
8. *Vers l'invisible 1958-1967*.   Paris, Plon, 1967; vols. 1-8 as *Journal 1928-1966*, 2 vols., 1969.
9. *Ce qui reste de jour 1966-1972*.   Paris, Plon, 1972.
10. *La Bouteille à la mer 1972-1976*.   Paris, Plon, 1976.
11. *La Terre est si belle 1976-1978*.   Paris, Seuil, 1982.
12. *La Lumière du monde 1978-1981*.   Paris, Seuil, 1983.

Memories of Happy Days.   New York, Harper, 1942; London, Dent, 1944.

Gide vivant, with Jean Cocteau.   Paris, Amiot Dumont, 1952.

Oeuvres complètes.   Paris, Plon, 10 vols., 1954-65.

Autobiographie:
   Partir avant le jour.   Paris, Grasset, 1963; revised edition, Paris, Seuil, 1984; as *To Leave Before Dawn*, New York, Harcourt Brace, 1967; London, Owen, 1969.
   Mille Chemins ouverts.   Paris, Grasset, 1964; revised edition, Paris, Seuil, 1984.
   Terre lointaine.   Paris, Grasset, 1966; revised edition, Paris, Seuil, 1984.
   Jeunesse.   Paris, Grasset, 1974; revised edition, Paris, Seuil, 1984.

Qui sommes-nous?   Paris, Plon, 1972.

Oeuvres complètes (Pléiade edition), edited by Jacques Petit.   Paris, Gallimard, 5 vols., 1973-77.

Liberté.   Paris, Julliard, 1974.

La Nuit des fantômes (juvenile).   Paris, Plon, 1976.

Memories of Evil Days, edited by Jean-Pierre Piriou.   Charlottesville, University Press of Virginia, 1976.

Ce qu'il faut d'amour à l'homme.   Paris, Plon, 1978.

Dans la gueule du temps (journal 1925-1976).   Paris, Plon, 1978.

Une Grande Amitié: Correspondance 1926-1972, with Jacques Maritain, edited by Henry Bars and Eric Jourdan.   Paris, Gallimard, 1979.

Frère François.   Paris, Seuil, 1983.

Paris.   Paris, Champ Vallon-Seuil, 1983.

Translator, with Anne Green, *Basic Verities: Prose and Poetry*, by Charles Péguy.   New

York, Pantheon, and London, Kegan Paul, 1943.
Translator, with Anne Green, *Men and Saints*, by Charles Péguy.   New York, Pantheon,
1944; London, Kegan Paul, 1947.
Translator, *God Speaks: Religious Poetry*, by Charles Péguy.   New York, Pantheon,
1945.
Translator, *The Mystery of the Charity of Joan of Arc*, by Charles Péguy.   New York,
Pantheon, 1949; London, Hollis and Carter, 1950.

*

Bibliography: *Green: Essai de bibliographie des études en langue française consacrées à Green 1923-1967* by Peter C. Hoy, Paris, Minard, 1970.

Critical Studies: *With Much Love* by Anne Green, New York, Harper, 1948; *Green and the Thorn of Puritanism* by Samuel Stokes, New York, Columbia University Press, 1955; *Hallucination and Death as Motifs of Escape in the Novels by Green* by M.G. Cooke, Washington, D.C., Catholic University of America Press, 1960; *Green* by Glenn S. Burne, New York, Twayne, 1972; *The Metamorphosis of the Self: The Mystic, The Sensualist, and the Artist in the Works of Green* by John M. Dunaway, Lexington, University Press of Kentucky, 1978.

*   *   *

Although Julien Green was born of American parents and has retained his American citizenship, his preferred language has always been French. His published works, with the exception of an early story and two volumes of "memories," have been written in French, and most have been translated into English. The central and unifying theme which runs through Green's writings is his sense of "duality," of a tension between strongly opposing spiritual and sensual impulses. For Green is devoutly religious, having been converted, at age 16, from a puritanical Protestantism to an equally puritanical Catholicism. Obsessed with the idea of purity he was horrified when he experienced strong sexual impulses directed exclusively toward his male schoolmates. For him, the flesh and the senses became the mortal enemy, the Devil incarnate, and he felt that his body was the battleground for a war between Satan—the Impure, the threat of damnation literally believed in—and God, Purity, and Salvation. His novels and plays are partially disguised autobiographies in which he strives to understand and reconcile these painful inner conflicts.

In his early works Green tended to disguise his "emotional bias." The novels *Avarice House*, *The Closed Garden*, and *The Dark Journey* have many female characters whose lives bear little resemblance to Green's, except that they were all victims of powerful emotions, obsessions, tending towards violence, insanity, and suicide. Writing, for Green, was itself an obsession and a necessity, the only means for him to maintain his psychological equilibrium, and he saw it as a means of exorcising the demons of his divided self. And so his plots moved ever closer to autobiography, as in *The Strange River*, which portrays characters incapable of violent actions—a novel dealing with a man who, in trying to discover his true identity, discovers his own baseness. During the 1930's and 40's, Green suffered a temporary loss of religious faith, and he sought escape by writing novels of fantasy such as *The Dreamer*, *Midnight*, *Then Shall the Dust Return*, and *If I Were You*. He then returned to the exploration of his emotional bias in the novel *Moïra* and the play *South*, both tragic stories played out against the violence of the American South, and in *The Transgressor*, *Each in His Darkness*, and *The Other One*.

While some critics have called him a "man of the Middle Ages," an anachronistic solitary obsessed by the temptations of the devil, Green has turned his spiritual-carnal conflicts into powerful and candid psychological studies, sharply focused within the sensibilities of its central figures, rich in vivid imagery with symbolic overtones, and expressed with an intensity which, at times, makes for painful reading. Some scholars believe, however, that Green's journals and autobiographies, which offer fascinating studies of the relations between life and art, will remain the most valuable of his works.

—Glenn S. Burne

GUILLÉN, (Pedro) Jorge. Spanish. Born in Valladolid, 18 January 1893. Educated at the Instituto de Valladolid, 1903-09; Maison Perreyre, Fribourg, Switzerland, 1909-11; University of Madrid, 1911-13; University of Granada, 1913, M.A.; Dr. of Letters (University of Madrid), 1924. Married 1) Germain Cahen in 1921 (died, 1947), one daughter and one son; 2) Irene Mochi-Sismondi in 1961. Lecturer in Spanish, the Sorbonne, Paris, 1917-23, and Oxford University, 1929-31; Professor, University of Murcia, 1926-29, and University of Seville, 1931-38; jailed in 1936, and left Spain, 1938: then taught at Middlebury College, Vermont, 1938-39, and McGill University, Montreal, 1939-40; Professor of Spanish, Wellesley College, Massachusetts, 1940-58, then emeritus. Charles Eliot Norton Lecturer, Harvard University, Cambridge, Massachusetts, 1957, 1958; also taught or lectured at Yale University, New Haven, Connecticut, 1947, Colegio de Mexico, 1950, University of California, Berkeley, 1951, Ohio State University, Columbus, 1952-53, University of the Andes, Bogota, 1961, University of Puerto Rico, Rio Piedras, 1962, 1964, University of Pittsburgh, 1966, and University of California, San Diego, 1968. Recipient: Guggenheim Fellowship, 1954; American Academy Award, 1955; City of Florence Poetry Prize, 1957; Etna-Taormina Prize, 1959; San Luca Prize, 1964; Bennett Prize (*Hudson Review*), 1975; Cervantes Prize, 1976; Feltrinelli Prize, 1977; Alfonso Reyes Prize (Mexico), 1977; Ollin Yoliztli Prize (Mexico), 1982. Address: 9 Windermere Park, Arlington, Massachusetts 02174, U.S.A. *Died 6 February 1984.*

PUBLICATIONS

Verse

Cántico. Madrid, Revista de Occidente, 1928; revised edition, Madrid, Cruz y Raya, 1936; revised edition, Mexico City, Litoral, 1945; complete edition, Buenos Aires, Sudamericana, 1950; as *Cántico: A Selection*, translated by Norman Thomas di Giovanni, London, Deutsch, and Boston, Little Brown, 1965.
Clamor (Maremágnum, ...que van a dar en la mar, A la altura de las circunstancias). Buenos Aires, Sudamericana, 3 vols., 1957-63.
Homenaje. Milan, All'Insegna del Pesce d'Oro, 1967.
Affirmation: A Bilingual Anthology, edited and translated by Julian Palley. Norman, University of Oklahoma Press, 1968.
Aire nuestro (Cántico, Clamor, Homenaje). Milan, All'Insegna del Pesce d'Oro, 1968.
Guirnalda civil. Cambridge, Massachusetts, Halty Ferguson, 1970.
Y otros poemas. Buenos Aires, Muchnik, 1973.
Guillén on Guillén: The Poetry and the Poet. Princeton, New Jersey, Princeton University Press, 1979.
Final. 1981.

Other

Federico en persona: Semblanza y epistolario (on García Lorca).   Buenos Aires, Emecé, 1959.
El argumento de la obra.   Milan, All'Insegna del Pesce d'Oro, 1961.
Lenguaje y poesía.   Madrid, Revista de Occidente, 1962; as *Language and Poetry: Some Poets of Spain*, Cambridge, Massachusetts, Harvard University Press, 1961.
En torno a Gabriel Miró: Breve epistolario.   Madrid, Arte y Bibliofilía, 1970.

Translator, *El cementerio marino*, by Paul Valéry.   1930.

*

Critical Studies: *A Generation of Spanish Poets* by C.B. Morris, London, Cambridge University Press, 1969; *Luminous Reality: The Poetry of Guillén* edited by Ivar Ivask and Juan Marichal, Norman, University of Oklahoma Press, 1969; *Poesía de Guillén* by Andrew P. Debicki, Madrid, Gredos, 1973; *The Vibrant Silence in Guillén's "Aire nuestro"* by Florence L. Yudin, Chapel Hill, University of North Carolina Department of Romance Languages, 1974; *Cántico de Guillén y aire nuestro* by Joaquin Casalduero, Madrid, Gredos, 1974; *La obra poética de Guillén* by Oreste Macrí, Barcelona, Ariel, 1976.

*   *   *

The poetry of Jorge Guillén is characterized by perspective, intelligence, and pluralism; its underpinnings—correlation, synthesis, contrast—support a dynamics which spans the gamut of human experience. The five volumes of collected poetry, *Aire nuestro I-V* (Our Common Air) sustain a masterful dialectic in which the air we breathe is Guillén's planetary metaphor for the fullest realization of individual and collective potential.

Guillén's poetic vision embraces esthetics, history, linguistics, and philosophy, from a focus which uncovers their hidden correspondences. His considerable journalistic writings and literary essays complement and explicate the poet's multi-faceted art.

Among the five books, *Cántico* has received the widest critical and popular attention. Its reception established Guillén as a major voice in contemporary Spanish poetry, and it remains the favorite of scholars and editors. In the present writer's opinion, this singular emphasis has delayed comprehensive studies of the entire opus; and it has also tended to distract attention from the magnitude of Guillén's achievement. While each volume published has its unique poetic climate, the complete works show an incontestable organic unity: both the poetic modes and their expression speak for continuity. In the lush weave of his poetry, Guillén explains the creative process as basically open and provisional. Similarly, life and death, harmony and chaos, speech and silence, seen from kaleidoscopic perspective, may only be dislodged facets of a sliding reality.

For Guillén, great poetry means the absence of an historical first-person; he demands an objective "I," who can filter and transpose lived experience. By situating his texts on multiple planes, from the quotidian to the epiphanic, Guillén's narrators dispose the mind and sensibility to experience the "maravilla suficiente" (sufficient marvel) of full physical existence. From this attentive, exultant observation, the "I" of *Cántico* postulates global sufficiency: "El mundo está bien/ Hecho" (The world is well made); some fifty years later, the narrator of *Final* recalls and amplifies: "El universo es quien 'está bien hecho' " (The universe is the one that is well made).

Love centers Guillén's world: it is the vital relationship which disposes reality for the poet's recreation.

¡Amor! Ni tú ni yo,
Nosotros, y por él
Todas las maravillas
En que el ser llega a ser.

(Love! Not you nor I, We, and for such love all the marvels with which one's being becomes existence.) Guillén celebrates liberated sexuality and erotic love with enthusiasm unmatched in Spanish poetry. Throughout 2,500 pages, the beloved is vibrantly present, physically and spiritually sharing a precious oasis, yet herself a full person. Complementing these hymns to love, Guillén represents writing as another co-existence of equals, whether in tribute to the poets of the past (*Homenaje*), or in creative complicity with his most real interlocutor—"Ese contemporáneo....El único lector que tiennes faz a faz" (That contemporary....The only reader whom you have face to face).

Past and present coalesce, bifurcate, and clash in Guillén's perspectivistic art: "La Historia es sólo voluntad del hombre" (History is only man's will). Of the five volumes, *Clamor* is the one which most forcefully addresses contemporary society; its dominant notes alternate between protest and satire; its message, uncompromising against tyranny, sympathizes with human limitations. But each of the other four books also examines critically the forces which undermine and diminish man's potential for creative survival on our planet, and in his particular historical moment ("Time of Crisis"). Most importarly, taken as a whole, Guillén's masterpiece orchestrates a global design in which the prospect for the future is a resounding commitment to re-humanization: "Paz, queramos paz" (Peace, let us wish for peace). While such an imperative has its bitter irony, the human values conveyed epitomize Jorge Guillén's unique accomplishment: a hopeful poetry of open time.

—Florence L. Yudin

HACKS, Peter. German. Born in Breslau, 21 March 1928. Educated at the University of Munich, Ph.D. 1951. Married Anna Elisabeth Wiede in 1955. Emigrated to East Germany: free-lance writer. Recipient: GDR Ministry of Culture Lessing Prize, 1956; Critics Prize (Germany), 1972; GDR National Prize, 1977. Address: c/o Akademie der Künste, 104 Berlin, East Germany.

PUBLICATIONS

Plays

Eröffnung des indischen Zeitalters (produced Munich, 1954). Included in *Theaterstücke*, 1957; revised version, as *Columbus*, in *Ausgewählte Dramen 1*, 1972.
Die Schlacht bei Lobositz (produced Berlin, 1956). Included in *Theaterstücke*, 1957.
Der Held der westlichen Welt, with Anna Wiede, from the play *The Playboy of the Western World* by J.M. Synge (produced Berlin, 1956). Included in *Stücke*, by Synge, Leipzig, Reclam, 1972.
Das Volksbuch vom Herzog Ernst (produced Mannheim, 1967). Included in *Theaterstücke*, 1957.
Theaterstücke. Berlin, Aufbau, 1957.
Der Müller von Sanssouci (produced Berlin, 1958). Included in *Fünf Stücke*, 1965.

Die Kindermörderin, from a play by H.L. Wagner (produced Wuppertal, 1959). Included in *Zwei Bearbeitungen*, 1963.

Die Sorgen und die Macht (produced Senftenberg, 1960; revised version, produced Berlin, 1962). Included in *Fünf Stücke*, 1965.

Der Frieden, from a play by Aristophanes (produced Berlin, 1962). Included in *Zwei Bearbeitungen*, 1963.

Zwei Bearbeitungen. Frankfurt, Suhrkamp, 1963.

Die schöne Helena, from the operetta libretto by Meilhac and Halévy (produced Berlin, 1964). Included in *Stücke nach Stücken*, 1965.

Fünf Stücke. Frankfurt, Suhrkamp, 1965.

Stücke nach Stücken. Berlin, Aufbau, 1965.

Polly; oder, Die Bataille am Bluewater Creek, from the play by John Gay (produced Halle, 1966). Included in *Stücke nach Stücken*, 1965.

Moritz Tassow (produced Berlin, 1965). Included in *Vier Komödien*, 1971.

Amphitryon (produced Göttingen, 1968; New York, 1970). Berlin, Eulenspiegel, 1969.

Margarete in Aix (produced Basel, 1969). Included in *Vier Komödien*, 1971.

Omphale (produced Frankfurt, 1970). Included in *Vier Komödien*, 1971; revised version, music by S. Matthus (produced Berlin, 1975).

Vier Komödien. Frankfurt, Suhrkamp, 1971.

Ausgewählte Dramen 1-3. Berlin, Aufbau, 3 vols., 1972-81.

Noch einen Löffel Gift, Liebling?, music by S. Matthus (produced Berlin, 1972). Included in *Oper*, 1975.

Adam und Eva (produced Dresden, 1973). Dusseldorf, Claassen, 1976.

Die Vögel, from the play by Aristophanes (produced Dresden, 1981). Included in *Oper*, 1975.

Oper. Berlin, Aufbau, 1975.

Prexaspes (produced Dresden, 1975). Included in *Ausgewählte Dramen 2*, 1976.

Das Jahrmarktsfest zu Plundersweilern, from the play by Goethe (produced Berlin 1975). With *Rosie träumt*, Berlin, Aufbau, 1976.

Rosie träumt, from the plays by Hroswitha von Gandersheim (produced Berlin, 1975). With *Das Jahrmarktsfest zu Plundersweilern*, Berlin, Aufbau, 1976.

Ein Gespräch im Hause Stein über den abwesenden Herrn von Goethe (produced Dresden, 1976). Included in *Ausgewählte Dramen 2*, 1976; as *Conversations about an Absent Lover* (produced Dublin, 1977; as *Charlotte*, produced New York, 1980).

Die Fische (produced Göttingen, 1978). Included in *Sechs Dramen*, 1978.

Sechs Dramen (includes *Numa*). Dusseldorf, Claassen, 1978.

Senecas Tod (produced Berlin, 1980). Included in *Sechs Dramen*, 1978.

Armer Ritter (juvenile; produced Göttingen, 1978). Included in *Märchendramen*, Berlin, Henschel, 1980.

Pandora, from a play by Goethe (produced Göttingen, 1982). Berlin, Aufbau, 1981.

Musen (produced Magdeburg, 1983). Included in *Ausgewählte Dramen 3*, 1981.

Barby, from a play by R. Strahl (produced Halle, 1983).

Die Kinder (juvenile; produced Greifswald, 1984).

Radio Plays: *Der gestoblene Ton*, 1953; *Das Fell der Zeit*, 1954; *Geschichte eines alten Wittibers in Jahre 1637*, 1957.

Television Plays: *Die unadlige Gräfin*, 1957-58; *Falsche Bärte und Nasen*, 1961.

Fiction

Der Schuhu und die fliegende Prinzessin. Berlin, Eulenspiegel, 1966.

Die Dinge in Buta. Berlin, Berliner Handpresse, 1974.

Verse

Lieder zur Stücken. Berlin, Eulenspiegel, 1968.
Poesiealbum. Berlin, Neues Leben, 1972.

Other

Das Windloch (juvenile). Gütersloh, Bertelsmann, 1956.
Das Turmverlies (juvenile). Berlin, Kinderbuch, 1962.
Der Flohmarkt (juvenile). Berlin, Kinderbuch, 1965.
Der Affe Oswald (juvenile). Munich, Parabel, 1971.
Der Bär auf dem Försterball (juvenile). Cologne, Middelhauve, 1972.
Die Katze wäscht den Omnibus (juvenile). Berlin, Kinderbuch, 1972.
Das Poetische: Ansätze zu einer postrevolutionären Dramaturgie. Frankfurt, Suhrkamp, 1972.
Kathrinchen ging spazieren (juvenile). Cologne, Middelhauve, 1973.
Lieder, Briefe, Gedichte. Wuppertal, Hammer, 1974.
Die Sonne (juvenile). Berlin, Kinderbuch, 1975.
Meta Morfoss (juvenile). Cologne, Middelhauve, 1975.
Die Massgaben der Kunst: Gesammelte Aufsätze. Berlin, Henschel, 1977.
Das musikalische Nashorn (juvenile). Berlin, Kinderbuch, 1978.
Armer Ritter (juvenile). Berlin, Kinderbuch, 1979.
Geschichten von Henriette und Onkel Titus (juvenile). Berlin, Kinderbuch, 1979.
Leberecht am schiefen Fenster (juvenile). Berlin, Kinderbuch, 1979.
Der Mann mit dem schwärzlichen Hintern (juvenile). Berlin, Kinderbuch, 1980.
Jules Ratte (juvenile). Berlin, Kinderbuch, 1981.
Essais. Leipzig, Reclam, 1983.

*

Critical Studies: *Hacks* by Peter Schütze, Kronberg, Scriptor, 1976; *Die Stücke von Hacks* by Winfried Schleyer, Stuttgart, Klett, 1976; *"Enfant Terrible" of Contemporary East German Drama: Hacks in His Role as Adaptor and Innovator* by Judith R. Scheid, Bonn, Bouvier, 1977; *Hacks: Leben und Werk* by Christoph Trilse, Berlin, Das Europäische Buch, 1980; "Hacks" by Michael Mitchell in *The Writer and Society in the GDR*, Tayport, Fife, Hurron Press, 1983.

* * *

Peter Hacks's first four plays, written both before and after he emigrated from West to East Germany in 1955, follow, although not slavishly, the Brechtian method of epic theatre, using historical figures to present models of historical processes seen from a Marxist perspective, while at the same time revealing the workings of class society. In them his commitment to Marxist theory is demonstrated both with an intellectual wit that has become the hallmark of his use of language and with an awareness of the possibilities, especially comic, of the stage. In his next two major plays he attacked contemporary subjects: the theme of *Die Sorgen und die Macht*, for example, is the conflict between the demands for quality and quantity in production during the GDR's reconstruction period. With its positive moral it looks like the kind of play the authorities were trying to encourage, but ran into criticism on a number of counts, in particular for the excessively subjective motivation of the hero, whose exemplary development is fuelled by the energy of his own temperament rather than by class consciousness. The other main criticism was aroused by his treatment of the contrast between ideal (= future communist society) and reality (= drab present of the GDR).

This contrast, in a more generalised and thus more acceptable form, is one of the central themes of his later "classical" plays for, since the early 1960's, Hacks has rejected epic theatre for a "proletarian classicism." He sees this as the aesthetic correlation of the GDR's own view of itself as a "developed socialist society": if the majority have been converted there is no longer any need to preach at them and, therefore, no need for epic theatre. These "classical" plays use mythical and historical material and fall roughly into two groups—strict ones observing the unities of time, place, and action and written throughout in verse (e.g., *Amphitryon, Adam und Eva, Senecas Tod*) and others with complex plots, a multiplicity of characters, and a mixture of prose and verse (e.g., *Margarete in Aix, Prexaspes, Numa*). The former concentrate on great characters as demonstrations of human potential while the latter deal with questions of society, history, and politics. All of Hacks's plays are basically in the comic mode which, with his proletarian classicism and the poetic theatre he has revived, he sees as an expression of the "self-confidence of the [working] class."

Highly respected in the East, he is still occasionally criticised for his somewhat abstract humanism; widely played in the West, his classicism is there sometimes seen as a retreat from the dangers, for an Eastern bloc writer, of contemporary subjects into a realm of highbrow entertainment. This is partly true, but only partly as he started to develop his classical theory before the contemporary plays which brought official displeasure, and his classicism is a style which clearly suits his nature and talents. These plays celebrate the richness of human creativity which only full emancipation will fully release. However, Hacks no longer sees that as happening at some real point of future historical development: it has receded into the mists of the ideal. But the conflicts he portrays between "emancipated individuals and a not yet fully emancipated society" are not tragic; the comic mode remains as evidence of his basically optimistic and materialist view of man.

—Michael Mitchell

HANDKE, Peter. Austrian. Born in Griffen, Carinthia, 6 December 1942. Educated at a school in Griffen, 1948-54; Marianum Catholic Boys School, Tanzenberg bei Klagenfurt, 1954-59; Klagenfurt Gymnasium, 1959-61; University of Graz, 1961-65. Married Libgart Schwarz in 1966 (separated, 1972), one daughter. Full-time writer since 1966; co-founder, Verlag der Autoren, 1969. Recipient: Free Theatre Hauptmann Prize (Berlin), 1967; Schiller Prize (Mannheim), 1972; Steiermark Prize, 1972; Büchner Prize, 1973; Kafka Prize (refused), 1979. Address: c/o Suhrkamp Verlag, Postfach 4229, 6000 Frankfurt am Main, Germany.

PUBLICATIONS

Plays

Publikumsbeschimpfung (produced Frankfurt, 1966).   Included in *Publikumsbeschimp-fung und andere Sprechstücke*, 1966; as *Offending the Audience* (produced London, 1970; New York, 1974), in *Kaspar and Other Plays*, 1969.
Selbstbezichtigung (produced Oberhausen, 1966).   Included in *Publikumsbeschimpfung und andere Sprechstücke*, 1966; as *Self-Accusation* (produced New York, 1970; Lon-

don, 1973), in *Kaspar and Other Plays*, 1969.

Weissagung (produced Oberhausen, 1966). Included in *Publikumsbeschimpfung und andere Sprechstücke*, 1966; as *Prophecy* (produced London, 1972), in *The Ride Across Lake Constance and Other Plays*, 1976.

Publikumsbeschimpfung und andere Sprechstücke. Frankfurt, Suhrkamp, 1966.

Hilferufe (produced Stockholm, 1967). Included in *Stücke 1*, 1972; as *Calling for Help* (produced London, 1972), in *The Ride Across Lake Constance and Other Plays*, 1976.

Kaspar (produced Frankfurt, 1968). Frankfurt, Suhrkamp, 1968; translated as *Kaspar* (produced New York and London, 1973), in *Kaspar and Other Plays*, 1969; published separately, London, Methuen, 1972.

Das Mündel will Vormund sein (produced Frankfurt, 1969). Included in *Prosa, Gedichte, Theaterstücke, Hörspiel, Aufsätze*, 1969; as *My Foot My Tutor* (produced London, 1971), in *The Ride Across Lake Constance and Other Plays*, 1976; in *Shakespeare the Sadist and Others*, London, Methuen, 1977.

Kaspar and Other Plays (includes *Offending the Audience* and *Self-Accusation*). New York, Farrar Straus, 1969; *Offending the Audience and Self-Accusation*, London, Methuen, 1971.

Quodlibet (produced Basel, 1970). Frankfurt, Verlag der Autoren, 1970; translated as *Quodlibet*, in *The Ride Across Lake Constance and Other Plays*, 1976.

Hörspiel No. 2, 3, und 4. Frankfurt, Verlag der Autoren, 1970.

Wind und Meer: 4 Hörspiele. Frankfurt, Suhrkamp, 1970.

Der Ritt über den Bodensee (produced Berlin, 1971). Frankfurt, Verlag der Autoren, 1970; as *The Ride Across Lake Constance* (produced New York, 1972; London, 1973), London, Methuen, 1973; in *The Ride Across Lake Constance and Other Plays*, 1976.

Stücke 1-2. Frankfurt, Suhrkamp, 2 vols., 1972-73.

Die Unvernünftigen sterben aus (produced Zurich, 1974). Frankfurt, Suhrkamp, 1973; as *They Are Dying Out* (produced London, 1976), London, Methuen, 1975; in *The Ride Across Lake Constance and Other Plays*, 1976.

Falsche Bewegung (screenplay). Frankfurt, Suhrkamp, 1975.

The Ride Across Lake Constance and Other Plays (includes *Prophecy*, *Calling for Help*, *My Foot My Tutor*, *Quodlibet*, *They Are Dying Out*). New York, Farrar Straus, 1976.

Über die Dörfer: Dramatisches Gedichte (produced Salzburg, 1982). Frankfurt, Suhrkamp, 1981.

Screenplays: *Falsche Bewegung*; *Die linkshändige Frau*, 1977; *Die Angst des Tormanns beim Elfmeter*; *Der kurze Brief zum langen Abschied*.

Fiction

Die Hornissen. Frankfurt, Suhrkamp, 1966.

Der Hausierer. Frankfurt, Suhrkamp, 1967.

Begrüssung des Aufsichtsrats: Prosatexte. Salzburg, Residenz, 1967.

Die Angst des Tormanns beim Elfmeter. Frankfurt, Suhrkamp, 1970; as *The Goalie's Anxiety at the Penalty Kick*, New York, Farrar Straus, 1972; London, Methuen, 1977.

Der kurze Brief zum langen Abschied. Frankfurt, Suhrkamp, 1972; as *Short Letter, Long Farewell*, New York, Farrar Straus, 1974; London, Methuen, 1977.

Wünschloses Unglück. Salzburg, Residenz, 1972; as *A Sorrow Beyond Dreams*, New York, Farrar Straus, 1975; London, Souvenir Press, 1976.

Die Stunde der wahren Empfindung. Frankfurt, Suhrkamp, 1975; as *A Moment of True Feeling*, New York, Farrar Straus, 1977.

Die linkshändige Frau. Frankfurt, Suhrkamp, 1976; as *The Left-Handed Woman*, New York, Farrar Straus, 1978; London, Methuen, 1980.

Langsame Heimkehr. Frankfurt, Suhrkamp, 1979; as *Slow Homecoming*, New York, Farrar Straus, 1983.
Kindergeschichte. Frankfurt, Suhrkamp, 1981.

Verse

Die Innenwelt der Aussenwelt der Innenwelt. Frankfurt, Suhrkamp, 1969; as *The Innerworld of the Outerworld of the Innerworld*, New York, Seabury Press, 1974.
Deutsche Gedichte. Frankfurt, Euphorion, 1969.
Das Ende des Flanierens. Vienna, Davidpress, 1976.

Other

Prosa, Gedichte, Theaterstücke, Hörspiel, Aufsätze. Frankfurt, Suhrkamp, 1969.
Chronik der laufenden Ereignisse. Frankfurt, Verlag der Autoren, 1971.
Ich bin ein Bewohner des Elfenbeinturms. Frankfurt, Suhrkamp, 1972.
Wiener Läden, illustrated by Didi Petrikat. Munich, Hanser, 1974.
Als das Wünschen noch geholfen hat. Frankfurt, Suhrkamp, 1974; as *Nonsense and Happiness*, New York, Urizen, 1976.
Der Rand der Wörter: Erzählungen, Gedichte, Stücke, edited by Heinz F. Schafroth. Stuttgart, Reclam, 1975.
Das Gewicht der Welt: Ein Journal (November 1975-März 1977). Salzburg, Residenz, 1977; as *The Weight of the World*, New York, Farrar Straus, 1983.
Die Lehre der Sainte-Victoire. Frankfurt, Suhrkamp, 1980.
Die Geschichte des Bleistifts. Salzburg, Residenz, 1982.

Editor, *Der gewöhnliche Schrecken: Neue Horrorgeschichten.* Salzburg, Residenz, 1969.
Editor, *Charakter; Der Schwur des Martin Krist, Dokument: Frühe Erzählung*, by Franz Nabl. Salzburg, Residenz, 1975.

*

Bibliography: *Handke: An Annotated Bibliography* by June Schlueter and Ellis Finger, New York, Garland, 1982.

Critical Studies: *Handke: Theatre and Anti-Theatre* by Nicholas Hern, London, Wolff, 1971, New York, Ungar, 1972; *Über Handke* edited by Michael Scharang, Frankfurt, Suhrkamp, 1972; *Handke* by R. Nagele and R. Voris, Munich, Beck, 1978; *Handke* edited by Heinz Ludwig Arnold, Munich, Text und Kritik, 1978; *Handke: Ansätze, Analysen, Anmerkungen* edited by Manfred Jurgensen, Bern, Francke, 1979; *The Plays and Novels of Handke* by June Schlueter, Pittsburgh, University of Pittsburgh Press, 1981; "The 'Grazer Gruppe': Handke and Wolfgang Bauer" by Hugh Rorrison, in *Modern Austrian Writing* edited by Alan Best and Hans Wolfschütz, London Wolff, 1980; *New German Dramatists* by Denis Calandra, London, Methuen, 1983.

*　　*　　*

Peter Handke is the most successful experimental writer of the generation that emerged in Germany in the late 1960's. Provocation was his early stock-in-trade. His first stage piece, *Offending the Audience*, was a diatribe for four voices—no plot, no characters, no setting—which attacked both conventional dramatic form and technique and the complacent assumptions of the normal middle-brow theatregoer. At the meeting of the "Gruppe 47" in 1966 in

Princeton he publicly diagnosed "description-impotence" in this group which included the major writers of the day, Heinrich Böll and Günter Grass among them. Excessive descriptive analysis of recent German history had, he suggested, made artistic eunuchs of them all. Handke signalled his rejection of public in favour of private concerns by claiming the ivory tower as his preferred domicile, and by advocating the intuitive atmospheric plays of Ödön von Horváth as an antidote to the pervasive influence of Brecht's political theatre.

His own plays are minimal, quirky, but effective pieces. *Kaspar* introduces a clown figure who can utter only one sentence. Voices on loudspeakers proceed to deconstruct that sentence and drill him in proper speech, and ideas to match. It is a theatrical metaphor for the danger of indoctrination by media. After the "speech-play" came a play without words, *My Foot My Tutor* in which two characters mime a series of actions from tying laces to topping turnips with a ferocious agricultural guillotine. Each act turns into a test in which the eager junior is vanquished by his smug superior, this time a metaphor for man's insatiable competitiveness. In *The Ride Across Lake Constance*, Handke equipped four old-time movie stars with a dialogue of disconnected clichés and left them to posture plotlessly on the stage. The result was stylish comedy.

Handke's novels too are experimental, tortuously fragmented and oblique at first, for example in *Die Hornissen*. This changes, and *A Sorrow Beyond Dreams* is a lucidly self-aware reflection on his mother's suicide at 51. Here the autobiographical stratum in his writing surfaces for the first time as he charts her life from the backwoods of Carinthia to bomb-devastated Berlin and back. Handke had escaped the pettiness and drudgery that slowly killed his mother and we can see his writing as a means of self-definition, his nomadic literary life as self-emancipation. *Short Letter, Long Farewell* strews fractured reflections of the break-up of his marriage through the account of a trip across the U.S.A. *The Left-Handed Woman* copes, like himself, with a single-parent family. The *enfant terrible* who left Graz for West Berlin and finally Paris has now returned to Salzburg, and a mellow, positive note resonates in his recent works. His last novel is called *Slow Homecoming*.

Über die Dörfer, a dramatic poem, brings Gregor, the gifted brother, back to his native valley to the brother and sister who stayed at home. There are confrontations but no real dialogue, just extended monologues on their hopes for and disappointments in each other. When all is said and acrimony complete, their enigmatic female mentor Nova points in a ten page peroration to the true reality. The blue of the mountains really exists, she says, the brown of the pistol-holster does not. "Heaven is great, the village is great....Eternal peace is possible....Go forth into the villages." Handke has returned to the world of Stifter and found in nature a truth beyond religion.

—Hugh Rorrison

HAVEL, Václav. Czech. Born in Prague, 5 October 1936. Educated at a technical college, 1955-57; Academy of Art, Prague, 1962-67. Military service, 1957-59. Married to Olga Splíchalová. Stagehand, Divadlo ABC theatre, Prague, 1959; stagehand, assistant to the artistic director, literary manager (dramaturge), and resident playwright, Theater Na zábradlí [Theatre on the Balustrade], Prague, 1960-69; worker at brewery, Trutnov, Bohemia, early 1970's; writings judged subversive: passport confiscated, 1969; imprisoned for brief terms 1977, 1978, and in 1979 sentenced to 4½ years imprisonment: released because of illness, 1983.

HAVEL

Recipient: Obie Award, 1968, 1970; Austrian State Prize, 1969; Palach Prize, 1980. Honorary doctorate: York University, Toronto, 1982. Address: U dejvického rybníčku 4, 16000 Prague 6, Czechoslovakia.

PUBLICATIONS

Plays

Autostop [The Hitchhike], with Ivan Vyskočil (produced Prague, 1961).   Prague, Dilia, 1961.
Nejlepší rocky pani Hermanové [The Best "Rock" of Mrs. Herman], with Miloš Macourek (produced Prague, 1962).
Zahradní slavnost (produced Prague, 1963).   Prague, Orbis, 1964; as *The Garden Party*, London, Cape, 1969.
Vyrozumění (produced Prague, 1965).   Prague, Dilia, 1965; as *The Memorandum* (produced New York, 1968; London, 1970), London, Cape, 1967; New York, Grove Press, 1980.
Ztížená možnost soustředění (produced Prague, 1968).   Prague, Orbis, 1968; as *The Increased Difficulty of Concentration* (produced New York, 1969; Richmond, Surrey, 1978), London, Cape, 1972.
Spiklenci [The Conspirators] (produced Baden-Baden, 1974).   Included in *Hry*, 1977.
Audience (produced Vienna, 1976).   Included in *Hry*, 1977; as *Conversation*, in *Index*, Autumn 1976.
Vernisáž (produced Vienna, 1976).   Included in *Hry*, 1977; as *Private View* (produced New York, 1984).
Zebrácká opera [The Beggar's Opera] (produced Terst, 1976).   Included in *Hry*, 1977.
Hry 1970-1976 (includes *Spiklenci, Zebrácká opera, Horský hotel* [A Mountain Hotel], *Audience, Vernisáž*).   Toronto, 68 Publishers, 1977.
Horský hotel (produced Vienna, 1981).   Included in *Hry*, 1977.
Protest (produced Hamburg, 1978; New York, 1983).   Excerpts in *Proměny 16, 3, 1979*.
Chyba [The Mistake] (produced Stockholm, 1983).   Published in *Svědectví 18*, 1983.

Radio Play: *Anděl strážný* [The Guardian Angel], 1969 (Germany).

Television Play: *Motýl na anténě* [Butterfly on the Antenna].

Other

Josef Capek, with Vera Ptáčková.   Prague, Divadelní Ústav, 1963.
Protokoly [Protokols] (miscellany).   Prague, Mladá Fronta, 1966.

*

Bibliography: in *Slovník ceskych spisovatelu*, Toronto, 68 Publishers, 1982.

Critical Studies: *Czech Drama since World War II* by Paul I. Trensky, White Plains, New York, Sharpe, 1978; *The Silenced Theatre: Czech Playwrights Without a Stage*, Toronto, University of Toronto Press, 1979, and "Havel, A Writer for Today's Season," in *World Literature Today 55*, Summer 1981, both by Marketa Goetz-Stankiewicz.

*   *   *

Ironically, recognition in the West of Václav Havel's status as a major contemporary dramatist has been partly obscured by the attention given to his political and personal experiences: his participation in the Charter 77 human rights movement, the official ban on publication of his works, and his harassment and imprisonment by the Czech authorities.

Havel's remarkable literary output nonetheless gives a highly individual shape to some of the most central literary, philosophical, and political subjects of our time, providing an acute and eloquent diagnosis of the problems of human social interaction, East or West. The work of this writer from the cross-roads of Europe uniquely combines fundamental ethical concern with high theatrical sophistication, profound political insights with sparkling humour, and engagement in contemporary issues with a classical sense of form. At the core of Havel's writings there is an analysis of three interrelated themes: the relationship between man and the system he lives under, the progressive alienation of the individual from himself and others, and language as a medium which both rules man and is his instrument of power. These serious socio-philosophic matters are dealt with, however, with humour and high entertainment, for Havel's plays carry their remarkable moral, intellectual, and political burden lightly. Their combination of original thought and striking wit has brought them success in the West, from London to Stockholm, from Vienna to New York.

Havel's plays up to the present can be seen as roughly forming three triads, each primarily focussed on one of the above issues. *The Garden Party*, *The Memorandum* and *Horský hotel* deal with the phenomenon of language. In *The Garden Party* the protagonist achieves a new consciousness by acquiring an "official" language. Scoring politico-linguistic victories over his colleagues, he rises to bureaucratic fame. In *The Memorandum* Havel explores language as an instrument of power in a more explicit way by actually inventing a synthetic language and then demonstrating how it acts to create and perpetuate a system that moulds man into a well-functioning machine-part, crushing any trace of the unpredictable, the imaginative, the non-mechanistic. By the time Havel writes *Horský hotel*, the total mechanization of communication has become the very subject of the play. A number of phrases are distributed regularly throughout the action but the characters who speak them are interchangeable. Language remains autonomous, personality disintegrates.

The second triad more fully reveals Havel's versatility, as well as his basic concern with ethics. *The Increased Difficulty of Concentration* (akin to Stoppard's *Jumpers*) presents a protagonist who has been selected as a sample of computerized behaviour patterns. As his actions become increasingly mechanical and predictable, the computer recording his experiences develops emotional "human" qualities. *Spiklenci* is a wry reflection on the cyclical nature of revolutions and the suspect motivations of its makers. In contrast to this, his dramatic adaptation of John Gay's ballad opera *The Beggar's Opera* moves the theme of power play into the twilight zone where representatives of the law and the underworld meet, seem to clash, then ambiguously collaborate. Here Havel stages a scintillating game of moral juggling.

The third triad (all one-act plays) was written between 1975 and 1978, just prior to Havel's prison sentence. Staged and televised all over the Western world, these plays are all built around the semi-autobiographical "dissident" writer Vaněk (a character since taken up by two other Czech playwrights, Pavel Kohout and Pavel Landovský), who gets into situations that are both absurd and—in the context of contemporary Czechoslovakia—utterly realistic. In each play Vaněk's ethical standards are put to the test. In *Audience* a cushier job is offered in return for information for the state police files. The promise of a less harassed existence in return for certain adjustments in harmony with "normalization" is the subject of *Private View*. *Protest*, the most significant of these plays, takes on directly the issue of freedom of speech and thought. A successful, "integrated" writer, defending his accommodation with the system confronts Vaněk with a brilliant demonstration of pseudo-reasoning, perhaps the best example of perverted rationality yet displayed in the modern theare.

It remains to be seen whether Havel will achieve comparable stature as a writer of prose. His "Open Letter to President Husak" (translated in *Encounter*, September 1975), his eloquent philosophical essay "The Power of the Powerless" (published in *O svobodě a moci*, Cologne, Index, 1980), humour, and other issues, show the depth of his perceptions, ranging from analyses of the effects of a coercive political system on artistic imagination to speculations on the nature of humour. His letters from prison are due to appear in 1984.

—Marketa Goetz-Stankiewicz

HÉBERT, Anne. Canadian. Born in Sainte-Catherine-de-Fossambault, Quebec, 1 August 1916. Educated at Collège Saint-Coeur de Marie, Merici, Quebec, and Collège Notre Dame, Bellevue, Quebec. Worked for Radio Canada, 1950-53, and the National Film Board of Canada, 1953-60. Recipient: Canadian Government grant, 1954; France-Canada Prize, 1957; Devernay Prize, 1958; Canada Council grant, 1960, 1961; Guggenheim grant, 1963; Province of Quebec grant, 1965; Molson Prize, 1967; French Booksellers Prize, 1971; Governor-General's Award, 1975; French Academy award, 1975; Monaco Grand Prize, 1976; David Prize, (Quebec), 1978; Fémina Prize, 1982 (France). D.Litt.: University of Toronto, 1967. Member, Royal Society of Canada, 1960. Address: 24 rue de Pontoise, 75005 Paris, France.

PUBLICATIONS

Fiction

> *Le Torrent*. Montreal, Beauchemin, 1950; as *Le Torrent suivi de deux nouvelles inédites*, Montreal, HMH, 1963; as *The Torrent: Novellas and Short Stories*, Montreal, Harvest House, 1973.
> *Les Chambres de bois*. Paris, Seuil, 1958; as *The Silent Rooms*, Don Mills, Ontario, Musson, 1974.
> *Kamouraska*. Paris, Seuil, 1970; translated as *Kamouraska*, Don Mills, Ontario, Musson, and New York, Crown, 1973.
> *Les Enfants du sabbat*. Paris, Seuil, 1975; as *Children of the Black Sabbath*, Don Mills, Ontario, Musson, and New York, Crown, 1977.
> *Héloïse*. Paris, Seuil, 1980.
> *Les Fous de bassan*. Paris, Seuil, 1982.

Plays

> *Le Temps sauvage, La Mercière assassinée, Les Invités au procès: Théâtre*. Montreal, HMH, 1967.

Screenplays and commentaries: *Les Indes parmi nous*, 1954; *Drôle de mic-mac*, 1954; *Le Médecin du nord*, 1954; *La Canne à pêche*, 1959; *Saint-Denys-Garneau*, 1960; *Le Déficient mental*, 1960.

Radio Play: *Les Invités au procès*.

Television Plays: *Le Temps sauvage*; *La Mercière assassinée*.

HÉBERT

Verse

Les Songes en équilibre.   Montreal, L'Arbre, 1942.
Le Tombeau des rois.   Quebec, Institut Littéraire, 1953; as *The Tomb of the Kings,*
Toronto, Contact Press, 1967.
Poèmes (includes *Le Tombeau des rois* and *Mystère de la parole*).   Paris, Seuil, 1960; as
Poems, Don Mills, Ontario, Musson, 1975.
Saint-Denys-Garneau and Hébert (selected poetry), translated by F.R. Scott.   Van-
couver, Klanak Press, 1962; revised edition, 1978.

Other

Dialogue sur la traduction, with F.R. Scott, edited by Jeanne Lapointe.   Montreal,
HMH, 1970.

*

Critical Studies: *Hébert* by René Lacôte, Paris, Poètes d'Aujourd'hui, 1969; *Hébert* by Pierre
Pagé, Montreal, Fides, 1971; *Hébert et le miracle de la parole* by Jean Louis Major, Montreal,
University of Montreal, 1976; *Entre songe et parole: Structure du Tombeau des rois de Hébert*
by Pierre-Hervé Lemieux, Ottawa, University of Ottawa, 1978; *La Quête de l'équilibre dans
l'oeuvre romanesque de Hébert* by Serge A. Thériault, Hull, Quebec, Asticou, 1980.

*   *   *

As a young woman in Quebec, Anne Hébert was involved with the group responsible for *La
Releve,* a journal founded by her cousin, Hector de Saint-Denys-Garneau, and dedicated to
renewing the spiritual, artistic, and intellectual life of a province isolated from the external
world by an all-powerful jansenist Church. Thanks to this coterie and her father, Maurice, a
well-known literary critic, Hébert enjoyed a broad literary culture not then available to the
majority of her compatriots. This is reflected in her first volume of verse, *Les Songes en
équilibre.* While this now appears to the author herself childish and derivative, a far cry from
the post-surrealist poetry of France, the directness of her language and the strength of her
imagery reveal a voice strikingly different from that of her predecessors and even her contemporaries in Quebec.

The ten years following this publication, marked by a series of personal losses, exercised a
profound influence on her work. Her most famous short story, "Le Torrent," first published in
1947 as "Au Bord du torrent" and revised for inclusion as the title-piece in a volume of collected
short stories, *The Torrent,* and now taken as a paradigm of Quebec itself, conveys the sense of
dispossession characteristic of all her later writing, although, in her second volume of poetry,
The Tomb of the Kings, devoted to her confrontation with death, the final allusion to dawn
(and to a possible rebirth) shows that some hope subsists. This is usually translated, however, as
in other short stories in *The Torrent* (e.g., "L'Ange de Dominique"), by the idea that "real life is
elsewhere."

In general, the universe she creates, one of physical or temporal isolation, is redolent of
violence and despair, both heightened by the sparse, even stark, style of the author. Betrayal,
murder, incest, madness are the themes she uses to explore the limits of our existence. In *The
Tomb of the Kings* she writes: "In an ordered world, The dead below, The quick above, The
dead weary me, The quick kill me" (my translation). Some of these lines reappear in ironic
repetition throughout her work, but her world knows no such order. For her characters, there is
no absolute distinction between life and death, here and there, present and past, natural and
supernatural. The past returns to kill us (*La Mercière assassinée*); vampires, symbolic and
"real," stalk their innocent victims in Paris (*The Silent Rooms, Héloïse*); the dead haunt us
(*Kamouraska*).

167

The author leads the readers on a mythical journey, for some into their individual being, for others into the collective self of Quebec, for all into the death encaged in the heart of human experience. The mythic quality is reinforced by two elements in particular: one, the meticulous reconstitution of those actual events in Quebec history she often uses as a springboard; two, the presence, the demystification even, of many elements from fairy and folktales, e.g., the Cinderella and Sleeping Beauty stories, the ogres that people a hostile land, the Underworld.

—Maïr Verthuy

HEINESEN, William. Danish. Born in Tórshavn, Faroe Islands, 15 January 1900. Educated in commercial school, Copenhagen, 1916-19. Married Elisa Johansen in 1932; three sons. Journalist in Ringsted and Copenhagen, 1919-32, then settled in Tórshavn. Also musician and artist: Chairman, Faroese Museum of Fine Art, 1969. Recipient: Nathansen Prize, 1956; Holberg Medal, 1960; Danish-Faroese Cultural Fund Prize, 1962; Nordic Council Prize, 1965; Scandinavian Literary Prize, 1965; Aarestrup Medal, 1968. Member, Danish Academy, 1961. Address: DK-3800 Tórshavn, Faroe Islands.

PUBLICATIONS

Fiction

Stjernerne Vaagner [The Stars Awaken]. Copenhagen, Levin & Munksgaard, 1930.
Blaesende Gry [Windswept Dawn]. Copenhagen, Levin & Munksgaard, 1934; revised edition, Copenhagen, Gyldendal, 1962.
Noatun. Copenhagen, Gyldendal, 1938; as *Niels Peter*, London, Routledge, 1939.
Den sorte Gryde [The Black Cauldron]. Copenhagen, Gyldendal, 1949.
De fortabte Spillemaend. Copenhagen, Gyldendal, 1950; as *The Lost Musicians*, New York, Twayne, 1971.
Moder Syvstjerne. Copenhagen, Gyldendal, 1952; as *The Kingdom of the Earth*, New York, Twayne, 1974.
Det fortryllede Lys [The Enchanted Light]. Copenhagen, Gyldendal, 1957.
Gamaliels Besaettelse [Gamaliel's Bewitchment]. Copenhagen, Gyldendal, 1960.
Det gode Håb [The Lively Hope]. Copenhagen, Gyldendal, 1964.
Kur mod onde Ånder [Cure Against Evil Spirits]. Copenhagen, Gyldendal, 1967.
Don Juan fra Tranhuset [Don Juan from the Blubber Works]. Copenhagen, Gyldendal, 1970.
Tårnet ved verdens ende. Copenhagen, Gyldendal, 1976; as *The Tower at the End of the World*, Findhorn, Morayshire, Thule, 1980; Forest Grove, Oregon, Hydra, 1981.
Her skal danses: seks fortaellinger [Let the Dance Go On: Six Stories]. Copenhagen, Gyldendal, 1980.
The Winged Darkness and Other Stories. New York, Irvington, 1982.

Play

Ranafelli, in *Varthin*. 1929.

Verse

Arktiske Elegier [Arctic Elegies]. Copenhagen, Levin & Munksgaard, 1921.
Høbjergning ved Havet [Haymaking by the Sea] Copenhagen, Levin & Munksgaard, 1924.
Sange mod Vaardybet [Songs at the Spring Deep]. Copenhagen, Levin & Munksgaard, 1927.
Den dunkle Sol [The Dark Sun]. Copenhagen, Levin & Munksgaard, 1936.
Digte i Udvalg [Selected Poems]. Copenhagen, Gyldendal, 1955.
Hymne og Harmsang [Hymn and Song of Indignation]. Copenhagen, Gyldendal, 1961.
Panorame med Regnbue [Panorama with Rainbow]. Copenhagen, Gyldendal, 1972.
Arctis, translated by Anne Born. Findhorn, Morayshire, Thule, and Forest Grove, Oregon, Hydra, 1980.

Other

Tann deiliga Havn [Fair Tórshavn]. Tórshavn, Jacobsens Bokahandil, 1953.
Det dyrebare Liv [Precious Life] (biography of J.F. Jacobsen). Copenhagen, Gyldendal, 1958.
Førayar, Gandaoyggjarnar/Faerøerne, de magiske Øer/The Faroe Islands, The Magic Islands, photographs by Gerard Franceschi. Copenhagen, Rhodos, 1971.

*

Critical Studies: *Three Faroese Novelists* by Hedin Brønner, New York, Twayne, 1973; *Heinesen* by W. Glyn Jones, New York, Twayne, 1974.

*   *   *

William Heinesen is one of the outstanding poets and novelists of Scandinavia this century, distinguished for the breadth of his imagination and for his linguistic and stylistic brilliance. After moving from his native Tórshavn to Copenhagen, he published exclusively lyric poetry in the 1920's, echoing the neo-Romantic and Symbolist poetry of the turn of the century, but clearly influenced by Johannes V. Jensen, a writer who has remained a major source of inspiration to him throughout his life. Originally elegiac and expressive of an awareness of the passage of time and the constant presence of death, the poems gradually develop a more optimistic and dynamic approach, though still bearing the traces of religious speculation caused by the death of the poet's brother in 1927. The 1930's saw a change, and Heinesen progressed to poems expressing political awareness, often painting satirical portraits of a society dominated by materialism and money. The later poems are often strikingly modernist in idiom, a mixture of the satirical and the more reflective youthful poetry.

Heinesen is, meanwhile, chiefly famed for his prose. His first published novel, *Blaesende Gry* (Windswept Dawn), was influenced by the Danish collective novel, but showed a greater interest in the individual personality than was usual in this genre. It was formless but powerful, and was completely recast for a second edition in 1962, in which the emphasis is moved from religious considerations to social questions. *Niels Peter* continued the collective genre, but towards the end of the 1940's Heinesen started on his major works, *Den sorte Gryde, The Lost Musicians, The Kingdom of the Earth, Det gode Håb*. Here he moves from a more or less sober account into the realm of fantasy and imagination, reflecting on man's place in the universe, the confrontation of life and death forces, the role of woman as the vehicle of life, the mystery of the human psyche. *Det gode Håb*, Heinesen's only historical novel, is an allegory of a fascist dictatorship as well as a penetrating study of human personality; full of conscious anachronisms and written in a language which smacks of the 17th century without any attempt to be authentic, it is considered by many to be Heinesen's masterpiece.

Since this novel, which took forty years to complete, Heinesen has concentrated on the short story, in which he has further explored the themes of his earlier years, though with increasing concentration on the mystery of human nature. His portraits of children are warm and sensitive, often humorous; in particular, he is fond of portraying puberty, revealing the incipient erotic instincts in children unaware of what is happening to them. In his latest volume of short stories, *Her skal danses*, he adds to these themes a moving story centred on the cultic significance of the Faroese chain dance, a profound homage to life, with violent death as its background.

It is a matter of regret to many Faroese that Heinesen has chosen to write in Danish, thereby becoming as much identified with Danish literature as with Faroese. His works are nevertheless intensely Faroese, and he presents the Faroe Islands as a microcosm in such a way that they are immediately intelligible to the outsider with no knowledge of them whatever. His combination of Faroeseness and universality is unique.

—W. Glyn Jones

HERBERT, Zbigniew. Polish. Born in Lvov, 29 October 1924. Educated at the University of Cracow, M.A. in economics 1947; Nicholas Copernicus University of Toruń, M.A. in law 1948; University of Warsaw, M.A. in philosophy 1950. Served in the Polish Resistance Home Army during World War II. Married Katarzyna Dzieduszycka in 1968. Worked as a bank clerk, manual laborer, and journalist; staff member, *Twórczość* literary review, Warsaw, 1955-76; Co-Editor, *Poezja*, Warsaw, 1965-68; Professor of Modern European Literature, California State College, Los Angeles, 1970; Visiting Professor, University of Gdańsk, 1972. Recipient: Polish Radio Competition prize, 1958; Polish Institute of Arts and Sciences (USA) Millennium Prize, 1964; Austrian State Prize for European Literature, 1965; Herder Prize (Hamburg), 1973; Petrarch Prize, 1979. Corresponding Member, Bavarian Academy. Address: Promenada 21 m. 4, 00 778 Warsaw, Poland.

Publications

Verse

Struna światla [A Chord of Light]. Warsaw, Czytelnik, 1956.
Hermes, pies i gwiazda [Hermes, A Dog, and a Star]. Warsaw, Czytelnik, 1957.
Studium przedmiotu [The Study of an Object]. Warsaw, Czytelnik, 1961.
Selected Poems, translated by Czeslaw Milosz and Peter Dale Scott. London, Penguin, 1968.
Napis [The Inscription]. Warsaw, Czytelnik, 1969.
Wiersze zebrane [Collected Verse]. Warsaw, Czytelnik, 1971.
Pan Cogito [Mr. Cogito]. Warsaw, Czytelnik, 1974.
Selected Poems, edited and translated by John and Bogdana Carpenter. London, and New York, Oxford University Press, 1977.
Raport z oblezonego miasta [Report from a Besieged Town]. Paris, Instytut Literacki, 1983.

Plays

Jaskinia filozofów, in *Dramaty*. 1970; as *The Philosopher's Den*, in *The Broken Mirror:*

A Collection of Writings from Contemporary Poland, New York, Random House, 1958.
Dramaty (includes *Jaskinia filozofów*; *Rekonstrukcja poety* [The Poet's Reconstruction]; *Drugi pokój* [The Other Room]; *Lalek*). Warsaw, PIW, 1970.

Other

Barbarzyńca w ogrodzie [A Barbarian in the Garden] (essays). Warsaw, Czytelnik, 1962.
Wybór poezji; Dramaty [Selected Poems, Plays]   Warsaw, Czytelnik, 1973.

*

Critical Study: "Herbert and Yevtushenko: On Whose Side Is History?" by George Gömöri, in *Mosaic 3*, 1969.

*   *   *

Zbigniew Herbert is among the best poets who emerged in the "new wave" of Polish literature in 1955-56. Although born in 1924 and not much younger than Rózewicz (with whom he shares wartime memories and experiences), Herbert is not an embittered "survivor" but an ironical moralist. It is mainly his critical attachment to history and his firm adherence to classical and Christian values that make Herbert's poetry different from most poets of his generation. While in his first two books of poetry, *Struna światla* and *Hermes, pies i gwiazda*, there are still a number of poems about the responsibility of the living towards the dead, and some caustic tales written in poetic prose which hold up to ridicule the absurd logic and Byzantine methods of Stalinism (e.g., "Cesarz," "Mur," "Bajka ruska"—"The Emperor," "The Wall," "Russian Tale"), in his later work Herbert often resorts to historical parable to express personal problems (e.g., in "Powrot prokonsula"—"The Return of the Proconsul"). In the late 1960's and early 1970's—which Herbert mostly spent traveling abroad—his concerns broadened to include meditations on the past and present of Western civilization, while he did not abandon his search for answers to specific Polish problems. The poetic harvest of these years was collected in *Pan Cogito* and *Raport z oblezonego miasta*. The latter collection also includes some "Cogito" poems; this fictitious character seems to be Herbert's wiser and more dispassionate alter-ego. Herbert writes on the whole in a rhymeless but vigorous free verse informed by a controlled, often sarcastic rhetoric. "Repeat great words repeat them stubbornly/like those crossing the desert who perished in the sand," he addresses himself in the poem "Przeslanie Pana Cogito," translated by John and Bogdana Carpenter as "The Envoy of Mr. Cogito." Herbert is a tortured classicist who has absorbed and overcome the temptation of the avant-garde with the help of a critically observed tradition.

Herbert's essays were collected in the volume *Barbarzyńca w ogrodzie*. They are mostly on medieval themes related to Italian and French art, architecture, and history, and are characterized by great lucidity of style and an effortless display of erudition. One of the best essays in this collection investigates the genocide of the Cathar heretics of France ("O Albigensach, inkwizytorach, i trubadurach"—"Albigenses, Inquisitors, and Troubadours")—a subject which has a strangely familiar ring for students of modern history. Herbert's plays collected in *Dramaty* deal with contemporary psychological and moral problems; these were written for radio and are probably less effective on stage.

—George Gömöri

HERMANS, Willem Frederik. Dutch. Born in Amsterdam, 1 September 1921. Educated at Barlaeus Gymnasium, Amsterdam; studied geography at University of Amsterdam, graduated 1950. Ph.D. 1955. Married Emelie Henriette Meurs in 1950. Staff member, *Criterium*, 1946-48, and *Podium*, 1949-50, and after 1963; reader in geography, University of Groningen, 1958-73; then full-time writer. Regular contributor, *NRC/Handelsblad* and *Het Parool* newspapers. Has lived in Paris since 1973. Recipient: Hooft Prize, 1971; Ministry of Culture Prize, 1977. Address: 86 avenue Niel, 75017 Paris, France; or, c/o De Bezige Bij, P.O. Box 5184, 1007 AD Amsterdam, Netherlands.

PUBLICATIONS

Fiction

Conserve [Preserves]. Amsterdam, Salm, 1947; revised edition in *Drie melodrama's*, 1957.
Moedwil en misverstand [Malice and Misunderstanding]. Amsterdam, Meulenhoff, 1948.
De Tranen der acacia's [The Tears of the Acacias]. Amsterdam, Van Oorschot, 1950.
Ik heb altijd gelijk [I Am Always Right]. Amsterdam, Van Oorschot, 1951.
Het behouden huis. Amsterdam, Bezige Bij, 1952; as "The House of Refuge," in *The World of Modern Fiction*, edited by Steven Marcus, New York, Simon and Schuster, 1966.
Paranoia. Amsterdam, Van Oorschot, 1953.
De god Denkbaar, Denkbaar de god [The God Conceivable, Conceivable the God]. Amsterdam, Van Oorschot, 1956.
Een landingspoging op Newfoundland en andere verhalen [An Attempted Landing on Newfoundland and Other Stories]. Amsterdam, Van Oorschot, 1957.
Drie melodrama's: Conserve, De leproos van Molokai, Hermans is hier geweest [Three Melodramas: Preserves, The Leper of Molokai, Hermans Was Here]. Amsterdam, Van Oorschot, 1957.
De donkere Kamer van Damocles. Amsterdam, Van Oorschot, 1959; as *The Dark Room of Damocles*, London, Heinemann, 1962.
Nooit meer slapen [Never Sleep Again]. Amsterdam, Bezige Bij, 1966.
Een wonderkind of een total loss [A Child Prodigy or a Total Loss]. Amsterdam, Bezige Bij, 1967.
Herinneringen van een engelbewaarden [Memoirs of a Guardian Angel]. Amsterdam, Bezige Bij, 1971.
Het evangelie van O. Dapper Dapper [The Gospel according to O. Dapper Dapper]. Amsterdam, Bezige Bij, 1973.
Onder professoren [Among Professors]. Amsterdam, Bezige Bij, 1975.
Vijf verhalen [Five Stories]. Utrecht, Knippenberg, 1980.
Dood en weggeraakt [Dead and Gone]. Antwerp Ziggurat, 1980.
Filip's sonatine. Amsterdam, Bezige Bij, 1980.
Homme's hoest [Homme's Cough]. Amsterdam, Bezige Bij, 1980.
Uit talloos veel miljoenen [From Countless Millions]. Amsterdam, Bezige Bij, 1981.
Geyerstein's dynamiek. Amsterdam, Bezige Bij, 1982.

Plays

Het omgekeerde pension [The Inverted Boarding House], in *Briefgeheim: Vier eenacters* [Confidential: Four One-Act Plays]. Amsterdam, Corvey, 1953.

De Woeste wandeling [The Wild Walk] (screenplay). Amsterdam, Bezige Bij, 1962.
Drie drama's [Three Plays]. Amsterdam, Bezige Bij, 1962.
King Kong. Amsterdam, Bezige Bij, 1972.
Periander. Amsterdam, Bezige Bij, 1974.

Verse

Kussen door een rag van woorden [Kissing Through a Web of Words]. Amsterdam, privately printed, 1944.
Horror coeli en andere gedichten [Horror Coeli and Other Poems]. Amsterdam, Meulenhoff, 1946.
Hypnodrome. The Hague, Stols, 1947.
Overgebleven gedichten [Poetic Remnants]. Amsterdam, Rap, 1968.

Other

Fenomenologie van de pin-up girl. Amsterdam, Van Oorschot, 1950.
Description et genèse des dépôts meubles de surface et du relief de l'Oesling. Luxembourg, Service Géologique, 1955.
Het zonale beginsel in de geografie [The Zonal Principle in Geography]. Groningen, Wolters, 1958.
Misdaad aan de Noordpool [Murder at the North Pole] (as Fjodor Klondyke). N.p., n.d.
De demon van ivoor [The Ivory Demon] (as Fjodor Klondyke). N.p., n.d.
Erosie [Erosion]. Zaandijk, Heijnis, 1960.
Mandarijnen op zwavelzuur [Mandarins in Sulphuric Acid]. Groningen, Mandarijnenpers, 1963.
Het sadistische Universum; Van Wittgenstein tot Weinreb [The Sadistic Universe: From Wittgenstein to Weinreb]. Amsterdam, Bezige Bij, 2 vols., 1964-76.
Wittgenstein in de mode en Kazemier niet [Wittgenstein in Fashion, But Not Kazemier]. Amsterdam, Bezige Bij, 1967.
Annum Veritatis (as Pater Anastase Prudhomme, S.J.). Amsterdam, Rap, 1968.
Fotobiografie. Amsterdam, Rap, 1969.
De laatste resten tropisch Nederland [The Last Remnants of Tropical Holland]. Amsterdam, Bezige Bij, 1969.
Hollywood. Amsterdam, Rap, 1970.
Machines in Bikini. Zandvoort, Eliance Pers, 1974.
De raadselachtige Multatuli [The Enigmatic Multatuli]. Amsterdam, Boelen, 1976.
Boze brieven van Bijkaart [Bijkaart's Angry Letters]. Amsterdam, Bezige Bij, 1977.
Bijzondere tekens [Special Signs]. Antwerp, Ziggurat, 1977.
Houten leeuwen en leeuwen van goud [Wooden Lions and Lions of Gold]. Amsterdam, Bezige Bij, 1979.
Ik draag geen helm met vederbos [I Wear No Helmet with a Plume]. Amsterdam, Bezige Bij, 1979.
Klaas kwam niet [Klaas Didn't Come]. Amsterdam, Bezige Bij, 1983.

Editor, *Focquenbroch: Bloemlezing uit zijn lyriek* [Focquenbroch: An Anthology of His Lyric Poetry]. Amsterdam, Van Oorschot, 1946.

Translator, *Zonlicht op zaterdag* [Daylight on Saturday], by J.B. Priestley. Amsterdam, Arbeiderspers, 1947.
Translator, *Kraters in lichterlaaie* [Craters Ablaze], by H. Tazieff. The Hague, Leopold, 1954.

Translator, *Tractatus logicus-philosophicus*, by Ludwig Wittgenstein. Amsterdam, Athenaeum-Polak & Van Gennep, 1975.
Translator, *De martelgang van de dikzak* [The Fat Man's Ordeal], by Henri Beraud. Amsterdam, 1981.
Translator, *Zeven gedichten* [Seven Poems], by O.V. de Milosz. Amsterdam, Cornamona Pers, 1981.

*

Bibliography: *Bibliografie van de verspreide publicaties van Hermans* by Frans A. Janssen and Rob Delvigne, Amsterdam, Rap, 1972.

Critical Studies: *Hermans* by Ed Popelier, Bruges, Orion, 1979; *Bedriegers en bedrogenen: Opstellen over het werk van Hermans* by Frans A. Janssen, Amsterdam, Bezige Bij, 1980.

*   *   *

Although he published some poetry during and just after the Second World War, Willem Frederik Hermans's favoured medium is fiction. His ten novels, five novellas, and six volumes of stories give him a pre-eminent place among living Dutch practitioners. In addition, he is a brilliant and feared polemical essayist, and has written a number of filmscripts and plays.

His fiction explores a universe essentially chaotic and unknowable, loveless, full of violence, hatred, and, above all, confusion. Hermans sees the novelist as engaged in a "science without proofs," and his own undertaking is bedevilled by a distrust of language he shares with the philosopher Wittgenstein, whom he has both translated and written of admiringly. "My greatest regret is that I cannot write with light like a camera," he sighed in his "Preamble" to the collection *Paranoia*, though this very frustration leads him to maximum precision of language, stark clarity of description, and a persistent, even obsessive concern with the visual (not surprisingly, one novel and one story have been filmed).

From his bizarre debut, *Conserve*, set in a Mormon community in Utah, to his recent novel *Uit talloos veel miljoenen*, in which he satirises his own former university, Groningen, Hermans presents us with a memorable array of anti-heroes, outsiders who struggle with a hostile world before succumbing to it. Sometimes their defeat is physically fatal, in other cases the battering is a spiritual and moral one.

In one of Hermans's most succinct and powerful evocations of chaos and futility, the novella "The House of Refuge," a partisan fighting in Eastern Europe at the end of the Second World War seeks to escape the horrors of the front line in a house left intact, whose owners he kills. However, the war catches up with him, and the "refuge" the house seemed to offer proves illusory.

The Dark Room of Damocles, arguably Hermans's masterpiece to date, has been praised by John le Carré as one of the best spy-stories of the period. The main protagonist, an insignificant tobacconist, becomes caught up in underground work during the German occupation, but is subsequently unable to prove the existence of a "double" who he claims recruited and instructed him, but who has since disappeared. Period, place, and atmosphere are vividly captured and the book can be read as an adventure yarn, but what is most impressive and disturbing is the way that the picture of reality shared by protagonist and reader for two-thirds of the novel cannot be substantiated when called into question in the final section.

Disorientation of character and reader is achieved by more radical means in the cryptic fantasy *De god Denkbaar, Denkbaar de god* and its satirical sequel *Het evangelie van O. Dapper Dapper*. In *Nooit meer slapen* Hermans uses a more familiar narrative mode to give a gripping first-person account of a young geologist's abortive expedition to northern Norway in search of meteor craters, which leads him to question the purpose of scientific enquiry.

Hermans's Swift-like onslaughts on the literary and intellectual establishment, in the essay collections *Mandarijnen op zwavelzuur* and *Van Wittgenstein tot Weinreb* and in a long succession of magazine and newspaper articles, have won him as many enemies as admirers and emulators, while allegedly slighting remarks against Roman Catholics placed in the mouth of a character in the novel *Ik heb altijd gelijk* resulted in (unsuccessful) prosecution. His polemical belligerence sometimes recalls Multatuli, author of the greatest Dutch prose classic, the colonial novel *Max Havelaar* (1860), to whom Hermans devoted a discerning and provocative study.

Some recent work, notably the novella *Filip's sonatine*, has been a disappointingly uneven reprise of earlier themes, in which the cynicism is occasionally facile, but such strictures are minor ones. Hermans has repeatedly shown, in the course of a distinguished career, the capacity to find new and powerful ways of rendering his familiar vision, and one looks forward eagerly to the next version of the "same book" he insists he has been writing all along.

—Paul Vincent

HEYM, Stefan. German. Born Helmut Flieg in Chemnitz, 10 April 1913; name legally changed to Stefan Heym, 1943. Educated at the University of Berlin; University of Chicago, M.A. 1935. Served in the United States Army, 1943-48: Bronze Star. Married 1) Gertrude Peltyn in 1944 (died, 1969); 2) Inge Hohn in 1971. Editor, *Deutsches Volksecho*, New York, 1937-39; since 1952, has lived in East Berlin: fined for publishing outside the GDR without government permission, 1979. Wrote all his books to and including *The King David Report* in English; later books written in German. Recipient: Heinrich Mann Prize 1953; GDR National Prize. Address: Rabindranath-Tagore-Strasse 9, 118 Berlin-Grünau, East Germany.

PUBLICATIONS

Fiction

Hostages. New York, Putnam, 1942; London, Putnam, 1943; as *The Glasenapp Case*, Berlin, Seven Seas, 1962; as *Der Fall Glasenapp*, Leipzig, List, 1958.
Of Smiling Peace. Boston, Little Brown, 1944; London, Skeffington, 1946.
The Crusaders. Boston, Little Brown, 1948; London, Cassell, 1950; as *Keruzfahre von heute*, Leipzig, List, 1950; as *Der bittere Lorbeer*, Munich, List, 1950.
The Eyes of Reason. Boston, Little Brown, 1951; London, Cassell, 1952; as *Die Augen der Vernunft*, Leipzig, List, 1955.
Goldsborough. Leipzig, List, 1953; translated as *Goldsborough*, New York, Blue Heron Press, 1954; London, Cassell, 1961.
Die Kannibalen und andere Erzählungen. Leipzig, List, 1953; as *The Cannibals and Other Stories*, Berlin, Seven Seas, 1958.
Schatten und Licht: Geschichten aus einem geteilten Lande. Leipzig, List, 1960; as *Shadows and Lights: Eight Short Stories*, London, Cassell, 1963.
Die Papiere des Andreas Lenz. Leipzig, List, 1963; as *Lenz; oder, Die Freiheit*, Munich, List, 1965; as *The Lenz Papers*, London, Cassell, 1964.
Lassalle. Munich, Bechtle, 1969; as *Uncertain Friend*, London, Cassell, 1969.
Die Schmähschrift; oder, Die Königin gegen Defoe. Zurich, Diogenes, 1970; as *The*

Queen Against Defoe and Other Stories, New York, Hill, 1974; London, Hodder and Stoughton, 1975.
Der König-David-Bericht. Munich, Kindler, 1972; as *The King David Report*, New York, Putnam, and London, Hodder and Stoughton, 1973.
Fünf Tage im Juni. Munich, Bertelsmann, 1974; as *Five Days in June*, London, Hodder and Stoughton, 1977; Buffalo, New York, Prometheus, 1978.
Die richtige Einstellung und andere Erzählungen. Munich, Bertelsmann, 1976.
Collin. Munich, Bertelsmann, 1979; as *Collin*, New York, Stuart, and London, Hodder and Stoughton, 1980.
Ahasver. Munich, Bertelsmann, 1981; as *The Wandering Jew*, New York, Holt Rinehart, 1984.
Schwarzenberg. Munich, Bertelsmann, 1984.

Play

Tom Sawyers grosses Abenteuer, with Hanus Burger. Berlin, Henschel, 1952.

Other

Nazis in U.S.A.: An Expose of Hitler's Aims and Agents in the U.S.A. New York, American Committee for Anti-Nazi Literature, 1938.
Forschungsreise ins Herz der deutschen Arbeiterklasse. Berlin, Tribune, 1953.
Reise ins Land der unbegrenzten Möglichkeiten. Berlin, Tribune, 1954; as *Keine Angst vor Russlands Bären*, Dusseldorf, Brücken, 1955.
Im Kopf sauber: Schriften zum Tage. Leipzig, List, 1954.
Offen Gesagt: Neue Schriften zum Tage. Berlin, Volk & Welt, 1957.
Das kosmische Zeitalter. Berlin, Tribune, 1959; as *A Visit to Soviet Science*, Marzani & Munsell, 1959; as *The Cosmic Age: A Report*, New Delhi, People's Publishing House, 1959.
Casimir und Cymbelinchen: Zwei Märchen (juvenile). Berlin, Kinderbuch, 1966.
Cymbelinchen; oder, Der Ernst des Lebens: Vier Märchen für kluge Kinder. Munich, Bertelsmann, 1975.
Die Wachsmuth-Syndrom. Berlin, Berliner Handpresse, 1975.
Erich Hückniesel, und das fortgesetzte Rotkäppchen. Berlin, Berliner Handpresse, 1977.
Wege und Umwege: Streitbare Schriften aus fünf Jahrzehnten, edited by Peter Mallwitz. Munich, Bertelsmann, 1980.

Editor, *Auskunft 1-2: Neue Prose aus der DDR*. Munich, Verlag der Autoren, 2 vols., 1974-78.

Translator, *King Leopold's Soliloquy*, by Mark Twain. Berlin, Tribune, 1961.

*   *   *

Stefan Heym's fiction owes much to his wide-ranging experience as a highly successful journalist. He is an unashamed realist, he has a fine eye for detail and for the gripping plot, and he can develop his themes through telling use of confrontation and dialogue. Throughout his literary career he has revealed considerable courage in his preparedness to stand against what he felt to be unacceptable in a succession of different societies (National Socialism, US imperialism, Stalinism, dogmatism), and he has repeatedly used the figure of the struggling intellectual as a focus for broad questions on the nature of truth, the influence (and corruption) of power, the reaction of individuals in crisis or revolution, and questions on death and dying.

Although his first language was German, exile in the USA led him to complete his first novel in English; thereafter he tended to use English as first language of literary composition until the 1970's. He has, however, proved to be one of the best self-translators of our age, and all his novels have appeared in two versions. Like many of his heroes, Heym has proved an outsider, a tireless campaigner, and a champion of the individual. Unlike his heroes, however, he has also proved a vigorous survivor, and he is currently one of the foremost writers of the German Democratic Republic.

Heym has achieved considerable success with short stories and investigative-reflective journalism, but his major achievement has been his novels. In all of these—from the detective story of the resistance movement in Prague (1942) to the historical, theological, and cultural interpretation-cum-satire of reformation Germany (1981)—Heym has always reached a mass audience through his ability to combine drama and tension with serious questioning of issues relevant to our own age. His works have also carried force through his ability to incorporate much historical detail, which sometimes takes the form of documents. In this respect his novels are thoroughly researched "investigations," and his scholarship has covered such different events as the pillorying of Daniel Defoe, the Baden revolution of 1849, the disturbances in East Germany in 1953, and even the biblical story of King David. The perspective is always socialist. Personal experience has regularly informed a number of his works, and dramatic moments of his career are as striking in his early panoramic treatment of the American advance in Europe (in one of the major novels of the Second World War, *The Crusaders*), as they are in his late study of Stalinist elements in the GDR (*Collin*).

Heym's most acclaimed work is *The King David Report*, which subtly exposes the contradictions of the Books of *Samuel* and *Kings*. The attempt by King Solomon to legitimise his own succession becomes a source of grim comedy in its own right, but Heym reconsiders the biblical evidence in a strikingly unorthodox manner and suggests the relevance of his interpretation for several societies beyond that of ancient Israel. Parody of the style of the Authorised Version enriches the humour of this troubling, and often moving, investigation of primitive totalitarianism.

—Peter Hutchinson

HOCHHUTH, Rolf. German.   Born in Eschwege, 1 April 1931.   Educated at Realgymnasium, Eschwege to 1948; studied bookselling at a technical school; attended universities of Heidelberg and Munich, 1952-55. Married Dana Pavic; three sons. Worked for mayor of Eschwege, after World War II; since 1955; staff member, Verlag C. Bertelsmann, Gütersloh. Resident dramatist, Basel Municipal Theater. Recipient: Young Generation Prize, 1963. Address: Postfach 661, 4002 Basel, Switzerland.

PUBLICATIONS

Plays

   Der Stellvertreter (produced Berlin, 1963).   Reinbek, Rowohlt, 1963; as *The Represen-*

tative (produced London, 1963), London, Methuen, 1963; as *The Deputy* (produced New York, 1964), New York, Grove Press, 1964.
Soldaten: Nekrolog auf Genf (produced Berlin, 1967). Reinbek, Rowohlt, 1967; as *Soldiers: An Obituary for Geneva* (produced New York, 1968), New York, Grove Press, 1968.
Guerillas (produced Stuttgart, 1970). Reinbek, Rowohlt, 1970.
Die Hebamme (produced Zurich, 1972). Reinbek, Rowohlt, 1971.
Lysistrate und die Nato (produced Vienna, 1974). Reinbek, Rowohlt, 1973..
Tod eines Jägers. Reinbek, Rowohlt, 1976.
Juristen (produced Hamburg, 1980). Reinbek, Rowohlt, 1979.
Ärztinnen (produced Mannheim, 1980). Reinbek, Rowohlt, 1980.

Fiction

Zwischenspiel in Baden-Baden. Reinbek, Rowohlt, 1959.
Die Berliner Antigone. Reinbek, Rowohlt, 1964.
Eine Liebe in Deutschland. Reinbek, Rowohlt, 1978; as *A German Love Story*, London, Weidenfeld and Nicolson, and Boston, Little Brown, 1980.

Other

Krieg und Klassenkrieg: Studien. Reinbek, Rowohlt, 1971.
Die Berliner Antigone: Prose und Verse. Reinbek, Rowohlt, 1975.
Dokumente zur politischen Wirkung, edited by Reinhart Hoffmeister. Munich, Kindler, 1980.

Editor, *Sämtliche Werke*, by Wilhelm Busch. Gütersloh, Mohn, 1959, and Munich, Bertelsmann, 1960.
Editor, *Lustige Streiche in Versen und Farben*, by Wilhelm Busch. Hamburg, Ruetten & Loening, 1961.
Editor, *Liebe in unserer Zeit: 16 Erzählungen.* Hamburg, Ruetten & Loening, 1961.
Editor, *Die Deutschen*, by Otto Flake. Frankfurt, Fischer, 1962.
Editor, *Am grauen Meer: Gesammelte Werke*, by Theodor Storm. Hamburg, Mosaik, 1963.
Editor, *Dichter und Herrscher*, by Thomas Mann. Munich, Bertelsmann, 1964.
Editor, *Die grossen Meister.* Cologne, Kiepenheuer & Witsch, 1966.
Editor, with Peter Härting, *Werke*, by Otto Flake. Frankfurt, Fischer, 1973.
Editor, with Hans Heinrich Koch, *Kaisers Zeiten: Bilder einer Epoche aus dem Archiv der Hofphotographen Oscar und Gustav Tellgmann.* Munich, Herbig, 1973.

*

Critical Studies: *The Storm over The Deputy* edited by Eric Bentley, New York, Grove Press, 1964; *Hochhuth* by M.E. Ward, Boston, Twayne, 1977; *Hochhuth* by Rainer Taëni, London, Wolff, 1977; *Hochhuth* edited by Walter Hinck, Reinbek, Rowohlt, 1981.

*   *   *

The German dramatist Rolf Hochhuth shot to fame in a welter of controversy aroused by his first play, *The Deputy*, 1963, which accused Pope Pius XII of condoning the extermination of the Jews in the Third Reich. Within a year a collection of essays and articles pro and contra Hochhuth's "explosive drama" was edited by Eric Bentley under the title *The Storm over The Deputy*. Produced by Erwin Piscator in Berlin this play ushered in the wave of documentary drama that was to make the theatre a forum of critical debate in Germany and elsewhere. Despite the topicality of theme and lengthy essayistic reflections by the author in the manner of Shaw—with whom Hochhuth shares a polemical indignation—there is little that is documentary in the play itself. Hochhuth writes in the tradition of the Schillerian historical tragedy where the individual is shown in the dilemma of a historical situation having to take the responsibility for decisive moral actions. The protagonist tends to heroic stature in both Schiller and Hochhuth, and the structure of *The Deputy* reflects the pattern of conflict and catastrophe inherent in classical tragedy. This pattern is only masked by the interspersed quotations from such sources as diaries, memoirs, and biographies.

Hochhuth maintained his controversial impact in his second play, *Soldiers*, in which he pleaded for the exclusion of civilian targets from modern aerial warfare. The focus of his attack was another "hero" of history, Winston Churchill, who was alleged by Hochhuth to have personally ordered the massive and militarily unnecessary bombing of Dresden as well as the sabotaging of the plane in which the Polish freedom leader, General Sikorski, was killed. (These allegations led to court cases and the banning of the play from the National Theatre.) Hochhuth does not resolve the uneasy marriage of these two themes with the depiction of Churchill as an instrument of destiny, so the central issues of fate and free will, historical necessity and individual moral responsibility remain confused and unfocussed.

As with *The Deputy*, which appeared as the war crimes trials in Germany gathered momentum and helped lift the taboos concealing the national past, Hochhuth showed a perfect sense of timing for topicality of theme by launching *Soldiers* at the height of the American bombings in Vietnam. Subsequent dramas also thematized up-to-the-minute topics: the possible scenario for a left-wing putsch in the U.S.A. (*Guerillas*); homeless underdogs struggling against a faceless bureaucracy (*Die Hebamme*); opposition to the building of a NATO base (*Lysistrate und die Nato*); indictment of the legal profession for active cooperation with the Nazis (*Juristen*).

Hochhuth's output over the past twenty years is significant as a touchstone of controversial issues that engender acute argument. Turning the stage into a political tribunal he probes the guilty conscience of a nation that has not yet been salved, and accurately reflects the provocative accusations levelled by a younger generation at those Germans who had carried the power and the responsibility from 1933 to 1945. His plays are often only loosely structured and diffuse, and the characters mouthpieces of abstract political programmes and slogans; it is less their cliché-ridden rhetorical speech and philosophical banalities than their fierce sense of outrage that carries an audience.

—Arrigo V. Subiotto

HOCHWÄLDER, Fritz. Austrian. Born in Vienna, 28 May 1911. Educated at Reform-Realgymnasium, Vienna, and in evening classes at Volkshochschule. Married 1) Ursula Buchi in 1951; 2) Susanne Schreiner in 1960, one daughter. Apprentice upholsterer in Vienna; moved to Switzerland in 1938, and free-lance writer in Zurich since 1945. Recipient: Vienna Prize, 1955, and Ehrenring, 1972; Grillparzer Prize, 1956; Wildgans Prize, 1963; Austrian State Prize, 1966; Austrian Ehrenkreunz für Kunst und Wissenschaft, 1971. Named Professor by Austrian government, 1963. Address: Am Oeschbrig 27, 8053 Zurich, Switzerland.

HOCHWÄLDER

Publications

Plays

Jehr (produced Vienna, 1933).
Liebe in Florenz; oder, Die unziemliche Neugier (produced Vienna, 1936).
Das heilige Experiment (produced Biel, 1943). Zurich, Elgg, 1947; as *The Strong Are Lonely* (as *Crown Colony*, produced New York, 1947; as *The Strong Are Lonely*, produced New York, 1953; London, 1955), New York, French, 1954.
Der Flüchtling, from a work by Georg Kaiser (produced Biel, 1945). Zurich, Elgg, 1954.
Hotel du commerce (produced Prague, 1946). Zurich, Elgg, 1954.
Meier Helmbrecht (produced Vienna, 1947). Zurich, Elgg, 1956.
Der öffentliche Ankläger (produced Stuttgart, 1948). Hamburg, Zsolnay, 1954; as *The Public Prosecutor* (produced London, 1957), London, French, 1958.
Virginia (produced Hamburg, 1951).
Der Unschuldige (produced Vienna, 1958). Privately printed, 1949; Zurich, Elgg, 1958.
Virginia (produced Hamburg, 1951).
Donadieu (produced Vienna, 1953). Hamburg, Zsolnay, 1953.
Die Herbege (produced Vienna, 1957). Zurich, Elgg, 1956; as *The Inn* (produced Liverpool, 1962.
Donnerstag (produced Salzburg, 1959). Included in *Dramen 1*, 1959.
Dramen 1-2. Munich, Langen-Müller, 2 vols., 1959-64.
Esther. Zurich, Elgg, 1960.
1003 (produced Vienna, 1964). Included in *Dramen 2*, 1964.
Der Himbeerpflücker (televised, 1965; produced Zurich, 1965). Munich, Langen-Müller, 1965; as *The Raspberry Picker* (produced London, 1967), in *The Public Prosecutor and Other Plays*, 1979.
Der Befehl (televised, 1967; produced Vienna, 1968). Graz, Stiasny, 1967; as *The Order*, in *Modern International Drama 3*, no. 2, 1970.
Dramen. Munich, Langen-Müller, 1968.
Dramen. Graz, Verlag Styria, 3 vols., 1975-79.
Lazaretti; oder, Der Säbeltiger (produced Salzburg, 1975). Graz, Verlag Styria, 1975; as *Lazaretti; or, the Saber-Toothed Tiger*, in *The Public Prosecutor and Other Plays*, 1979.
The Public Prosecutor and Other Plays. New York, Ungar, 1979.
Die Prinzessin von Chimay. Graz, Verlag Styria, 1982.

Radio Plays: *Der Reigen*, from the play by Schnitzler; *Weinsberger Ostern 1525*.

Television Plays: *Der Himbeerpflücker*, 1965; *Der Befehl*, 1967.

Other

Im Wechsel der Zeit: Autobiographische Skizzen und Essays. Graz, Verlag Styria, 1980.

*

Critical Studies: *The Theater of Protest and Paradox* by George E. Wellwarth, New York, New York University Press, and London, MacGibbon and Kee, 1964; "The Theatre of Hochwälder" by James Schmitt, in *Modern Austrian Literature 11*, no. 1, 1978 (includes bibliography); *Der Dramatiker Hochwälder* by Wilhelm Bortenschlager, Innsbruck, Wagner, 1979.

*   *   *

Fritz Hochwälder was born in Vienna in 1911. Like so many other prominent theatre people in Austria and Germany, he fled to Switzerland when the Nazis came to power. It was there that Hochwälder wrote his first important play. *Das heilige Experiment* was written while Hochwälder was on leave of absence from the labour camp in which he and many other political refugees had been interned by the Swiss. The play was first performed in Switzerland in 1943 and was subsequently produced at the Burgtheater in Hochwälder's native Vienna, as well as in Germany, France, Holland, Sweden, Finland, Norway, Argentina, Brazil, and Greece.

Hochwälder's dramas deal with conflict within the human mind. A dramatist ideally raises a conflict in the mind of the protagonist and lets us see him grow to an awareness of it. The purest drama is condensed into that moment in which the character sees himself as he is for the first time, when he becomes conscious of the difference between the illusion he has lived and the reality he should have lived. It is a moment of self-realization for the character and for the audience watching him. This destruction of illusion and rearrangement of personal values is the basis of Hochwälder's drama.

Hochwälder's plays are representative of the genre that has come to be known as "exile" literature. It can safely be said that all of the writers of any talent in Austria and Germany (with the possible exception of the by then superannuated Gerhart Hauptmann) were either silenced, killed, or exiled by the Nazis. As might be expected, the principal theme that these writers concerned themselves with in exile with an almost obsessive tenacity was the nature of guilt. With the exception of *Das heilige Experiment*, an attempt to write a modern tragedy based on a conflict of ideas, all of Hochwälder's plays are concerned with the question of where to place the guilt. In *Meier Helmbrecht* he argues that the fathers are responsible for the children. In *Der Flüchtling* he argues that a man is responsible for his own integrity—that the plea that he is only a cog in the machine is valueless. The plea that "orders are orders" and one has no choice but to follow them was, of course, one that became almost an automatic, rhythmic refrain after the war, when every German chanted it like a daily prayer. Hochwälder deals with the justice of this plea on the part of the older generation in *Meier Helmbrecht*, on the part of the man in the street in *Der Flüchtling*, and in *The Public Prosecutor*, a melodrama about the French Revolution, he deals with the leaders of the people. Fouquier-Tinville, the cold-blooded prosecutor who engineered the Reign of Terror, pleads that he is a servant of the state and that it is his duty to obey orders: "Here we only obey our orders.... We follow whoever is in power.... I obey the law and carry out such orders as may come to me. I don't question whether they are good or bad.... I was merely employing the means I was given—carrying out my orders. That is why I feel I can reject any personal responsibility." At the end of the play Fouquier-Tinville falls into the trap he has been tricked into setting for himself. Hochwälder makes it clear that his explanations are consciously specious and that his actions are dictated by cynical opportunism and an insane thirst for power.

Guilt is also the subject of *The Raspberry Picker*, Hochwälder's best play so far and certainly one of the peaks of exile literature. In this play Hochwälder takes aim at his own countrymen specifically for the first time as he tells the story of a petty crook on the lam in a remote Austrian village who is mistaken for a former officer in a concentration camp that brought prosperity and employment to the village under the Nazis. The petty crook, "Levantine" in appearance, is mistaken for the mass-murdering "Raspberry Picker," so named because of his habit of shooting prisoners while they are picking the fruit, and is fawned upon and honored by the leading citizens of the village, all of whom look back to the Nazi regime as a Golden Age.

Like so many of his contemporaries, Hochwälder has lived the irony of having to use the attempted destruction of his culture and the uprooting of his life as the source of his art.

—George E. Wellwarth

HOLUB, Miroslav. Czech. Born in Plzeň13 September 1923. Educated at Charles University School of Medicine, Prague, 1947-53, M.D. 1953; Czechoslovak Academy of Sciences, Institute of Microbiology, Prague, 1954-57, Ph.D. in immunology 1958. Married 1) Věra Koktová in 1948; 2) Marta Svikruhová in 1963; 3) Jitka Langrová in 1969; two sons and one daughter. Railway worker, 1942-45; Clinical Pathologist, Bulovka Hospital, Prague, 1953-54; Junior Scientific Worker, 1954-65, and Senior Scientific Worker, 1968-71, Institute of Microbiology; visiting investigator, Public Health Research Institute, New York, 1965-67; worked at Max Planck Institute, Freiburg, 1968-69. Since 1972, Senior Scientific Worker, Institute for Clinical and Experimental Medicine, Prague. Visiting Professor of Creative Writing, Oberlin College, Ohio, 1979 and 1982. Editor, *Vesmír* (popular science magazine), Prague, 1951-65. Member, Bavarian Academy of Arts, 1969. Address: Svépomocná 107, Hrnčíře, 149 00 Prague 4, Czechoslovakia.

PUBLICATIONS

Verse

Denní služba [Day Duty]. Prague, Ceskoslovenský Spisovatel, 1958.
Achilles a želva [Achilles and the Tortoise]. Prague, Mladá Fronta, 1960.
Slavikář [Primer]. Prague, Ceskoslovenský Spisovatel, 1961.
Jdi a otevři dveře [Go and Open the Door]. Prague, Mladá Fronta, 1962.
Kam teče krev [Where the Blood Flows]. Prague, Ceskoslovenský Spisovatel, 1963.
Zcela nesoustavná zoologie [A Completely Unsystematic Zoology]. Prague, Mladá Fronta, 1963.
Tak zvané srdce [The So-Called Heart]. Prague, Mladá Fronta, 1963.
Anamneza: Výbor z poezie 1958-1963 [Anamnesis]. Prague, Mladá Fronta, 1964.
Selected Poems, translated by Ian Milner and George Theiner. London, Penguin, 1967.
Ačkoli. Prague, Ceskoslovenský Spisovatel, 1969; as *Although*, London, Cape, 1971.
Beton: Verše z New Yorku a z Prahy [Concrete]. Prague, Mladá Fronta, 1970.
Události [Events]. Prague, VSUP, 1971.
Notes of a Clay Pigeon. London, Secker and Warburg, 1977.
Sagittal Section, translated by Stuart Friebert and Dana Hábová. Oberlin, Ohio, Oberlin College Press, 1980.
Naopal. Prague, Mladá Fronta, 1982; as *On the Contrary*, Newcastle upon Tyne, Bloodaxe, 1984.
Interferon; or, On the Theatre, translated by Dana Hábová and David Young. Oberlin, Ohio, Oberlin College Press, 1982.

Other

Anděl na kolečkách: Poloreportáž z USA [Angel on Wheels: Sketches from the USA]. Prague, Ceskoslovenský Spisovatel, 1963.
Tři kroky po zemi [Three Steps on the Earth]. Prague, Naše Vojsko, 1965.
Zít v New Yorku [To Live in New York]. Prague, Melantrich, 1969.

Translator, *Poe čili údolí neklidu* [Poe; or, The Valley of Unrest]. Prague, Ceskoslovenský Spisovatel, 1971.
Translator, *Zivé hodiny* [The Living Clock], by L.M. Ward. Prague, Mladá Fronta, 1979.
Translator, *Buňka, medúza, a ja* [The Cell, The Medusa, and I], by L. Thomas. Prague, Mladá Fronta, 1982.

Author of more than 120 scientific papers and monographs.

* * *

In the context of Czech poetry, Miroslav Holub is almost an anomaly. Czech, a language in which the primary role is played by the verb, capable of expressing through a system of aspects fine nuances of action, a tongue that can by the use of diminutives convey both affection and dislike, naturally tempts those inclined to pour out their heart in verse to surrender to a lyricism in which the sheer linguistic beauty of the message may obscure a paucity of ideas. There has never been a dearth of lyrical poets in Czech literature and the multitudes have helped to produce great talents.

However, to Holub a sensual intoxication with a flow of incandescent associations or with pure sound and melody would be completely alien. His is an unromantic lyricism of the intellect that does not allow itself to be carried away by spontaneity. The word is under strict control, traditional literary devices are avoided, poetry is a spectacular way to demonstrate the human being's most important characteristic—the capacity to think.

It was no coincidence that Holub's work first appeared in the mid-1950's when it still seemed that with more effort, knowledge would prevail upon ignorance and the world could be made into a reasonably inhabitable place. Even in Eastern Europe after Stalin's death the rigidity of dogma was being timidly replaced with more civilized attitudes. In art, cardboard heroes set in ideologically devised situations were making way for more credible living people existing in circumstances of everyday life. Intimacy and an unhurried, calm observation of the little miracles, ironies, and puzzles that the world offers on every step were substituted for the artificially induced grandiose gestures of the "struggle for socialism."

The examination of details well suited Holub, a scientist by profession. The penetrating incisive mind summed up its vision in poems that, although they sometimes used the language of laboratory reports, reached the core of the subject by means of a short cut such as only a powerful verbal image can provide. Very much in the spirit of the times, Holub's analytical skepticism served as a scalpel that would cut out any diseased tissue so that the flesh—and the body politic—would heal and progress toward a scientifically founded rational future.

His poetry, refined, intricate, sober and sophisticated, ultimately proclaimed a self-assured confidence in the limitless power of human endeavour. Poetry itself was considered to be a means of expanding the realm of intelligence rising ever higher from the primeval bog of superstition and ignorance. "A Marathon runner is more free than a vagabond, and a cosmonaut than a sage in the state of levitation."

While he was regarded by most of his compatriots with admiration rather than affection, the cerebral, emotionless style of Holub's poetry appealed in the 1960's particularly to those in the English-speaking world who were familiar with the work of similarly oriented modern American poets, e.g., Lawrence Ferlinghetti. Perhaps it was the essential optimism, the trust in the near omnipotence of science, the identification of freedom with self-regulation that caused certain reservations at home. Optimism, once officially decreed, had been discredited, science had often been seen to fail, self-regulation and discipline could be easily turned into regimentation, some must have felt, despite assurances to the contrary. Would a world from which all irrationality had been eradicated still be a place fit for humans. And, paradoxically, for poetry?

After a decade of partly enforced silence, Holub seems less assured that progress and enlightenment are unquestionable values. He treats his subjects now with a grain of wry doubt, and, rather than submitting exact answers, in his recent poetry, as concise and pointed as ever, he tries to define and voice some very complex philosophical questions.

—Igor Hájek

HRABAL, Bohumil. Czech. Born near Brno, 28 March 1914. Educated at grammar school, and at Charles University, Prague, law degree 1946. Has worked as lawyer's clerk, railwayman, salesman, steel worker in Kladno foundries, laborer, stage hand and extra. Recipient: Gottwald State Prize, 1968. Address: Na Hrázi 24, Prague 8—Liben, Czechoslovakia.

PUBLICATIONS

Fiction

Hovory lidí [People's Conversations]. Prague, Spolek Ceských Bibliofilu, 1956.
Perlička na dně [A Pearl at the Bottom]. Prague, Ceskoslovenský Spisovatel, 1963.
Pábitelé [Palaverers]. Prague, Mladá Fronta, 1964.
Taneční hodiny pro starší a pokročilé [Advanced Dancing Lessons]. Prague, Ceskoslovenský Spisovatel, 1964.
Ostře sledované vlaky. Prague, Ceskoslovenský Spisovatel, 1965; as *A Close Watch on the Trains*, London, Cape, 1968; as *Closely Watched Trains*, New York, Grove Press, 1968.
Inzerát na dum, ve kterém už nechci bydlet [Advertising a House I Don't Want to Live In Anymore]. Prague, Mladá Fronta, 1965.
Automat svět. Prague, Mladá Fronta, 1966; as *The Death of Mr. Baltisberger*, New York, Doubleday, 1975.
Morytáty a legendy [Fair Ditties and Legends]. Prague, Ceskoslovenský Spisovatel, 1968.
Postřižiny [The Shorn]. Prague, Ceskoslovenský Spisovatel, 1976.
Krasosmutnění [Lovely Wistfulness]. Prague, Ceskoslovenský Spisovatel, 1977.
Mestecko ve kterém se zastavil čas [The Town Where Time Stood Still]. Innsbruck, Comenius, 1978.
Příliš hlucná samota [A Too Noisy Loneliness]. Cologne, Index, 1980.
Jak jsem obsluhoval anglického krále [I Who Have Served the English King]. Cologne, Index, 1980.
Kluby poezie [The Poetry Club]. Prague, Mladá Fronta, 1981.
Harlekýnovy milióny [The Harlequin's Millions]. Prague, Ceskoslovenský Spisovatel, 1981.

Plays

Closely Watched Trains (translation of screenplay), with Jiří Menzel. New York, Simon and Schuster, 1971; as *Closely Observed Trains*, London, Lorrimer, 1971.

Screenplays: *Fadni odpoledne (A Boring Afternoon)*, with Ivan Passer, 1965; *Ostře sledované vlaky (Closely Watched Trains; Closely Observed Trains)*, with Jiří Menzel, 1967; *Postriziny* (The Cutting), 1980.

Other

Toto město je ve společné péči obyvatel [This Town Is in the Joint Care of All Its Inhabitants]. Prague, Ceskoslovenský Spisovatel, 1967.
Slavnosti sněženek [Celebration of Snowdrops]. Prague, Ceskoslovenský Spisovatel, 1978.
Domaci ukoly z pilnosti [Voluntary Homework] (miscellany). Prague, Ceskoslovenský Spisovatel, 1982.

Editor, *Výbor z ceske prczy* [Selected Czech Prose].   Prague, Mladá Fronta, 1967.

*   *   *

Bohumil Hrabal is not an intellectual writer. To a possible career in law he preferred to try his hand at a dozen different jobs and trades, mostly of the kind that sedate and respectable people would avoid if they could. But it was the ever changing environment that satisfied his thirst for the illuminating experience, for movement, for the sudden flash of beauty. Long years spent in the company of compulsive talkers, more often than not fortified by Czech beer, provided him with a treasure of tales and anecdotes, and he claims that all that he does is to transcribe, arrange, and collate them.

The claim cannot be taken seriously. The raw material that Hrabal had collected would never have achieved a literary significance had it not been exposed to the spotlight of his talent and shaped by his perception. The latter, in turn, has been very much influenced by an admiration for and fervent assimilation of an almost indiscriminately wide range of masterworks of world literature, particularly of the modern period.

Something like that, however, could be said of nearly all serious fiction writers. Wherein lies then Hrabal's originality and the enormous appeal of his work? No doubt in his personal vision, zany and grotesque, and equally in the choice of his characters. They are mostly people from the periphery of life, the misfits, the failures, those who did not quite make it. They compensate for their lack in worldly success with fantasy, fuelled by drink and congenial company. In their bragging, imagination lends magic even to the greyness of everyday life so that it glows with vivid and unexpected colours. Obsessed with the delight and pain of life, they endow their personal histories with meaning by recreating them from discarded bits and pieces. Even in the lowliest and most pathetic of them a "pearl at the bottom" can be found, a spark of humanity that is never quite extinguished.

Hrabal's stories seldom have any real plot. Events, episodes, scraps of observation are either related in a stream of talk, as in *Taneční hodiny pro starší a pokročilé*, written in a single unfinished sentence, or assembled by a technique reminiscent of a surrealist collage. Quite often they are reminiscent of the pictures of Sunday painters that are filled with seemingly unconnected action on every plane and in every corner of the canvas, yet present in fact a unified and integrated view. The similarity does not end here. Although some critics have found in Hrabal's work the application of refined literary skills, it seems that they have been adopted without much conscious effort and that Hrabal's method is really intuitive.

Such opinion may find support in the fact that whenever he has attempted to adjust his work to more conventional standards, e.g., in *A Close Watch on the Trains*, the result has proved to be inferior to his less self-conscious writing. In recent years, when he has been exposed to particular pressures from a political system that frowns upon any artistic eccentricity and non-conformity, he unfortunately on several occasions mutilated or consented to the mutilation of his work in order to assure its publication. Comparison with the original manuscript versions which circulate in the West suggests that a work of art need not only be protected from the censor, but sometimes from its creator as well.

—Igor Hájek

INFANTE, Guillermo Cabrera.   *See* CABRERA INFANTE, Guillermo.

IONESCO, Eugène. French. Born in Slatina, Romania, 26 November 1912; grew up in France. Educated at the University of Bucharest, graduated 1936; the Sorbonne, agrégation de Lettres. Married Rodica Burileanu in 1936; one daughter. Taught French in Bucharest from age 18; worked as a proofreader in Paris, 1938; then free-lance writer. Recipient: Tours Festival Prize, for film, 1959; Italia Prize, 1963; Society of Authors theatre prize (France), 1966; National Grand Prize for Theatre, 1969; Monaco Grand Prize, 1969; Austrian State Prize for European Literature, 1970; Jerusalem Prize, 1973. Honorary doctorate: New York University, 1971; universities of Louvain, Warwick, Tel Aviv. Chevalier, Legion of Honor, 1970. Member, French Academy, 1971. Agent: Société des Auteurs Dramatiques, 9-11 rue Ballu, 75009 Paris. Address: 96 boulevard du Montparnasse, 75014 Paris, France.

Publications

Plays

La Cantatrice chauve (produced Paris, 1950). Included in *Théâtre I*, 1954; as *The Bald Soprano* (produced London, 1956; New York, 1958), in *Plays I*, 1958.
La Leçon (produced Paris, 1951). Included in *Théâtre I*, 1954; as *The Lesson* (produced London and New York, 1958), in *Plays I*, 1958.
Les Chaises (produced Paris, 1952). Included in *Théâtre I*, 1954; as *The Chairs* (produced London, 1957; New York, 1958), in *Plays I*, 1958.
Sept petits sketches (*Les Grandes Chaleurs, Le connaissez-vous?, Le Rhume onirique, La Jeune Fille à marier, Le Maître, Le Nièce-Épouse, Le Salon de l'automobile*) (produced Paris, 1953). *La Jeune Fille à marier* included in *Théâtre II*, 1958, as *Maid to Marry*, in *Plays III*, 1960; *Le Maître* included in *Théâtre II*, 1958, as *The Leader*, in *Plays IV*, 1960; *La Nièce-Épouse* translated as *The Niece-Wife*, in *Ionesco* by Richard N. Coe, 1971; *Le Salon de l'automobile* included in *Théâtre IV*, 1966, as *The Motor Show* in *Plays V*, 1963.
Victimes du devoir (produced Paris, 1953). Included in *Théâtre I*, 1954; as *Victims of Duty* (produced New York, 1960), in *Plays II*, 1958.
Théâtre I (*La Cantatrice chauve; La Leçon; Jacques, ou, La Soumission; Les Chaises; Victimes du devoir; Amédée, ou, Comment s'en débarrasser*). Paris, Gallimard, 1954.
Amédée; ou, Comment s'en débarrasser (produced Paris, 1954). Included in *Théâtre I*, 1954; as *Amedee* (produced New York, 1955), in *Plays II*, 1958.
Jacques; ou, La Soumission (produced Paris, 1955). Included in *Théâtre I*, 1954; as *Jack* (produced New York, 1958), in *Plays I*, 1958.
Le Nouveau Locataire (produced Helsinki, 1955; Paris, 1957). Included in *Théâtre II*, 1958; as *The New Tenant* (produced London, 1956; New York, 1960), in *Plays II*, 1958.
Le Tableau (produced Paris, 1955). Included in *Théâtre III*, 1963; as *The Picture* (produced New York, 1969), in *Plays VII*, 1968.
L'Impromptu de l'Alma; ou, Le Caméléon du berger (produced Paris, 1956). Included in *Théâtre II*, 1958; as *Improvisation; or, The Shepherd's Chameleon* (produced New York, 1960), in *Plays III*, 1960.
L'Avenir est dans les oeufs; ou, Il faut tout pour faire un monde (produced Paris, 1957). Included in *Théâtre II*, 1958; as *The Future Is in Eggs; or, It Takes All Sorts to Make a World*, in *Plays IV*, 1960.
Impromptu pour la Duchesse de Windsor (produced Paris, 1957).
Plays I (*The Chairs; The Bald Soprano; The Lesson; Jack, or, Obedience*). London, Calder, 1958; as *Four Plays*, New York, Grove Press, 1958.
Théâtre II (*L'Impromptu de l'Alma, ou, Le Caméléon du berger; Tueur sans gages; Le Nouveau Locataire; L'Avenir est dans les oeufs, ou, Il faut tout pour faire un monde; Le Maître; La Jeune Fille à marier*). Paris, Gallimard, 1958.

Tueur sans gages (produced Paris, 1959). Included in *Théâtre II*, 1958; as *The Killer* (produced New York, 1960), in *Plays III*, 1960.

Plays II (*Amedee, or, How to Get Rid of It*; *The New Tenant*; *Victims of Duty*). New York, Grove Press, 1958; London, Calder, 1961.

Rhinocéros (produced Dusseldorf, 1959; Paris, 1960). Included in *Théâtre III*, 1963; translated as *Rhinoceros* (produced London, 1960; New York, 1961), in *Plays IV*, 1960.

Scène à quatre (produced Spoleto, 1959). Included in *Théâtre III*, 1963; as *Foursome* (produced London, 1970), in *Plays V*, 1963.

Apprendre à marcher (ballet scenario; produced Paris, 1960). Included in *Théâtre IV*, 1966; as *Learning to Walk*, in *Plays IX*, 1973.

Plays III (*The Killer*; *Improvisation, or, The Shepherd's Chameleon*; *Maid to Marry*). New York, Grove Press, 1960; London, Calder, 1962.

Plays IV (*Rhinoceros*; *The Leader*; *The Future Is in Eggs, or, It Takes All Sorts to Make a World*). New York, Grove Press, 1960; London, Calder, 1963.

Délire à deux (produced Paris, 1962). Included in *Théâtre III*, 1963; as *Frenzy for Two*, in *Plays VI*, 1965.

Le Roi se meurt (produced Paris, 1962). Paris, Gallimard, 1963; as *Exit the King* (produced London, 1963; Ann Arbor, Michigan, 1967), New York, Grove Press, 1963; in *Plays V*, 1963.

Le Piéton de l'air (produced Dusseldorf, 1962; Paris, 1963). Included in *Théâtre III*, 1963; as *A Stroll in the Air* (produced New York, 1964), in *Plays VI*, 1965.

Théâtre III (*Rhinocéros*; *Le Piéton de l'air*; *Délire à deux*; *Le Tableau*; *Scène à quatre*; *Les Salutations*; *La Colère*). Paris, Gallimard, 1963.

Plays V (*Exit the King, The Motor Show, Foursome*). London, Calder, 1963.

Les Salutations (produced London, 1970). Included in *Théâtre III*, 1963; as *Salutations*, in *Plays VII*, 1968.

La Soif et la faim (produced Dusseldorf, 1964; Paris, 1966). Included in *Théâtre IV*, 1966; as *Hunger and Thirst* (produced Stockbridge, Massachusetts, 1969), in *Plays VII*, 1968.

La Lacune (produced Paris, 1965). Included in *Théâtre IV*, 1966.

Plays VI (*A Stroll in the Air, Frenzy for Two*). London, Calder, 1965; New York, Grove Press, 1968.

Pour préparer un oeuf dur (produced Paris, 1966). Included in *Théâtre IV*, 1966.

Théâtre IV (*Le Roi se meurt*, *La Soif et la faim*; *La Lacune*; *Le Salon de l'automobile*; *L'Oeuf dur*; *Pour préparer un oeuf dur*; *Le Jeune Homme à marier*; *Apprendre à marcher*). Paris, Gallimard, 1966.

Plays VII (*Hunger and Thirst, The Picture, Anger, Salutations*). London, Calder, 1968; New York, Grove Press, 1969.

Jeux de massacre (produced Dusseldorf and Paris, 1970). Paris, Gallimard, 1970; as *Killing Game* (as *Wipe-Out Game*, produced Washington, D.C. 1971), New York, Grove Press, 1974.

Plays VIII (*Here Comes a Chopper, The Oversight, The Foot of the Wall*). London, Calder and Boyars, 1971.

Macbett (produced Paris, 1972). Paris, Gallimard, 1972; translated as *Macbett*, in *Plays IX*, 1973.

Plays IX (*Macbett, The Mire, Learning to Walk*). London, Calder and Boyars, 1973.

Ce formidable bordel (produced Paris, 1973). Paris, Gallimard, 1973.

Théâtre V (*Jeux de massacre, Macbett, La Vase, Exercices de conversation et de diction françaises pour étudiants américains*). Paris, Gallimard, 1974.

L'Homme aux valises (produced Paris, 1975). Paris, Gallimard, 1975; as *Man with Bags* (produced Baltimore, 1977), New York, Grove Press, 1977; as *The Man with the Luggage*, in *Plays XI*, 1979.

A Hell of a Mess. New York, Grove Press, 1975.

Plays X (*Oh What a Bloody Circus, The Hard-Boiled Egg*). London, Calder and Boyars,

1976.
Plays XI (The Man with the Luggage, The Duel, Double Act). London, Calder, 1979.
Théâtre VII (Voyages chez les morts: Thèmes et variations). Paris, Gallimard, 1981; as *Plays XII (Journey among the Dead),* London, Calder, 1983.

Screenplays: "La Colère" episode in *Les Sept Péchés capitaux,* 1962; *Monsieur Tête* (animated film), 1970.

Ballet Scenarios for Television, with Fleming Flindt: *La Leçon,* 1963; *Le Jeune Homme à marier,* 1965; *The Triumph of Death,* 1971.

Fiction

La Photo du Colonel. Paris, Gallimard, 1962; as *The Colonel's Photograph,* London, Faber, 1967; New York, Grove Press, 1969.
Le Solitaire. Paris, Mercure de France, 1973; as *The Hermit,* New York, Viking Press, 1974; London, Deutsch, 1975.

Other

Elegii pentru fiinti mici. Craiova, Romania, Scirsul Romanesc, 1931.
Nu! Bucharest, Vremea, 1934.
Notes et contre-notes. Paris, Gallimard, 1962; revised edition, 1966; as *Notes and Counter-Notes,* New York, Grove Press, 1964.
Entretiens avec Claude Bonnefoy. Paris, Belfond, 1966; as *Conversations with Ionesco,* London, Faber, 1970; New York, Holt Rinehart, 1971.
Journal en miettes. Paris, Mercure de France, 1967; as *Fragments of a Journal,* New York, Grove Press, 1968.
Présent passé, passé présent. Paris, Mercure de France, 1968; as *Present Past, Past Present,* New York, Grove Press, 1971; London, Calder and Boyars, 1972.
Conte pour enfants. Paris, Quist, 4 vols., 1969-75; as *Story for Children,* New York, Quist, 1968-75.
Découvertes, illustrated by the author. Geneva, Skira, 1969.
Mise en train: Première année de français, with Michael Benamou. New York, Macmillan, 1969.
Monsieur Tête (animated film text). Munich, Bruckmann, 1970.
Discours de réception à l'Académie française.... Paris, Gallimard, 1971.
Entre la vie et la rêve: Entretiens avec Claude Bonnefoy. Paris, Belfond, 1977.
Antidotes. Paris, Gallimard, 1977.
Un Homme en question. Paris, Gallimard, 1979.
Le Noir et le blanc. St. Gallen, Erker, 1980.
Hugoliade. Paris, Gallimard, 1982.

*

Bibliography: *Ionesco: A Bibliography* by Griffith R. Hughes and Ruth Bury, Cardiff, University of Wales Press, 1974; *Bibliographie et index thématique des études sur Ionesco* by Wolfgang Leiner, Fribourg, Editions Universitaires, 1980.

Critical Studies: *Ionesco* by Richard N. Coe, New York, Grove Press, 1961, revised edition, London, Methuen, 1971; *Ionesco* by Leonard C. Pronko, New York, Columbia University Press, 1965; *Ionesco and Genet* by Josephine Jacobsen and William Randolph Mueller, New York, Hill and Wang, 1968; *Brecht and Ionesco: Commitment in Context* by J.H. Wulbern,

Urbana, University of Illinois Press, 1971; *Ionesco* by Ronald Hayman, London, Heinemann, 1972; *Ionesco* by Allan Lewis, New York, Twayne, 1972; *Ionesco: A Collection of Critical Essays* edited by Rose C. Lamont, Englewood Cliffs, New Jersey, Prentice Hall, 1973, and *The Two Faces of Ionesco* edited by Lamont and M.J. Friedman, Troy, New York, Whitston, 1978.

*   *   *

Like some other members of the new drama movement which burst on the French stage in the early 1950's, such as Beckett and Adamov, Eugène Ionesco was an outsider: a Romanian who did not come from an orthodox French literary background. His first play, *The Bald Soprano*, created a sensation when it was put on in a small theatre in Paris, and the so-called "theatre of the absurd" was suddenly born. At least, not quite suddenly; there had been a few lone forerunners, like *Ubu Roi*, Jarry's iconoclastic play of 1896, or Apollinaire's *Les Mamelles de Tirésias*, a quixotic plea for repopulation uttered in the darkest years of World War I, but they remained without much of a following. Ionesco's dazzling comedy about a couple who discover, after a long and increasingly zany conversation, that they are man and wife, changed all that. It came like a bolt from the blue, not surprisingly, since it was not based on anything which had gone before in the theatre, but on the eminently actable exchanges on a Linguaphone record which Ionesco had bought in an attempt to teach himself English conversation.

That simple initial stroke of genius—to perceive theatricality where no one else had thought to look for it—launched Ionesco on a controversial but lucrative career which has brought him many honours, of which the one he most prizes is perhaps election to that élite literary establishment in France, the Académie Française. He has, however, missed the Nobel Prize— Beckett won it instead—which indicates no doubt the extent and limitations of his achievement: that he is a prolific and inventive writer but not a great one, whose best work was done in the earlier part of his career.

The Lesson, for instance, is a superb piece of theatre, in which a girl's private lesson turns into ritual rape and murder as the tutor "assaults" her with words which pour unstoppably from his lips. *The Chairs* is also concerned with proliferation, something of an Ionesco trade mark: in this case chairs fill the stage as an elderly couple welcome an invisible audience to listen to the wisdom of an orator who turns out to be dumb. In *Victims of Duty* one character is stuffed with food he does not want and another dies a "victim of duty" in a black comedy which disturbs and amuses the audience simultaneously. This gift—of treating serious matters with unsettling levity—is exercised to perfection in *Amedee*, perhaps Ionesco's finest work. Amedee is host to a corpse which he cannot rid his flat of (hence the subtitle "how to get rid of it"); indeed, it starts instead to grow, and mushrooms spring up from his floors. Hilariously incapable of disposing of the suffocating nuisance, Amedee (who, it is revealed, is a failed playwright) floats away from it all to the consternation of his long-suffering wife and the dismay of a passing policeman, who laments the loss to literature of such a promising writer.

There is a unique charm about the plays which Ionesco wrote in the early 1950's that disappears from *The Killer* (1958) onwards, when the writing becomes more didactic and less dramatically inventive. *The Killer* is about a character called Bérenger, who stands for Ionesco himself and all decent, ordinary people; this man is overwhelmed by evil he cannot control in the shape of an assassin who ignores all his honest and liberal words and bears down mercilessly upon him as the curtain falls. Bérenger is also the protagonist in *Rhinoceros*, a play about crowds and power, the gullibility of the masses and the insidiousness of propaganda, and becomes a kind of spokesman for Ionesco's own anti-totalitarian political position. This is all very worthy, but it makes for tiresome watching in the theatre. The same applies to the long plays which followed, *Exit the King, Hunger and Thirst*, and *Macbett*, the last of which is in the same line as Edward Bond's *Lear* or Stoppard's *Rosencrantz and Guildenstern Are Dead*, all meditations upon or adaptations of Shakespeare.

The recent plays have been put on in major theatres by prestige companies—a far cry from the pocket theatres which launched Ionesco in the early 1950's—but the critics' reaction has been mixed. There was always a tendency in this playwright to verbosity, but whereas in *The Lesson* the exuberant language was almost a character in its own right, in the later plays it becomes mere windy rhetoric. This should not, however, detract from the magnitude of the achievement represented by the sheer theatrical inventiveness of the early work; besides, Ionesco is not merely a playwright. His meditations on the art of theatre, collected in *Notes and Counter-Notes*, are a major contribution to the theory of drama, a not unworthy successor to Artaud's *The Theatre and Its Double* (1938) which has had such an important influence on the sort of theatre which Ionesco took a leading part in creating, a theatre in which traditional notions of stagecraft are abandoned in favour of a more dream-like conception of plot and character.

Ionesco is also a poet (his earliest writings are in Romanian), a short story writer of some power (especially in tales which deal in concentrated form with the dream situations subsequently elaborated into full-length stage works), and a charming autobiographer and essayist. He is just the sort of prolific, elegant, and versatile writer whom the French Academy likes to recruit, and it is very much to his credit that he achieved election to this body notwithstanding his foreign origins. He is a fine if not a great writer, and thanks to *The Bald Soprano*, which so astonished Paris first-nighters on May 11, 1950, he is assured for ever of an honourable place in theatre history.

—John Fletcher

JACCOTTET, Philippe. Born in Moudon, Switzerland, 30 June 1925. Educated at the University of Lausanne, 1944-46, graduated 1946. Married Anne-Marie Haesler in 1953; one son and one daughter. Translator for Mermod publishers, Lausanne, 1946-53. Since 1953 has lived in Grignan, France. Recipient: Hermès Prize, 1962; Voss Prize, for translation, 1966; Lausanne Prize, 1970; Ramuz Prize, 1970; Montaigne Prize (Hamburg), 1972; Halpérine-Kaminsky Prize, for translation, 1973; Larbaud Prize, 1978. Address: c/o Maeght, 13 Rue de Téhéran, 75008 Paris, France.

PUBLICATIONS

Verse

Requiem. Lausanne, Mermod, 1947.
L'Effraie et autres poésies. Paris, Gallimard, 1953.
L'Ignorant: Poèmes 1952-1956. Paris, Gallimard, 1958.
Airs: Poèmes 1961-1964. Paris, Gallimard, 1967.
Leçons. Lausanne, Payot, 1969.
Poésie 1946-1967. Paris, Gallimard, 1971.
Chants d'en bas. Lausanne, Payot, 1974.
Breathings, translated by Cid Corman. New York, Grossman, 1974.

Fiction

L'Obscurité: Récit. Paris, Gallimard, 1961.

Other

La Promenade sous les arbres: Proses. Lausanne, Mermod, 1957.
Éléments d'un songe: Proses. Paris, Gallimard, 1961.
La Semaison: Carnets 1954-1962. Lausanne, Payot, 1963; revised edition, as *La Semaison: Carnets 1954-1967*, Paris, Gallimard, 1971; as *Seedtime*, New York, New Directions, 1977.
Paysages de Grignan. Lausanne, Bibliothèque des Arts, 1964.
Autriche. Lausanne, Rencontre, 1966.
L'Entretien des muses: Chroniques de poésie. Paris, Gallimard, 1968.
Paysages avec figures absentes: Proses. Paris, Gallimard, 1970.
Rilke par lui-même. Paris, Seuil, 1971.
À travers un verger. Montpellier, Fata Morgana, 1975; as *Through an Orchard*, Portree, Isle of Skye, Aquila, 1978.
Adieu à Gustave Roud, with Maurice Chappaz and Jacques Chessex. Vevey, Switzerland, Galland, 1977.
Beauregard. Paris, Maeght, 1981.

Editor, *Élégies et autres vers*, by Francis Jammes. Lausanne, Mermod, 1946.
Editor, *Gustave Roud.* Paris, Seghers, 1968.

Translator, *La Mort à Venise*, by Mann. Lausanne, Mermod, 1946.
Translator, *L'Odyssée*, by Homer. Paris, Club Français du Livre, 1955.
Translator, *L'Homme sans qualités*, by Musil. Paris, Seuil, 1957.
Translator, *Les Désarrois de l'élève Törless*, by Musil. Paris, Livre de Poche, 1967.
Translator, *Le Vaisseau des morts*, by B. Traven. Paris, Livre de Poche, 1967.
Translator, *Oeuvres complètes*, by Hölderlin. Paris, Gallimard, 1967.
Translator, *Correspondance*, by Rilke. Paris, Seuil, 1976.
Translator, *Le Banquet*, by Plato. Lausanne, L'Aire, 1979.

Also translator of novels by Carlo Cassola and others.

*

Critical Study: *Jaccottet* by Alain Clerval, Paris, Seghers, 1976.

*   *   *

Philippe Jaccottet is one of the more interesting poets writing in French who emerged in the postwar period. He is a French writer in the same sense that Rousseau is: he remains closer to the natural world than his Parisian counterparts, and his Swiss origins find their way into his poetry even though he has long since taken up residence in rural Southern France. The parallel with Rousseau is, moreover, suggested by Jaccottet's 1957 book *Promenade sous les arbres*, a solitary meditation on nature and poetry. His notebooks for the period 1954 to 1967 likewise take their title from a rural, agricultural image: *Seedtime*. The notes in *Seeedtime* are in fact the best introduction to Jaccottet's collected poetry, a sizable part of which Cid Corman has ably translated as *Breathings*.

The four major collections of Jaccottet's poetic maturity show a relatively clear evolution of his craft. *L'Effraie* features regular alexandrines in rhymed couplets, as in "Portovenere," and very competent and sensitive sonnets: "Comme je suis un étranger dans notre vie" (As I am a stranger in our life), "Comme un homme qui se plairait dans la tristesse" (Like a man who would take pleasure in sadness), and others, none of which is translated in *Breathings*. The overall mood is somewhat sombre and austere. The dominant tone is suggested by the title poem: the screech-owl's call announces an imminent death. By the time of his third collection, *Airs*, which groups poems written from 1961 to 1964, Jaccottet had moved away from the regular versification of his beginnings. A loose octosyllabic line provides a basic rhythm that is frequently quickened by seven- or five-syllable lines. Along with this formal evolution, one notes a gradual disappearance of the lyrical I.

Jaccottet's preferred imagery includes the extinguished lamp and the mysterious, yet awaited, voice. His privileged moment is the darkness just before daybreak, his seasons, autumn and winter: "There where the earth ends/lifted very near air/(in the light where the invisible/dream of God roams)//between rock and reverie//that snow: ermine escapes" (*Airs*). The first poem of *Leçons* constitutes a remarkable criticism of Jaccottet's earlier verse in *L'Effraie* and *L'Ignorant*, a lesson is poetic humility: "Once/I, the frightened, the ignorant, hardly alive,/covering my eyes with images,/pretended to guide the dying and dead.//I, the sheltered,/spared, hardly suffering poet,/dared trace paths in the abyss.//Now, lamp blown out,/hand more errant, trembling,/I start again slowly in the air" (from *Breathings*). The new discontinuities and breaks in both rhythm and imagery attempt, often with great success, to move ever closer to the precarious uncertainties of human life.

In France Jaccottet is probably better known as a translator than as a poet. His translations from the German are especially good and, in the case of Musil and Mann, have played a significant role in the dissemination of their novels among readers of French. His translations of Hölderlin and Rilke are also worthy of note.

—A. James Arnold

JANSSON, Tove (Marika). Finnish. Born in Helsinki, 9 August 1914. Studied at art schools in Stockholm, Helsinki, and Paris. Writer (in Swedish), and artist: creator of the Moomins in cartoon and book form; cartoon strip *Moomin* appeared in *Evening News*, London, 1953-60; several individual shows. Recipient: Lagerlöf Medal, 1942, 1972; Finnish Academy Award, 1959; Andersen Medal, 1966; Finnish State Prize, 1971; Swedish Academy Prize, 1972. Address: c/o Schildts Förlagsaktiebolag, Annegatan 16, 90120 Helsinki 12, Finland.

PUBLICATIONS

Fiction

Lyssnerskan [The Listener]. Stockholm, Bonnier, 1971.
Sommarboken. Stockholm, Bonnier, 1972; as *The Summer Book*, New York, Pantheon, and London, Hutchinson, 1975.
Solstaden. Stockholm, Bonnier, 1974; as *Sun City*, New York, Pantheon, 1976; London, Hutchinson, 1977.
Dockskåpet och andra berättelser [The Doll's House and Other Stories]. Stockholm, Bonnier, 1978.
Den ärliga bedragaren [The Honest Cheat]. Stockholm, Bonnier, 1982.

Other

Mumintrollet och Kometen. Helsinki, Söderstrom, 1946; as *Comet in Moominland*, London, Benn, 1951; New York, Walck, 1967.

Trollkarlens Hatt. Helsinki, Schildt, 1949; as *Finn Family Moomintroll,* London, Benn, 1950; as *The Happy Moomins,* Indianapolis, Bobbs Merrill, 1951.
Muminpappans Bravader. Helsinki, Schildt, 1950; as *The Exploits of Moominpappa,* London, Benn, 1952; New York, Walck, 1966.
Hur Gick det Sen? Helsinki, Schildt, 1952; as *Moomin Mymble and Little My,* London, Benn, 1953.
Farlig Midsommar. Helsinki, Schildt, 1954; as *Moominsummer Madness,* London, Benn, 1955; New York, Walck, 1961.
Trollvinter. Helsinki, Schildt, 1957; as *Moominland Midwinter,* London, Benn, 1958; New York, Walck, 1962.
Vem Ska trösta knyttet? Helsinki, Schildt, 1960; as *Who Will Comfort Toffle?,* London, Benn, 1960.
Det Osynliga Barnet och andra berättelser. Helsinki, Schildt, 1962; as *Tales from Moominvalley,* London, Benn, 1963; New York, Walck, 1964.
Pappan och Havet. Helsinki, Schildt, 1965; as *Moomin Pappa at Sea,* London, Benn, 1966; New York, Walck, 1967.
Muminpappans memoarer. Stockholm, Gebers, 1968.
Bildhuggarens Dotter (autobiography). Stockholm, Almqvist & Wiksell, 1968; as *Sculptor's Daughter,* London, Benn, 1969.
Sent i November. Helsinki, Schildt, 1970; as *Moominvalley in November,* London, Benn, and New York, Walck, 1971.
Den farliga resan. Stockholm, Bonnier, 1977; as *The Dangerous Journey,* London, Benn, 1978.

*

Critical Studies: *Jansson: Pappan och Havet* (in English), Hull, University of Hull Department of Scandinavian Studies, 1979, and *Jansson,* Boston, Twayne, 1984, both by W. Glyn Jones.

*   *   *

As the author of the Moomin books, Tove Jansson is internationally famous. However, even at an early stage in the Moomin stories, an adult element begins to emerge, centred on obsession, the limit to contact between different creatures, the problems of the artist. In *Moominland Midwinter* the childish element is already beginning to recede, and Tove Jansson is concerned with the phenomenon of change in living beings and with the question of establishing the nature of reality. The collection of short stories entitled *Tales from Moominvalley* moves directly into these central themes in stories which are only superficially for children. The last two of the Moomin books continue this process, and it is doubtful whether children can any longer really understand them. The themes are adult, though they are presented in the guise of children's stories.

Tove Jansson now takes the logical step of moving into adult literature proper, originally with semi-autobiographical stories with a simple charm which should not blind the reader to the deeper implications. The account of her childhood as a sculptor's daughter gives scope for consideration of the artist's problem, while the account of a child's relationship with an ageing grandmother allows an exploration of the extent and limit of human contact.

Subsequent works show an increasing interest in the abnormal sides of human nature, in the frightening power of the imagination, and in the loneliness of the individual. The most important volume of short stories, *Dockskåpet* (The Doll's House), moves yet further into the realm of the abnormal in a series of gripping and disturbing stories in which the predatory nature of artistic inspiration is added to the earlier themes. One particular aspect of Tove Jansson's psychological preoccupations is senility, and this she makes the central motif in a novel about life in an American community for the aged, *Sun City.* All the old people living in one house are portrayed with both humour and warm sympathy. The symbolism in this novel seems to imply the need for some kind of dream on which to survive.

The latest novel, *Den ärliga bedragaren* (The Honest Cheat), returns to the themes of the predatory nature of certain human relationships and the difficulty of establishing contact between two radically different and unusual personalities; the problems of the artist form a dramatic background.

Tove Jansson is now established as a major writer of penetrating and highly idiosyncratic adult fiction, an author who has made the very difficult transition from a writer of children's fantasies to books completely beyond the comprehension of children. Taken as a whole, her work shows an impressive thematic unity transcending the two genres in which she has excelled. The honours bestowed on her betoken the esteem in which she is held both at home and abroad.

—W. Glyn Jones

JOHNSON, Uwe. German. Born in Kämmin, Pomerania (now in Poland), 20 July 1934. Educated at a school in Güstrow; University of Rostock, 1952-54; University of Leipzig, 1954-56, diploma in philology 1956. Married Elizabeth Schmidt in 1962; one daughter. Free-lance writer: lived in Güstrow to 1959, in West Berlin, 1959-74, and in England since 1975. Lecturer, Wayne State University, Detroit, and Harvard University, Cambridge, Massachusetts, 1961; editor of German writing, Harcourt Brace, publishers, New York, 1966-67. Recipient: Berlin Academy Fontane Prize, 1960; International Publishers Prize, 1962; Villa Massino grant, 1962; Büchner Prize, 1971; Raabe Prize, 1975; Thomas Mann Prize (Lübeck), 1978. Address: c/o Suhrkamp Verlag, Lindenstrasse 29-35, Postfach 4229, 6000 Frankfurt am Main, Germany. *Died in March 1984.*

PUBLICATIONS

Fiction

Mutmassungen über Jakob. Frankfurt, Suhrkamp, 1959; as *Speculations about Jakob*, New York, Grove Press, and London, Cape, 1963.
Das dritte Buch über Achim. Frankfurt, Suhrkamp, 1961; as *The Third Book about Achim*, New York, Harper, 1967.
Karsch und andere Prosa. Frankfurt, Suhrkamp, 1964; translated in part as *An Absence*, London, Cape, 1969.
Zwei Ansichten. Frankfurt, Suhrkamp, 1965; as *Two Views*, New York, Harcourt Brace, 1966; London, Cape, 1967.
Jahrestage: Aus dem Leben von Gesine Cresspahl. Frankfurt, Suhrkamp, 4 vols., 1970-83; vols. 1-2 translated as *Anniversaries: From the Life of Gesine Cresspahl*, New York, Harcourt Brace, 1975.
Von dem Fischer un syner Fru: Ein Märchen nach Philipp Otto Runge. Frankfurt, Insel, 1976.
Skizze eines Verunglückten. Frankfurt, Suhrkamp, 1982.

Other

Eine Reise nach Klagenfurt. Frankfurt, Suhrkamp, 1974.

Berliner Sachen: Aufsätze. Frankfurt, Suhrkamp, 1975.
Begleitumstände: Frankfurter Vorlesungen. Frankfurt, Suhrkamp, 1980.

Editor, *Me-ti: Buch der Wendungen*, by Brecht. Frankfurt, Suhrkamp, 1965.
Editor, with Hans Mayer, *Das Werk von Samuel Beckett—Berliner Colloquium.* Frankfurt, Suhrkamp, 1975.
Editor, *Stich-Worte*, by Max Frisch, Frankfurt, Suhrkamp, 1975.

Translator, *Israel Potter*, by Herman Melville. Leipzig, Dieterich, 1960.
Translator, *In diesem Land*, by John Knowles. Frankfurt, Suhrkamp, 1963.

*

Bibliography: *Johnson: Bibliographie* by Nicolai Riedel, Bonn, Bouvier, 1981.

Critical Studies: *Über Johnson* edited by Reinhart Baumgart, Frankfurt, Suhrkamp, 1970; *Johnson* by Mark Boulby, New York, Ungar, 1974; *Ich und Er: First and Third Person Self-Reference and Problems of Identity in Three Contemporary German-Language Novels* by Paul F. Botheroyd, The Hague, Mouton, 1976.

*   *   *

Uwe Johnson's first novel, *Speculations about Jakob*, both acclaimed for its originality and condemned for its puzzling intricacy, was one of the first literary evocations of life in divided Germany. Its indirect approach indeed requires hard work from the reader to reconstruct even the sequence of events from its montage of action, conversation, and memory. Nevertheless it is now unquestionably one of the subtlest presentations of an often trivialised theme. Johnson's picture of the two Germanys avoids all political sensationalism and attempts instead to capture the depth of division by revealing two differing concepts of personality. Jakob is their focus, his death an expression of their irreconcilability. One system sees history as an inevitable socio-political progression, to which the individual Jakob must subordinate all personal moral values. The other prizes individuality, and the novel's complex form presents a view of Jakob's personality as the nexus of many strands of human experience; yet "freedom" can also mean lack of orientation, and Jakob's death derives not from political pressure but the impossibility of choosing between two imperfect worlds.

After this remarkable first novel Johnson's subsequent works seem perhaps less challenging. In *The Third Book about Achim* he covers similar thematic ground. A Western reporter's inability to write a book on an East German sporting hero highlights again the two states' radically different conceptions of personality, the one subsumed in function, the other presup-posing some "truth" behind it. The novel is thought-provoking, particularly in its exploration of two different German languages; yet precisely because the quest leads to emptiness, *The Third Book about Achim* leave a necessarily flat impression, quite unlike Johnson's first novel. The same might be said about *Two Views*, in which he takes an "obvious" starting point, a Romeo and Juliet love story across the Berlin Wall, and shows ironically that the separation is not in the end physical but emotional, that the relationship is indeed sustained only by shared resentment of the Wall.

Since then Johnson has published few works in number, but the four volumes of *Anniversaries* are a major achievement. Taking up characters from his first novel, he follows their histories back into Nazi Germany and forward into modern US society, but this is no popular sequel for curiosity's sake. On one level he is strongly reinforcing his view of individuality as supremely important, by granting his figures extended personal histories; on another he is emphasising that personality means the responsible exercising of moral choices. Both aspects fascinate by the vivid detail of their depiction, but perhaps most fascinating of all is the sustained counter-point of past and present. The past holds lessons for the great issues of today, and involvement in current moral debate points up the ambiguities of the past. Nazi Germany to Vietnam and beyond: personal views of Western history, and historical consciousness as a major part of the continuous development that is personality. Time, memory, the processes of perception, the emancipation of personal judgement—these are themes which should ensure Johnson's magnum opus a lasting reputation.

—Mary E. Stewart

KEMAL, Yashar (Yasar Kemal Gokçeli). Turkish. Born in Adana, in autumn 1923. Educated at schools in Kadirli. Married Thilda Serrero in 1952; one son. Worked as farmhand, cobbler's apprentice, construction worker, clerk, and petition writer in southern Turkey; reporter, *Cumhuriyet* newspaper, Istanbul, 1951-63; then full-time writer. Editor, *Ant* Marxist weekly, in 1960's; on Central Committee of Turkish Labor Party; arrested and tried for communist propaganda, 1950, and imprisoned briefly for political views, 1971. Former President, Turkish Writers Union. Recipient: Varlik Prize, 1956; Iskender Award, 1966; International Theatre Festival Prize, (Nancy), 1966; Madarali Award, 1973; Foreign Book Prize (France), 1979; Cino del Duca Prize (France), 1982. Commander, Legion of Honor, 1984. Address: P.K. 14, Basinköy, Istanbul, Turkey.

PUBLICATIONS

Fiction

Sari Sicak [Yellow Heat]. Istanbul, Varlik, 1952.
Ince Memed. Istanbul, Remzi, 1955; as *Memed, My Hawk*, New York, Pantheon, and London, Collins, 1961.
Teneke [The Drumming-Out]. Istanbul, Varlik, 1955.
Ortadirek. Istanbul, Remzi, 1960; as *The Wind from the Plain*, London, Collins, 1963; New York, Dodd Mead, 1969.
Yer Demir, Gök Bakir. Istanbul, Guven, 1963; as *Iron Earth, Copper Sky*, London, Collins, 1974; New York, Morrow, 1979.
Üç Anadolu Efsanesi [Three Anatolian Legends]. Istanbul, Ararat, 1967.
Bütün Hikâyeler. Istanbul, Ararat, 1967; translated in part as *Anatolian Tales*, London, Collins, 1968; New York, Dodd Mead, 1969.
Ince Memed II. Istanbul, Ant, 1969; as *They Burn the Thistles*, London, Collins, 1973; New York, Morrow, 1977.
Ölmez Otu. Istanbul, Ant, 1969; as *The Undying Grass*, London, Collins, 1977; New York, Morrow, 1978.
Ağridaği Efsanesi. Istanbul, Cem, 1970; as *The Legend of Ararat*, London, Collins, 1975.
Binboğalar Efsanesi. Istanbul, Cem, 1971; as *The Legend of the Thousand Bulls*, London, Collins, 1976.
Çakircale efe [The Bandit Çakircali]. Istanbul, Ararat, 1972.
Akçasazin Ağalari [The Lords of Akchasaz]:

1. *Demirciler Çarsisi Cinayeti.* Istanbul, Cem, 1974; as *Murder in the Ironsmiths Market*, London, Collins, 1979; New York, Morrow, 1980.
2. *Yusufçuk Yusuf* [Yusuf, Little Yusuf]. Istanbul, Cem, 1975.
Yilani Öldürseler [Kill the Serpent]. Istanbul, Cem, 1976.
Al Gözüm Seyreyle Salih. Istanbul, Cem, 1976; as *The Saga of a Seagull*, London, Collins, 1981; as *Seagull*, New York, Pantheon, 1981.
Kuslar da Gitti [The Birds Are Gone]. Istanbul, Milliyet, 1978.
Deniz Küstü [The Sea Is Sullen]. Istanbul, Milliyet, 1978.
Kimsecik [A Little Nobody]. Istanbul, Tekin, 1980.
Hüyükteki nar Ağaci [Pomegranate on the Knoll]. Istanbul, Toros, 1982.
Ince Memed III. Istanbul, Toros, 1984.

Plays

Teneke [The Drumming-Out], from his own play (produced Istanbul, 1965).
Yer Demir, Gök Bakir [Iron Earth, Copper Sky], from his own play (produced Nancy, 1966; Istanbul, 1967).

Other

Yanan Ormanlarda Elli Gün [Fifty Days in Burning Forests]. Istanbul, Türkiye Ormancilar Cemiyeti, 1955.
Çukurova Yana Yana [Chukurova Up in Flames]. Istanbul, Yeditepe, 1955.
Peri Bacalari [Fairy Chimneys]. Istanbul, Varlik, 1957.
Tas Çatlassa [The Stones Cry Out]. Istanbul, Ataç, 1961.
Bu Diyai Bastan Basa [This Country from Top to Bottom]. Istanbul, Cem, 1972.
Bir Bulut Kayniyor [A Cloud Is Churning]. Istanbul, Cem, 1974.
Baldaki Tuz [Salt in the Honey]. Istanbul, Cem, 1974.
Filler Sultani ile Kirmizki Sakalli Topal Karinca [The Sultan of the Elephants and the Red-Bearded Lame Ant]. Istanbul, Cem, 1977.
Allahin Askerleri [God's Soldiers]. Istanbul, Milliyet, 1978.
Ağacin Çürüğü [Dry Rot in the Tree]. Istanbul, Milliyet, 1980.

*

Critical Studies: "Kemal Issue" of *Edebiyat: A Journal of Middle Eastern Literatures 5*, nos. 1-2, 1980.

*   *   *

"Traditionally and temperamentally," Yashar Kemal wrote in the early 1970's, "I feel drawn to the art of Homer and Cervantes." Although it is difficult to detect any links between him and Cervantes, an imaginative critic can divine Kemal's aspiration to create a modern saga in the spirit of the Homeric epic. Aspects of his fiction invite comparison with Tolstoy, Hardy, Steinbeck, Silone, and Faulkner. Kemal himself has often paid tribute to "Father Faulkner," drawing analogies between Yoknapatawpha County and his own Chukurova, the fertile plains of southern Turkey where the dramatic events of most of Kemal's major novels take place.

Frequently mentioned as a candidate for the Nobel Prize for Literature, Kemal enjoys immense popularity in Turkey. He has been extensively translated into all major and some minor languages (his first novel, *Memed, My Hawk*, is available in no less than 25 languages). Particularly in France, the Scandinavian countries, and many Socialist nations, his works have drawn critical praise and achieved wide circulation.

Kemal's youthful literary interests were molded by poetry and oral narrative. His first publication was a collection of elegies from southern Turkey, and his earliest writings that brought him to national attention were short vivid reportorial pieces published in the influential daily *Cumhuriyet*. His early predilections are discernible in his fiction in many refined and compelling ways: the narrative style has a strong affinity to the Turkish oral tradition and a penchant for poetic devices, often dominated by an elegiac tone. Many of the scenes are suffused with the heightened effects that had characterized the author's early journalistic writing—sharp focus on events and characters, an unmistaking ear for rhythms of speech, and a masterful description of locale and action.

Memed, My Hawk, made into a film by Peter Ustinov (premiered in 1984), is an action-filled novel about a brigand who becomes a folk hero by taking up arms against the exploiters of the poor. This novel, and virtually all the other works of fiction Kemal published until the mid-1970's, are among the masterworks of Turkey's so-called "Village Literature" which depicts the plight of peasants living in abject poverty in the grip of a feudal system. His second novel, *The Wind from the Plain*, although less popular than *Memed, My Hawk*, is likely to endure as the author's best. Compared by some critics to Steinbeck's *Grapes of Wrath*, it is a moving saga of destitute peasants trudging along in search of work. The trilogy comprising *The Wind from the Plain*, *Iron Earth*, *Copper Sky*, and *The Undying Grass* represents the zenith of Kemal's achievement and has somewhat overshadowed his other multi-volume novels as well as his fiction about coastal towns and city life since the mid-1970's.

Kemal's later novels display a stronger reliance on the lyrical style and stream-of-consciousness techniques and a tendency to blend realistic depictions with myth and fantasy. In some, sprawling narration tends to lose the power that characterizes his earlier crisp style.

Raymond Williams describes Kemal as a prime example of a novelist of social change. In an intensely personal formulation, Kemal unfurls, almost in poetic terms, the harsh reality of the countryside, with its beauties and brutalities, with its myths and passions. His entire work stands as an indictment of an archaic unjust system and reaffirms his faith and optimism in the eventual triumph of the human spirit.

—Talat S. Halman

KIS, Danilo. Yugoslav. Born in Subotica, 22 February 1935. Educated at Belgrade University, degree in comparative literature 1958. Editor, *Vidici*. Spent several years in France as lecturer in Serbo-Croat at various universities. Recipient: NIN Prize, 1973; Goran Prize, 1977. Address: c/o Nolit Publishing House, Terazijie 27/II, Postanski fah 369, 11000 Belgrade, Yugoslavia.

PUBLICATIONS

Fiction

Mansarda; Psalam 44 [The Garret, Psalm 44]. Belgrade, Kosmos, 1962.
Bašta, pepeo. Belgrade, Prosveta, 1965; as *Garden, Ashes*, New York, Harcourt Brace, 1976.

Rani jadi [Early Sorrows]. Belgrade, Nolit, 1970.
Peščanik [Sand-Glass]. Belgrade, Prosveta, 1972.
Grobnica za Borisa Davidoviča. Belgrade, Beogradski izdavačko-grafički zavod-Zagreb, Liber, 1976; as *A Tomb for Boris Davidovich*, New York, Harcourt Brace, 1978; London, Penguin, 1980.
Enciklopedija mrtvih [The Encyclopedia of the Dead]. Belgrade, Prosveta-Zagreb, Globus, 1983.

Plays

Elektra (produced 1969).
Noć i magla [Night and Mist] (includes *Papagaj* [The Parrot], *Drveni sanduk Tomasa Vulfa* [The Wooden Chest of Thomas Wolfe], *Mehanički lavovi* [The Mechanical Lions]). Belgrade, Prosveta-Zagreb, Globus, 1983.

Other

Po-etika [Poetics]. Belgrade, Nolit, 2 vols., 1972-74.
Čaš anatomije [The Anatomy Lesson]. Belgrade, Nolit, 1978.
Homo poeticus. Belgrade, Prosveta-Zagreb, Globus, 1983.
Sabrana dela [Collected Works]. Belgrade, Prosveta-Zagreb, Globus, 10 vols., 1983.

Editor, with Mirjana Miočinović, *Sabrana dela* [Collected Works], by Lautréamont. 1964.

*   *   *

Danilo Kiš occupies a pre-eminent position among contemporary Yugoslav writers on the strength of his carefully crafted ficiton, but his other literary ventures—plays for radio and television, essays and translations from French, Hungarian and Russian—are also held in high esteem. His early novels, *Mansarda* and *Psalam 44*, have clearly indicated two important features of Kiš as a fiction writer: his keen interest in the themes of human suffering and his lack of interest in the vestiges of traditional realistic narrative and classical psychological analysis.

Mansarda is basically a story of the youthful love patterned on the myth of Orpheus and Eurydice, but one of the things the novel captures best is the garret atmosphere of the hero's juvenile world of capricious daydreams, hallucinations, paradoxical reasoning, and cynicism from which he is "dethroned" and brought down to be faced with the demanding banalities of everyday life. Many quotations and literary and mythological allusions give the novel a strong intellectual edge. The author's concern with the contrasting facets of existence and the playful dance of his language make this story of how innocence changes into experience one of the most original first novels published in Yugoslavia after the World War II.

Psalam 44 is Kiš's attempt at the literature of the holocaust. It is a stream-of-consciousness novel in which a young Jewish girl reveals her distressing history in the tense moments preceding her escape from the Birkenau concentration camp with her newborn baby and her French girl friend. The account of her desperate efforts to survive after the escape is concluded with a qualified happy ending: the re-united family visit the camp six years afterwards in order to hand down to the child "the joy of those who, out of death and love, were able to create life." The most impressive feature of the novel is the dispassionate, almost lethargic calmness of the narrative which recaptures in most grisly detail the abyss of human agony.

Kiš's next novel, *Garden, Ashes*, has a strong autobiographical element. The narrator-protagonist is the Jewish boy Andreas Sam, who grows up in the Danubian plains in the 1940's, before, during, and after the war. His memories concentrate on a small, tightly knit group of characters, but are dominated by the overpowering personality of his father, Eduard, a railway official who has compiled a gigantic Universal Timetable and who disappeared during the holocaust. The book is in large measure the search of a son for the father (a hypochondriac, lunatic dreamer, drunkard, and loner) he lost even before his death, in an attempt to establish distant and unnoticed connections which in his childhood he could not believe existed. A skilful interweaving of introspective poetic strands, striking intellectual displays, and reminiscences almost sensuously brought to life makes this book a particular kind of creative autobiography, clothed in a fine net of soft lyrical weave. Kiš followed it with a sequel, *Rani jadi*, a collection of short stories where the Sam family appear again portrayed in the same tone of melancholic lyricism and psychological subtlety.

Peščanik, where the same father figure turns up under the initials E.S., is a novel which seemingly lacks all thematic and narrative coherence. It is composed of various texts referring to E.S., his motivations and actions, but the key to understanding these diverse writings (letters, documents, reports, and notes), which demand the reader's utmost concentration and patience, is given at the end of the book, in a letter written by E.S. to his sister. It casts a revealing light on Kiš's apparently chaotic narrative and discloses its moral seriousness in the history of a man who, in the inferno of history and amid the atmosphere of selfishness and indifference, tries to secure the survival of his family.

A Tomb for Boris Davidovich, a collection of short stories concerned with the theme of suffering of the innocent, makes a new departure. All the stories except one, which takes place in southern France in 1330, describe the misfortunes of several characters (mostly Jewish) who perished in the Soviet labour camps or died in the USSR as the victims of forces of terror. The stories, based on authentic documents and case histories, are an original hybrid of fiction and "faction" and bear a general resemblance to Arthur Koestler's *Darkness at Noon*, "although surpassing it in both horrifying detail and narrative skill," as Joseph Brodsky said in his introduction to the English translation. Accused for plagiarism by some Yugoslav critics, Kiš refuted their allegations in a highly polemic *Čas anatomije*, turning his defence into a virulent satire of his critics.

In his latest volume of short stories, *Enciklopedija mrtvih*, Kiš widens his thematic range through his interest in ancient legends and metaphysical strata of existence. His paramount concern for human suffering caused by forces of history, however, has preserved its centrality in his writing.

—Dušan Puvačić

KONWICKI, Tadeusz. Polish. Born in Nowa Wilejka, near Vilnius, 22 June 1926. Educated at the University of Warsaw, and the Jagellonian University, Cracow, 1945-49. Served in the resistance during World War II. Married Danuta Lenica in 1949; two daughters. Full-time writer and journalist; also screenwriter and film director. Recipient: State Prize for Literature, 1950, 1954, 1966; (for films): Venice Festival prize, 1958; Mannheim Festival prize, 1962; San Remo Festival prize, 1972; Mondello Prize (Italy), 1980. Address: Górskiego, 1 m. 68, 00-033 Warsaw, Poland.

PUBLICATIONS

Fiction

Przy budowie [At the Building Site]. Warsaw, Czytelnik, 1950.
Godzina smutku [The Hour of Sadness]. Warsaw, Czytelnik, 1954.

Wladza [Power]. Warsaw, Czytelnik, 1954.
Z oblezonego miasta [From the Besieged Town]. Warsaw, Iskry, 1956.
Rojsty [The Marshes]. Warsaw, Czytelnik, 1956.
Dziura w niebie [A Hole in the Sky]. Warsaw, Iskry, 1959.
Sennik wspolczesny. Warsaw, Iskry, 1963; as *A Dreambook for Our Time*, Cambridge, Massachusetts, MIT Press, 1969.
Wniebowstapienie [Ascension]. Warsaw, Iskry, 1967.
Nic albo nic [Nothing or Nothing]. Warsaw, Czytelnik, 1971.
Kronika wypadków milosnych [The Chronicle of Love Events]. Warsaw, Czytelnik, 1974.
Kalendarz i klepsydra [A Calendar and a Water-Clock]. Warsaw, Czytelnik, 1976.
Kompleks polski, in *Zapis 3*. 1977; as *The Polish Complex*, New York, Farrar Straus, 1982.
Mala apokalipsa, in *Zapis 10*. 1979; as *A Minor Apocalypse*, London, Faber, and New York, Farrar Straus, 1983.
Wschody i zachody kziezyca [Setting and Rising of the Moon], in *Zapis 21*. 1982.

Plays (screenplays)

Ostatni dzień lata [The Last Day of Summer] (includes *Zadnuszki* [Halloween], *Salto*, *Matura* [Entrance Examination], *Zimowy zmlerzch* [Winter Dusk]). Warsaw, Iskry, 1966; augmented edition (includes *Jak daleko stad, jak blisko* [So Far, So Near]), 1973.

Screenplays: *Zimowy zmlerzch*, 1957; *Ostatni dzień lata*, 1958; *Matka Joanna od Aniolów* (*Joan of the Angels?*), with Jerzy Kawalerowicz, 1961; *Zaduszki*, 1961; *Faraon* [Pharaoh], with Jerzy Kawalerowicz, 1965; *Salto*, 1965; *Matura*, 1965; *Jowita* (*Jovita*), 1967; *Jak daleko stad, jak blisko*, 1971.

Other

Zwierzoczlekoupiór. Warsaw, Czytelnik, 1969; as *The Anthropos-Specter-Beast*, New York, Phillips, and London, Oxford University Press, 1977.
Dlaczego kot jest kot [Why a Cat Is a Cat]. Warsaw, KAW, 1976.

*

Critical Studies: *Konwicki* (in French) by Jacek Wegner, Warsaw, Agence des Auteurs, 1973; "The Haunted World of Konwicki" by J.R. Krzyzanowski, in *Books Abroad 48*, 1974.

*   *   *

All Tadeusz Konwicki's major fiction up to and including *A Dreambook for Our Time* derives ultimately from the few months in 1944 when he served (at the age of 18) in the Home Army (AK) in the marshes and forests of his native Lithuania. After the end of World War II, the AK was an unmentionable subject in Poland, only rehabilitated along with many of its former members in the late 1950's. In all the novels the same imagery recurs obsessively: a forest or wilderness "filled with accursed spirits," dead bodies of troops being carted off somewhere; church bells in the distance, "chaotic feverish dreams which come just before dawn," and the Polish martyrs of the 1863 Insurrection put down by the Muscovites, and whose graves are to be found scattered all over Eastern Poland (the Russian zone). In *A Dreambook for Our Time* itself, Oldster, the protagonist, after a suicide attempt, revisits the valley where, as a partisan, he had been ordered to kill a fellow countryman who had betrayed other partisans to the Germans. His attempt to assuage his guilt is not complete, but at the end of the novel, "I would scramble with the remains of my strength out of the seething depths to the edge of reality, and would get up to an ordinary, commonplace day, with its usual troubles, its everyday toil, its so well-known familiar drudgery."

But starting with *Wniebowstapienie*, much of his fiction has been rejected by publishers, or censors, or perhaps someone even more elevated, and has been published abroad (London). The later novels have become increasingly self-indulgent, stylistically repetitive (everything comes in groups of three—nouns, adjectives, verbs), and consists largely of semi-autobiographical communing with himself.

—David Welsh

KROETZ, Franz Xaver. German. Born in Munich, 25 February 1946. Studied acting in Munich and at Reinhardt Seminar, Vienna; actor in Munich, 1966-70; playwright-in-residence, Heidelberg Theater, 1972-73. Recipient: Thoma Medal, 1970; Fontane Prize, 1972; Critics Prize (Germany), 1973; Hanover Drama Prize, 1974; Lübke Prize, 1975. Address: Keyserling-strasse 10, 8000 Munich 60, Germany.

PUBLICATIONS

Plays

Wildwechsel (produced Dortmund, 1971). Wollerau, Lentz, 1973.
Michis Blut (produced Munich, 1971). Included in *Gesammelte Stücke*, 1975; as *Michi's Blood* (produced New Haven, Connecticut, 1975), in *Farmyard and Four Plays*, 1976.
Heimarbeit, und Hartnäckig (produced Munich, 1971). Included in *Drei Stücke*, 1971; *Heimarbeit* translated as *Homeworker* (produced London, 1974).
Drei Stücke. Frankfurt, Suhrkamp, 1971.
Männersache (produced Darmstadt, 1972). Included in *Drei Stücke*, 1971; revised version, as *Ein Mann, ein Wörterbuch* (produced Vienna, 1977); as *A Man, A Dictionary*, in *Farmyard and Four Plays*, 1976.
Dolomitenstadt Lienz (produced Bochum, 1972). Frankfurt, Suhrkamp, 1974.
Globales Interesse (produced Munich, 1972).
Herzliche Grüsse aus Grado (televised, 1972; produced Dusseldorf, 1976).
Stallerhof (produced Hamburg, 1972). Included in *Vier Stücke*, 1972; translated as *Stallerhof* (produced London, 1974), in *Bauer, Fassbinder, Handke, Kroetz*, London, Eyre Methuen, 1977; as *Farmyard*, in *Farmyard and Four Plays*, 1976.
Oberösterreich (produced Heidelberg, 1972). Frankfurt, Suhrkamp, 1974; as *Morecambe* (produced Edinburgh and London, 1975).
Vier Stücke. Frankfurt, Suhrkamp, 1972.
Wunschkonzert (produced Stuttgart, 1973). Included in *Vier Stücke*, 1972; as *Request Concert* (as *Request Programme*, produced Edinburgh, 1974; as *Request Concert*, produced New York, 1981), in *Farmyard and Four Plays*, 1976.
Geisterbahn (produced Vienna, 1975). Included in *Vier Stücke*, 1972; as *Geisterbahn*

(produced London, 1975).
Lieber Fritz (produced Darmstadt, 1975).   Included in *Vier Stücke*, 1972.
Münchner Kindl (produced Munich, 1973).   Frankfurt, Suhrkamp, 1974.
Maria Magdalena, from the play by Hebbel (produced Heidelberg, 1973).   Frankfurt, Suhrkamp, 1974.
Die Wahl fürs Leben (broadcast, 1973; produced Munich, 1980).   Included in *Weitere Aussichten*, 1976.
Weitere Aussichten (televised, 1974; produced Karl-Marx-Stadt, 1975).   Included in *Weitere Aussichten*, 1976.
Das Nest (produced Munich, 1975).   Included in *Weitere Aussichten*, 1976.
Reise ins Glück (broadcast, 1975; produced Zurich, 1976).   Included in *Weitere Aussichten*, 1976.
Gesammelte Stücke.   Frankfurt, Suhrkamp, 1975.
Weitere Aussichten: Ein Lesebuch, edited by Thomas Thieringer.   Cologne, Kiepenheuer & Witsch, 1976.
Farmyard and Four Plays.   New York, Urizen, 1976.
Agnes Bernauer, from the play by Hebbel (produced Leipzig, 1977).   Included in *Weitere Aussichten*, 1976.
Sterntaler (produced Braunschweig, 1977).
Mensch Meier (produced Dusseldorf, 1978).   Included in *Drei neue Stücke*, 1979.
Drei neue Stücke.   Frankfurt, Suhrkamp, 1979.
Der stramme Max (produced Recklinghausen, 1980).   Included in *Drei neue Stücke*, 1979.
Wer durchs Laub geht...(produced Marburg, 1981).   Included in *Drei neue Stücke*, 1979.
Nicht Fisch nicht Fleisch (produced Dusseldorf, 1981).   With *Verfassungsfeinde* and *Jumbo-Track*, Frankfurt, Suhrkamp, 1981.

Radio Plays: *Inklusive*, 1972; *Bilanz*, 1972; *Gute Besserung*, 1972; *Die Wahl fürs Leben*, 1973.

Television Plays: *Herzliche Grüsse aus Grado*, 1972; *Weitere Aussichten*, 1974; *Der Mensch Adam Deigl und die Obrigkeit*, from a work by Josef Martin Bauer, 1974.

Fiction

Der Mondscheinknecht.   Frankfurt, Suhrkamp, 1981.

Other

Chiemgauer Geschichten: Bayerische Menschen erzählen.   Cologne, Kiepenheuer & Witsch, 1977.
Ein Lesebuch: Stücke, Polemik, Gespräche, Filme, Hörspiele, Analysen.   Reinbek, Rowohlt, 1982.
Frühe Stücke, Frühe Prosa.   Frankfurt, Suhrkamp, 1983.

*

Critical Studies: "Kroetz Checklist" by Hugh Rorrison, in *Theatrefacts 3*, no. 2, 1976; *Kroetz* by Rolf-Peter Carl, Munich, Beck, 1978; *Kroetz* edited by Heinz Ludwig Arnold, Munich, Text & Kritik, 1978; *Kroetz: The Emergence of a Political Playwright* by R.W. Blevins, Las Vegas, Nevada, Lang, 1983.

*   *   *

Franz Xaver Kroetz emerged in the 1970's as the new realist of the German theatre. The development of the New Left after 1968 and the revival of Ödön von Horváth's folk plays about the "little man" (and woman) in the Weimar Republic paved the way for him, but it was clear from his first small-scale dialect pieces that his was a new and individual voice on the West German stage which, unlike East Germany's, had never been strong on the presentation of lower-class figures. His first play, *Wildwechsel*, charts the course of an adolescent love affair between a young factory hand and the 13-year-old daughter of an ordinary couple. It ends with the father murdered and the pair in prison. *Farmyard* shows an even more sensational coupling: Sepp, a lonely old farm labourer, seduces his employer's under-age, retarded daughter and is summarily sent packing. Kroetz brings out the tender attachment of the unprepossessing pair. The sequel, *Geisterbahn*, shows their brief marriage which ends with Sepp's death from cancer, whereupon Beppi suffocates their baby. These one-acters are built round marginal figures whom the German economic miracle has by-passed, and whose uncomprehending frustration erupts into violence towards those close to them. They derive their power from the intense yet halting and laconic stage dialogue of Kroetz's inarticulate subjects.

Kroetz left school at sixteen and took various unskilled jobs. When his ambition to be an actor was frustrated he turned to writing. His sympathy with the underdog led him to join the German Communist Party in 1972, and he developed an interest in East Germany, where he was one of the few West German dramatists to be performed. (His interest cooled and he resigned from the GCP in 1980.) The focus of his work shifted from fringe figures to ordinary wage-earners trying to make ends meet in the consumer society. This was to be a more central assault on capitalism, and television versions brought his plays to a wide audience. *Morecambe* shows how a working couple face a future on one wage when the wife accidentally becomes pregnant. *Das Nest* shows how a truck driver decides to bring charges against his employer when the "harmless liquid" he has been asked to dump in a pond turns out to be toxic. In these plays, and in *Mensch Meier*, the characters come to recognise their economic dependency and the attendant family constraints, and a process of emancipation begins. Kroetz's attempt to modernize two classics by Friedrich Hebbel, *Maria Magdalena* and *Agnes Bernauer*, was only partially successful, but he is still trying to extend his range.

Nicht Fisch nicht Fleisch uses two contrasting couples to present differentiated responses to technological change at the workplace, and it has a surreal nude bathing scene in which the redundant compositors as it were touch the bottom, before resurfacing to face the future in the last scene. Kroetz's work has become less powerful and universal as his subjects have become more typical of West German society, but he is still the most acute and accomplished observer of the working-class scene in the German theatre.

—Hugh Rorrison

KUNDERA, Milan. French. Born in Brno, Czechoslovakia, 1 April 1929; became French citizen, 1981. Educated at Charles University, Prague; Academy of Music and Dramatic Arts Film Faculty, Prague, 1956. Married Věra Hrabánková in 1967. Worker, and pianist in jazz band, 1950-56; Assistant Professor of Film, Academy of Music and Dramatic Arts, 1959-69; Professor of Comparative Literature, University of Rennes, France, 1975-80. Since 1980, Professor, École des Hautes Études, Paris. Member of the Editorial Board, *Literární Noviny*, 1956-59, 1963-68, and *Listy*, 1968-69. Recipient: Writers' Publishing House prize, 1961, 1969;

Klement Lukeš Prize, 1963; Union of Czechoslovak Writers' Prize, 1968; Médicis Prize (France), 1973; Mondello Prize (Italy), 1978; Common Wealth Award (USA), 1981; Europa Prize, 1982. Honorary doctorate: University of Michigan, Ann Arbor, 1983. Address: École des Hautes Études, 54 Boulevard Raspail, 75006 Paris, France.

PUBLICATIONS

Fiction

Zert. Prague, Czechoslovak Writers' Union, 1967; as *The Joke*, New York, Coward McCann, and London, Macdonald, 1969.
Směšné lásky (short stories). Prague, Czechoslovak Writers' Union, 1970; as *Laughable Loves*, New York, Knopf, 1974; London, Murray, 1977.
Zivot de jinde. Toronto, 68 Publishers, 1979; as *Life Is Elsewhere*, New York, Knopf, 1974.
Valčik na rozloučenou. Toronto, 68 Publishers, 1979; as *The Farewell Party*, New York, Knopf, 1976; London, Murray, 1977.
Kniha smichu a zapomnění. Toronto, 68 Publishers, 1981; as *The Book of Laughter and Forgetting*, New York, Knopf, 1980; London, Faber, 1982.
Nesnesitelná lehkost bytí, as *The Unbearable Lightness of Being*. New York, Harper, and London, Faber, 1984.

Plays

Majitelé klíču [The Owners of the Keys] (produced Prague, 1962). Prague, Czechoslovak Writers' Union, 1962.
Dvě usi dvě svatby [Double Wedding] (as *Ptákovina* [Cock-a-Doodle-Do], produced Prague, 1969). Prague, Dilia, 1968.
Jacques et son maître: Hommage à Denis Diderot (produced Paris, 1981). Paris, Gallimard, 1981.

Verse

Clověk zahrada širá [Man: A Broad Garden]. Prague, Czechoslovak Writers' Union, 1953.
Poslední máj [The Last May]. Prague, Czechoslovak Writers' Union, 1955; revised edition, 1963.
Monology [Monologues]. Prague, Czechoslovak Writers' Union, 1957.

Other

Umění romanu [The Art of the Novel]. Prague, Czechoslovak Writers' Union, 1960.

*

Critical Studies: "Kundera Issue" of *Liberté*, January 1979; *Kundera: A Voice from Central Europe* by Robert Porter, Aarhus, Denmark, Arkona, 1981; "Kundera Issue" of *L'Infini*, 1984.

*   *   *

Milan Kundera has published work in all genres: literary essays, lyric poetry, short stories, plays, and especially novels. His three volumes of short stories, *Laughable Loves*, which appeared in the 1960's and were later reworked into one volume, provide the key to his novels. Sex, humour, and politics intertwine to ensnare young heroes in ironic twists. The stories are all about the freedom of the individual. Kundera's first novel, *The Joke*, is narrated from four viewpoints; the hero Ludvik, a victim of political denunciation as a result of his untimely sense of humour, is seeking years later to revenge himself on an old adversary, only to discover that now his revenge is untimely. The joke is on the hero.

Kundera is a healthy sceptic whose novels are all anti-something. *The Joke* challenged the messianic seriousness of ideology. *Life Is Elsewhere* attacks lyricism (Kundera gave up writing verse in 1964 after publishing a revised edition of his earlier poetic collection *Monology*). The lyric poet, talented and dangerously sincere, is also an egoist, and in *Life Is Elsewhere* the poet turns political informer and his vanity invites his own death. The biographies of Rimbaud and Wolker, as well as many other lyric poets, have clearly influenced this novel. If *Life Is Elsewhere* is "anti-poetry" *The Farewell Party* plays with the very concept of the novel, at times presenting the reader with flesh and blood characters, at times introducing a touch of the supernatural. *The Book of Laughter and Forgetting*, regarded by some as Kundera's finest achievement, is his first work written in exile in France and can only with qualification be termed a novel. Blending short story, autobiography, memoir, and political comment, the work is none the less cohesive and dynamic. The author once commented that all his books now, given the revised seven-story version of *Laughable Loves*, are made up of odd numbers of units and are thus not easily divided up.

Clearly from that comic doubting school of Central Europe which spawned Hašek, Kafka, and Musil, Kundera now enjoys a prominent place in European letters, a place attained by literary prowess rather than political engagement. In his publicist works, he has been anxious to draw attention to the cultural riches of a Central Europe, which has been all but destroyed by the Yalta agreement. The term Eastern Europe is meaningless in cultural terms.

Kundera was a highly regarded writer in Czechoslovakia in the 1960's, but his speech at the 1967 writers congress led to official censure, and after the 1968 Soviet-led invasion his works were banned and he was unable to work officially. He was allowed to emigrate to France in 1975 where his writing has always had most appeal outside his homeland. Of his three plays *Jacques et son maître*, a genial genuflexion to Diderot and the Enlightenment, has possibly been the most popular, though he remains primarily a novelist and would seem to have demonstrated in his own work his contention that the genre of the novel is far from dead.

—Robert Porter

KUNERT, Günter. German. Born in Berlin, 6 March 1929. Studied at Academy of Applied Arts, Berlin-Weissensee, 1946-49. Married Marianne Todten in 1951. Staff member, *Ulenspiegel*, 1949; expelled from the Communist Party, 1977, and has lived in West Germany since 1979. Lecturer, University of Texas, Fall 1972; writer-in-residence, University of Warwick, Coventry, 1975. Recipient: Heinrich Mann Prize, 1962; Becher Prize, 1973; Confederation of German Industry award, 1980. Address: Schulstrasse 7, 2216 Kaisborstel, Germany.

PUBLICATIONS

Verse

Wegschilder und Mauerinschriften. Berlin, Aufbau, 1950.

Unter diesem Himmel. Berlin, Neues Leben, 1955.
Tagwerke. Halle, Middeldeutschen Verlag, 1960.
Das kreuzbrave Liederbuch. Berlin, Aufbau, 1961.
Erinnerung an einen Planeten. Munich, Hanser, 1963.
Der ungebetene Gast. Berlin, Aufbau, 1965.
Verkündigung des Wetters. Munich, Hanser, 1966.
Unschuld der Natur. Berlin, Aufbau, 1966.
Poesiealbum acht. Berlin, Neues Leben, 1968.
Warnung vor Spiegeln. Munich, Hanser, 1970.
Notizen in Kreide. Leipzig, Reclam, 1970.
Offener Ausgang. Berlin, Aufbau, 1972.
Im weiteren Fortgang. Munich, Hanser, 1974.
Das kleine Aber. Berlin, Aufbau, 1976.
Unterwegs nach Utopia. Munich, Hanser, 1977.
Verlangen nach Bomarzo: Reisegedichte. Munich, Hanser, 1978.
Unruhiger Schlaf. Munich, Deutscher Taschenbuch Verlag, 1979.
Abtötungsverfahren. Munich, Hanser, 1980.
Stilleben. Munich, Hanser, 1983.

Plays

Der Kaiser von Hondu. Berlin, Aufbau, 1959.
Ein anderer K: Hörspiele. Berlin, Aufau, 1977.

Radio Plays: *Mit der Zeit ein Feuer*; *Ehrenhändel*; *Ein anderer K.*

Television Play: *Fetzers Flucht*, 1962.

Fiction

Der ewige Detektiv und andere Geschichten. Berlin, Eulenspiegel, 1954.
Tagträume. Munich, Hanser, 1964.
Im Namen der Hüte. Munich, Hanser, 1967.
Die Beerdigung findet in aller Stille statt. Munich, Hanser, 1968.
Kramen in Fächern. Berlin, Aufbau, 1969.
Tagträume in Berlin und andernorts. Munich, Hanser, 1972.
Gast aus England. Munich, Hanser, 1973.
Kinobesuch. Leipzig, Insel, 1977.
Drei Berliner Geschichten. Berlin, Aufbau, 1979.

Other

Kunerts lästerliche Leinwand. Berlin, Eulenspiegel, 1965.
Betonformen, Ortsangabel. Berlin, Literarisches Colloquium, 1969.
Die geheime Bibliothek. Berlin, Aufbau, 1973.
Der andere Planet: Ansichten von Amerika. Munich, Hanser, 1975.
Der Mittelpunkt der Erde. Berlin, Eulenspiegel, 1975.
Warum schreiben: Notizen zur Literatur. Munich, Hanser, 1976.
Jeder Wunsch ein Treffler (juvenile). Cologne, Middelhauve, 1976.
Berliner Wände, photographs by Thomas Höpker. Munich, Hanser, 1976.
Camera obscura. Munich, Hanser, 1978.
Heinrich von Kleist: Ein Modell. Berlin, Akademie der Kunst, 1978.

Ein englisches Tagebuch. Berlin, Aufbau, 1978.
Die Schreie der Fledermäuse (miscellany), edited by D.R. Zimmer. Munich, Hanser, 1979.
Ziellose Umtriebe. Berlin, Aufbau, 1979.
Ulenspiegel: Zeitschrift für Literatur, Kunst, und Satire, edited by Kunert and H. Sandberg. Munich, Hanser, 1979.
Kurze Beschreibung eines Momentes der Ewigkeit. Leipzig, Reclam, 1980.
Verspätete Monologe. Munich, Hanser, 1981.
Diesseits des Erinnerns. Munich, Hanser, 1982.
Die letzten Indianer Europas. Hauzenberg, Pongratz, 1983.
Leben und Schreiben. Pfaffenweiler, Pfaffenweiler Press, 1983.
Windy Times (verse and prose). New York, Red Dust, 1983.

Editor, *Kriegsfibel,* by Brecht. Berlin, Eulenspiegel, 1955.
Editor, *Gedichte,* by Nikolaus Lenau. Frankfurt, Fischer, 1969.
Editor, *Über die irdische Liebe und andere gewisse Welträtsel in Liedern und Balladen,* by Brecht. Berlin, Eulenspiegel, 1970.
Editor, *Dimension* (East German literature). Austin, University of Texas Press, 1973.
Editor, *Mein Lesebuch.* Frankfurt, Fischer, 1983.

*

Critical Study: *Kunert Lesen* edited by Michael Krüger, Munich, Hanser, 1979.

* * *

Poetry and literary criticism, short stories and television plays—Günter Kunert has written in almost every genre. His real talent undoubtedly lies in the more concise forms: his one novel is of uneven quality. In his best poems and short stories, on the other hand, Kunert achieves a stylistic virtuosity and intellectual sharpness hardly rivalled in East German writing.

Kunert's often biting irony, his command of the aphorism, and his extensive use of the parable all reveal the influence of Bertolt Brecht on his work. He has taken the latter's dialectical approach to reality a step further, however, in according the concept of the paradox an important place in much of his poetry. Kunert demonstrated its function in the essay "Paradoxie als Prinzip" by analyzing one of his first poems to employ the technique: in "Ikarus 64" the reader is encouraged to "spread his arms" and fly—and then told this is, of course, impossible. "Flight," Kunert explains, is here a metaphor for flight from the past—which in fact cannot be escaped, but whose baleful influence can be lessened if the attempt is nonetheless made. The paradoxical formulation of this problem is intended to provoke the reader into looking more critically at society.

Kunert's negative view of the past, engendered by his experience of fascism and the war, forms a leitmotif in his work. His first collection of poems, *Wegschilder und Mauerinschriften,* contains a number which warn against the danger of the recent war being repeated: in one, a survivor crawls from a bombed house vowing "never again"—only to add (in an ironic afterthought typical of Kunert) "at least, not straightaway." The tenor of these so-called "warning poems" changed, however, in the 1960's from one of admonition to growing disillusionment. In poems from the collection *Der ungebetene Gast* to *Warnung vor Spiegeln,* Kunert insisted with growing emphasis that far from being dead the past was still at work in the distortions of East German socialism. Thus in "Hoffnungsvolle Entdeckung" he shows the emergence of a soulless bureaucracy, in which mountains of files squeeze the blood from the citizens registered in them. Above all, Kunert began to depict in both poems and stories an insidious alienation of the individual in society, extending from the work-place to his private life.

This trend in Kunert's work inevitably led to repeated attacks on him from Party critics in the GDR. In 1963 some of his poems were described as "lumps of dirt"; in 1966 he was accused of displaying un-Marxist "despair"; and in 1969 a volume of short stories was similarly condemned. His situation worsened in the 1970's as his poems became more pessimistic (the utopia aspired to by socialism reveals itself in one poem to be an "El Dorado," a chimera) and their irony more vitriolic. His involvement in a series of cultural-political controversies further strained his relations with the Party, so that in 1979 he finally left East Germany. His most recent work is informed by an uncompromisingly resigned tone which, although it can verge on affectation, more frequently displays both formal and philosophical subtlety.

—Neil Jackson

LANGEVIN, André. Canadian. Born in Montreal, Quebec, in 1927. Worked for the Canadian Broadcasting Corporation. Recipient: Cercle du Livre de France Prize, 1951, 1953; Canada Council Senior Fellowship, 1959; Liberté Prize, 1967. Address: c/o McClelland and Stewart Ltd., 25 Hollinger Road, Toronto, Ontario M4B 3G2, Canada.

PUBLICATIONS

Fiction

L'Évadé de la nuit. Montreal, Cercle du Livre de France, 1951.
Poussière sur la ville. Montreal, Cercle du Livre de France, 1953; as Dust over the City, Toronto, McClelland and Stewart, 1954.
Le Temps des hommes. Montreal, Cercle du Livre de France, 1956.
L'Élan d'Amérique. Montreal, Cercle du Livre de France, 1972.
Une Chaîne dans le parc. Paris, Julliard, 1974; as Orphan Street, Toronto, McClelland and Stewart, 1976; Philadelphia, Lippincott, 1977.

Plays

Une Nuit d'amour (produced Montreal, 1954).
L'Oeil du peuple (produced Montreal, 1958). Montreal, Cercle du Livre de France, 1958.

*

Critical Studies: "Time and Space in Langevin's L'Élan d'Amérique" by Richard G. Hodgson, in Canadian Literature, Spring 1981; The Temptation of Despair: A Study of the Quebec Novelist Langevin by David J. Bond, Fredericton, New Brunswick, York Press, 1982.

*   *   *

Although his last novel was published in 1974, André Langevin is one of contemporary Quebec's most important novelists. Using such basic themes of Quebec literature as isolation, suffering, and death, Langevin has produced two major novels, *Dust over the City* and *L'Élan d'Amérique*, three other novels (which have unfortunately received very little critical attention), three short stories, and two plays. The evolution of Langevin's novelistic technique from *Dust over the City* to *L'Élan d'Amérique* illustrates very graphically the fundamental changes which have occurred in the Quebec novel since the 1950's.

In *Dust over the City*, Langevin used the first-person narrative of a young doctor practicing in an asbestos-mining town whose wife's adulterous affair leads to tragedy as the framework for an extremely moving examination of some of the metaphysical and other problems of modern man. In addition to the fundamental themes of solitude and alienation, *Dust over the City* poses the question of the meaning of physical suffering and of "the burning sense of inner anguish" felt by the doctor in a way which is very reminiscent of the novels of Albert Camus. Indeed, Langevin refers explicitly to the existentialist concepts of absurdity, divine injustice, and revolt. But it is not just because of its treatment of such themes that Langevin's novel is one of the major landmarks in Quebec fiction since the Second World War. Langevin's mastery of the first-person narrative form and his highly effective symbolic use of space to reflect the innermost feelings of the human heart make *Dust over the City* one of the best novels ever published in Canada.

Langevin's other major contribution to the contemporary Quebec novel, *L'Élan d'Amérique*, is a very different work, both in form and in content. Borrowing heavily from the stream-of-consciousness techniques of the French "new" novelists, Langevin set out, in writing this novel, to study the disillusionment and frustration felt by the Quebec people in the period immediately following the October crisis of 1970, during which the Ottawa government invoked the War Measures Act to suppress a separatist uprising. As in *Dust over the City*, space has a vitally important symbolic function in this novel, which consists of the interior monologues of the two main characters, Claire Peabody, the Franco-American wife of an American industrialist, and Antoine, a modern version of the archetypal *coureur de bois* ("woods man"). Like most of Langevin's characters, Claire and Antoine are orphans, but their lack of family is but one form of their isolation and alienation, which take on, as in all of Langevin's novels, both a physical and a spiritual dimension. Startlingly innovative at the level of narrative techniques and structures, *L'Élan d'Amérique* also marks an important stage in the awakening of the Quebec consciousnesss and in the process of self-realization currently going on in Quebec.

In these two novels, and in the other three (*L'Évadé de la nuit*, *Le Temps des hommes*, and *Orphan Street*), Langevin seeks to provide answers to some of the fundamental questions concerning the human condition which have always been his chief preoccupation. His novels are firmly rooted in the context of modern Quebec culture but at the same time they deal eloquently with universal literary themes centering around the social and metaphysical dilemmas facing modern man.

—Richard G. Hodgson

LAXNESS, Halldór. Pseudonym for Halldór Kiljan Gudjónsson. Icelandic. Born in Reykjavik, 23 April 1902. Attended grammar school, Reykjavik; lived in Benedictine monastery, Luxembourg; Jesuit school, Champion House, Osterley, England, 1923-24. Married 1) Ingibjörg Einarsdóttir in 1930, one son; 2) Audur Sveinsdóttir in 1945, two daughters. Lived in Europe, then in the USA, 1927-29, and in Iceland since 1930. Recipient: International Peace Movement Prize, 1953; Nobel Prize for Literature, 1955; Sonning Prize, 1969. Address: P.O. Box 664, Reykjavik, Iceland.

Fiction

Barn Náttúrunnar [Child of Nature]. Reykjavik, Höfundarin, 1919.
Nokkrar sógur [Several Stories]. Reykjavik, Isafoldarprentsmidja, 1923.
Undir Helgahnúk [Under the Holy Mountain]. Reykjavik, Arnasonar, 1924.
Vefarinn mikli frá Kasmír [The Great Weaver from Kashmir]. Reykjavik, Prentsmidjan Acta, 1927.
Salka Valka (Thu vínvidur hreini, Fuglinn í fjörunni). Reykjavik, Bokádeild Menningarsjods, 2 vols., 1931-32; translated as *Salka Valka*, Boston, Houghton Mifflin, 1936; London, Allen and Unwin, 1963.
Fótatak manna [Footsteps of Men]. Akureyri, Jónsson, 1933.
Sjálfstoett fólk. Reykjavik, Briem, 2 vols., 1934-35; as *Independent People*, London, Allen and Unwin, 1945; New York, Knopf, 1946.
Thordur gamli halti [Old Thordur the Lame]. 1935.
Heimsljós. Reykjavik, Helgafell, 2 vols., 1955; as *World Light*, Madison, University of Wisconsin Press, 1969.
   1. *Ljós heimsins* [The Light of the World]. Reykjavik, Heimskringla, 1937.
   2. *Höll sumarlandsins* [The Palace of the Summerland]. Reykjavik, Heimskringla, 1938.
   3. *Hús skáldsins* [The Poet's House]. Reykjavik, Heimskringla, 1939.
   4. *Fegurd himinsins* [The Beauty of the Sky]. Reykjavik, Heimskringla, 1940.
Gerska aefintýrid [The Russian Adventure]. Reykjavik, Heimskringla, 1938.
Sjö töframenn [Seven Magicians]. Reykjavik, Heimskringla, 1942.
Trilogy:
   1. *Íslandsklukkan* [Iceland's Bell]. Reykjavik, Helgafell, 1943.
   2. *Hid ljósa man* [The Bright Maiden]. Reykjavik, Helgafell, 1944.
   3. *Eldur í Kaupinhafn* [Fire in Copenhagen]. Reykjavik, Helgafell, 1946.
Atómstödin. Reykjavik, Helgafell, 1948; as *The Atom Station*, London, Methuen, 1961; Sag Harbor, New York, Second Chance Press, 1982.
Gerpla. Reykjavik, Helgafell, 1952; as *The Happy Warriors*, London, Methuen, 1958.
Brekkukotsannáll. Reykjavik, Helgafell, 1957; as *The Fish Can Sing*, London, Methuen, 1966, New York, Crowell, 1967.
Jomfruin goda og husid [The Honor of the House]. Reykjavik, Helgafell, 1959.
Paradísarheimt. Reykjavik, Helgafell, 1960; as *Paradise Reclaimed*, London, Methuen, and New York, Crowell, 1962.
Sjöstafakverid. Reykjavik, Helgafell, 1964; as *A Quire of Seven*, Reykjavik, Iceland Review, 1974; Forest Grove, Oregon, Hydra, 1981.
Kristnihald undir Jökli. Reykjavik, Helgafell, 1968; as *Christianity at the Glacier*, 1972.
Gudsgjafathula [A Narration of God's Gift]. Reykjavik, Helgafell, 1972.
Seiseijú, mikil ósköp [Oh Yea! By Jove]. Reykjavik, Helgafell, 1977.

Plays

Straumrof [Short Circuit]. Reykjavik, Heimskringla, 1934.
Snaefrídur Islandssól [Snaefrídur, Iceland's Sun]. Reykjavik, Helgafell, 1950.
Silfurtúnglid [The Silver Moon]. Reykjavik, Helgafell, 1954.
Strompleikurinn [The Chimney Play]. Reykjavik, Helgafell, 1961.
Prjónastofan Sólin [The Sun Knitting Shop]. Reykjavik, Helgafell, 1962.
Dúfnaveislan. Reykjavik, Helgafell, 1966; as *The Pigeon Banquet*, 1973.
Úa. Reykjavik, Helgafell, 1970.
Nordanstulkan [The Girl from the North]. Reykjavik, Helgafell, 1972.

Verse

Kvaedakver [A Sheaf of Poems]. Reykjavik, Prentsmidjan Acta, 1930.

Other

Kathólsk vidhorf [A Catholic View]. Reykjavik, Arnasonar, 1925.
Althýdubókin [The Book of the Plain People]. Reykjavik, Althyduprentsmidjan, 1929.
I austurvegi [On the Eastern Road]. Reykjavik, Sovétvinafélag Islands, 1933.
Dagleid á fjöllum: Greinar [Day's Journey in the Mountains]. Reykjavik, Heimskringla, 1937.
Vettvangur dagsins [Forum of the Day]. Reykjavik, Heimskringla, 1942.
Sjálfsagdir hlutir [Things Taken for Granted]. Reykjavik, Helgafell, 1946.
Reisubókarkorn [A Little Travel Book]. Reykjavik, Helgafell, 1950.
Heiman eg fór [I Went from Home]. Reykjavik, Helgafell, 1952.
Dagur í senn [A Day at a Time]. Reykjavik, Helgafell, 1955.
Gjörningabók [Miscellany]. Reykjavik, Helgafell, 1959.
Skáldatími [Poets' Time]. Reykjavik, Helgafell, 1963.
Upphaf mannúdarstefnu [The Origin of Humanism]. Reykjavik, Helgafell, 1965.
Íslendíngaspjall [Talk of Icelanders]. Reykjavik, Helgafell, 1967.
Vínlandspúnktar [Vineland Notes]. Reykjavik, Helgafell, 1969.
Innansveitarkronika [A Parish Chronicle]. Reykjavik, Helgafell, 1970.
Yfirskygdir staoir [Overshadowed Places]. Reykjavik, Helgafell, 1971.
Thjodhatidarrolla [Book of National Celebration]. Reykjavik, Helgafell, 1974.
Í túninu heima [In the Hayfields of Home]. Reykjavik, Helgafell, 1975.
Úngur eg var [Young I Was]. Reykjavik, Helgafell, 1976.
Sjömeistarasagan [The Story of the Seven Masters]. Reykjavik, Helgafell, 1978.
Grikklandsárid [The Year in Greece]. Reykjavik, Helgafell, 1980.
Vid heygardshornid. Reykjavik, Helgafell, 1981.

Editor, *Grettissaga.* Reykjavik, Helgafell, 1946.
Editor, *Laxdaela saga.* Reykjavik, Helgafell, 1973.

Translator, *Adventa*, by Gunnar Gunnarsson. Reykjavik, Heimskringla, 1939.
Translator, *Alexandreis; thad, Er Alexanders Saga Mikla.* Reykjavik, Helgafell, 1945.

Also translator of *A Farewell to Arms* and *A Moveable Feast* by Hemingway and *Candide* by Voltaire.

*

Bibliography: by Haraldur Sigurdsson, in *Landsbokasafn Islands: Arbok*, 1971, and in *Skirnir 146*, 1972.

Critical Studies: *Den store vävaren*, Stockholm, Raben & Sjögren, 1954, *Skaldens hus*, Stockholm, Raben & Sjögren, 1956, and *Laxness*, New York, Twayne, 1971, all by Peter Hallberg; "Laxness Issue" of *Scandinavica 11*, no. 1, 1972.

*   *   *

Halldór Laxness made his breakthrough in 1923 with the novel *Vefarinn mikli frá Kasmír*. It is a conversion novel, inspired by the spirit if not the facts, of Laxness's own conversion to Roman Catholicism. It confronts a baffling number of conflicting views of the world with each other, and makes clear that in turning to religion, Stein Ellidi is renouncing human claims.

Thus it represents an important element in Laxness's work: the problem of the individual vis-à-vis a monolithic authority, the claims of the individual conscience as opposed to the conformative nature of the major ideologies.

Laxness subsequently spent a period in America where under the influence of Upton Sinclair and Sinclair Lewis he developed a sense of social injustice resulting in his becoming a Communist. One fruit was the major novel *Salka Valka* concerning the establishment of a trade union in a fishing village and describing the effect this has on the environment, and in particular on Salka Valka herself. Social novels continued with *Independent People*, portraying the individualist peasant who believes he is free but is in fact being exploited by society, and *World Light* about a visionary pauper persecuted by his fellows.

In 1943-46 Laxness turned to the historical novel with *Íslandsklukkan*, about Jón Hreggvidsson's battle with the authorities. Unjustly condemned to death, he pursues a prolonged and finally successful struggle against bureaucracy. There are distinct national overtones, but also a poetical element centred on the main female character. The novel can be seen as a glorification of the Icelandic character, but it also represents the individual confronted with an impersonal bureaucracy. Similar ideas are found in *The Atom Station* and *The Happy Warriors*.

The national theme, though with universal overtones, appears in *Paradise Reclaimed*, about a poor Icelandic farmer tempted by a Mormon bishop to emigrate to the earthly paradise of Salt Lake City. In a touching, but sometimes bitingly satirical novel, Steinar experiences the unswerving faith of an ideology, but fails to accept it fully himself, and he returns to his home in Iceland, *his* paradise.

Recently, Laxness has moved from the long epic to the more concentrated, pithy novel, closely related to the plays with which he has also experimented. Outstanding is *Christianity at the Glacier*, a humorous but nevertheless serious and philosophical novel about a bishop who sends an assistant to examine the state of Christianity in an outlying village. The result, when he finds a priest who cannot be bothered burying the dead, preferring to shoe horses and offer his congregation practical help, a doctor who has given up a brilliant career to study the skies, and a pastor's wife who has been both nun and prostitute, is a picture of humankind in all its diversity.

In portraying the individual's confrontation with societies and ideologies, Laxness constantly takes the side of the individual. He examines both Catholicism and Communism, but ultimately it is probably Taoism, with its demand for tolerance and humanity, that attracts him most. He weds his philosophical considerations to his intense national feeling and gives the two a universal significance.

—W. Glyn Jones

LE CLÉZIO, J(ean)-M(arie) G(ustave).   French.   Born in Nice, 13 April 1940.   Educated at schools in Africa, 1947-50, and Nice, 1950-57; Bristol University, England, 1958-59; in London, 1960-61; Institut d'Études Littéraires, Nice, 1959-63, licence-ès-lettres 1963; University of Aix-en-Provence, M.A. 1964. Married Rosalie Piquemal in 1961; one daughter. Teacher, Buddhist University, Bangkok, 1966-67, University of Mexico, Mexico City, 1967; lived with Embera Indians, Panama, 1969-73. Since 1973 has lived in Nice. Recipient: Renaudot Prize, 1963; Larbaud Prize, 1972; French Academy Morand Prize, 1980. Address: c/o Gallimard, 5 rue Sébastien-Bottin, 75007 Paris, France.

LE CLÉZIO

PUBLICATIONS

Fiction

Le Procès-Verbal. Paris, Gallimard, 1963; as *The Interrogation*, London, Hamish Hamilton, 1964.
Le Jour; ou, Beaumont fit connaissance avec sa doleur. Paris, Mercure, 1964.
La Fièvre. Paris, Gallimard, 1965; as *Fever*, New York, Atheneum, 1966.
Le Déluge. Paris, Gallimard, 1966; as *The Flood*, New York, Atheneum, 1968.
Terra amata. Paris, Gallimard, 1968; translated as *Terra Amata*, London, Hamish Hamilton, 1969.
Le Livre des fuites. Paris, Gallimard, 1969; as *The Book of Flights*, London, Cape, 1971; New York, Atheneum, 1972.
La Guerre. Paris, Gallimard, 1970; as *War*, London, Cape, 1973.
Les Géants. Paris, Gallimard, 1973; as *The Giants*, London, Cape, and New York, Atheneum, 1975.
Voyages de l'autre côté. Paris, Gallimard, 1975.
Voyage aux pays des arbres. Paris, Gallimard, 1978.
Mondo et autres histoires. Paris, Gallimard, 1978.
Désert. Paris, Gallimard, 1980.
La Ronde et autres faits divers. Paris, Gallimard, 1982.

Other

L'Extase matérielle. Paris, Gallimard, 1966.
Haï. Geneva, Skira, 1971.
Mydriase. Montpellier, Fata Morgana, 1973.
L'Inconnu sur la terre. Paris, Gallimard, 1978.
Trois villes saintes. Paris, Gallimard, 1980.

Translator, *Les Prophéties du chilam Balam.* Paris, Gallimard, 1976.

*

Critical Studies: *Conversations avec Le Clézio* by P. Lhoste, Paris, Mercure, 1971; *Le Clézio* by Jennifer Waelti-Walters, Boston, Twayne, 1977.

*   *   *

J.-M.G. Le Clézio is connected to none of the modern movements in French literature. He stands by himself, expressing his anguish and his quest in powerfully lyric prose which breaks the traditional bounds of the novel and creates an epic of consciousness rather than of deeds. His world is a mysterious place that man must struggle to understand but from which he is separated by a growing multitude of man-made objects, which is rapidly becoming intolerable and from which his characters try to escape. They do this by flight: flight from the city in quest of the natural world; flight from everyday perception in quest of a greater understanding (by meditation, walking, emotion, drugs), in a series of books that become progressively less violent until the flight leads into the world of the imagination, the world of children, and of very simple happenings.

An alteration of quest and flight controls the works which are built on a series of juxtapositions of opposites: the city and the natural world, the sun and the sea, male and female. All man's thought is centred on the sun for it is the source of revelation and around its image Le Clézio creates his structures. The complementary influence is water, symbol both of woman and of death. Indeed the books express a version of the Icarus myth for the metaphors that dominate them when taken chronologially are the sea and death, falling, the sun, soaring up to the light, and the city as labyrinth and womb.

Juxtaposition of alternatives provides the form as well as the content of the works. The use of subject pronouns is unstable; narration moves frequently from "I" to "you" to "he" without apparent motivation—a technique which both alienates the reader and forces him to share the alienation of narrator and protagonist. It should be noted that there is a strong vein of humour running through the novels also. Many of the novels have little or no plot, and in many cases the sections within a book have no apparent order, yet they are very clear to read as they are made up of a series of situations which illustrate a major theme from different angles. These can be complementary or contradictory, developing the theme further or offering another possibility, a different interpretation, so that the effect is that of a number of tableaux rather than of continuous narration. The same effect is created between the books, for each is complete in itself and yet is linked to the world of the other books by a system of recurrent detail, repetition of images, new or further treatment of themes and problems. Hence all Le Clézio's writings are woven together into a single growing structure in which each strand reinforces the others, and adds to their combined impact and power.

—Jennifer Waelti-Walters

LEM, Stanislaw. Polish. Born in Lvov, 12 September 1921. Studied medicine in Lvov, 1939-41, 1944-46, and at Jagellonian University, Cracow, 1946-48. Married Barbara Lem in 1953; one son. Garage assistant during World War II; assistant in Science Circle, Jagellonian University, Cracow, 1947-49; Contributor, *Zycie Nauki* [Life of Science] magazine, 1947-49; full-time writer from 1949. Co-Founder, Polish Astronautical Society. Recipient: Polish State Prize, 1976. Agent: Franz Rottensteiner, Marchettigasse 9/17, 1060 Vienna, Austria. Address: Ulitsa Narwik 21, 30436 Cracow, Poland.

PUBLICATIONS

Fiction

Astronauci [The Astronauts]. Warsaw, Czytelnik, 1951.
Sezam i inne opowiadania [Sesame and Other Stories]. Warsaw, Iskry, 1954.
Oblok Magellana [The Magellan Nebula]. Warsaw, Iskry, 1955.
Dzienniki gwiazdowe. Warsaw, Iskry, 1957; as *The Star Diaries*, London, Secker and Warburg, and New York, Seabury Press, 1976; as *Memoirs of a Space Traveller*, Secker and Warburg, and New York, Harcourt Brace, 1982.
Czas nieutracony [Time Not Wasted]: *Szpital przemienienia* [Hospital of the Blessed]; *Wsrod umarlych* [Among the Dead]; *Powrót* [Return]. Cracow, Literackie, 3 vols., 1957.
Śledztwo. Warsaw, Ministerstwa Obrony Narodowej, 1959; as *The Investigation*, New York, Seabury Press, 1974.

Powrót z gwiazd. Warsaw, Czytelnik, 1961; as *Return from the Stars*, London, Secker and Warburg, and New York, Harcourt Brace, 1980.
Solaris. Warsaw, Ministerstwa Obrony Narodowej, 1961; translated as *Solaris*, London, Faber, and New York, Walker, 1971.
Pamietnik znaleziony w wannie. Cracow, Literackie, 1961; as *Memoirs Found in a Bathtub*, New York, Seabury Press, 1973.
Ksiega robotow [Book of Robots]. Cracow, Literackie, 1961.
Noc ksiezycowa [Lunar Night]. Cracow, Literackie, 1963.
Niezwyciezony i inne opowiadania. Warsaw, Ministerstwa Obrony Narodowej, 1964; as *The Invincible*, London, Sidgwick and Jackson, and New York, Seabury Press, 1973.
Bajki robotów [Robot Fables]. Cracow, Literackie, 1964.
Cyberiada. Cracow, Literackie, 1965; as *The Cyberiad*, New York, Seabury Press, 1974; London, Secker and Warburg, 1975.
Polowanie [The Hunt]. Cracow, Literackie, 1965.
Wysoki zamek [The High Castle]. Warsaw, Ministerstwa Obrony Narodowej, 1966.
Ratujmy Kosmos i inne opowiadania [Let Us Save the Cosmos and Other Stories]. Cracow, Literackie, 1966.
Opowieści o pilocie Pirxie. Cracow, Literackie, 1968; as *Tales of Pirx the Pilot*, New York, Harcourt Brace, 1979; London, Secker and Warburg, 1980.
Glos Pana [The Voice of the Master]. Warsaw, Czytelnik, 1968.
Ze wspomnień Ijona Tichego: Kongres futurologiczny. 1971; as *The Futurological Congress*, New York, Seabury Press, 1974; London, Secker and Warburg, 1975.
Bezsenność [Insomnia]. Cracow, Literackie, 1971.
Doskonala próznia. Warsaw, Czytelnik, 1971; as *A Perfect Vacuum*, London, Secker and Warburg, and New York, Harcourt Brace, 1979.
Wielkość urojona. Warsaw, Czytelnik, 1973; as *Imaginary Magnitude*, New York, Harcourt Brace, 1984.
Maska [The Mask]. Cracow, Literackie, 1976.
Suplement [Supplement]. Cracow, Literackie, 1976.
Katar. Cracow, Literackie, 1976; as *The Chain of Chance*, London, Secker and Warburg, and New York, Harcourt Brace, 1978.
Mortal Engines. New York, Seabury Press, 1977.
Powtórka [Repetition]. Warsaw, Iskry, 1979.
Golem XIV. Warsaw, Iskry, 1981.
The Cosmic Carnival of Lem, edited by Michael Kandel. New York, Continuum, 1981.
More Tales of Pirx the Pilot. New York, Harcourt Brace, 1982; London, Secker and Warburg, 1983.
Wizja lokalna [Eyewitness Account]. Cracow, Literackie, 1982.

Plays

Jacht Paradise, with Roman Hussarski. Warsaw, Czytelnik, 1951.

Screenplay: *Przekledaniec* [Roly Poly].

Television Play: *Maska*, from his own novel.

Other

Dialogi [Dialogues]. Cracow, Literackie, 1957.
Wejscie na orbite [Getting into Orbit]. Cracow, Literackie, 1962.
Summa technologiae. Cracow, Literackie, 1964.
Filozofia przypadku [The Philosophy of Chance]. Cracow, Literackie, 1968.

Fantastyka i futurologia [Science Fiction and Futurology]. Cracow, Literackie, 1970.
Rozprawy i szkice [Essays and Sketches]. Cracow, Literackie, 1975.

*

Critical Studies: *Lem: Ein moderner Revisionist* by Frank Rainer Scheck, Essen, Arbeiterkulturverlag, 1974; *Lem: Der dialektische Weise aus Kraków*, Frankfurt, Insel, 1976, and *Über Lem*, Frankfurt, Suhrkamp, 1981, both edited by Werner Berthel; *Lem* by Richard E. Ziegfeld, New York, Ungar, 1983.

* * *

Stanislaw Lem was trained in medicine. He argued theology with Karol Wojtlay, now better known as Pope John-Paul II. He is among the most widely read writers in the world and is certainly the most important writer of science fiction.

Had René Descartes written fiction, it may well have resembled that of Stanislaw Lem. Descartes first called attention to the importance of separating the activity or process of consciousness from its products. Lem's work is largely centered on this epistemological tension: that as rational agents we are condemned to build models to discover the truth that always eludes us: we seek "the Cause of the Effect, the Effect that in turn causes Action, and so a continuity is established...the chains that bind us." But Lem is no pessimist. He finds great joy in building "new and better kinds of game." In any case, Lem never lets readers forget that truth is model-relative, the result of a process at least as fundamental as its product. This is the thesis of *Solaris, The Investigation,* and *The Invincible.* Thus in the broadest view, his work is interested in the nature of consciousness. More specifically, he explains that science is an activity, a game, that constructs models to reveal truths that would otherwise not exist; and that this activity is not often self-conscious about its limits. Focusing this even more narrowly, Lem considers cybernetics and computer-generated artificial intelligence (AI). Thus in *The Cyberiad* he says, "Sometimes men build robots, sometimes robots build men. What does it matter, really, whether one thinks with metal or with protoplasm?" Much of his humorous work, including *The Star Diaries* and *The Futurological Congress*, uses robots to speculate on this and similar questions implicit in a cybernetic definition of consciousness. Treated with Lem's great erudition and creativity, these topics distinguish his work as central to contemporary science, politics, technology, and values.

Lem also turns his epistemological technique on literature itself to suggest how fictional worlds are built, how myth functions, and how criticism operates. In *Memoirs Found in a Bathtub* he demonstrates how various models can be used to interpret a text without ever finding *the* truth. In *A Perfect Vacuum*, a collection of reviews of nonexistent books, he shows how criticism or model-building can become an end in itself so that truth is sacrificed to method.

Lem eclipses most of the phenomenologists, structuralists, and New Novelists—with whom he has much in common—by suggesting that their adherence to a single epistemological model is no more liberated than the adherence of those they oppose to a single metaphysical model. Lem's work refutes their glib predictions about the death of the novel by demonstrating a sophisticated, popular, informed, and significant literature fulfilling its classical task of model-building to clarify values and offer choices so that, as Lem writes in *The Cyberiad*, future historians can say of us: "they didn't own the machine, neither did the machine own them."

—John Rothfork

LLOSA, Mario Vargas. *See* **VARGAS LLOSA, Mario.**

LO-JOHANSSON, (Karl) Ivar. Swedish. Born in Ösmo, 23 February 1901. Self-educated. Worked as stonecutter, farmhand, journalist, workman in France, England, and Hungary, 1925-29; then full-time writer. Recipient: Dobloug Prize, 1953, 1973; Nordic Council Prize, 1979. Ph.D.: University of Uppsala, 1964. Address: Bastugatan 21, 11725 Stockholm, Sweden.

PUBLICATIONS

Fiction

Måna är död [Mana Is Dead]. Stockholm, Bonnier, 1932.
Godnatt, jord [Goodnight, Earth]. Stockholm, Bonnier, 1933.
Kungsgatan [King's Street]. Stockholm, Bonnier, 1935.
Statarna [The Farm Laborers]. Stockholm, Bonnier, 2 vols., 1936-37.
Bara en mor [Only a Mother]. Stockholm, Bonnier, 1939.
Jordproletärerna [Proletarians of the Soil]. Stockholm, Bonnier, 1941.
Traktorn [The Tractor]. Stockholm, Bonnier, 1943.
Geniet: En roman om pubertet [The Genius: A Novel of Puberty]. Stockholm, Bonnier, 1947.
Ungdomsnoveller [Stories of Youth]. Stockholm, Bonnier, 1948.
Autobiographical Series: *Analfabeten* [The Illiterate], *Gårdfarihandlaren* [The Peddler], *Stockholmaren* [The Stockholmer], *Journalisten* [The Journalist], *Författaren* [The Writer], *Socialisten* [The Socialist], *Soldaten* [The Soldier], *Proletärförtfattaren* [The Proletarian Writer]. Stockholm, Bonnier, 8 vols., 1951-60.
Lyckan. Stockholm, Bonnier, 1962; as *Bodies of Love*, London, Souvenir Press, 1971.
Astronomens hus [Astronomer's House]. Stockholm, Bonnier, 1966.
Elektra, kvinna år 2070 [Woman of the Year 2070]. Stockholm, Bonnier, 1967.
Passionerna: Älskog. Stockholm, Bonnier, 1968.
Martyrerna [The Martyrs]. Stockholm, Bonnier, 1968.
Girigbukarna [The Misers]. Stockholm, Bonnier, 1969.
Karriäristerna [The Careerists]. Stockholm, Bonnier, 1969.
Vällustingarna [The Libertines]. Stockholm, Bonnier, 1970.
Lögnhalsarna [The Liars]. Stockholm, Bonnier, 1971.
Vishetslärarna [Teachers of Wisdom]. Stockholm, Bonnier, 1972.
Ordets makt: Historien om språket [The Power of Words]. Stockholm, Bonnier, 1973.
Nunnan i Vadstena: Sedeskildringar [The Nun of Vadstena]. Stockholm, Bonnier, 1973.
Folket och herrarna [The People and the Masters]. Stockholm, Norstedt, 1973.
Furstarna: en krönika från Gustav Vasa till Karl XII [The Rulers]. Stockholm, Bonnier, 1974.
Lastbara berättelser [Stories of Vice]. Stockholm, Bonnier, 1974.
Passionsnoveller I-II [Stories of Passion] (selection). Stockholm, Aldus, 2 vols., 1974.
En arbetares liv: Proletärnoveller [A Worker's Life: Proletarian Stories]. Stockholm, Bonnier, 1977.

Verse

Ur klyvnadens tid [The Splitting Time]. Stockholm, FIB, 1958.

Other

Vagabondliv i Frankrike [Vagabondage in France]. Stockholm, Wahlström & Widstrand, 1927.
Kolet i våld [The Coal's Power]. Stockholm, Wahlström & Widstrand, 1928.
Statarliv [Farm Laborers' Lives]. Stockholm, Folket i Bild, 1941.
Stridsskrifter. Stockholm, Bonnier, 1946.
Statarna i bild [Farm Laborers in Pictures], illustrated by Gunnar Lundh. Stockholm, KF, 1948.
Monism. Stockholm, Bonnier, 1948.
Ålderdom [Old Age], illustrated by Sven Järlås. Stockholm, KF, 1949.
Vagabondliv [Vagabondage]. Stockholm, Bonnier, 1949.
Ålderdoms-Sverige [Sweden for the Aged]. Stockholm, Bonnier, 1952.
Okänt Paris [Unknown Paris], illustrated by Tore Johnson. Stockholm, Bonnier, 1954.
Zigenarväg [Gypsy Ways], illustrated by Anna Riwkin-Brick. Stockholm, Bonnier, 1955.
Att skriva en roman [Writing a Novel]. Stockholm, Bonnier, 1957.
Zigenare [Gypsies]. Stockholm, Bonnier, 1963.
Statarnas liv och död [Farm Laborers Alive and Dead] (selection). Stockholm, Bonnier, 1963.
Statarskolan i litteraturen [Farm Laborers Literary School]. Gothenberg, Författarförlaget, 1972.
Dagbok fron 20-talet I-II [Diary from the Twenties]. Lund, Corona, 1974.
Stridsskrifter I-II [Polemical Pamphlets]. Lund, Fax, 1974.
Dagar och dagsverken: Debatter och memoarer [Days and Days' Work]. Stockholm, Bonnier, 1975.
Under de gröna ekarna i Sörmland [Under the Green Oaks in Sörmland]. Stockholm, Forum, 1976.
Passioner i urval (selection). Stockholm, Bra, 1976.
Den sociala fotobildboken [The Social Photograph Book]. Stockholm, Rabén & Sjoegren, 1977.
Pubertet [Puberty] (memoirs). Stockholm, Bonnier, 1978.
Asfalt [Asphalt] (memoirs). Stockholm, Bonnier, 1979.
Tröskeln [The Threshold] (memoirs). Stockholm, Bonnier, 1982.

*

Critical Studies: *Lo-Johansson* by Mauritz Edström, Stockholm, Bonnier, 1954, revised edition as *Åvan, kärleken, klassen: En bok om Lo-Johanssons författarskap*, Stockholm, Forum, 1976; *Lo-Johansson* by Ragnar Oldberg, Stockholm, Bonnier, 1957, and *Lo-Johansson i trycksvärtans ljus* by Oldberg and Lars Furuland, Stockholm, Bonnier, 1961; *Om Lo-Johansson* by Bertil Palmqvist, Lund, Fax, 1974; *Kärlek och ära* by Ola Holmgren, Stockholm, Liber, 1978.

*   *   *

Inevitably Ivar Lo-Johansson is associated with the generation of largely self-educated proletarian writers whose work has been a prominent feature of modern Swedish literature. Like Eyvind Johnson, Harry Martinson, or Jan Fridegård, he first achieved recognition in the 1930's with the portrayal of lower-class characters and milieux, often in the form of large-scale autobiographical novels in which the writer traced the relationship between a gifted and imaginative child and the oppressed and oppressive world in which he grew up.

Lo-Johansson's contribution to this genre, *Godnatt, jord* (Goodnight, Earth) is one of a series of books in which he describes the life and history of the *statare*, an impoverished class of tied farm labourers paid in kind ("stat") rather than cash. Partly as a result of the impassioned realism of these books, which included *Bara en mor* (Only a Mother) and the collections of sharply etched stories, *Statarna* (The Statare) and *Jordproletärerna* (Proletarians of the Soil), as well as through his active propaganda on their behalf, the statare system was abolished in 1945. Only recently, however, has the literary achievement of these works in their fusion of personal experience with the objectivity of an epic narrative been fully appreciated.

After experimenting with the collective novel in *Traktorn* (The Tractor) and the outspoken sexual polemic of *Geniet* (The Genius), Lo-Johansson confounded his readers' preconceptions by writing a series of eight wryly humorous autobiographical novels in which, in the earlier volumes at least, he succeeded in combining realistic detail with central organizing images of great imaginative power. *Analfabetan* (The Illiterate) is a compassionate account of his childhood home, while in *Gårdfarihandlaren* (The Peddler) and *Stockholmaren* (The Stockholmer), the strain of romanticism inherent in the narrative of his proletarian *Wanderjahre* is filtered through a lens of self-deflating irony.

Having brought what he described as the story "of an I the narrator has decided to call his own" down to the point at which he writes it, Lo-Johansson then embarked upon several volumes of short stories (145 stories in all), at least half of them on historical subjects. This was again in keeping with the development of the other Swedish proletarian writers, as if, having described their childhoods and documented the often painful process of emancipation from their background, they all felt a need to broaden their perspective and explore their roots in history. But unlike several of his contemporaries, Lo-Johansson did not abandon his earlier material permanently. Just when it appeared he might have mellowed into a respectable old man of letters, he returned to the past with renewed vigour in *Pubertet* (Puberty), the first volume in a further autobiographical sequence. In the three works which have appeared so far, he takes up once again what has been his most constant theme, the conflict between what he recognizes as his own deeply rooted individualism and his solidarity with the collective whose feelings and history he has continually sought to express. But if the events he relates are inevitably less urgently immediate than before, the apparent detachment of age now invests his material with a clarity that is both artistically effective and psychologically perceptive.

—Michael Robinson

LUCEBERT. Pseudonym for Lubertus Jacobus Swaanswijk. Dutch. Born in Amsterdam, 15 September 1924. Educated at Institute for Arts and Crafts, Amsterdam, 1938. Artist: member of Dutch Experimental Group, 1949, and Cobra, 1949; group and individual shows since 1948; retrospective exhibition, Stedelijk Museum, Amsterdam, 1969. Has lived in Bergen, North Holland, since 1953. Recipient: Anut Poetry Prize, 1954; Biennale de la Jeunesse Prize, 1959; Biennale Internazionale di Scultura prize, 1959; Marzotto Prize, 1962; Venice Biennale Cardazzo Prize, 1964; Hooft Prize, 1967; Triennial State Literary Prize, 1983. Address: Boendermakerhof 10, 1861 TB Bergen, Netherlands.

PUBLICATIONS

Verse

Triangel in de jungle [Triangle in the Jungle]. The Hague, Stols, 1951.
Apocrief [Apocryphal]. Amsterdam, Bezige Bij, 1952.
Van de afground en de luchtmens [Of the Abyss and the Airman]. The Hague, Stols, 1953.
Alfabel. Amsterdam, Bezige Bij, 1955.
De Amsterdamse school. The Hague, Stols, 1955.
Amulet. Amsterdam, Bezige Bij, 1957.
Val voor vliegengod [A Trap for a God of the Flies]. Amsterdam, Bezige Bij, 1959.
Lithologie: Tien gedichten, tien litho's. Hilversum, De Jong, 1959.
De gebroken rietlijn. Amsterdam, Instituut voor Kunstnijverheidsonderwijs, 1959.
Dag en nacht [Day and Night]. Hilversum, van Saane, 1959.
Januari. Amsterdam, Bezige Bij, 1964.
Gedichten 1948-1963 [Poems]. Amsterdam, Bezige Bij, 1965.
Seizoen [Season]. Amsterdam, Wereldbibliotheek, 1968.
Drie lagen diep [Three Layers Deep]. Amsterdam, Stedelijk Museum, 1969.
Verzamelde gedichten [Collected Poems], edited by C.W. van der Watering. Amsterdam, Bezige Bij, 1974.
The Tired Lovers They Are Machines, translated by Peter Nijmeijer. Deal Kent, Transgravity, 1974.
Beelden in het heden [Pictures in the Present]. Utrecht, Knippenberg, 1977.
Chambre-Antichambre, with Bert Schierbeek. The Hague, BZZTôH, 1978.
Mooi uitzicht en andere kurioziteiten [Nice View and Other Curiosities]. Amsterdam, Bezige Bij, 1980.
Oogsten in de dwaaltuin [Harvesting in the Maze]. Amsterdam, Bezige Bij, 1981.
De moerasruiter uit het paradÿs. Ambsterdam, Bezige Bij, 1983.

Play

De perfekte misdaad [The Perfect Crime]. The Hague, Bert Bakkar, 1968.

Other

Dames en heren [Ladies and Gentlemen]. Amsterdam, Bezige Bij, 1976.

*

Critical Studies: *Lucebert* edited by Lucebert, London, Marlborough Art, 1963; *The Experimental Artists* by Bert Schierbeek, Amsterdam, Meulenhoff, 1963; *Lucebert* (in English) by J. Eijkelboom, Amsterdam, Meulenhoff, 1964; *Met de ogen dicht* by C.W. Van de Watering, Muiderberg, Continho, 1979.

*   *   *

Lucebert's distinctiveness and stature as a poet have become clearer with the passage of time. As "Emperor" and principal spokesman of the 1950's generation of experimentalists, the *Vijftigers*, he was to some a standard-bearer in the iconoclastic assault on pre-war complacency and provincialism in much Dutch poetry, to others a pretentious and often incoherent literary vandal and demagogue. Neither image did justice to Lucebert's richly synthetic craftsmanship,

221

which, despite the startling and seemingly impenetrable "newness" of parts of it in a Dutch context, was informed from the first by a profound sense of literary and intellectual continuity.

The early collections bear the clear traces of his involvement as a painter with the Cobra movement, whose dislike of abstractions and admiration of the primitive directness of children's art he shares. Kaleidoscopically suggestive images, bewildering associative leaps, multilayered neologisms and ambiguous syntax assail and challenge the reader one moment, suggesting links with surrealism and Dada (Hans Arp is cited as a revered master), while the next a naively transparent, programmatic pronouncement proclaims that the poet's goal is to use "simplicity's enlightened waters/to give expression to the whole expanse and fulness of life" ("School of Poetry"). His poetry does indeed evoke the great themes of birth, love, death, war, destruction, and regeneration and simplicity and complexity co-exist in it. To achieve his stated aim, he draws on sources as diverse as Dutch predecessors like Herman Gorter (who is echoed in the title of the poem quoted), Hölderlin, Brecht, and Chinese classical verse (as in the serene "Fisherman by Ma Yuan").

Though unashamedly and often scathingly anti-elitist and anti-bourgeois, Lucebert's political and lyrical subversiveness is never simplistic propaganda; the irony and self-mockery of the "nimble con-man" reeling off his "little revolution" are apt to escape many of his critics. At the level of form, his break with the past is less radical than may appear from his abandonment of punctuation, capitalisation, and regular line-length in much of his work: his are not arbitrary word-clusters, but are bound together by such traditional elements as assonance, alliteration, and even internal rhyme—for all his dismissal of the "rhyme rats" of a previous generation. The poet himself regards the ultimate determinant of line-structure as the pattern of the breath, and his poems' resonance is best felt when they are read aloud.

His very choice of pseudonym is a revealing example of the way in which by dismantling and reassembling morphological units he transforms the familiar and banal—in this case his own Christian name—and achieves dense allusiveness: both its roots, one Latin and one Germanic, mean "light," while the combination evokes the fallen angel Lucifer. Both associations are very relevant; light, both literal and figurative, is a constant preoccupation for this painter-poet, who, moreover, like the great modernist Paul van Ostaijen (1898-1928), sees poetry as "a game with words anchored in metaphysics," an heroic mystical journey finally doomed because of human imperfection.

Some disillusion with the medium of language, at a time when experimentalism had lost much of its freshness and had itself become, in the hands of lesser imitators, the mannerism of an elite, may account for Lucebert's relatively small poetic output in the 1960's and 1970's, during which period he devoted himself mainly to painting. However, the collection *Oogsten in de dwaaltuin*, though sober, somber and even bleak in comparison with earlier work, showed the hand of a mature master, and hopefully heralds a new phase of productivity.

—Paul Vincent

LUNDKVIST, (Nils) Artur. Swedish. Born in Oderljunga, 3 March 1905. Self-educated. Married Maria Wine in 1936. Recipient: Lenin Prize, 1958; Dobloug Prize, 1958; Little Nobel Prize, 1961; Prize of the Nine, 1963; Bellman Prize, 1964. Honorary doctorate: Stockholm University, 1968. Member, Swedish Academy, 1968. Address: c/o Albert Bonniers Förlag, Sveavägen 56, Box 3159, 103 63 Stockholm, Sweden.

PUBLICATIONS

Verse

Glöd [Fervor of Embers]. Stockholm, Bonnier, 1928.
Fem unga [Five Young Men], with others. 1929.
Naket liv [Naked Life]. Stockholm, Bonnier, 1929.
Svart stad [Black City]. Stockholm, Bonnier, 1930.
Vit man [White Man]. Stockholm, Bonnier, 1932.
Nattens broar [The Bridges of Night]. Stockholm, Bonnier, 1936.
Sirensång [Siren Song]. Stockholm, Bonnier, 1937.
Eldtema [Fire Theme]. Stockholm, Bonnier, 1939.
Korsväg [Crossway]. Stockholm, Bonnier, 1942.
Dikter mellan djur och Gud [Poems Between Animal and God]. Stockholm, Bonnier, 1944.
Skinn över sten [Skin over Stone]. Stockholm, Bonnier, 1947.
Fotspår i vattnet [Footprints in the Water]. Stockholm, Bonnier, 1949.
Liv som gräs [Lives as Grass]. Stockholm, Bonnier, 1954.
Vindrosor, moteld [Wind Roses, Counterfire]. Stockholm, Bonnier, 1955.
Dikter 1928-1954. Stockholm, Bonnier, 1956.
Agadir. Stockholm, Bonnier, 1961; as *Agadir*, translated by William Jay Smith and Leif Sjöberg, Pittsburgh, International Poetry Forum, 1979.
Ogonblick och vågor [Moments and Waves]. Stockholm, Bonnier, 1962.
Texter i snön [Texts in the Snow]. Stockholm, Bonnier, 1964.
Besvärjelser till tröst [Incantations for Consolation]. Stockholm, Bonnier, 1969.
Världens härlighet: Prosadikter och andra texter följda av elegi för Pablo Neruda [The Splendour of the World: Prose Poems and Other Texts Followed by an Elegy for Pablo Neruda]. Stockholm, Bonnier, 1975.

Fiction

Jordisk prosa [Earthly Prose]. Stockholm, Bonnier, 1930.
Floderna flyter mot havet [The Rivers Flow to the Sea]. Stockholm, Bonnier, 1934.
Himmelsfärd [Ascension]. Stockholm, Bonnier, 1935.
Vandrarens träd [The Tree of the Wanderer]. Stockholm, Bonnier, 1941.
Vindingevals [Vindinge Waltz]. Stockholm, Tiden, 1956.
Berget och svalorna [The Mountain and the Swallows]. Stockholm, Tiden, 1957.
Ur en befolkad ensamhet [From a Peopled Loneliness]. Stockholm, Tiden, 1958.
Komedi i hägerskog [Comedy in the Heron Wood]. Stockholm, Tiden, 1959.
Orians upplevelser [Orian's Experiences]. Stockholm, Tiden, 1960.
Det talande trädet. Stockholm, Bonnier, 1960; as *The Talking Tree*, Salt Lake City, Utah, Brigham Young University Press, 1982.
Berättelser för vilsekomna [Stories for Lost Persons]. Stockholm, Tiden, 1961.
Sida vad sida [Side by Side]. Stockholm, Tiden, 1962.
Drömmar i ovädrens tid [Dreams in the Time of Storms]. Stockholm, Bonnier, 1963.
Darunga; eller, Varginnans mjölk [Darunga; or, The Milk of the She-Wolf]. Stockholm, Bonnier, 1964.
Sällskap för natten [Company for the Night]. Stockholm, Bonnier, 1965.
Mörkskogen [The Dark Forest]. Stockholm, Bonnier, 1967.
Snapphanens liv och död [Life and Death of the Marauder]. Stockholm, Bonnier, 1968.
Historier mellan åsarna [Stories Between the Ridges]. Stockholm, Bonnier, 1969.
Långt borta, mycket nära [Far Away, Very Near]. Gothenberg, Författarförlaget, 1970.

Himlens vilja [The Will of Heaven]. Stockholm, Bonnier, 1970.
Tvivla, korsfarare! En sannolik berättelse [Doubt, Crusader! A Probable Story].
 Stockholm, Bonnier, 1972.
Lustgårdens demoni [The Gardens of Delight]. Stockholm, Bonnier, 1973.
Livsälskare, svartmalåre [One Who Loves Life and Paints in Black]. Stockholm,
 Bonnier, 1974.
Fantasins slott och vardagens stenar [Fantasy Castle and Everyday Stones]. Gothen-
 berg, Författarförlaget, 1974.
Slavar för Särkland [Slaves for Särkland]. Stockholm, Bonnier, 1977.
Flykten och överlevandet [Flight and Survival]. Stockholm, Bonnier, 1977.
En gång i Nineve [Once in Nineveh] (selection). Stockholm, Coeckelbergh, 1978.
Utvandring till paradiset [Emigration to Paradise]. Stockholm, Bonnier, 1979.
Babylon—gudarnas sköka [Babylon—Whore of the Gods]. Stockholm, Bonnier, 1981.

Other

Atlantvind [Ocean Winds]. Stockholm, Bonnier, 1932.
Negerkust [Negro Coast]. Stockholm, Bonnier, 1933.
Drakblod [Dragon's Blood]. Stockholm, Bonnier, 1936.
Ikarus flykt [The Flight of Icarus]. Stockholm, Bonnier, 1939.
Tre Amerikaner: Dreiser, Lewis, Anderson. Stockholm, Bonnier, 1939.
Amerikas nya författare [America's New Writers]. Stockholm, Bonnier, 1940.
Diktare och avslöjare i Amerikas moderna litteratur [Authors and Informers in Modern
 American Literature]. Stockholm, Kooperativa Förbundets, 1942.
Jan Fridegard, with Lars Forssell. Stockholm, Frilansen, 1949.
Negerland [Negro Land]. Stockholm, Bonnier, 1949.
Indiabrand [India Fire]. Stockholm, Bonnier, 1950.
Vallmor från Taschkent [Poppies from Tashkent]. Stockholm, Bonnier, 1952.
Malinga. Stockholm, Bonnier, 1952.
Spegel för dag och natt [Mirror for Day and Night]. Stockholm, Bonnier, 1953.
Den förvandlade draken: En resa i Kina [The Transformed Dragon: A Trip to China].
 Stockholm, Tiden, 1955.
Vulkanisk kontinent: En resa i Sydamerika [Volcanic Continent: A Trip to South Ame-
 rica]. Stockholm, Tiden, 1957.
Poeter i profil [Poets in Profile]. Stockholm, FIB, 1958.
Utsikter över utländsk prosa [Views on Foreign Prose]. Stockholm, Bonnier, 1959.
Från utsiktstornet [From the Lookout Tower]. Stockholm, Kronos-Tiden, 1963.
Hägringar i handen: En resa i Israel [Mirages in Hand: A Trip to Israel]. Stockholm,
 Tiden, 1964.
Så lever Kuba [How Cuba Lives]. Stockholm, Tiden, 1965.
Självporträtt av en drömmare med öppna ögon [Self-Portrait of a Dreamer with Open
 Eyes]. Stockholm, Bonnier, 1966.
Buñuel. Stockholm, Norstedt, 1968.
Gunnar Ekelöf. Stockholm, Norstedt, 1968.
Brottställen [Fractures]. Stockholm, Bonnier, 1968.
Utflykter med utländska författare [Excursions with Foreign Authors]. Stockholm,
 Bonnier, 1969.
Antipodien [The Antipodes]. Stockholm, Bonnier, 1971.
Läsefrukter [Fruits of Reading]. Stockholm, Bonnier, 1973.
*Krigarens dikt: En sannolik framställning av Alexander den Stores hadlingar och lev-
 nadsöden* [The Warrior's Poem: A Probable Description of Alexander the Great's
 Actions and Fate]. Stockholm, Bonnier, 1976.
Sett i det strömmande vattnet och hört i den viskande vinden [Seen in the Flowing Water

and Heard on the Whispering Wind]. Stockholm, Bonnier, 1978.
Fantansi med realism: Om nutida utländsk skönlitterature [Fantasy with Realism: On Modern Foreign Literature]. Stockholm, Liber, 1979.
Skrivet mot Kvällen [Written Towards Evening]. Stockholm, Bonnier, 1980.
Gustav Hendenvind-Eriksson. Stockholm, Norstedt, 1982.
Sinnebilder [Symbols]. Stockholm, Bonnier, 1982.

Editor, *Twelve Modern Poets: An Anthology.* Stockholm, Continental, 1946.
Editor, *Europas litteraturhistoria 1918-1939.* Stockholm, Forum, 1946.
Editor, *90-tal: En lyrisk antologi.* Stockholm, Bonnier, 1956.
Editor, *Den mörke brodern: En antologi negerlyrik i urval.* Stockholm, FIB, 1957.
Editor, *Författare tar standpunkt.* Stockholm, Tiden, 1960.
Editor, *Stora Amerikanska berättare.* Stockholm, Folket i Bild, 1962.
Editor, *30-tal: En prosaantologi.* Stockholm, Rabén och Sjögren, 1963.
Editor, with Asa Scherdin-Lambert, *Vithariga revolvar.* Stockholm, FIB, 1966.

Translator, *Den stora oceanen,* by Pablo Neruda. Stockholm, FIB, 1956.
Translator, *Poet i New York,* by García Lorca. Stockholm, FIB, 1959.
Translator, *Den valdsamma arstiden,* by Octavio Paz. Stockholm, FIB, 1960.
Translator, with Francisco J. Uríz, *Kondor och Kolibri* (Spanish-American verse). Stockholm, FIB, 1962.
Translator, with Francisco J. Uríz, *Lampan på marken,* by Pablo Neruda. Stockholm, Bonnier, 1963.
Translator, with Francisco J. Uríz, *Vredgade vittnen: Sex moderna Spanska poeter.* Stockholm, FIB, 1966.
Translator, with Marina Torres, *Vårlig klarvaka,* by M.A. Asturias. Stockholm, FIB, 1967.
Translator, with Marina Torres, *Vargen som föds av kärleken: Latinamerikansk kärlekslyrik.* Stockholm, Gidlund, 1968.
Translator, with Dagmar Chvojkova-Pallasová, *Mellan regnets fingrar,* by Vítêzlav Nezval. Stockholm, FIB, 1968.
Translator, with Gun Bergman, *Elegier,* by Léopold Senghor. Stockholm, Bonnier, 1969.
Translator, *Ett skrik är ett skrik är ett,* by Francisco J. Uríz. Stockholm, Rabén och Sjögren, 1969.

*

Critical Studies: *Livsdykraren Lundkvist* by Kjell Espmark, Stockholm, Bonnier, 1964; interview with Leif Sjöberg, in *Books Abroad 50,* 1976; *Lundkvist i en föränderlig värld* by P. Lindblom, Stockholm, Tiden, 1976.

*   *   *

Artur Lundkvist has always been the most eclectic of writers. He was one of the first to introduce modernism into Swedish poetry, and a little later came under the influence of the French surrealists. In his early verse—much influenced by the Americans Carl Sandburg and Walt Whitman, by the Finn Elmer Diktonius, and by the ideas of Freud and D.H. Lawrence— he proclaims an ecstatic primitivist acceptance of life in all its forms: "Anything as long as it is life and fire, beauty and cursing, anything that tears us up, lights us to flames or hits us in the gob and makes us humble, miserable." Sexual mysticism and an aggressive critique of civilisation are tied into an uneasy but fruitful union with machine-worship and a belief in urbanisation. By the end of the 1930's such an outlook had become less tenable and his views became more pessimistic, more resigned: "And you who have believed in life to the uttermost, now say: Life is not possible." He nevertheless retained his belief in the power of art to destroy and renew, and he followed the surrealists in their desire to act as spokesmen for the unconscious, even the Jungian collective unconscious.

Lundkvist's poetry is visual rather than intellectual. Particular image follows particular image—sometimes logically, sometimes by association—to create an all-embracing collage in which the individual elements are submerged. The sheer visual richness of his imagination can, on occasion, lead to an undisciplined naming of parts; at best it leads to an unusually concrete universality.

Lundkvist's considerable prose production falls into three main categories. From his early days he has been a world traveller and, beginning in *Negerkust*, he has recorded his impressions in travel-book form. Travel also forms one element in a mixed genre with which he is particularly associated: in works such as *Malinga* prose-sketches join with travel pieces, short short-stories with prose-poems and aphorisms. The result is again collage, "sliding between reality and fantasy." Since *Himlens vilja* he has concentrated on historical novels. Through figures ranging from Alexander the Great through Genghis Khan to Goya he portrays the same restlessness, the same urge to change civilisation, the same intensity, and the same richness of visual image that characterise his poetry.

No less important than Lundkvist's own creative writing has been his role as intermediary. Right from the beginning of his career he has acted as critic, translator, and introducer of writers and literary trends from the rest of the world, especially (though certainly not exclusively) from the Anglo-Saxon and Hispanic areas. Through both his own work and his introduction of that of others, Lundkvist has had a potent stimulating and internationalising effect on modern Swedish writing.

—Peter Graves

LUZI, Mario. Italian. Born in Castello, near Florence, 20 October 1914. Educated at schools in Florence and Siena; University of Florence, 1930-36; Ph.D. 1936. Married Elena Monazi in 1942; one child. Teacher in Florence, San Miniato, Rome, and in Florence, 1945-55. Since 1955, Professor of French, University of Florence. Recipient: Carducci Prize, 1953; Marzotto Prize, 1957; Etna-Taorima Prize, 1964; Fiuggi Prize, 1971; Viareggio Prize, 1978. Address: Via Bellaziva 20, 50136 Florence, Italy.

PUBLICATIONS

Verse

La barca. Modena, Guanda, 1935.
Avvento notturno. Florence, Vallecchi, 1940.
Un brindisi. Florence, Sansoni, 1946.
Quanderno gotico. Florence, Vallecchi, 1947.
Primizie del deserto. Milan, Schwarz, 1952.
Onore del vero. Venice, Pozza, 1957.
Il giusto della vita. Milan, Garzanti, 1960.

Nel magma. Milan, Scheiwiller, 1963; revised edition, 1966.
Dal fondo delle campagne. Turin, Einaudi, 1965.
Su fondamenti invisibili. Milan, Rizzoli, 1971.
Poesie. Milan, Garzanti, 1974.
In the Dark Body of Metamorphosis and Other Poems, translated by Isidore Lawrence Salomon. New York, Norton, 1975.
Al fuoco della controversia. Milan, Garzanti, 1978.
Tutti le poesie. Milan, Garzanti, 2 vols., 1979.

Plays

Ipazia. Milan, Scheiwiller, 1973.
Libro di Ipazia. Milan, Rizzoli, 1979.
Rosales. Milan, Rizzoli, 1983.

Other

L'opium chrétien. Modena, Guanda, 1938.
Un'illusione platonica e altri saggi. Florence, Edizioni di Rivoluzione, 1941; revised edition, Bologna, Boni, 1972.
Biografia a Ebe. Florence, Vallecchi, 1942.
L'inferno e il limbo. Florence, Marzocco, 1949; revised edition, Milan, Il Saggiatore, 1964.
Studio su Mallarmé. Florence, Sansoni, 1952.
Aspetti della generazione napoleonica ed altri saggi di letteratura francese. Modena, Guanda, 1956.
Lo stile di Constant. Milan, Il Saggiatore, 1962.
Trame. Lecce, Quaderni del Critone, 1963; revised edition, Milan, Rizzoli, 1982.
Tutto in questione. Florence, Vallecchi, 1965.
Vicissitudine e forma. Milan, Rizzoli, 1974.
Discorso naturale. Milan, Garzanti, 1984.

Editor, with Tommaso Landolfi, *Anthologie de la poésie lyrique française.* Florence, Sansoni, 1950.
Editor, *L'idea simbolista.* Milan, Garzanti, 1959.

Translator, *Vita e letteratura,* by Charles du Bos. Padua, Cedam, 1943.
Translator, *Poesia e prose,* by Coleridge. Milan, Cederna, 1949.
Translator, *Andromaca,* by Racine, in *Teatro francese del Grande Secolo.* Rome, ERI, 1960.
Translator, *La fonte,* by Jorge Guillén. Milan, Scheiwiller, 1961.
Translator, *Riccardo II,* by Shakespeare. Turin, Einaudi, 1966.
Translator, *La cordigliera delle Ande.* Turin, Einaudi, 1983.

*

Critical Studies: "Luzi" by W. Craft, in *Books Abroad,* Winter 1975; "The Dark Body of Metamorphosis" by Radcliffe Squires, in *Michigan Quarterly Review,* Winter 1975; *Il fuoco e la metamorfosi* by Giancarlo Quiziconi, Bologna, Cappelli, 1980.

*   *   *

Since Montale's death, Mario Luzi is commonly regarded—and with some justification—as the most important living Italian poet. Since 1935, when he published his first volume of poetry—*La barca*—he has written a quite substantial body of both verse and criticism that is impressive for its individuality and, at times, for its originality. During the lifetime of Ungaretti, Montale, and Quasimodo, Luzi had succeeded in creating a particularly personal line of poetry, with a characteristic vein and timbre. For all his admiration of Ungaretti and Montale, who may have to some extent influenced him, Luzi is something more than a continuator of what these poets represent.

Because he is an admirer of such culturally and artistically diverse poets as Cavalcanti, D'Annunzio, and Cardarelli on the one hand, and Coleridge and Eluard on the other, and of Oriental philosophy and mysticism as well as the religious philosophy of the West, Luzi's poetry achieves a fruitful synthesis between what is symbolic and realistic, mystical and experimental, and the very tone of his poetry, at its most characteristic, registers a perfect fusion between the reflective and the discursive, the lyrical and the philosophical, the subjective and the universal.

It is due to this synthesis that Luzi's poetic imagery too has the evocative potency it has, exploiting both what is conventional and what the poet arrives at by exploratory thought and creative perception, which serves to underline the intrinsically reflective and meditative, if not wholly mystical and philosophical character of Luzi's poetry, with its creative interplay between what is within time and what is timeless, what is contingent and what is eternal, what is empirically realized and what is beyond experience. Thus a certain symbolism underlies much of Luzi's poetry—a symbolism owing more to Eliot than to the French Symbolists, as his later and most mature volumes of poetry—*Onore del vero, Il giusto della vita, Nel magma*, and *Dal fondo della campagne*—amply illustrate. In these volumes Luzi's strength and individuality are revealed through such qualities as his neo-religio-philosophical humanism, the moral intensity of his thought expressed by means of a discursive lyricism, his inner calm and self-control that are both moral and creative, and his artistic and technical mastery which is synonymous with a rare kind of sincerity and integrity.

In one of his earlier poems ("A un compagno," 1944) Luzi said: "per me essere è non dimenticare" (for me to live means not to forget), which may be taken as an epigraph for all his poetic *oeuvre*, summing up, as it does, the introspective, morally charged, and poetically realized existentialism underlying his verse and his temperament.

—G. Singh

MAHFOUZ, Naguib. Egyptian. Born in Cairo, 11 December 1911. Educated at the University of Cairo, 1930-34, degree in philosophy 1934. Married; has children. Worked in secretarial post at University of Cairo to 1938; journalist: staff member, *Ar-Risala*, and contributor to *al-Hilal* and *al-Ahram*. Civil servant: joined Ministry of Islamic Affairs, 1939, and later in Department of Art: head of State Cinema Organization; adviser to Minister of Culture; retired, 1971. Recipient: Egyptian State Prize, 1956. Address: 172 Nile Street, Agouza, Cairo, Egypt.

PUBLICATIONS

Fiction

Hams al-junun [The Whisper of Madness].   Cairo, 1939.

Abath al aqdar [The Mockery of Fate].   Cairo, 1939.
Radubis.   Cairo, Misr, 1943.
Kifah Tiba [Thebes's Struggle].   Cairo, Misr, 1944.
Khan al-Khalili.   Cairo, 1945.
Al-Qahira al-jadida [New Cairo].   Cairo, Misr, 1946.
Zuqaq al-Midaqq.   Cairo, Misr, 1947; as *Midaq Alley*, Beirut, Khayyat, 1966; revised
    edition, London, Heinemann, and Washington, D.C., Three Continents, 1975.
Al-Sarab [Mirage].   Cairo, 1949(?).
Bidaya wa-nihaya [A Beginning and an End].   Cairo, Misr, 1949.
Al-Thulathiya [The Trilogy]:
    Bayn al-Qasrayn.   Cairo, Misr, 1956.
    Qasr al-Shawq.   Cairo, Misr, 1957.
    Al-Sukkariya.   Cairo, Misr, 1957.
Al-Liss wa-l-Kilab [The Thief and the Dogs].   Cairo, Misr, 1961.
Al-Summan wa-l-Kharif [Quail and Autumn].   Cairo, Misr, 1962.
Dunya Allah [The World of God].   Cairo, Misr, 1963.
Al-Tariq [The Way].   Cairo, Misr, 1964.
Al-Shahhadh [The Beggar].   Cairo, Misr, 1965.
Bayt sayyi al-suma [A House of Ill-Repute].   Cairo, Misr, 1965.
Tharthara fawq al-Nil [Chit-Chat on the Nile].   Cairo, Misr, 1966.
Awlad Haratina.   Beirut, Al-Adab, 1967; as *Children of Gebelawi*, London, Heinemann,
    and Washington, D.C., Three Continents, 1981.
Miramar.   Cairo, Misr, 1967; translated as *Miramar*, Cairo, American University in
    Cairo Press, London, Heinemann, and Washington, D.C., Three Continents, 1978.
Khammarat al-qitt al-aswad [The Black Cat Tavern].   Cairo, Misr, 1968.
Taht al-mizalla [Under the Awning].   Cairo, Misr, 1969.
Hikaya bila bidaya wala nihaya [A Story Without Beginning or End].   Cairo, Misr, 1971.
Shahr al-asal [Honeymoon].   Cairo, Misr, 1971.
Al-Maraya.   Cairo, Misr, 1972; as *Mirrors*, Minneapolis, Bibliotheca Islamica, 1977.
Al-Hubb Tahta al-Matar [Love in the Rain].   Cairo, Misr, 1973.
God's World: An Anthology of Short Stories, edited by Akef Abadir and Roger Allen.
    Minneapolis, Bibliotheca Islamica, 1973.
Al-Jarima [The Crime].   Cairo, Misr, 1973.
Al-Karnak [Karnak].   Cairo, Misr, 1974.
Hikayat Haratina [Stories of Our District].   Cairo, Misr, 1975.
Qalb al-Layl [In the Heart of the Night].   Cairo, Misr, 1975.
Hadrat al-Muhtaram [Honorable Sir].   Cairo, Misr, 1975.
Al-Hubb fawqa Hadabat al-Haram [Love on Pyramid Mount].   Cairo, Misr, 1979.
Al-Shaytan ya'iz [Satan Preaches].   Cairo, Misr, 1979.

Other

Nagib Mahfuz-yatadhakkar [Mahfouz Remembers], edited by Gamal al-Gaytani.   Beirut,
    Al-Masirah, 1980.

*

Critical Study: *The Changing Rhythm: A Study of Mahfuz's Novels* by Sasson Somekh,
Leiden, Brill, 1973.

*   *   *

Naguib Mahfouz is the dominant novelist of Egypt of the 20th century to date and one of the
most influential of the Arab novelists. With the exception of his first three novels, set in ancient

Egypt, and a few recent allegorical works, the bulk of his writing has been devoted to chronicling modern Egyptian life, and particularly that of Cairo.

Mahfouz is an exceptional product of the Egyptian system. He graduated from Cairo University and has worked in journalism in addition to a career in government service. One of his most typical heroes is the government bureaucrat. This choice is appropriate, since in modern Egypt the civil service has often been the employer of both first and last resort. The great period of Arabic classical prose literature, moreover, in the 8th and 9th centuries A.D. was a civil service literature, by and for government secretaries.

His historical novels were not simply romances but also political statements put in a covert form. The message of *Kifah Tiba*, for example, is: foreign colonialists, go home. His reputation is based primarily on his later novels, however, and in particular on his masterful trilogy. The trilogy, with its volumes named after sections of Cairo, is composed of *Bayn al-Qasrayn*, *Qasr al-Shawq*, and *Al-Sukkariya*. The first volume traces the fortunes of a Cairo merchant's family through the period climaxed by the 1919 revolution. The two other volumes take the family respectively through the middle 1920's and then up to 1944. A lesser but comparable work, *Midaq Alley*, had attempted in one volume to provide a slice of Cairo life cut horizontally through space down a Cairo alley rather than the trilogy's vertical cut through a family's life and times. The residents of Midaq Alley were set into motion when the most beautiful woman has to decide whether to marry the alley barber or become a prostitute for British soldiers. Critics have suggested that she represents the plight of Egypt at that time.

Mahfouz has not been afraid in his works to scratch at the human crust. He has allowed the lusts and muck concealed within to ooze out in a panorama of local colour. In *Qasr al-Shawq*, for example, a family crisis is created when Yasin marries his father's favourite prostitute.

In his more recent fiction, Mahfouz has substituted introspection for some of the local colour and experimented with stream of consciousness passages. In *Al-Liss wa-l-Kilab* he provides a grim and sleek account of a thief who, having attempted to take revenge on a powerful foe, is hunted down. *Miramar* features the psychological clash between the old and new in Egypt following the 1952 revolution. The residents of a boarding house in Alexandria which has seen better days react in ways which reflect their outlook on life and their backgrounds when a beautiful woman joins the staff.

One of the themes that runs throughout these different periods is human ambition: that lust which cannot be satisfied. In some of his recent works Mahfouz has also dealt allegorically with religion. In his short story "Za balawi" (in *Dunya Allah*) a Sufi healer on the lam from the police seems the only path left open to the narrator who is seeking a cure from an unnamed malady which may even be the insipid nature of the world today. *Children of Gebelawi* draws on Jewish, Christian, and Islamic history for inspiration for the plot in an allegory recounting the lives of the offspring of one man. Although this work contains the pessimism of many of his works, it holds out hope that mankind can through free enquiry make progress in social justice.

—William M. Hutchins

MALLET-JORIS, Françoise. Pseudonym for Françoise Lilar. French. Born in Antwerp, Belgium, 6 July 1930; now a French citizen. Educated in Antwerp; at Bryn Mawr College, Pennsylvania, 1947-48; the Sorbonne, Paris, 1949. Married 1) Robert Amadou in 1947 (divorced, 1948), one son; 2) Alain Joxe in 1952 (marriage dissolved), one son and one daughter; 3) Jacques Delfau in 1958, one daughter. Reader for Julliard publishers, Paris, from

1952, and for Grasset publishers, Paris, from 1965; since 1980, Member of the Board of Directors, Television Network 1, Paris. Songwriter for Marie-Paule Belle. Recipient: French Booksellers Prize, 1957; Fémina Prize, 1958; Julliard Prize, 1963; Monaco Grand Prize, 1965. Member, 1970, and since 1973 Vice President, Goncourt Academy. Address: c/o Grasset, 61 rue des Saints-Pères, 75006 Paris, France.

PUBLICATIONS

Fiction

Le Rempart des Béguines. Paris, Julliard, 1951; as *The Illusionist*, New York, Farrar Straus, 1952; as *Into the Labyrinth*, London, W.H. Allen, 1953.
La Chambre rouge. Paris, Julliard, 1955; as *The Red Room*, New York, Farrar Straus, and London, W.H. Allen, 1956.
Cordélia. Paris, Julliard, 1956; as *Cordelia and Other Stories*, New York, Farrar Straus, and London, W.H. Allen, 1965.
Les Mensonges. Paris, Julliard, 1956; as *House of Lies*, New York, Farrar Straus, 1957; London, W.H. Allen, 1958.
L'Empire Céleste. Paris, Julliard, 1958; as *Café Céleste*, New York, Farrar Straus, and London, W.H. Allen, 1959.
Les Personnages. Paris, Julliard, 1961; as *The Favourite*, New York, Farrar Straus, and London, W.H. Allen, 1962.
Les Signes et les prodiges. Paris, Grasset, 1966; as *Signs and Wonders*, New York, Farrar Straus, 1966; London, W.H. Allen, 1967.
Trois âges de la nuit: Histoires de sorcellerie. Paris, Grasset, 1968; as *The Witches: Three Tales of Sorcery*, New York, Farrar Straus, 1969; London, W.H. Allen, 1970.
Le Jeu du souterrain. Paris, Grasset, 1973; as *The Underground Game*, London, W.H. Allen, 1974; New York, Dutton, 1975.
Allegra. Paris, Grasset, 1976.
Dickie-Roi. Paris, Grasset, 1979.
Un Chagrin d'amour et d'ailleurs. Paris, Grasset, 1981.
Le Clin d'oeil de l'ange. Paris, Gallimard, 1983.

Plays

Un Gout de miel, with G. Arout, from play by Shelagh Delaney. Paris, L'Avant-Scène, 1960.

Screenplays: *Le Gigolo*, 1962; *Le Rempart des Béguines*, 1972.

Verse

Poèmes du dimanche. Brussels, Artistes, 1947.

Other

Lettre à moi-même. Paris, Julliard, 1963; as *A Letter to Myself*, New York, Farrar Straus, and London, W.H. Allen, 1964.
Marie Mancini: Le Premier amour de Louis XIV. Paris, Hachette, 1964; as *The Uncompromising Heart: A Life of Marie Mancini, Louis XIV's First Love*, New York,

Farrar Straus, and London, W.H. Allen, 1966.
Enfance, ton regard. Paris, Hachette, 1966.
La Maison de papier. Paris, Grasset, 1970; as *The Paper House*, New York, Farrar Straus, and London, W.H. Allen, 1971.
Le Roi qui aimait trop les fleurs (juvenile). Paris, Casterman, 1971.
Les Feuilles mortes d'un bel été (juvenile). Paris, Grasset, 1973.
J'aurais voulu jouer de l'accordéon. Paris, Julliard, 1975.
Juliette Greco, with Michel Grisolia. Paris, Seghers, 1975.
Jeanne Guyon. Paris, Flammarion, 1978.

Editor, *Nouvelles.* Paris, Julliard, 1957.
Editor, *Le Rendez-vous donne par Mallet-Joris à quelques jeunes écrivains.* Paris, Julliard, 1962.
Editor, *Lettres*, by Madame de Sévigné. Paris, Rombaldi, 1969.

*

Critical Studies: "Mallet-Joris and the Anatomy of the Will" by Rima Drell Reck, in *Yale French Studies* (New Haven, Connecticut), Summer 1959; "Mirrors and Masks in the World of Mallet-Joris" by Geneviève Delattre, in *Yale French Studies* Spring 1961; *Mallet-Joris* (in French) by Michel Géoris, Brussels, Méyère, 1964; *Mallet-Joris* (in French) edited by Monique Détry, Paris, Grasset, 1976.

*   *   *

The eminent French critic Pierre-Henri Simon called Françoise Mallet-Joris one of the most gifted writers of her generation. Her first novel, *Le Rempart des Béguines*, published in 1951 when the author was 21 years old, is the story of an adolescent who enters into a lesbian relationship with her father's mistress. The protagonist of the novel is the prototype of all of the author's subsequent heroines; she is an independent, brave, and resolute young girl, created in the author's own image, who refuses to play the role assigned to her by society and who revolts against the hypocrisy and constraints of her milieu. Her rebellion is directed solely against family and society without reference to the human condition.

While the behavior of the heroines of *Le Rempart des Béguines*, of its sequel *La Chambre rouge*, and of the short stories of *Cordélia* is motivated by a search for truth, that of the males is characterized by a flight from truth. The men in Mallet-Joris's work are, for the most part, inauthentic beings who have directed their efforts towards creating an image of themselves that will free them from the existentialist imperative of creating their own essence. The danger of such behavior is made manifest in *Les Mensonges* and *L'Empire Céleste*, where the male protagonists find ultimately that the personas they have created have destroyed their authentic being, leaving nothing in its stead. In these two novels, the author changes from first- to third-person narration. Interior monologues, dialogues, and individual perceptions provide the multiple points of view that were lacking in the preceding works.

Mallet-Joris presents her prototypical heroine against historical backgrounds in two novels, *Les Personnages* and *Trois âges de la nuit*, and two biographical works, *Marie Mancini* and *Jeanne Guyon*. The women who are the protagonists of these works are called "personnes" (authentic beings) by the author because they remain true to their inner selves. She contrasts them with characters she refers to as "personnages" (personae), because they hide behind masks and play prescribed roles. While each of the heroines revolts in a different way against society, all of them are similarly conspired against and attacked on all sides by hostile forces. In these works, the author's denunciation of the plight of the heroine develops into a more sweeping indictment of the condition of women in general, expressing a feminine bias that will become more pronounced in her subsequent novels. Emphasis is also placed in these works on spiritual preoccupations which often take precedence over social concerns and which will constitute the essence of Mallet-Joris's later works.

Lettre à moi-même is an autobiographical work in which the author tells the story of her search for God and her religious conversion. This work provides the key to all of Mallet-Joris's later works, for it is the search for an absolute that motivates the characters of the novels *Les Signes et les prodiges*, *Allegra*, *Dickie-Roi*, and *Un Chagrin d'amour et d'ailleurs* as well as of the short stories of *Le Clin d'oeil de l'ange*.

Françoise Mallet-Joris's novels remain within the framework of the traditional novel with their emphasis on plot and characterization. At the same time, her emphasis on visual detail and her use of certain techniques of the new novel place her within the mainstream of modern fiction.

—Lucille Frackman Becker

MANDIARGUES, André Pieyre de. *See* **PIEYRE DE MANDIARGUES, André.**

MÁRQUEZ, Gabriel García. *See* **GARCÍA MÁRQUEZ, Gabriel.**

MATUTE (Ausejo), Ana María. Spanish. Born in Barcelona, 26 July 1926. Educated at Damas Negras French Nuns College and schools in Barcelona and Madrid. Married Ramón Eugenio de Goicoechea in 1952 (separated, 1963), one son. Member of the Turia literary group, with Juan Goytisolo and others, Barcelona, 1951. Visiting professor, Indiana University, Bloomington, 1965-66, and University of Oklahoma, Norman, 1969; Writer-in-Residence, University of Virginia, Charlottesville, 1978-79. Recipient: Café Gijón Prize, 1952; Planeta Prize, 1954; Critics Prize (Spain), 1959; March Foundation grant, 1959; Ministry of Information Cervantes Prize, 1959; Nadal Prize, 1960; Lazarillo Prize, for children's writing, 1965; Fastenrath Prize, 1969. Honorary Fellow, American Association of Teachers of Spanish and Portuguese; Corresponding Member, Hispanic Society of America, 1960. Address: c/o Ediciones Destino, Consejo de Ciento 425, Barcelona 9, Spain.

PUBLICATIONS

Fiction

Los Abel. Barcelona, Destino, 1948.
Fiesta al noroeste. Madrid, Aguado, 1953.

La pequeña vida. Madrid, Prensa Española, 1953.
Pequeño teatro. Barcelona, Planeta, 1954.
En esta tierra. Barcelona, Exito, 1955.
Los cuentos, Vagabundos. Barcelona, G.P., 1956.
Los niños tontos. Madrid, Arion, 1956.
El tiempo. Barcelona, Mateu, 1957.
Los hijos muertos. Barcelona, Planeta, 1958; as *The Lost Children,* New York, Macmillan, 1965.
Los mercaderes:
   1. *Primera memoria.* Barcelona, Destino, 1959; as *Awakening,* London, Hutchinson, 1963; as *School of the Sun,* New York, Pantheon, 1963.
   2. *Los soldados lloran de noche.* Barcelona, Destino, 1964.
   3. *La trampa.* Barcelona, Destino, 1969.
Tres y un sueño. Barcelona, Destino, 1961.
A la mitad del camino. Barcelona, Rocas, 1961.
Historias de la Artámila. Barcelona, Destino, 1961.
El arrepentido. Barcelona, Rocas, 1961.
El río. Barcelona, Argos, 1963.
Algunos muchachos. Barcelona, Destino, 1968.
La torre vigía. Barcelona, Lumen, 1971.
Olvidado rey Gudú. Barcelona, Lumen, 1980.
Diablo vuelve a casa. Barcelona, Destino, 1980.

Other

El país de la pizarra (juvenile). Barcelona, Molino, 1957.
Paulina, el mundo, y las estrellas (juvenile). Barcelona, Garbo, 1960.
El saltamontes verde: El aprendiz (juvenile). Barcelona, Lumen, 1960.
Libro de juegos para los niños de los otros, photographs by Jaime Buesa. Barcelona, Lumen, 1961.
Caballito loco; Carnivalito (juvenile). Barcelona, Lumen, 1962.
El polizón del "Ulises" (juvenile). Barcelona, Lumen, 1965.
Obra completa. Barcelona, Destino, 1971— .

*

Critical Studies: *The World of Matute* by M. Weitzner, Lexington, University Press of Kentucky, 1970; *The Literary World of Matute* by Margaret E.W. Jones, Lexington, University Press of Kentucky, 1970; *Matute* by Janet Díaz, New York, Twayne, 1971; *Matute* by Rosa Roma, Madrid, Espesa, 1971.

*   *   *

Ana María Matute has written a number of major prize-winning novels as well as collections of short stories and fiction for juveniles. Her major emphasis concerns the process of growing up and the loss of illusion and innocence by anguished adolescents who seek in vain for love and beauty in an ugly and terrifying adult world. Fusing fantasy and reality, Matute paints a portrait of a materialistic, petrified Spain, filled with social and ethical problems and victimized by fratricidal strife, but she evinces great maternal tenderness toward alienated orphan children.

In many of her novels Matute deforms nature to reflect the fatalistic elements of a hateful, violent world and its citizens. At times she affects an involuted, baroque style; at others she overwhelms the reader with a rich and delicate sensory imagery. She uses interior monologue, flashbacks, first-person narrative, free association, and temporal jumps, fusing subjective lyricism with committed literature much as she dichotomizes and coalesces fantasy and reality.

In one of her best early novels, *Fiesta al noroeste*, an excellent psychological analysis of the all-powerful local overlord, Juan Midinao, she exposes the hypocrisy of traditional Spanish values and explores the need for freedom from political oppression, the Cain-Abel theme, the plight of brutalized children, and existential loneliness and inability to communicate.

Los hijos muertos, her most complex and ambitious novel, deals with the generation gap, the tragic legacy of the Civil War, and the lack of love and charity. The protagonist, Daniel Corvo, loses his life, like so many others in his idealistic generation which dreams of justice in the face of a repressive, decadent, and sterile tradition.

School of the Sun, the first volume of a trilogy, *Los mercaderes*, achieved an even greater critical acclaim. Matia, the young protagonist, loses her innocence, remaining silent in the face of injustice. In the second volume the merchants of this world continue to exploit others, and Manuel, a victim earlier of adult hypocrisy, fruitlessly sacrifices himself in the last days of the war. Bourgeois mentality, fear, and hatred continue in the final volume, set some thirty years later. Matia, guilt-ridden, betrayed by those she loved, nonetheless hopes for the future even in a degraded world of sexual repression which denies woman her moral and psychological liberty.

Typical of Matute's many short story collections, *Historias de la Artámila* contains sketches of childhood, real and imagined, in a fantasy town between the Pyrenees and the Ebro. Her everyday scenes do not disguise the existential isolation found in an unjust world.

Matute's protagonists, trapped by time, unable to communicate, often dream of a lost Paradise. But the author's world of oppressed children lacks Christian charity, and sooner or later, abandoning fantasy, they must react to false values and lack of comprehension and learn to explore the disparate values of a brutalized and tragic world.

—Kessel Schwartz

MAURIAC, Claude. French. Born in Paris, 25 April 1914; son of the writer François Mauriac. Educated at Lycée Janson-de-Sailly; University of Paris, doctorate in law. Married Marie-Claude Monte in 1951; two sons and one daughter. Private secretary to de Gaulle, 1944-49; founding director, *Liberté de l'Esprit* magazine, Paris, 1949-53; critic and columnist ("La Vie des Lettres"), *Le Figaro*, Paris, 1946-77, and film critic, *Figaro Littéraire*, 1947-72. Since 1977, film critic, *Vendredi Samedi Dimanche*, Paris. Recipient: Sainte Beuve Prize, 1949; Médicis Prize, 1959. Chevalier, Legion of Honor. Address: 24 Quai de Béthune, 75004 Paris, France.

PUBLICATIONS

Fiction

Le Dialogue intérieur:
  Toutes les femmes sont fatales. Paris, Michel, 1951; as *All Women Are Fatal*, New York, Braziller, 1964; as *Femmes fatales*, London, Calder and Boyars, 1966.
  Le Dîner en ville. Paris, Michel, 1959; as *The Dinner Party*, New York, Braziller,

1960; as *Dinner in Town*, London, Calder, 1963.
Le Marquise sortit à cinq heures. Paris, Michel, 1961; as *The Marquise Went Out at Five*, New York, Braziller, 1962; London, Calder and Boyars, 1967.
L'Agrandissement. Paris, Michel, 1963.
L'Oubli. Paris, Grasset, 1966.
Le Bouddha s'est mis à trembler. Paris, Grasset, 1979.
Un Coeur tout neuf. Paris, Grasset, 1980.
Radio nuit. Paris, Grasset, 1982.

Plays

La Conversation (produced Paris, 1966). Paris, Grasset, 1964.
Les Parisiens du dimanche (produced Montreal, 1967). In *Théâtre*, 1968.
Théâtre (includes *La Conversation*; *Ici, maintenant*; *Le Cirque*; *Les Parisiens du dimanche*; *Le Hun*). Paris, Grasset, 1968.

Screenplays: *Les Sept péchés capitaux* (*The Seven Deadly Sins*), with others, 1962; *Thérèse*, with François Mauriac and Georges Franju, 1963.

Other

Introduction à une mystique de l'enfer. Paris, Grasset, 1938.
La corporation dans l'état. Bordeaux, Bière, 1941.
Aimer Balzac. Paris, Table Ronde, 1945.
Jean Cocteau; ou, La Vérité du mensonge. Paris, Lieutier, 1945.
Malraux; ou, Le Mal du héros. Paris, Grasset, 1946.
André Breton: Essai. Paris, Flore, 1949.
Conversations avec André Gide: Extraits d'un journal. Paris, Michel, 1951; as *Conversations with André Gide*, New York, Braziller, 1965.
Hommes et idées d'aujourd'hui. Paris, Michel, 1953.
L'Amour du cinéma. Paris, Michel, 1954.
Petite littérature du cinéma. Paris, Cerf, 1957.
L'Alittérature contemporaine. Paris, Michel, 1958; revised edition, 1969; as *The New Literature*, New York, Braziller, 1959.
De la littérature à l'alittérature. Paris, Grasset, 1969.
Le Temps immobile:
   1. *Une amitié contrariée.* Paris, Grasset, 1970.
   2. *Les Espaces imaginaires.* Paris, Grasset, 1975.
   3. *Et comme l'espérance est violente.* Paris, Grasset, 1976.
   4. *La Terrasse de Malagar.* Paris, Grasset, 1977.
   5. *Aimer de Gaulle.* Paris, Grasset, 1978.
   6. *L'Éternité parfois.* Paris, Grasset, 1978.
   7. *Le Rire des pères dans les yeux des enfants.* Paris, Grasset, 1981.
Un autre de Gaulle: Journal 1944-1954. Paris, Hachette, 1971; as *Aimer de Gaulle*, Paris, Grasset, 1978; as *The Other de Gaulle: Diaries 1944-1954*, New York, Day, and London, Angus and Robertson, 1973.
Une Certaine Rage. Paris, Laffont, 1977.
Laurent Terzieff. Paris, Stock, 1980.

Editor, *Proust*. Paris, Seuil, 1953.

*

MELO NETO

Critical Studies: "Structure in the Novels of Mauriac" by S. Johnston, in *French Review 38*, February 1965.

* * *

Writing in the limelight of the fascinating problems and techniques underscored by the French New Novel, and by the 20th-century novel in general, Claude Mauriac is largely concerned in his work with the conception and incubation of creative inspiration, along with the dilemma of choice resulting from the infringement of multiple subject matter upon any delimitation of time and space. Beyond the ontological, psychological, and moral planes, Mauriac measures his art against metaphysical dimensions. For Mauriac communication has become buried under an almost unsupportable burden of self-consciousness. Language is experienced not merely as something shared but as something corrupted, weighted down by historical accumulation. There is a devaluation of language and character in Mauriac's work. Characters who in the hands of former writers had some fictional relief now lose artistic dimension.

In his tetralogy, titled significantly *Le Dialogue intérieur*, Mauriac examines silence as an element of dialogue, of communication and knowledge. Silence for Mauriac is merely the furthest extension of that reluctance to communicate, that ambivalence about making contact with an audience or a character, which is a leading motif of modern art, with its tireless commitment to the new and esoteric. *L'Agrandissement* (The Enlargement or The Blow-up, a term borrowed from photography) is the last novel of the series, which, like the preceding ones, is "nouveaux" by virtue of its technical similarities with the work of Nathalie Sarraute and Michel Butor, among others. But in *L'Agrandissement*, Mauriac becomes for the first time a pioneer by writing what may be described as an essay on the novel in the form of a novel. The tetralogy has been compared to Samuel Beckett's trilogy (*Molloy, Malone Dies, The Unnamable*) in the single respect that each successive novel narrows the scope allowed to its predecessor. In Beckett's series there is a progressive constriction of space and number of characters; in Mauriac's, the narrowing affects only time. *L'Agrandissement* is not only an absorbing picture of a novelist's mind at work and a fascinating commentary on the three preceding novels, but an entertainment full of humorous quirks. To indicate that it forms an uninterrupted interior monologue, the book, although conventionally punctuated, consists of a single enormous paragraph—some two-hundred pages in length!

Claude Mauriac, borrowing from the New Novelists, is concerned primarily with art and fiction as means of grasping reality. He is preoccupied with depicting a reality consisting of simultaneous thoughts, spoken words, and tacit communication. As an introverted essayist and literary theorist who disguises his form as "novelistic," Claude Mauriac prefigures what some critics have recently observed: that most art in our time has been experienced by audiences as a move into silence, unintelligibility, invisibility, or inaudibility.

—Sandra María Boschetto

MELO NETO, João Cabral de. Brazilian. Born in Recife, 9 January 1920. Married Stella Barbosa de Oliveira in 1947. Entered diplomatic service, 1945: posts in Spain, England, and Switzerland; dismissed, 1952, but reinstated; since 1960, administrative officer in Ministry of

Agriculture. Recipient: Anchieta Prize, 1954; Brazilian Academy of Letters Prize, 1955. Member, Brazilian Academy of Letters, 1969. Address: Ministry of Agriculture, Esplanada dos Minesterios, Block D, 8th Floor, 70043 Brasilia D.F., Brazil.

PUBLICATIONS

Verse

Pedro do Sono.   Privately printed, 1942.
O Engenheiro.   Rio de Janeiro, Amigos da Poesia, 1945.
Psicologia da composição, com a Fábula de Anfion e Antiode.   Barcelona, O Livro Inconsútil, 1947.
O Ção sem Plumas.   Privately printed, 1950.
Poemas Reunidos.   Rio de Janeiro, Orfeu, 1954.
O Rio.   São Paulo, Comissão do IV Centenário da Cidade de São Paulo, 1954.
Pregão Turístico.   Recife, Magalhães, 1955.
Duas Águas.   Rio de Janeiro, Olympio, 1956.
Aniki Bobó.   Recife, Magalhães, 1958.
Quaderna 1956-1959.   Lisbon, Guimarães, 1960.
Dois Parlamentos 1958-1960.   Privately printed, 1961.
Terceira feira.   Rio de Janeiro, Editôra do Autor, 1961.
Poemas Escolhidos.   Lisbon, Portugalia, 1963.
Antologia Poética.   Rio de Janeiro, Editôra do Autor, 1963; revised edition, Rio de Janeiro, Sabiá, 1967, 1973.
Morte e Vida Severina.   São Paulo, Teatro da Universidade Católica de São Paulo, 1965.
A Educacão pela Pedra.   Rio de Janeiro, Editôra do Áutor, 1966.
Morte e Vida Severina, e outros poemas em voz alta.   Privately printed, 1966; revised edition, Rio de Janeiro, Sabiá, 1967, 1973.
The Rebounding Stone, translated by A.B.M. Cadaxa.   London, Outposts, 1967.
Funeral de um Lavrador.   São Paulo, Musical Arlequim, 1967.
Poesias completas 1940-1965.   Rio de Janeiro, Sabiá, 1968; revised edition, 1975, 1979.
Museu de tudo: Poesia 1966-74.   Rio de Janeiro, Olympio, 1975.
Escola das facas.   Rio de Janeiro, Olympio, 1980.
Poesia crítica: Antologia.   Rio de Janeiro, Olympio, 1982.
[Selections] in *Modern Brazilian Poetry* edited by John Nist, Bloomington, Indiana University Press, 1962, and *An Anthology of Twentieth Century Brazilian Poetry* edited by Elizabeth Bishop, Middletown, Connecticut, Wesleyan University Press, 1972.

Other

Joan Miró.   Barcelona, Edicions de 10c, 1950.
O Arquivo das Índias e o Brasil.   Rio de Janeiro, Min. de Relacões Exteriores, 1966.

*

Critical Studies: *Melo Neto* edited by Benedito Nunes, Petrópolis, Vozes, 1971; *A pedra e o rio: Uma interpretação de poesia de Melo Neto* by Lauro Escorel, São Paulo, Duas Cidades, 1973; *A Imitação da forma* by João Alexandre Barbosa, São Paulo, Duas Cidades, 1975; *A poética do silêncio: Melo Neto* by Modesto Carone, São Paulo, Perspectiva, 1979; *João Cabral: Tempo e memória* by Marta de Senna, Rio de Janeiro, Antares, 1980.

*   *   *

As the acknowledged leader of the Generation of 1945, João Cabral de Melo Neto began by reacting against the verbosity, vehemence, and ethnocentrism of the 1922 Modernists; he was, however, strongly influenced by two older Brazilian poets, Manuel Bandeira and Carlos Drummond de Andrade, as well as by Marianne Moore and Valéry. His first collection of verse, *Pedra do Sono*, contained highly personal and frequently surrealistic poems based primarily upon free association.

During the next five years, Melo Neto moved rather rapidly towards a quite different poetic stance, striving to create a new theory of the poetic process and to describe and exemplify that theory in his works. As the title of his 1945 book, *Engenheiro*, suggests, he defined poetry as an intensely conscious and self-conscious enterprise, in which all personal associations and all traditional poetic connotations are painstakingly chiseled off the surfaces of every word, revealing the Platonic essence—the elemental force whose expression is the word's paramount function; these basic building-blocks of discourse are then carefully arranged in patterns designed, as Melo Neto put it, to recreate "the indifferent perfection of geometry, like magazine reproductions of Mondrian, seen from a distance."

Melo Neto was very much aware, however, that this kind of intellectualized poetic minimalism could lead to an amoral, socially exclusive hermeticism; his physical isolation from the reality of Brazilian life during his years of diplomatic service abroad may well have intensified his disquiet about an ivory-tower aesthetics far removed from the dust-dry landscapes and the over-crowded shanty-towns and cemeteries of his ancestral and spiritual homeland, the Brazilian Northeast. One result of this preoccupation is Melo Neto's best-known work, *Morte e Vida Severina*, a verse drama drawn from Northeastern folk traditions. He has attempted to synthesize minimalist aesthetics and social consciousness in other ways, however, and his efforts have provided important models for a number of younger Brazilian poets.

The basis for synthesis, as Melo Neto sees it, is the image and the reality of the stone. His own "Education by Stone," his effort to strip away superficiality of thought and discourse in order to reach the elemental, simply parallels a process which occurs naturally and inevitably among the poorest inhabitants of the Northeast's barren and stony landscapes: "you don't learn the stone, there; there, the stone/born stone, penetrates the soul." As a result of this convergence through the stone, the painfully purified language of the poet and the painfully experienced life of the Northeastern peasant meet on common ground, and both identification and communication are possible:

> That's why the man from up-country says little:
> the stone words ulcerate the mouth
> and it hurts to speak in the stone language;
> those to whom it's native speak by main force.
> Furthermore, that's why he speaks slowly:
> he has to take up the words carefully,
> he has to sweeten them with his tongue, candy them;
> well, all this work takes time.

(Trans. W.S. Merwin)

—David T. Haberly

MICHAUX, Henri. French. Born in Namur, Belgium, 24 May 1899; became French citizen, 1955. Educated at Putte-Grasheide, 1906-11; Jesuit College, Brussels, 1911-17; studied medicine in Brussels, 1919. Married Marie Louise Ferdière in 1941 (died, 1948). Ship's stoker in French merchant marines, in Europe and North and South America, 1920-21. Free-lance writer, Brussels, 1922-24, and since 1924, in Paris; painter: numerous individual exhibitions since 1937, including retrospectives at Musée d'Art Moderne, Paris, 1978, and Guggenheim Museum, New York, 1978. Editor, *Hermès* review, Paris, 1937-39. Recipient: Einaudi Prize, 1960; National Grand Prize for Letters (France), 1965. Address: c/o Gallimard, 5 rue Sébastien-Bottin, 75007 Paris, France.

PUBLICATIONS

Verse

Qui je fus. Paris, Gallimard, 1927.
Mes propriétés (includes prose). Paris, Fourcade, 1929.
Un Certain Plume. Paris, Carrefour, 1930.
La Nuit remue. Paris, Gallimard, 1935; revised edition, 1967.
Plume, précédé de Lointain intérieur. Paris, Gallimard, 1938; revised edition, 1967.
Au pays de la magie (includes prose poems). Paris, Gallimard, 1941; edited by Peter Broome, London Athlone Press, 1977.
Épreuves, exorcismes 1940-44. Paris, Gallimard, 1945.
Liberté d'Action. Paris, Fontaine, 1945.
Apparitions, illustrated by the author. Paris, Point du Jour, 1946.
Ici Poddema. Lausanne, Mermod, 1946.
Ailleurs (includes prose). Paris, Gallimard, 1948, revised edition, 1967.
La Vie dans les plis. Paris, Gallimard, 1949.
Poésie pour pouvoir. Paris, Drouin, 1949.
Passages 1937-1950. Paris, Gallimard, 1950; revised edition, 1963.
Mouvements, illustrated by the author. Paris, Gallimard, 1952.
Face aux verrous. Paris, Gallimard, 1954; revised edition, 1967.
Paix dans les brisements, illustrated by the author. Paris, Flinker, 1959.
Vers la complétude (Saisie et dessaisies). Paris, GLM, 1967.
(Selections), translated by Teo Savory. Santa Barbara, California, Unicorn Press, 1967.
Moments: Traversées du temps. Paris, Gallimard, 1973.
Choix de poèmes. Paris, Gallimard, 1976.

Plays

Quand tombent les toits. Paris, GLM, 1973.

Screenplay: *Images du monde visionnaire,* with Eric Duvivier, 1963.

Fiction

Voyage en Grande Garabagne. Paris, Gallimard, 1936.

Other

Ecuador: Journal de voyage. Paris, Gallimard, 1929; revised edition, 1968; as *Ecuador: A Travel Journal,* Seattle, University of Washington Press, 1968; London, Owen, 1970.
Un Barbare en Asie. Paris, Gallimard, 1933; revised edition, 1967; as *A Barbarian in*

Asia, New York, New Directions, 1949.

Entre centre et absence, illustrated by the author. Paris, Matarasso, 1936.

Sifflets dans le temple. Paris, GLM, 1936.

Peintures. Paris, GLM, 1939.

Arbres des tropiques, illustrated by the author. Paris, Gallimard, 1941.

Exorcismes, illustrated by the author. Paris, Godet, 1943.

Tu vas être père (published anonymously). Privately printed, 1943.

Labyrinthes, illustrated by the author. Paris, Godet, 1944.

Le Lobe des monstres, illustrated by the author. Paris, L'Arbalète, 1944.

L'Espace du dedans. Paris, Gallimard, 1944; revised edition, 1966; as *Selected Writings: The Space Within*, New York, New Directions, 1951.

Peintures et dessins. Paris, Point du Jour, 1946.

Arriver à se réveiller. Paris, L'Air du Temps, 1947.

Nous deux encore. Paris, Lambert, 1948.

Meidosems, illustrated by the author. Paris, Point du Jour, 1948.

Lecture. Paris, Euros, 1950.

Tranches de savoir. Paris, Les Pas Perdus, 1950.

Veille. Paris, Universelle, 1951.

Nouvelles de l'étranger. Paris, Mercure, 1952.

Quatre cents hommes en croix, illustrated by the author. Paris, Bettencourt, 1956.

Misérable miracle, illustrated by the author. Monaco, Rocher, 1956; revised edition, Paris, Gallimard, 1972; as *Miserable Miracle: Mescaline*, San Francisco, City Lights, 1963.

L'Infini turbulent, illustrated by the author. Paris, Mercure, 1957; revised edition, 1964; as *Infinite Turbulence*, London, Calder and Boyars, 1975; New York, Riverrun, 1980.

Vigies sur cible. Paris, Dragon, 1959.

Connaissance par les gouffres. Paris, Gallimard, 1961; as *Light Through Darkness: Explorations Through Drugs*, New York, Orion Press, 1963; London, Bodley Head, 1964.

Vents et poussières 1955-1962, illustrated by the author. Paris, Flinker, 1962.

Les Grandes Épreuves de l'esprit et les innombrables petites (autobiography). Paris, Gallimard, 1966; as *The Major Ordeals of the Mind and the Countless Minor Ones*, New York, Harcourt Brace, and London, Secker and Warburg, 1974.

Parcours, edited by René Bertelé. Paris, Point Cardinal, 1967.

Façons d'endormi, façons d'éveillé. Paris, Gallimard, 1969.

Poteaux d'angle. Paris, Herne, 1971; revised edition, Paris, Gallimard, 1981.

Emergences-Résurgences, illustrated by the author. Geneva, Skira, 1972.

En rêvant à partir de peintures énigmatiques. Montpellier, Fata Morgana, 1972.

Bras cassé. Montpellier, Fata Morgana, 1973.

Par la voie des rythmes. Montpellier, Fata Morgana, 1974.

Moriturus. Montpellier, Fata Morgana, 1974.

Idéogrammes en Chine. Montpellier, Fata Morgana, 1975.

Coups d'arrêt. Paris, Collet de Buffle, 1975.

Face à ce qui se dérobe. Paris, Gallimard, 1975.

Les Ravagés. Montpellier, Fata Morgana, 1976.

Jours de silence. Montpellier, Fata Morgana, 1978.

Saisir. Montpellier, Fata Morgana, 1979.

Une Voie pour l'insubordination. Montpellier, Fata Morgana, 1980.

Comme un ensablement. Montpellier, Fata Morgana, 1981.

Affrontements. Montpellier, Fata Morgana, 1981.

Chemins cherchés, Chemins perdus, Transgressions. Paris, Gallimard, 1981.

Les Commencements. Montpellier, Fata Morgana, 1983.

Par surprise. Montpellier, Fata Morgana, 1983.

Michaux's work defies traditional categorization, and some of the above works include verse or "poetic texts."

*

Critical Studies: *Michaux* by René Bertelé, Paris, Seghers, 1946, revised edition, 1980; *Michaux* by Robert Bréchon, Paris, Gallimard, 1959; *Michaux; ou, Une Mesure de l'être* by Raymond Bellour, Paris, Gallimard, 1965; *Michaux* by Kurt Leonhard, London, Thames and Hudson, 1967; *Michaux: A Study of His Literary Works* by Malcolm Bowie, Oxford, Clarendon Press, 1973; *Michaux* by Peter Broome, London, Athlone Press, 1977; *Michaux* by Virginia La Charité, Boston, Twayne, 1977; *Creatures Within* by Frederic Shepler, Bloomington, Indiana, Physsardt, 1977.

*　　*　　*

Henri Michaux, rebel against literary stereotypes and clichés of vision, ruthless explorer of his own restless and deceptive inner movements, dark and disturbing artist of a poetics of the metamorphic and the imperfect, ingenious technician in the seams of the unconscious, penetrating humorist deft at exposing the absurdities of human behaviour, and stylist of an uncanny balance poised between the lucid and the hallucinatory, the harmless and the horrific, the controlled and the uncontrollable, has stamped himself as one of the great original spirits of 20th-century French writing.

The title of Michaux's first collection, *Qui je fus*, touches the theme of the divisions and dispersion of the self: a moving ground of enigmas, oddities, and threatening contradictions. It was followed in 1929 by *Mes propriétés*, where a groping protagonist, precursor of Beckett's alienated derelicts, seeks to appropriate the intractable and senseless matter of reality; where the author, by a quirkish humour and a private psychological magic, grapples with the unpredictabilities of a hostile or unaccommodating world. This humour of the absurd takes full flight in *Un Certain Plume* in the creation of the character Plume, a featherweight *étranger* in the family of Kafka's K. or Camus's Meursault, embodying what Camus calls the "divorce between the actor and his decor, man and his life" but rebounding, Chaplin-like, through the caprices and incomprehensibilities of a foreign order.

One of the century's most wilful *déracinés*, Michaux has been tempted by the disruptive trajectories of travel. His travel journal *Ecuador*, spasmodically charting a year's arduous descent from the Andes to the Amazon estuary, is an abrasive antidote to romanticism and exoticism: curt, unillusioned, denuded. The travelogue which followed, *Un Barbare en Asie*, is by contrast receptive, effervescent, and stylistically provocative as it flits dexterously and with probing analysis through the mentality and curiosities of habit of the Indians, Malays, Chinese, Indonesians, and Japanese. Their conclusion, however, is the same: that the answer lies not in the outside world or external movement, but in the infinite mobility and unexplored expanses of the *lointain intérieur*, that *espace du dedans* which gives its title to the major collective anthology of Michaux's work.

Just as the displaced person Plume was already a buffer-character wedged comically between hostile powers, so the imaginary lands, Grande Garabagne, the Pays de la Magie and Poddema, depicted in Michaux's great trilogy *Ailleurs* are described by the author as "buffer-states," situated disconcertingly between external observation and inner obsession, the enchanting and the grotesque, entertaining fancy and the most biting satirical and moral diagnosis. Here, in weird utopias reminiscent of *Gulliver's Travels*, *Erewhon*, or Huxley's *Brave New World*, the author and the world, the ideal and the real, play out a balance of power in a no-man's land which is fascinating and at times unnerving.

Michaux's "resistance" poetry of the Second World War is collected in *Épreuves, exorcismes*, famous for its idiosyncratic definition of poetry as exorcism and notable for its resourceful counter-measures against intuitions and nightmares of monstrosity.

La Vie dans les plis and *Face aux verrous* invite us into the full display of the ingenuities of the poet's inner workshop: philosophical maxims that freeze, long poems whipping up ungovernable energies, tongue-in-cheek prose analyses that hold reality in check, turn it topsy-turvy or twist its neck, strange metaphorical configurations depicting the deepest dualities of human nature, flexible lyrical forays into zones of spiritual movement that defy identification. These texts lead in turn to Michaux's vast explorations, in the wake of De Quincey, Baudelaire, and Aldous Huxley, of the furthermost reaches of the human mind as revealed through drugs: its rhythms and tempos, its visions and blanks, its incurable ambivalences, its dazzling captures and clumsy impotences, its euphoric joys and unbearable tortures, as evoked in *Misérable miracle*, *L'Infini turbulent*, *Connaissance par les gouffres*, or *Les Grandes Épreuves de l'esprit*. One should mention, finally, the remarkable poetry of a collection such as *Moments*: transcendental intuitions of a cleansing purity, precariously held in space and almost beyond expression, which act as a reminder that Michaux, endlessly inventive, has never ceased to shape new definitions of poetic language.

—Peter Broome

MILOSZ, Czeslaw. American. Born in Szetejnie, Lithuania, 30 June 1911; came to the United States in 1960; naturalized citizen, 1970. Educated at the High School, Wilno (now Vilnius); University of Stephan Batory, Wilno, M. Juris. 1934; studied in Paris, 1934-35. Took part in the Polish resistance during World War II. Programmer, Polish National Radio, 1935-39; Member of the Polish Diplomatic Service, Washington, D.C., and Paris, 1945-50; free-lance writer, Paris, 1951-60; Visiting Lecturer, 1960-61, Professor of Slavic Languages and Literatures, 1961-78, and since 1978 Professor Emeritus, University of California, Berkeley. Co-Founder of the literary periodical *Zagary*, 1931. Recipient: European Literary prize, 1953; Kister Award, 1967; Jurzykowski Foundation Award, 1968; Creative Arts Fellowship, 1968, and University Citation, 1978, University of California; Polish P.E.N. Club award, for translation, 1974; Guggenheim Fellowship, 1976; Neustadt International Prize, 1978; Nobel Prize for Literature, 1980. Litt.D.: University of Michigan, Ann Arbor, 1977; honorary doctorate: Catholic University, Lublin, 1981; Brandeis University, Waltham, Massachusetts, 1983. Address: 978 Grizzly Peak Boulevard, Berkeley, California 94708, U.S.A.

PUBLICATIONS

Verse

Poemat o czasie zastyglym [A Poem on Time Frozen]. Vilnius, 1933.
Trzy zimy [Three Winters]. Vilnius, Union of Polish Writers, 1936.
Wiersze [Poems] (as J. Syruć). Warsaw, 1940.
Ocalenie [Rescue]. Warsaw, Czytelnik, 1945.
Światlo dzienne [Daylight]. Paris, Instytut Literacki, 1953.
Traktat poetycki [Treatise on Poetry]. Paris, Instytut Literacki, 1957.
Kontynenty [Continents]. Paris, Instytut Literacki, 1958.
Król Popiel i inne wiersze [King Popiel and Other Poems]. Paris, Instytut Literacki,

1962.

Gucio zaczarowany [Bobo's Metamorphosis]. Paris, Instytut Literacki, 1965.

Wiersze [Poems]. London, Oficyna Poetow i Malarzy, 1967.

Miasto bez imienia [City Without a Name]. Paris, Instytut Literacki, 1969.

Selected Poems. New York, Seabury Press, 1973; revised edition, New York, Ecco Press, 1981.

Gdzie wschodzi slonce i kedy zapada [From Where the Sun Rises to Where It Sets]. Paris, Instytut Literacki, 1974.

Utwory poetyckie [Selected Poems]. Ann Arbor, University of Michigan Slavic Publications, 1976.

Bells in Winter, translated by the author and Lillian Vallee. New York, Ecco Press, 1978; Manchester, Carcanet Press, 1980.

Hymn o perle [Hymn to the Pearl]. Ann Arbor, University of Michigan Slavic Publications, 1982.

The Separate Notebook. New York, Ecco Press, 1984.

Fiction

Zdobycie wladzy. Paris, Instytut Literacki, 1955; as *The Seizure of Power*, New York, Criterion, 1955; as *The Usurpers*, London, Faber, 1955.

Dolina Issy. Paris, Instytut Literacki, 1955; as *The Issa Valley*, London, Sidgwick and Jackson, and New York, Farrar Straus, 1981.

Other

Zniewolony umysl (essays). Paris, Instytut Literacki, 1953; as *The Captive Mind*, New York, Knopf, and London, Secker and Warburg, 1953.

Rodzinna Europa. Paris, Instytut Literacki, 1959; as *Native Realm: A Search for Self-Definition*, New York, Doubleday, 1968; London, Sidgwick and Jackson, 1981.

Czlowiek wsród skorpionów: Studium o Stanislawie Brzozowskim [A Man Among Scorpions: A Study of Stanislaw Brzozowski]. Paris, Instytut Literacki, 1962.

The History of Polish Literature. New York, Macmillan, and London, Collier Macmillan, 1969.

Widzenia nad Zatoka San Francisco. Paris, Instytut Literacki, 1969; as *Visions from San Francisco Bay*, Manchester, Carcanet Press, and New York, Farrar Straus, 1982.

Prywatne obowiazki [Private Obligations]. Paris, Instytut Literacki, 1972.

Mój wiek: Pamietnik nówiony [My Century: An Oral Diary] (interview with Alexander Wat), edited by Lidia Ciolkoszowa. London, Polonia Book Fund, 2 vols., 1977.

Emperor of the Earth: Modes of Eccentric Vision. Berkeley, University of California Press, 1977.

Ziemia Ulro. Paris, Instytut Literacki, 1977; as *The Land of Ulro*, New York, Farrar Straus, 1983.

Ogród nauk [The Garden of Knowledge]. Paris, Instytut Literacki, 1980.

Dziela zbiorowe [Collected Works]. Paris, Instytut Literacki, 1980— .

Nobel Lecture. New York, Farrar Straus, 1981.

The Witness of Poetry (lectures). Cambridge, Massachusetts, Harvard University Press, 1983.

Editor, with Zbigniew Folejewski, *Antologia poezji spolecznej* [Anthology of Social Poetry]. Vilnius, 1933.

Editor, *Pieśń niepodlegla* [Invincible Song]. Warsaw, 1942.

Editor and Translator, *Drogami kleski* [On the Roads of Defeat], by Jacques Maritain. Warsaw, 1942.

Editor and Translator, *Polityka i rzeczywistość* [Politics and Reality], by Jeanne Hersch. Paris, Instytut Literacki, 1955.

Editor and Translator, *Praca i jej gorycze* [Work and Its Discontents], by Daniel Bell. Paris, Instytut Literacki, 1957.

Editor and Translator, *Wybór pism* [Selected Works], by Simone Weil. Paris, Instytut Literacki, 1958.

Editor, *Kultura masowa* [Mass Culture]. Paris, Instytut Literacki, 1959.

Editor, *Wegry* [Hungary]. Paris, Instytut Literacki, 1960.

Editor and Translator, *Postwar Polish Poetry: An Anthology.* New York, Doubleday, 1965; revised edition, Berkeley, University of California Press, 1983.

Editor, *Lettres inédites de O.V. de L. Milosz à Christian Gauss.* Paris, Silvaire, 1976.

Translator, with Peter Dale Scott, *Selected Poems*, by Zbigniew Herbert. London, Penguin, 1968.

Translator, *Mediterranean Poems*, by Alexander Wat. Ann Arbor, Michigan, Ardis, 1977.

Translator, *Ewangelia wedlug sw. Marka* [The Gospel According to St. Mark]. Cracow, Znak, 1978.

Translator, *Ksiega Hioba* [The Book of Job]. Paris, Dialogue, 1980.

*

Critical Studies: "Milosz Issue" of *World Literature Today 52*, Summer 1978, and of *Ironwood 18*, 1981; *Rozmowy z Czeslawem Miloszem* by Alexander Fiut, Cracow, Wydawnictwo Literackie, 1981; *Prdrozny swiata: Rozmowy z Czeslawem Miloszem, Komentane* by Ewe Czarnecha, New York, Bicentennial, 1983.

*   *   *

Czeslaw Milosz is an outstanding figure of 20th-century Polish literature. In his youth he belonged to the so-called "Second Vanguard," the poetry of which was characterized by neo-symbolistic tendencies of a "catastrophist" kind. Milosz's poetry before the Second World War suggests the nearness of some kind of a cataclysm; there is a "thorn of prophecy" in these otherwise carefully structured, distant, and allusive poems. During the war the poet's perception of reality and with it his poetic language underwent a substantial change—in the cycle "Świat" (World) and even more so in the collection *Ocalenie*, he dropped many of his poetic adornments of the 1930's and tried to redefine the world in terms of compassion and hope. At the same time he was profoundly disturbed by the brutality of totalitarianism and the savagery of war, as in "Dedication":

> What is poetry which does not save
> Nations or people?
> A connivance with official lies,
> A song of drunkards whose throats
> will be cut in a moment.

The antinomies of Milosz's poetry are between "immoral" beauty and "moral" truth, between chaos and order, nature and civilization. His poetry is pervaded by a strong historicism and a constant awareness of transcience, and the poet himself seems to oscillate between his "private cares" and contemplations and his historical, even social preoccupations. This is reflected by the "polyphony" of Milosz's poetic voices, stressed by Jan Blonski in his essay in *World Literature Today* (Summer 1978); he sometimes speaks with different voices within the same poem. Nevertheless, his longer poems "Traktat moralny" (A Moral Treatise) and *Traktat poetycki* are didactic in a way which has not been attempted since Norwid. *Traktat poetycki* is a multi-faceted, ironic survey of Polish literature since the end of the 19th century. In California

Milosz's poetry became more introspective and absorbed elements of Surrealism in poems such as "Album snów" (Album of Dreams) and "Po ziemi naszej" (Throughout Our Lands). The most representative piece of his Californian period, the long polyphonic poem *Gdzie wschodzi słonce i kedy zapada* blends memories of the poet's childhood and youth with the imagery of American nature and with eschatological expectations of the Last Judgement.

Milosz's reputation as a writer of fiction rests on a number of novels of which the compelling *The Issa Valley*, a Manichean tale of the poet's childhood in densely wooded Lithuania, is the most accomplished. *Native Realm* is also written in the autobiographical vein but with the purpose of tracing the author's intellectual development from his university years in Wilno (through Paris) to his settling down in Warsaw. None the less, it was *The Captive Mind* that made Milosz best known outside Poland. Written soon after his break with the Communist Polish authorities in 1951, this book is an incisive and rather pessimistic analysis of the intricate mechanism of the Polish intelligentsia's adaptation to Communist ideology. Milosz has also written several books of essays on Polish and American themes—of these *Visions from San Francisco Bay*, written "to exorcise the evil spirit of contemporary times," should have the greatest appeal to the general reader.

Milosz is the author of a comprehensive and challenging history of Polish literature, *The History of Polish Literature*, and an excellent translator. He has translated into Polish among other things T.S. Eliot's and Simone Weil's writings and published an anthology of Polish poetry in English translation, *Postwar Polish Poetry*.

—George Gömöri

MORANTE, Elsa. Italian. Born in Rome, 18 August 1918. Married Alberto Moravia, *q.v.*, in 1941 (divorced). Recipient: Viareggio Prize, 1948; Strega Prize, 1957; Séguier Prize, 1977. Lives in Rome. Address: c/o Einaudi, Via Umberto Biancamano, CP 245, 10121 Turin, Italy.

PUBLICATIONS

Fiction

Il gioco segreto (short stories). Milan, Garzanti, 1941.
Menzogna e sortilegio. Turin, Einaudi, 1948; abridged translation, as *House of Liars*, New York, Harcourt Brace, 1951.
L'isola di Arturo. Turin, Einaudi, 1957; as *Arturo's Island*, New York, Knopf, and London, Collins, 1959.
Lo scialle andaluso (short stories). Turin, Einaudi, 1963.
La storia. Turin, Einaudi, 1974; as *History: A Novel*, New York, Knopf, 1977; London, Allen Lane, 1978.
Aracoeli. Turin, Einaudi, 1982.

Verse

Alibi. Milan, Longanesi, 1958.
Il mondo salvato dai ragazzini e altri poemi. Turin, Einaudi, 1968.

Other

Le bellissime avventure di Caterì dalla trecciolina (juvenile).   Turin, Einaudi, 1941; revised edition, as *Le straordinarie avventure di Caterina*, 1959.

Translator, *Il libro degli appunti*, by Katherine Mansfield.   Milan, Rizzoli, 1945.
Translator, with Marcella Hannau, *Il meglio di Katherine Mansfield*.   Milan, Longanesi, 1957.

*

Critical Studies: *Struttura e stile nella narrativa di Morante* by A.R. Pupino, Ravenna, Longo, 1968; *Morante* (in Italian) by Gianni Venturi, Florence, La Nuova Italia, 1977; *Scrittura e follia nei romanzi di Morante* by Donatella Ravanello, Venice, Marsilio, 1980.

*   *   *

Elsa Morante has been one of the most influential and most controversial writers in postwar Italian letters. She began her career writing children's stories (published as *Le bellissime avventure di Caterì dalla trecciolina*); but in time her literary activities expanded to other fields, and to date her work includes two volumes of poetry, various essays and translations, two collections of short stories, and four novels. Of all her works, the most notable have been her novels, *House of Liars, Arturo's Island, History*, and the recent *Aracoeli*. The importance of these books derives in part from Morante's extraordinary gifts as a storyteller and in part from the vigorous response that certain of them, and particularly *History*, elicited both from the Italian literary establishment and from the reading public at large.

House of Liars, Morante's first novel, won the Viareggio Prize in 1948. It treats one of Morante's most consistent themes, the conflict between the enticing distractions of fantasy and the bleak reality of the day-to-day world. The novel is a family saga of three generations narrated by the orphaned Elisa, the last of the line. All of her predecessors had been drawn away from their everyday lives by madness and fantasy, and they all met their ruin when they tried to conduct themselves as though their fantasies were actually true. Elisa's solitary retracing of the past should logically help her to evade a similar fate, but even at the seemingly happy end of the story, her relationship with reality is far from certain. The novel's lyrical qualities and poetic language, while impressive, do not conceal Morante's underlying critique of the current crisis of Western bourgeois life and values. Morante's next novel, *Arturo's Island* (subtitled "Memories of a Child"), is in some respects equally poetic. But it is also more trenchant in its depiction of the opposition between illusion and the finally undeniable facts of reality. The book, which won the Strega Prize in 1957, begins with the title character lost amid his idealized memories of his dead mother and the fabulous tales of romance and adventure recounted to him by his father. Arturo's utopian world on the island of Procida is shattered, however, by his treatment at the hands of his father, who betrays him in favor of a petty criminal encountered as a consequence of the father's supposedly "fantastical" excursions around the homosexual circuit. Arturo's disillusionment is compounded, moreover, by his realization of his own potentially incestuous desire for his young stepmother. At the novel's conclusion Arturo's disenchantment is complete, and he leaves the island for the world outside.

The theme of utopian hope in open combat with worldly despair is also at the center of Morante's book of poetry of the late 1960's, *Il mondo salvato dai ragazzini*. In the poems making up this volume, the lyrical qualities of her earlier verse (collected in *Alibi*) are dominated by the social concerns of her utopian/distopian view of the world. This world view is apparent, too, in Morante's most ambitious work, the lengthy historical novel, *History*.

History is narrated in straightforward Italian and laced with the effects of both *romanesco* dialect and the jargon of contemporary journalism. The bulk of the novel is concerned with characters and events in Rome during the period of World War II. It concentrates on the fortunes and (mostly) misfortunes of a half-Jewish epileptic school teacher, Ida Almagià, her two children, and their assortment of eccentric familial acquaintances, animals included. Perhaps because of her affliction or perhaps because of fate, Ida is not only poor but also extremely simple. One result of her limitations is a narrative that focuses on the little people of "history," as opposed to the machinations of the official "History" of international politics, which the narrator treats—disparagingly, to say the least—in the intrusive segments introducing and concluding the entire text and interspersed between the chapters. Of the two children, Nino, the elder one, is among the book's most forceful and energetic characters (if also the most ideologically confused, switching from Fascist to partisan to black marketeer without apparent hesitation), whereas Useppe, the miraculously innocent fruit of a lonely German soldier's rape, is at once the story's most strikingly original figure and its most poetically engaging. The narrative takes the family from the arrival of the Germans and the imposition of racial laws to displacement and a period of communal life amid Rome's wartime rubble. It continues with the appearance and subsequent adventures of a troubled young drug addict named Davide Segre and finally leads to the family's dissolution and to the miserable deaths of all of the main characters.

Despite its status as an *historical* novel, *History* is cast in the mold of the uneasy union of Marxist and Christian ideals that characterized the *current* social beliefs and interests not only of Morante but also of many other social and political commentators during the postwar period in general, and particularly in the mid-1970's. Due to the novel's obvious concern for contemporary social problems as well as its publication by a major editorial house (Einaudi) capable of undertaking a publicity campaign on a national scale, *History* received more thorough—and more bitterly divided—discussion in the popular press than any Italian novel ever had. The debate incited by the book fragmented both the Italian left and right, and at the same time it resulted in phenomenal sales, making *History* the best-selling new novel in the history of Italian publishing. Other factors also contributed to the response to the novel, including Morante's stature as a writer, her previous association with political groups in Rome, and her marriage to Alberto Moravia (from whom, however, she had been estranged for some time). But in the end, the reason for the vigor of the book's reception was no doubt the power of the narrative itself, both in its technical complexity and its social engagement. Unfortunately, Morante's latest novel, *Aracoeli*, does not continue along the line initiated by *History* either in social or in literary terms. Among all of her literary endeavors, then, *History* remains, at least for the time being, Morante's masterwork.

—Gregory L. Lucente

MORAVIA, Alberto. Pseudonym for Alberto Pincherle. Italian. Born in Rome, 28 November 1907. Educated at home; received high school equivalency diploma 1967. Contracted tuberculosis in 1916 and spent much time in sanatoriums. Married 1) Elsa Morante, *q.v.*, in 1941 (divorced); 2) Dacia Maraini in 1963. Foreign correspondent, *La Stampa*, Milan, and *Gazzetta del Popolo*, Turin, in the 1930's; film critic, *La Nuova Europa*, 1944-46. Since 1953, Editor, with Alberto Carocci, *Nuovi Argomenti*, Milan; since 1955, film critic, *L'Espresso*, Milan. State Department Lecturer in the United States, 1955; President, International P.E.N., 1959. Recipient: Corriere Lombardo prize, 1945; Strega Prize, 1952; Marzotto Prize, 1954; Viareggio Prize, 1961. Honorary Member, American Academy; Chevalier, 1952, and Commander, 1984, Legion of Honor (France). Address: Lungotevere della Vittoria 1, Rome, Italy.

PUBLICATIONS

Fiction

Gli indifferenti.   Milan, Alpes, 1929; as *The Indifferent Ones*, New York, Dutton, 1932; as *The Time of Indifference*, New York, Farrar Straus, and London, Secker and Warburg, 1953.

Le ambizioni sbagliate.   Milan, Mondadori, 1935; as *The Wheel of Fortune*, New York, Viking Press, 1937; London, Cassell, 1938; as *Mistaken Ambitions*, New York, Farrar Straus, 1955.

La bella vita.   Lanciano, Carabba, 1935.

L'imbroglio.   Milan, Bompiani, 1937.

I sogni del pigro.   Milan, Bompiani, 1940.

La mascherata.   Milan, Bompiani, 1941; as *The Fancy Dress Party*, London, Secker and Warburg, 1947.

L'amante infelice.   Milan, Bompiani, 1943.

L'epidemia: Racconti surrealistici e satirici.   Rome, Documento, 1944.

Agostino.   Milan, Bompiani, 1944; translated as *Agostino*, London, Secker and Warburg, 1947.

Due cortigiane; Serata di Don Giovanni.   Rome, L'Acquario, 1945.

La romana.   Milan, Bompiani, 1947; as *The Woman of Rome*, New York, Farrar Straus, and London, Secker and Warburg, 1949.

La disubbidienza.   Milan, Bompiani, 1948; as *Disobedience*, London, Secker and Warburg, 1950.

L'amore coniugale e altri racconti.   Milan, Bompiani, 1949; selection as *Conjugal Love*, London, Secker and Warburg, 1951; in *Five Novels*, 1955.

Two Adolescents: The Stories of Agostino and Luca (includes *Agostino* and *Disobedience*).   New York, Farrar Straus, 1950; London, Secker and Warburg, 1952.

Il conformista.   Milan, Bompiani, 1951; as *The Conformist*, New York, Farrar Straus, 1951; London, Secker and Warburg, 1952.

I racconti.   Milan, Bompiani, 1952; selections as *Bitter Honeymoon and Other Stories*, London, Secker and Warburg, 1954; New York, Farrar Straus, 1956; and *The Wayward Wife and Other Stories*, Secker and Warburg, 1960.

Racconti romani.   Milan, Bompiani, 1954; translated in part as *Roman Tales*, London, Secker and Warburg, 1956; New York, Farrar Straus, 1957.

Il disprezzo.   Milan, Bompiani, 1954; as *A Ghost at Noon*, New York, Farrar Straus, and London, Secker and Warburg, 1955.

Five Novels.   New York, Farrar Straus, 1955.

La ciociara.   Milan, Bompiani, 1957; as *Two Women*, New York, Farrar Straus, and London, Secker and Warburg, 1958.

Nuovi racconti romani.   Milan, Bompiani, 1959; selection as *More Roman Tales*, London, Secker and Warburg, 1963.

La noia.   Milan, Bompiani, 1960; as *The Empty Canvas*, New York, Farrar Straus, and London, Secker and Warburg, 1961.

L'automa.   Milan, Bompiani, 1963; as *The Fetish and Other Stories*, London, Secker and Warburg, 1964; New York, Farrar Straus, 1965.

Cortigiana stanca.   Milan, Bompiani, 1965.

L'attenzione.   Milan, Bompiani, 1965; as *The Lie*, New York, Farrar Straus, and London, Secker and Warburg, 1966.

Una cosa è una cosa.   Milan, Bompiani, 1967; selection as *Command and I Will Obey You*, New York, Farrar Straus, 1969.

Il paradiso.   Milan, Bompiani, 1970; as *Paradise and Other Stories*, London, Secker and Warburg, 1971; as *Bought and Sold*, New York, Farrar Straus, 1973.

Io e lui. Milan, Bompiani, 1971; as *Two: A Phallic Novel,* New York, Farrar Straus, 1972; as *The Two of Us,* London, Secker and Warburg, 1972.

Un'altra vita. Milan, Bompiani, 1973; as *Lady Godiva and Other Stories,* London, Secker and Warburg, 1975.

Boh. Milan, Bompiani, 1976; as *The Voice of the Sea and Other Stories,* London, Secker and Warburg, 1978.

La vita interiore. Milan, Bompiani, 1978; as *Time of Desecration,* New York, Farrar Straus, and London, Secker and Warburg, 1980.

1934. Milan, Bompiani, 1982; translated as *1934,* New York, Farrar Straus, and London, Secker and Warburg, 1983.

La cosa e altri racconti. Milan, Bompiani, 1983.

Storie della preistoria Favole. Milan, Bompiani, 1983.

Plays

Gli indifferenti, with Luigi Squarzini, from the novel by Moravia (produced Rome, 1948). In *Sipario,* 1948.

Il provino (produced Milan, 1955).

Non approfondire (produced 1957).

Teatro (includes *Beatrice Cenci* and *La mascherata,* from his own novel). Milan, Bompiani, 1958; *Beatrice Cenci* (in English), London, Secker and Warburg, 1965; New York, Farrar Straus, 1966.

Il mondo è quello che è (produced Venice, 1966). Milan, Bompiani, 1966.

Il dio Kurt (produced Rome, 1969). Milan, Bompiani, 1968.

La vita è gioco (produced Rome, 1970). Milan, Bompiani, 1969.

Screenplays: *Un colpo di pistola,* 1941; *Zazà,* 1942; *Ultimo incontro,* 1951; *Sensualità,* 1951; *Tempi nostri,* 1952; *La provinciale (The Wayward Wife),* 1952; *Villa Borghese,* 1953; *La donna del Fiume,* 1954; *La romana (The Woman of Rome),* 1955; *Racconti romani (Roman Tales),* 1956; *Racconti d'estate (Love on the Riviera),* 1958; *I delfini (The Dauphins),* 1960; *La giornata balorda (From a Roman Balcony),* 1960; *Una domenica d'estate,* 1961; *Agostino,* 1962; *Ieri oggi domani (Yesterday, Today, and Tomorrow),* 1963; *Le ore nude,* 1964; *L'occhio selvaggio (The Wild Eye),* 1967.

Other

La speranza: Ossia cristianesimo e comunismo. Rome, Documento, 1944.

Opere complete. Milan, Bompiani, 17 vols., 1952-67.

Un mese in U.R.S.S. Milan, Bompiani, 1958.

I moralisti moderni, with Elemire Zolla. Milan, Garzanti, 1960.

Women of Rome, photographs by Sam Waagenaar. Utrecht, Bruno, 1960.

Un' idea dell' India. Milan, Bompiani, 1962.

Claudia Cardinale. Milan, Lerici, 1963.

L'uomo come fine e altri saggi. Milan, Bompiani, 1964; as *Man as an End: A Defence of Humanism,* London, Secker and Warburg, 1965; New York, Farrar Straus, 1966.

La rivoluzione culturale in Cina ovvero il convitato di pietra. Milan, Bompiani, 1967; as *The Red Book and the Great Wall: An Impression of Mao's China,* New York, Farrar Straus, and London, Secker and Warburg, 1968.

A quale tribù appartieni? Milan, Bompiani, 1972; as *Which Tribe Do You Belong To?,* New York, Farrar Straus, and London, Secker and Warburg, 1974.

Al cinema: Centoquarantotto film d'autore. Milan, Bompiani, 1975.

La mutazione femminile: Conversazione con Moravia sulla donna, by Carla Ravaiola. Milan, Bompiani, 1975.
Intervista sullo scrittore scomodo, edited by Nello Ajello. Rome, Laterza, 1978.
Quando Ba Lena era tanto piccola. Teramo, Lisciani e Zampetti, 1978.
Cosma e i briganti. Palermo, Sellerio, 1980.
Impegno controvoglia: Saggi, articoli, interviste, edited by Renzo Paris. Milan, Bompiani, 1980.
Lettere del Sahara. Milan, Bompiani, 1981.

Editor, with Elemire Zolla, *Saggi italiani*. Milan, Bompiani, 1960.

*

Bibliography: *An Annotated Bibliography of Moravia Criticism in Italy and in the English-Speaking World (1929-1975)* by Ferdinando Alfonsi, New York, Garland, 1976.

Critical Studies: *Moravia* by Giuliano Dego, Edinburgh, Oliver and Boyd, 1966, New York, Barnes and Noble, 1967; *Three Italian Novelists* by Donald W. Heiney, Ann Arbor, University of Michigan Press, 1968; *The Existentialism of Moravia* by Joan Ross and D. Freed, Carbondale, Southern Illinois University Press, 1972; *Moravia* by Jane E. Cottrell, New York, Ungar, 1974.

*   *   *

Alberto Moravia's first novel, *The Time of Indifference*, raised him to prominence, and it has remained his most significant work. Although many critics have regarded it primarily as a condemnation of Italian society under Fascism, the import of the work is much broader: it was one of the first European novels to depict the existential crisis of the generation between the wars, that new *mal de siècle* which was to find its chief literary apologists in Sartre, Beauvoir, and Camus. *The Time of Indifference* is also fundamental to Moravia's development as a writer, for it contains most of the themes treated in his later works: the superficiality of the bourgeoisie, the importance of money and sexuality in the conduct of human affairs, and the rapport (or lack of it) between man and reality.

Like *The Time of Indifference*, most of Moravia's early fiction is set in middle-class Roman society. Toward the end of World War II, however, his attention shifted to the lower classes, a milieu with which he had become familiar while hiding from the Nazis in 1943-44. This new interest in the people can in part be attributed to the populist tendencies that were so widespread among anti-fascists of the period, but it also seemed to Moravia that there was an authentic relation between the people and reality. Consequently, the Roman tales and his most significant novels of the next fifteen years all deal with the working class and the *petite bourgeoisie*. Of particular interest is *The Woman of Rome* because, in addition to its being his first novel set among the people, it also initiates a new narrative perspective, that of a woman who recounts her story in the first person. Moravia will eventually abandon completely traditional third-person narration on the grounds that, since objective reality is unknowable, only a subjective point of view can approximate reality. Moreover, many of the protagonists of his later works are female, as is the narrator of *Two Women*, usually considered his best novel.

Toward the end of the 1950's Moravia returned to his bourgeois characters. Without denying that the people may have a more authentic rapport with reality, the author recognized that the problem of the intellectual was still unresolved. His philosophical interests and especially his reading of the works of Ludwig Wittgenstein inclined him toward a new genre constructed on ideological bases, which he called the "essay-novel." *The Empty Canvas* and *The Lie* explored, respectively, the painter's and the writer's relation to reality, while his short stories treated a variety of questions, among them the linguistic, semiotic, and phenomenological aspects of reality. The author's conclusions seem slight, but they were perhaps inevitable. Like Pirandello before him, Moravia determined that a material rapport with reality through painting or writing is not possible; the best that can be achieved is a contemplative stance. Moravia's fiction in the 1970's veered sharply away from the "philosophical" works of the preceding decade. The comic *Two: A Phallic Novel* mocks the intellectual pretensions of a writer who hopes to create a literary masterpiece by sublimating his sexual urges. More representative of this period, however, is *Time of Desecration*, whose female protagonist rebels against her family and her society by becoming active in a revolutionary movement. The short stories of this decade are told from the point of view of a woman narrator, and they deal with feminist issues in the modern world. Despite Moravia's conspicuous narrative skill and the topical interest of the themes, his fiction during the 1970's lacks the substantial force of his earlier work.

Moravia's most recent novel, *1934*, is more typical of his best work. The story of a young man of letters enamored of a girl with a dual personality, *1934* poses the question of whether it is possible to live without hope and not desire death. Beyond the questions of individual human values lie the political issues of our century—it is significant that the novel takes place during Mussolini's regime. Indeed, although most of Moravia's novels are set in a time period contemporaneous with the writing of the works, he has returned in several of his novels (*The Woman of Rome*, *The Conformist*, *Two Women*, and now *1934*) to Fascist Italy. By the author's own admission, his experience under Fascism was one of the two most important events in his life (the other was his long bout with tuberculosis). In a more general way, one can conclude that Moravia considers fascism and communism (both as political systems and as mental attitudes) to be the determining forces in 20th-century civilization.

Although he is best known as a writer of prose fiction, Moravia's work spans several genres. He has written hundreds of movie reviews, and in recent years several works of children's literature have appeared. Numerous essays on art, literature, and politics reveal his intelligence and broad interests; especially noteworthy is "Man as an End" (1954), which is a forceful plea for humanistic values. Despite Moravia's lifelong interest in the theatre and the dramatic qualities inherent in much of his fiction, none of his half dozen plays has enhanced his reputation. On the other hand, the accounts of his travels in the U.S.S.R., India, China, and Africa are testimony to the author's powers of observation and his deep appreciation of diverse cultures.

The breadth of Moravia's endeavors and his commitment to intellectual, social, and political concerns have made him a potent cultural force in 20th-century Italy and, to a lesser extent, elsewhere. Although his fiction has enjoyed both popular and critical acclaim for more than half a century, two aspects of his work have been frequently criticized; some have objected to the graphic depiction of sexuality in his novels, and many critics have lamented his stylistic and technical conservatism: most of his fiction can be situated in the current of literary realism begun by the great novelists of the 19th century. Like them, Moravia is a consummate teller of stories who, in the course of a long career, has achieved a substantial literary production with only occasional lapses of quality. Considered in its totality, Moravia's work constitutes an unrivaled panorama of Italian life in the 20th century.

—Louis Kibler

MROZEK, Slawomir. Polish. Born in Borzecin, 26 June 1930. Studied architecture in Cracow. Married Maria Obremba in 1959. Cartoonist and journalist; then full-time writer;

lived in Western Europe, 1963-72, and since 1975: now lives in Paris. Recipient: Austrian State Prize for European Literature, 1972. Address: c/o Instytut Literacki, 91 Avenue de Poissy, 78600 Mesnil le Roi, France.

PUBLICATIONS

Plays

Utwory Sceniczne (includes *Policja, Meczenstwo Piotra O'Heya, Indyk, Na pelnym morzu, Karol, Striptease, Zabawa, Kynolog w Rozterce, Czarowna noc, Smierc Prucznika, Tango, Testarium, Drugie danie, Woda, Dom na granicy*). Cracow, Wydawnictwo Literackie, 2 vols., 1963-73.

Policja, in *Utwory Sceniczne 1.* 1963; as *The Policeman* (produced New York, 1961; London, 1964), in *Six Plays,* 1967.

Na pelnym morzu, in *Utwory Sceniczne 1.* 1963; as *Out at Sea* (produced New York, 1962; Edinburgh, 1965), in *Six Plays,* 1967.

Karol, in *Utwory Sceniczne 1.* 1963; as *Charlie* (produced Edinburgh, 1964) in *Six Plays,* 1967.

Zabawa, in *Utwory Sceniczne 1.* 1963; as *The Party* (produced Edinburgh, 1964; London, 1975), in *Six Plays,* 1967.

Czarowna noc, in *Utwory Sceniczne 1.* 1963; as *Enchanted Night* (produced Edinburgh, 1964; London, 1971), in *Six Plays,* 1967.

Striptease, in *Utwory Sceniczne 1.* 1963; translated as *Striptease* (produced Lawrence, Kansas, 1964; London, 1969), in *Three Plays,* 1972.

Meczenstwo Piotra O'Heya, in *Utwory Sceniczne 1.* 1963; as *The Martyrdom of Piotr Ohey,* in *Six Plays,* 1967.

Tango, in *Utwory Sceniczne 2.* 1973; translated as *Tango* (produced London, 1966; New York, 1969), London, Cape, and New York, Grove Press, 1968.

Six Plays (includes *The Policeman, The Martyrdom of Piotr Ohey, Out at Sea, Charlie, The Party, Enchanted Night*). London, Cape, and New York, Grove Press, 1967.

Watzlaw. 1970; translated as *Vatzlav* (produced Stratford, Ontario, 1970; London, 1973), New York, Grove Press, 1970; London, Cape, 1972.

Testarium, in *Utwory Sceniczne 2.* 1973; as *The Prophets* (produced Glasgow, 1970), in *Three Plays,* 1972.

Three Plays (includes *Striptease, Repeat Performance, The Prophets*). New York, Grove Press, 1972.

Drugie danie, in *Utwory Sceniczne 2.* 1973; as *Repeat Performance,* in *Three Plays,* 1972.

Utwory Sceniczne nowe (includes *Rzeznia, Emigranci, Wyspa roz*). Cracow, Wydawnictwo Literackie, 1975.

Emigranci, in *Utwory Sceniczne nowe.* 1975; as *The Emigrés* (produced London, 1976; New York, 1979).

Fiction

Malenkie lato. Cracow, 1956.

Polska w Obrazach. Cracow, 1957.

Slon. Cracow, Wydawnictwo Literackie, 1958; as *The Elephant,* London, Macdonald, 1962; New York, Grove Press, 1963.

Wesele w Atomicach [A Wedding in Atomtown]. Cracow, Wydawnictwo Literackie, 1959.

Postepowiec. Warsaw, Iskry, 1960.

Ucieczka na poludnie [Escape Southward].   Warsaw, Iskry, 1961.
Deszcz.   Cracow, Wydawnictwo Literackie, 1962.
Polpancerze praktyczne.   Cracow, 1963.
Opowiadania [Stories].   Cracow, Wydawnictwo Literackie, 2 vols., 1964-74.
The Ugupu Bird (selection).   London, Macdonald, 1968.
Dwa listy i inne opowiadania [Two Letters and Other Stories].   Paris, Instytut Literacki, 1970.

Other

Przez Okulary (cartoons).   Warsaw, Iskry, 1968.

*

Critical Study: *Zurück zu Form: Strukturanalysen zu Mrozek* by Alek Pohl, Berlin, Henssel, 1972.

*   *   *

Slawomir Mrozek is contemporary Poland's most penetrating and popular writer. He combines steely, precise language with sharp irony and surrealism, and thus elevates the absurd situations that typify a modern totalitarian state to more than just benign or malignant satire. As a product of the limited thawing of intellectual life following the 1956 "Polish October," Mrozek's work is published intermittently, when the censor feels like proving his tolerance. As a result of such state anti-patronage the Polish public has seen staged plays dealing with areas of enormous sensitivity, such as the police, exile, or the state bureaucracy, but in a way that no direct references are made to specific national figures or countries. That the Polish political status quo also actively interferes with people's lives is purely "coincidental." His other main target is his disaffected but apathetic audience whose neuroses and phobias he dissects and blames for the continuing malaise, in conceding so much to "Big Brother."

Mrozek's obvious success rests particularly with his plays, hitting a suppressed nerve again and again: *The Policeman* first found that nerve as it depicted the mind-boggling inanity of the thugs elevated to the guardianship of law and order. While the characters are stereotyped and the plot absurd, Mrozek's technique is clear: he invites comparison between the universal (policja) and the particular (the Polish "milicja obywatelska"). The audience reads these many levels into such works, used as it is to many decades of censorship.

Tango firmly established Mrozek's reputation. It is a witty representation of the problems of the generation gap, and "revolting" children. Artur, son of the family, fights for the re-establishment of traditional values and ambitions in the face of his parents' dated ideals of spontaneous performance art, free love, and revolutionary freedom. *Tango* reveals the forces willing to profit from such "power struggles" when the mother's boorish lover stages a *coup d'état* and imposes his vision of social progress on his hosts—dancing the tango. While the intellectuals argue, the workers seize the freedoms promised.

Despite other plays, his dramatic work was extended again by his experiences during his brief exiles abroad. The product of these travels was *The Emigrés*, where the plot centres around two exiles, living in constant conflict, a rapacious *gastarbeiter* of peasant stock and a cynical, disillusioned intellectual. The tension between them leads to a murder attempt, and the acceptance of the immutability of their sentences to—exile, economic and political.

In all his plays, his collections of short stories (particularly *The Elephant* and *Deszcz*), and even in his irreverent cartoons published in the weekly *Szpilki*, Mrozek paints a bleak picture of humanity and, by implication, of his fellow Poles. These snapshots of personal or national obsessions have imprisoned people in a deadly logic of action (or inaction). While that logic (which is absurd) may be humorous when represented, Mrozek is warning his audiences that a break has to be made in the vicious circle of survival and power. For that reason, Mrozek is one of the few Polish writers today whose work is relevant even to non-Polish audiences.

—Donald Pirie

MULISCH, Harry (Kurt Victor). Dutch. Born in Haarlem, 29 July 1927. Educated at Haarlem Lyceum. Married Sjoerdje Woudenberg in 1971; two daughters. Writer: Founder-Editor, *Randstad* magazine; Member of the Board, De Bezige Bij, publishers, Amsterdam. Recipient: Reina Prinsen Geerligs Prize, 1951; Bijenkorf Prize, 1957; Anne Frank Prize, 1957; Visser Neerlandia Prize, 1960; Athos Prize, 1961; Constantijn Huygens Prize, 1977; Hooft Prize, 1979. Address: Leidsekade 103, 1017 PP Amsterdam, Netherlands.

PUBLICATIONS

Fiction

Tussen hamer en aambeeld [Between Hammer and Anvil]. Amsterdam, Arbeiderspers, 1952.
Archibald Strohalm. Amsterdam, Bezige Bij, 1952.
Chantage op het leven [Blackmailing Life]. Amsterdam, Bezige Bij, 1953.
Di diamant [The Diamond]. Amsterdam, Bezige Bij, 1954.
De sprong der paarden en de zoute zee [The Horses' Leap and the Salt Sea]. Amsterdam, De Beuk, 1955.
Het mirakel [The Miracle]. Amsterdam, Arbeiderspers, 1956.
Het zwarte licht [The Black Light]. Amsterdam, Bezige Bij, 1956.
De versierde mens [The Decorated Man]. Amsterdam, Bezige Bij, 1957.
Het stenen bruidsbed. Amsterdam, Bezige Bij, 1959; as *The Stone Bridal Bed*, New York and London, Abelard Schuman, 1962.
Quauhquauhtinchan in den vreemde: Een sprookje [Quauhquauhtinchan Abroad: A Fairy Tale]. Amsterdam, Bezige Bij, 1962.
Wat gebeurde er met Sergeant Massuro?. Amsterdam, Bezige Bij, 1972; as "What Happened to Sergeant Massuro," in *The Modern Image: Outstanding Stories from the Hudson Review*, edited by Frederick Morgan, New York, Norton, 1965.
De verteller [The Narrator]. Amsterdam, Bezige Bij, 1970.
De grens [The Limit]. Amsterdam, Loeb, 1975.
Twee vrouwen. Amsterdam, Bezige Bij, 1975; as *Two Women*, London, Calder, 1980; New York, Riverrun, 1981.
Verzamelde verhalen 1947-1977 [Collected Stories]. Amsterdam, Anthenaeum-Polak & Van Gennep, 1977.
Oude lucht: Drie verhalen [Stale Air: Three Stories]. Amsterdam, Bezige Bij, 1977.
De aanslag [The Attack]. Amsterdam, Bezige Bij, 1982.
De gezochte spiegel [The Sought Mirror]. Zutphen, Ten Bosch, 1983.
The Decorated Man (7 novellas). London, Calder, 1984.

Plays

Tanchelijn: Kroniek van een ketter [Tanchelijn: Chronicle of a Heretic]. Amsterdam, Bezige Bij, 1960.
De knop: Gevolgd door Stan Laurel & Oliver Hardy [The Button: Followed by Stan Laurel & Oliver Hardy]. Amsterdam, Bezige Bij, 1961.
Reconstructie, with others (produced Amsterdam, 1969). Amsterdam, Bezige Bij, 1969.
Oidipous Oidipous, from the play by Sophocles. Amsterdam, Bezige Bij, 1972.
Bezoekuur [Visiting Time]. Amsterdam, Bezige Bij, 1974.
Volk en vaderliefde: Een koningskomedie [The People and Paternal Love: A Royal Comedy]. Amsterdam, Bezige Bij, 1975.
Axel, from the play by Villiers de l'Isle-Adam. Amsterdam, Bezige Bij, 1977.

Verse

Woorden, woorden, woorden [Words, Words, Words]. Amsterdam, Bezige Bij, 1973.
De vogels: Drie balladen [The Birds: Three Ballads]. Amsterdam, Athenaeum-Polak & Van Gennep, 1974.
Tegenlicht [Light in the Eyes]. Amsterdam, Athenaeum-Polak & Van Gennep, 1975.
Kind en kraai [Kinfolk]. Amsterdam, Eliance Pers, 1975.
De wijn is drinkbaar dank zij her glas [The Wine Is Drinkable Because of the Glass]. Amsterdam, Bezige Bij, 1976.
De taal is een ei [Language Is an Egg]. Amsterdam, Athenaeum, 1976.
Wat poëzie is: Een leerdicht. Amsterdam, Athenaeum, 1978; as *What Poetry Is*, Merrick, New York, Cross Cutltural, 1981.
Opus gran. Amsterdam, De Harmonie, 1982.

Other

Manifesten [Manifestoes]. Zaandijk, Heijnis, 1958.
Voer voor psychologen [Fodder for Psychologists]. Amsterdam, Bezige Bij, 1961.
Wenken voor de bescherming van uw gezin en uzelf, tijdens de jongste dag [Tips for the Protection of Your Family and Yourself, at the Day of Judgement]. Amsterdam, Bezige Bij, 1961.
De zaak 40/61: Een reportage [The Eichmann Case: A Report]. Amsterdam, Bezige Bij, 1962.
Bericht aan de rattenkoning [Report to King Rat]. Amsterdam, Bezige Bij, 1966.
Wenken voor de Jongste Dag [Tips for the Day of Judgement]. Amsterdam, Bezige Bij, 1967.
Het woord bij de daad: Getuigenissen van de revolutie op Cuba [Words after Deeds: Testimony on the Cuban Revolution]. Amsterdam, Bezige Bij, 1968.
Israël is zelf een mens [Israel Is Human Too]. The Hague, Bakker, 1969.
Paralipomena Orphica. Amsterdam, Bezige Bij, 1970.
Over de affaire Padilla [The Padilla Affair]. Amsterdam, Bezige Bij, 1971.
De verteler verteld [The Story of "The Narrator"]. Amsterdam, Bezige Bij, 1971.
De toekomst van gisteren [The Future of Yesterday]. Amsterdam, Bezige Bij, 1972.
Soep lepelen met een vork [Eating Soup with a Fork]. Amsterdam, Bezige Bij, 1972.
Het sexuele bolwerk [The Sexual Bastion]. Amsterdam, Bezige Bij, 1973.
Mijn getijdenboek [My Book of Hours]. Amsterdam, Landshoff, 1975.
Het ironische van de ironie: Over het geval G.K. van het Reve [The Irony of Irony: On the Case of G.K. van het Reve]. Amsterdam, Manteau, 1976.
Vergrote raadsels: Verklaringen, paradoxen, mulischesken [Magnified Riddles: Explanations, Paradoxes, Mulischesques], edited by Gerd de Ley. Nijmegen, Gottmer,

1976.
Paniek der onschuld [Panic of Innocence]. Amsterdam, Bezige Bij, 1979.
De compositie van de wereld[The Composition of the World]. Amsterdam, Bezige Bij, 1980.
De mythische formule: Dertig gesprekken 1951-1981 [The Mythical Formula: Thirty Conversations 1951-1981]. Amsterdam, Bezige Bij, 1981.

*

Bibliography: *Mulisch: Een bibliografie* by Marita Mathijsen, The Hague, BZZTôH, 1979.

Critical Studies: *Mulisch* by Johannes van Ham, Bruges, Desclée de Brouwer, 1969; *Mulisch, naar ik veronderstel* by Jan H. Donner, Amsterdam, Bezige Bij, 1971; *Mulisch* by J.H. Caspers, N.S. Huisman, and J.G.M. Weck, Amsterdam, Versluys, 1971.

*　　*　　*

Though chronologically Harry Mulisch belongs to the "war generation" which also produced Hermans, Reve, and Wolkers, his wide-ranging output of fiction, drama, autobiographical and philosophical essays, superior political journalism, and, more recently, poetry distinguishes itself from the essential naturalism and introverted pessimism of these contemporaries by its playful life-assertiveness and its magico-mythical vision of man, history, and art.

A collection of autobiographical pieces and artistic manifestoes, published in 1961 under the typically provocative title *Voer voor psychologen* (Fodder for Psychologists), illuminates his underlying motivations and concerns as an artist. For Mulisch the act of writing is akin to alchemy, at once a transformatory rather than a descriptive process, and a quest for the Philosophers' Stone of an all-embracing explanatory principle underlying the surface chaos of existence. In his novels, stories, and plays of the 1950's, with their bizarre juxtapositions of banal realism and supernatural flights of fancy, that principle is often his very personal reading of the Oedipus myth (he was later to adapt Sophocles's version for the Dutch stage), in which God-the-Father represents the tyranny of death and time. Many of his protagonists, like the visionary puppeteer and charlatan Archibald Strohalm in his first novel (1952) or the heretical title-figure of the play *Tanchelijn* (1960), are also significantly themselves artists of a kind, who try to usurp the authority of that God and are destroyed, though their very destruction is a form of identification.

In *The Stone Bridal Bed* (1959), arguably the most successful work of Mulisch's "first period," in which an American participant in the Allied bombing of Dresden returns to the city after the war and is caught up in a nightmare of guilt and retribution, the realistic surface is disturbed by mythical and historical undercurrents, most strikingly in the typographically distinct passages of Homeric prose-poetry.

During the 1960's fiction took a back seat, as Mulisch became increasingly involved with contemporary political reality, in turn warning against the dehumanising effect of runaway technology (*De zaak 40/61*), extolling the anarchistic Dutch Provo movement (*Bericht aan de rattenkoning*), attacking the nuclear arms race (*Wenken voor de Jongste Dag*), celebrating the first heady days of the Cuban revolution (*Het woord bij de daad*), and participating in a collaborative opera-project on the life of Che Guevara, performed as *Reconstructie* in 1969. His subsequent disillusion with utopianism of all kinds is recorded in *De toekomst van gisteren*, an account of a significantly unwritten work on the fate of Europe after a Nazi victory.

De verteller, a bewildering collage of narrative fragments, riddles, formulae, etc., so cryptic as to require its own key, marked a return to the author's perennial concern with his own creative processes as a story-teller, for whom, he succinctly and dogmatically put it, "the problem is never *what* to write about, but *how* to write about it." By comparison the best-selling *Two Women*, which was later filmed, has a deceptively conventional, even trite, story-line, featuring a love-triangle and a violent denouement, but subtly evokes a mythical dimension:

here that of the Orpheus legend.

Some of Mulisch's recent poetry, often dream-like and tantalisingly hermetic, is reminiscent of his admired predecessor Gerrit Achterberg.

The ambitious and long-gestated philosophical study *De compositie van de wereld*, which attempts to account for the whole of human existence and history in terms of the musical octave, met with a mixed reception, and was criticised as pretentious and simplistic. However, if read primarily as literature, the work is entirely consistent with the oeuvre of this eternal enthusiast and dilettante, whose next publication may be (or may not be, since he has been repeatedly distracted in the past) an historical-philosophical novel on which he has worked for twenty years, to be called *The Discovery of Moscow*.

Reading Mulisch is a constant imaginative and intellectual adventure—one may often dissent, but one is seldom bored.

—Paul Vincent

MÜLLER, Heiner. German. Born in Eppendorf, Saxony, 9 January 1929. Bookshop worker, then journalist and free-lance writer: editor, *Junge Kunst* magazine; staff member, Berliner-Maxim-Gorki-Theater, 1958-59. Recipient: Heinrich Mann Prize, 1959; Erich Weinert Medal, 1964; BZ Critics Prize, 1970, 1976; GDR Ministry of Culture Lessing Prize, 1975. Address: c/o Rotbuch Verlag, Potsdamer strasse 98, 1000 Berlin 30, Germany.

PUBLICATIONS

Plays

Zehn Tage, die die Welt Erschütterten, with Hagen Müller-Stahl, from a work by John Reed (produced Berlin, 1957).   Leipzig, Hofmeister, 1958.
Der Lohndrücker (produced Leipzig, 1958).   Berlin, Henschel, 1958.
Die Korrektur (produced Berlin, 1958).   Berlin, Henschel, 1959.
Die Umsiedlerin (produced Berlin, 1961).   Berlin, Rotbuch, 1975; revised version, as *Die Baueren* (produced Berlin, 1975), in *Stücke*, 1975.
Herakles 5 (produced Berlin, 1974).   With *Philoktet*, Frankfurt, Suhrkamp, 1966.
Philoktet (produced Munich, 1968).   With *Herakles 5*, Frankfurt, Suhrkamp, 1966, translated as *Philoctetes*, Lincoln, University of Nebraska Press, 1981.
Ödipus Tyrann, from the work by Hölderlin (produced Berlin, 1967).   Berlin, Aufbau, 1968.
Die Aristokraten, with Benno Besson (produced Berlin, 1968).
Wie es such gefällt, from the play *As You Like It* by Shakespeare (produced Munich, 1968).   Included in *Kopien*, 1977.
Drachenoper, from the opera *Lancelot* by Paul Dessau (produced Berlin, 1969).   Included in *Theater-Arbeit*, 1975.
Horizonte, from a work by Gerhart Winterlich (produced Berlin, 1969).   Included in *Theater-Arbeit*, 1975.

MÜLLER

Prometheus (produced Zurich, 1969). Included in *Geschichten aus der Produktion 2*, 1974.
Weiberkomödie, from a radio play by Inge Müller (produced Magdeburg, 1970). Included in *Theater-Arbeit*, 1975.
Arzt wider Willen, with Benno Besson (produced Berlin, 1970).
Die Möwe, with Ginka Tscholakowa, from a work by Chekhov (produced Berlin, 1972).
Macbeth, from the play by Shakespeare (produced Magdeburg, 1972). Included in *Stücke*, 1975.
Die Horatier (produced Berlin, 1972). Included in *Stücke*, 1975; as *The Horatians*, in *Minnesota Review*, 1976.
Zement, from a work by Fyodor Gladkov (produced Berlin, 1973). Included in *Geschichten aus der Produktion 2*, 1974; as *Cement* (produced Wivenhoe Park, Essex, 1981), in *New German Critique 16*, Winter 1979.
Traktor (produced Neustrelitz, 1974-75). Included in *Geschichten aus der Produktion 2*, 1974.
Geschichten aus der Produktion 1-2. Berlin, Rotbuch, 2 vols., 1974.
Der Bau (produced Berlin, 1980). Included in *Geschichten aus der Producktion 1*, 1974.
Die Schlacht (produced Berlin, 1975). Berlin, Henschel, 1977.
Mauser, from the novel *And Quiet Flows the Don* by Sholokhov (produced Austin, Texas, 1975). Included in *Mauser* (collection), 1978.
Theater-Arbeit. Berlin, Rotbuch, 1975.
Stücke. Berlin, Henschel, 1975.
Kopien: 3 Versuche, Shakespeare zu töten. Frankfurt, Suhrkamp, 1977.
Leben Gundlings Friedrich von Preussen Lessings Schlaf Traum Schrei (produced Frankfurt, 1979). With *Die Schlacht*, 1977; as *The Life of Gundling*, New York, Performing Arts Journal, 1984.
Hamlet, with Matthias Langhoff, from the play by Shakespeare (produced Berlin, 1977). Included in *Shakespeare Factory 2*, 1980.
Germania Tod in Berlin (produced Munich, 1978). Berlin, Rotbuch, 1977.
Fatzer (produced Hamburg, 1978).
Mauser (collection). Berlin, Rotbuch, 1978.
Die Hamletmaschine (produced Paris, 1979). Included in *Mauser*, 1978; translation published New York, Performing Arts Journal, 1984.
Shakespeare Factory 2. Frankfurt, Suhrkamp, 1980.
Der Auftrag (produced Berlin, 1980). Published in *Theater Heute*, March 1980; as *The Assignment*, New York, Performing Arts Journal, 1984.
Quartett, from the novel *Les Liaisons dangereuses* by Laclos. Frankfurt, Verlag der Autoren, 1981; as *Quartet* (produced London, 1983).
Verkommenes Ufer Medeamaterial Landschaft mit Argonauten (produced Vienna, 1983). Translation published New York, Performing Arts Journal, 1984.

*

Critical Studies: *Müller* by Genia Schulz, Stuttgart, Metzler, 1980; *Müller* edited by Heinz Ludwig Arnold, Munich, Text & Kritik, 1982; *New German Dramatists* by Denis Calandra, London, Macmillan, 1983.

*   *   *

The plays of Heiner Müller could be organized within two basic periods: the Brechtian period from 1956-1968 and the avant-garde period from 1968 to the present. As "the new Brecht" (a title Müller bears in both East and West zones), Müller concentrated on the historical development of state socialism in the GDR. These early plays are composed of character types and classical verse forms, depicting the move of history through contradiction

259

and error, a style regarded as both formative and unacceptable by the official Cultural Policy in the East and as Marxist model as well as pessimistic individualism in the West.

In 1968, concurrent with the Soviet invasion of Czechoslovakia, Müller's plays adopt a darker tone. History is no longer their subject matter, but merely a theatrical element, mixed with classical themes, horrifying fantasies and personal dreams. *Cement* provides an example of this style: set in the Soviet Revolution, fantasy scenes of Prometheus and Heracles are interspersed with those of historical events. The play ends in scenes of Party expulsions. Subsequent to *Cement*, the plays of the late 1970's are composed of fragmentary scenes and sentences, cast in a postmodern text of metaphor and allusion. These plays indict theatrical conventions as allies of state politics. *Die Hamletmaschine* illustrates this indictment: Hamlet is a prince of both state and theatrical imperialistic organizations with the playwright as the hidden power behind the throne. The language of the stage is portrayed as exclusionary and oppressive. The play calls for a revolution against its own production.

Müller's avant-garde plays require a new production style, combining the stage traditions of the Absurdists with those of Performance Art. The plays suggest visual spectacles which clarify their basic meanings, but which have an obtuse relationship with the words of the text. The process of discovering the production elements is both aesthetic and political in its technique. Because of this unique sense of production, Müller has begun to direct his own plays in the 1980's. In production, he combines the elements of Piscator's and Brecht's political theaters with those of Beckett and Robert Wilson.

In spite of the major change in Müller's work from his early to his late plays, certain themes run through his entire opus. The theme of sexual politics develops throughout his plays, allied with themes of the sexual ownership of women and the sexual roles in which both theater and state have cast them. The theme of imperialism develops through capitalism, state socialism to theatrical convention. The theme of the individual as subject or object of the political process is portrayed through early collectives to postmodern autobiographical dreams.

Presently, Müller enjoys an international reputation as an innovator of dramatic form, a master of German dramatic language, and a crucial political voice on the stage.

—Sue-Ellen Case

OE Kenzaburo. Japanese. Born in Ehime, Shikoku, 31 January 1935. Educated at Tokyo University, degree in French 1959. Married; two children. Free-lance writer. Recipient: Akutagawa Prize, 1958; Shinchosha Prize, 1964; Tanizaki Prize, 1967. Address: 585 Seijo-machi, Steagaya-ku, Tokyo, Japan.

PUBLICATIONS

Fiction

Shisha no Ogori [The Arrogance of the Dead].   Tokyo, Bungei Shunju Shinsha, 1958.
Miru maeni Tobe [Leap Before You Look].   Tokyo, Shinchosha, 1958.
Memushiri kouchi [Pluck the Flowers, Gun the Kids],   Tokyo, Kodansha, 1958.

Warera no jidai [Our Age]. Tokyo, Chuo Koransha, 1959.
Kodoku na seinen no kyuka. 1960.
Okurete kita seinen [Born Too Late]. Tokyo, Shinchosha, 1962.
Sakebigoe [Screams]. Tokyo, Kodansha, 1962.
Seiteki ningen [The Sexual Man]. Tokyo, Shinchosha, 1963.
Kojinteki na taiken. Tokyo, Shinchosha, 1964; as *A Personal Matter*, New York, Grove Press, 1968; London, Weidenfeld and Nicolson, 1969.
Man'en gannen no futtoboru. Tokyo, Kodansha, 1967; as *The Silent Cry*, Tokyo, Kodansha, 1974.
Warera no kyoki o ikinobiru michi o sheieyo. 1969; augmented edition, 1975.
Nichijo seikatsu no boken. 1971.
Mizukara waga namida o nugui-tamau hi. Tokyo, Kodansha, 1972; as *The Day He Himself Shall Wipe My Tears Away*, in *Teach Us to Outgrow Our Madness*, 1977.
Sora no kaibutsu Agui. 1972.
Kozui wa waga tamashii ni oyobi [The Flood Has Reached My Soul]. Tokyo, Shinchosha, 1973.
Seinen no omei. 1974.
Pinchi ranna chosho [A Report on a Pinch-Runner]. Tokyo, Shinchosha, 1976.
Teach Us to Outgrow Our Madness: Four Short Novels (includes *Teach Us to Outgrow Our Madness, The Day He Himself Shall Wipe My Tears Away, Prize Stock, Aghwee the Sky Monster*). New York, Grove Press, 1977; London, Boyars, 1978.
Dojidai gemu [Coeval Games]. 1979.

Other

Sekai no wakamonotachi. 1962.
Hiroshima noto [Hiroshima Notes]. Tokyo, Iwanami Shoten, 1965.
Zensakuhin [Collected Works]. Tokyo, Shinchosha, 6 vols., 1966-67; 2nd series, 1977—.
Jizokusuru kokorozashi. 1968.
Kowaremono to shite no ningen. 1970.
Okinawa noto [Okinawa Notes]. Tokyo, Iwanami Shoten, 1970.
Kujira no shimetsusuru hi. 1972.
Dojidai to shite no sengo. 1973.
Joyko e. 1974.
Bungaku noto. 1974.
Genshuku na tsunawatari. 1974.
Kotoba no votte. 1976.

Editor, *Itami Mansaku essei shu*, by Mansaku Itami. 1971.

*

Critical Study: *The Search for Authenticity in Modern Japanese Literature* by Hisaaki Yamanouchi, Cambridge, Cambridge University Press, 1978.

*   *   *

Oe Kenzaburo acknowledges that when he started writing fiction he was indebted to Abe Kobo's works as his models. Oe's earliest works such as "A Strange Job" and *Shisha no Ogori* depict a sterile and insecure life of alienation somewhat resembling that in Abe's works.

In "The Catch" Oe creates a world of his own: in a remote countryside during World War II the village boys attain an almost prelapsarian pastoral sense of felicity through their sympathy towards a captured black American fighter-pilot but are eventually baffled by the adults who demand the handing over of the captive. These boys are transformed into juvenile delinquents, a kind of fallen angels, in *Memushiri kouchi*. Oe's aspiration to the innocence embodied in pastoral is overshadowed by the harsh realities of life in *Miru maeni Tobe*, *Warera no jidai*, and *Okurete kita seinen*. In works such as *Sakebigoe* and *Seiteki ningen* sexual behaviour functions as a means of making up for salvation.

In 1963 Oe went through two important experiences: first, the birth of his eldest son with an abnormal outgrowth in his skull that needed a surgical operation; second, his visit to Hiroshima. These experiences resulted in his writing *A Personal Matter* and *Hiroshima noto* respectively, the latter leading to *Okinawa noto*.

In *The Silent Cry*, the best of Oe's works so far, the past and the present are synchronized. In 1960 the protagonist, an ineffectual intellectual, and his active younger brother are each suffering from the aftermath of the Security Treaty turmoil. In their quest for identity they go back to the country seat of the Nedokoros (literally meaning "where the root is"). What they discover is the truth about a domestic conflict in 1860 between the family patriarch and his younger brother, the latter leading a peasants' revolt. The brothers' quest for the *genius loci* of the countryside is, however, beyond them as city-dwellers of 1960.

Throughout the 1970's Oe was prolific, producing *The Day He Himself Shall Wipe My Tears Away*, *Kozui wa waga tamashii ni oyobi*, *Pinchi ranna chosho*, and other works. Since the beginning of the 1980's Oe has been exploring new possibilities for prose fiction. In *Dojidai gemu* Oe uses anthropological concepts for a framework. Other recent works experiment with an ingenious first-person narrative. One of them is in a sense a sequel to *A Personal Matter* in narrating how the author copes with the problems posed by his handicapped son and how the latter is indispensable for his own survival. This work also demonstrates the more than scholarly capacity with which he reads foreign literature (in this case William Blake) and the infinite potential to cultivate new ground in the decades to come.

—Hisaaki Yamanouchi

ONETTI, Juan Carlos. Uruguayan. Born in Montevideo, 1 July 1909. Married Dolly Muhr in 1955; one son and one daughter. Editor for Reuters, Montevideo, 1942-43, and Buenos Aires, 1943-46; manager of an advertising firm, Montevideo, 1955-57; director of municipal libraries, Montevideo, after 1957. Editor, *Marcha*, Montevideo, 1939-42, and *Vea y Lea*, Buenos Aires, 1946-55. Recipient: National Literature Prize, 1963; William Faulkner Foundation Ibero-American Award, 1963; Casa de las Américas Prize, 1965; Italian-Latin American Institute Prize, 1972. Address: Gonzalo Ramfrez 1497, Montevideo, Uruguay.

PUBLICATIONS

Fiction

El pozo. Montevideo, Signo, 1939.
Tierra de nadie. Buenos Aires, Losada, 1941.
Para esta noche. Buenos Aires, Poseidon, 1943.
La vida breve. Buenos Aires, Sudamericana, 1950; as *A Brief Life*, New York, Grossman, 1976.

Un sueño realizado y otros cuentos. Montevideo, Número, 1951.
Los adioses. Buenos Aires, Sur, 1954.
Una tumba sin nombre. Montevideo, Marcha, 1959.
La cara de la desgracia. Montevideo, Alfa, 1960.
El astillero. Buenos Aires, Fabirl, 1961; as *The Shipyard*, New York, Scribner, 1968.
El infierno tan temido. Montevideo, Asir, 1962.
Tan triste como ella. Montevideo, Alfa, 1963.
Juntacadáveres. Montevideo, Alfa, 1964.
Cuentos completos. Buenos Aires, Centro Editor de America Latina, 1967; revised edition, 1973.
Novelas [and *Cuentos*]*cortas completas.* Caracas, Monte Avila, 2 vols., 1968.
La novia robada y otros cuentos. Buenos Aires, Centro Editor de America Latina, 1968.
Los rostros del amor. Buenos Aires, Centro Editor de America Latina, 1968.
Obras completas. Mexico City, Aguilar, 1970.
La muerte y la niña. Buenos Aires, Corregidor, 1973.
Tiempo de abrazar y los cuentos de 1933 a 1950. Montevideo, Arca, 1974.
Tan triste como ella y otros cuentos. Barcelona, Lumen, 1976.
Dejemos hablar al viento. Barcelona, Bruguera, 1980.

Other

Requiem por Faulkner. Montevideo, Arca, 1976.

*

Critical Studies: *The Formal Expression of Meaning in Onetti's Narrative Art* by Yvonne P. Jones, Cuernavaca, Cidoc, 1971; *Three Authors of Alienation: Bombal, Onetti, Carpentier* by M. Ian Adams, Austin, University of Texas Press, 1975; *Onetti: El ritual de la impostura* by Hugo J. Verani, Caracas, Monte Avila, 1981.

*　　　*　　　*

The many difficulties involved in reading Juan Carlos Onetti are responsible for his relative obscurity. His literary creation is permeated at all levels with ambiguity. Human actions become difficult to define, frequently having multiple and contradictory results. Characters can be created by other characters with, at times, the creations taking over from the creator, as in *A Brief Life*, or there can be multiple characters in which the number of possibilities of definition are gradually reduced, as in the first part of *Dejemos hablar al viento*. Even when the characters are clearly defined, as occurs in *The Shipyard*, or in some of the short stories, the motives and meanings of their actions are nebulous. The world these shadowy creations inhabit is a nightmare of sordidness and hopelessness, filled with drugs, alcohol, perversion, and promiscuity. To read Onetti is to wander among the ruins of human aspiration.

Onetti's most visible literary origins are Dos Passos, Céline and Faulkner. The influence of the first two is evident in two of his early novels, *Tierra de nadie* and *Para esta noche*. Onetti's major literary creation begins with *A Brief Life*, where he follows the Faulknerian technique of creating a literary landscape. The riverside town of Santa María, actually imagined by the protagonist, Juan María Brausen, is the device that allows Onetti in *A Brief Life*, and all later works, to free his creativity and to communicate his unique vision. His use of a fictitious landscape is not an imitation of Faulkner. The development of Yoknapatawpha County is centrifugal, while that of Santa María is centripetal. Santa María is literary creation turned upon itself. Brausen creates the town as one of several escapes from his failing personal and professional life. Later, there is a statue in the plaza of Brausen, the Founder. In later works Brausen becomes the Creator and, at one point is prayed to as though he were God. The final stage of the process is seen in Onetti's last novel, *Dejemos hablar al viento*, where the protagonist, knowing that he was created by Brausen, probably recreates or reimagines Brausen's Santa María, only finally to destroy it.

Within the involuted world of the town, whether seen in novels or stories, several characters emerge, gradually acquiring dimensions and life beyond the individual works. Through these figures the reader has the clearest presentation of Onetti's view of life.

Díaz-Grey, created by Brausen in *A Brief Life*, is a doctor, addicted to morphine, who impinges on the lives of most of Onetti's other important characters. Totally cynical and corrupt, Díaz-Grey has broad experience with what he views as the hopelessness and absurdity of the human situation. He rises above the wreckage because of his desire to observe and to attempt to understand, even though he knows the latter to be a meaningless task.

Larsen is the opposite of Díaz-Grey. He is cunning rather than intelligent. A pimp whose failed attempt to establish a whorehouse is the subject of *Juntacadáveres*, he arrives at the greatest vision of the absurdity of life of all of Onetti's characters.

These and other figures provide the reader with a searing vision of man's ability to survive in a meaningless world. The reader who can tolerate Onetti's ambiguity and complexity is, in the end, forced by the struggle with those characteristics to become a participant, not an observer.

—M. Ian Adams

PARRA, Nicanor. Chilean. Born in Chillán, 5 September 1914. Educated at the University of Chile, Santiago, degree in mathematics and physics 1938; studied advanced mechanics, Brown University, Providence, Rhode Island, 1943-45; studied cosmology at Oxford University (British Council grant), 1949-51. Married 1) Ana Troncoso in 1948 (marriage dissolved); 2) Inga Palmen; seven children. Taught in secondary school, 1938-43, since 1948, Director of School of Engineering, and since 1952, Professor of Theoretical Physics, University of Chile. Visiting Professor, Louisiana State University, Baton Rouge, 1966, and New York, Columbia, and Yale universities, 1971. Recipient: City of Santiago Prize, 1937, 1955; Writers Union Prize, 1954; National Literature Prize, 1969.

PUBLICATIONS

Verse

Cancionero sin nombre. Santiago, Nascimento, 1937.
Poemas y antipoemas. Santiago, Nascimento, 1954, 3rd. edition, 1964.
La cueca larga. Santiago, Editorial Universitaria, 1958.
Anti-Poems. San Francisco, City Lights, 1960.
Versos de salón. Santiago, Nascimento, 1962.
La cueca larga y otros poemas, edited by Margarita Aguirre and Juan Agustín Palazuelos. Buenos Aires, Editorial Universitaria, 1964.
Poems and Antipoems, edited by Miller Williams. New York, New Directions, 1967; London, Cape, 1968.
Canciones rusas. Santiago, Editorial Universitaria, 1967.

Poesía rusa contemporanea. Santiago, Ediciones Nueva Universidad, 1967.
Obra gruesa. Santiago, Editorial Universitaria, 1969; as *Emergency Poems*, translated by Miller Williams, New York, New Directions, 1972; London, Boyars, 1977.
Los profesores. New York, Antiediciones Villa Miseria, 1971.
Antipoemas: Antologia 1944-1969. Barcelona, Seix Barral, 1972.
Artefactos. Santiago, Universidad Católica de Chile, 1972.
Sermones y prédicas del Cristo de Elqui. Santiago, Universidad de Chile Estudios Humanisticos, 1977.
Nuevos sermones y prédicas del Cristo de Elqui. Valparaiso, Ganymedes, 1979.

Other

Discursos, with Pablo Neruda. Santiago, Nascimento, 1962.

*

Critical Studies: *Parra y la poesía de lo cotidiano* by Hugo Montes, Santiago, Pacifico, 2nd edition, 1974; *The Antipoetry of Parra* by Edith Grossman, New York, New York University Press, 1975; *No se termina nunca de nacer: La poesía de Parra* by Marlene Gottlieb, Madrid, Playor, 1977.

*   *   *

Nicanor Parra, the creator of antipoetry, has brought to Hispanic literature a new vision of the expressive possibilities of colloquial Spanish. His writing attacks most of our esthetic sensibilities by undermining traditional expectations of what poetry is and means, and it consequently has had an important liberating impact on the world of Latin American letters. As a purely domestic phenomenon, antipoetry is a prime example of a generational reaction to the styles and concerns of earlier poets: it negates the highly metaphorical, surrealistic style of the 1930's, and it intensifies those currents and tendencies that pointed toward simplification and the increasing accessibility of poetry to a mass-educated urban audience. From a more cosmopolitan point of view, Parra's achievement may well be due to his strong and continuing interest in and knowledge of poetry written in English, both British and North American (Parra is fluent in English, and he readily admits to the profound influence of English-language poets such as Donne and Eliot on his artistic development). In this sense, antipoetry is a kind of anglicization of poetry in Spanish.

For those more familiar with the English-language poetic tradition than with the Hispanic, Parra's effort to communicate directly with the reader in an accessible language is no great novelty, for we have seen it in practice over and over again in the work of poets who write in English, from William Wordsworth to Walt Whitman to William Carlos Williams. But ordinary practice in English is extraordinary in Spanish, and when Parra relegates what he calls "poetry" to an ash heap of purposeful obscurity or trite sentimentality, he is laying the theoretical groundwork for the Hispanic reader's acceptance of antipoetry as the long overdue cleaning of poetry's house.

One of the most significant characteristics of Parra's writing is the view of poetry as an extension of ordinary language rather than a special form of discourse. It is this use of the spoken idiom, liberally laced with ironic humor, that Parra has called antipoetry; he arbitrarily defines "poetry" as everything that he finds alien in literature: pomposity, rhetoric, and self-conscious lyricism, metaphor, and imagery. Parra consistently refuses to give an exact definition of antipoetry, however, or to demarcate its limits with precision. He claims that he chose the term for purely "strategic reasons," and calls his work a "professional secret." In an interview with Patricio Lerzundi, "In Defense of Antipoetry: An Interview with Nicanor Parra," *Review* (Winter 1971/Spring 1972), he stated: "If you put me up against the wall and say 'OK, tell us once and for all what anitpoetry is,' I'll tell you I haven't the slightest idea—go

PARRA

ahead, frisk me." Parra tends to turn efforts at eliciting more precise definitions into anti-interviews, changing his statements about himself and his writing according to whim, or possibly according to what he thinks will most distract his audience and his interviewer. His best known answer to those who insist on exact definitions (and an excellent example of how he uses familiar language in his writing) is from the antipoem "Test":

> What is antipoetry
> A tempest in a teapot?
> A bit of snow on a rock?
> A container full of human excrement
> as Father Salvatierra believes?
> A mirror that tells the truth?
> A woman with her legs spread?
> A slap in the face
> of the president of the Writer's Society?
> (May God have mercy on his soul)
> A warning to young poets?
> A jet-propelled coffin?
> A coffin run by centrifugal force?
> A kerosene coffin?
> A funeral chapel without a body?
> Place an X beside
> the definition that you consider correct.

—Edith Grossman

PAZ, Octavio. Mexican. Born in Mexico City, 31 March 1914. Educated at the National University of Mexico, Mexico City. Married Marie José Tramini in 1964; one daughter. Writer: founder or editor of literary reviews *Barandal*, 1931, *El Popular*, late 1930's, *Taller*, 1938-41, *El Hijo Pródigo*, 1943-46, and since 1976, *Plural*, later called *Vuelta*. Secretary, Mexican Embassy, Paris, 1946; Chargé d'Affaires, 1951, later posted to Secretariat for External Affairs, Mexican Embassy, Tokyo; Mexican Ambassador to India, 1962-68 (resigned). Taught at University of Texas; Simón Bolívar Professor of Latin American Studies, 1970, and Fellow of Churchill College, 1970-71, Cambridge University; Charles Eliot Norton Professor of Poetry, Harvard University, Cambridge, Massachusetts, 1971-72. Recipient: Guggenheim Fellowship, 1944; International Grand Prize for Poetry, 1963; Jerusalem Prize, 1977; Critics Prize (Spain), 1977; National Prize for Letters, 1977; Grand Aigle d'Or (Nice), 1979; Neustadt International Prize, 1982. Member, American Academy. Address: Revista Vuelta, Leonardo da Vinci 17, Mexico 19, D.F., Mexico.

PUBLICATIONS

Verse

Luna silvestre. Mexico City, Fabula, 1933.
Raíz del hombre. Mexico City, Simbad, 1937.

266

¡No pasarán! Mexico City, Simbad, 1937.

Bajo tu clara sombra y otros poemas sobre España. Valencia, Españolas, 1937; revised edition, Valencia, Tierra Nueva, 1941.

Entre la piedra y la flor. Mexico City, Nueva Voz, 1941.

A la orilla del mundo y primer día: Bajo tu clara sombra, Raíz del hombre, Noche de resurrecciones. Mexico City, Companía Editora y Librera Ars, 1942.

Libertad bajo palabra. Mexico City, Tezontle, 1949.

¿Aquila o sol? Mexico City, Tezontle, 1951; as *Eagle or Sun?*, translated by Eliot Weinberger, New York, October House, 1970.

Semillas para un himno. Mexico City, Tezontle, 1954.

Piedra de sol. Mexico City, Tezontle, 1957; as *Sun Stone*, translated by Muriel Rukeyser, New York, New Directions, 1963; as *The Sun Stone*, translated by Donald Gardner, York, Cosmos, 1969.

La estación violenta. Mexico City, Fondo de Cultura Económica, 1958.

Agua y viento. Bogota, Mito, 1959.

Libertad bajo palabra: Obra poética 1935-1958. Mexico City, Fondo de Cultura Económica, 1960; revised edition, 1968.

Salamandra 1958-1961. Mexico City, Mortiz, 1962.

Selected Poems, translated by Muriel Rukeyser. Bloomington, Indiana University Press, 1963.

Viento entero. New Delhi, Laxton Press, 1965.

Vrinidiban, Madurai. New Delhi, Laxton Press, 1965.

Blanco. Mexico City, Mortiz, 1967; as *Blanco*, translated by Eliot Weinberger, New York, The Press, 1974.

Ladera este (1962-1968). Mexico City, Mortiz, 1969.

La centana: Poemas 1935-1968. Barcelona, Seix Barral, 1969.

Configurations. New York, New Directions, and London, Cape, 1971.

Renga, with others. Paris, Gallimard, 1971; as *Renga*, translated by Charles Tomlinson, New York, Braziller, 1972; London, Penguin, 1980.

Early Poems 1935-1955. New York, New Directions, 1973.

Pasado en claro. Mexico City, Fondo de Cultura Económica, 1975.

Vuelta. Barcelona, Seix Barral, 1976.

A Draft of Shadows and Other Poems. New York, New Directions, 1979.

Selected Poems, translated by Charles Tomlinson. London, Penguin, 1979.

Airborn/Hijos del aire, with Charles Tomlinson. London, Anvil Press, 1981.

Play

La hija de Rappaccini, from the story by Nathaniel Hawthorne (produced Mexico, 1956). Published in *Primera antología de obras en un acto*, edited by Maruxa Vilalta, Mexico City, Collección Teatro Mexicano, 1959.

Other

El laberinto de la soledad. Mexico City, Cuadernos Americanos, 1950; revised edition, Mexico City, Fondo de Cultura Económica, 1959; as *The Labyrinth of Solitude*, New York, Grove Press, 1962; London, Allen Lane, 1967.

El arco y la lire: El poema, la revelación poética, poésia e historia. Mexico City, Fondo de Cultura Económica, 1956; revised edition, 1967; as *The Bow and the Lyre: The Poem, The Poetic Revelation, Poetry and History*, Austin, University of Texas Press, 1973.

Las peras del olmo. Mexico City, Universidad Nacional Autónoma de México, 1957.

Cuadrivio (on Darío, Lopez Verlarde, Pessoa, Cernuda). Mexico City, Mortiz, 1965.

PAZ

Los signos en rotación. Buenos Aires, Sur, 1965.
Puertas al campo. Mexico City, Universidad Nacional Autónoma de México, 1966.
Claude Lévi-Strauss; o, El nuevo festín de Esopo. Mexico City, Mortiz, 1967; as *Claude Lévi-Strauss: An Introduction,* Ithaca, New York, Cornell University Press, 1970; as *On Lévi-Strauss,* London, Cape, 1970.
Corriente alterna. Mexico City, Siglo Veintiuno, 1967; as *Alternating Current,* New York, Viking Press, 1973; London, Wildwood House, 1974.
Marcel Duchamp; o, El castillo de la pureza. Mexico City, Era, 1968; as *Marcel Duchamp; or, The Castle of Purity,* New York, Grossman, and London, Cape Goliard, 1970.
Conjunciones y disyunciones. Mexico City, Mortiz, 1969; as *Conjunctions and Disjunctions,* New York, Viking Press, 1974; London, Wildwood House, 1975.
Posdata. Mexico City, Siglo Veintiuno, 1970; as *The Other Mexico: Critique of the Pyramid,* New York, Grove Press, 1972.
Las cosas en su sitio: Sobre la literatura española del siglo XX, with Juan Marichal. Mexico City, Finisterre, 1971.
Los signos en rotación y otros ensayos, edited by Carlos Fuentes. Madrid, Alianza, 1971.
Traducción: Literatura y literalidad. Barcelona, Tusquets, 1971.
Apariencia desnuda: La obra de Marcel Duchamp. Mexico City, Era, 1973; as *Marcel Duchamp: Appearance Stripped Bare,* New York, Viking Press, 1979.
El signo y el garabato. Mexico City, Mortiz, 1973.
Solo a dos voces, with Julián Ríos. Barcelona, Lumen, 1973.
Teatro de signos/transparencias, edited by Julián Ríos. Madrid, Fundamentos, 1974.
Versiones y diversiones (translations). Mexico City, Mortiz, 1974.
Los hijos del limo: Del romanticismo a la vanguardia (lectures). Barcelona, Seix Barral, 1974; as *Children of the Mire: Modern Poetry from Romanticism to the Avant-Garde,* Cambridge, Massachusetts, Harvard University Press, 1974.
El mono gramático. Barcelona, Seix Barral, 1974; as *The Monkey Grammarian,* New York, Seaver, 1981.
The Siren and the Seashells and Other Essays on Poets and Poetry. Austin, University of Texas Press, 1976.
Xavier Villaurrutia en persona y en obra. Mexico City, Fondo de Cultura Económica, 1978.
El ogro filantrópico: Historia y política 1971-1978. Barcelona, Seix Barral, 1979.
Rufino Tamayo: Myth and Magic. New York, Guggenheim Foundation, 1979.

Editor, *Voces de España.* Mexico City, Letras de Mexico, 1938.
Editor, with others, *Laurel: Antología de la poésia moderna en lengua española.* Mexico City, Séneca, 1941.
Editor, *Anthologie de la poésie mexicaine.* Paris, Nagel, 1952.
Editor, *Antología poética.* Mexico City, Revista Panoramas, 1956.
Editor, *Anthology of Mexican Poetry,* translated by Samuel Beckett. Bloomington, Indiana University Press, 1958; London, Thames and Hudson, 1959.
Editor, *Tamayo en la pintura mexicana.* Mexico City, Imprenta Universitaria, 1959.
Editor, *Magia de la risa.* Xalapa, Universidad Veracruzana, 1962.
Editor, *Antología,* by Fernando Pessoa. Mexico City, Universidad Nacional Autónoma de México, 1962.
Editor, with Pedro Zekeli, *Cuatro poetas contemporáneos de Suecia: Martinson, Lundkvist, Ekelöf, y Lindegren.* Mexico City, Universidad Nacional Autónoma de México, 1963.
Editor, with others, *Poésia en movimiento: Mexico 1915-1966.* Mexico City, Siglo Veintiuno, 1966; as *New Poetry of Mexico,* edited by Mark Strand, New York, Dutton, 1970; London, Secker and Warburg, 1972.

Translator, with E. Hayashiya, *Sendas de Oku*, by Basho.   Mexico City, Universidad
Nacional Autónoma de México, 1957.
Translator, *Veinte poemas*, by William Carlos Williams.   Mexico City, Era, 1973.
Translator, *15 poemas*, by Apollinaire.   Mexico City, Latitudes, 1979.

*

Bibliography: *Paz: Bibliografía crítica* by Hugo J. Verani, Mexico City, Universidad Nacional
Autónoma de México, 1983.

Critical Studies: *The Poetic Modes of Paz* by Rachel Phillips, London, Oxford University
Press, 1972; *The Perpetual Present: The Poetry and Prose of Paz* edited by Ivar Ivask, Norman,
University of Oklahoma Press, 1973; *Paz: A Study of His Poetics* by Jason Wilson, Cambridge,
Cambridge University Press, 1979.

*   *   *

Within the intellectual landscape of the 20th century, in an increasingly specialized and
divided world, Octavio Paz is a writer of exceptional and diverse interests, of prodigious
versatility, unusual erudition and imagination, recognized as one of the major poets of our time
and as a lucid interpreter of modernity. His critical thought includes a bewildering number of
fields of human activity—art, aesthetics, philosophy, Oreintal religion, anthropology, psychology, political ideology. The preoccupations that cross the writing of Octavio Paz—the
search for lost unity and the reconciliation of man with himself and the universe, the celebration
of love and of freedom of thinking, the merging of contraries, the reviving of the poetic
word—converge in the reflexive prose of his essays and in a poetry that assumes the form of
self-criticism and incessant interrogation, two sides of an organic whole of inseparable unity in
its diversity, that constitutes an uncommon and passionate testimony of humanity.
   Paz is primarily a poet, considered (along with Neruda and Vallejo) as one of the truly
outstanding Spanish-American poets of the century. Paz sees poetry as a path towards the
revelation of man, as a means to restore authenticity. Poetic creation and erotic love are the
only ways to reconcile the opposing forces of the world, the only ways to transcend solitude and
reach spiritual fulfillment.
   The extensive travels of Octavio Paz throughout the world have affected the many phases
and transformations of his poetry. His first trip to Spain in 1937, during the Civil War,
introduced him to the Spanish tradition, particularly the Baroque world of Quevedo and
Góngora, poets who left a deep mark on his early writing. His stay in the United States
(1944-45) enabled him to read the great poets of the Anglo-American tradition (Eliot, Pound,
Cummings); he came to share with them the representation of the dissociated image of the
world and the self through fragmentation and simultaneity, through the suppression of logical
ties. During the five years that he lived in France (1946-51), he participated in the surrealist
movement and developed a lifelong affinity with its tenets. Paz sees surrealism as an activity of
the human spirit based on the idea of rebellion, love, and freedom, as a total subversion, as a
movement meant to recapture the natural innocence of man. His debt to surrealism can best be
found in *La estación violenta*, where his poetry becomes more hermetic, and indulges in
complex oneiric images and occasional automatic writing. The conjunction of ancient Mexican
mythology and surrealism ("telluric surrealism," as termed by the French poet Benjamin Péret)
guides his quest for eternal values, his desire to transcend the contradictions of humanity.
"Hymn among the Ruins" and, above all, *Sun Stone* are the masterpieces of this period of his
poetry. In Japan (1952) he was ready to explore Japanese poetry, primarily the Haiku, a form
of poetry that stresses condensation, ellipsis, and imagery. After a stay in Mexico (1953-58) he
resided in France again (1959-62), where he deepened his interest in structuralism. Finally, he
became Ambassador to India (1962-68), a country that profoundly affected his vision of the
world and his approach to poetry. Many concepts of Oriental thought were incorporated into

his poetics: detachment from the outside world, the illusory nature of the world, the stress on natural man, the illusion of the ego, sudden illumination, transcendence through the senses, rebellion against all systems. *Ladera este* and *Blanco* include the major poems of this period.

Since the early 1960's the most significant constants of Paz's poetic work are experimentation with space and the use of visual effects. Faced with the disconcerting, fragmentary, and dissociated character of reality, he questions all certainty and converts natural relationships into multiple, unconnected moments, which are regrouped in a space that reveals the fragmented consciousness of modern man, the loss of cosmic harmony and the ancient, coherent image of reality. The most important poems of the 1960's ("Whole Wind," *Blanco*) are constellations of juxtaposed fragments and of voices in perpetual rotation in which the simultaneity of times and spaces is the point of confluence in an inexhaustible net of relations that enrich the analytical reading of the text. In his poetry the spatial-temporal markings disappear, and all ages converge in a privileged moment, in that evanescent and fleeting, atemporal and archetypal present. Paz liberates language from the illusion of representing an empirical reality: spaces, times, and distant cultures interweave without explicit transition and give the poem a plural meaning.

Paz is also a major essayist. Few Spanish-American writers, if any, have developed a critical system that encompasses the main intellectual currents of modern times. In twenty volumes of essays, from his early reflections on Mexican society (*The Labyrinth of Solitude*) and on poetic theory (*The Bow and the Lyre*), his studies on structuralism and modern art (the books on Lévi-Strauss and Marcel Duchamp), the meditations on eroticism (*Conjunctions and Disjunctions*), and on diverse artistic manifestations (five books), to the revision of the modern poetic tradition (*Children of the Mire*), of political ideology (*El ogro filantrópico*), and his monumental book on Sor Juana Inés de la Cruz, critical reflexion is one of the central preoccupations of Octavio Paz, a product of a lucid and passionate meditation on the culture of the modern times. Paz sees himself, and all writers, as dissidents, as outsiders: "Our civilization has been founded on the notion of criticism: there is nothing sacred or untouchable except the freedom to think. Without criticism, that is to say, without rigor and without experimentation, there is no science; without criticism there is no art or literature. I would also say that without criticism there is no healthy society. The writer is not the servant of the Church, the State, a political party, a country, the people, or social morals: he is the servant of language. But he really serves it only when he questions it: modern literature is above all criticism of language."

During almost half a century Octavio Paz has adhered, then, to two fundamental premises: the questioning of all established truths and, above all, the passionate search for human dignity and the defense of the freedom of the human being, principles whose aim is always in Paz a recovery of the essential values of humanism.

—Hugo J. Verani

PIEYRE DE MANDIARGUES, André (Paul Édouard). French. Born in Paris, 14 March 1909. Educated at the Lycée Carnot, Paris; École des Hautes Études Commerciales, Paris, one year; the Sorbonne, Paris. Married Bona Tibertelli in 1950 (divorced), one daughter; remarried, 1967. Recipient: Critics Prize (France), 1951; *Figaro Littéraire* Prize, 1963; Goncourt Prize, 1967; French Academy Grand Prize for Poetry, 1979; Nice Festival award, 1981. Address: 36 rue de Sévigné, 75003 Paris, France.

PUBLICATIONS

Fiction

Le Musée noir. Paris, Laffont, 1946.
L'Etudiante. Paris, Fontaine, 1946.
Soleil des loups. Paris, Laffont, 1951.
Marbre. Paris, Laffont, 1953.
L'Anglais décrit dans le château fermé (as Pierre Morien). N.p., Oxford and Cambridge, 1953; revised edition, as André Pieyre de Mandiargues, Paris, Gallimard, 1979.
Le Lis de mer. Paris, Laffont, 1956; as *The Girl Beneath the Lion*, New York, Grove Press, 1958.
Feu de braise. Paris, Grasset, 1959; as *Blaze of Embers*, London, Calder and Boyars, 1971.
Sabine. Paris, Mercure, 1963.
La Motocyclette. Paris, Gallimard, 1963; as *The Motorcycle*, New York, Grove Press, 1966; as *The Girl on the Motorcycle*, London, Calder and Boyars, 1966.
Porte dévergondée. Paris, Gallimard, 1965.
La Marge. Paris, Gallimard, 1967; as *The Margin*, New York, Grove Press, 1969.
Le Marronnier. Paris, Mercure, 1968.
La Nuit de mil neuf cent quatorze; ou, Le Style liberty. Paris, Herne, 1970.
Mascarets. Paris, Gallimard, 1971.
Sous la lame. Paris, Gallimard, 1976.
Crachefeu. Paris, Nouveau Cercle Parisien du Livre, 1980.
Des Cobras à Paris. Montpellier, Fata Morgana, 1982.
Le Deuil des roses. Paris, Gallimard, 1983.

Plays

Isabella Morra (produced Paris, 1973). Paris, Gallimard, 1973.
La Nuit séculaire. Paris, Gallimard, 1979.
Arsène et Cléopâtre. Paris, Gallimard, 1981.

Verse

Dans les années sordides. Monaco, APM, 1943.
Hedera; ou, La Persistance de l'amour pendant une rêverie. Monaco, Hommage, 1945.
Astyanax. Paris, Terrain Vague, 1956.
Cartolines et dédicaces. Paris, Terrain Vague, 1960.
L'Âge de craie, suivi de Hedera. Paris, Gallimard, 1961.
La Nuit l'amour. Paris, Loeb, 1962.
Le Point où j'en suis, suivi de Dalila exaltée et de La Nuit d'amour l'amour. Paris, Gallimard, 1964.
Jacinthes. Paris, Lazar Vernet, 1967; as *Hyacinthes*, Paris, Olv, 1967.
Ruisseau des solitudes, suivi de Jacinthes et de Chapeaugaga. Paris, Gallimard, 1968.
Croiseur noir. Paris, Lazar Vernet, 1972.
Parapapilloneries. Paris, Casset, 1976.
L'Ivre oeil, suivi de Croiseur noir et de Passage de l'Egyptienne. Paris Gallimard, 1979.

Other

Les Incongruités monumentales.   Paris, Laffont, 1946.
Les Septs Périls spectraux.   Paris, Les Pas Perdus, 1950.
Les Masques de Léonor Fini.   Paris, La Parade, 1951.
Les Monstres de Bomarzo.   Paris, Grasset, 1958.
Le Cadran lunaire.   Paris, Laffont, 1958.
Le Belvédère.   Paris, Grasset, 1958; *Deuxième Belvédère*, Grasset, 1962; *Troisième Belvédère*, Paris, Gallimard, 1971.
Sugaï.   Paris, Fall, 1960.
Beylamour.   Paris, Pauvert, 1965.
Les Corps illuminés.   Paris, Mercure, 1965.
Larmes de généraux.   Stockholm, Igell, 1965.
Critiquettes.   Montpellier, Fata Morgana, 1967.
Le Lièvre de la lune.   Milan, M'Arte, 1970.
Eros solaire.   Paris, Tchou, 1970.
Bona: L'Amour et la peinture.   Geneva, Skira, 1971.
Terre érotique.   Paris, Tchou, 1974.
Chagall.   Paris, Maeght, 1975.
Le Désordre de la mémoire: Entretiens avec Francine Mallet.   Paris, Gallimard, 1975.
Arcimboldo le merveilleux.   Paris, Laffont, 1977; as *Arcimboldo the Marvelous*, New York, Abrams, 1978.
Le Trésor cruel de Hans Bellmer.   Paris, Sphinx, 1979.
Un Saturne gai.   Paris, Gallimard, 1982.
Sept jardins fantastiques.   Tokyo, Muleta, 1983.

Translator, *La Femme de Gogol*, by Tommaso Landolfi.   Paris, Gallimard, 1969.
Translator, *Le Fille de Rappuccini*, by Octavio Paz.   Paris, Mercure, 1972.
Translator, *Le Vent parmi les roseaux*, by W.B. Yeats.   Paris, Lazar Vernet, 1972.
Translator, *La Petite Bassaride*, by F. de Pisis.   Paris, L'Herne, 1972.
Translator, *Onze plus un*, by F. de Pisis.   Rome, Bestetti, 1975.
Translator, *Madame de Sade*, by Mishima Yukio.   Paris, Gallimard, 1976.

*

Critical Studies: "Pieyre de Mandiargues Issue" of *Cahiers Renaud-Barrault 86*, 1974; *Pieyre de Mandiargues* (in French) by Salah Stétié, Paris, Seghers, 1978; *The Fiction of Pieyre de Mandiargues* by David J. Bond, Syracuse, New York, Syracuse University Press, 1982.

*   *   *

André Pieyre de Mandiargues has engaged in an impressively wide range of writing: poetry, fiction, plays, and essays on art and literature. His work shows an obvious affinity with surrealism, and he was, in fact, associated with the surrealists for about six years immediately after the Second World War. Surrealism confirmed him in the belief that art should reveal the hidden aspects of reality, the surprising behind the banal, and, in the preface to his first volume of short stories, *Le Musée noir*, he claims that the marvellous is everywhere, and that it is revealed once there is "an atmosphere favourable to the trans-figuration of phenomena felt by the senses."

It is precisely such an atmosphere that Mandiargues attempts to create in his work. His fiction especially is full of fantasy, the unexpected and the mysterious: characters change shape or size; dream projects into reality; strangely beautiful women lure men to their destruction; the flow of time is disturbed or halted. There are also strongly mythical overtones in several works. Rebecca, travelling to her lover on her motorcycle in *The Motorcycle*, Sigismond, wandering around Barcelona in *The Margin*, Vanina, meeting her lover in a dark wood in *The Girl*

Beneath the Lion, and many characters undergoing strange experiences in the short stories, may all be seen as mythical heroes or heroines in search of the source of life. These characters are not psychological studies or fully rounded people, but epiphanies, beings through whom mysterious forces flow. In moments of erotic ecstasy, and in their daily relations with the natural world, they commune with what Mandiargues calls the "panic"—the very forces of life inherent in nature.

Mandiargues's fiction is marked by a cruel eroticism, and scenes of flagellation, rape, and violent coupling are not uncommon. While there is a typically surrealist desire to shock in such scenes, there is also another purpose. Constantly associated with eroticism is death, for Mandiargues believes that the powers of life, expressed in the sexual urge, are also encountered in death, and he tries to show that life and death are two aspects of the same forces.

The style of these works is highly poetic, baroque yet precise, and based on detailed observation of the physical world. Jean d'Ormesson calls Mandiargues "one of the rare stylists of our contemporary literature" (*Les Nouvelles Littéraires*, 14 May 1971), and Mark Temmer says that he produces "prose cadences worthy of Bossuet or Bourdaloue, rhythmic forms into which are poured, like gold and silver, the verbal counterpart of his sensations" (*Yale French Studies 31*, 1964).

Mandiargues attaches great importance to poetry, saying that it is "as marvellous as love" (*Le Désordre de la mémoire*). His own poetry has woman, seen as the incarnation of the marvellous, at its centre. Like his fiction, it reveals the hidden beauty of the world, the presence of "panic" forces, and the importance of dream. His critical work is far-ranging, but it shows a predilection for surrealism, the baroque, and anything that is unusual or innovative in art and literature. Mandiargues's plays are the least successful artistically of his works. They lack dramatic interest, and only *Isabella Morra* is noteworthy for a certain poetry.

—David J. Bond

PINGET, Robert. Swiss. Born in Geneva, 19 July 1919. Educated in Geneva, received law degree; studied at École des Beaux-Arts, Paris. Practiced law, 1944-46; moved to France in 1946, and worked as painter; taught drawing and French in England. Since 1951, free-lance writer in Paris. Recipient: Ford Foundation grant, 1960; Critics Prize (France), 1963; Fémina Prize, 1965. Address: c/o Editions de Minuit, 7 rue Bernard-Palissy, 75006 Paris, France.

PUBLICATIONS

Fiction

Entre Fantoine et Agapa (stories). Jarnac, Tour d Feu, 1951; as *Between Fantoine and Agapa*, New York, Red Dust, 1982.
Mahu; ou, Le matériau. Paris, Laffont, 1952; as *Mahu; or, The Material*, London, Calder and Boyars, 1966.
Le Renard et la boussole. Paris, Gallimard, 1953.
Graal Flibuste. Paris, Minuit, 1956; revised edition, 1966.

Baga. Paris, Minuit, 1958; translated as *Baga*, London, Calder and Boyars, 1967.
Le Fiston. Paris, Minuit, 1959; as *No Answer*, London, Calder, 1961; as *Monsieur Levert*, New York, Grove Press, 1961.
Clope au dossier. Paris, Minuit, 1961.
L'Inquisitoire. Paris, Minuit, 1962; as *The Inquisitory*, London, Calder and Boyars, and New York, Grove Press, 1966.
Quelqu'un. Paris, Minuit, 1965; as *Someone*, New York, Red Dust, 1984.
Le Libéra. Paris, Minuit, 1968; as *The Libera Me Domine*, London, Calder and Boyars, 1972; New York, Red Dust, 1978.
Passacaille. Paris, Minuit, 1969; as *Recurrent Melody*, London, Calder and Boyars, 1975; as *Passacaglia*, New York, Red Dust, 1978.
Fable. Paris, Minuit, 1971; translated as *Fable*, London, Calder, and New York, Red Dust, 1980.
Cette voix. Paris, Minuit, 1975; as *That Voice*, New York, Red Dust, 1982.
L'Apocryphe. Paris, Minuit, 1980.
Monsieur Songe. Paris, Minuit, 1982.

Plays

Lettre morte, from his novel *Le Fiston* (produced Paris, 1960). Paris, Minuit, 1959; as *Dead Letter* (produced Bromley, Kent, 1961), in *Plays 1*, 1963.
La Manivelle/The Old Tune (radio play; bilingual edition). Paris, Minuit, 1960; *The Old Tune* (produced Edinburgh, 1964; London, 1972), in *Plays 1*, 1963.
Ici ou ailleurs, suivi de Architruc et de L'Hypothèse. Paris, Minuit, 1961.
Ici ou ailleurs, from his novel *Clope au dossier*, in *Ici ou ailleurs* (collection). 1961; as *Clope* (produced London, 1964), in *Plays 1*, 1963.
Architruc, in *Ici ou ailleurs* (collection). 1961; as *Architruc* (produced London, 1967), in *Plays 2*, 1967.
L'Hypothèse, in *Ici ou ailleurs* (collection). 1961; as *The Hypothesis* (produced London, 1967), in *Plays 2*, 1967.
Plays 1. London, Calder, 1963; as *Three Plays*, New York, Hill and Wang, 1966.
Autour de Mortin (radio play). Paris, Minuit, 1965; as *About Mortin*, in *Plays 2*, 1967.
Plays 2. London, Calder and Boyars, 1967; as *Three Plays*, New York, Hill and Wang, 1968.
Identité, suivi de Abel et Bela. Paris, Minuit, 1971.
Paralchimie, suivi de Architruc, L'Hypothèse, Nuit. Paris, Minuit, 1973.
Lubie (radio play), in *Présence Francophone 22*, Spring 1981.

*

Critical Study: *Pinget: The Novel as Quest* by Robert M. Henkels, Jr., University, University of Alabama Press, 1979.

*   *   *

Robert Pinget brings to life a world whose every aspect—from its people, places, and things to the literary conventions and the very words used to describe it—strike the reader as curiously and simultaneously familiar and strange. In achieving this paradoxical accomplishment Pinget has succeeded brilliantly in bringing to stage and page the arbitrary limitations and the poetic potential of the spoken word.

As in the works of other practitioners of the cyclical novel (Balzac, Zola, Romains, Faulkner), many elements from Pinget's pseudo-chronicle of French country life reappear from one book to the next. But instead of bringing the contours of life in the author's evocative hamlets "between Fantoine and Agapa" into clearer focus, the recurring material contradicts, alters, or calls into question assertions that have appeared previously. To imagine a verbal analogue to the constantly shifting patterns of a kaleidoscope is to approximate in visual terms the challenges and delights of Pinget's writings. Both depend extensively for their effects on the alternation of repetition and variation.

Although remarkably consistent in its aims and techniques, Pinget's work has evolved through three distinct (if somewhat overlapping) chronological stages or manners. His first books, from *Between Fantoine and Agapa* through *Le Renard et la boussole*, revel in verbal acrobatics that recall the Surrealists and serve as warm-up exercises for the works to come. Pinget parodies the presuppositions and mannerisms of popular fiction (the mystery novel, the travel novel, the gothic novel) in the fiction from *Graal Flibuste* through *Someone*. The novels and plays of this period are the most accessible to readers accustomed to the conventions of the 19th-century "well-made" novel. In his most recent work (from *The Libera Me Domine* through *That Voice*), Pinget experiments with permutations and combinations of words, phrases, and themes developed contrapuntally. Here the joys and trials of writing, the indignities of aging, the passing of the seasons, and the tittle-tattle of the village gain pathos and profundity in fugue-like verbal arabesques. Words and the tone of the voice speaking them become the novelist-playwright's subject and object.

The "new novels" of Robbe-Grillet, Beckett, Simon, Sarraute have done much to challenge outdated literary forms and replace them with modes of expression that reflect more accurately our relativistic, unsettled consciousness. Unique among his Editions de Minuit colleagues because of an alert sense of humor and a keen listening ear, Pinget has become one of the new novels' most arresting and fluent voices.

—Robert M. Henkels, Jr.

PONGE, Francis (Jean Gaston Alfred). French. Born in Montpellier, 27 March 1899. Educated at Lycée Malherbe, Caen, 1909-16; Lycée Louis-le-Grand, Paris, 1916-17; studied philosophy at the Sorbonne and law at École de Droit, Paris, 1917-18. In French military service, 1918-19. Married Odette Chabanel in 1931; one child. Secretary, Gallimard publishers, Paris, 1923, and Hachette publishers, Paris, 1931-37; member of the Communist Party, 1937-47; insurance salesman, 1937-39; on staff of Resistance paper *Progrès de Lyon*, Bourg-en-Bresse, 1942; worked for National Committee of Journalists, 1942-44; Literary and Artistic Director, Action, 1944-46; taught at Alliance Française, Paris, 1952-64; Gildersleeve Visiting Professor, Barnard College and Columbia University, New York, 1966-67. Recipient: International poetry prize, 1959; Ingram Merrill Foundation award, 1972; Neustadt International Prize, 1974. Corresponding Member, Bavarian Academy, 1969; Officer, Legion of Honor. Address: 34 rue Lhomond, 75005 Paris, France.

PUBLICATIONS

Verse

Douze Petits Écrits. Paris, Gallimard, 1926.

Le Parti Pris des choses. Paris, Gallimard, 1942; revised edition, 1949; edited by Ian Higgins, 1979; as *The Voice of Things*, New York, McGraw Hill, 1972.
L'Oeillet, La Guêpe, Le Mimosa. Lausanne, Mermod, 1946.
Le Carnet du bois de pins. Lausanne, Mermod, 1947.
Liasse: Vingt-et-un Textes suivis d'une bibliographie. Lyons, Écrivains Réunis, 1948.
Le Peintre a l'étude. Paris, Gallimard, 1948.
Proêmes. Paris, Gallimard, 1948.
La Crevette dans tous ses états. Paris, Vrille, 1948.
La Seine. Lausanne, Guilde du Livre, 1950.
L'Araignée. Paris, Aubier, 1952.
La Rage de l'expression. Lausanne, Mermod, 1952.
Des Cristaux naturels. Saint-Maurice-d'Ételan, Bettencourt, 1952(?).
Ponge (selection), edited by Philippe Sollers. Paris, Seghers, 1963.
Tome premier. Paris, Gallimard, 1965.
Nouveau Recueil. Paris, Gallimard, 1967.
Ponge (selection), edited by Jean Thibaudeau. Paris, Gallimard, 1967.
Two Prose Poems translated by Peter Hoy. Leicester, Black Knight Press, 1968.
Rain: A Prose Poem, translated by Peter Hoy. London, Poet and Printer, 1969.
Ici haute. Privately printed, 1971.
Things, translated by Cid Corman. Tokyo, Mushinsha, and New York, Grossman, 1971.
Ponge: Inventeur et classique. Paris, Union Générale d'Éditions, 1977.
The Sun Placed in the Abyss and Other Texts, translated by Serge Gavronsky. New York, SUN, 1977.
The Power of Language: Texts and Translations, edited and translated by Serge Gavronsky. Berkeley, University of California Press, 1979.

Other

Le Grand Recueil: Lyres, Méthodes, Pièces. Paris, Gallimard, 3 vols., 1961; revised edition, 1976-78.
De la nature morte et de Chardin. Paris, Hermann, 1964(?).
Pour un Malherbe. Paris, Gallimard, 1965; revised edition, 1977.
La Savon. Paris, Gallimard, 1967; as *Soap*, London, Cape, 1969.
Entretiens de Ponge avec Philippe Sollers, edited by Sollers. Paris, Gallimard, 1970.
La Fabrique du "pré". Geneva, Skira, 1971; as *The Making of the "Pré"*, Columbia, University of Missouri Press, 1979.
Méthodes. Paris, Gallimard, 1971.
Georges Braque, de Draeger, with Pierre Descargues and André Malraux. Montrouge, Draeger, 1971; translated as *Georges Braque*, New York, Abrams, 1971.
Picasso de Draeger, with Pierre Descargues and Edward Quinn. Montrouge, Draeger, 1974.
L'Atelier contemporain. Paris, Gallimard, 1977.
Comment une figue de paroles et pourquoi. Paris, Flammarion, 1977.
L'Écrit Beaubourg. Paris, Centre Pompidou, 1977.
Nioque de l'avant-printemps. Paris, Gallimard, 1983.

*

Critical Studies: "Ponge Issue" of *Nouvelle Revue Française*, 1956; *Testimony of the Invisible Man: William Carlos Williams, Ponge, Rainer Maria Rilke, Pablo Neruda* by Nancy Willard, Columbia, University of Missouri Press, 1970; *Ponge* by Ian Higgins, London, Athlone Press, 1979; *Ponge* by Martin Sorrell, Boston, Twayne, 1981.

*   *   *

It is difficult to describe the work of Francis Ponge without making him sound like a philosopher. His writing certainly contains threads of materialism, existentialism, phenomenology. But Ponge is far from being a theorist. Chary of over-conceptualization, he sums himself up as an artist "whose intuitions rule his intellect, someone for whom everything starts with a sensation, an emotion."

For Ponge, "sensation" means a sensuous response to "Things." He often depicts this using erotic or gastronomic imagery, and he openly relishes the gradual savouring and voluptuous possession of a delectable object. In "The Pleasures of the Door," one of the pieces in *Le Parti Pris des choses*, we find the startling phrase "tenir dans ses bras une porte," "to embrace a door." Similarly he writes of a desire to "hug" the River Seine. In some ways, Ponge limits the accessibility of his writing by avoiding conventional symbolism, but, by doing so, he presents the reader with sharp shifts in perspective. These are thought-provoking and, even now, refreshingly novel. Inspired by the physicality of "Things," he instills in his reader the same "...ardour which comes from the depths...the Eros which makes me write...". Instead of the Sartrean "Hell is other people," Ponge, stressing the importance of the relationship between the poet and the world, writes "Notre *Paradis*, en somme, ne serait-ce pas les autres?" And where Sartre's nauseating pebble triggers off depths of metaphysical "Angst," Ponge's pebble is one of the objects "on the outside of the soul, of course, and yet at the same time, anchorage or the mind...". Their material presence affirms the reality of the world.

Ponge's writing, reflecting this, is a positive and humorous antidote to Existentialist "Angst." It is the vitality of the writing, and its understated, gleeful mirth which first strike the reader. "Escargots," another piece from *Le Parti Pris*, is a good example of Ponge's adroit manipulation of both his subject and the reader. The hero is a snail, whose virtues are enumerated at length, a ridiculous catalogue of incongruities. Only the occasional pathetic remark undermines the surge of the mock-heroic.

But even this masterpiece of absurdity contains some important notions concerning man and language. As in "Le Mollusque," Ponge compares language to the secretions of the creature housed and protected, and restricted, by its hardening shell. Sartre called Ponge a "rat caught in a trap," and criticized his futile attempt to attain perfection of expression. Ponge would not deny the charge. But, imprisoned, he is also housed and protected, and if his writing represents a vicious circle, it is also a vital circle.

Language, organic, growing, is exactly analogous to the living organism. Ponge commented that, to reach the essence of a fruit, the poet has to create a text possessing the qualities of that fruit. This is illustrated practically in the bizarre work, *Comment une figue de paroles et pourquoi* (How a fig of words and why). Here the fig of words grows and ripens throughout the book until the "thickness of the words has accumulated...". Ponge's work is dense, ripe, and ready to be savoured by the reader.

—Sally McMullen (Croft)

POPA, Vasko. Yugoslavian. Born in Grebenac, Vojvodina, Serbia, 29 July 1922. Educated at the universities of Vienna, Bucharest, and Belgrade, degree in French literature 1949. Served in the partisan forces during World War II. Since 1949, Editor, Nolit Publishing House, Belgrade. Recipient: Branko Radičević Prize, 1953; Zmaj Prize, 1956; Austrian State Prize for European Literature, 1967. Address: Bulevar Revolucije 26, 11000 Belgrade, Yugoslavia.

PUBLICATIONS

Verse

Kora [Bark]. Belgrade, Nolit, 1953.
Nepočin-polje [Unrest-Field]. Novi Sad, Matica srpska, 1956.
Pesme [Poems]. Belgrade, Srpska književna zadruga, 1965.
Sporedno nebo [Secondary Heaven]. Belgrade, Nolit, 1968.
Selected Poems, translated by Anne Pennington. London, Penguin, 1969.
The Little Box, translated by Charles Simic. Washington, D.C., Charioteer Press, 1970.
Uspravna zemlja. Belgrade, Vuk Karadžić, 1972; as *Earth Erect*, translated by Anne Pennington, London, Anvil Press Poetry, 1973.
Vučja so [Wolf-Salt]. Belgrade, Vuk Karadžić, 1975.
Zivo meso [Raw Flesh]. Belgrade, Vuk Karadžić, 1975.
Kuća nasred druma [The House in the Middle of the Highway]. Belgrade, Vuk Karadžić, 1975.
Izabrane pesme [Selected Poems]. Belgrade, Rad, 1975.
Collected Poems, translated by Anne Pennington. Manchester, Carcanet, 1978; New York, Persea, 1979.
Homage to the Lame Wolf: Selected Poems 1956-1975, edited and translated by Charles Simic. Oberlin, Ohio, Oberlin College, 1979.
Rez [Cut]. Belgrade, Nolit, 1981.

Other

Editor, *Od zlata jabuka: Rukovet narodnih umotvorina* [The Golden Apple: A Collection of Folk Literature]. Belgrade, Nolit, 1958; selection, as *The Golden Apple*, London, Anvil Press Poetry, 1980.
Editor, *Urnebesnik: Zbornik pesničkog humora* [Bawler: A Collection of Poetic Humor]. Belgrade, Nolit, 1960.
Editor, *Ponočno sunce: Zbornik pesničkih snovidenja* [Midnight Sun: A Collection of Poetic Dreams]. Belgrade, Nolit, 1962.

*

Critical Studies: "The Poetry of Popa" by Ted Hughes, in *Critical Survey 2*, 1966; "Popa: The Poetry of Things in a Void" by V.D. Mihailovich, in *Books Abroad 43*, 1969; "Fertile Fire: The Poetry of Popa" by B. Johnson, in *Journal of British-Yugoslav Society 2*, 1979.

*   *   *

Vasko Popa is not only one of Yugoslavia's finest poets, but he is also the one who is most internationally known. Although stylistic and other debts do show in his poetry, his voice is uniquely his own. Popa's first collection, *Kora*, hints at some grafting from surrealism, expressionism, and symbolism, but he never seems imitative because he has developed a highly personalized poetical idiom rooted in the poetical traditions of the Balkans and their folklore. As a Yugoslav critic said, he was "the first post-war modernist who began to explore the symbols of national culture and history in an original way."

Already in his first collection some of the lasting features of his poetry have emerged. The poems are arranged in thematically coherent cycles made of a few poems which are composed of a limited number of concise, elliptical free-verses without any punctuation and with frequent repetitions. Most of the poems consist of images organized around concepts or objects observed from Popa's highly original and unusually daring point of view, forcing the reader to approach the common things of everyday life in a way he has never seen them before. The result is an innocent astonishment which joins a freshness of original approach with the realization that the common is being put into a more complex and controlled use which, however, is not too difficult to "decipher" because of Popa's firm grip of the real and the rational. "I am not dreaming," he says. By the use of black humour, grotesque paradox, and wit Popa portrays a world where an extensive sense of unrest, alarm, torment, and menace prevails and where a man's only defence is his humanity.

His fellow poet Miodrag Pavlović described Popa's poetry as a merger of "lexical abundance and syntactical strictness." In his idiom live side by side the linguistic traditions of medieval and folk literature and the colloquial, urban language of contemporary communication. On the other hand, his language is trimmed of almost all rhetorical decorations, laconic, succinct, verging on the epigrammatic and the aphoristic.

Just as the objects, animals, and plants from his first book were suggestive of some facets of the general condition of man, so did the poems from his second book, *Nepočin-polje*, describing everyday children's games, help Popa to transpose the same or similar situations into a series of mutually related dramas of existence taking place on the "unrest-field" of the real world (using here an expression from a folk riddle as a kind of global metaphor). The cycles "Games," "Give Me Back My Rags," and "One Bone to Another" uncover the complex and contradictory possibilities of life compressed within them, and disclose the adult existential traumas lying beneath the humorous, folkloristic surface of juvenile playfulness.

Sporedno nebo, a collection consisting of seven sections, each comprising seven poems, is full of new energy directed towards an exploration of symbols. Motifs from ancient myths, fairy tales, folk epics, alchemy, and esoteric medieval doctrines combine to portray a drama of cosmic misunderstandings and paradoxes, of "primary and final questions," where human beings play only an unsignificant part.

In *Earth Erect* Popa turns to the most dramatic periods of the Serbian past looking for symbols relevant for the collective destiny of his country in the present and the future. He finds them in the medieval monasteries and their founding fathers, in legends, myths, and historical truths based on Serbian triumphs and disasters. In the most natural way the idiom of these poems acquires some of the qualities of the language of the traditional folk epic and of the liturgy of the Serbian Orthodox Church.

Vučja so reiterates some of the themes from the previous book through his interest in various superstitions and legends surrounding the image of the wolf in Serbian folklore. The image of the wolf still lingers in some of the poems of *Živo meso*, but in this collection the emphasis is shifted to the poet himself. Popa's earlier poetry was shorn of all private, personal references; however, the larger part of *Živo meso* is inspired by his memories of his native town of Vršac. His childhood and his early youth are revived in a series of nostalgic, bitter-sweet flash-backs. This new poetry is brief, lyrical, touching on love, family relations, occasionally social and historical comments. Popa has continued to introduce an increasing number of new themes in his latest collection, *Rez*. The book is an untypical mixture of urban occasional verse, socially and politically committed poems, and versified responses to natural disasters, travels, and encounters all over the world. Most critics have found these two collections highly disappointing and have complained that Popa's later poems, neither in their themes nor in their language, regain the concentration, intensity, and significance of his earlier verse. Nevertheless, in spite of all their shortcomings, they indicate Popa's praiseworthy desire for change.

—Dušan Puvačić

PRATOLINI, Vasco. Italian. Born in Florence, 19 October 1913. Printer's apprentice and street vendor in Florence; in tuberculosis sanatorium, 1935-37; founded *Campo di Marte* magazine, 1939 (closed by Fascist government); film and art critic, 1943-45; screenwriter and journalist, 1946-50. Recipient: *Libera Stampa* Prize, 1947; Foreign Book Prize (France), 1950; Viareggio Prize, 1955; Feltrinelli Prize, 1957; Veillon Prize, 1961; Marzotto Prize, 1963. Address: Via Tolmino 12, Rome, Italy.

PUBLICATIONS

Fiction

Il tappeto verde. Florence, Vallecchi, 1941.
Via de' Magazzini. Florence, Vallecchi, 1942.
Le amiche. Florence, Vallecchi, 1943.
Il quartiere. Rome, La Nuova Biblioteca, 1944; as *The Naked Streets*, New York, Wyn, 1952; as *A Tale of Santa Croce*, London, Owen, 1952.
Cronaca familiare. Florence, Vallecchi, 1947; as *Two Brothers*, New York, Orion Press, 1962.
Mestiere da vagabondo. Milan, Mondadori, 1947.
Cronache di povere amanti. Florence, Vallecchi, 1947; as *A Tale of Poor Lovers*, New York, Viking Press, and London, Hamish Hamilton, 1949.
Un eroe del nostro tempo. Milan, Bompiani, 1949; as *A Hero of Our Time*, New York, Prentice Hall, 1951; as *A Hero of Today*, London, Hamish Hamilton, 1951.
Le ragazze di Sanfrediano. Florence, Vallecchi, 1953.
Il mio cuore a Ponte Milvio: Vecchie carte. Rome, Cultura Sociale, 1954.
Una storia italiana
   Metello. Florence, Vallecchi, 1955; translated as *Metello*, Boston, Little Brown, and London, Chatto and Windus, 1968.
   Lo scialo. Milan, Mondadori, 1960; revised edition, 1976.
   Allegoria e derisione. Milan, Mondadori, 1966.
Diario sentimentale. Florence, Vallecchi, 1956.
La costanza della ragione. Milan, Mondadori, 1963; as *Bruno Santini*, Boston, Little Brown, and London, Chatto and Windus, 1965.

Plays

La domenica della buona gente (radio play), with Giandomenica Giagni, in *Sipario 76*, 1952.
Lungo viaggio di Natale, from his own story, in *Teatro d'Oggi 11-12*, 1954.

Verse

La città ha i miei trent'anni. Milan, Scheiwiller, 1967.
Calendario del '67. Salerno, Il Catalogo, 1978.

Other

Gli uomini che si voltano: Diario di Villa Rosa. Rome, Atlante, 1952.
Il mannello di Natascia. Salerno, Il Catalogo, 1980.

Editor, *L'Eredità*, by Mario Pratesi. Milan, Bompiani, 1965.

*

Critical Studies: *Pratolini* by Alberto Asor Rosa, Rome, Edizioni Moderne, 1958; *Pratolini* by Fulvio Longobardi, Milan, Mursia, 1964; *Pratolini: The Development of a Social Novelist* by Frank Rosengarten, Carbondale, Southern Illinois University Press, 1965; *Pratolini* by Francesco Paolo Memmo, Florence, La Nuova Italia, 1977.

*　　*　　*

During the 1930's and early 1940's, Vasco Pratolini wrote a series of short stories and novelettes based largely on memories of childhood and adolescence, and characterized by constant wavering between fragmentary lyricism and objective narrative. The delicate vignettes of *Il tappeto verde* exemplify the former tendency, while the short story "Una giornata memorabile" and the autobiographical novel *Via de' Magazzini* give clear indication of a capacity to depict character against the background of a specific social milieu, that of working-class districts in his native Florence.

With the publication of *The Naked Streets* in 1944 and especially of *A Tale of Poor Lovers* in 1947, Pratolini moved resolutely to the forefront of Italy's postwar revival of realistic fiction. His conception of realism was influenced by French and Russian antecedents, yet he achieved a distinctive and original style of his own. *A Tale of Poor Lovers* is a complex, Ariostesque description of Florentine society during the mid-1920's. The interaction of the private and the public, of the intimate and the political aspects of life as experienced by people belonging to the lower-middle and working classes, is presented in such a way as to give the reader an understanding of the fascist epoch from diverse points of view. Pratolini's tale or "chronicle," as it was called in Italian, also contains several excursuses on Florentine history and customs which enliven and enrich the novel.

Pratolini's major project during the 1950's and 1960's was a trilogy of historical novels bearing the general title *Una storia italiana*. Although conceived and written as autonomous works, the three volumes comprising the trilogy—*Metello*, *Lo scialo*, and *Allegoria e derisione*—form part of an organic narrative enterprise whose principal aim is to highlight, through the depiction of "typical" characters, the dominant trends and tendencies of Italian society from 1875 to 1945. The protagonists of the three volumes are intended to represent the attitudes, the mentality, the virtues and defects of entire social strata. Pratolini's point of view is not impartial, since his conception of Italian history has been shaped by his communist beliefs and in particular by the historical and political writings of the Italian Marxist thinker Antonio Gramsci. But Pratolini's highly cultivated sense of literary artistry and his interest in the emotional as well as social and political sources of human behavior save him from simplistic reductionism and dogmatism. He aspires in this trilogy, and succeeds in good measure, to offer an imaginative recreation of Italian history by using a wide variety of techniques, from journalistic documentation reminiscent of Dreiser and Dos Passos to symbolic imagery and psychoanalytic probing characteristic of literary modernism.

During the 1970's, Pratolini published small collections of already published writings. But he is currently at work on a new novel, provisionally entitled *Malattia infantile*. Despite diminished productivity as a novelist, he has continued to be active as an essayist, screen writer, art critic, and journalist.

—Frank Rosengarten

PRISCO, Michele. Italian. Born in Torre Annunziata, 18 January 1920. Educated at the University of Naples, degree in law 1942. Served in Scuola Allievi Ufficiali di Complemento,

1942-43. Married Sarah Buonomo in 1951; two daughters. Free-lance writer: founding director, *Le Ragioni Narrative*, Naples, 1961-62; Vice President, National Union of Writers, from 1959. Recipient: Naples Prize, 1962; Strega Prize, 1966. Address: c/o Rizzoli, Via Rizzoli 2, 20132 Milan, Italy.

PUBLICATIONS

Fiction

La provincia addormentata, Milan, Mondadori, 1949, revised edition, Milan, Rizzoli, 1969.
Gli eredi del vento. Milan, Rizzoli, 1950; as *Heirs to the Wind*, London, Verschoyle, 1953.
Figli difficili. Milan, Rizzoli, 1954.
Fuochi a mare. Milan, Rizzoli, 1957.
La dama di piazza. Milan, Rizzoli, 1961.
Punto franco. Milan, Rizzoli, 1965.
Una spirale di nebbia. Milan, Rizzoli, 1966; as *A Spiral of Mist*, New York, Dutton, and London, Chatto and Windus, 1969.
I cieli della sera. Milan, Rizzoli, 1970.
Inventario della memoria. Milan, Rizzoli, 1970.
Gli ermellini neri. Milan, Rizzoli, 1975.
Il colore del cristallo. Milan, Rizzoli, 1977.
Le parole del silenzio. Milan, Rizzoli, 1981.

*

Critical Studies: *Invito alla lettura di Prisco* by Pompeo Giannantonio, Milan, Mursia, 1977; *Prisco* by Giuseppe Amoroso, Florence, La Nuova Italia, 1980.

*   *   *

In spite of the privileged status enjoyed by experimentation in postwar Italian narrative, Michele Prisco has remained faithful to a mimetic concept of writing in the tradition of the 19th-century novel. Eschewing the modes of structural innovation identified with the avant-garde, Prisco has won recognition as the author of finely wrought symmetrical narratives marked by solid characterization and psychological depth. Lending further substance to his work is the fact that much of it is set in his native environment, Naples and the small towns in the outlying province.

Prisco began his career with *La provincia addormentata*, a collection of short stories in which are prefigured *in nuce* the basic coordinates of his early narrative: the microcosm of provincial life typified by a middle class holding to its rancid conformism as it struggles with the primeval forces of hatred, violence, and hidden remorse; the family as a value-shaping locus threatened by conflicts and dissension; the attention to social interactions which, more often than not, are based on vested interests, hypocrisy, and mistrust. From this thematic core spring such works as *Heirs to the Wind* where the biblical passage, "He that troubleth his own house shall inherit the wind," is exemplified by the downfall of a prosperous family, a downfall caused by the egotism of five sisters effectively exploited by a greedy and unscrupulous outsider through the expedient of marriage. In *la dama di piazza* Prisco broadens somewhat his narrative scope, offering, together with the customary plot structure and skillful character treatment, a valuable account of socio-political life in Naples in the 1930's.

I cieli della sera betrays a fresh orientation in Prisco's work, evidenced by a dominant concern with abnormal and evil-prone manifestations of human nature. In a narrative vein of intense introspective analysis that brings to mind Dostoevsky and Bernanos, the author penetrates the darkest spheres of the mind, shedding light, and in the process posing cogent moral questions, on the forces of evil that assert themselves in unsuspecting individuals. In *I cieli della sera* the narrator sets out to investigate the mysterious death of his parents and, in doing so, seeks to understand, to use Prisco's words, "the expressions of evil in the world and the reasons for its uncontrolled, widespread presence." *Gli ermellini neri*, perhaps Prisco's best novel, is a compelling study in psychological subjugation masterminded with satanic zeal by a young man intent, in his exalted narcissism, on erasing the dichotomy between good and evil, morality and perversion. In Prisco's latest work, *Le parole del silenzio*, a man's tragic death in an automobile accident serves as the focus of a narrative effort which, eschewing explicitness, relies on muted tones and the reverberations of past memories to reconstitute the strands of a moving and revealing experience.

Far from representing an involution in the light of contemporary Italian fiction, Prisco's work offers exemplary evidence that the traditional novel can withstand the test of time, indeed can renew itself through the resourcefulness of writers like Prisco whose receptivity to technical innovation is superseded by a deeper concern with moral and philosophical questions of lasting value.

—Augustus Pallotta

QIAN ZHONGSHU. *See* CH'IEN CHUNG-SHU.

RASPUTIN, Valentin (Grigorevich). Russian. Born in Ust-Uda, Irkutsk Oblast, 15 March 1937. Educated at Irkutsk University, graduated in literature and history, 1959. Journalist, then full-time writer. Lives in Irkutsk.

Publications

Fiction

Kray vozle samovo neba [The Land at the Edge of Heaven Itself]. Irkutsk, Vostochno-Sibirskoe Knizhnoe Izdatel'stvo, 1966.
Den'gi dlya Marii [Money for Maria]. Moscow, Molodaya Gvardia, 1968.
Povesti [Stories]. Moscow, Molodaya Gvardia, 1976.
Zhivi i pomni. Moscow, Sovremennik, 1975; as *Live and Remember*, New York, Mac-

millan, 1978.
Posledny srok [Borrowed Time]. Moscow, Molodaya Gvardia, 1976.
Farewell to Matyora. New York, Macmillan, 1979.
Money for Maria, and Borrowed Time: Two Village Tales. St. Lucia, University of
Queensland Press, 1981; London, Quartet, 1983.

*

Critical Studies: "For Truth and Goodness: The Stories of Rasputin" by Vladimir Vasil'ev, in
Soviet Studies in Literature 14, 1978; "To Live and to Remember: Comments on Rasputin's
Prose" by E. Starikova, in *Soviet Studies in Literature 14*, 1978, *Beyond Socialist Realism:
Soviet Fiction since "Ivan Denisovich"* by Geoffrey Hosking, New York, Holmes and Meier,
1980; "Matera—Farewells and Encounters" by Boris Pankin, in *Soviet Studies in Literature
18*, 1981.

*　　*　　*

Valentin Rasputin has emerged as one of the leading figures in the so-called "village prose"
movement, which arose in the late 1950's and by the following decade had come to include
much of the best contemporary writing in the Soviet Union. Rasputin's first stories, from the
early and mid-1960's, originally appeared in local Siberian publications, but his work quickly
attracted national interest; since 1970 his writings have appeared regularly in the Moscow
journal *Our Contemporary* (*Nash Sovremennik*), which has maintained a strong commitment
to the village writers. As is the case with the other authors to whom this label has been applied
(such as Abramov, Belov, Nosov, Shukshin, Zalygin, and at times Solzhenitsyn), Rasputin
belongs to the movement not just because his own origins and the settings for his stories happen
to be outside the main urban centers but also because a particular set of themes recurs
throughout his work. Either explicitly or implicitly, Rasputin constantly compares life in the
village with that in the city, to the usual detriment of the latter, and shows those in the country
victimized by the complexities and demands of modern society. Thus in his first major work,
the novella *Money for Maria*, the central figure is a semi-literate peasant woman, in charge of a
village store, who somehow must come up with a thousand rubles that an inspector has found
to be missing or face jail. If the story begins with this contrast between implacable authority and
the simple honesty of Maria, it goes on to draw equally sharp distinctions between peasants and
city dwellers in its later scenes. There appears to be no bridge between the two worlds, and,
typically for Rasputin, the question of whether or not the needed money will be obtained is left
open.

That village life is changing irrevocably becomes clear in *Borrowed Time*, where a dying
peasant woman comes to realize that the countryside has changed greatly during her lifetime
and that the four children who come to visit her (two from the city and two who have remained
in the country) no longer share her values—and indeed the four end up leaving before she dies.
A sign of Rasputin's growng maturity as a writer was his ability to present the divergent
personalities and the web of relationships among the five central characters at the same time
that he offered a psychological study of how imminent death affects not just the dying but also
others in a family. The depth of Rasputin's concern for village life is revealed in *Farewell to
Matyora*, which depicts the period just before a small island village is to be flooded as part of a
huge hydro-electric project. The story is permeated with nostalgia, not just for an older way of
life, but also for an older set of values, when people lived more in accordance with their
conscience. Both the modern bureaucrats and the new settlement of apartments to which the
villagers are to be moved are depicted as cold and lacking the spirit of the peasants and their
beloved village. By questioning the cost of progress Rasputin has brought himself into conflict
with part of the Soviet critical establishment, which has never been totally at ease with the
concerns raised by the village prose writers.

In some ways Rasputin's current reputation seems surprising. He has never been a prolific
writer, especially by Soviet standards. Residing in Irkutsk, he is far from the centers of Russian

literary activity. And the locales of his stories, which are most often set near the banks of the Angara river flowing northward from Irkutsk, are hardly likely to be familiar to the majority of his readers. Yet his themes have struck a nerve in the popular imagination, and he has also come to display considerable literary skills. Nowhere is that talent more in evidence than in his novella *Live and Remember*. In it a Siberian soldier, wounded during the waning days of World War II, decides after his recovery to return to his native village instead of to the front. But the work is less about him than his wife, who aids him in his hiding, eventually becomes pregnant, and, tortured by the suspicions of her fellow villagers, finally commits suicide. Rasputin's ability to capture the nuances of Siberian peasant speech, the subtlety with which he renders a psychological portrayal of his protagonists, the sympathy and depth he lends to his depiction of the wife (here as in most of his important works the central and most sympathetic character is a woman), the mastery with which he weaves a complex yet gripping narrative that includes shifting points of view as well as the use of flashbacks and dreams—all these are the mark of a fine literary craftsman.

—Barry P. Scherr

REVE, Gerard (Kornelis van het). Dutch. Born in Amsterdam, 14 December 1923. Educated at Vossius Gymnasium, Amsterdam; school for graphic design. Reporter, *Het Parool*, Amsterdam, 1945-47; lived in London, studying drama and working as a mental nurse, 1952-57; since 1957, Editor, *Tirade* magazine; has lived in France since 1969. Recipient: Hooft Prize, 1968. Address: La Grâce, Le Poët-Laval, 26160 La Bégude de Mazenc, France.

PUBLICATIONS

Fiction

De avonden: Een winterverhaal [The Evenings: A Winter's Tale]. Amsterdam, Bezige Bij, 1947.
Werther Nieland. Amsterdam, Bezige Bij, 1949.
De ondergang van de familie Boslowits [The Downfall of the Boslowits Family]. Amsterdam, Bezige Bij, 1950.
The Acrobat and Other Stories (written in English). Amsterdam and London, Van Oorschot, 1956; as *Vier wintervertellingen* [Four Winter Tales], Amsterdam, Van Oorschot, 1963.
Tien vrolijke verhalen [Ten Cheerful Stories]. Amsterdam, Van Oorschot, 1961.
Op weg naar het einde [Approaching the End]. Amsterdam, Van Oorschot, 1963.
Nader tot U [Nearer to You]. Amsterdam, Van Oorschot, 1966.
A Prison Song in Prose (written in English). Amsterdam, Athenaeum-Polak & Van Gennep, 1968.
De taal der liefde [The Language of Love]. Amsterdam, Athenaeum-Polak & Van Gennep, 1972.
Onze vrienden [Our Friends]. Amsterdam, Athenaeum-Polak & Van Gennep, 1972.

285

Lieve jongens [Dear Boys]. Amsterdam, Athenaeum-Polak & Van Gennep, 1973.
Lekker kerstbrood [Lovely Christmas Cake]. Amstelveen, Peter Loeb, 1973.
Rietsuiker [Cane Sugar]. Amstelveen, Peter Loeb, 1974.
Het lieve leven [Dear Life]. Amsterdam, Athenaeum-Polak & Van Gennep, 1974.
Ik had hem lief [I Loved Him]. Amsterdam, Elsevier, 1975.
Een circusjongen [A Circus Boy]. Amsterdam, Athenaeum-Polak & Van Gennep, 1975.
Oud en eenzaam [Old and Alone]. Amsterdam, Elsevier, 1978.
Moeder en zoon [Mother and Son]. Amsterdam, Elsevier Manteau, 1980.
De vierde man [The Fourth Man]. Amsterdam, Elsevier Manteau, 1981.
Wolf. Amsterdam, Elsevier Manteau, 1983.

Play

Commissaris Fennedy. Amsterdam, Bezige Bij, 1962.

Verse

Zes gedichten [Six Poems]. Amsterdam, Polak & Van Gennep, 1965.
Gezicht op Kerstmis, en andere geestelijke liederen [Prospect of Christmas, and Other Spiritual Poems]. Amsterdam, Fritz Boer, 1965.
Credo. Zandvoort, Eliance Pers, 1973.
Trouw. Zandvoort, Eliance Pers, 1973.
Het zingend hart [The Singing Heart]. Amsterdam, Athenaeum-Polak & Van Gennep, 1973.
Elf gedichten [Eleven Poems]. Amsterdam, The Publishers, 1973.
Cubaans bidprentje. Amsterdam, Loeb & Van der Velden, 1978.
Vergeten gedichten [Forgotten Poems]. Amsterdam, Bibliotheca Reviana, 1979.
(Selection in English), in *DutchCrossing 12*, December 1980.

Other

Verzameld werk [Collected Work]. Amsterdam, Van Oorschot, 1956.
Veertien etsen van Frans Lodewijk Pannekoek [Fourteen Etchings by Frans Lodewijk Pannekoek]. Amsterdam, Rap, 1967.
Uit de kunst: Brieven aan Simon Carmiggelt [A Work of Art: Letters to Simon Carmiggelt]. Zandvoort, Eliance Pers, 1970.
Vier pleidooien [Four Pleas]. Amsterdam, Athenaeum-Polak & Van Gennep, 1971.
Drie toespraken [Three Public Addresses]. Amsterdam, Peter Loeb, 1976.
Brieven aan kandidaat katholiek A 1962-1969 [Letters to Prospective Catholic A]. Amsterdam, Rap, 1976.
Een eigen huis [A House of One's Own]. Amsterdam, Elsevier Manteau, 1979.
Brieven aan Wimie 1959-1963 [Letters to Wimie]. Utrecht, Veen, 1980.
Brieven aan Josine M 1959-1975 [Letters to Josine M]. Amsterdam, Van Oorschot, 1981.
Brieven aan Bernard S 1965-1975 [Letters to Bernard S], edited by Sjaak Hubregtse. Utrecht, Veen, 1981.
Archief Reve 1931-1980, edited by Pierre H. Dubois, annotated by Sjaak Hubregtse. Baarn, Prom, 2 vols., 1981-82.
Brieven aan Simon C 1971-1976 [Letters to Simon C]. Amsterdam, Van Oorschot, 1982.
Album Reve, edited by Joost Schafthuizen. Amsterdam, Elsevier, 1983.

*

Bibliography: *Bibliografie van Reve* by Gerrit Heuvelman and Peter Willems, privately printed, 1980.

Critical Studies: *Reve* by Mia Meijer and Klaus Beekman, Bruges, Orion, 1973, revised edition, 1978; *Over "De avonden" van Reve* by E. Kummer, Amsterdam, Wetenschappelijke, 1976; *Tussen chaos en orde: Essays over het werk van Reve* edited by Sjaak Hubregtse, Amsterdam, Peter Loeb, 1981.

*   *   *

Gerard Reve is widely regarded as the supreme stylist among living Dutch prose-writers, though his literary career since the 1960's has made him, artistically, morally, and politically, a controversial figure.

His early, naturalistic, work derives its impact from an understated, deadpan formality of tone, used to telling effect in his first novel, *De avonden*, which became a classic of the war generation and has enjoyed enduring popularity since. The book, whose "hero," a school dropout in his early twenties still living at home, spends an aimless ten days between Christmas and New Year conversing but not communicating with family and friends, reflecting on his lot, and finally appealing *de profundis* to a God he may or may not believe in, is punctuated by a series of nightmares in which his repressed anxieties surface. Equally impressive is the novella *Werther Nieland*, a study of boyhood obsession and ritual.

A period spent in England (where his contacts included Angus Wilson), produced a collection of eerie stories in English, *The Acrobat*, and an involvement with English theatre as student, critic, and translator (of, among others, Pinter, Albee, and Brendan Behan). His own activity as a playwright was short-lived: only one play, reminiscent of Tennessee Williams, was performed, while a second, called *Moorlandshuis*, though commissioned and awarded a literary prize, was never published.

Two widely acclaimed books of "open letters," *Op weg naar het einde* and *Nader tot u* (the latter containing a number of striking poems), mark a major turning-point. Freed from the constraints of a traditional plot, Reve blurs the boundaries of fiction and autobiography (the explicit treatment of his own homosexuality broke an important taboo in the post-war Netherlands), in a style switching constantly from the solemnly exalted and archaic to the grossly colloquial, often to riotous effect. In *Nader tot u*, under the influence of Mario Praz's work, he finds his mission as a Romantic Decadent dedicated to celebrating the sacred trinity of Love, Sex, and Death (such capitalising of key concepts is to become a hallmark) in the context of a very individual brand of Roman Catholicism, to which he was converted in 1966. The much-publicised conversion, exploited with the flair of a natural showman, helped make him a national figure with a mass readership, as well as incurring the disapproval of some of the literary establishment and a conviction for blasphemy, against which he appealed eloquently and successfully.

The cult of "Revism" (a play on the shortened form of his name and its associations with *rêve*), using frame narrative to weave a bizarre tapestry of fact and fantasy, was carried further in *De taal der liefde*, in which a queen figure strongly suggestive of the actual Dutch monarch acts as confidante and muse, and in its sequel *Lieve jongens*, which was subsequently filmed. *Een circusjongen* made virtuoso use of kitsch elements, but in lesser books his writing tended to become overly mannered and repetitive.

Reve made a comeback in a more sober vein with *Oud en eenzaam*, in which he ingeniously combines an account of a homosexual pursuit in present-day France with a flashback to a heterosexual episode in the London of the 1950's, and confirmed it two years later in *Moerder en zoon*, which traces his religious development, culminating, in a sublimely comic passage, in his improbable acceptance into the Catholic Church.

For Reve, the self-professed Romantic, the outer world is ultimately mere decor, and as such to be treated with appropriate scepticism. His conservative political stance, as expressed both in his work and in a notorious recent newspaper interview, have led to widespread public outrage and to charges of fascism and racialism. His pronouncements in this field may be seen as reactions partly to a childhood spent in a fanatically Communist family and partly to the rhetoric of progressive conformism which attended the post-1960's wave of "democratisation" in the Netherlands. Admirers would claim that the element of irony and self-parody is as difficult to gauge as it is with a writer like Jorge Luis Borges.

Certainly, Reve continues to have as many adherents as detractors, witness the growth in recent years of a veritable "Reve industry" of secondary literature, archive material and letters, a monument during the author's own lifetime to thirty years' diverse and often distinguished literary achievement.

—Paul Vincent

RIFBJERG, Klaus. Danish. Born in Copenhagen, 15 December 1931. Educated at Princeton University, New Jersey, 1950-51; University of Copenhagen, 1951-55. Married Inge Gerner Andersen in 1955; one son and two daughters. Film director, 1955-57; critic and columnist, *Information* newspaper, 1955, and *Politiken*, 1957-59, both in Copenhagen; Editor, with Villy Sorensen, *Vindrosen*, 1959-63. Recipient: Aarestup Medal, 1964; Danish Critics Award, 1965; Danish Academy Prize, 1966; Nordic Council Prize, 1970. Address: c/o Gyldendalske Boghandel, Klareboderne 3, 1148 Copenhagen, Denmark.

PUBLICATIONS

Verse

Under vejr med mig selv [Getting Wind of Myself].   Copenhagen, Schønberg, 1956.
Efterkrig [Postwar].   Copenhagen, Schønberg, 1957.
Konfrontation   Copenhagen, Schønberg, 1960.
Camouflage.   Copenhagen, Gyldendal, 1961.
Voliere.   Copenhagen, Gyldendal, 1962.
Portraet.   Copenhagen, Gyldendal, 1963.
Amagerdigte [Poems from Amager].   Copenhagen, Gyldendal, 1965.
Drømmen om København of andre digte fra byen.   Copenhagen, Gyldendal, 1967.
Faedrelandssange.   Copenhagen, Gyldendal, 1967.
(Selection), photographs by Flemming Arnholm.   Copenhagen, Rhodos, 1969.
I skyttens tegn: Digte i udvalg 1956-67.   Copenhagen, Gyldendal, 1970.
Mytologier [Mythologies].   Copenhagen, Gyldendal, 1970.
Scener fra det daglige liv [Scenes from Daily Life].   Copenhagen, Gyldendal, 1973.
25 desperate digte [25 Desperate Poems].   Copenhagen, Gyldendal, 1974.
En hugorm i solen.   Copenhagen, Gyldendal, 1974.
Selected Poems, translated by Nadia Christensen and Alexander Taylor.   Willimantic, Connecticut, Curbstone Press, 1975.
Den søndag.   Copenhagen, Brøndum, 1975.

Stranden [The Beach]. Copenhagen, Sommersko, 1976.
Livsfrisen [The Frieze of Life]. Copenhagen, Gyldendal, 1979.
Spansk motiv [Spanish Motif]. Copenhagen, Gyldendal, 1980.
Landet Atlantis [The Land of Atlantis]. Copenhagen, Gyldendal, 1981.

Plays

Weekend (Filmmanuskript). Copenhagen, Danske Filmmuseum, 1962.
Hvá skal vi lave?, with Jesper Jensen. Copenhagen, Gyldendal, 1963.
Diskret ophold, with Jesper Jensen. Copenhagen, Gyldendal, 1965.
Udviklinger: Et skuespil for fire jazz-musikere, fire skueskillere, og lille teater (produced Stockholm,1965). Copenhagen, Gyldendal, 1965; as *Developments: A Play for Four Jazz Musicians, Four Actors, and a Little Theater*, in *Modern Nordic Plays*, Oslo, Universitetsforlaget, 1974.
Hvad en mand har brug for. Copenhagen, Gyldendal, 1966.
Der var engang en krig: En film, with Palle Kjaerulff-Schmidt. Copenhagen, Gyldendal, 1966.
Voks. Copenhagen, Gyldendal, 1968.
År. Copenhagen, Gyldendal, 1970.
Narrene [Fools]. Copenhagen, Gyldendal, 1971.
Svaret blaeser i vinden. Copenhagen, Gyldendal, 1971.
Privatlivets fred: Et filmmanuskript. Copenhagen, Gyldendal, 1974.

Fiction

Den kroniske uskyld [Chronic Innocence]. Copenhagen, Schønberg, 1958.
Og andre historier [And Other Stories]. Copenhagen, Gyldendal, 1964.
Operaelskeren [The Opera Lover]. Copenhagen, Gyldendal, 1966.
Arkivet [The Archives]. Copenhagen, Gyldendal, 1967.
Lonni og Karl [Lonni and Karl]. Copenhagen, Gyldendal, 1968.
Anna (jeg) Anna. Copenhagen, Gyldendal, 1969; as *Anna (I) Anna*, Willimantic, Connecticut, Curbstone Press, 1982.
Rejsende. Copenhagen, Gyldendal, 1969.
Marts 1970 [March]. Copenhagen, Gyldendal, 1970.
Brevet til Gerda [The Letter to Gerda]. Copenhagen, Gyldendal, 1972.
R.R. Copenhagen, Gyldendal, 1972.
Den syende jomfru og andre noveller [The Sewing Virgin and Other Stories]. Copenhagen, Gyldendal, 1972.
Dilettanterne [The Dilettantes]. Copenhagen, Gyldendal, 1973.
Sommer [Summer]. Copenhagen, Gyldendal, 1974.
En hugorm i Solen [A Viper in the Sun]. Copenhagen, Gyldendal, 1974.
Vejen ad hvilken [The Road along Which]. Copenhagen, Gyldendal, 1975.
Det korte af det lange [In Short]. Copenhagen, Gyldendal, 1976.
Twist. Copenhagen, Gyldendal, 1976.
Kiks [Miss]. Copenhagen, Gyldendal, 1976.
De beskedne: En familiekrønike [The Modest: A Family Chronicle]. Copenhagen, Gyldendal, 4 vols., 1976.
Et bortvendt ansigt. Copenhagen, Gyldendal, 1977.
Drengene. Copenhagen, Gyldendal, 1977.
Tango. Copenhagen, Gyldendal, 1978.
Joker. Copenhagen, Gyldendal, 1979.
De hellige aber [The Sacred Monkeys]. Copenhagen, Gyldendal, 1981.

Other

Rifbjerg: KR-journalistik, edited by Hanne Marie Svendsen. Copenhagen, Gyldendal, 1967.
I medgang of modgang, illustrated by Lilli Friis. Copenhagen, Gyldendal, 1970.
Leif den Lykkelige jun. Copenhagen, Gyldendal, 1971.
Lena Jørgensen, Klintevej 4, 2650 Hvidovre. Copenhagen, Gyldendal, 1971.
Dengang det var før: Syn kronikker. Copenhagen, Gyldendal, 1971.
Til Spanien [To Spain]. Copenhagen, Gyldendal, 1971.
Rifbjergs lytterroman, edited by Ole Larsen and others. Copenhagen, Gyldendal, 1972.
Tak for turen. Copenhagen, Gyldendal, 1975.
Deres Majestaet! Åbent brev til Dronning Margrethe II af Danmark. Copenhagen, Corsaren, 1977.
Dobbeltgaenger; eller, Den Korte, inderlige men fuldstaendig sande beretning om Klaus Rifbjergs liv. Copenhagen, Gyldendal, 1978.
Det sorte hul. Copenhagen, Gyldendal, 1980.
Vores år. Copenhagen, Gyldendal, 2 vols., 1980.

Editor, *Boi—ii-ng '64!* Copenhagen, Gyldendal, 1964.
Editor, *Min yndlingslaesning.* Copenhagen, Vendelkaer, 1965.
Editor, with Jørgen Gustava Brandt and Uffe Harder, *Anthologie de la poésie danoise contemporaine.* Paris, Gallimard, 1975.

*

Critical Studies: *Rifbjerg* by Torben Brostrøm, Copenhagen, Gyldendal, 1970; "Rifbjerg" by Charlotte Schiander Gray, in *Books Abroad*, Winter, 1975.

* * *

To many Danes Klaus Rifbjerg embodies the "Modern" literary movement. Although he is active and confident in all genres, it is his poetry that most clearly reveals his fundamental concerns and his original contribution to Danish post-war literature; his ability to forge a new poetic language, capable of expressing the experience of life in a modern, secular, materialistic world, and his exploration of his personal experience in such a way that universal significance is not lost sight of. *Konfrontation* (1960) marked the breakthrough not only of Rifbjerg himself as a major poet but also of the new, international Modernist movement in Denmark. In a direct, almost physical language his poetry confronts the reality of a world "empty, empty, empty—blissfully empty...of all but objects" ("Frihavnen"—Free Port). In *Camouflage* and *Portraet* he further explored the associative and creative force of language to the point where he seemed to break the limits of what language could contain, and *Amagerdigte*, 1965, signalled a new approach. Dealing—like *Camouflage*—with personal experience, its more straightforward style invites the reader to share the poet's recollections of childhood rather than experiencing their poetic expression. As later collections make clear—e.g., *Mytologier* and *Livsfrisen*—this change implied no rejection of experiment. Rather, it showed his ability to develop his medium and respond to the mood of his time.

Although he has written drama—his first original work was *Udviklinger* a Pirandellian play on illusion and identity—the novel has increasingly become Rifbjerg's preferred medium. His first novel, *Den kroniske uskyld*, is typical of his prose work in that its formative artistic impulse derives from a central theme: the formative processes and points of crisis in life, the—often tortuous—development of individual identity. His awareness of the deceptive nature of surface realism and of his own position as a creator of fiction is evident in his first collection of short stories, *Og andre historier* where his playing with points-of-view and varying degrees of identification with characters successfully expresses the complexity of human experience. Rifbjerg's mastery of language ensures that in the best of his prose and poetry language is no mere vehicle through which to express experience: it *becomes* that experience itself.

Gradually, Rifbjerg has moved away from the subjective view of childhood and youth to a more objective treatment of the whole of life. A late novel, *De hellige aber*, shows that when he deals with the experience of childhood, the original search for meaning in his own life has become a search for human values in an increasingly de-humanized world. Although clearly a "political" novel, written in the style of surface realism, its foundation in fantasy saves it from abstract dogmaticism. There is more to art than the expression of opinion, and even where humanity is threatened with total destruction this writer can glimpse a faint ray of hope.

—Hans Christian Andersen

RITSOS, Yannis. Greek. Born in Monemvasia, 1 May 1909. Married Fallitasa Georgiades in 1954; one child. Law clerk, Angepoulos law firm, Athens, 1925; clerk, Mitsopoulos-Oeconomopoulos, notaries, Athens, 1925-26; assistant librarian, Lawyers Association, Athens, 1926; in a tuberculosis sanatorium, 1927-31; worked for a music theatre in the 1930's; member of the Chorus of Ancient Tragedies, National Theatre of Greece, 1938-45, and actor and dancer for Athens Opera House; editor and proofreader, Govostis, publishers, Athens, 1945-48, 1952-56. Since 1956, full-time writer. Recipient: Greek State Prize, 1956; International Grand Prize for Poetry, 1972; Dimitroff International Prize (Bulgaria), 1974; de Vigny Prize (France), 1975; Etna-Taormina Prize, 1976; Seregno-Brianza International Prize, 1976; Lenin Prize, 1977; Mondello Prize (Italy), 1978. Honorary doctorate: Salonica University, 1975; University of Birmingham, 1978. Address: 39 M. Koraka Street, Athens 219, Greece.

PUBLICATIONS

Verse

Trakter [Tractors]. Athens, Govostis, 1934.
Pyramides [Pyramids]. Athens, Govostis, 1935.
Epitafios. Athens, Rizospastis, 1936.
To tragoudi tes adelfis mou [The Song of My Sister]. Athens, Govostis, 1937.
Earini Symfonia [Spring Symphony]. Athens, Govostis, 1938.
To emvatirio tou okeanou [The March of the Ocean]. Athens, Govostis, 1940.
Palia Mazurka se rythmo vrohis [An Old Mazurka in the Rhythm of the Rain]. Athens, Govostis, 1943.
Dokimasia [Trial]. Athens, Govostis, 1943.
O syntrofos [Our Comrade]. Athens, Govostis, 1945.
A anthropos me to garyfallo [The Man with the Carnation]. Bucharest, Ekdotiko Nea Ellada, 1952.
Agrypnia [Vigil]. Athens, Pyxida, 1954.
Proino astro [Morning Star]. Athens, 1955.
He sonata tou selenofotos. Athens, Kedros, 1956; as *The Moonlight Sonata*, translated by John Stathatos, New Malden, Surrey, Tangent, 1975.

Chroniko [Chronicle]. Athens, Kedros, 1957.

Hydria [The Urn]. Athens, 1957.

Apoheretismos [Farewell]. Athens, Kedros, 1957.

Cheimerine diavgeia [Winter Limpidity]. Athens, Kedros, 1957.

Petrinos Chronos [Stony Time]. Bucharest, Politikes Ke Logotechnikes Ekdoseis, 1957.

He Geitonies tou Kosmou [The Neighborhoods of the World]. Bucharest, Politikes Ke Logotechnikes Ekdoseis, 1957.

Otan erchetai ho xenos [When the Stranger Comes]. Athens, Kedros, 1958.

Any potachti Politeia [Unsubjugated City]. Bucharest, Politikes Ke Logotechnikes Ekdoseis, 1958.

He architectoniki ton dentron [The Architecture of the Trees]. Bucharest, Politikes Ke Logotechnikes Ekdoseis, 1958.

Hoi gerontisses k'he thalassa [The Old Women and the Sea]. Athens, Kedros, 1959.

To parathyro [The Window]. Athens, Kedros, 1960.

He gefyra [The Bridge]. Athens, Kedros, 1960.

Ho mavros Hagios [The Black Saint]. Athens, Kedros, 1961.

Poiemata [Poems]. Athens, Kedros, 4 vols., 1961-75.

To nekro spiti [The Dead House]. Athens, Kedros, 1962.

Kato ap'ton iskio tou vounou [Beneath the Shadow of the Mountain]. Athens, Kedros, 1962.

To dentro tis fylakis kai he gynaikes [The Prison Tree and the Women]. Athens, Kedros, 1963.

Martyries [Testimonies]. Athens, Kedros, 2 vols., 1963-66.

Dodeka poiemata gia ton Kavafe [Twelve Poems for Cavafy]. Athens, Kedros, 1963.

Paichnidia t'ouranou kai tou nerou [Playful Games of the Sky and the Water]. Athens, Kedros, 1964.

Philoctetes. Athens, Kedros, 1965.

Orestes. Athens, Kedros, 1966.

Ostrava. Athens, Kedros, 1967.

Romiossini: The Story of the Greeks. Paradise, California, Dustbooks, 1969.

Poems, translated by Alan Page. Oxford, Oxonian Press, 1969.

Romiossini and Other Poems. Madison, Wisconsin, Quixote Press, 1969.

Gestures and Other Poems 1968-1970, translated by Nikos Stangos. London, Cape Goliard Press, and New York, Grossman, 1971.

Petres, Epanalepseis, Kinglidoma [Stones, Repetitions, Railings]. Athens, Kedros, 1972.

He epistrofe tes Iphigeneias [The Return of Iphigenia]. Athens, Kedros, 1972.

He Helene [Helen]. Athens, Kedros, 1972.

Cheironomies [Gestures]. Athens, Kedros, 1972.

Tetarte diastase [Fourth Dimension]. Athens, Kedros, 1972.

Chrysothemis. Athens, Kedros, 1972.

Ismene. Athens, Kedros, 1972.

Dekaochto lianotragouda tes pikres patridas. Athens, Kedros, 1973; as *Eighteen Short Songs of the Bitter Motherland*, translated by Amy Mims, St. Paul, Minnesota, North Central, 1974.

Diadromos kai skala. Athens, Kedros, 1973; as *Corridor and Stairs*, translated by Nikos Germanacos, Curragh, Ireland, Goldsmith Press, 1976.

Contradictions, translated by John Stathatos. Rushden, Northamptonshire, Sceptre Press, 1973.

Graganda. Athens, Kedros, 1973.

Ho afanismos tis Milos [The Annihilation of Milos]. Athens, Kedros, 1974.

Hymnos kai threnos gia tin Kypro [Hymn and Lament for Cyprus]. Athens, Kedros, 1974.

Kapnismeno tsoukali [The Soot-Black Pot]. Athens, Kedros, 1974.

Kodonostasio [Belfry]. Athens, Kedros, 1974.
Ho tikhos mesa ston kathrefti [The Wall in the Mirror]. Athens, Kedros, 1974.
Chartina [Papermade]. Athens, Kedros, 1974.
Selected Poems, translated by Nikos Stangos. London, Penguin, 1974.
He Kyra ton Ambelion. Athens, Kedros, 1975; as *The Lady of the Vineyards*, translated by Apostolos N. Athanassakis, New York, Pella, 1981.
Ta Epikairika 1945-1969 [Topical Verse]. Athens, Kedros, 1975.
He teleftea pro Anthropou hekatontaetia [The Last Century Before Man]. Athens, Kedros, 1975.
Hemerologhia exorias [Diaries in Exile]. Athens, Kedros, 1975.
To hysterografo tis doxas [The Postscript of Glory]. Athens, Kedros, 1975.
Mantatoforos. Athens, Kedros, 1975.
To thyroreio [Conciergerie]. Athens, Kedros, 1976.
The Fourth Dimension: Selected Poems, translated by Rae Dalven. Boston, Godine, 1976.
To makrino [Remote]. Athens, Kedros, 1977.
Gignesthai [Becoming]. Athens, Kedros, 1977.
Epitome (selection), edited by G. Veloudis. Athens, Kedros, 1977.
Chronicle of Exile, translated by Minas Savvas. San Francisco, Wire Press, 1977.
Loipon? [Well Then?]. Athens, Kedros, 1978.
Volidoskopos [Sounding Lead]. Athens, Kedros, 1978.
Toichokolletes [Bill Poster]. Athens, Kedros, 1978.
To soma kai to haima [Body and Blood]. Athens, Kedros, 1978.
Trochonomos [The Traffic-Regulator]. Athens, Kedros, 1978.
He pyle [The Gate]. Athens, Kedros, 1978.
Monemvassiotisses [Monemvassia Women]. Athens, Kedros, 1978.
To teratodes aristourghima [The Monstrous Masterpiece]. Athens, Kedros, 1978.
Phaedra. Athens, Kedros, 1978.
To roptro [The Knocker]. Athens, Kedros, 1978.
Mia pygolampida fotizei ti nychta. Athens, Kedros, 1978.
Grafe tyflou [Scripture of the Blind]. Athens, Kedros, 1979.
Ritsos in Parenthesis, translated by Kimon Friar. Princeton, New Jersey, Princeton University Press, 1979.
Scripture of the Blind, translated by Kimon Friar and Kostas Myrsiades. Columbus, Ohio State University Press, 1979.
Subterranean Horses, translated by Minas Savvas. Columbus, Ohio State University Press, 1980.
'Oneiro kalokerinou messimeriou [A Midsummer's Noon Dream]. Athens, Kedros, 1980.
Diafaneia [Transparency]. Athens, Kedros, 1980.
Parodos [Parody]. Athens, Kedros, 1980.
Monochorda. Athens, Kedros, 1980.
Ta erotica. Athens, Kedros, 1981.
Syntrofica tragoudia [Comradeship Songs]. Athens, Synchroni Epochi, 1981.
Hypokofa [Muffled]. Athens, Kedros, 1982.
Italiko triptycho. Athens, Kedros, 1982.
Moyovassia. Athens, Kedros, 1982.
Erotica: Small Suite in Red Major, Naked Body, Carnal Word, translated by Kimon Friar. Old Chatham, New York, Sachem Press, 1982.
Selected Poems, translated by Edmund Keeley. New York, Ecco Press, 1983.
To choriko ton sfougarhadon [The Sponge-Divers' Chorale]. Athens, Kedros, 1983.
Teiresias. Athens, Kedros, 1983.

Plays

Pera ap'ton iskio ton Kyparission [Beyond the Shadow of the Cypress Trees] (produced Bucharest, 1959). Bucharest, Politikes Ke Logotechnikes Ekdoseis, 1958.
Mia gynaika plai sti thalassa [A Woman by the Sea] (produced Bucharest, 1959). Bucharest, Politikes Ke Logotechnikes Ekdoseis, 1959.

Other

Ariostos ho prosechtikos afhighite stigmes tou viou tou ke tou hypnou tou. Athens, Kedros, 1982.
Ti paraxena pragmata [Strange Things]. Athens, Kedros, 1983.

*

Critical Studies: *Ritsos: Étude, choix de texte, et bibliographie* by Chrysa Papandréou, Paris, Seghers, 1968; "Ritsos' *Romiosini*: Style as Historical Memory" by W. V. Spanos, in *American Poetry Review*, September-October 1973.

* * *

Yannis Ritsos is widely hailed as the foremost poet of the Greek left. He is also one of the most prolific poets in any language, with more than two thousand pages of published verse to his name. Two strands run through all his work—his Marxist commitment and a vein of pessimistic introspection. In Ritsos's earliest collections of poetry, such as *Trakter* (1934), we find poems which explore personal grief alongside others stridently proclaiming the future liberation of the masses. The first poem in which these two moods are combined constructively into a synthesis in *Epitafios* (1936), a lyrical lament for a young man shot down by police at a demonstration, in which however the lamentation is not that of the poet himself but is dramatically projected: it is the victim's mother who speaks. By this means Ritsos was able to subordinate his talent for expressive grief within a poetic structure in which a harsh optimism prevails.

Ill-health and frequent imprisonment for his political beliefs combined to keep Ritsos at a distance from public life, and for a time in the 1940's and early 1950's, in the aftermath of the Greek civil war, he was unable to publish freely. He wrote prolifically throughout this period, however, and in 1954 published as part of the collection *Agrypnia* his best-known poem, "Romiosini," a long poem celebrating the historical essence of the Greek identity (the *romiosíni* of the title) as an age-old struggle against the harsh elements that comprise the Greek landscape, but still more against human oppressors. From this time on the political optimism of Ritsos's early poems has been subsumed into a political and universal sense of tragedy. These poems affirm a deep faith, not so much directly in the outcome of the political struggle, but rather in the ultimate triumph of the noble and free in human nature.

In the 1950's and 1960's, Ritsos's output is characterised by the juxtaposition of long poems with very short poems. In both, the mood of introspection continues to appear, but by this time it is either placed in a dramatic context, as it is in the long poems, or refined by an ironic sharpness of detail that in the short poems converts a natural melancholy into epigrammatic surprise. Although his political commitment remains unchanged, Ritsos depicts life as tragic, but at the same time containing heroic hope in the face of the odds, and with its own beauty, even in defeat. It is often been pointed out that Ritsos is a gifted painter, and that many of his short poems, in particular, reveal the painter's eye: the poem is a juxtaposition of colours, perhaps, or of shapes. In contrast to these very short poems, with the tight structure of an epigram or of an artist's miniature, Ritsos's long poems are discursive, loosely constructed pieces. Their long, strongly rhythmical free-verse lines allow the poet to explore changing moods and to develop a theme, not consequentially, but in extended form—again rather as a painter works, but this time on a large canvas.

Many of Ritsos's poems have achieved wide popularity through being set to music by popular composers such as Mikis Theodorakis, and much of his recent production seems to be directed toward this outlet.

—Roderick Beaton

ROBBE-GRILLET, Alain. French. Born in Brest, 18 August 1922. Educated at Lycée de Brest, and Lycées Buffon and St. Louis, Paris; National Institute of Agronomy, Paris, diploma 1944. Sent to work in German tank factory during World War II. Married Catherine Rstakian in 1957. Engineer, National Statistical Institute, Paris, 1945-49, and Institute of Colonial Fruits and Crops, Morocco, French Guinea, and Martinique, 1949-51; then full-time writer: since 1955, literary consultant, Éditions de Minuit, Paris. Recipient: Fénéon Prize, 1954; Critics Prize (France), 1955; del Duca bursary, 1956; Delluc Prize, 1963; Mondello Prize, 1982. Officer, Order of Merit; Chevalier, Legion of Honor. Address: 18 Boulevard Maillot, 92200 Neuilly-sur-Seine, France.

PUBLICATIONS

Fiction

Les Gommes. Paris, Minuit, 1953; as *The Erasers*, New York, Grove Press, 1964; London, Calder and Boyars, 1966.

Le Voyeur. Paris, Minuit, 1955; as *The Voyeur*, New York, Grove Press, 1958; London, Calder, 1959.

La Jalousie. Paris, Minuit, 1957; as *Jealousy*, New York, Grove Press, and London, Calder, 1959.

Dans le labyrinthe. Paris, Minuit, 1959; as *In the Labyrinth*, New York, Grove Press, 1960; London, Calder and Boyars, 1968.

L'Année dernière à Marienbad. Paris, Minuit, 1961; as *Last Year at Marienbad*, New York, Grove Press, and London, Calder and Boyars, 1962.

Instantanés. Paris, Minuit, 1962; as *Snapshots*, with *Towards a New Novel*, London, Calder and Boyars, 1965; published separately, New York, Grove Press, 1968.

L'Immortelle. Paris, Minuit, 1963; as *The Immortal One*, London, Calder and Boyars, 1971.

La Maison de rendez-vous. Paris, Minuit, 1965; translated as *La Maison de Rendez-vous*, New York, Grove Press, 1966; as *The House of Assignation*, London, Calder and Boyars, 1970.

Projet pour une révolution à New York. Paris, Minuit, 1970; as *Project for a Revolution in New York*, New York, Grove Press, 1972; London, Calder and Boyars, 1973.

Glissements progressifs du plaisir. Paris, Minuit, 1974.

Topologie d'une cité fantôme. Paris, Minuit, 1976; as *Topology of a Phantom City*, New York, Grove Press, 1977; London, Calder and Boyars, 1978.

Souvenirs du triangle d'or. Paris, Minuit, 1978; as *Memories of the Golden Triangle*, London, Calder, 1984.
Un Régicide. Paris, Minuit, 1978.
Djinn. Paris, Minuit, 1981; translated as *Djinn*, New York, Grove Press, 1982; London, Calder, 1983.

Plays

Screenplays: *L'Année dernière à Marienbad* (*Last Year at Marienbad*), 1961; *L'Immortelle*, 1963; *Trans-Europ-Express*, 1967; *L'Homme qui ment* (*The Man Who Lies*), 1968; *L'Eden et après*, 1970; *Glissements progressifs du plaisir*, 1973; *Le Jeu avec le feu*, 1975; *La Belle Captive*, 1983.

Other

Pour un nouveau roman. Paris, Minuit, 1963; revised edition, 1970; as *Towards a New Novel*, with *Snapshots*, London, Calder and Boyars, 1965; as *For a New Novel: Essays on Fiction*, New York, Grove Press, 1966.
Rêves de jeunes filles, photographs by David Hamilton. Paris, Laffont, 1971; as *Dreams of a Young Girl*, New York, Morrow, 1971; as *Dreams of Young Girls*, London, Collins, 1971.
Les Demoiselles d'Hamilton, photographs by David Hamilton. Paris, Laffont, 1972; as *Sisters*, New York, Morrow, 1973; London, Collins, 1976.
La Belle Captive, with René Magritte. Paris, Bibliotheque des Arts, 1976.
Temple aux miroirs, with Irina Ionesco. Paris, Seghers, 1977.

*

Bibliography: *Robbe-Grillet: An Annotated Bibliography of Critical Studies 1953-1972* by Dale W. Fraizer, Metuchen, New Jersey, Scarecrow Press, 1973.

Critical Studies: *Robbe-Grillet and the New French Novel* by Ben Frank Stoltzfus, Carbondale, Southern Illinois University Press, 1964; *The French New Novel: Claude Simon, Michel Butor, Robbe-Grillet* by John Sturrock, London, Oxford University Press, 1969; *Les Gommes* edited by J.S. Wood, Englewood Cliffs, New Jersey, Prentice Hall, 1970; *Narrative Consciousness: Structure and Perception in the Fiction of Kafka, Beckett, and Robbe-Grillet* by G.H. Szanto, Austin, University of Texas Press, 1972; *The Novels of Robbe-Grillet* by Bruce Morrissette, Ithaca, New York, Cornell University Press, 1975; *The Film Career of Robbe-Grillet* by William F. Van Wert, London, Prior, 1977; *The Films of Robbe-Grillet* by Roy Armes, Amsterdam, Benjamins, 1981; *Robbe-Grillet* by John Fletcher, London, Methuen, 1983.

*   *   *

The best-known of the so-called *nouveaux romanciers* in France—writers who have attempted to find a new path for the novel in radical distinction to the methods of classic authors like Balzac—Alain Robbe-Grillet began life as an agricultural scientist, and turned to literature only after illness brought his research career in the field to an end. He thus comes from a background which is different to that of the normal French person of letters, and explains to some extent the iconoclastic impact he made on the literary scene when his second novel, *Les Gommes*, was published in Paris in 1953 (his first novel, *Un Régicide*, appeared only in 1978).

Les Gommes is a detective story based on the legend of Oedipus. A sleuth called Wallas arrives in a provincial town to investigate a murder which, twenty-four hours to the second later, he himself commits: and the man he accidentally shoots is his own father who had managed to survive a similar attack the previous evening. This complex, enigmatic story is typical of Robbe-Grillet, who followed it, in *Le Voyeur*, with a novel about a travelling salesman who visits the offshore island of his birth and (perhaps) commits a sadistic rape and murder before leaving scot-free some days later; the reason why it is necessary to say "perhaps" is because the crime may have been enacted in the protagonist's sick mind only.

La Jalousie turns on a French pun: *jalousie* means both jealousy and slatted blinds. The workings of the sick mind of the protagonist now actually become the text, so that the novel itself constitutes a fit of jealousy in which the narrator watches his wife obsessively through slatted blinds as she plans (or so he believes) a night away from home in the company of a neighbouring planter who is a frequent visitor to the house. The jealous frenzy subsides—and the novel ends—only with the return of the (errant?) wife and the (apparent) discomfiture of the neighbour, whom the wife teases for his clumsiness as a motor mechanic, a remark the narrator naturally interprets in a bawdy sense.

Robbe-Grillet has declared on a number of occasions how much he owes to Kafka, and so it is not surprising that *Dans le labyrinthe* should be Kafkaesque in inspiration. A soldier is wandering in a snow-covered town looking for a man to whom he wants to deliver the effects of a dead comrade after a major military disaster, and he ends up dying from wounds himself. What is not clear is how far the whole story is elaborated by the narrator on the basis of a picture called "The Defeat at Reichenfels," that is to what extent, like jealousy in the previous novel, it is a construct of the fantasising consciousness.

During the next few years Robbe-Grillet concentrated on making or helping to make a number of films, of which the best-known is *L'Année dernière à Marienbad* (directed by Alain Resnais), the story of a man who succeeds in persuading a woman that she agreed, the year before in Marienbad, to meet him in the resort where they presently are staying and leave her husband for him. As in *Jealousy*, there is at the heart of *Marienbad* ambiguity about what precisely is real, what exactly happened, and who is mesmerising whom. Robbe-Grillet then proceeded to make a number of films himself, one of which, *L'Immortelle* (based on the Orpheus and Eurydice legend; a man dies with the woman he loves after he has already succeeded once in "resurrecting" her from the dead) is, for all its amateurish clumsiness of technique, a considerable work of art.

Robbe-Grillet returned to the novel in *La Maison de rendez-vous*, a witty parody of James Bond stories set in an exotic Hong Kong where women's flesh "plays a large part" in the protagonist's dreams, and *Projet pour une révolution à New York*, a more self-indulgently sadistic fantasy about an imaginary wave of terrorism in Manhattan. Since then the preoccupation with sadism and voyeurism has become almost totally obsessive, and the recent novels and films are tedious reading and viewing, as are the "soft-porn" books like *Les Demoiselles d'Hamilton* and *Temple aux miroirs* with which he has been closely associated. The detachment which characterised the analysis of the diseased or tortured mind in *Le Voyeur* and *La Jalousie* is replaced in the latest work by a modish and self-indulgent exhibition of something disturbingly close to the fantasies which the protagonist of *Le Voyeur* luxuriated in.

Robbe-Grillet has also made a considerable reputation for himself as a theorist of fiction, and his collected articles in *Pour un nouveau roman* are widely admired. They contain a clear statement of his position, which is that in a world without God, in which the universe is not hostile to mankind (as Camus tended to suppose) but merely indifferent, the novelist should avoid what he stigmatises as anthropomorphism, that is, the illusion that there is a sly complicity between humanity and things, which leads to writing overladen with sentimental metaphors such as "the lowering sky" or "the cruel sea." People who steer clear of this sort of thing, Robbe-Grillet argues, write fiction which makes none of the outworn and even discredited assumptions about coherence of plot and solidity of character, and which accepts that time is a fluid, not stable medium.

It is clear why his novels, based as they are on this philosophy, seemed so radical, even iconoclastic, when they first appeared. Now that many of his theoretical arguments have been accepted—it was no less a writer than John Fowles who said that we live in the age of

Robbe-Grillet—the genuine part of his achievement can more easily be separated from the spurious, and on that basis it is clear that his best work is contained in the three mature novels of his middle period, *Le Voyeur*, *La Jalousie*, and *Dans le labyrinthe*, works which will remain important in the history of 20th-century literature long after the polemics which surrounded their publication have been forgotten.

—John Fletcher

RÓZEWICZ, Tadeusz. Polish. Born in Radomsko, 9 October 1921. Educated at Jagellonian University, Cracow, 1948-53. Served in the Polish resistance Home Army during World War II. Married; two sons. Lived in Gliwice until 1968, then in Wroclaw. Recipient: State Prize, 1955, 1966; Cracow Prize, 1959; Minister of Culture Prize, 1962; Wroclaw Prize, 1972; Austrian State Prize, 1982. Commander of the Cross, Order Polonia Restituta. Address: Ulitsa Janus zewicka 13 m. 14, 53-136 Wroclaw, Poland.

PUBLICATIONS

Plays

Kartoteka. With *Zielona róza*, Warsaw, PIW, 1961; as *The Card Index* (as *The Dossier*, produced New York, 1961; as *The Card Index*, produced Oxford, 1967; London, 1968), in *The Card Index and Other Plays*, 1969.
Świadkowie, in *Nic w plaszczu Prospera*. 1962; as *The Witnesses*, in *The Witnesses and Other Plays*, 1970.
Grupa Laokoona [Laocoon Group], in *Nic w plaszczu Prospera*. 1962.
Utwory dramatyczne (includes *Kartoteka*, *Grupa Laokoona*, *Śmieszny staruszek*, *Spaghetti i Miecz* [Spaghetti and the Sword], *Wyszedl z domu*, *Akt przerywany*). Cracow, Wydawnictwo Literackie, 1966.
Stara kobieta wysiaduje, in *Dialog 8*. 1968; as *The Old Woman Broods*, in *The Witnesses and Other Plays*, 1970.
The Card Index and Other Plays. London, Calder and Boyars, 1969; New York, Grove Press, 1970.
Wyszedl z domu, as *Gone Out*, in *The Card Index and Other Plays*. 1969.
Akt przerywany, as *The Interrupted Act*, in *The Card Index and Other Plays*. 1969.
Śmieszny staruszek, as *The Funny Old Man* (produced London, 1973), in *The Witnesses and Other Plays*, 1970.
The Witnesses and Other Plays. London, Calder and Boyars, 1970.
Na czworakach [On All Fours], in *Dialog 9*, 1971.
Sztuki teatralne [Theatrical Plays]. Wroclaw, Ossolineum, 1972.
Biale malzeństwo, i inne utwory sceniczne [White Marriage and Other Plays]. Cracow, Wydawnictwo Literackie, 1975; *Biale malzeństwo* translated as *Mariage Blanc*, in *Mariage Blanc, and the Hungry Artist Departs*, 1983.
Teatr niekonsekwencji [The Inconsistent Theatre]. Wroclaw, Ossolineum, 1979.
Mariage Blanc, and The Hungry Artist Departs. London, Boyars, 1983.

Fiction

Opadly liście z drzew [The Leaves Have Fallen from the Trees].   Warsaw, PIW, 1955.
Przerwany egzamin [The Interrupted Examination].   Warsaw, PIW, 1960.
Wycieczka do muzeum [An Excursion to a Museum].   Warsaw, Czytelnik, 1966.
Opowiadania wybrane [Selected Stories].   Warsaw, Czytelnik, 1968.
Śmierć w starych dekoracjach [Death amid Old Stage Props].   Warsaw, PIW, 1970.
Opowiadania traumatyczne [Traumatic Stories].   Cracow, Wydawnictwo Literackie,
   1979.

Verse

Niepokój [Anxiety].   Cracow, Przetom, 1947.
Czerwona rekawiczka [The Red Glove].   Cracow, Wydawnictwo Ksiazka, 1948.
Czas który idzie [The Time Which Goes By].   Warsaw, Czytelnik, 1951.
Wiersze i obrazy [Poems and Images].   Warsaw, Czytelnik, 1952.
Równina [The Plain].   Cracow, Wydawnictwo Literackie, 1954.
Uśmiechy [Smiles].   Warsaw, Czytelnik, 1955.
Srebrny klos [Silver Grain].   Warsaw, Czytelnik, 1955.
Poemat otwarty [An Open Room].   Cracow, Wydawnictwo Literackie, 1956.
Poezje zebrane [Selected Poems].   Cracow, Wydawnictwo Literackie, 1957.
Formy [Forms].   Warsaw, Czytelnik, 1958.
Rozmowa z ksieciem [Conversation with a Prince].   Warsaw, PIW, 1960.
Glos anonima [The Anonymous Voice].   Katowice, Ślask, 1961.
Zielona róza; Kartoteka [Green Rose; Card Index].   Warsaw, PIW, 1961; *Zielona róza*
   translated as *Green Rose*, Darlington, Western Australia, John Michael, 1982.
Nic w plaszczu Prospera [Nothing in Prospero's Cloak] (includes the plays *Świadkowie*
   and *Grupa Laokoona*).   Warsaw, PIW, 1962.
Niepokój: Wybór wierszy 1945-1961.   Warsaw, PIW, 1963.
Twarz [The Face].   Warsaw, Czytelnik, 1964.
Twarz trzecia [The Third Face].   Warsaw, Czytelnik, 1968.
Regio [That Area].   Warsaw, PIW, 1969.
Faces of Anxiety, translated by Adam Czerniawski.   London, Rapp and Whiting, 1969.
Wiersze [Poems].   Warsaw, PIW, 1974.
The Survivor and Other Poems, translated by Magnus I. Krynski and Robert A.
   Maguire.   Princeton, New Jersey, Princeton University Press, 1976.
Selected Poems, translated by Adam Czerniawski.   London, Penguin, 1976.
Conversation with a Prince and Other Poems, translated by Adam Czerniawski.   Lon-
   don, Anvil Press Poetry, 1982.

Other

Kartki z Wegier [Notes from Hungary].   Warsaw, Czytelnik, 1953.
Przygotowanie do wieczoru autorskiego [Preparations for a Poetry Reading].   Warsaw,
   PIW, 1971.
Proza [Prose].   Wroclaw, Ossolineum, 1973.
Duszyczka [A Little Soul].   Cracow, Wydawnictwo Literackie, 1977.
Próba rekonstrukcji [A Trial of Reconstruction].   Wroclaw, Ossolineum, 1979.

*

Critical Study: *Rósewicz* (in English) by Henryk Vogler, Warsaw, Authors' Agency and
Czytelnik, 1976.

*   *   *

Tadeusz Rózewicz is one of those poets whose artistic development was shaped by history in a decisive way. He was under twenty when the Second World War broke out and his war experiences—he belonged to the underground Home Army and fought in the Resistance—set the tone of the early poetry. His first collections of verse, *Niepokój* and *Czerwona rekawiczka*, were characterized by a stark, almost bare style of great simplicity dispensing with rhymes and metaphors; in these books Rózewicz created an anti-poetic model. His style reflected his conviction that the wartime collapse of traditional values led to a situation in which the poet had to re-establish the meaning of ordinary words and had to start building from the foundations: "Create a new [poetry]/which builds/from common feelings/from simple words/ Let it take away from man/all that is animal/and divine." After writing a number of anti-war poems and trying to force upon himself an optimistic mood in accordance with the expectations of the post-war Communist regime, in the 1960's Rózewicz's attention became focused on what he saw as the crisis of European culture and civilization. While aware of the bankruptcy of certain Socialist ideals ("the new man/that's him there/yes it's that/sewage pipe/which lets through/ everything"), he attacked the mindless consumerism of the West in equally bitter terms. In his mature poetry—as Magnus Krynski and Robert Maguire point out in their introduction to an English selection of his work—there is a tension "between a highly emotional tone...and the 'objective' presentation of seemingly factual data." Especially in the collections *Twarz* and *Regio* Rózewicz made frequent use of the collage-technique, sprinkling his poems with foreign names and quotations, often in another language.

For all his distinction as a poet, Rózewicz is probably better known as a playwright both in and outside Poland. His first two plays, *The Dossier* (*The Card Index*) and *The Witnesses*, were hailed as—apart from Mrozek—the most interesting examples of the Polish theatre of the absurd. In *The Dossier* the life of the nameless hero is simultaneously intersected by people who knew him at different ages and in various roles; *The Witnesses* (subtitled "Our Little Stabilization") begins with a dialogue recited by a nameless man and a woman which reflects the author's unease about the post-1956 adaptation of Polish society to "normal" petty-bourgeois standards, an adaptation which is in any case illusory: "Perhaps our little stabilization/is nothing but a dream." *The Interrupted Act* consists mainly of stage directions and the author's self-mocking commentaries on the subject of his stagecraft. Already here a note of admiration for Samuel Beckett can be detected which becomes even more obvious in *The Old Woman Broods*. Part of this play takes place on a huge rubbish heap after a devastating war or cataclysm of the future, while another part is filled with the gluttonous old woman's endless (and largely meaningless) monologues. In recent years Rózewicz scored his greatest theatrical success with the play *Mariage Blanc*, an amusing, and heavily Freudian, interpretation of young girls' fears and phantasies. Rózewicz's prose fiction is, by and large, restricted to short stories written in a terse, laconic style; his *Śmierć w starych dekoracjach* is a longer story which takes place in a Rome polluted by vulgarity and consumerism.

—George Gömöri

RUIBAL (Argibay), José. Spanish. Born near Pontevedra, Galicia, 27 October 1925. Military service in Madrid. Married to Consuelo Vazquez de Parga; two children. Lived in Argentina and Uruguay in the 1950's and 1960's; has taught at the State University of New York, Albany, 1972, 1973, University of Minnesota, Minneapolis, 1973, 1974, 1976, and Syracuse University, New York, 1978. Recipient: Modern International Drama prize, 1969; March Foundation grant, 1972. Address: Olivar 3, 3D, Madrid 12, Spain.

Plays

Los mendigos y seis piezas de café-teatro (includes *La secretaria, Los mutantes, El rabo, Los ojos, El padre, El supergerente*). Madrid, Escelicer, 1969; book was almost immediately banned, and reissued as *El mono piadoso y seis piezas de café-teatro*, 1969; *Los mendigos* translated as *The Beggars*, in *Drama and Theatre 7*, no. 1, 1968; *El rabo* translated as *Tails*, in *Drama Review*, Summer 1969; *El mono piadoso* (produced 1970).
La máquina de pedir, El asno, La ciencia de birlibirloque. Madrid, Siglo Veintiuno, 1970; *El asno* translated as *The Jackass* (produced Binghamton, New York, 1971; New York City, 1972), in *The New Wave Spanish Drama*, edited by George E. Wellwarth, New York, New York University Press, 1970; *La máquina de pedir* translated as *The Begging Machine*, in *Modern International Drama*, 1975.
Teatro difícil (includes *Curriculum vitae, El bacalao*). Madrid, Escelicer, 1971; *El bacalao* translated as *The Codfish*, in *Modern International Drama*, 1972.
Teatro sobre teatro. Madrid, Catedra, 1975.
El hombre y la mosca. Madrid, Fundamentos, 1977; as *The Man and the Fly* (produced Binghamton, New York, 1971), in *The New Wave Spanish Drama*, edited by George E. Wellwarth, New York, New York University Press, 1970.

*

Critical Study: *Spanish Underground Drama* by George E. Wellwarth, University Park, Pennsylvania State University Press, 1972.

*   *   *

José Ruibal first achieved prominence outside Spain during the latter years of the Franco regime. He and a group of other dramatists, principally Antonio Martínez Ballesteros, José María Bellido, and the late Juan Antonio Castro, founded what came to be known as the "Spanish Underground Drama." This was a catch-all term that was first used in the United States and shortly afterwards in England, West Germany, and other European countries to describe drama that was considered politically subversive by the Franco regime and was consequently censored in Spain, where it could neither be published nor performed.

The principal characteristic of Ruibal's theatre was its use of symbolism and a technique of deliberately distancing the audience from the action by setting it in mythical countries and by giving the characters non-Hispanic names. This was done partially in the hope of fooling the censors, never very intelligent readers of literature, into thinking that the play lacked direct references to the Spanish situation, partially in order to universalize the plays (the demise of Spanish totalitarianism has by no means caused them to lose their pertinence), and partially in order to enable the spectator to think about the action)—i.e., objectify it—rather than be emotionally caught up in it.

Ruibal's initial success, like that of his fellow dramatists of the "underground" such as, in addition to those mentioned above, Miguel Romero Esteo, Luis Matilla, Jerónimo López Mozo, Angel García Pintado, Eduardo Quiles, Luis Riaza, and the very important Catalan writers Manuel de Pedrolo and Josep Benet, came in the United States through publication in various anthologies (e.g., *Modern Spanish Theatre, New Wave Spanish Drama, New Generation Spanish Drama, Three Catalan Dramatists*) and in journals such as *Modern International Drama* as well as through productions in university theatres. Subsequently Ruibal spent several years in the United States as a guest lecturer at numerous colleges and universities.

Ruibal's major works are *The Man and the Fly* and *The Begging Machine*. Although he had written a number of interesting plays prior to the former, such as *Tails*, *The Beggars*, and *The Jackass*, it is with *The Man and the Fly* that Ruibal created the most trenchant satire of totalitarianism that the Spanish Underground Drama has produced. The focus of the play is on the tendency—as Lord Acton put it—of absolute power to become absolutely corrupt, in this case through an attempt at self-deification by means of a putatively eternal series of doubles. The fragility and ridiculousness of the attempt is depicted by a setting almost overloaded with symbolism: a crystal dome decorated with stained-glass panels and hunting trophies on a foundation of skulls, indestructible from the outside, fragile on the inside, and incapable of ever being completed.

Ruibal's other major play, *The Begging Machine*, concerns the hypocrisy of charity and the mechanization of life. Its principal symbol is a Begging Machine that not only begs but steals as well. Ruibal makes use of surrealistic techniques by making one of his chief characters a yellow octopus that gives birth constantly to oil tankers and by showing the ruling powers of the world as hybrid machine-men, their heads in the form of miniature computers if they are civilians and in the form of weapons if they are in uniform.

It is hard to predict Ruibal's future as a dramatist at this point. He has the talent and the versatility to accomplish almost anything in the theatre and the maturity and insight to treat any subject. Of that there can be no question.

—George E. Wellwarth

RULFO (Vizcaíno), Juan. Mexican. Born in Sayula, Jalisco, 16 May 1918. Educated at the universities of Guadalajara and Mexico City. Director of the Editorial Department, National Institute for Indigenous Studies, Mexico City. Adviser, and Fellow, Centro Mexicano de Escritores. Address: Centro Mexicano de Escritores, Valle Arizpe, 18 Mexico, D.F. 12, Mexico.

PUBLICATIONS

Fiction

El llano en llamas. Mexico City, Fondo de Cultura Económica, 1953; revised edition, 1970; as *The Burning Plain and Other Stories*, Austin, University of Texas Press, 1967.
Pedro Páramo. Mexico City, Fondo de Cultura Económica, 1955; translated as *Pedro Páramo*, New York, Grove Press, 1959.
El gallo de oro y otros textos para cine. Mexico City, Era, 1980.

Other

Autobiografía armada, edited by Reina Roffé. Buenos Aires, Corregidor, 1973.
Obra completa, edited by Jorge Ruffinelli. Caracas, Ayacucho, 1977.

Editor, *Antología personal*. Rio Piedras, Puerto Rico, Huracan, 1978.

*

Critical Studies: *El arte de Rulfo: Historios de vivos y fiduntos* by Hugo Rodríguez Alcalá, Mexico City, Instituto Nacional de Bellas Artes, 1965; *Paradise and Fall in Rulfo's Pedro Páramo* by George Ronald Freeman, Cuernavaca, Cidoc, 1970; *El laberinto mexicano en/de Rulfo* by Manuel Ferrer Chivite, Mexico City, Novaro, 1972; *Las cuentos de Rulfo* by Donald K. Gordon, Madrid, Playor, 1976.

*　　*　　*

Juan Rulfo's literary fame rests on two small volumes: *The Burning Plain*, a collection of 15 short stories, and his novel *Pedro Páramo*. He has also written movie scripts, but they are not generally considered part of his literary achievement.

The most obvious external characteristic of his art is regionalism. Almost everything takes place in his native state of Jalisco. The time framework is before, during, and immediately after the Revolution. But Rulfo uses regionalism only as a tool to achieve goals far different from those of any regionalist writer. His focus is on the universal meaning of the passions, suffering, and failures of rural inhabitants.

Rulfo's style dominates his artistic creation. He uses simple structures, eliminating all inessential elements. action patterns are reduced to one or two central actions which carry the meaning for the entire situation. Speech dominates. It is generally the direct expression of uneducated peasants. The frequent result is the poetization of verbal communication, as the connotations of what is expressed become more important than the expression itself.

All the stories in *The Burning Plain* have a common theme: human failure. Each work examines one or several ways in which failure occurs. Nature itself in "We're Very Poor," in the form of a flood, destroys a young girl's only dowry, a cow and calf. With the animals her family had hoped for a marriage that would keep her from a life of prostitution, which had been her sister's fate. An almost supernatural malignant atmosphere of an entire town, Luvina (also the title), allows only a miserable existence for the inhabitants, and destroys the life and hopes of a teacher who comes to work there. Guilt shared by an adulterous couple for hastening the natural death of their brother and husband withers their passion and denies them the possibility of happiness. The insensitivity of the government in giving useless land to peasants deprives them of any hope for a future in the story "They Gave Us the Land."

Pedro Páramo depicts the same world as that of the short stories, but differs considerably in other ways. The stories are generally simple in structure and narrative viewpoint. Ambiguity, multiplicity of viewpoints, and complexity of structure characterize the novel. The stylized naturalistic realism of *The Burning Plain* is present in *Pedro Páramo*, but is secondary to and controlled by another element: the supernatural. All, or almost all of the novel takes place in the world of the dead. Through the voices and memories of the dead, talking to each other or to themselves, the reader haltingly reconstructs the brutal life of Pedro Páramo, a small town cacique who will do anything to increase his power.

The thematic structure of *Pedro Páramo* is also significantly different from that of the stories. The human suffering and failure are the same, but several themes that were hidden or non-existent come to the foreground in the novel. The failure of paternity, generally implied in the stories, is dominant in the novel, both as a theme and as a structural element. The plot is concerned with Juan Preciado's search for his father, Pedro Páramo, who is described as a "living hatred." Pedro fails as a father both to his acknowledged son Miguel, and as a father figure for his town. When angered he lets the town die. The one ennobling feature of the man is his life-long unrequited love for the woman who, insane, eventually becomes his wife. The lyrical presentation of love in *Pedro Páramo* is unique in Rulfo's work.

Rulfo's achievement is the creation of a stark and yet strangely attractive vision of simple Mexican lives that come to have universal meaning.

—M. Ian Adams

SALACROU, Armand (Camille). French. Born in Rouen, 9 August 1899. Educated at Lycée du Havre; studied medicine and philosophy in Paris, from 1918. Served in the French Army, 1939-40; taken prisoner, 1940, but escaped to Vichy France. Married Jeanne Jeandet in 1922; two daughters. Journalist in the 1920's; founded an advertising agency, 1931. President, Society of Dramatic Authors; President, Unesco International Institute of the Theatre. Member, Goncourt Academy 1949-71. Grand officer, Legion of Honor. Address: Villa Maritime, 76600 Le Havre, France.

PUBLICATIONS

Plays

Le Casseur d'assiettes (produced Leiden, Netherlands, 1954). Paris, Galérie Simon, 1924.
Tour à terre (produced Paris, 1925). With *Le Pont de l'Europe*, Paris, Gallimard, 1929.
Le Pont de l'Europe (produced Paris, 1927). With *Tour à terre*, Paris, Gallimard, 1929.
Patchouli (produced Paris, 1930). Paris, Gallimard, 1930.
Atlas-Hôtel (produced Paris, 1931). Paris, Bravo, 1931.
La Vie en rose (produced Paris, 1931). Paris, Cahiers du Sud, 1936.
Les Frénétiques (produced Paris, 1934). Paris, Fayard, 1935.
Une Femme libre (produced Paris, 1934). With *Atlas-Hôtel*, Paris, Gallimard, 1934.
L'Inconnue d'Arras (produced Paris, 1935). Paris, Gallimard, 1936; as *The Unknown Woman of Arras* (produced London, 1948; Stanford, California, 1952).
Un Homme comme les autres (produced Paris, 1936). Paris, Fayard, 1937.
La Terre est ronde (produced Paris, 1938). With *Un Homme comme les autres*, Paris, Gallimard, 1938; as *The World Is Round*, in *Three Plays*, 1967.
Histoire de rire (produced Paris, 1939). Paris, Fayard, 1940; as *No Laughing Matter* (produced Long Island, New York, 1957); as *When the Music Stops* (produced London, 1957), in *Three Plays*, 1967.
La Marguerite (produced Paris, 1944). With *Histoire de rire* and *Le Casseur d'assiettes*, Paris, Gallimard, 1941; as *Marguerite* (produced Urbana, Illinois, 1951; Edinburgh, 1958), London, French, 1967; in *Three Plays*, 1967.
Théâtre. Paris, Gallimard, 8 vols., 1943-66; revised edition, 1977— .
Les Fiancés du Havre (produced Paris, 1944). Paris, Gallimard, 1944.
Le Soldat et la sorcière (produced Paris, 1945). Paris, Fayard, 1946.
Les Nuits de la colère (produced Paris, 1946). Paris, Gallimard, 1946; as *Men of Darkness* (produced New York, 1948).
L'Archipel Lenoir (produced Paris, 1947). Paris, Gallimard, 1948; as *Never Say Die* (produced London, 1966).
Pourquoi pas moi? (produced Brussels, 1948). With *Poof*, Paris, Bordas, 1948.
Poof (produced Paris, 1950). With *Pourquoi pas moi?*, Paris, Bordas, 1948.
Dieu le savait (produced Paris, 1951). With *Pourquoi pas moi?*, Paris, Gallimard, 1951.
Sens interdit (produced Paris, 1953). Paris, Gallimard, 1953.
Les Invités du Bon Dieu (produced Paris, 1953). Paris, Gallimard, 1953.
Le Miroir (produced Paris, 1956). In *L'Avant-Scène 139*, 1956.
Une Femme trop honnête (produced Paris, 1956). Paris, Gallimard, 1956.
La Boule de verre.Paris, Estienne, 1958.
La Beauté du diable (screenplay), with René Clair, in *Comédies*, by Clair. Paris, Gallimard, 1959.
Boulevard Durand. Paris, Gallimard, 1960; edited by Colin Radford, London, Hutchinson, 1975; translated as *Boulevard Durand* (produced Liverpool, 1963).
Comme les chardons. Paris, Gallimard, 1964.

La Rue noire. Paris, Gallimard, 1967.
Three Plays (includes *Marguerite, The World Is Round, When the Music Stops*). Minneapolis, University of Minnesota Press, 1967.

Screenplays: *Histoire de rire*, with Georges Neveux, 1941; *La Beauté du diable*, with René Clair, 1950.

Other

Les Idées de la nuit. Paris, Fayard, 1960.
Impromptu délibéré: Entretiens avec Paul-Louis Mignon. Paris, Gallimard, 1966.
Dans la salle des pas perdus. Paris, Gallimard, 2 vols., 1974-76.

*

Critical Studies: *Salacrou* by Paul-Louis Mignon, Paris, Gallimard, 1960; *Modern French Theatre* by Jacques Guicharnand, New Haven, Connecticut, Yale University Press, 1961; *French Drama of the Inter-War Years* by Dorothy Knowles, London, Harrap, 1967.

*   *   *

Over a period of more than forty years, Armand Salacrou wrote some twenty plays. The variety is bewildering, ranging from farce to documentary tragedy and from historical drama with a clear contemporary message to closely observed and very funny social comedy full of acerbic satire. Some of the plays were addressed to theatre-goers with advanced tastes, others were intended for the Parisian boulevard audience, by whom they were received enthusiastically, and *Boulevard Durand* was designed to speak straight to the working classes. Salacrou acquired a mastery of stage craft and dialogue, yet it would be tempting to describe him as a playwright in search of a medium flexible enough for the presentation of his views and looking for a public with whose aspiration he could relate satisfactorily. But beneath the surface of his works there are certain constant preoccupations.

Attracted by Communism from his early years, Salacrou regularly used drama to probe the contemporary political and social problems which demanded his attention. He adapted the story of Savanarola's activities in Renaissance Florence as a commentary on fascism in *The World Is Round*. First produced by Charles Dullin in 1938, the play was revived with great success just after World War II. *L'Archipel Lenoir* of 1948 is a comedy of bitter humour and rich characterisation which delivers a scathing attack on bourgeois values. *Les Nuits de la colère*, Salacrou's tragedy of the French Resistance movement against the German occupation, went far beyond facile patriotism and conventional heroics. Jean-Louis Barrault's 1946 production made a deep impression. In *Boulevard Durand* in 1960 Salacrou dramatised in Brechtian style an episode from the trade-union history of his home town of Le Havre. The story of a flagrant miscarriage of justice in 1910 is presented very directly, and the political tendency is perhaps rather obvious. But the poignancy of the personal tragedies of those involved is also brought out powerfully, and Salacrou felt that he had succeeded in creating authentic popular theatre.

Except when occasionally tempted into caricaturing the bourgeoisie, Salacrou presents humanity and human relationships with deep sympathy, though that often goes with sardonic humour as well, as in *When the Music Stops*. The thought that death is both inevitable and incomprehensible haunts him, and it has been argued that his metaphysical anguish may be related to his never-ending search for a satisfying substitute for the Catholic faith he lost in his youth. To convey an all-pervading sense of malaise about the meaning of life, Salacrou often uses the image of the nightmare.

Fascination with the problem of the nature of time is another marked characteristic of Salacrou's outlook. For instance, in a number of his plays, such as *L'Inconnue d'Arras* and *Les*

Nuits de la colère, the flashback is employed. No doubt Salacrou, who worked in films for a while, was influenced by cinematic techniques, as were many of his contemporaries, and the device has obvious advantages for the analytic dramatisation of moral issues. But unlike those who exploited the flashback simply for its convenience, Salacrou finds the contemplation of irreversibility of time truly disquieting.

—C.N. Smith

SARRAUTE, Nathalie (née Tcherniak). Born in Ivanovo, Russia, 18 July 1900. Educated at Lycée Fénelon, Paris; the Sorbonne, Paris, Licence in English 1920; Oxford University, 1921; École de Droit, Paris, law degree 1925. Married Raymond Sarraute in 1925; three daughters. Member of the French Bar, 1926-41. Since 1941, full-time writer. Recipient: International Publishers Prize, 1964. Address: 12 Avenue Pierre I de Serbie, 75116 Paris, France.

PUBLICATIONS

Fiction

Tropismes. Paris, Denoël, 1939; revised edition, Paris, Minuit, 1957; as *Tropisms*, with *The Age of Suspicion*, London, Calder, 1963; published separately, New York, Braziller, 1967.
Portrait d'un inconnu. Paris, Marin, 1948; as *Portrait of a Man Unknown*, New York, Braziller, 1958; London, Calder, 1959.
Martereau. Paris, Gallimard, 1953; translated as *Martereau*, New York, Braziller, 1959; London, Calder, 1964.
Le Planétarium. Paris, Gallimard, 1959; as *The Planetarium*, New York, Braziller, 1960; London, Calder, 1961.
Les Fruits d'or. Paris, Gallimard, 1963; as *The Golden Fruits*, New York, Braziller, 1964; London, Calder, 1965.
Entre la vie et la mort. Paris, Gallimard, 1968; as *Between Life and Death*, New York, Braziller, 1969; London, Calder and Boyars, 1970.
Vous les entendez? Paris, Gallimard, 1972; as *Do You Hear Them?*, New York, Braziller, 1973; London, Calder and Boyars, 1975.
"disent les imbéciles." Paris, Gallimard, 1976; as *"fools say,"* New York, Braziller, and London, Calder, 1977.
L'Usage de la parole. Paris, Gallimard, 1980; as *The Use of Speech*, New York, Braziller, 1980.

Plays

Le Silence, suivi de Le Mensonge (produced Paris, 1967). Paris, Gallimard, 1967; as *Silence, and The Lie* (produced London, 1972), London, Calder and Boyars, 1969.

Isma (produced Paris, 1973).   With *Le Silence* and *Le Mensonge*, Paris, Gallimard, 1970;
as *Izzuma*, in *Collected Plays*, 1980.
C'est beau (produced Paris, 1975).   In *Théâtre*, 1978; as *It's Beautiful*, in *Collected Plays*,
1980.
Elle est là (produced Paris, 1978).   In *Théâtre*, 1978; as *It Is There*, in *Collected Plays*,
1980.
Théâtre (includes *Elle est là, C'est beau, Isma, Le Mensonge, Le Silence*).   Paris, Galli-
mard, 1978.
Collected Plays (includes *It Is There, It's Beautiful, Izzuma, The Lie, Silence*).   London,
Calder, 1980; New York, Braziller, 1981.

Other

L'Ère du soupçon.   Paris, Gallimard, 1956; as *The Age of Suspicion*, New York, Braziller, 1963; with *Tropisms*, London, Calder and Boyars, 1963.
Enfance (autobiography).   Paris, Gallimard, 1983; as *Childhood*, New York, Braziller,
1984.

*

Critical Studies: *Sarraute* by Ruth Z. Temple, New York, Columbia University Press, 1968;
Sarraute by Gretchen Rous Besser, Boston, Twayne, 1979; *Sarraute and the War of the Words:
A Study of Five Novels* by Valerie Minogue, Edinburgh, Edinburgh University Press, 1981;
The Novels of Sarraute: Towards an Aesthetic by Helen Watson-Williams, Amsterdam,
Rodopi, 1981.

*   *   *

Not a prolific writer, Nathalie Sarraute has produced seven novels, two volumes of studies
rather like prose poems, six short plays, an autobiographical volume, and many influential
critical essays. The essays collected in *The Age of Suspicion* (1956) provided an early manifesto
for the literary movement dubbed the New Novel, or *nouveau roman*, in whose emergence in
the late 1950's Sarraute played a leading role. The essays, deriving not from abstract theorising
but from the demands of a new subject-matter, reject the conventions of the traditional novel
and defend the novelist's need for formal experimentation. Her first work, *Tropisms*, begun in
1932, was first published in 1939 and republished in the more welcoming climate of 1957; these
evocative sketches already show the preoccupation with the unspoken undertow of human
discourse which makes Sarraute's work quite distinct from that of other New Novelists and
keeps it, for all its radical innovations, more fundamentally attached to the realist mimetic
tradition. This undertow she has variously termed "tropisms" (taking the word from the
Natural Sciences where it denotes movement in response to stimulus), "sub-conversation,"
"infra-psychology," "pre-language," and "le ressenti" (the "felt" or "experienced").
     The plays, originally written for radio and broadcast in many countries, have also been
successfully performed on stage: like *Tropisms*, they enlarge specific moments in human
encounters, so that the actors speak words which would normally remain unspoken, and
formulate feelings that would normally be no more than the twitching of a muscle or a tiny
eye-movement. *The Use of Speech* returns to the prose-poem form of *Tropisms*, and with its
intricate unfurlings of the movements preceding and following speech, testifies to the constancy
of Sarraute's attention to tropistic undercurrents. Finding traces of similar undercurrents in
many literary predecessors, notably Dostoevsky and Proust, Sarraute acknowledges her
decision to follow a Proustian direction, discarding the conventional demands of the novel to
give herself space and time enough to slow down, enlarge, and deepen the subterranean feelings
Proust briefly suggests or retrospectively analyses. In Sarrautean fiction, they do not occur in
the interstices of the action, nor are they viewed in retrospect, but constitute the action, and the

poetic prose which recreates rather than describes them invites the reader to participate in their immediacy. Sarraute's option for the microscopic inevitably excludes large-scale frames of reference—to broad social, political or moral issues—but offers a penetrating view of inter-personal encounters at a universal level.

Communication of these elusive particles of feeling demanded not only a style able to defeat the petrifying and categorising tendency inherent in language, but a new approach to the novel-form. Sarraute's fictional works reflect, along with a maturing stylistic technique, a critique of, and progressive liberation from, the conventions of the novel. The boundaries between "observation" and creation are shown to be uncertain; the relation between "observer" and "observed" is problematic; certain sequences are "replayed" with different tonalities, and the authority of the narrator is radically undermined; each new voice becomes a suspect narrative source, striving to impose its own plot and characterisation on the world about it. In *Portrait of a Man Unknown* an unnamed first-person narrator struggles to observe an old man and his daughter (inspired by Balzac's Eugénie Grandet and her miserly father), but the constantly changing figures refuse to be converted into consistent characters, and the narrator refuses to "cheat" by giving them names. The narrative of *Martereau* takes up where *Portrait* leaves off. Starting with the seemingly defined and solid character of Martereau, it subjects him to scrutiny and speculation till he is only a perplexing bundle of possibilities. *The Planetarium* sees the dispossession of the first-person narrator: an aspiring writer becomes only one among a number of voices relating domestic conflicts and the clashes of bourgeois and intellectual attitudes. *The Golden Fruits* is a discussion by many voices of the changing fortunes of a novel called "The Golden Fruits": in a mixture of self-definition and literary comment they not only provide a brilliantly funny satire of Parisian literary circles but show the fundamental uncer-tainty of all literary values. *Between Life and Death* takes the reader into the consciousness of the writer in the act of writing, oscillating between the self-abnegation of creativity and the self-consciousness that intrudes to make him "play the writer." *Do You Hear Them?*, the most tenderly ironic of the novels, focuses on the love, anger, hopes, exasperations, and doubts of a father hearing, interpreting, and reinterpreting his chldren's laughter. *Fools say...* again centres on characterisation and categorisation. The most recent and least "difficult" work, *Childhood*, is autobiographical in origin and is arguably the summit of Sarraute's later work. It submits the novelist's early memories to the same probing scrutiny found in the novels, with a similar insistence on the fluidity of experience: it is a richly poetic patchwork of childhood fragments. From Sarraute's ironic attacks on narrative features (the meshing of events into "plot," the reduction of fluctuating beings to "characters") that bedevil literature and life alike, the positive values that emerge are humility, compassion, and humour. They are the qualities that make Sarraute one of France's greatest living writers.

In Sarraute's hesitant pages with their question-marks, trails of dots, and broken syntax, the trivia of everyday life—an unexplained silence, a mispronunciation, a bar of soap, marks of screw-holes in a door, and intrusive "My dear" in a conversation—become focal points for doubt and mortal anguish, but the ironic disproportion between the trivia and the feelings they carry maintains a precarious and poetic balance between the tragic and the comic.

—Valerie Minogue

SASTRE (Salvador), Alfonso. Spanish. Born in Madrid, 20 February 1926. Educated at the universities of Madrid and Murcia. Married Eva Forest in 1955; two sons and one daughter.

Co-Founding Director, Arte Nuevo theatre group, 1945-48, Founder, Teatro de Agitación Social (often censored; imprisoned, 1956, 1961), and Founder, with José María de Quinto, Realistic Theatre Group, 1960. Theatre Editor, *La Hora*, 1948-50. Recipient: Viareggio-Versilia Prize, 1976. Address: c/o Aguilar, Juan Bravo 38, Madrid 6, Spain

PUBLICATIONS

Plays

Uranio 235 (produced Madrid, 1946). Included in *Teatro de vanguardia*, 1949.
Ha sonado la muerte, with Medardo Fraile (produced Madrid, 1946). Included in *Teatre de vanguardia*, 1949.
Cargamento de sueños (produced Madrid, 1948). Included in *Teatro de vanguardia*, 1949.
Teatro de vanguardia (includes *Uranio 235, Cargamento de sueños*, and, with Medardo Fraile, *Ha sonado de muerte* and *Comedia sonámbula*). Madrid, Permán, 1949.
Escuadra hacia la muerte (produced Madrid, 1953). Included in *Teatro*, 1960; edited by Farris Anderson, with *La mordaza*, Madrid, Clásicos Castalia, 1975.
La mordaza (produced Madrid, 1954). Madrid, Escelicer, 1965; edited by Farris Anderson, with *Escuadra hacia la muerte*, Madrid, Clásicos Castalia, 1975.
La sangre de Dios (produced Valencia, 1955). Madrid, Escelicer, 1959.
Ana Kleiber (produced Athens, 1960). Madrid, Escelicer, 1957; translated as *Anna Kleiber* (produced Belfast, 1967), in *The New Theatre of Europe*, edited by Robert W. Corrigan, New York, Dell, 1962.
El pan de todos (produced Barcelona, 1957). Madrid, Escelicer, 1960.
El cuervo (produced Madrid, 1957). Madrid, Escelicer, 1960.
Medea (produced 1958). Madrid, Escelicer, 1963.
Muerte en el barrio (produced Madrid, 1959). Included in *Teatro*, 1960.
La cornada (produced Madrid, 1960). Madrid, Escelicer, 1965; as *Death Thrust*, in *Masterpieces of the Modern Spanish Theatre*, edited by Robert W. Corrigan, New York, Collier, 1967.
Teatro (includes *Escuadra hacia la muerte, Tierra roja, Ana Kleiber, Muerte en el barrio, Guillermo Tell tiene los ojos tristes, El cuervo*). Buenos Aires, Losada, 1960.
Tierra roja (produced Montevideo). Included in *Teatro*, 1960.
Guillermo Tell tiene los ojos tristes (produced Madrid, 1965). Included in *Teatro*, 1960; as *Sad Are the Eyes of William Tell*, in *The New Wave Spanish Drama*, edited by George E. Wellwarth, New York, New York University Press, 1970.
En la red (produced Madrid, 1961). Madrid, Escelicer, 1961.
Cuatro dramas de la revolución. Madrid, Bullon, 1963.
Cargamento de sueños, Prólogo patético, Asalto nocturno. Madrid, Taurus, 1964.
Asalto nocturno (produced Barcelona, 1965). With *Cargamento de sueños*, 1964.
Prólogo patético, with *Cargamento de sueños*. 1964; as *Pathetic Prologue*, in *Modern International Drama*, March 1968.
Teatro selecto. Madrid, Escelicer, 1966.
Obras completas (plays). Madrid, Aguilar, 1967.
Oficio de tinieblas (produced Madrid, 1967). Madrid, Alfil, 1967.
El circulito de tiza (produced in part, Alicante, 1969). Included in *Obras completas*, 1967.
El escenario diabólico: El cuervo, Ejercicios de terror, Las cintas magnéticas. Barcelona, Saturno, 1973.
Las cintas magnéticas (produced Lyons, France, 1973). Included in *El escenario diabólico*, 1973.

Ejercicios de terror (produced in part, Murcia, 1981). Included in *El escenario diabólico*, 1973.
Askatasuna! (televised, 1974). Included in *Teatro político*, 1979.
M.S.V.; o, La sangre y la ceniza (produced Barcelona, 1976). With *Crónicas romanas*, Madrid, Cátedra, 1979.
Teatro político (includes *Askatasuna!, El camarada oscuro, Análisis espectral de un Comando al servicio de la Revolución Proletaria*). Donostia, Hordago, 1979.
Crónicas romanas (produced Avignon, France, 1982). With *M.S.V.*, Madrid, Cátedra, 1979.
Ahola no es de leil (produced Madrid, 1979). Madrid, Vox, 1980.
Tragedia fantástica de la gitana Celestina (produced Rome, 1979). Published in *Primer Acto 192*, January-February 1982.
El hijo único de Guillermo Tell, in *Estreno 9*, Spring 1983.
La taberna fantástica, edited by Mariano de Paco. Murcia, Cuadernos de la Cátedra de Teatro de la Universidad de Murcia, 1983.

Television Play: *Askatasuna!*, 1974.

Fiction

Las noches lúgubres. Madrid, Horizonte, 1964.
El paralelo 38. Madrid, Alfaguara, 1965.
Flores rojas para Miguel Servet. Madrid, Rivadeneyra, 1967.
Lumpen, marginacion, y jerigonca. Madrid, Legasa, 1980.
El lugar del crimen—Unheimlich. Barcelona, Vergara, 1982.

Verse

Balada de Carabanchel y otros poemas celulares. Paris, Ruedo Ibérico, 1976.
El español al alcance de todos. Madrid, Sensemayá Chororó, 1978.
TBO. Madrid, Zero Zyx, 1978.

Other

Drama y sociedad. Madrid, Taurus, 1956.
Anatomía del realismo. Barcelona, Seix Barral, 1965; revised edition, 1974.
La revolución y la crítica de la cultura. Barcelona, Grijalbo, 1970.
Crítica de la imaginación. Madrid, Cátedra, 1978.
Escrito en Euskadi. Madrid, Revolución, 1982.

*

Critical Studies: *Sastre* by Farris Anderson, New York, Twayne, 1971; *Sastre, dramaturgo de la revolución* by Anje C. van der Naald, New York, Las Américas, 1973; *Il teatro de Sastre* by Magda Ruggeri Marchetti, Rome, Bulzoni, 1975; *The Contemporary Spanish Theatre (1949-1972)* by Marion Holt, Boston, Twayne, 1975.

* * *

Alfonso Sastre represents an almost clinically objective case of the creative dramatist in absolute conflict with the demands of popular taste and the limitations which severe political censorship have imposed on his work. His dedication to a revolutionary view of theatre dates from his early university affiliation with young radical groups, his wide reading of French, German, and American plays and dramatic theory, and his own unyielding vision of theatre as a social and existentialist statement. The writer was not yet twenty years old when he began to write short plays of somewhat cryptic social message (*Uranio 235* and *Cargamento de sueños*) and participated in the founding of a theatrical group, Arte Nuevo. In 1950, the playwright helped draft and co-signed a manifesto proclaiming the establishment of a "Theatre of Social Agitation." This creative movement failed to attract much interest save that of the police and the censors of Spain's socially repressive government. Sastre was effectively prohibited from producing the plays he continued to write, except in the most restricted media: small university groups, with inadequate staging and inexperienced actors and directors.

Three years later his best-known work, *Escuadra hacia la muerte*, was produced by a student group in a major theatre in Madrid, but censorship closed the play after three performances. This was sufficient to attract international attention to Sastre's theatre and to originate the legend of the dramatic genius denied voice by a repressive dictatorship. The author has indeed suffered incarceration and other civil indignities for no more aggressive acts than the expression of his ideas, and he has generally been denied access in Spain to the major theatres and professional companies that would certainly have produced his work. He continued to write, and most of his plays have by now been published in Spain and abroad. Several of his works were produced initially outside Spain: in France, Italy, Greece, Czechoslovakia, and despite frequent revocation of his passport by Spanish authorities, the author has traveled to openings of his work abroad and to literary congresses as distant as Sweden and Cuba. He has frequently been invited to lecture and teach courses in American universities, but has invariably been denied the necessary visa for entry into the United States.

Sastre is as much a critical theorist of contemporary drama as he is a playwright; he has written as much *about* theatre as he has written theatre, and a great deal on his own work and creative revolutionary stance. His guiding principle is a sort of analytic social realism. For Sastre, revolution must and will come to pass, but it will create as many problems of human conscience and coexistence as it corrects or eliminates. His many articles on dramatic theory, some incorporated in two books (*Drama y sociedad* and *Anatomía del realismo*) detail dramatic and social esthetics that are often contradictory and at times close to unintelligible. A lack of linear coherence is found in much of his recent drama. Sastre's international success is based on his more straightforward plays (*Escuadra hacia la muerte, La mordaza, Guillermo Tell tiene los ojos tristes, Tierra roja*), all written in the early and mid-1950's. An important facet of his work has been the adaptation of plays by Strindberg, Weiss, Ibsen, O'Casey, and Sartre. This activity, along with his foreign productions, places Sastre in a European milieu, and it is difficult to think of him now as an exclusively Spanish dramatist.

In the last decade, Sastre has moved ever farther from the structure of a traditional "bourgeois" theatre. The author had never modeled his work on the three-act formula typical of both classical and modern Spanish drama. He has preferred to write in *cuadros*, relatively short scenes of varying number. He frequently complicates his dramatic exposition with flashbacks, overlapping of time, enforced audience participation, taped sounds and voices, disruptive use of lights and music, and calculated interruptions of the action.

Sastre is undeniably a major intellectual and artistic figure in contemporary European theatre, and we can only surmise what his work would have been, conceived in a more open, less frustrating social context. As it is, his has been the most persistently contentious dramatic voice raised in four decades of post-war Spain.

—James Russell Stamm

SCIASCIA, Leonardo. Born in Racalmuto, Sicily, 8 January 1921. Educated at Istituto Magistrale, Caltanissetta, Sicily. Teacher in elementary schools, Caltanissetta, 1949-57, and Palermo, 1957-68. Since 1979, Radical Party Deputy, European parliament, Brussels. Recipient: Libera Stampa Prize, 1957; Prato Prize, 1960; Crotone Prize, 1961; Séguier Prize, 1975; Foreign Book Prize (France), 1976. Address: Via Scaduto 10/B, 90144 Palermo, Italy.

PUBLICATIONS

Fiction

Favole della dittatura. Rome, Bardi, 1950.
Le parrocchie di Regalpetra. Bari, Laterza, 1956; as *Salt in the Wound*, New York, Orion Press, 1969.
Gli zii di Sicilia. Turin, Einaudi, 1958.
Il giorno della civetta. Turin, Einaudi, 1961; as *Mafia Vendetta*, London, Cape, 1963; New York, Knopf, 1964.
Il consiglio d'Egitto. Turin, Einaudi, 1963; as *The Council of Egypt*, New York, Knopf, and London, Cape, 1966.
Morte dell'inquisitore. Bari, Laterza, 1964; as *Death of the Inquisitor*, in *Salt in the Wound*, 1967.
A ciascuno il suo. Turin, Einaudi, 1966; as *A Man's Blessing*, New York, Harper, 1968; London, Cape, 1969.
Il contesto. Turin, Einaudi, 1971; as *Equal Danger*, New York, Harper, 1973; London, Cape, 1974.
Il mare colore del vino. Turin, Einaudi, 1973.
Todo modo. Turin, Einaudi, 1974; as *One Way or Another*, New York, Harper, 1977.
Candido; ovvero, Un sogno fatto in Sicilia. Turin, Einaudi, 1977; as *Candido; or, A Dream Dreamed in Sicily*, New York, Harcourt Brace, 1979; Manchester, Carcanet Press, 1982.

Plays

L'onorevole. Turin, Einaudi, 1965.
L'onorevole, Recitazione della controversia liparitana, I mafiosi. Turin, Einaudi, 1976.

Verse

La Sicilia, il suo cuore. Rome, Bardi, 1952.

Other

Pirandello e il pirandellismo. Rome, Caltanissetta, 1953.
Pirandello e la Sicilia. Rome, Caltanissetta, 1961.
Feste religiose in Sicilia. Bari, Leonardo da Vinci Editrice, 1965.
La corda pazza: Scrittori e cose della Sicilia. Turin, Einaudi, 1970.
Palermo felicissima, with Rosario La Duca. Palermo, Il Punto, 1973.
La scomparsa di Majorana. Turin, Einaudi, 1975.
I pugnalatori. Turin, Einaudi, 1976.
I Siciliani, with Dominique Fernandez, illustrated by Ferdinando Scianna. Turin, Einaudi, 1977.

L'affaire Moro. Palermo, Sellerio, 1978.
Delle parti degli infedeli. Palermo, Sellerio, 1979.
La Sicilia come metafora: Intervista, with Marcelle Padovani. Milan, Mondadori, 1979.
Nero su nero. Turin, Einaudi, 1980.
Il teatro della memoria. Turin, Einaudi, 1981.
La sentenza memorabile. Palermo, Sellerio, 1982.
Kermesse. Palermo, Sellerio, 1982.
Cruciverba. Turin, Einaudi, 1984.

Editor, *Torre di guardia*, by Alberto Savinio. Palermo, Sellerio, 1977.
Editor, *Delle cose di Sicilia.* Palermo, Sellerio, 1980.

*

Critical Studies: *Sciascia* by Walter Mauro, Florence, La Nuova Italia, 1970; *Invito alla lettura di Sciascia* by Claude Ambroise, Milan, Mursia, 1974; *Sciascia* by Luigi Cattanei, Flroence, Le Monnier, 1979; "Sciascia Issue" of *L'Arc 77* (Paris), 1979; *Sciascia: A Thematic and Structural Study* by Giovanni Jackson, Ravenna, Longo, 1981; "Sciascia" by Verina Jones, in *Writers and Society in Contemporary Italy* edited by Michael Caesar and Peters Hainsworth, Leamington Spa, Berg, 1984.

*   *   *

Leonardo Sciascia is above all a Sicilian writer. This is reflected not only in the settings and plots of his books, but, more particularly, in his preoccupation with themes that reflect the Spanish and even the Arab influence on the island: the Mafia, inquisitions, and power. He is not, however, a regional writer, and he would not be so successful if he did not convey a universal meaning in his work.

He began in the neo-realist manner with "School Reports" which describe the problems of an elementary school teacher faced with swearing, spitting 12-year-olds. To these were added other pieces about the fictional town of Regalpietra to make up *Salt in the Wound*. Sciascia has agreed that all his themes are already present in this book, and has described his work as "the continuous story of the defeat of reason and those who have been overwhelmed and annihilated in that defeat." As author he clings to the Enlightenment position of the man of reason, the investigator who is trying to get at the truth both in fiction and documentary works. It is not always easy to draw a clear line between the two: "My subject-matter is that of the essayist, which then assumes the 'modes' of literature." The research for his documentary legal investigations is always very thorough but their appeal lies in the narrator's way with suspense and the final exposure of the institution under investigation.

Gli zii di Sicilia deals, in four stories, with proposed solutions to the Sicilian problem, discarding in turn America, communism, the ideals of the Risorgimento, and fascism. In *Mafia Vendetta* Sciascia uses for the first time the form of the detective story in an investigation of the methods of the Mafia and the ills of Sicily. By making his detective a policeman from Parma he raises his sights outside the Sicilian world. *The Council of Egypt* is set in the 18th century and examines the questions of the writing and faking of history and of the idealists' faking of the future. *A Man's Blessing* returns to the detective story, but with less optimism about the power of reason to solve a crime and deal with the Mafia. *Equal Danger* is set in an imaginary South American state and finds the detective investigating the murders of a number of judges. He is stalemated by opposing and conniving political parties. *One Way or Another* is set in Sicily in a hermitage run as a Christian-Democrat hotel. The narrator, a detective, is embroiled in the intrigues of the Party as Church and State. In *Candido* Sciascia attempts the speed and lightness of Voltaire in dealing with Italian politics since the arrival of the Americans and their support of the Mafia in 1945. Young Candido runs the political gamut, finally renouncing even the clear eye of Voltaire, and, having twice tried unsuccessfully to cultivate his lands, sets out at

SCIASCIA

the end as the child of fortune.
Having taken on the roles of judge and prophet, Sciascia was challenged by the Moro affair in 1978 when life seemed to be taking over from literature with the kidnapping and execution of the President of the Christian-Democrat Party by the Red Brigades. He wrote *L'affaire Moro* four months after the event; it reads like a confirmation of the political stalemate in *Equal Danger*.
As well as being a writer and journalist Sciascia has become an active politician. He stood as an Independent on the Communist list in the Palermo municipal elections of 1975, but soon resigned because of the delays and compromises of office. Since 1979 he has been an Italian and European Deputy as a member of the Radical Party.

—Judy Rawson

SENGHOR, Léopold (Sédar). Senegalese. Born in Joal, 9 October 1906. Educated at a Catholic elementary school, Ngasobil, 1914-23; Libermann Junior Seminary, Dakar, 1923-26; secondary school in Dakar (later Lycée Van Vollenhoven), 1926-28; Lycée Louis-le-Grand, Paris, 1928-31; the Sorbonne, agrégation 1935. French military service, 1934-35; served in the French Army, 1939-42: prisoner of war, 1940-42; later active in Resistance. Married 1) Ginette Eboué in 1946, two sons; 2) Colette Hubert in 1957, one son. Teacher, Lycée Descartes, Tours, 1935-38, and Lycée Marcelin-Berthelot, Saint-Maur des Fossés, 1938 and 1942-45; Professor, École Nationale de la France d'Outremer, 1944-60; member of the two French constituent assemblies, 1945-46, and Deputy for Senegal in the French National Assembly, 1946-59: Government Minister, 1955-56; First President of Republic of Senegal, 1960-80. Founder, with Aimé Césaire and Léon Damas, *L'Etudiant Noir*, Paris, 1934. Recipient: German Book Trade Freedom Prize, 1968; International Grand Prize for Poetry, 1970; Apollinaire Prize, 1974; Monaco Grand Prize, 1977; Cino del Duca Prize, 1978; Unesco International Book Award, 1979. Grand Cross, Legion of Honor, Member, French Academy, 1984, and many honorary memberships and degrees. Agent: Editions du Seuil, 27 rue Jacob, 75006 Paris, France. Address: BP 5106, Dakar-Fann, Senegal.

PUBLICATIONS

Verse

Chants d'ombre. Paris, Seuil, 1945.
Hosties noires. Paris, Seuil, 1948.
Chants pour Naëtt. Paris, Seghers, 1949.
Éthiopiques. Paris, Seuil, 1956.
Nocturnes. Paris, Seuil, 1961; translated as *Nocturnes*, London, Heinemann, 1969.
Poèmes. Paris, Seuil, 1964.
Selected Poems, edited by John Reed and Clive Wake. London, Oxford University Press, and New York, Atheneum, 1964.
Elégie pour Alizés. Paris, Seuil, 1969.

314

Lettres d'hivernage. Paris, Seuil, 1973.
Selected Poems, translated by Craig Williamson. London, Rex Collings, 1976.
Selected Poems, edited by Abiola Irele. London, Cambridge University Press, 1977.
Poems of a Black Orpheus, translated by William Oxley. London, Menard, 1981.

Other

Pierre Teilhard de Chardin et la politique africaine. Paris, Seuil, 1952.
La Belle Histoire de Leuk-le-lièvre, with Abdoulaye Sadji. Paris, Hachette, 1953.
Liberté:
1. *Négritude et humanisme.* Paris, Seuil, 1964.
2. *Nation et voie africaine du socialisme.* Paris, Seuil, 1971; as *Nationhood and the African Road to Socialism*, Paris, Présence Africaine, 1962; as *On African Socialism*, London, Pall Mall Press, 1964.
3. *Négritude et civilisation de l'universel.* Paris, Seuil, 1977.
4. *Socialisme et planification.* Paris, Seuil, 1983.
Prose and Poetry, edited and translated by John Reed and Clive Wake. London, Oxford University Press, 1965.
La Parole chez Paul Claudel et chez les négro-africains. Dakar, Nouvelles Editions Africaines, 1973.
Africa. Montrouge, Draeger, 1976.
Pour une relecture africaine de Marx et d'Engels. Dakar, Nouvelles Editions Africaines, 1976.
La Poésie de l'action, with Mohamed Aziza. Paris, Stock, 1980.

Editor, *Anthologie de la nouvelle poésie nègre et malgache.* Paris, Presses Universitaires de France, 1948.

*

Bibliography: *Senghor: Bibliographie* by Bureau de Documentation de la Présidence de la République, Dakar, Fondation L.S. Senghor, 1982.

Critical Studies: *Senghor and the Politics of Negritude* by Irving L. Markovitz, London, Heinemann, 1969; *The African Image in the Work of Senghor* by Barend Van Niekerk, Cape Town, Balkema, 1970; *Senghor: An Intellectual Biography* by Jack Hymans, Edinburgh, Edinburgh University Press, 1971; *The Poetry of Senghor* by S. Okechukwu Mezu, London, Heinemann, 1973; *The Concept of Négritude in the Poetry of Senghor* by Sylvia Washington Bâ, Princeton, New Jersey, Princeton University Press, 1973; *Senghor; ou, La Poésie du royaume d'enfance* by Geneviève Lebaud, Dakar, Nouvelles Editions Africaines, 1976.

*   *   *

A man who made distinguished contributions in the sphere of politics in Africa during the era of decolonisation as well as in the world of literature, Léopold Senghor reveals in his literary works the complex interplay of cultural forces which makes *négritude* such a problematic concept. After a childhood in Senegal in an environment where Catholicism was dominant and French values were rated highly, he completed his education in Paris and continued to move in French intellectual circles until the outbreak of the war. He came under the influence of Paul Claudel's sensuous mystic lyricism. He was also attracted by the religious and philosophical speculations of Emmanuel Mounier and Pierre Teilhard de Chardin. Ironically enough, it was also a French novel—*Les Déracinés* (The Uprooted) which Maurice Barrès had written in 1897 to stir up French public opinion over the Prussian occupation of Lorraine—which brought Senghor to an appreciation of his own need to preserve and develop his cultural identity as a black African. He was by no means persuaded that he should jettison all that he had learned to respect and cherish in metropolitan France, but rather sought to assimilate it with the insights and attitudes of his homeland.

Interest in Africa, aroused by the publication of André Gide's *Voyage au Congo* (Journey to the Congo) in 1927 and *Le Retour du Tchad* (Return from Chad) a year later, was further stimulated by the Paris Colonial Exhibition in 1931. The time was ripe for the black intellectuals in Paris to assert themselves, and Senghor, along with Aimé Césaire from Martinique who is credited with coining the word *négritude*, played a leading part. In particular he became associated with *L'Etudiant Noir* (The Black Student) which aimed at raising black consciousness while at the same time breaking down barriers between writers and students from different colonies, whether in Africa or the West Indies. The culmination of Senghor's efforts to demonstrate the vitality of black literature in French came with the publication in 1940 of his *Anthologie de la nouvelle poésie nègre et malgache de langue française*. With an important introduction with the title "Orphée noir" (Black Orpheus) by Jean-Paul Sartre, the anthology made a strong impact and has been reprinted several times.

As well as an advocate of black poetry, Senghor is a gifted poet in his own right. "Chaka" is an extended poem on the theme of Shaka, a more or less legendary Zulu king from pre-colonial days; though not properly a dramatic work, it has been staged and broadcast with some success. Generally Senghor did not work on such a large scale, producing a number of collections of lyric poems in which the influence of Paul Claudel and Saint-John Perse are unmistakeable, *Chants d'ombre*, *Hosties noires*, *Éthiopiques*, and *Nocturnes*. As the titles themselves hint, Senghor is a poet of twilight and darkness, which he explores in every manifestation, from womb to grave, as the reservoir of true energy. He takes the primordial themes of love and nature and expresses them with rich vocabulary and the grand rhetoric which Claudel reintroduced into French poetry with his *Odes*. Lyric in the traditional senses of the term, Senghor's poems are often conceived as for recitation or chanting to the accompaniment of an African drum or stringed or wind instrument.

—C.N. Smith

SHOLOKHOV, Mikhail (Alexandrovich). Russian. Born in Kruzhilin, 24 May 1905. Educated at schools in Moscow, Boguchar, and Veshenskaya. Served in the army, 1920-22. Married Maria Petrovna Gromoslavskaya in 1923; four children. Teacher, clerk, tax inspector, laborer, playwright, actor, journalist: war correspondent during World War II. Member of the Communist Party of the Soviet Union, 1932, of the Central Committee, 1961, and of the Presidium of the 23rd to 26th Party Congress, 1966-81. Elected Deputy of the Supreme Soviet, 1937. Member of the Presidium, Union of Soviet Writers, 1934. Recipient: Stalin Prize, 1941; Lenin Prize, 1960; Nobel Prize for Literature, 1965; Hero of Socialist Labor, 1967, 1980; Fadeyev Medal, 1974. LL.D.: University of St. Andrews, 1962; Ph.D.: University of Rostov, 1965; University of Leipzig, 1965. Member, Academy of Sciences, 1939. Address: Stanitsa Veshenskaya, Rostov Region, USSR; or, USSR Union of Writers, Ulitsa Vorovskogo 20, Moscow 69, USSR. *Died 20 February 1984.*

Fiction

Dvukhmuzhnyaya [The Woman Who Had Two Husbands]. Moscow, Gosizdat, 1925.
Krasnogvardeitsy [Red Guards]. Moscow, Gosizdat, 1925.
Donskiye rasskazy. Moscow, Novaya Moskva, 1926; as *Tales from the Don*, London,
Putnam, 1961; New York, Knopf, 1962.
Lazorevaya step [The Azure Steppe]. Moscow, Novaya Moskva, 1926; augmented
edition, Moscow, Moskovskoye Tovarishchestvo Pisaletey, 1931.
Tikhy Don. 4 vols., 1928-40; revised edition, 1953; as *And Quiet Flows the Don* and *The
Don Flows Home to the Sea*, London, Putnam, 2 vols., 1934-40; New York, Knopf, 2
vols., 1935-41; as *The Silent Don*, Knopf, 1 vol., 1941.
Podnyataya tselina. 1932-60; revised edition, 1952; as *Virgin Soil Upturned* and *Harvest
on the Don*, London, Putnam, 2 vols., 1935-60; as *Seeds of Tomorrow* and *Harvest on
the Don*, New York, Knopf, 2 vols., 1935-61.
Nauka nenavisti; Oni srazhalis' za rodinu; Sud'ba cheloveka. Moscow, Sovremennik,
1971; translated in part as *Hate*, Moscow, Foreign Languages Publishing House, 1942,
and as *The Science of Hatred*, New York, New Age, 1943; as *The Fate of a Man*,
Moscow, Foreign Languages Publishing House, 1957; Princeton, New Jersey, Van
Nostrand, 1960.
Rannie rasskazy [Early Stories]. Moscow, Sovetskaya Rossiya, 1961.
Fierce and Gentle Warriors. New York, Doubleday, 1967.

Other

Sobraniye sochineniy [Collected Works]. Moscow, Molodaya Gvardia, 8 vols., 1956-60.
Put'-dorozhen'ka [The Way and the Road]. Moscow, Molodaya Gvardia, 1962.
Slovo o Rodine. Moscow, 1965; as *One Man's Destiny and Other Stories, Articles, and
Sketches 1923-1962*, London, Putnam, and New York, Knopf, 1967.
Po veleniyu dushi. Moscow, 1970; as *At the Bidding of the Heart: Essays, Sketches,
Papers*, Moscow, Progress, 1973.

*

Critical Studies: *Sholokhov: A Critical Introduction* by D.H. Stewart, Ann Arbor, University
of Michigan Press, 1967; *Russian Fiction and Soviet Ideology: Introduction to Fedin, Leonov,
and Sholokhov* by Ernest J. Simmons, New York, Columbia University Press, 1968; *Sholokhov* by C.G. Bearne, Edinburgh, Oliver and Boyd, 1969; *The World of Young Sholokhov:
Vision of Violence* by Michael Klimenko, North Quincy, Massachusetts, Christopher, 1972;
Problems in the Literary Biography of Sholokhov by Roy A. Medvedev, Cambridge, Cambridge University Press, 1977; *Sholokhov and His Art* by Herman Ermolaev, Princeton, New
Jersey, Princeton University Press, 1982; *The Authorship of "The Quiet Don"* by Geir Kjestsaa
and others, Oslo, Solum, and Atlantic Highlands, New Jersey, Humanities Press, 1984.

* * *

Mikhail Sholokhov began his literary career with some thirty short stories written between
1923 and 1927. Most of these stories focus on the merciless socio-political struggle within Don
Cossack families and villages during the civil war and the early years of Soviet rule. Although
the stories are artistically uneven, they demonstrate Sholokhov's rapid development from an
imitative apprentice into an original craftsman with a keen eye for striking detail, a bent for
dramatic collisions, an earthy sense of humor, and the ability to use effectively the juicy

Cossack dialect.

Sholokhov's major work is the epic novel *And Quiet Flows the Don*. Set in the years 1912-22, this monument to the Don Cossacks offers a panoramic view of their life in time of peace and during the turbulent years of war and revolution. Sholokhov treats man as a part of nature, with love, procreation, and perpetual renewal forming the very core of existence. Human emotions and actions are frequently related to processes occurring in nature, whose vivid descriptions bespeak an acute perception of form, color, sound, smell, and movement. The novel occupies a unique place in Soviet literature in that it portrays the fighting of the Whites against the Reds and does it with considerable objectivity. Its protagonist is ideologically uncommitted; his search for a political truth is overshadowed by his passionate and tragic love, illustrating the author's belief that almost every true love ends in separation or loss. The novel abounds in tense situations arising from personal and political conflicts. The Cossack characters are portrayed as full-blooded individuals and their dialogues are superb. In his own narrative Sholokhov liberally employs dialecticisms and the imagery of Cossack folk poetry. In its prolific use of color, figures of speech, and bold syntactical constructions, the novel reveals a kinship with the Soviet ornamental prose of the 1920's. Since 1928 Sholokhov's authorship of the novel has been questioned on the grounds that he could not have written such a vast and unbiased epic because of his youth or because of his pro-Soviet persuasion. There is no convincing evidence to support these allegations.

Sholokhov's second novel, *Virgin Soil Upturned*, portraying collectivization in a Don Cossack village, marks the beginning of his artistic decline, attributable to his growing adherence to official interpretations of events, alcoholism, and an exhaustion of his creativity. While volume 1 gives a fairly accurate and dynamic account of the initial stage of collectivization, the static volume 2 does not go beyond the summer of 1930, avoiding the terrorism and famine of the years 1932-33.

During World War II Sholokhov produced several agitational sketches and a story, *The Science of Hatred*, showing real and imagined atrocities of the German army. He also started the war novel *They Fought for Their Country*, which remains unfinished. Its published chapters describe a battle in the Don region and provide flashbacks into the characters' past.

Sholokhov's last completed work, the story *The Fate of a Man*, blends propaganda of Soviet patriotism with the theme of personal grief caused by the war.

—Herman Ermolaev

SIMENON, Georges (Joseph Christian). Belgian. Born in Liège 13 February 1903. Educated at convent nursery school, Liège; Collège St. Louis and Collège St. Servais, Liège, to age 15. Served in the Belgian cavalry, 1921-22; High Commissioner for Belgian refugees in La Rochelle during World War II. Married 1) Régine Renchon in 1923 (divorced, 1950), one son; 2) Denise Ouimet in 1950, two sons and one daughter (deceased). Apprenticed to a pastry chef and bookseller, 1918-19; reporter and columnist, Liège *Gazette*, 1919-21; secretary to the writers Henri Binet-Valmer, 1922-23, and the Marquis de Tracy, 1923-24; then free-lance writer in Paris; lived in the U.S.A. and Canada after World War II, and in Switzerland after 1955. Recipient: Mystery Writers of America Grand Master Award, 1965. Member, Royal Academy of French Language and Literature (Belgium), 1953. Address: Secrétariat de Georges Simenon, avenue du Temple 19B, 1012 Lausanne, Switzerland.

Fiction

Étoile de cinéma (as Georges d'Isly). Paris, Rouff, 1925.
Volupteuses étreintes (as Plick et Plock). Paris, Prima, 1925.
Le Chéri de Tantine (as Plick et Plock). Paris, Prima, 1925.
Bobette et ses satyres (as Bobette). Paris, Ferenczi, 1928.
Un Petit Poison (as Kim). Paris, Ferenczi, 1928.
Helas! (as Germain d'Antibes). Paris, Ferenczi, 1929.
Des Deux Maîtresses (as Jean Dossage). Paris, Ferenczi, 1929.
Trop belle pour elle! (as G. Violis). Paris, Ferenczi, 1929.
Pietr-le-Letton. Paris, Fayard, 1931; as *The Strange Case of Peter the Lett*, New York, Covici Friede, 1933; as *The Case of Peter the Lett*, in *Inspector Maigret Investigates*, London, Hurst and Blackett, 1934.
Au rendez-vous des Terre-Neuvas. Paris, Fayard, 1931; as *The Sailor's Rendezvous*, in *Maigret Keeps a Rendezvous*, London, Routledge, 1940; New York, Harcourt Brace, 1941.
Le Charretier de "La Providence." Paris, Fayard, 1931; as *The Crime at Lock 14*, with *The Shadow on the Courtyard*, New York, Covici Friede, 1934; in *The Triumph of Inspector Maigret*, London, Hurst and Blackett, 1934; as *Maigret Meets a Milord*, London, Penguin, 1963.
Le Chien jaune. Paris, Fayard, 1931; as *A Face for a Clue*, in *The Patience of Maigret*, London, Routledge, 1939; New York, Harcourt Brace, 1940.
La Danseuse de Gai-Moulin. Paris, Fayard, 1931; as *At the Gai-Moulin*, in *Maigret Abroad*, New York, Harcourt Brace, 1940; with *A Battle of Nerves*, London, Penguin, 1951.
M. Gallet décédé. Paris, Fayard, 1931; as *The Death of Monsieur Gallet*, New York, Covici Friede, 1932; in *Introducing Inspector Maigret*, London, Hurst and Blackett, 1933; as *Maigret Stonewalled*, London, Penguin, 1963.
La Nuit de carrefour. Paris, Fayard, 1931; as *The Crossroad Murders*, in *Inspector Maigret Investigates*, London, Hurst and Blackett, 1934; as *Maigret at the Crossroads*, London, Penguin, 1963.
Le Pendu de Saint-Pholien. Paris, Fayard, 1931; as *The Crime of Inspector Maigret*, New York, Covici Friede, 1933; in *Introducing Inspector Maigret*, London, Hurst and Blackett, 1933; as *Maigret and the Hundred Gibbets*, London, Penguin, 1963.
Un Crime en Hollande. Paris, Fayard, 1931; as *A Crime in Holland*, in *Maigret Abroad*, New York, Harcourt Brace, 1940; with *A Face for a Clue*, London, Penguin, 1952.
La Tête d'un homme. Paris, Fayard, 1931; as *L'Homme de la Tour Eiffel*, 1950; as *A Battle of Nerves*, in *The Patience of Maigret*, London, Routledge, 1939; New York, Harcourt Brace, 1940.
Le Relais d'Alsace. Paris, Fayard, 1931; as *The Man from Everywhere*, in *Maigret and M. L'Abbé*, London, Routledge, 1941; New York, Harcourt Brace, 1942.
L'Affaire Saint-Fiacre. Paris, Fayard, 1932; as *The Saint-Fiacre Affair*, in *Maigret Keeps a Rendezvous*, London, Routledge, 1940; New York, Harcourt Brace, 1941; as *Maigret Goes Home*, London, Penguin, 1967.
Chez les Flamands. Paris, Fayard, 1932; as *The Flemish Shop*, in *Maigret to the Rescue*, London, Routledge, 1940; New York, Harcourt Brace, 1941.
Le Fou de Bergerac. Paris, Fayard, 1932; as *The Madman of Bergerac*, in *Maigret Travels South*, New York, Harcourt Brace, 1940.
La Guinguette à deux sous. Paris, Fayard, 1932; as *Guinguette by the Seine*, in *Maigret to the Rescue*, London, Routledge, 1940; New York, Harcourt Brace, 1941.
Liberty Bar. Paris, Fayard, 1932; as *Liberty Bar*, in *Maigret Travels South*, New York,

Harcourt Brace, 1940.

L'Ombre chinoise. Paris, Fayard, 1932; as *The Shadow in the Courtyard*, with *The Crime at Lock 14*, New York, Covici Friede, 1934; in *The Triumph of Inspector Maigret*, London, Hurst and Blackett, 1934; as *Maigret Mystified*, London, Penguin, 1965.

Le Port des brumes. Paris, Fayard, 1932; as *Death of a Harbor Master*, in *Maigret and M. L'Abbé*, London, Routledge, 1941; New York, Harcourt Brace, 1942.

Le Passageur du "Polarlys." Paris, Fayard, 1932; as *The Mystery of the Polarlys*, in *In Two Latitudes*, London, Routledge, 1942; New York, Harcourt Brace, 1943; as *Danger at Sea*, in *On Land and Sea*, New York, Hanover House, 1954.

Les Treize Mystères. Paris, Fayard, 1932.

Les Treize Enigmes. Paris, Fayard, 1932.

Les Treize Coupables. Paris, Fayard, 1932.

L'Ecluse no. 1. Paris, Fayard, 1933; as *The Lock at Charenton*, in *Maigret Sits It Out*, New York, Harcourt Brace, 1941.

L'Âne rouge. Paris, Fayard, 1933; as *The Night-Club*, London, Hamish Hamilton, 1979.

Le Coup de lune. Paris, Fayard, 1933; as *Tropic Moon*, in *In Two Latitudes*, London, Routledge, 1942; New York, Harcourt Brace, 1943.

Les Fiançailles de Mr. Hire. Paris, Fayard, 1933; as *Mr. Hire's Engagement*, in *The Sacrifice*, London, Hamish Hamilton, 1958.

Les Gens d'en face. Paris, Fayard, 1933; as *The Window over the Way*, with *The Gendarme's Report*, London, Routledge, 1951; as *Danger Ashore*, in *On Land and Sea*, New York, Hanover House, 1954.

Le Haut mal. Paris, Fayard, 1933; as *The Woman in the Grey House*, in *Affairs of Destiny*, London, Routledge, 1942; New York, Harcourt Brace, 1944.

La Maison du canal. Paris, Fayard, 1933; as *The House by the Canal*, with *The Ostenders*, London, Routledge, 1952.

L'Homme de Londres. Paris, Fayard, 1934; as *Newhaven-Dieppe*, in *Affairs of Destiny*, London, Routledge, 1942; New York, Harcourt Brace, 1944.

Maigret. Paris, Fayard, 1934; as *Maigret Returns*, in *Maigret Sits It Out*, New York, Harcourt Brace, 1941.

Les Suicidés. Paris, Gallimard, 1934; as *One Way Out*, in *Escape in Vain*, London, Routledge, 1943; New York, Harcourt Brace, 1944.

Le Locataire. Paris, Gallimard, 1934; as *The Lodger*, in *Escape in Vain*, London, Routledge, 1943; New York, Harcourt Brace, 1944.

Les Clients d'Avrenos. Paris, Gallimard, 1935.

Les Pitard. Paris, Gallimard, 1935; as *A Wife at Sea*, with *The Murderer*, London, Routledge, 1949.

Quartier Nègre. Paris, Gallimard, 1935.

Les Demoiselles de Concarneau. Paris, Gallimard, 1936; as *The Breton Sisters*, in *Havoc by Accident*, New York, Harcourt Brace, 1943; London, Penguin, 1952.

L'Evadé. Paris, Gallimard, 1936; as *The Disintegration of J.P.G.*, London, Routledge, 1937.

Long cours. Paris, Gallimard, 1936; as *The Long Exile*, New York, Harcourt Brace, 1982; London, Hamish Hamilton, 1983.

45° à l'ombre. Paris, Gallimard, 1936.

L'Assassin. Paris, Gallimard, 1937; as *The Murderer*, with *A Wife at Sea*, London, Routledge, 1949.

Le Blanc à lunettes. Paris, Gallimard, 1937; as *Tatala*, in *Havoc by Accident*, New York, Harcourt Brace, 1943; London, Penguin, 1952.

Faubourg. Paris, Gallimard, 1937; as *Home Town*, in *On the Danger Line*, New York, Harcourt Brace, 1944; London, Penguin, 1952.

Le Testament Donadieu. Paris, Gallimard, 1937; as *The Shadow Falls*, New York,

Harcourt Brace, 1945.

Les Sept Minutes. Paris, Gallimard, 1938.

Ceux de la soif. Paris, Gallimard, 1938.

Chemin sans issue. Paris, Gallimard, 1938; as *Blind Alley*, New York, Reynal, 1946; in *Lost Moorings*, London, Routledge, 1946.

Le Cheval blanc. Paris, Gallimard, 1938.

L'Homme qui regardait passer les trains. Paris, Gallimard, 1938; as *The Man Who Watched the Trains Go By*, London, Routledge, 1942; New York, Reynal, 1946.

Le Marie du port. Paris, Gallimard, 1938; as *A Chit of a Girl*, with *Justice*, London, Routledge, 1949; as *The Girl in Waiting*, with *Justice*, 1957.

Monsieur La Souris. Paris, Gallimard, 1938; as *Monsieur La Souris*, with *Poisoned Relations*, London, Routledge, 1950; as *The Mouse*, London, Penguin, 1966.

Les Rescapés du Télémaque. Paris, Gallimard, 1938; as *The Survivors*, with *Black Rain* London, Routledge, 1949.

Les Soeurs Lacroix. Paris, Gallimard, 1938; as *Poisoned Relations*, with *Monsieur La Souris*, London, Routledge, 1950.

Le Suspect. Paris, Gallimard, 1938; as *The Green Thermos*, in *On the Danger Line*, New York, Harcourt Brace, 1944; London, Penguin, 1952.

Touriste de bananes. Paris, Gallimard, 1938; as *Banana Tourist*, in *Lost Moorings*, London, Routledge, 1946.

Le Bourgmestre de Furnes. Paris, Gallimard, 1939; as *The Bourgomaster of Furnes*, London, Routledge, 1952.

Chez Krull. Paris, Gallimard, 1939; as *Chez Krull*, in *A Sense of Guilt*, London, Hamish Hamilton, 1955.

Les Inconnus dans la maison. Paris, Gallimard, 1940; as *Stranger in the House*, London, Routledge, 1951; New York, Doubleday, 1954.

Malempin. Paris, Gallimard, 1940; as *The Family Lie*, London, Hamish Hamilton, 1978.

Bergelon. Paris, Gallimard, 1941.

Cour d'assises. Paris, Gallimard, 1941; as *Justice*, with *A Chit of a Girl*, London, Routledge, 1949.

Il pleut bergère. Paris, Gallimard, 1941; as *Black Rain*, New York, Reynal, 1947; with *The Survivors*, London, Routledge, 1949.

La Maison des sept jeunes filles. Paris, Gallimard, 1941.

L'Outlaw. Paris, Gallimard, 1941.

Le Voyageur de la Toussaint. Paris, Gallimard, 1941; as *Strange Inheritance*, London, Routledge, 1950.

Le Fils Cardinaud. Paris, Gallimard, 1942; as *Young Cardinaud*, in *The Sacrifice*, London, Hamish Hamilton, 1956.

Oncle Charles s'est enfermé. Paris, Gallimard, 1942.

La Vérité sur Bébé Donge. Paris, Gallimard, 1942; as *The Trial of Bebe Donge*, London, Routledge, 1952; as *I Take This Woman*, in *Satan's Children*, New York, Prentice Hall, 1953.

La Veuve Couderc. Paris, Gallimard, 1942; as *Ticket of Leave*, London, Routledge, 1954; as *The Widow*, with *Magician*, New York, Doubleday, 1955.

Maigret revient. Paris, Gallimard, 1942; translated in part as *Maigret and the Spinster*, New York, Harcourt Brace, and London, Hamish Hamilton, 1977; *Maigret and the Hotel Majestic*, Hamish Hamilton, 1977, New York, Harcourt Brace, 1978.

Le Petit Docteur. Paris, Gallimard, 1943; as *The Little Doctor*, London, Hamish Hamilton, 1978.

Les Nouvelles Enquêtes de Maigret. Paris, Gallimard, 1944.

La Rapport du gendarme. Paris, Gallimard, 1944; as *The Gendarme's Report*, with *The Window over the Way*, London, Routledge, 1951.

Signe Picpus. Paris, Gallimard, 1944; as *To Any Lengths*, London, Penguin, 1958.

Les Dossiers de l'Agence O. Paris, Gallimard, 1945.

L'Aîné des ferchaux. Paris, Gallimard, 1945; as *Magnet of Doom*, London, Routledge, 1948; as *The First Born*, New York, Reynal, 1949.

Le Fenêtre des Rouet. Paris, Jeune Parque, 1945; as *Across the Street*, London, Routledge, 1954.

La Fuite de M. Monde. Paris, Jeune Parque, 1945; as *Monsieur Monde Vanishes*, London, Hamish Hamilton, 1967; New York, Harcourt Brace, 1977.

Le Cercle des Mahé. Paris, Gallimard, 1946.

Les Noces de Poitiers. Paris, Gallimard, 1946.

Trois Chambres à Manhattan. Paris, Cité, 1947; as *Three Beds in Manhattan*, New York, Doubleday, 1964; London, Hamish Hamilton, 1976.

Au Bout du rouleau. Paris, Cité, 1947.

Le Clan des Ostendais. Paris, Gallimard, 1947; as *The Ostenders*, with *The House by the Canal*, London, Routledge, 1952.

Lettre à mon juge. Paris, Cité, 1947; as *Act of Passion*, New York, Prentice Hall, 1952; London, Routledge, 1953.

Le Passager clandestin. Paris, Jeune Parque, 1947; as *The Stowaway*, London, Hamish Hamilton, 1957.

Maigret et l'inspecteur malchanceux. Paris, Cité, 1947.

Maigret à New York. Paris, Cité, 1947; as *Maigret in New York's Underworld*, New York, New American Library, 1956.

Maigret se fache, suivi de Le Pipe de Maigret. Paris, Cité, 1948.

Maigret et son mort. Paris, Cité, 1948; as *Maigret's Dead Man*, New York, Doubleday, 1964; as *Maigret's Special Murder*, London, Hamish Hamilton, 1964.

Les Vacances de Maigret. Paris, Cité, 1948; as *Maigret on Holiday*, London, Routledge, 1950; as *No Vacation for Maigret*, New York, Doubleday, 1953.

Le Bilan maletras. Paris, Gallimard, 1948.

Le Destin des Malou. Paris, Cité 1948; as *The Fate of the Malous*, London, Hamish Hamilton, 1948.

La Jument perdue. Paris, Cité 1948.

La Neige était sale. Paris, Cité 1948; as *The Snow Was Black*, New York, Prentice Hall, 1950; as *The Stain on the Snow*, London, Routledge, 1953.

Pedigree. Paris, Cité 1948; as *Pedigree*, London, Hamish Hamilton, 1962.

Maigret chez le coroner. Paris, Cité 1949; as *Maigret and the Coroner*, London, Hamish Hamilton, 1980.

Maigret et la vieille dame. Paris, Cité 1949; as *Maigret and the Old Lady*, London, Hamish Hamilton, 1958; in *Maigret Cinq*, New York, Harcourt Brace, 1965.

Mon ami Maigret. Paris, Cité 1949; as *My Friend Maigret*, in *The Methods of Maigret*, New York, Doubleday, 1957; London, Hamish Hamilton, 1957.

La Première Enquête de Maigret, 1913. Paris, Cité 1949; as *Maigret's First Case*, London, Hamish Hamilton, 1965; in *Maigret Cinq*, New York, Harcourt Brace, 1965.

Les Fantômes du chapelier. Paris, Cité 1949; as *The Hatter's Ghost*, in *The Judge and the Hatter*, London, Hamish Hamilton, 1956; as *The Hatter's Phantom*, New York, Harcourt Brace, 1976.

Le Fond de la bouteille. Paris, Cité 1949; as *The Bottom of the Bottle*, in *Tidal Wave*, New York, Doubleday, 1954; London, Hamish Hamilton, 1977.

Les Quatre Jours du pauvre homme. Paris, Cité 1949; as *Four Days in a Lifetime*, in *Satan's Children*, New York, Prentice Hall, 1953; London, Hamish Hamilton, 1977.

L'Amie de Mme. Maigret. Paris, Cité 1950; as *Madame Maigret's Own Case*, New York, Doubleday, 1959; as *Madame Maigret's Friend*, London, Hamish Hamilton, 1960.

Les Petits Cochons sans queues. Paris, Cité 1950.

L'Enterrement de Monsieur Bouvet. Paris, Cité 1950; as *The Burial of Monsieur Bouvet*, in *Destinations*, New York, Doubleday, 1955; as *Inquest on Bouvet*, London, Hamish Hamilton, 1958.

Les Volets verts. Paris, Cité, 1950; as *The Heart of a Man*, New York, Prentice Hall, 1951; in *A Sense of Guilt*, London, Hamish Hamilton, 1955.

Un Nouveau dans la ville. Paris, Cité, 1951.

Tante Jeanne. Paris, Cité, 1951; as *Aunt Jeanne*, London, Routledge, 1953; New York, Harcourt Brace, 1983.

Le Temps d'Anaïs. Paris, Cité, 1951; as *The Girl in His Past*, New York, Prentice Hall, 1952; London, Hamish Hamilton, 1976.

Une Vie comme neuve. Paris, Cité, 1951; as *A New Lease on Life*, New York, Doubleday, and London, Hamish Hamilton, 1963.

Un Noël de Maigret. Paris, Cité, 1951; as *Maigret's Christmas*. London, Hamish Hamilton, 1976; New York, Harcourt Brace, 1977.

Maigret au Picratt's. Paris, Cité, 1951; as *Maigret in Montmartre*, in *Maigret Right and Wrong*, London, Hamish Hamilton, 1954; as *Inspector Maigret and the Strangled Stripper*, New York, Doubleday, 1956.

Maigret en meuble. Paris, Cité, 1951; as *Maigret Takes a Room*, London, Hamish Hamilton, 1960; as *Maigret Rents a Room*, New York, Doubleday, 1961.

Maigret et la grande perche. Paris, Cité, 1951; as *Maigret and the Burglar's Wife*, London, Hamish Hamilton, 1955; New York, Doubleday, 1956.

Les Mémoires de Maigret. Paris, Cité, 1951; as *Maigret's Memories*, London, Hamish Hamilton, 1963.

Maigret, Lognon, et les gangsters. Paris, Cité, 1952; as *Maigret and the Killers*, New York, Doubleday, 1954; as *Maigret and the Gangsters*, London, Hamish Hamilton, 1974.

Le Revolver de Maigret. Paris, Cité, 1952; as *Maigret's Revolver*, New York, Doubleday, 1956.

Marie qui louche. Paris, Cité, 1952; as *The Girl with a Squint*, London, Hamish Hamilton, and New York, Harcourt Brace, 1978.

Les Frères Rico. Paris, Cité, 1952; as *The Brothers Rico*, in *Tidal Wave*, New York, Doubleday, 1954; in *Violent Ends*, London, Hamish Hamilton, 1954.

La Mort de Belle. Paris, Cité, 1952; as *Belle*, in *Tidal Wave*, New York, Doubleday, 1954; in *Violent Ends*, London, Hamish Hamilton, 1954.

Antoine et Julie. Paris, Cité, 1953; as *Magician*, with *The Widow*, New York, Doubleday, 1955; as *The Magician*, London, Hamish Hamilton, 1974.

L'Escalier de fer. Paris, Cité, 1953; as *The Iron Staircase*, London, Hamish Hamilton, 1963; New York, Harcourt Brace, 1977.

Feux rouges. Paris, Cité, 1953; as *The Hitchhiker*, in *Destinations*, New York, Doubleday, 1955; as *Red Lights*, in *Danger Ahead*, London, Hamish Hamilton, 1955.

Maigret et l'homme du banc. Paris, Cité, 1953; as *Maigret and the Man on the Bench*, New York, Harcourt Brace, 1975; as *Maigret and the Man on the Boulevard*, London, Hamish Hamilton, 1975.

Maigret a peur. Paris, Cité, 1953; as *Maigret Afraid*, London, Hamish Hamilton, 1961.

Maigret se trompe. Paris, Cité, 1953; as *Maigret's Mistake*, in *Maigret Right and Wrong*, London, Hamish Hamilton, 1957; in *Five Times Maigret*, New York, Harcourt Brace, 1964.

Le Bateau d'Émile. Paris, Gallimard, 1954.

Maigret à l'école. Paris, Cité, 1954; as *Maigret Goes to School*, London, Hamish Hamilton, 1957; in *Five Times Maigret*, New York, Harcourt Brace, 1964.

Maigret et la jeune morte. Paris, Cité, 1954; as *Maigret and the Young Girl*, London, Hamish Hamilton, 1955; as *Inspector Maigret and the Dead Girl*, New York, Doubleday, 1955.

Crime impuni. Paris, Cité, 1954; as *Fugitive*, New York, Doubleday, 1955; as *Account Unsettled*, London, Hamish Hamilton, 1962.

Le Grand Bob. Paris, Cité, 1954; as *Big Bob*, London, Hamish Hamilton, 1969.

L'Horloger d'Everton. Paris, Cité, 1954; as *The Watchmaker of Everton*, in *Danger*

Ahead, London, Hamish Hamilton, 1955; with *Witnesses*, New York, Doubleday, 1956.

Les Témoins. Paris, Cité, 1955; as *Witnesses*, with *The Watchmaker of Everton*, New York, Doubleday, 1956; in *The Judge and the Hatter*, London, Hamish Hamilton, 1956.

La Boule noire. Paris, Cité, 1955.

Maigret tend un piège. Paris, Cité, 1955; as *Maigret Sets a Trap*, London, Hamish Hamilton, 1965; New York, Harcourt Brace, 1972.

Maigret chez le ministre. Paris, Cité, 1955; as *Maigret and the Calame Report*, New York, Harcourt Brace, 1969; as *Maigret and the Minister*, London, Hamish Hamilton, 1969.

Maigret et le corps sans tête. Paris, Cité, 1955; as *Maigret and the Headless Corpse*, London, Hamish Hamilton, 1967; New York, Harcourt Brace, 1968.

Les Complices. Paris, Cité, 1956; as *The Accomplices*, with *The Blue Room*, New York, Harcourt Brace, 1964; London, Hamish Hamilton, 1966.

En case de malheur. Paris, Cité, 1956; as *In Case of Emergency*, New York, Doubleday, 1958; London, Hamish Hamilton, 1960.

Le Petit Homme d'Arkhangelsk. Paris, Cité, 1956; as *The Little Man from Arkangel*, London, Hamish Hamilton, 1957; with *Sunday*, New York, Harcourt Brace, 1966.

Un Échec de Maigret. Paris, Cité, 1957; as *Maigret's Failure*, London, Hamish Hamilton, 1962.

Maigret s'amuse. Paris, Cité, 1957; as *Maigret's Little Joke*, London, Hamish Hamilton, 1957; as *None of Maigret's Business*, New York, Doubleday, 1958.

Maigret voyage. Paris, Cité, 1957; as *Maigret and the Millionairess*, New York, Harcourt Brace, and London, Hamish Hamilton, 1974.

Le Fils. Paris, Cité, 1957; as *The Son*, London, Hamish Hamilton, 1958.

Le Nègre. Paris, Cité, 1957; as *The Negro*, London, Hamish Hamilton, 1959.

Le Passage de la ligne. Paris, Cité, 1958.

Le Président. Paris, Cité, 1958; as *The Premier*, London, Hamish Hamilton, 1961; with *The Train*, New York, Harcourt Brace, 1966.

Strip-Tease. Paris, Cité, 1958; as *Striptease*, London, Hamish Hamilton, 1959.

Dimanche. Paris, Cité, 1958; as *Sunday*, London, Hamish Hamilton, 1960; with *The Little Man from Arkangel*, New York, Harcourt Brace, 1966.

Les Scruples de Maigret. Paris, Cité, 1958; as *Maigret Has Scruples*, London, Hamish Hamilton, 1959; with *Versus Inspector Maigret*, New York, Doubleday, 1960.

La Vieille. Paris, Cité, 1959.

Une Confidence de Maigret. Paris, Cité, 1959; as *Maigret Has Doubts*, London, Hamish Hamilton, 1968.

Maigret et les témoins recalcitrants. Paris, Cité, 1959; as *Maigret and the Reluctant Witness*, London, Hamish Hamilton, 1959; in *Versus Inspector Maigret*, New York, Doubleday, 1960.

The Short Cases of Inspector Maigret. New York, Doubleday, 1959.

L'Ours en peluche. Paris, Cité, 1960; as *Teddy Bear*, London, Hamish Hamilton, 1971; New York, Harcourt Brace, 1972.

Le Veuf. Paris, Cité, 1960; as *The Widower*, London, Hamish Hamilton, 1961.

Maigret aux assises. Paris, Cité, 1960; as *Maigret in Court*, London, Hamish Hamilton, 1961; New York, Harcourt Brace, 1973.

Maigret et les vieillards. Paris, Cité, 1960; as *Maigret in Society*, London, Hamish Hamilton, 1962.

Betty. Paris, Cité, 1961; as *Betty*, New York, Harcourt Brace, and London, Hamish Hamilton, 1975.

Le Train. Paris, Cité, 1961; as *The Train*, London, Hamish Hamilton, 1964; with *The Premier*, New York, Harcourt Brace, 1966.

Maigret et le voleur paresseux. Paris, Cité, 1961; as *Maigret and the Lazy Burglar*,

London, Hamish Hamilton, 1963; in *A Maigret Trio*, New York, Harcourt Brace, 1973.

Maigret et les braves gens. Paris, Cité, 1962; as *Maigret and the Black Sheep*, London, Hamish Hamilton, and New York, Harcourt Brace, 1976.

Maigret et le client du samedi. Paris, Cité, 1962; as *Maigret and the Saturday Caller*, London, Hamish Hamilton, 1964.

Les Autres. Paris, Cité, 1962; as *The House on Quai Notre Dame*, New York, Harcourt Brace, 1975; as *The Others*, London, Hamish Hamilton, 1975.

La Porte. Paris, Cité, 1962; as *The Door*, London, Hamish Hamilton, 1964.

Maigret et le clochard. Paris, Cité, 1962; as *Maigret and the Bum*, New York, Harcourt Brace, 1973; as *Maigret and the Dosser*, London, Hamish Hamilton, 1973.

Le Rue aux trois poussins. Paris, Cité, 1963.

Les Anneaux de Bicetre. Paris, Cité, 1963; as *The Patient*, London, Hamish Hamilton, 1963; as *The Bells of Bicetre*, New York, Harcourt Brace, 1964.

La Colère de Maigret. Paris, Cité, 1963; as *Maigret Loses His Temper*, London, Hamish Hamilton, 1965; New York, Harcourt Brace, 1974.

La Chambre bleue. Paris, Cité, 1964; as *The Blue Room*, with *The Accomplices*, New York, Harcourt Brace, 1964; London, Hamish Hamilton, 1965.

L'Homme au petit chien. Paris, Cité, 1964; as *The Man with the Little Dog*, London, Hamish Hamilton, 1965.

Maigret et le fantôme. Paris, Cité, 1964; as *Maigret and the Ghost*, London, Hamish Hamilton, 1976; as *Maigret and the Apparition*, New York, Harcourt Brace, 1976.

Maigret se défend. Paris, Cité, 1964; as *Maigret on the Defensive*, London, Hamish Hamilton, 1966.

La Patience de Maigret. Paris, Cité, 1965; as *The Patience of Maigret*. London, Hamish Hamilton, 1966.

Le Petit Saint. Paris, Cité, 1965; as *The Little Saint*, New York, Harcourt Brace, 1965; London, Hamish Hamilton, 1976.

Le Train de Venise. Paris, Cité, 1965; as *The Venice Train*, New York, Harcourt Brace, and London, Hamish Hamilton, 1974.

Les Enquêtes du Commissaire Maigret. Paris, Cité, 2 vols., 1966-67.

Le Confessionnal. Paris, Cité, 1966; as *The Confessional*, London, Hamish Hamilton, 1967; New York, Harcourt Brace, 1968.

La Mort d'Auguste. Paris, Cité, 1966; as *The Old Man Dies*, New York, Harcourt Brace, 1967; London, Hamish Hamilton, 1968.

Maigret et l'affaire Nahour. Paris, Cité, 1966; as *Maigret and the Nahour Case*, London, Hamish Hamilton, 1967.

Le Voleur de Maigret. Paris, Cité, 1967; as *Maigret's Pickpocket*, New York, Harcourt Brace, and London, Hamish Hamilton, 1968.

Le Chat. Paris, Cité, 1967; as *The Cat*, New York, Harcourt Brace, 1967; London, Hamish Hamilton, 1972.

Le Deménagement. Paris, Cité, 1967; as *The Neighbours*, London, Hamish Hamilton, 1968; as *The Move*, New York, Harcourt Brace, 1968.

La Main. Paris, Cité, 1968; as *The Man on the Bench in the Barn*, New York, Harcourt Brace, and London, Hamish Hamilton, 1970.

La Prison. Paris, Cité, 1968; as *The Prison*, New York, Harcourt Brace, and London, Hamish Hamilton, 1969.

L'Ami d'enfance de Maigret. Paris, Cité, 1968; as *Maigret's Boyhood Friend*, New York, Harcourt Brace, and London, Hamish Hamilton, 1970.

Maigret à Vichy. Paris, Cité, 1968; as *Maigret Takes the Waters*, London, Hamish Hamilton, 1969; as *Maigret in Vichy*, New York, Harcourt Brace, 1969.

Maigret hésite. Paris, Cité, 1968; as *Maigret Hesitates*, New York, Harcourt Brace, and London, Hamish Hamilton, 1970.

Il y a encore des noisetiers. Paris, Cité, 1969.

Novembre. Paris, Cité, 1969; as *November*, New York, Harcourt Brace, and London,

Hamish Hamilton, 1970.

Maigret et le tueur. Paris, Cité, 1969; as *Maigret and the Killer*, New York, Harcourt Brace, and London, Hamish Hamilton, 1971.

Le Riche Homme. Paris, Cité, 1970; as *The Rich Man*, New York, Harcourt Brace, and London, Hamish Hamilton, 1971.

La Folle de Maigret. Paris, Cité, 1970; as *Maigret and the Madwoman*, New York, Harcourt Brace, and London, Hamish Hamilton, 1972.

Maigret et le marchand de vin. Paris, Cité, 1970; as *Maigret and the Wine Merchant*, New York, Harcourt Brace, and London, Hamish Hamilton, 1971.

Le Cage de verre. Paris, Cité, 1971; as *The Glass Cage*, New York, Harcourt Brace, and London, Hamish Hamilton, 1973.

La Disparition d'Odile. Paris, Cité, 1971; as *The Disappearance of Odile*, New York, Harcourt Brace, and London, Hamish Hamilton, 1972.

Maigret et l'homme tout seul. Paris, Cité, 1971; as *Maigret and the Loner*, New York, Harcourt Brace, and London, Hamish Hamilton, 1975.

Maigret et l'indicateur. Paris, Cité, 1971; as *Maigret and the Informer*, New York, Harcourt Brace, 1972; as *Maigret and the Flea*, London, Hamish Hamilton, 1972.

Les Innocents. Paris, Cité, 1972; as *The Innocents*, London, Hamish Hamilton, 1973; New York, Harcourt Brace, 1974.

Maigret et Monsieur Charles. Paris, Cité, 1972; as *Maigret and Monsieur Charles*, London, Hamish Hamilton, 1973.

Complete Maigret Short Stories. London, Hamish Hamilton, 2 vols., and New York, Harcourt Brace, 2 vols., 1976.

Fiction as Georges Sim

Au pont des arches. Liège, Bénard, 1921.
Les Ridicules. Liège, n.p., 1921.
Les Larmes avant le bonheur. Paris, Ferenczi, 1925.
Le Feu s'éteint. Paris, Fayard, 1927.
Les Voleurs de navires. Paris, Tallandier, 1927.
Défense d'aimer. Paris, Ferenczi, 1927.
Le Cercle de la soif. Paris, Ferenczi, 1927.
Paris-Leste. Paris, Paris Plaisirs, 1927.
Un Monsieur libidineux. Paris, Prima, 1927.
Les Coeurs perdus. Paris, Tallandier, 1928.
Le secret des Lamas. Paris, Tallandier, 1928.
Les Maudits du Pacifique. Paris, Tallandier, 1928.
Le Monstre blanc de la terre de feu. Paris, Ferenczi, 1928; as *L'Île de la désolation* (as Christian Brulls), 1933.
Miss Baby. Paris, Fayard, 1928.
Le Semeur de larmes. Paris, Ferenczi, 1928.
Le Roi des glaces. Paris, Tallandier, 1928.
Le Sous-Marin dans la forêt. Paris, Tallandier, 1928.
La Maison sans soleil. Paris, Fayard, 1928.
Aimer l'amour. Paris, Ferenczi, 1928.
Songes d'été. Paris, Ferenczi, 1928.
Les Nains des cataractes. Paris, Tallandier, 1928.
Le Lac d'angoisse. Paris, Ferenczi, 1928; as *Le Lac des esclaves* (as Christian Brulls), 1933.
Le Sang des gitanes. Paris, Ferenczi, 1928.
Chair de beauté. Paris, Fayard, 1928.
Les Mémoires d'un prostitué. Paris, Prima, 1929.

En robe de mariée. Paris, Tallandier, 1929.
La Panthère borgne. Paris, Tallandier, 1929.
La Fiancée aux mains de glace. Paris, Fayard, 1929.
Les Bandits de Chicago. Paris, Fayard, 1929.
L'Île des hommes roux. Paris, Tallandier, 1929.
Le Roi du Pacifique. Paris, Ferenczi, 1929; as Le Bateau d'or, 1935.
Le Gorille-Roi. Paris, Tallandier, 1929.
Les Contrabandiers de l'alcool. Paris, Fayard, 1929.
La Femme qui tue. Paris, Fayard, 1929.
Destinées. Paris, Fayard, 1929.
L'Île des maudits. Paris, Ferenczi, 1929; as Naufrage du "Pelican," 1933.
La Femme en deuil. Paris, Tallandier, 1929.
L'Oeil de l'Utah. Paris, Tallandier, 1930.
L'Homme qui tremble. Paris, Tallandier, 1930.
Nez d'argent. Paris, Ferenczi, 1930; as Le Paria des bois sauvages, 1933.
Mademoiselle Million. Paris, Fayard, 1930; as Les Ruses de l'amour, 1954.
Le Pêcheur de Bouées. Paris, Tallandier, 1930.
Le Chinois de San-Francisco. Paris, Tallandier, 1930.
La Femme 47. Paris, Fayard, 1930.
Katia, acrobate. Paris, Fayard, 1931.
L'Homme à la cigarette. Paris, Tallandier, 1931.
L'Homme de proie. Paris, Fayard, 1931.
Les Errants. Paris, Fayard, 1931.
La Maison de l'inquietude. Paris, Tallandier, 1932.
L'Épave. Paris, Fayard, 1932.
Matricule 12. Paris, Tallandier, 1932.
La Fiancée du diable. Paris, Fayard, 1932.
La Femme rousse. Paris, Tallandier, 1933.
Le Château des sables rouges. Paris, Tallandier, 1933.
Deuxième bureau. Paris, Tallandier, 1933.

Fiction as Jean du Perry

Le Roman d'une dactylo. Paris, Ferenczi, 1924.
Amour d'exilée. Paris, Ferenczi, 1925.
L'Oiseau blessé. Paris, Ferenczi, 1925.
L'Heureuse Fin. Paris, Ferenzci, 1925.
La Fiancée fugitive. Paris, Ferenczi, 1925.
Entre deux haines. Paris, Ferenczi, 1925.
Pour le sauver. Paris, Ferenczi, 1925.
Ceux qu'on avait oubliés.... Paris, Ferenczi, 1925.
Pour qu'il soit heureux. Paris, Ferenczi, 1925.
Amour d'Afrique. Paris, Ferenczi, 1925.
A l'assaut d'un coeur. Paris, Ferenczi, 1925.
L'Orgueil d'aimer. Paris, Ferenczi, 1926.
Celle qui est aimée. Paris, Ferenczi, 1926.
Les Yeux qui ordonnent. Paris, Ferenczi, 1926.
Que ma mère l'ignore! Paris, Ferenczi, 1926.
De la rue au bonheur. Paris, Ferenczi, 1926.
Un Péché de jeunesse. Paris, Ferenczi, 1926.
Lili Tristesse. Paris, Ferenczi, 1927.
Un tout petit coeur. Paris, Editions du Livre National, 1927.
Le Fou d'amour. Paris, Ferenczi, 1928.

Coeur exalté. Paris, Ferenczi, 1928.
Trois coeurs dans la tempête. Paris, Ferenczi, 1928.
Les Amants de la mansarde. Paris, Ferenczi, 1928.
Un Jour de soleil. Paris, Ferenczi, 1928.
La Fille de l'autre. Paris, Ferenczi, 1929.
L'Amour et l'argent. Paris, Ferenczi, 1929.
Coeur de poupée. Paris, Ferenczi, 1929.
Une Femme a tué. Paris, Ferenczi, 1929.
Deux Coeurs de femme. Paris, Ferenczi, 1929.
L'Épave d'amour. Paris, Ferenczi, 1929.
Le Mirage de Paris. Paris, Ferenczi, 1929.
Celle qui passe. Paris, Ferenczi, 1930.
Petite Exilée. Paris, Ferenczi, 1930.
Les Amants du malheur. Paris, Ferenczi, 1930.
La Femme ardente. Paris, Ferenczi, 1930.
La Porte close. Paris, Ferenczi, 1930.
Le Poupée brisée. Paris, Ferenczi, 1930.
Pauvre Amante! Paris, Ferenczi, 1931.
Le Rêve qui meurt. Paris, Rouff, 1931.
Marie-Mystère. Paris, Fayard, 1931.

Fiction as Georges-Martin Georges

L'Orgueil qui meurt. Paris, Editions du Livre National, 1925.
Un Soir de vertige. Paris, Ferenczi, 1928.
Brin d'amour. Paris, Ferenczi, 1928.
Les Coeurs vides. Paris, Ferenczi, 1928.
Cabotine.... Paris, Ferenczi, 1928.
Aimer, mourir. Paris, Ferenczi, 1928.
Voleuse d'amour. Paris, Ferenczi, 1929.
Une Ombre dans la nuit. Paris, Ferenczi, 1929.
Nuit de Paris. Paris, Ferenczi, 1929.
La Victime. Paris, Ferenczi, 1929.
Un Nid d'amour. Paris, Ferenczi, 1930.
Bobette, mannequin. Paris, Ferenczi, 1930.
La Puissance du souvenir. Paris, Ferenczi, 1930.
Le Bonheur de Lili. Paris, Ferenczi, 1930.
Le Double Vie. Paris, Ferenczi, 1931.

Fiction as Christian Brulls

La Pretresse des vaudoux. Paris, Tallandier, 1925.
Nox l'insaissable. Paris, Ferenczi, 1926.
Se Ma Tsien, le sacrificateur. Paris, Tallandier, 1926.
Le Désert du froid qui tue. Paris, Ferenczi, 1928; as *Le Yacht fantôme* (as Georges Sim), Paris, Tallandier, 1933.
Mademoiselle X. Paris, Fayard, 1928.
Annie, danseuse. Paris, Ferenczi, 1928.
Dolorosa. Paris, Fayard, 1928.
Les Adolescents passionnés. Paris, Fayard, 1929.
L'Amant sans nom. Paris, Fayard, 1929.
Un Drame au Pôle Sud. Paris, Fayard, 1929.
Les Pirates du Texas. Paris, Fayard, 1929; as *La Chasse au whiskey*, 1934.

Captain, S.O.S. Paris, Fayard, 1929.
Jacques d'Antifer, roi des Iles du Vent. Paris, Fayard, 1930; as *L'Heritier du corsaire*, 1934.
L'Inconnue. Paris, Fayard, 1930.
Train de nuit. Paris, Fayard, 1930.
Pour venger son père. Paris, Ferenczi, 1931.
La Maison de la haine. Paris, Fayard, 1931.
La Maison des disparus. Paris, Fayard, 1931.
Les Forçats de Paris. Paris, Fayard, 1932.
La Figurante. Paris, Fayard, 1932.
Fièvre. Paris, Fayard, 1932.
L'Evasion. Paris, Fayard, 1934.
L'Île empoisonnée. Paris, Ferenczi, 1937.
Seul parmi les gorilles. Paris, Ferenczi, 1937.

Fiction as Gom Gut

Un Viol aux quat'z'arts. Paris, Prima, 1925.
Perversités frivoles. Paris, Prima, 1925.
Au grand 13. Paris, Prima, 1925.
Plaisirs charnels. Paris, Prima, 1925.
Aux vingt-huit négresses. Paris, Prima, 1925.
La Noce à Montmartre. Paris, Prima, 1925.
Liquettes au vent. Paris, Prima, 1926.
Une Petite très sensuelle. Paris, Prima, 1926.
Orgies bourgeoises. Paris, Prima, 1926.
L'Homme aux douze étreintes. Paris, Prima, 1927.
Étreintes passionnées. Paris, Prima, 1927.
Une Môme dessalée. Paris, Prima, 1927.
L'Amant fantôme. Paris, Prima, 1928.
L'Amour à Montparnasse. Paris, Prima, 1928.
Les Distractions d'Hélène. Paris, Prima, 1928.

Fiction as Luc Dorsan

Histoire d'un pantalon. Paris, Prima, 1926.
Nine violée. Paris, Prima, 1926.
Nichonnette. Paris, Prima, 1926.
Mémoires d'un vieux suiveur. Paris, Prima, 1926.
Nuit de noces, doubles noces, les noces ardentes. Paris, Prima, 1926.
La Pucelle de Benouville. Paris, Prima, 1927.
Une Petite dessalée. Paris, Ferenczi, 1928.
Un Drôle de Coco. Paris, Prima, 1929.

Fiction as Jean Dorsage

L'Amour méconnu. Paris, Ferenczi, 1928.
Celle qui revient. Paris, Ferenczi, 1929.
Coeur de jeune fille. Paris, Ferenczi, 1930.
Soeurette. Paris, Ferenczi, 1930.
Les Chercheurs de bonheur. Paris, Ferenczi, 1930.

Fiction as Gaston Vialis

Un Petit Corps blessé. Paris, Ferenczi, 1928.
Haïr à force d'aimer. Paris, Ferenczi, 1928.
Le Parfum du passé. Paris, Ferenczi, 1929.
Lili-sourire. Paris, Ferenczi, 1930.
Folie d'un soir. Paris, Ferenczi, 1930.
Âme de jeune fille. Paris, Ferenczi, 1931.

Fiction as Jacques Dersonne

Un Seul Baiser.... Paris, Ferenczi, 1928.
La Merveilleuse Aventure. Paris, Ferenczi, 1929.
Les Étapes du mensonge. Paris, Ferenczi, 1930.
Baisers mortels. Paris, Ferenczi, 1930.
Victime de son fils. Paris, Ferenczi, 1931.

Plays

Quartier nègre (also director: produced Brussels, 1936).
La Neige était sale, with Frédéric Dard, from the novel by Simenon (produced Paris, 1950). In *Oeuvres Libres 57,* Paris, Fayard, 1951.

Ballet scenario: *La Chambre,* music by Georges Auric, 1955.

Other

Les Trois Crimes de mes amis. Paris, Gallimard, 1938.
Le Mauvaise Etoile. Paris, Gallimard, 1938.
Je me souviens.... Paris, Cité, 1945.
Long cours sur les rivières et canaux. Liège, Dynamo, 1952.
Le Roman de l'homme. Paris, Cité, 1960; as *The Novel of Man,* New York, Harcourt Brace, 1964.
La Femme en France. Paris, Cité, 1960.
Entretiens avec Roger Stéphane. Paris, RTF, 1963.
Ma Conviction profonde. Paris, Callier, 1963.
Oeuvres complètes, edited by Gilbert Sigaux. Lausanne, Rencontre, 72 vols., 1967-75.
Le Paris de Simenon. Paris, Tehou, 1969; as *Simenon's Paris,* London, Ebury Press, and New York, Dial Press, 1970.
Quand j'étais vieux. Paris, Cité, 1970; as *When I Was Old,* New York, Harcourt Brace, 1971; London, Hamish Hamilton, 1972.
Lettre à ma mère. Paris, Cité, 1974; as *Letter to My Mother,* London, Hamish Hamilton, and New York, Harcourt Brace, 1976.
Un Homme comme un autre. Paris, Cité, 1975.
Des Traces de pas. Paris, Cité, 1975.
Vent du nord, vent du sud. Paris, Cité, 1976.
Les Petits Hommes. Paris, Cité, 1976.
Mes Apprentissages: À la decouverte de la France, À la recherche de l'homme nu, edited by Francis Lacassin and Gilbert Sigaux. Paris, Union Général d'Editions, 2 vols., 1976.
De la cave au grenier. Paris, Cité, 1977.
À l'abri de notre arbre. Paris, Cité, 1977.

Un Banc au soleil. Paris, Cité, 1977.
Tant que je suis vivant. Paris, Cité, 1978.
Vacances obligatoires. Paris, Cité, 1978.
La Main dans la main. Paris, Cité, 1978.
Au-delà de ma porte-fenêtre. Paris, Cité, 1978.
Point-virgule. Paris, Cité, 1979.
À quoi bon jurer? Paris, Cité, 1979.
Je suis resté un enfant de choeur. Paris, Cité, 1979.
Le Prix d'un homme. Paris, Cité, 1980.
On dit que j'ai soixante-quinze ans. Paris, Cité, 1980.
Quand vient le froid. Paris, Cité, 1980.
Les Libertés qu'il nous reste. Paris, Cité, 1981.
La Femme endormie. Paris, Cité, 1981.
Jour et nuit. Paris, Cité, 1981.
Destinées. Paris, Cité, 1981.
Mémoires intimes. Paris, Cité, 1981.

*

Bibliography: *Simenon* by Bernard de Fallois, Paris, Gallimard, 1961, revised edition, 1971; *Simenon: A Checklist of His "Maigret" and Other Mystery Novels and Short Stories in French and English Translations* by Trudee Young, Metuchen, New Jersey, Scarecrow Press, 1976.

Critical Studies: *The Art of Simenon* by Thomas Narcejac, London, Routledge, 1952; *Simenon in Court* by John Raymond, London, Hamish Hamilton, 1968; *Simenon's Paris* by Frederick Frank, New York, Dial Press, 1970; *Simenon* by Lucille Frackman Becker, Boston, Twayne, 1977; *The Mystery of Simenon: A Biography* by Fenton Bresler, London, Heinemann-Quixote Press, and New York, Beaufort, 1983; *L'Univers de Simenon* (includes bibliography) by Maurice Piron, Paris, Cité, 1983.

*   *   *

Georges Simenon's productivity has been a source of amazement to critics and has often diverted them from a consideration of the literary merits of his work. But even more remarkable than the quantity of Simenon's work is its generally superior quality. His novels are marked by an extraordinary blend of narrative skill and psychological insight. Considered as a whole, Simenon's work is unique in modern literature. There are few contemporary writers who have recreated an entire period as completely as Simenon. He has evoked the atmosphere of France in the first half of the 20th century, portraying its provinces and cities, its people and customs on a vast canvas that can be compared to Balzac's *Comédie humaine*, while, at the same time, imbuing the characters with a universality that transcends time and geographical boundaries. His novels form a bridge between the traditional novel, which sought merely to tell a story, and the modern novel, which has more ambitious goals.

Like the traditional novelists, Simenon keeps to chronological plot structure; his novels start at the moment of crisis—the past is evoked by a series of flashbacks—and work directly to a conclusion. Simenon employs many traditional plot situations in his novels, such as conflict over an inheritance, desperate actions to maintain a privileged position, or sibling rivalry leading to murder. The novels range in mood from tragedy to tragicomedy, to drama, to melodrama. That none of them is a comedy may be attributed to Simenon's view of life, summed up in the words: "It's a difficult job to be a man."

Unlike many novelists of the post-World War II era, Simenon excludes from his work religion, politics, war, history, and metaphysical speculation. His aim, using a contemporary, timeless background, is to explore the eternal problems of man's destiny. For Simenon, success as a novelist implies being understood by people in all walks of life at all times. Nevertheless,

Simenon's novels are very distinctly products of the 20th century. His impatience with language, his belief that language is a means, not an end, are attitudes shared by the majority of his peers. His novels also express the anguish of the 20th century, the feelings of alienation, guilt, and expatriation to which the novels of Kafka, Camus, and Sartre have accustomed us. Like their protagonists, Simenon's characters find themselves alone in a world without transcendent values and without the social structure and hierarchy that formerly gave order, stability, and meaning to life. They are existentialists inadvertently, for they must find in themselves the answers that were formerly supplied by society and religion; they must act instinctively as they encounter each new situation, for nothing in their past dictates their actions.

Yet, Simenon's protagonists go beyond those of Sartre and Camus to join those of Beckett. Unlike the existentialist heroes, Simenon's characters lack lucidity, they are unable to understand their desperate situation. While the existentialist hero assumes his role, and, by choosing, creates his essence, Simenon's characters do not choose, but are carried along by forces stronger than themselves; they watch helplessly as they are crushed beneath the weight of pressures too heavy to bear. Like Beckett's characters, they are the object, not the subject, of the dramas in which they are involved. Led only by vague forces, Simenon's characters do not initiate their actions, but merely carry them out. As a result, they are not responsible for what they do, a concept that brings with it the concomitant contemporary thesis, the banality of evil. Simenon's characters murder without thought, instinctively, as they breathe. Their lack of lucidity, their subservience to blind forces epitomize the sickness of the 20th-century concentration camp and gulag mentality. The type of man portrayed in Simenon's work, other than Maigret, the comforting old-fashioned father figure, lacks distinctive characteristics or positive values which explains why there are no great thoughts, ambitions, or passions in Simenon's work.

—Lucille Frackman Becker

SIMON, Claude (Eugène Henri). French. Born in Tananarive, Madagascar, 10 October 1913. Educated at Collège Stanislas, Paris; at Cambridge and Oxford universities for a short time; studied painting with André Lhote. Served in the French Cavalry, 1934-35 and 1939-40: captured, but escaped, 1940; joined resistance movement in Perpignan. Married 1) Yvonne Ducuing in 1951 (marriage dissolved); 2) Rea Karavas in 1978. Lives in Paris and in Salses, Pyrenees, where he is a wine-grower. Recipient: Nouvelle Vague Prize, 1960; Médicis Prize, 1967. D.Litt.: University of East Anglia, Norwich. Address: Salses, 66600 Rivesaltes, France.

PUBLICATIONS

Fiction

Le Tricheur. Paris, Sagittaire, 1945.
Gulliver. Paris, Calmann Lévy, 1952.
Le Sacre du printemps. Paris, Calmann Lévy, 1954.
Le Vent: Tentative de restitution d'un rétable baroque. Paris, Minuit, 1957; as *The Wind: Attempted Restoration of a Baroque Masterpiece,* New York, Braziller, 1959.

L'Herbe. Paris, Minuit, 1958; as *The Grass*, New York, Braziller, 1960; London, Cape, 1961.

La Route des Flandres. Paris, Minuit, 1960; as *The Flanders Road*, New York, Braziller, 1961; London, Cape, 1962.

Le Palace. Paris, Minuit, 1962; as *The Palace*, New York, Braziller, 1963; London, Cape, 1964.

Histoire. Paris, Minuit, 1967; translated as *Histoire*, New York, Braziller, 1968; London, Cape, 1969.

La Bataille de Pharsale. Paris, Minuit, 1969; as *The Battle of Pharsalus*, New York, Braziller, and London, Cape, 1971.

Les Corps conducteurs. Paris, Minuit, 1971; as *Conducting Bodies*, New York, Viking Press, 1974; London, Calder and Boyars, 1975.

Triptyque. Paris, Minuit, 1973; as *Triptych*, New York, Viking Press, 1976; London, Calder, 1977.

Leçon de choses. Paris, Minuit, 1975; as *The World about Us*, Princeton, New Jersey, Ontario Review Press, 1983.

Les Géorgiques. Paris, Minuit, 1981.

Play

La Séparation, from his novel *L'Herbe* (produced Paris, 1963).

Other

La Corde raide. Paris, Sagittaire, 1947.
Femmes, illustrated by Joan Miró. Paris, Maeght, 1966; as *La Chevelure de Bérénice*, Paris, Minuit, 1984.
Orion aveugle. Geneva, Skira, 1970.

*

Critical Studies: *The French New Novel: Simon, Michel Butor, Alain Robbe-Grillet* by John Sturrock, London, Oxford University Press, 1969; *Simon* by Salvador Jimenez-Fajardo, Boston, Twayne, 1975; *The Novels of Simon* by J.A.E. Loubère, Ithaca, New York, Cornell University Press, 1975; *Simon and Fiction Now* by John Fletcher, London, Calder and Boyars, 1975; *Simon's Mythic Muse* by Karen Gould, York, South Carolina, French Literature Publications, 1979; *Orion Blinded: Essays on Simon* edited by Gould and Randi Birn, Lewisburg, Pennsylvania, Bucknell University Press, 1981; *John Fowles, John Hawkes, Simon: Problems of Self and Form in the Post-Modernist Novel* by Robert Burden, Würzburg, Königshausen Neumann, 1980.

*   *   *

Considered by many to be the greatest of the group of writers loosely linked by the French literary movement known as the *nouveau roman*, Claude Simon took longer than some of the others to achieve prominence. His first novel, *Le Tricheur*, written about the same time as Albert Camus's much more famous book *L'Etranger*, although published a few years later, reflects a similar world of chance and absurdity; the title refers to the fact that mankind struggles in vain to correct ("cheat") destiny. In its overt imitation of the style of "hard-boiled" American novels, and in its bold use of sudden time shifts, it foreshadows major features of Simon's later, more mature writing.

He then wrote two very different works. *Gulliver* represented an unsuccessful attempt to produce a popular book in the Faulkner manner, and *Le Sacre du printemps* explored for the first time Simon's experiences in the Spanish civil war when he engaged in some gun-running for the republican side. With *The Wind* he joined the lists of Robbe-Grillet's publisher, the Editions de Minuit, with whom he has remained ever since. *The Wind*, set in the wind-swept Pyrenean region where he spends part of every year, is the first work of his which has clear affinities with the *nouveau roman* style of narrative, but *The Grass* represents a more powerful breakthrough into a personal idiom. The title, taken from a remark made by Pasternak to the effect that it is no more possible to watch history unfolding than it is to observe the grass growing, introduces the story of a woman who changes her mind about leaving her husband and running off with her lover, although neither she nor the reader is able to pinpoint the moment when her decision was taken.

The action of *The Flanders Road* (the death of a cavalry officer on a country road during the Battle of the Meuse in 1940) occupies only a few minutes of real time, but the narrating voice which explores and develops this simple incident weaves a fabric which fills the entire book. *The Palace* returns to personal memories of civil war Barcelona deployed to more tragic effect than in *La Sacre du printemps*, and *Histoire* is a dense, sombre story of a family and its misfortunes which "grows" out of a collection of postcards which the narrator's mother received during her protracted engagement to the man who was to become the narrator's father. Since this book Simon has relied heavily on objective materials of this kind; *The Battle of Pharsalus* is constructed around extracts from Roman historians and novelists, and *Conducting Bodies* and *The World about Us* are based on real objects like cigar-box labels and snapshots. *Triptych* and *Les Géorgiques* exploit in addition personal memories or family history, such as the true story of one of Simon's ancestors who took an active part in the French revolution and served as a general under Napoleon.

Simon writes in a rich and sensuous style, composed of long, complex sentences with a higher-than-average proportion of present participles, which owes a lot to American writing, Faulkner's in particular, in its attempt to encompass the bewildering flux of life. Like Faulkner's, too, Simon's vision is pessimistic, even tragic; he shows mankind powerless to compete with the continually renewed vigour of the natural world. In *Les Géorgiques*, for instance, the alternation of the seasons, of rain and sun and springtime, continue as if indifferent to human tragedy, and men attempt in vain to transcend their condition through frenetic military and political activity.

—John Fletcher

SKVORECKÝ, Josef. Canadian. Born in Náchod, Czechoslovakia, 27 September 1924; became Canadian citizen, 1976. Educated at Charles University, Prague, Ph.D. 1951. Served in the Czechoslovak Army Tank Corps, 1951-53. Married Zdena Salivarová in 1958. Editor, State Publishing House, Prague, 1953-56 and 1959-63, and *Světová Literatura* [World Literature] magazine, Prague, 1956-59; free-lance writer, Prague, 1963-68. Visiting Lecturer, 1969-70, Writer-in-Residence, 1970-71, Associate Professor of English, 1971-75, and since 1975, Professor of English, University of Toronto. Since 1973, Editor, 68 Publishers, Toronto. Recipient: Czechoslovak Writers Union award, 1967; Canada Council grant, 1978; Neustadt International prize, 1980; Guggenheim Fellowship, 1980. Agent: Louise Dennys, Lester Orpen Dennys Inc., 78 Sullivan Street, Toronto, Ontario M5T 1C1. Address: 487 Sackville Street, Toronto, Ontario M4X 1T6, Canada.

PUBLICATIONS

Fiction

Zbabělci. Prague, Ceskoslovenský Spisovatel, 1958; as *The Cowards*, New York, Grove Press, and London, Gollancz, 1970.
Legenda Emöke. Prague, Ceskoslovenský Spisovatel, 1963; as *Emöke* in *The Bass Saxophone*, 1977.
Sedmiramenný svícen [The Menorah]. Prague, Naše Vojsko, 1964.
Ze života lepší společnosti [The Life of Better People]. Prague, Mladá Fronta, 1965.
Smutek poručíka Boruvky. Prague, Mladá Fronta, 1966; as *The Mournful Demeanour of Lieutenant Boruvka*, London, Gollancz, 1973.
Bassaxofon. Prague, Svobodné Slovo, 1967; as *The Bass Saxophone* (includes *Emöke*), Toronto, Anson Cartwright, 1977; London, Chatto and Windus, 1978; New York, Knopf, 1979.
Babylónský příběh [A Babylonian Story]. Prague, Svobodné Slovo, 1967.
Konec nylonového věku [The End of the Nylon Age]. Prague, Ceskoslovenský Spisovatel, 1967.
Farářuv konec [End of a Priest] (novelization of screenplay). Hradec Králové, Kruh, 1969.
Lvíče. Prague, Ceskoslovenský Spisovatel, 1969; as *Miss Silver's Past*, New York, Grove Press, 1974; London, Bodley Head, 1976.
Hořkej svět: Povídky z let 1946-1967 [The Bitter World: Selected Stories 1946-1967]. Prague, Odeon, 1969.
Tankový prapor [The Tank Corps]. Toronto, 68 Publishers, 1971.
Mirákl [Miracle]. Toronto, 68 Publishers, 1972.
Hříchy pro pátera Knoxe [Sins for Father Knox]. Toronto, 68 Publishers, 1973.
Prima sezóna. Toronto, 68 Publishers, 1975; as *The Swell Season: A Text on the Most Important Things in Life*, Toronto, Dennys, and London, Chatto and Windus, 1983.
Konec poručíka Boruvky [The End of Lieutenant Boruvka]. Toronto, 68 Publishers, 1975.
Příběh inženýra lidských duší. Toronto, 68 Publishers, 2 vols., 1977; as *The Engineer of Human Souls*, Toronto, Dennys, and New York, Knopf, 1984.
Navrat poručíka Boruvky [The Return of Lieutenant Boruvka]. Toronto, 68 Publishers, 1981.
Scherzo capriccioso. Toronto, 68 Publishers, 1984.

Plays

Buh do domu [God in Your House] (produced Toronto, 1980). Toronto, 68 Publishers, 1980.

Screenplays: *Zločin v dívčí škole* [Crime in a Girls School], 1966; *Zločin v šantánu* [Crime in a Nightclub], 1968; *Farářuv konec* [End of a Priest], 1968; *Flirt se slečnou Stříbrnou* [Flirtations with Miss Silver], 1969; *Sest černých dívek* [Six Brunettes], 1969.

Radio Play: *The New Men and Women*, 1977 (Canada).

Verse

Nezoufejte! [Do Not Despair!]. Munich, Poezie mimo Domov, 1980.
Divka z Chicaga a jiné hříchy mládí: Básně z let 1940-1945 [The Girl from

Chicago...]. Munich, Poezie mimo Domov, 1980.

Other

Nápady čtenáře detektivek [Reading Detective Stories]. Prague, Ceskoslovenský Spisovatel, 1965.
O nich—o nás [They—Which Is We] (essays on American literature). Hradec Králové, Kruh, 1968.
All the Bright Young Men and Women: A Personal History of the Czech Cinema. Toronto, Peter Martin Associates, 1971.
Na brigádě [Working Overtime] (essays on contemporary Czech writers), with Antonín Brousek. Toronto, 68 Publishers, 1979.
Velká povídka o Americe (1969) [A Tall Tale about America]. Toronto, 68 Publishers, 1980.
Jiří Menzel and the History of the Closely Watched Trains. Boulder, Colorado, East European Monographs, 1982.
Útěky [Escapes] (ghostwritten autobiography of Lída Baarová). Toronto, 68 Publishers, 1983.

Editor, with P.L. Doružka, *Tvář jazzu* [The Face of Jazz]. Prague, Státní Hudební Vydavatelství, 2 vols., 1964-66.
Editor, with P.L. Doružka, *Jazz ová inspirace* [The Jazz Inspiration]. Prague, Odeon, 1966.

Translator of works by Ray Bradbury, Henry James, Hemingway, Faulkner, Sinclair Lewis, Alan Sillitoe, Dashiell Hammett, Raymond Chandler, and William Styron.

*

Bibliography: by Ivar Ivask, in *World Literature Today*, Autumn 1980.

*   *   *

"You're playing about the same thing all the time," a mother is said to have complained to her saxophonist son. Unwittingly, she pronounced a comment that fits jazz as well as nearly all literature. It certainly applies to the work of Josef Skvorecký. Since his earliest and perhaps most successful novel, *The Cowards*, written in 1948 but published only ten years later, he has pursued an ever elusive main theme: the magic of the world when it is young and the eternal game of love that the equally young men and women play in it. Even when he deviated from his preoccupation to examine other subjects, the throbbing of it could still be felt under the surface.

Over the years, Skvorecký has explored the theme in many contexts and circumstances. The backbone of his work is several novels which follow the adventures of Danny Smiřický, in whom it is not difficult to recognize the author's alter ego, made up of both reality and fantasy. In these books, Danny ages, but his principal attitudes remain those of a young man. He first appears in *The Cowards*, just turned twenty, and views with irreverence and cynicism, quite natural and appropriate to his age, the hypocritical antics of his senior fellow-citizens as they struggle to keep their respectability and positions at the end of the Second World War. Following in the author's footsteps, he turns up in his latest incarnation, in *The Engineer of Human Souls*, far from his native Czechoslovakia as a middle-aged professor of American literature at a Canadian university.

In between lies a historical epoch, nearly three decades of the turbulent 20th century. Danny has had his share of it: soon after the end of the Nazi occupation came the Stalinist years, then new hope in the 1960's cut short by the Soviet invasion in 1968, and then exile in Canada. The entire period comes to life in Skvorecký's novels. Service in the People's Army in the 1950's has been recorded in the hilariously satirical *Tankový prapor* and the sadly failed attempt to combine socialism and freedom has been captured in *Mirákl*.

Those, however, are only the surface features of the social, temporal and physical landscapes through which Danny passes on his pilgrimage. Deceptive as the great *Theatrum mundi* may be, Danny is endowed with a perception which allows him to uncover the true nature of the roles that people play in it. Retold by him, it sounds more like a farce than a drama. Skvorecký is an author who does not deny his readers the right to enjoy a laugh. But only a very inexperienced reader would miss the serious note, the bitter-sweet and sometimes tragic ostinato under the thrilling, joyful tones. The world is wonderful, but deadly.

On the other hand, there are ways to deal with this inevitability. In the midst of all cruelty, betrayal, baseness, and simple stupidity that corrupt the beauty that should be forever, Skvorecký finds several points of reassurance and security, to which he keeps returning. He is particularly attached to the times and space where we first meet young Danny, and he revisits those years in many of his stories, notably in *The Swell Season*. It is treated with a nostalgia that touches upon sentimentality. It permeates even those novels and short stories where Danny is replaced with other characters as the central figure or the narrator.

Another source of reassurance is jazz. *The Cowards* is a jazz novel not just because it turns around a youthful jazz band. Even *The Bass Saxophone* is not exclusively the story of one musical instrument. It is the spirit of the music that underlies Skvorecký's work. His style has been affected by the clipped phrases of the trumpet and the smooth runs of the saxophone, and his outlook has been shaped by the yearning and the ecstasy that can both be heard in jazz. In Nazi-occupied Europe it was the symbol of freedom; in the the Stalinist years it signified irrepressible creativity; in happier times it has been the provider of elation. In the words of the composer George Handy, "jazz originated as the outgrowths of the emotions of a frustrated people; but these emotions belong to all of us." Indeed they do: even when transformed into prose.

—Igor Hájek

SOLDATI, Mario. Italian. Born in Turin, 17 November 1906. Educated at Jesuit schools in Turin; Istituto Superiore di Storia dell'Arte, Rome; University of Turin, 1927; Columbia University, New York, 1929-31. Married twice; three children. Full-time writer; also film director; regular contributor, *Il Giorno* and *Il Corriere della Sera*. Recipient: Strega D'Annunzio Prize, 1972; Bagutta Prize, 1976; Naples Prize, 1978. Address: Via Moriggi 7, 20123 Milan, Italy.

PUBLICATIONS

Fiction

Salmace. Novara, La Libra, 1929.
La verità sul casa Motta. Milan, Rizzoli, 1941.
L'amico gesuita. Milan, Rizzoli, 1943.
A cena col commendatore. Milan, Garzanti, 1950; as *The Commander Comes to Dine,*

London, Lehmann, 1952; as *Dinner with the Commendatore*, New York, Knopf, 1953.
Le lettere da Capri. Milan, Garzanti, 1954; as *The Capri Letters*, London, Hamish Hamilton, 1955; New York, Knopf, 1956; as *Affair in Capri*, New York, Berkley, 1957.
La confessione. Milan, Garzanti, 1955; as *The Confession*, New York, Knopf, and London, Deutsch, 1958.
Il vero Silvestri. Milan, Garzanti, 1957; as *The Real Silvestri*, London, Deutsch, 1960; New York, Knopf, 1961.
I racconti. Milan, Garzanti, 1957.
La messa dei villeggianti. Milan, Mondadori, 1959.
I racconti (1927-1947). Milan, Mondadori, 1961.
Storie di spettri. Milan, Mondadori, 1962.
Le due città. Milan, Garzanti, 1964; as *The Malacca Cane*, London, Deutsch, and New York, St. Martin's Press, 1973.
La busta orancione. Milan, Mondadori, 1966; as *The Orange Envelope*, London, Deutsch, and New York, Harcourt Brace, 1969.
I racconti del Maresciallo. Milan, Mondadori, 1967.
Fuori. Milan, Mondadori, 1968.
L'attore. Milan, Mondadori, 1970.
55 novelle per l'inverno. Milan, Mondadori, 1971.
Lo smeraldo. Milan, Mondadori, 1974; as *The Emerald*, New York, Harcourt Brace, 1977.
La sposa americana. Milan, Mondadori, 1978; as *The American Bride*, Hodder and Stoughton, 1979.
44 novelle per l'estate. Milan, Mondadori, 1979.
Addio diletta Amelia. Milan, Mondadori, 1979.
La carta del cielo: Racconti. Turin, Einaudi, 1980.
L'incendio. Milan, Mondadori, 1981.
La casa del perchè. Milan, Mondadori, 1982.
Nuovi racconti del Maresciallo. Milan, Rizzoli 1984.

Plays

Pilato. Turin, SEI, 1925.

Screenplays: *Gli uomini, che mascalzoni!*, 1932; *La Principessa Tarakanova*, 1938; *La signora di Montecarlo*, 1938; *Due milioni per un sorriso*, 1939; *Dora Nelson*, 1939; *Tutto per la donna*, 1940; *Piccolo mondo antico (Old-Fashioned World)*, 1941; *Tragica notte*, 1941; *Malombra*, 1942; *Quartieri alti*, 1943; *Le miserie del signor Travet (His Young Wife)*, 1945; *Eugenia Grandet*, 1946; *Daniele Cortis*, 1947; *Fuga in Francia (Flight into France)*, 1948; *Quel bandito sono io!*, 1949; *Botta e risposta*, 1950; *Donne e briganti (Of Love and Bandits)*, 1950; *Il sogno di Zorro*, 1951; *E l'amor che mi rovina*, 1951; *O.K. Nerone (O.K. Nero)*, 1951; *Le avventure di Mandrin*, 1952; *I tre corsari*, 1952; *Jolanda— La figlia del corsaro nero*, 1952; *La provinciale (The Wayward Wife)*, 1953; *La mano dello straniero (The Stranger's Hand)*, 1953; *Questa è la vita (Of Life and Love)*, 1954; *La donna del Fiume (Woman of the River)*, 1955; *Era di venerdi 17 (The Virtuous Bigamist)*, 1957; *Italia piccola*, 1957; *Policarpo—Ufficiale di scrittura*, 1959.

Other

America, primo amore. Florence, Bemporad, 1935.
Ventiquattro ore in uno studio cinematografico. Milan, Corticelli, 1945.
Fuga in Italia, Milan, Longanesi, 1947.
L'accalappiacani. Rome, Atlante, 1953.
Canzonette e viaggio televisivo. Milan, Mondadori, 1962.

Vino al vino. Milan, Mondadori, 1969.
I disperati del benessere: Viaggio in Svezia. Milan, Mondadori, 1970.
Gloria dell'uomo, with Colomba Russo. Florence, Cremonese, 1973.
Da spettatore. Milan, Mondadori, 1973.
Un prato di papaveri: Diario 1947-1964. Milan, Mondadori, 1973.
The Octopus and the Pirates (juvenile). London, Deutsch, 1974.
Lo specchio inclinato: Diario 1965-1971. Milan, Mondadori, 1975.
Piemonte e Valle d'Aosta, illustrated by Folco Quilici. Milan, Silvana, 1978.
Lo scopone, with Maurizio Corgnati. Milan, Mondadori, 1982.

*

Critical Studies: *Soldati* by Massimo Grillandi, Florence, La Nuova Italia, 1979; *Letterato al cinema: Soldati anni '40* edited by Orio Caldiron, Rome, Cineteca Nazionale, 1979; *Invito alla lettura di Soldati* by Walter Mauro, Milan, Mursia, 1981.

*   *   *

Mario Soldati's career has been divided between fiction and filmmaking. His films have gained a respectable following, though he has never achieved the international regard of several of his near-contemporaries (De Sica, Rossellini, Visconti), but as a writer of fiction he has over the years come to be seen as the master of an elegant and cultured style. Although he has written long novels (e.g., *The Malacca Cane*), his best and most famous work is his short fiction, and especially his novellas.

Other than a similarity in subject matter—often religious education, music or opera, academic life, World War II—what comes to be seen as central to Soldati's fiction is a specific sort of viewpoint. The stories are usually, though not always, presented from a point in the future: the narrator is looking back on an episode from his own past, or that of a friend or aquaintance; there is sometimes a complexity in the time sequence, though the material is always presented with lucidity and no attempt at obscurity.

The Real Silvestri, for instance, reveals how an intimate friend of the recently dead Silvestri, because of the unexpected revelation by another of Silvestri's friends that he was a blackmailer, has to re-evaluate his feelings about him. What seems to begin as a simple after-dinner story takes a turn for the complex: the narrator's feelings for the dead man are changed, and not negatively. Silvertri's character comes to take on an added dimension (and an added humanity) because of his failings. *The American Bride*, a recent work, also seems a simple story told in the present, but on the last page we realize it occurred eight years before. What had seemed a relatively ordinary triangular relationship between an Italian professor, his American wife, and an Americanized Sicilian girl takes on an additional complexity as the confrontation between Italian and American values. An even more complicated story of the necessary re-evaluation of one's attitudes is "The Green Jacket" (in *The Commander Comes to Dine*). A now-famous orchestra conductor is led to relate his experience during the war when he and another musician (a tympanist) were in hiding from the Germans. Because of circumstances, the obviously talented conductor has to play the musical fool to the tympanist, a pompous buffoon. Yet during this crisis the little man shows such a depth of character and humanity that even after 20 years the conductor is still in awe of him. Like the conductor, the reader is forced to revise his attitudes with each incident in the story.

The narrator of "The Green Jacket" also tells the other two stories in the collection *The Commander Comes to Dine*. "The Father of the Orphans" is itself a highly complex story, even though it hinges on what at first seems a simple case of a sophisticated man about town successfully hiding his true sexual preference (young men)—but the implications of self-awareness, guilt, and atonement are both logical and moving. The third story, "The Window," makes the commander himself one of the central characters, since he is in love with the English woman around whom the story is arranged. Essentially it is the story of her love for a young artist, an "Italian Italian, the bungling, idling, brilliant, unreliable Italian" feared by foreign men and adored by foreign women. The story shows the complexity of the Italian's nature and the strength of the English woman's love; there is also a picture of two other English women, retired prostitutes, who are themselves worthy of a story of their own.

Of Soldati's stories with a strong religious theme, the most impressive is perhaps *The Orange Envelope*. Here the narrator, years after the events took place, is viewing his own sadly mishandled life. His sexual nature has been haunted by the over-rich love of his religiose mother and has consequently taken on a tinge of masochism; his first and deepest love has been lost because of his mother's machinations; another woman has managed to swindle him by playing on his feelings of sexual and religious guilt; and he is ending his life by devoting his attentions to his feeble-minded brother. The book is honest and subtle.

Soldati is a traditional writer, and he brings to his fiction strong values of tolerance (even if presented with an often highly ironic tang) and compassion. If religion is often presented in a negative light, it adds merely a darker shadow to a picture of life generally seen in neutral colors.

—George Walsh

SOLZHENITSYN, Alexander (Isayevich). Born in Kislovodsk, 11 December 1918. Educated at school in Rostov-on-Don; University of Rostov, 1936-41, degree in mathematics and physics 1941; correspondence course in philology, Moscow University, 1939-41. Served in the Soviet Army, 1941-45: captain; decorated twice; arrested and stripped of rank, 1945. Married 1) Natalya Alexeevna Reshetovskaya in 1940 (divorced), remarried in 1957 (divorced, 1973), three sons; 2) Natalya Svetlova in 1973, one stepson. Physics teacher, secondary school, Morozovsk, 1941; sentenced to 8 years imprisonment for anti-Soviet agitation, 1945: in prisons in Moscow, 1945-50, and labor camp in Kazakhstan, 1950-53; released from prison, and exiled to Kok-Terek: mathematics teacher, 1953-56; released from exile, 1956, and settled in Ryazan, 1957, as teacher, then full-time writer; unable to publish from 1966; expelled from USSR, 1974; lived in Zurich, 1974-76, and in Vermont since 1976. Recipient: Foreign Book Prize (France), 1969; Nobel Prize for Literature, 1970. Member, American Academy of Arts and Sciences, 1969; Honorary Fellow, Hoover Institution on War, Revolution, and Peace, 1975. Address: c/o Harper and Row, 10 East 53rd Street, New York, New York 10022, U.S.A.

PUBLICATIONS

Fiction

Odin den' Ivana Denisovicha. London, Flegon Press, 1962; as *One Day in the Life of Ivan Denisovich*, New York, Praeger, and London, Gollancz, 1963.
Dlya pol'zy dela. Chicago, Russian Language Specialties, 1963; as *For the Good of the Cause*, New York, Praeger, 1964; London, Bodley Head, 1971.
Sluchay na stantsii Krechetvoka; Matryonin dvor. London, Flegon Press, 1963; as *We Never Make Mistakes*, Columbia, University of South Carolina Press, 1963.

Etudy i krokhotnye rasskazy. Frankfurt, Posev, 1964; as *Stories and Prose Poems*, New York, Farrar Straus, 1971; as *Prose Poems*, London, Bodley Head, 1971; as *Matryona's House and Other Stories*, London, Penguin, 1975.

V kruge pervom. Frankfurt, Fischer, 1968; as *The First Circle*, New York, Harper, and London, Harvill Press, 1968.

Rakovy korpus. Milan, Mondadori, 1968; complete version, London, Bodley Head, 1968; as *Cancer Ward*, Bodley Head, 2 vols., 1968-69; as *The Cancer Ward*, New York, Farrar Straus, 1969.

Six Etudes. Northfield, Minnesota, College City Press, 1971.

Avgust chetyrnadtsatovo. London, Flegon Press, 1971; expanded version, as *Krasnoe koleso 1* [The Red Wheel], in *Sobraniye sochineniy 11-12*, 1983; as *August 1914*, New York, Farrar Straus, and London, Bodley Head, 1972.

Plays

Olen' i shalashovka. London, Flegon Press, 1968; as *Respublika truda*, in *Sobraniye sochineniy 8*, 1981; as *The Love-Girl and the Innocent*, London, Bodley Head, and New York, Farrar Straus, 1969.

Svecha na vetru. London, Flegon Press, 1968; as *Svet, koroty, v tebe*, in *Sobraniye sochineniy 8*, 1981; as *Candle in the Wind*, Minneapolis, University of Minnesota Press, and London, Bodley Head-Oxford University Press, 1973.

Pir podebiteley, in *Sobraniye sochineniy 8*. 1981; as *Victory Celebrations*, London, Bodley Head, 1983; New York, Farrar Straus, 1984.

Plenniki, in *Sobraniye sochineniy 8*. 1981; as *Prisoners*, London, Bodley Head, 1983; New York, Farrar Straus, 1984.

Verse

Prusskiye nochi: Poema napisannaya v lagere v 1950. Paris, YMCA Press, 1974; as *Prussian Nights*, New York, Farrar Straus, and London, Collins, 1977.

Other

Sobraniye sochineniy [Collected Works]. Frankfurt, Posev, 6 vols., 1969-70.

Les Droits de l'écrivain. Paris, Seuil, 1969.

Nobelevskaya lektsiya po literature. Paris, YMCA Press, 1972; as *Nobel Lecture*, edited by F.D. Reeve, New York, Farrar Straus, 1972; as *One Word of Truth*, London, Bodley Head, 1972.

Arkhipelag Gulag. Paris, YMCA Press, 3 vols., 1973-76; as *The Gulag Archipelago*, New York, Harper, 3 vols., and London, Collins, 3 vols., 1974-78.

Mir i nasiliye [Peace and Violence]. Frankfurt, Posev, 1974.

Pis'mo vozhdyam Sovetskovo soyuza. Paris, YMCA Press, 1974; as *Letter to the Soviet Leaders*, New York, Harper, and London, Collins, 1974.

A Pictorial Autobiography. New York, Farrar Straus, 1974.

Bodalsya telyonok s dubom (autobiography). Paris, YMCA Press, 1975; as *The Oak and the Calf*, London, Collins, and New York, Harper, 1980.

Lenin v Tsyurikhe. Paris, YMCA Press, 1975; as *Lenin in Zurich*, New York, Farrar Straus, and London, Bodley Head, 1976.

Detente: Prospects for Democracy and Dictatorship. New Brunswick, New Jersey, Transaction, 1975.

Warning to the Western World (interview). New York, Farrar Straus, and London, BBC Publications, 1976.

A World Split Apart (address). New York, Harper, 1978.
Sobraniye sochineniy [Collected Works]. Paris, YMCA Press, 1978— .
The Mortal Danger: How Misconceptions about Russia Imperil the West. New York, Harper, and London, Bodley Head, 1980.
East and West (miscellany). New York, Harper, 1980.

*

Bibliography: *Solzhenitsyn: An International Bibliography of Writings by and about Him* by Donald M. Fiene, Ann Arbor, Michigan, Ardis, 1973.

Critical Studies: *Solzhenitsyn* by Georg Lukács, London, Merlin, 1970, Cambridge, Massachusetts, M.I.T. Press, 1971; *Solzhenitsyn: The Major Novels* by Abraham Rothberg, Ithaca, New York, Cornell University Press, 1971; *Solzhenitsyn* by David Burg and George Feifer, New York, Stein and Day, 1973; *Solzhenitsyn: Critical Essays and Documentary Materials* edited by John B. Dunlop and others, Belmont, Massachusetts, Nordland, 1973, revised edition, 1975; *Solzhenitsyn* by Christopher Moody, Edinburgh, Oliver and Boyd, 1973, revised edition, Oliver and Boyd, and New York, Harper, 1976; *Solzhenitsyn: A Collection of Critical Essays* edited by Kathryn Feuer, Englewood Cliffs, New Jersey, Prentice Hall, 1976; *Solzhenitsyn: Politics and Form* by Francis Barker, London, Macmillan, 1977; *Solzhenitsyn* by Steven Allaback, New York, Taplinger, 1978; *Solzhenitsyn and the Secret Circle* by Olga Andreyev Carlisle, New York, Holt Rinehart, and London, Routledge, 1978; *Solzhenitsyn and Dostoevsky: A Study in the Polyphonic Novel* by Vladislav Krasnov, London, Prior, 1980.

*   *   *

Alexander Solzhenitsyn's literary ambitions were already manifested in 1937 when he conceived the idea of creating a long novel about the Russian revolution and wrote several chapters of it. At that time Solzhenitsyn believed in Leninism, approving of the October Revolution. His experience in Soviet prisons and forced labor camps made him change his political orientation, and he took upon himself the messianic task of exposing the brutality, the mendacity, and the illegitimacy of the Communist rule in Russia.

In the early 1950's, while serving his sentence in a camp, Solzhenitsyn composed and memorized the poem *Prussian Nights* and the verse plays *Victory Celebrations* and *Prisoners* (originally, *Decembrists Without December*). These works show the devastating invasion of East Prussia by the Red Army and the treatment of Russian officers and soldiers by the Soviet counter-intelligence.

Upon his release from the camps, Solzhenitsyn turned to prose. He wrote the play *The Republic of Labor* (also known as *The Love-Girl and the Innocent*) and the film script *Znayut istinu tanki!* (The Tanks Know the Truth!) which depict Soviet camps and employ devices aimed at visual and aural effects. In *The Light That Is in You* (also known as *Candle in the Wind*) he concentrates on the moral vices common to the civilized world, but his dramatis personae turn out to be illustrations of his ideas rather than living individuals. He is more successful in a humorous reproduction of provincial ways in the film script *Tuneyadets* (A Parasite). (Both scripts are published in *Sobraniye sochineniy 8*, 1981.)

One Day in the Life of Ivan Denisovich, called a novel in the West but a short story by Solzhenitsyn, was his first published work. Written tersely and effectively, it presents a Soviet camp through the eyes of a peasant prisoner who manages to preserve his integrity in dehumanizing conditions. The story came out only because Khrushchev considered it useful for his anti-Stalin campaign. This fact facilitated the publication of "An Incident at Krechetovka Station," "Matryona's Home," and "For the Good of the Cause." The first story demonstrates how a young lieutenant is corrupted by the intense propaganda of vigilance designed to justify domestic repression. In the second story Solzhenitsyn draws an impressive portrait of a kind and unselfish peasant woman, a type of the righteous person that forms Russia's moral foundation. The third story, showing a callous bureaucratic disregard for ordinary Soviet citizens, lacks depth and poignancy. Solzhenitsyn's fifth, and last, work published in his homeland is the short story "Zakhar the Pouch," concerned with the preservation of historic monuments. No Soviet publisher could be found for "The Right Hand," "Kak zhal" (What a Pity), "The Easter Procession," and some fifteen poems in prose—tiny masterpieces containing Solzhenitsyn's philosophical observations.

The novels *The First Circle* and *Cancer Ward* draw much upon Solzhenitsyn's personal experiences—the one upon his life in a special prison for scientists and the other upon his stay in a cancer clinic. In both novels Solzhenitsyn raises questions of human destiny, morality, freedom, happiness, love, death, faith, social injustice, and the political purges. Man is seen in non-materialist terms as a repository of the image of eternity. He must guide himself by his own conscience. The full 96-chapter version of *The First Circle*, published for the first time in Russian in 1978, has a stronger political coloration than its 87-chapter version which was translated into many languages.

As in all of Solzhenitsyn's fiction, the action in both novels takes place within a very brief period of time. The characters are well individualized. In transmitting different viewpoints, Solzhenitsyn relies heavily on heated dialogues, enhancing their dynamism by the use of short interrogative and exclamatory sentences and by references to the characters' gestures, eyes, tone of voice, and facial expressions. Solzhenitsyn is fond of refreshing the Russian literary language with racy folk locutions, sayings, and proverbs. The novels are rich in metaphors, notably *Cancer Ward*, in which the animal imagery takes on symbolic significance. At the end of the novels the reader is left in the dark about the ultimate fate of the characters. But this does not matter much for Solzhenitsyn. What counts is the moral behavior of a character at the critical point in his life, where he reveals his true value.

August 1914 is the first published "knot" in what should be a multi-volume cycle of novels intitled *Krasnoe koleso* (The Red Wheel) and intended to depict the history of the Russian revolution by focusing on its crucial events. In *August 1914* such an event is the defeat of the Russian troops in East Prussia, which, in Solzhenitsyn's view, was the first in a series of military disasters that eventually led to the revolution. Solzhenitsyn equates the revolution with the senseless destruction of Russia, whose salvation lay in a gradual socio-economic evolution with the emphasis on individual morality. Among the structural innovations in *August 1914* are chapters giving factual accounts of military situations or consisting of various excerpts from contemporary newspapers. There are also passages in the form of film scripts, aiming at visual effects. The "knot" is overloaded with military details; even more structural damage was done in its 1983 Russian edition where it was split into two volumes, with the second volume incorporating over three hundred pages devoted to events preceding 1914 by several years. Much of the insertion is composed of factual information about the statesman Petr Stolypin, whom Solzhenitsyn admires for his firm handling of revolutionary violence and for his agrarian policy. Some of the new scenes and characterizations are artistically superb, but there is a feeling that Solzhenitsyn the historian, however stimulating and valid his historical concepts might be, encroaches upon Solzhenitsyn the artist.

Outside the imaginative literature Solzhenitsyn's unique achievement is *The Gulag Archipelago*, a comprehensive picture of the Soviet penal system from its inception to the mid-1960's. Resorting to metaphors and irony, Solzhenitsyn tells the story of arrests, interrogations, executions, camps, and exile. He rejects the principle of survival at any price. Moral decline caused by materialism and the appeasement of the Soviet Union by the West are the dominant themes of his speeches and journalistic writings. His literary autobiogaphy, *The Oak and the Calf*, is essential for an understanding of his personality.

—Herman Ermolaev

SØRENSEN, Villy. Danish. Born in Copenhagen, 13 January 1929. Studied philosophy and psychology at the universities of Copenhagen and Freiburg. Writer: Editor, with Klaus Rifbjerg, *Vindrosen*, 1959-63. Recipient: Critics' Prize, 1959; Danish Academy Prize, 1962; Søren Gyldendal Prize, 1965; Henri Nathansen Prize, 1969; Holberg Medal, 1973; Nordic Council Prize, 1974; Steffens Prize (Hamburg), 1974. Honorary doctorate: University of Copenhagen, 1979. Address: Skovvej 6, Taarbaek, 2930 Klampenborg, Denmark.

PUBLICATIONS

Fiction

Saere historier. Copenhagen, Gyldendal, 1953; as *Strange Stories*, London, Secker and Warburg, 1956; as *Tiger in the Kitchen and Other Strange Stories*, New York, Abelard Schuman, 1957.
Ufarlige historier [Safe Stories]. Copenhagen, Gyldendal, 1955.
Formynderfortaellinger [Tales of Guardianship]. Copenhagen, Gyldendal, 1964.
Vejrdage [Weather Days]. Copenhagen, Gyldendal, 1980.
Ragnarok. Aarhus, Centrum, 1982.

Other

Digtere og daemoner: Fortolkninger of vurderinger [Poets and Demons: Interpretation and Criticism]. Copenhagen, Gyldendal, 1959.
Hverken-eller: Kritiske betragninger [Neither-Nor: Critical Reflections]. Copenhagen, Gyldendal, 1961.
Friedrich Nietzsche. Copenhagen, Gads, 1963.
Kafkas digting [Kafka's Work]. Copenhagen, Gyldendal, 1968.
Mellem Fortid og fremtid [Between Past and Future]. Copenhagen, Gyldendal, 1969.
Schopenhauer. Copenhagen, Gyldendal, 1969.
Seneca: Humanisten ved Neros hof. Copenhagen, Gyldendal, 1976; as *Seneca: The Humanist at the Court of Nero*, Edinburgh, Canongate, 1984.
Oprørfra Midten, with Niels I. Meyer and K. Helveg Petersen. Copenhagen, Gyldendal, 1978; as *Revolt from the Middle*, London, Boyars, 1981.
Den gyldne middelvej og andre debatinglaeg fra 70erne [The Golden Mean and Other Contributions to Debate in the 1970's]. Copenhagen, Gyldendal, 1978.

Editor, *Eventyr og historier* [Tales and Stories], by H.C. Andersen. Copenhagen, Gyldendal, 1955.
Editor, *Begrebet angst* [The Concept of Dread], by Søren Kierkegaard. Copenhagen, Gyldendal, 1960.
Editor, *Midler uden mål* [Means Without Object]. Copenhagen, Spektrum, 1971.

Also translator of works by Broch, Kafka, Wagner, Seneca, and Erasmus.

*

Critical Studies: *Haabløse slaegter: Udgivet med indledning af Sørensen* by Herman J. Bang, Copenhagen, Gyldendal, 1965; *Saere fortaellere* by Thomas Bredsdorff, Copenhagen, Gyldendal, 1967; *Sørensen: En ideologikritisk analyse* by Ebbe Sønderiis, Grenå, GMT, 1972.

*   *   *

When Villy Sørensen made his debut in 1953, he went relatively unnoticed. Today, he is established as one of Denmark's most distinguished writers.

Although his work can be divided into two categories, the fiction and the philosophy, Sørensen himself has refused to distinguish between the two, preferring to see them as complementary. Nor does the literary historian find it easy to make an absolute distinction: the short stories *are* fiction, but they also express a philosophy, while some of the philosophical writings are at times close to the work of a creative writer. In both categories Sørensen stands as a linguistic innovator making frequent play on words, less for the sake of the immediate effect than to emphasise and to create a new perspective by using an expression that at first appears to be a cliché, but turns out to be innovatory.

With the early short stories, *Saere historier* and *Ufarlige historier*, Sørensen introduces the absurd into Danish literature. Kafka's influence is particularly obvious in "Mordsagen" ("The Murder Case"), about a police commissioner seeking to solve a murder which concerns him closely, but about which he knows absolutely nothing. The force of these stories taken as a whole is that man is subject to a disharmony which it is useless to seek to suppress. Rather, a way must be found of living with it. The innocence of childhood must give way to adult lack of innocence, as in the story of the two little boys who, in an effort to save the life of another child, saw off his leg and thus kill him. Death has entered their world, and reality has to be interpreted in a different way. Evil in man must be accepted, as is demonstrated in "Duo," in which Siamese twins have an operation to remove one half, the evil half, with a resultant disharmony in the "good" half, the implications being that both were necessary.

Disharmony in human nature extends to cultural and social disharmony, receiving philosophical treatment in *Digtere og daemoner* and ultimately in *Oprør fra Midten*.

The 1960's saw the publication of commentaries and translations, in which Sørensen's own philosophical purpose is apparent—an introduction to Kierkegaard's *Concept of Dread*, a translation of Kafka's short stories, and works on Nietzsche and Schopenhauer, as well as eager participation in the social and political debate of that time.

In 1976 came *Seneca*, pursuing further the examination of the myth as expressing man's disharmony, and at the same time interpreting a complex personality and culture. It is at once a scholarly examination of Seneca and his work and an explanation of the apparent contradiction between Seneca's principles and actions. Nero's court is a mirror of modern society, and no one reading this impressive book can fail to see its application to the present century.

In *Vejrdage*, in a series of brief, poetical pieces, Sørensen gives a direct expression to his philosophy, while in *Ragnarok* he retells the old Nordic myths in such a way as to make the futility of the Gods' behaviour relevant to the modern world.

—W. Glyn Jones

TARDIEU, Jean. French. Born in Saint-Germain-de-Joux, 1 November 1903; raised in Paris from 1905. Educated at Lycée Condorcet and the Sorbonne, both Paris. Married Marie-Laure Blot in 1932; one child. Joined Radiodiffusion-Télévision Française (RTF), Paris, 1944: Head of Drama, 1944-45; Director, "Club d'Essai" experimental drama studios, 1945-60; Program Director, 1954-64; Council Member, 1964-74. Recipient: French Academy Grand Prize for Poetry, 1972; Critics Prize (France), 1976. Chevalier, Legion of Honor. Address: 72 Boulevard Arago, 75013 Paris, France.

PUBLICATIONS

Plays

Qui est là (produced Anvers, 1949). Included in *Théâtre de chambre*, 1966; as *Who Goes There?*, in *The Underground Lovers*, 1968.
La Politesse inutile (produced Brussels, 1950). Included in *Théâtre de chambre*, 1966; as *Courtesy Doesn't Pay*, in *The Underground Lovers*, 1968.
Un mot pour un autre (produced Paris, 1950). Included in *Théâtre de chambre*, 1966.
Faust et Yorick (as *Mi-figure, mi-raisin*, produced Paris, 1951). Included in *Théâtre de chambre*, 1966; as *Faust and Yorick*, in *The Underground Lovers*, 1968.
Oswald et Zénaïde (produced Paris, 1951). Included in *Théâtre de chambre*, 1966.
Ce que parler veut dire (produced Paris, 1951). Included in *Théâtre de chambre*, 1966.
Il y avait foule au manoir (produced Paris, 1951). Included in *Théâtre de chambre*, 1966; as *The Crowd up at the Manor*, in *The Underground Lovers*, 1968.
Un Geste pour un autre (produced Paris, 1951). Included in *Théâtre de chambre*, 1966.
Conversation-sinfonietta (produced Paris, 1951). Included in *Théâtre de chambre*, 1966; as *Conversation-Sinfonietta*, in *The Underground Lovers*, 1968.
Eux seuls le savent (produced Paris, 1952). Included in *Théâtre de chambre*, 1966; as *They Alone Knew*, in *The Underground Lovers*, 1968.
Les Amants du métro (produced Paris, 1952). Included in *Poèmes à jouer*, 1969; as *The Underground lovers* (as *The Lovers in the Metro*, produced New York, 1962; as *The Underground Lovers*, produced London, 1969), in *The Underground Lovers* (collection), 1968.
Le Meuble (produced Bienne, 1954). Included in *Théâtre de chambre*, 1966; as *The Contraption* (produced Edinburgh, 1980), in *The Underground Lovers*, 1968.
La Serrure (produced Paris, 1955). Included in *Théâtre de chambre*, 1966; as *The Keyhole* (produced New York, 1962; London, 1980).
Le Guichet (produced Paris, 1955). Included in *Théâtre de chambre*, 1966 as *The Enquiry Office* (as *The Information Bureau*, produced New York, 1962), in *The Underground Lovers*, 1968.
La Société Apollon (produced Paris, 1955). Included in *Théâtre de chambre*, 1966; as *The Apollo Society*, in *The Underground Lovers*, 1968.
Théâtre de chambre. Paris, Gallimard, 1955; augmented edition (includes *Qui est là?, La Politesse inutile, Le Sacre de la nuit, Le Meuble, La Serrure, Le Guichet, Monsieur Moi, Faust et Yorick, La Sonate et les trois messieurs, La Société Apollon, Oswald et Zénaïde, Ce que parler veut dire, Il y avait foule au manoir, Eux seuls le savent, Un mot pour un autre, Un Geste pour un autre, Conversation-sinfonietta*), 1966.
Une Voix sans personne (produced Paris, 1956). Included in *Poèmes à jouer*, 1969.
Les Temps du verbe (produced Paris, 1956). Included in *Poèmes à jouer*, 1969.
Rythme à trois temps (produced Paris, 1959). Included in *Poèmes à jouer*, 1969.
Poèmes à jouer. Paris, Gallimard, 1960; augmented edition (includes *L'A.B.C. de notre vie, Rythme à trois temps, Une Voix sans personne, Les Temps du verbe, Les Amants du métro, Tonnerre sans orage, Des Arbres et des hommes, Trois personnes entrées dans des tableaux, Maledictions d'une Furie*), 1969.
Monsieur Moi, in *Théâtre de chambre*. 1966; as *Mr. Me* (produced London, 1972), in *The Underground Lovers*, 1968.
La Sonate et les trois messieurs, in *Théâtre de chambre*. 1966; as *The Sonata and the Three Gentlemen* (produced London, 1972), in *The Underground Lovers*, 1968.
The Underground Lovers and Other Experimental Plays (includes *Who Goes There?, Courtesy Doesn't Pay, The Contraption, The Enquiry Office, Mr. Me, Faust and Yorick, The Sonata and the Three Gentlemen, The Apollo Society, The Crowd up at the Manor, They Alone Knew, Conversation-Sinfonietta*). London, Allen and Unwin, 1968.

Une Soirée en Provence (includes *Une Soirée en Provence*; *Un Clavier un autre*, music by
Claude Arrieu; *Joyeux retour*; *Souper*, music by Marius Constant; *Le Club Archi-
mède*). Paris, Gallimard, 1975.
Le Professeur Froeppel. Paris, Gallimard, 1978.

Verse

Le Fleuve caché. Paris, Schiffrin, 1933.
Accents. Paris, Gallimard, 1939.
Le Témoin invisible. Paris, Gallimard, 1943.
Poèmes. Paris, Seuil, 1944.
Figures. Paris, Gallimard, 1944.
Les Dieux étouffés. Paris, Seghers, 1946.
Le Démon de l'irréalité. Neuchatel, Ides et Calendes, 1946.
Jours pétrifiés. Paris, Gallimard, 1948.
Monsieur monsieur. Paris, Gallimard, 1951.
Une Voix sans personne (includes prose). Paris, Gallimard, 1954.
L'Espace et la flûte, illustrated by Picasso. Paris, Gallimard, 1958.
Histoires obscures. Paris, Gallimard, 1961.
Choix de poèmes 1924-1954. Paris, Gallimard, 1961.
Le Fleuve caché: Poésies 1938-1961. Paris, Gallimard, 1968.
Formeries. Paris, Gallimard, 1976; translated as *Formeries*, Ann Arbor, Michigan,
Translation Press, 1982.
Comme ceci, comme cela. Paris, Gallimard, 1979.

Other

Bazaine, Estève, Lapicque, with André Frénaud and Jean Lescure. Paris, Carré, 1945.
Il était une fois, deux fois, trois fois. Paris, Gallimard, 1947.
Un Mot pour un autre. Paris, Gallimard, 1951.
La Première Personne du singulier. Paris, Gallimard, 1952.
Farouche à quatre feuilles, with others. Paris, Grasset, 1954.
De la peinture abstraite. Lausanne, Mermod, 1960.
Hollande. Paris, Maeght, 1963.
Pages d'écriture. Paris, Gallimard, 1967.
Les Portes de toiles. Paris, Gallimard, 1969.
Grandeurs et faiblesses de la radio. Paris, Unesco, 1969.
La Part de l'ombre. Paris, Gallimard, 1972.
Obscurité du jour. Geneva, Skira, 1974.
Bazaine, with Jean-Claude Schneider and Viveca Bosson. Paris, Maeght, 1975.

*

Critical Studies: *The Theatre of the Absurd* by Martin Esslin, New York, Doubleday, 1961,
London, Eyre and Spottiswoode, 1962, revised edition, London, Penguin, 1968, Doubleday,
1969; *The Theater of Protest and Paradox* by George E. Wellwarth, New York, New York
University Press, and London, MacGibbon and Kee, 1964; *Tardieu* by E. Nowlet, Paris,
Seghers, 1964, revised edition, 1978; *Le Dramaturgie poétique de Tardieu* by Paul Vernois,
Paris, Klincksieck, 1981.

*   *   *

Jean Tardieu is a writer who belongs to no literary movement and is identified with no
particular philosophy, a position unusual for any writer and peculiarly so for a French one. If

Tardieu may be said to have an intellectual position in his plays it is a tongue-in-cheek satiric attitude toward the arbitrary illogicalities of social intercourse. Combined with this is a sardonic tendency to follow situations to their ultimate logical conclusions. Both of these attitudes lead to the production of some outlandishly witty scenes that bear a stamp that is unmistakably Tardieu's. His principal contribution to dramatic literature, however, consists of his use of language as form rather than as semantic instrument. Words provide atmosphere and feeling instead of analyzable meaning.

Tardieu's use of language as form is best seen in *The Sonata and the Three Gentlemen*. In this play Tardieu tries to imitate the musical sonata form, using words as sounds. Three players sit on stools on a bare stage and talk dreamily, rhythmically, meaninglessly as they use speech to simulate the cadences of music. Tardieu's other experiments of this kind are *The Lovers in the Metro*, *Rythme à trois temps*, *Une Voix sans personne*, and *Conversation-Sinfonietta*.

In *The Keyhole* Tardieu plays with the concept of logic taken to its ultimate conclusion. *The Keyhole* is a sophisticated *grand guignol* skit shot through with a macabre humour. A timid little pervert comes to a whorehouse in order to see a woman undress. He is strictly a voyeur—personal contact with the woman does not interest him. The madam arranges matters so that he can watch one of her girls undress through a huge keyhole. We are given to understand that this occasion is the culminating point of the man's life—something he has been looking forward to and working for since an early age. Ecstatically the man watches the woman strip naked, but she does not stop. She takes out her eyes, pulls off her lips, peels off her flesh. Finally, when only a skeleton is left, the man drops dead. Other plays in this genre include *The Enquiry Office* and *The Contraption*.

Tardieu's satire of the conventions of social behaviour finds its high point in *Un Geste pour un autre*, where he exposes the basic meaninglessness of the little automatic gestures required by society by simply inventing a society the same as ours in all respects except that these gestures are reversed. In the Nameless Archipelago, where the play takes place, when a guest arrives at a party he puts his hat on and takes his shoes and socks off, making the hostess a present of the latter. Then he kisses her foot. During the party the guests amuse themselves by coughing and spitting and insulting each other.

Most of Tardieu's plays are a satiric protest against the enslavement of the human mind by social pressure. The theme of human helplessness in the face of authority—an authority that is, ironically, also purely human—appears again and again in his works. Tardieu sees the human race as pressed down flat by the weight of the social institutions that it has itself built up. Mentally, man has no initiative anymore; physically, he is timid and ulcer-ridden. The tragedy is that he has been brought to a state where his one wish is not to break the ring that he has put through his own nose but to hook it to something—anything. Tardieu's vision is of a world where logic leads to death, language is as semantically ephemeral as music, and everyday behaviour is grotesquely pointless and arbitrary.

—George E. Wellwarth

TAWFIQ AL-HAKIM. Egyptian. Born Husayn Tawfiq Isma'il Ahmad al-Hakim in Alexandria, 9 October 1898 (or possibly 1902 or 1903). Educated at Damanhur infant school; Muhammad Ali Secondary School, Cairo to 1921; Law school at University of Cairo, 1921-25; the Sorbonne, Paris, 1925-28. Married in 1946; one son and one daughter. Apprentice public prosecutor, in Alexandria, 1928-29, then public prosecutor in small towns, 1929-34; Director of Investigation Bureau, Ministry of Education, 1934-39; Director of Social Guidance, Ministry of Social Affairs, 1939-43; then full-time writer: associated with the newspapers *Akhbar al-Yawm* and *Al-Ahram*. Director general of Egyptian National Library, 1951; Member of the

Egyptian Higher Council of Arts, Literature, and Social Sciences, 1956-59, 1960— ; Egyptian representative, Unesco, Paris, 1959-60. President, Nadi al-Qissa, 1974. Recipient: State Literature Prize, 1961. Awarded Cordon of the Republic, 1958. Member, Academy of the Arabic Language, 1954. Address: c/o Al-Ahram, Al-Galaa Street, Cairo, Egypt.

PUBLICATIONS

Plays

Ahl al-Kahf [The People of the Cave]. Cairo, Misr, 1933.
Shahrazad. Cairo, Al-Masri, 1934; translated as *Shahrazad*, in *Plays, Prefaces, and Postscripts*, 1981.
Muhammad. Cairo, Lajna at-Ta'lif wa't-Tarjama wa'n-Nashr, 1936.
Masrahiyat [Plays]. Cairo, Al-Masri, 2 vols., 1937; *Nahr al-Junun* translated as *The River of Madness*, in *Islamic Literature*, New York, Washington Square Press, 1963.
Praxagora. Cairo, Al-Adab, 1939.
Nashid al-Anshad [The Song of Songs]. Cairo, Misr, 1940.
Pygmalion. Cairo, Al-Adab, 1942.
Sulayman al-Hakim; as *The Wisdom of Solomon*, in *Plays, Prefaces, and Postscripts*, 1981. Cairo, Al-Adab, 1943.
Shajarat al-Hukm [The Rulership Tree]. Cairo, Al-Adab, 1945.
Al-Malik Udib. Cairo, Al-Adab, 1949; as *King Oedipus*, in *Plays, Prefaces, and Postscripts*, 1981.
Masrah al-Mujtama [The Theatre of Society] (collection). Cairo, Al-Adab, 1950.
Al-Aydi an-Na'ima. Cairo, Al-Adab, 1954; as *Tender Hands*, in *Plays, Prefaces, and Postscripts*, 1981.
Isis. Cairo, Al-Adab, 1955.
Al-Masrah al-Munawwa' [The Diverse Theatre] (collection). Cairo, Al-Adab, 1956.
As-Safqa [The Deal]. Cairo, Al-Adab, 1956.
Rihla ila al-Ghad [Voyage to Tomorrow]. Cairo, Al-Adab, 1957; as *Al-'Alam al-Majhul* [The Unknown World], Beirut, Al-Kitab, 1973; as *Voyage to Tomorrow*, in *Plays, Prefaces, and Postscripts*, 1981.
La'bat al-Mawt [Death Game]. Cairo, Al-Adab, 1957.
Ashwak as-Salam [The Thorns of Peace]. Cairo, Al-Adab, 1957.
As-Sultan al-Ha'ir. Cairo, Al-Adab, 1960; as *The Sultan's Dilemma*, in *Fate of a Cockroach and Other Plays*, 1973.
Ya Tali' ash-Shajara. Cairo, Al-Adab, 1962; as *The Tree Climber*, London, Oxford University Press, 1966.
At-Ta'am li-Kull Fam [Food for the Millions]. Cairo, Al-Adab, 1963; as *Samira wa Hamdi*, Beirut, Al-Kitab, 1973; as *Food for the Millions*, in *Plays, Prefaces, and Postscripts*, 1981.
Rihla ar-Rabi' wa-l-Kharif [Spring and Autumn Journeys] (includes verse). Cairo, Al-Ma'arif, 1964; as *Ma'a az-Zaman* [Over the Years], Beirut, Al-Kitab, 1973.
Shams an-Nahar. Cairo, Al-Adab, 1965; as *Shams wa Qamar*, Beirut, Al-Kitab, 1973; as *Princess Sunshine*, in *Plays Prefaces, and Postscripts*, 1981.
Al-Warta. Cairo, Al-Adab, 1966; as *Incrimination*, in *Plays, Prefaces, and Postscripts*, 1981.
Bank al-Qalaq [Anxiety Bank]. Cairo, Al-Ma'arif, 1966.
Masir Sarsar. Cairo, Al-Adab, 1966; as *Fate of a Cockroach*, in *Fate of a Cockroach and Other Plays*, 1973.
Majlis al-'Adl [Council of Justice]. Cairo, Al-Adab, 1972.
Fate of a Cockroach and Other Plays (includes *The Song of Death, The Sultan's*

Dilemma, Not a Thing Out of Place). London, Heinemann, 1973.
Al-Hubb [Love] (collection). Beirut, Al-Kitab, 1973.
Ad-Dunya Riwaya Hazaliya [Life Is a Farce]. Beirut, Al-Kitab, 1974.
Al-Hamir [Donkeys]. Cairo, ash-Shuruq, 1975.
Plays, Prefaces, and Postscripts. Washington, D.C., Three Continents Press, 2 vols., 1981-84.
Ashab as-Sa'ada az-Zawjiya [Happily Married] (collection). Cairo, Ad-Dawliya lil-Intaj ath-Thaqafi, 1981.
Imsik Harami [Catch a Thief]. Cairo, Ad-Dawliyz lil-Intaj ath-Thaqafi, 1981.
Ah...Law 'Arifa ash-Shabab [Oh...If Only Youth Knew]. Cairo, Ad-Dawliya lil-Intaj ath-Thaqafi, 1981.
'Imarat al-Mu'allim Kanduz [The Building of Master Kanduz] (collection). Cairo, Ad-Dawliya lil-Intaj ath-Thaqafi, 1981.

Fiction

Awdat al-Ruh [Return of the Spirit]. Cairo, Ar-Ragha'ib, 1933.
Ahl al-Fann [Artistes]. Cairo, Al-Hilal, 1934.
Al-Qasr al-Mashur [The Enchanted Castle], with Taha Husayn. Cairo, Dar an-Nashr al-Hadith, 1936.
Yawmiyat Na'ib fi al-Aryaf. Cairo, Lajna at-Ta'lif wa't-Tarjama wa'n-Nashr, 1937; as *The Maze of Justice*, London, Harvill Press, 1947.
Tarikh Hayat Ma'ida [Biography of a Stomach]. Cairo, Lajna at-Ta'lif wa't-Tarjama wa'n-Nashr, 1938; as *Malik at-Tufayliyin* [King of the Moochers], Cairo, Dar Sa'd, 1946; as *Ash'ab, Amir at-Tufayliyin* [Ash'ab, Prince of Moochers], Cairo, Al-Adab, 1963.
'Usfur min ash-Sharq. Cairo, Lajna at-Ta'lif wa't-Tarjama wa'n-Nashr, 1938; as *Bird of the East*, Beirut, Khayats, 1966.
'Ahd ash-Shaytan [Pact with Satan]. Cairo, Lajna at-Ta'lif wa't-Tarjama wa'n-Nashr, 1938; as *Madrasa ash-Shaytan* [Satan's School], Cairo, Al-Hilal, 1955.
Raqisa al-Ma'bad [The Temple Dancer]. Cairo, Misr, 1939.
Ar-Ribat al-Muqaddas [The Sacred Bond]. Cairo, Misr, 1944.
Qisas [Stories]. Cairo, Sa'd Masr, 2 vols., 1949.
'Adala wa Fann [Justice and Art]. Cairo, Al-Adab, 1953; as *Ana wa'l-Qanun wal'Fann* [The Law, Art, and I], Cairo, Akhbar al-Yawm, 1973.
Arini Allah [Show Me God]. Cairo, Al-Adab, 1953.
Min Dhikrayat al-Fann wa'l-Qada' [Memories of Art and Justice]. Cairo, Al-Ma'arif, 1953.
Madrasa al-Mughaffalin [School for Fools]. Cairo, Al-Hilal, 1953.
Laylat az-Zifaf [Wedding Night]. Cairo, Al-Adab, 1966.
Al-Amira al-Bayda aw Bayad an-Nahar [Snow White]. Cairo, Al-Hay'a al-Misriya al-'Ama lil-Kitab, 1978.

Other

Tahta Shams al-Fikr [By the Light of the Sun of Thought]. Cairo, Lajna at-Ta'lif wa't-Tarjama wa'n-Nashr, 1938.
Himar al-Hakim [Al-Hakim's Ass]. Cairo, Al-Adab, 1940.
Sultan az-Zalam [The Reign of Darkness]. Cairo, Al-Adab, 1941.
Taht al-Misbah al-Akhdar [By the Light of the Green Lamp]. Cairo, Al-Adab, 1941.
Min al-Burj al-'Aji [From the Ivory Tower]. Cairo, Al-Adab, 1941.
Zahrat al-'Umr [The Flower of Life]. Cairo, Al-Adab, 1943.
Himari Qala li [My Donkey Told Me]. Cairo, Al-Ma'arif, 1945.

Fann al-Adab [The Art of Literature].   Cairo, Al-Adab, 1952.
'Asa al-Hakim [Al-Hakim's Staff].   Cairo, Al-Adab, 1954.
Ta'ammulat fi as-Siyasa [Reflections on Politics].   Cairo, Dar Ruz al-Yusuf, 1954.
At-Ta'aduliya [The Art of Balance].   Cairo, Al-Adab, 1955.
Adab al-Hayat [The Literature of Life].   Cairo, Ash-Sharika al-'Arabiya lit-Tiba'a, 1959.
Sijn al-'Umr [The Prison of Life].   Cairo, Al-Adab, 1964.
Qalibuna al-Masrahi [Our Theatrical Form].   Cairo, Al-Adab, 1967.
Qult...dhat Yawm [I Said...One Day].   Cairo, Akhbar al'Yawm, 1970.
Tawfiq al-Hakim yatahaddath [Tawfiq Al-Hakim Discusses].   Cairo, Al-Ahram, 1971.
Thawrat ash-Shabab [Revolt of the Young].   Cairo, Al-Ahram, 1971.
Ahadith ma'a Tawfiq al-Hakim min sana 1951-1971 [Conversations with Tawfiq al-Hakim], edited by Salah Tahir.   Cairo, Al-Ahram, 1971.
Rahib bayna Nisa' [A Monk among Women].   Cairo, Al-Kitab, 1972.
Rihla bayna 'Asrayn [Journey Between Two Ages].   Cairo, Al-Ahram, 1972.
Himari wa'Asaya wa'l-Akharun [My Donkey and Stick and the Others].   Cairo, Akhbar Al-Yawm, 1972.
Hadith ma'a al-Kawkab [Conversation with the Planet].   Beirut, Al-Kitab, 1974.
'Awdat al-Wa'y [Return of Consciousness].   Beirut, Dar ash-Shuruq, 1974.
Safahat min at-Tarikh al-Adabi min Waqi' Rasa'il wa-Watha'iq [Pages from Literary History: Selected Letters and Documents].   Cairo, Al-Ma'arif, 1975.
Bayn al-Fikr wa'l-Fann [Between Thought and Art].   Beirut (?), Al-Watan al-'Arabi, 1976.
Ta'am al-Fann wa'r-Ruh wa'l-Aql [Food for Art, Spirit, and Intellect].   Cairo, Al-Ma'arif, 1977.
Malamih Dakhiliya [Inner Features].   Cairo, Al-Adab, 1982.
Equilibrium and Islam.   Cairo, Al-Adab, 1983.

*

Critical Study: *Tawfiq al Hakim, Playwright of Egypt* by Richard Long, London, Ithaca Press, 1979.

*   *   *

Tawfiq al-Hakim is a widely read and influential 20th-century Arab author. His career has spanned the greater part of this century. He has made major and pioneering contributions to the Arab novel and especially to the theatre. Some of his plays are, however, better suited for reading than acting, according to his critics. Al-Hakim has also made a significant contribution by the example of his works to the development of modern literary Arabic.

Even before he went to France for advanced legal studies he had done some writing for the Egyptian theatre. In Paris he was soon smitten by the French theatre. It was there that he began his serious commitment to literature.

Al-Hakim's first novel was *Awdat al-Ruh*. It is the portrait of a young artist who is an Egyptian awakening to love and revolution at the same time, during the 1919 uprising against British control of Egypt. It is said to have influenced Nasser and the subsequent Egyptian revolution of 1952. The play *Shahrazad* is another early and important work. It investigates what may have happened after the heroine of the *Thousand and One Nights* married the king. Instead of living happily ever after, she drives him insane by the enigma of her existence: an ingenue who is also a goddess of story telling.

The third in al-Hakim's series of autobiographical novels was *The Maze of Justice*. It is one of his most convincing works with a rural setting. *Awdat al-Ruh* had also been in part a celebration of rural Egypt and its inhabitants whom al-Hakim saw then as the custodians of the spirit of Egypt passed down generation by generation from pharaonic times. *The Maze of Justice* was based on al-Hakim's own experiences as a rural prosecutor. Some desperate acts are recorded in it but the most desperate of all is the attempt to impose an urban elite's European-style legal system on the rural people.

In describing his own works, al-Hakim has called them spiritual, reformist, and diverse. Diverse he certainly has been, given the number and range of his works: plays, novels, published correspondence and interviews, short stories and political commentary. Some of his subjects have been completely Egyptian and full of local colour while others have been of international inspiration, like his version of *Oedipus*.

Although a consistent voice for social justice in his books, al-Hakim has been criticized for staying too long in an ivory tower. In his play *Princess Sunshine* the lovely princess is taunted to leave her castle by a free-lance guru. He shows her the suffering of the common people and gives her a crash course in wilderness survival. In the original ending, although they have fallen in love they renounce marriage so she can reform society while he resumes his career as a wandering artist. The response to critics is that an artist's role is to voice the concerns of the people and thereby reform the ruler who will reform society. For the artist to marry the ruler would be a short circuit, not a short cut.

To some critics al-Hakim has seemed to represent his generation and its international-minded Egyptian middle-class elite. He has therefore been thought a secular author almost by definition. Yet, by his own standards, al-Hakim has remained throughout his career a writer much concerned with religious and spiritual topics. In one of his early plays, which is more important for its time and message and influence than its dramatic appeal, *Ahl al-Kahf*, the main characters are Christian saints who have miraculously slept through centuries of paganism to awaken in a new Christian world. The inspiration for the play comes from Quranic sura number XVIII, "al-Kahf" (the Cave). As handled by al-Hakim, however, the play—while remaining faithful to the details of the Quran account—became a commentary on change and modernization. Is it still possible to live the way people did three hundred years ago, and particularly if you are a woman? Al-Hakim's most overtly Islamic work is *Muhammad*. It is a play or sequence of numerous scenes, and is based meticulously on the standard Islamic sources. Following up on his early pharaonism, al-Hakim devoted one play to the Isis story: *Isis*. In his book of popular Islamic philosophy, *Equilibrium and Islam*, al-Hakim has observed that religion is composed of two parts: the light and the lamp, the former divine, the latter human. The lamp, he suggests, since it is human will change. In other words, critics should not judge his dedication to Islam by a superficial reading of his works.

Al-Hakim's style is remarkable for its straightforward simplicity in a language known for its possible complexities. He makes some use of "Biblical" parallelism also found in earlier Arabic literature. He has shown a special taste for humorous situations based on misunderstandings and double meanings.

Although al-Hakim has received his share of criticism throughout his career, some of it political, he is recognized as an important pioneer in all phases of Arabic literature.

—William M. Hutchins

TORGA, Miguel. Pseudonym for Adolfo Correia da Rocha. Portuguese. Born in São Martinho da Anta, 12 August 1907. Educated at schools in Brazil, 1920-25; University of Coimbra, graduated as doctor 1933. Practicing physician: in São Martinho da Anta, Vila Nova de Miranda do Corvo, Leiria, and since 1940, in Coimbra. Recipient: International Grand Prize for Poetry, 1976. International Miguel Torga Prize named for him. Address: Rua Fernando Pessoa 3, Coimbra, Portugal.

PUBLICATIONS (privately printed unless otherwise noted)

Verse

Ansiedade (as Adolfo Correia da Rocha).   Coimbra, Imprensa Académica, 1928.
Rampa. Coimbra, Presença, 1930.
Tributo. 1931.
Abismo. 1932.
O outro livro de Job. 1936.
Lamentação. 1942.
Libertação. 1944.
Odes. 1946; revised edition, 1951, 1956.
Nihil Sibi. 1948.
Cântico do homen. 1950.
Alguns poemas ibéricos. 1952.
Penas do Purgatório. 1954.
Orfeu rebelde. 1958; revised edition, 1970.
Câmara ardente. 1962.
Poemas ibéricos. 1965.

Plays

Teatro: Terra firme, Mar. 1941; revised edition of *Mar*, 1970.
Terra firme (produced Coimbra, 1947).   Included in *Teatro*, 1941.
Sinfonia. 1947.
O Paraíso. 1949.

Fiction

Pão ázimo. 1931.
A criação do mundo: Os dois primeiros dias.   1937; revised edition, 1948.
O terceiro dia da Criação do mundo. 1938; revised edition, 1952.
O quarto dia da Criação do mundo. 1939.
Bichos. 1940; revised edition, 1970; as *Farrusco the Blackbird and Other Stories*, London, Allen and Unwin, 1950; New York, Arts Inc., 1951.
Montanha: Contos. 1941; augmented edition, as *Contos da montanha*, 1955, 1969.
Rua: Contos. 1942.
O senhor Ventura. 1943.
Novos contos da montanha. 1944; augmented edition, 1952, 1959, 1967, 1975.
Vindima. 1945; revised edition, 1965, 1971.
Pedras lavradas. 1951; revised edition, 1958.
O quinto dia da Criação do mundo. 1974.

Other

A terceira voz. 1934.
Diário 1-12. 1941-77.
Portugal. 1950; revised edition, 1967.
Traço de uniâo. 1955; revised edition, 1969.
Fogo preso. 1976.

*

Bibliography: in *Biblos*, 1979.

Critical Studies: *Humanist Despair in Miguel Torga* by Eduardo Lourenço, Coimbra, 1955; "The Art and Poetry of Torga" by Denis Brass, in *Sillages 2*, 1973; *Torga, Poeta Ibérico* by Jesús Herrero, Lisbon, 1979.

* * *

Miguel Torga, the *doyen* of Portuguese letters, and Portuguese candidate for the Nobel Prize, has shown over fifty years a consistency of courage and artistic purpose rarely equalled among his national contemporaries. This has led him into clashes with authority during the Salazar period, and he did his stint in prison. His early experience in a seminary, from which he fled to Brazil as a poor peasant boy to eke out an existence as a menial on a coffee estate, has marked his writing. He has rejected his childhood catholicism, but retained the imagery. With the Revolution of 1974 he achieved almost guru status with the new socialist government, and he published his political writings under the title *Fogo preso*. His fame rests, however, on a substantial corpus of poetry, and on his several collections of short stories which have been acclaimed as some of the finest in the language. "Torga found himself with a twofold problem. On the one hand he wanted to find real living types, that, while keeping the peninsular fire of their own condition, would have a universal message and at the same time remain Portuguese. On the other hand he had to create a style that could interpret this message in the drama and dynamism of our own times. And so he took the language to pieces and built it anew, taking in idioms and vocabulary of his own region, charged with dramatic content. And so, his is the short sentence and the significant word. An approach to cine technique" (introduction by Denis Brass to *Farrusco the Blackbird*).

The key to his work is his intense, even sensual relationship with his birth-place in Trás-os-Montes. His anguish is that the people there, for whom he wrote in the first place, are, many of them, illiterate, and cannot appreciate his work. Torga is a passionate traveller in his own and in other countries; many journeys are recorded in his *Diaries*. He recognizes the importance of the sea for the history and the economy of his country, and in his *Poemas ibéricos* he addresses the peninsular explorers who set out to till the sea against an uncertain harvest. The sea is also the title of one of his theatre pieces, *Mar*, where he treats a favourite theme of the prodigal, the man who is lost in shipwreck, or who goes overseas abandoning family, and who may or may not return. Torga sees himself as a kind of smuggler on the frontier between two worlds—Agarez (his birth-place)—and the rest. Agarez symbolizes the whole Iberian peninsula. He set out to explore that other world—Europe. But he always returned to "my hot peninsular night." He is very conscious of his mission as a peninsular writer. His world, he says, finishes only at the Pyrenees, that great barrier that saves his Don Quixote from the temptations of the *Folies Bergères*.

Torga has the "uncontaminated vision" of the countryman and the hunter. Hunting is his recreation and it informs several of his stories. He is a practising doctor, and his observation has been helped by his experience in the consulting room. He sees a link between the healing mission of the doctor, the priest, and the poet, all intent on saving or praising life, a mission wonderfully portrayed in the short story "Viaticum" (*O senhor Ventura*). The poet's alternating moods of hope and despair find utterance in the two longer poems *Lamentação* and *Libertação*. His poet's faith and optimism are boldly proclaimed in the title poem of the collection *Orfeu rebelde* (Orpheus in revolt).

—Denis Brass

TOURNIER, Michel (Edouard). French. Born in Paris, 19 December 1924. Educated at Collège Saint-Erembert and Collège Municipal, Saint-Germain-en-Laye; University of Paris; University of Tübingen. Producer and director, Radiodiffusion-Télévision Française (RTF), Paris, 1949-54; press attaché, 1955-58; director of literary services, Plon publishers, Paris, 1958-68. Recipient: French Academy Grand Prize for Novel, 1967; Goncourt Prize, 1970. Chevalier, Legion of Honor. Address: Le Presbytère, Choisel, 78460 Chevreuse, France.

PUBLICATIONS

Fiction

Vendredi; ou, Les Limbes du Pacifique. Paris, Gallimard, 1967; revised edition, 1978; as *Friday; or, The Other Island,* London, Collins, and New York, Doubleday, 1969; juvenile edition as *Vendredi; ou, La Vie sauvage,* Paris, Flammarion, 1971; as *Friday and Robinson: Life on Esperanza Island,* New York, Knopf, and London, Aldus, 1972.
Le Roi des Aulnes. Paris, Gallimard, 1970; as *The Erl-King,* London, Collins, 1972; as *The Ogre,* New York, Doubleday, 1972.
Les Météores. Paris, Gallimard, 1975; as *Gemini,* London, Collins, and New York, Doubleday, 1981.
Le Coq de bruyère (stories). Paris, Gallimard, 1978; as *The Fetishist and Other Tales,* London, Collins, 1983.
Gaspard, Melchior et Balthazar. Paris, Gallimard, 1980; as *The Four Wise Men,* London, Collins, and New York, Doubleday, 1982.
Gilles et Jeanne. Paris, Gallimard, 1983.

Other

Le Nain rouge. Montpellier, Fata Morgana, 1975.
Le Vent Paraclet. Paris, Gallimard, 1977.
Canada: Journal de voyage. Montreal, La Presse, 1977.
Des Clefs et des serrures. Paris, Chêne, 1979.
Le Vol du vampire. Paris, Mercure, 1981.
Pierrot et les secrets de la nuit (juvenile). Paris, Gallimard, 1981.
Vues de dos, photographs by Edouard Boubat. Paris, Gallimard, 1981.
Barbedor (juvenile). Paris, Gallimard, 1982.
Le Vagabond immobile, designs by Jean-Max-Tombeau. Paris, Gallimard, 1984.

*

Critical Study: *Tourniers "Le Roi des Aulnes" in deutsch-französischen Kontext* by Manfred S. Fischer, Bonn, Bouvier, 1977.

*   *   *

Michel Tournier's novels are all based on existing stories which have acquired mythical value, or on myths which he sees as forming part of the Western imagination. *Friday; or, The Other Island* tells the story of Robinson Crusoe—always a favourite with the French ever since Jean-Jacques Rousseau allowed Defoe's novel as the one book which his pupil Emile was permitted to read—from the point of view of Man Friday. In the end, it is Friday's values of spontaneity, leisure, and of man's natural harmony with nature that prevail over what Tournier presents as Robinson's autocratic colonialism, and the book has obvious links with the philosophy underlying the ecological movement. His most famous book so far, and probably his best, is *The Erl-King*, as a translation into the Europe of the 1940's of two pagan legends: the medieval one of the Erl King who steals children; and, ultimately, the Christian one of Saint Christopher who carries them to salvation. Its main character, Abel Tiffauges, is a French garage mechanic suffering from micromorphogenitalism who becomes involved in the Hitlerian enterprise of bringing together into the breeding centres known as Napas all available children fulfilling the exact norms laid down by the criteria of Aryan racialism. Like all Tournier's work, *The Erl-King* is characterised by an extreme wealth of poetic vocabulary, and Tournier is rightly regarded as having introduced into French literature an acute awareness of the physical world in all its manifestations which both contrasts with the French tendency to abstract intellectualism and corrects and complements it. *Gemini* describes the adventures of two brothers who are identical twins, a theme which Tournier presents in his autobiographical *Le Vent Paraclet* as having always obsessed him. It also contains, in the character of Alexandre, one of the most intriguing and attractive homosexuals in French literature. *The Four Wise Men* introduces into the story of the Nativity a fourth King, Taor, from Africa, whose role in the events provides an unexpected illustration of a major Christian virtue. *Gilles et Jeanne* is Tournier's shortest novel so far. It explores Gilles de Rais's homosexuality, and attempts an explanation of his later cruelties in the light of his failure to save Joan from the stake. Tournier has announced his intention of writing a novel on the theme of migrant workers from the Third World who come to live in Europe, and the autobiographical essays in *Le Vent Paraclet* frequently return to the view that the greatest problem facing Western man is his loneliness and refusal to enter into contact with his fellows. Tournier has also written a number of books for children, and adapted *Vendredi* for younger readers.

—Philip Thody

TRANSTRÖMER, Tomas (Gösta). Swedish. Born in Stockholm, 15 April 1931. Educated at the University of Stockholm, graduated 1956. Married Monica Bladh in 1958; two daughters. Psychologist at a prison for young people in Roxtuna, then in Linköping, 1960-66, and since 1967, in Västerås on a part-time basis. Address: c/o Bonniers, Sveavägen 56, Box 3159, 103 63 Stockholm, Sweden.

PUBLICATIONS

Verse

17 dikter [Poems]. Stockholm, Bonnier, 1954.
Hemligheter på vägen [Secrets on the Way]. Stockholm, Bonnier, 1958.
Den halvfärdiga himlen [The Half-finished Heaven]. Stockholm, Bonnier, 1962.
Klanger och spår [Soundings and Tracks]. Stockholm, Bonnier, 1966.
Three Poems. Lawrence, Kansas, Williams, 1966.
Kvartett [Quartet]. Stockholm, Bonnier, 1967.
Mörkerseende. Gothenburg, Författarförlaget, 1970; as *Night Vision*, Ithaca, New York, Lillabulero Press, 1971; London, London Magazine Editions, 1972.
Twenty Poems, translated by Robert Bly. Madison, Minnesota, Seventies Press, 1971.
Windows and Stones: Selected Poems, translated by May Swenson and Leif Sjöberg.

Pittsburgh, University of Pittsburgh Press, 1972.
Stigar [Paths]. Gothenburg, Författarförlaget, 1973.
Elegy, Some October Notes, translated by Robert Bly. Rushden, Northamptonshire, Sceptre Press, 1973.
Östersjöar. Stockholm, Bonnier, 1974; as *Baltics*, translated by Samuel Charters, Berkeley, California, Oyez, 1975; also translated by Robin Fulton, London, Oasis, 1980.
Selected Poems, translated by Robin Fulton. London, Penguin, 1974; Ann Arbor, Michigan, Ardis, 1981.
Citoyens, translated by Robin Fulton. Rushden, Northamptonshire, Sceptre Press, 1974.
Friends, You Drank Some Darkness, with Harry Martinson and Gunnar Ekelöf, translated by Robert Bly. Boston, Beacon Press, 1975.
Sanningsbarriären. Stockholm, Bonnier, 1978; as *Truth Barriers*, translated by Robert Bly, San Francisco, Sierra Club, 1980.
Dikter 1954-1978. Stockholm, Bonnier, 1979.
How the Late Autumn Night Novel Begins, translated by Robin Fulton. Knotting, Bedfordshire, Sceptre Press, 1980.
Det vilda torget [The Wild Market Square]. Stockholm, Bonnier, 1983.

*

Critical Studies: by B. Steene, in *Scandinavian Studies 37*, 1965; by Robin Fulton, in *Lines Review 35*, December 1970; "Tranströmer" by Gavin Orton, in *Essays on Swedish Literature from 1880 to the Present Day*, edited by Irene Scobbie, Aberdeen, University of Aberdeen, 1978; *Resans formler: En studie i Tranströmers poesi* by Kjell Espmark, 1983.

* * *

On the strength of two slim volumes of poetry Tomas Tranströmer became almost a cult figure in the 1950's. Although he followed in the Swedish tradition of nature poetry and was a successor to the surrealists, his metaphorical virtuosity inclined not to romantic ambiguity nor the absurd but to clarity, precision, and striking images—a giant oak is a "petrified elk"; "a dog's bark hangs like a hieroglyph over the garden"; at midnight "the spruce stands like the hand of a clock, spiked." Tranströmer stated in an interview that he viewed existence as a great mystery which in certain moments has a religious character, and it is this mystery he attempts to capture in his poetry. In the state between dreaming and waking he suggests a vision of the world experienced fleetingly: "In the first hours of the day our consciousness enfolds the world/like a hand holding a sun-warmed stone." As a psychologist he can use the dream to reach our subconscious but it also becomes the entrance to a visionary transcendental world: "But the writer is halfway into his image, there/he travels, at the same time eagle and mole." The tensions of his world are reflected often in antithesis: movement—stasis; light—darkness; interior—exterior ("Under the buzzard's hovering point of stillness/the roaring sea surges forward in the light"; or "There is peace in the forging prow"). There are often religious overtones—God is "unchanging and thus seldom noticed here" (*17 dikter*), or in *Hemligheter på vägen* we can feel "God's energy rolled up in the dark." The dreamer at the point of waking, the lover, and the musician come closest to realising the vision of cosmic harmony. For the lovers in *Den halvfärdiga himlen* "all questionmarks began to sing about God's existence," and in *Det vilda torget* the night sky lows and they "secretly milk the cosmos."

Activists criticised Tranströmer in the 1960's for lack of political commitment. Several of his poems bear political references—the Berlin Wall, the Algerian War, for instance—but as part of the flow of history. Man's role is to observe, listen, and sympathise with the victims; only the faces of the victims change. French atrocities in Algeria conjure up Dreyfus. A newspaper "full of events" lying outside for months is "on the way to becoming a plant...to being united with the earth. Just as a memory is slowly transmuted into your own self." Even urban pollution can be assimilated on this time scale. "Factories brood/the buildings sink two millimetres/per year—the ground is devouring them slowly." In *Baltics* the Baltic symbolises peoples of many ages co-existing in the present. It unites and divides countries and social systems but has wider connotations of eternity, solitude, and, in magic moments, of peace. At his best Tranströmer conjures up clear contours of our world in a new perspective making it familiar and yet strange and can convey his sense of wonder at our universe.

—Irene Scobbie

VALLEJO, Antonio Buero. *See* **BUERO VALLEJO, Antonio.**

VARGAS LLOSA, (Jorge) Mario (Pedro). Peruvian. Born in Arequipa, 28 March 1936. Educated in Bolivia to 1945; Leoncio Prado Military Academy, Lima, 1950-52; a school in Piura, 1952-53; University of San Marcos, Lima, B.A. 1957; University of Madrid, 1957-59. Married 1) Julia Urquidi in 1955 (divorced); 2) Patricia Llosa, three children. Journalist, *La Industria*, Piura, and for La Radio Panamericana and *La Cronica*, both in Lima; journalist, Agence-France-Presse, and broadcaster, French National Radio Network, in 1960's; lecturer or visiting professor, Queen Mary College and King's College, University of London, 1966-68, University of Washington, Seattle, 1968, University of Puerto Rico, Rio Piedras, 1969, and Columbia University, New York, 1975. Co-Founder, *Libre*, Paris, 1971. Recipient: Alas Prize, 1959; Biblioteca Breve Prize, 1962; Gallegos Prize (Venezuela), 1962; Critics Prize (Spain), 1964, 1967; National Prize, 1967. Address: c/o Editorial Seix Barral, Apdo de Correos 31, Tambor del Bruch s/n, Sant Joan Despi, Barcelona, Spain.

PUBLICATIONS

Fiction

Los jefes. Barcelona, Rocas, 1959.
La ciudad y los perros. Barcelona, Seix Barral, 1963; as *The Time of the Hero*, New York, Grove Press, 1966; London, Cape, 1967.
La casa verde. Barcelona, Seix Barral, 1966; as *The Green House*, New York, Harper, 1968; London, Cape, 1969.
Los cachorros. Barcelona, Lumen, 1967.

Conversación en la catedral. Barcelona, Seix Barral, 1969; as *Conversation in the Cathedral*, New York, Harper, 1975.
Lletra de batalla per "Tirant lo Blanc." Barcelona, Edicions 62, 1969.
Obras escogidas. Madrid, Aguilar, 1973.
Pantaleón y las visitadoras. Barcelona, Seix Barral, 1973; as *Captain Pantoja and the Special Service*, New York, Harper, and London, Cape, 1978.
La tía Julia y el escribidor. Barcelona, Seix Barral, 1977; as *Aunt Julia and the Scriptwriter*, New York, Farrar Straus, 1982; London, Faber, 1983.
The Cubs and Other Stories. New York, Harper, 1979.
La guerra del fin del mundo. Barcelona, Seix Barral, 1981.

Play

La señorita de Tacna. Barcelona, Seix Barral, 1981; as *The Senorita from Tacna* (produced New York, 1983).

Other

Literatura en la revolución y revolución en la literatura, with Julio Cortázar and Oscar Collazos. Mexico City, Siglo Veintiuno, 1970.
La historia secreta de una novela. Barcelona, Tusquets, 1971.
Gabriel García Márquez: Historia de un deicidio. Barcelona, Seix Barral, 1971.
La novela y el problema de la expresión literaria en Peru. Buenos Aires, América Nueva, 1974.
La orgía perpetua: Flaubert y "Madame Bovary." Madrid, Taurus, 1975.
José María Arguedas: Entre sapos y halcones. Madrid, Cultura Hispánica del Centro Iberoamericano de Cooperación, 1978.
La utopia arcaica. Cambridge, Cambridge University Centre of Latin American Studies, 1978.

Editor, with Gordon Brotherston, *Seven Stories from Spanish America.* Oxford, Pergamon Press, 1968.

*

Critical Studies: *Vargas Llosa's Pursuit of the Total Novel* by Luis A. Diez, Cuernavaca, Cidoc, 1970; *Homenaje a Vargas Llosa* edited by Helmy F. Giacomon and José Miguel Oviedo, New York, Las Américas, 1972; *Vargas Llosa: A Collection of Critical Essays* edited by Charles Rossman and Alan Warren Friedman, Austin, University of Texas Press, 1978.

*　　*　　*

Of the writers associated with "the boom" in Latin American literature in the 1960's, Mario Vargas Llosa was the youngest and the principal Peruvian. Attentive to the lessons of European and Anglo-American modernism, Vargas Llosa fused the panoramic realism characteristic of the 19th-century novel with the dynamic techniques characteristic of the 20th-century novel: multiple points of view; interior monologues and internalized dialogues; suspended identification of characters; montage effects; discontinous, fragmented, and intertwined narrative lines. His themes echo his narrative experiments. A promise of freedom, exhilarating and tantalizing, ends with the fiction as those established in power reimpose their authority by violence or as those devoid of power adopt and accept more tacit but no less forceful social constraints.

From his first published work, a collection of short stories spare in style and dramatic in construction, *Los jefes*, to his masterwork, *Conversation in the Cathedral*, Vargas Llosa's fictions pursue a trajectory of increasing narrative complexity. His first novel, *The Time of the Hero*, set in Lima's Colegio Militar Leoncio Prado, where the author had been a student, was doubly distinguished by a Spanish literary prize and a public burning in the school's courtyard. Using the school as a claustrophobic microcosm of Peruvian society, the novel explores the brutalizing effects of the military discipline of the school and the codes of honor imposed by the students on themselves and each other. His second novel, *The Green House*, extended the opposition between city and school geographically to an opposition between the green freedoms of the Amazonian jungle and the dusty constraints of Piura. A temporal contrast compounded the physical contrast, with both locations possessed of a mythic past invaded and altered by the present, an effect achieved by the shuffling of five interconnected narratives taking place over a forty-year span. In *Conversation in the Cathedral*, Vargas Llosa returned to Lima and, still intercutting narrative lines, elaborated an unwinding, circular structure affined to the detective story. Masterly in its narrative coherence, the novel ranges through social, sexual, and political corruption at all levels during the Odría regime of the 1950's with the unaccountable murder of a prostitute as the absent center on which the narrative turns.

Two comic novels and an historical novel followed: *Captain Pantoja and the Special Service*, derived from news stories about army-organized prostitution in the Amazon region, and *Aunt Julia and the Scriptwriter*, which approaches the finish of *Conversation in the Cathedral* in a comic mode. Not corruption, but the paradoxes of daily life, love, and writing play into and against one another as Vargas Llosa intercuts "Marito's" courtship of his own Aunt Julia and the extravagant, but socially representative soap-operas of Pedro Camacho. *La guerra del fin del mundo*, set in northeast Brazil at the end of the 19th century, explores the paradox of an insurrection led by religious reactionaries that inspires secular radicals.

Most recently, Vargas Llosa has turned playwright again to examine the linkages and fissures among life as it is lived, life as it is reconstructed by memory and desire, and the mysterious alchemy of art that uses and transforms those materials. The plays dramatize the relation between biography and art that has long been a theme of Vargas Llosa's criticism, whether with reference to his own work, as in *La historia secreta de una novela*, i.e., his own *Green House*, or to that of others, as in his massive and important study *Gabriel García Márquez: Historia de un deicidio*.

—Regina Janes

VOINOVICH, Vladimir (Nikolaevich). Born in Dushanbe, 26 September 1932. Educated at Moscow Pedagogical Institute, 1957-59. Served in the Soviet Army, 1951-55. Married 1) Valentina in 1957; one daughter and one son; 2) Irina Braude in 1965, one daughter. Worked as herdsman, factory hand, locksmith; construction and railroad worker; carpenter, aircraft mechanic; editor of radio programs; since 1956, free-lance writer in Moscow: expelled from Union of Soviet Writers, 1974; went to the West, 1980, and deprived of Soviet citizenship, 1981; taught Russian literature, Princeton University, New Jersey, 1982-83. Member, Bavarian Academy of Fine Arts. Agent: Georges Borchardt, 136 East 57th Street, New York, New York 10022, U.S.A. Address: Hans-Carossastrasse 5, 8035 Stokdorf, Germany.

PUBLICATIONS

Fiction

Pervye lastochki dnevnik derevenskogo uchitelya. Gorky, Gorkovskoye knizhnoye, 1962.

Stepen' doveriya [A Degree of Trust]. Moscow, Politizdat, 1972.
Povesti [Novellas]. Moscow, Sovietsky Pisatel, 1972.
Zhizn' i neobychaynye priklyucheniya soldata Ivana Chonkina. Paris, YMCA Press, 1975; as *The Life and Extraordinary Adventures of Private Ivan Chonkin*, New York, Farrar Straus, and London, Cape, 1977.
Putyom vzaimnoy perepiski. Paris, YMCA Press, 1979; as *In Plain Russian*, London, Cape, 1980.
Pretendent na prestol: Novye priklyucheniya soldata Ivana Chonkina. Paris, YMCA Press, 1979; as *Pretender to the Throne: The Further Adventures of Private Ivan Chonkin*, New York, Farrar Straus, and London, Cape, 1981.

Other

Ivankiada: Ili rasskaz o vselenii pisatelya Voinovicha v novuyu kvartiru. Ann Arbor, Michigan, Ardis, 1976; as *The Ivankiad: The Tale of the Writer Voinovich's Installation in His New Apartment*, New York, Farrar Straus, 1977; London, Cape, 1978.

*

Critical Study: "Voinovich and the Comedy of Innocence" by Robert Porter in *Forum for Modern Language Studies*, April 1980.

*   *   *

Vladimir Voinovich was highly regarded in the 1960's for stories such as "I Want to Be Honest" and "Two Comrades," which showed a high degree of frankness regarding urban life, the pressures on the individual to conform, and the unorthodox values of some unsophisticated characters. Wit, perception, and vigorous moral awareness are the hallmarks of Voinovich's work. Occasional light-hearted verse, the lyrics to a song about astronauts, an historical novel about Vera Figner, illustrate the writer's wide range and show him to be at once entertaining and serious. Highly irreverent satire is his *forte*, and his literary lineage might include Zoshchenko and Ilf and Petrov from the Soviet period. In his most mature work the legacy of Gogol is clearly in evidence.

Voinovich's masterpiece is the as-yet-unfinished novel about Private Ivan Chonkin. Utterly at variance with the mainstream of Soviet literature on the Second World War, this hilarious work shows Russia more at war with itself than the Germans. Hitler and Stalin are strikingly similar and the Soviet Union seems to be run by self-deluding incompetents, duped by ideology, pseudo-science, and myopic self-interest. Chonkin, the village simpleton and willy-nilly red-army-man, manages to confound all the institutions he comes into contact with by his uncomprehending innocence. Thus the Ivan-the-Fool of Russian folk stories becomes extremely subversive. The work has not been published legally in the Soviet Union, and Voinovich was forced into exile to the West in 1980. His style is earthy and racy, owing something to the literary device of *skaz* (the narrator adopting the tone of voice of some of his characters). In the time-honoured fashion of comic writers, the author frequently denigrates his own story and his own abilities to tell it. His "Russianness" of style may prove difficult to sustain in emigration.

Superstition, the animal world, folk wisdom all play a prominent part in Voinovich's work and often these gain the ascendency over officially sanctioned notions and values. In Voinovich the official myths are the most dangerous. Dreams, daydreams, naivety, and spontaneity are ultimately more valid and moral.

Voinovich's army service after the war has clearly influenced his writing in such stories as "By Means of Mutual Correspondence." Authority is persistently challenged and the small man sticking to his guns more out of simple-mindedness and simple-heartedness than out of lofty abstract ideals occurs frequently in Voinovich. One of the clearest short examples of this is the autobiographical *The Ivankiad*, which tells the story of the author's acquisition of a promised flat despite repeated attempts by a greedy big-wig to have it for himself.

Insistence on small obvious truths opens up yawning gaps between appearance and reality. Such discrepancies might be best glimpsed in the story "A Circle of Friends," where Stalin and his cronies burn the midnight oil in the Kremlin, arguing over a crossword as Hitler launches operation Barbarossa. Stalin has a dummy of himself placed at the one lit Kremlin window—to further the myth of his working while his people rest.

—Robert Porter

VOLPONI, Paolo. Italian. Born in Urbino, 6 February 1924. Educated at schools in Urbino; University of Urbino, 1943-47, law degree. Social services consultant, Calabria and Sicily, 1950-53, and Rome, 1953-55, and for Olivetti, Ivrea, 1956-71. Associated with *Officina* magazine in 1950's. Recipient: Viareggio Prize, for poetry, 1960, for fiction, 1975; Strega Prize, 1965. Address: c/o Einaudi, Via Umberto Biancamano, CP 245, 10121 Turin, Italy.

PUBLICATIONS

Fiction

Memoriale. Milan, Garzanti, 1962; as *My Troubles Began*, New York, Grossman, 1964; as *The Memorandum*, London, Calder and Boyars, 1967.
La macchina mondiale. Milan, Garzanti, 1965; as *The Worldwide Machine*, New York, Grossman, 1967; London, Calder and Boyars, 1969.
Corporale. Turin, Einaudi, 1974.
Il sipario ducale. Milan, Garzanti, 1975.
Il pianeta irritabile. Turin, Einaudi, 1978.
Il lanciatore del giavellotto. Turin, Einaudi, 1981.

Verse

Il ramarro. Urbino, Istituto d'Arte, 1948.
L'antica moneta. Florence, Vallecchi, 1955.
Le porte dell'Appennino. Milan, Feltrinelli, 1960.
Poesie e poemetti 1946-66, edited by Gualtiero De Santi. Turin, Einaudi, 1980.
(Selection) in English, in *The New Italian Poetry*, edited and translated by Lawrence R. Smith. Berkeley, University of California Press, 1981.

Other

Pier Paolo Pasolini nel dibattito culturale contemporaneo, with others. Pavia, Amministrazione Provinciale di Pavia, 1977.

*

Critical Studies: *Volponi* by Gian Carlo Ferretti, Florence, La Nuova Italia, 1972; "The Narrator-Protagonist and the Divided Self in Volponi's *Corporale*" by Rocco Capozzi, in *Forum Italicum 10*, 1976; "Note sul più recente Volponi: *Il lanciatore del giavellotto*" by Guido Santato, in *Otto-Novecento 7*, 1983.

* * *

In Paolo Volponi's development as a writer two factors are of particular interest: his association, from 1956 to 1971, with the firm Olivetti as a social services consultant; and his involvement, in the late 1950's, with *Officina*, an avant-garde review which advocated a close relationship between literature and the social sciences, consistent with Marxian thought mediated and brought into the context of Italian culture through the writings of Antonio Gramsci. Both experiences are discernible in Volponi's early narrative which draws attention to the changes in the fabric of Italian society stemming from the rapid industrial expansion of the early 1960's—the years of the "economic miracle."

Significant, in this respect, are the novels *The Memorandum* and *The Worldwide Machine* in which the impetus of industrialization is viewed in problematic terms, essentially as a dehumanizing force tied to the advances of neo-capitalism. Yet these works can hardly be characterized as a simplistic condemnation of technology. Volponi's heightened realism and his projection of contemporary life through the vicissitudes of eccentric, neurotic characters essentially unrepresentative of the working class point chiefly, and in a quasi-Orwellian fashion, to the abuses and potential consequences of misguided scientific progress. It is more accurate to say that Volponi's early fiction suggests a reformist view of technology, implicit in his concern for an equilibrium between human needs (freedom, individuality, creativity) and the rigid, impersonal make-up of the industrial system.

The social content of Volponi's work unfolds in unison with lucid character studies of disoriented individuals afflicted with various forms of mental disorders. Their opposition to the regimented structure of factory life gives rise to extreme reactions: defeatist sentiments leading to withdrawal and suicide in *The Memorandum*; an anthropocentric approach to technology which, in *The Worldwide Machine*, is translated into utopian designs for the betterment of humanity. This sociological perspective plays a lesser role in *Corporale* where the main focus is on introspective analysis and the narrative process that generates it. The condition of a schizoid character wrestling with deep anxieties is examined within a structural context in which the act of writing, through a skillful progression from first- to third-person narrative, tests its own resources and limitations as it subjects the divided self of the protagonist to intense psychoanalytical scrutiny.

The prospect of a nuclear cataclysm, foreshadowed in *Il sipario ducale*, takes on the semblance of a factual occurrence in *Il pianeta irritabile*. The work, an allegorical fable with foreboding allusions to the present, is set in 2293 in the aftermath of a nuclear conflagration which has destroyed virtually all forms of life on earth. Moving against the background of a ravaged landscape, four survivors—a gorilla, an elephant, a goose, and a circus midget—undertake the difficult journey toward a new land blessed with "harmonious living."

Il lanciatore del giavellotto marks a return to the familiar grounds of socially deviant behavior and psychological analysis, placed in evidence here by the story of an adolescent whose feelings of sexual inadequacy and the progressive manifestation of a tormenting Oedipus complex pave the way for a tragic ending. While the frame of Volponi's fiction rests on the constants of social consciousness and introspection, the constituent structures point to consistent renewal and diversity. Thus the work in question, departing from the problematic of industrial life, examines with discerning ability the experience of Fascism in a provincial town. What is reiterated with systematic and disturbing frequency in Volponi's novels is the pathological condition of his characters—a leitmotif through which the metaphor of disease asserts its value as the emblematic sign of our time.

Volponi's verse, collected in the volume *Poesie e poemetti 1946-66*, draws its strength from a process of renewal and intellectual maturity attested by a fluid dialectical interaction between the poetic persona and his native countryside. Youthful impressionism, structured with sensual and idyllic images of rural living, gives way in the course of time to the projection of an alienated, pensive self drawn time and again to the privileged place of his birth to examine the contingencies of life in the light of immanent, ancestral forms of a primitive culture.

—Augustus Pallotta

VOZNESENSKY, Andrei (Andreevich). Born in Moscow, 12 May 1933. Educated at Institute of Architecture, Moscow, degree 1957. Married Zoya Boguslavskaya; one son. Writer and painter. Member, American Academy and Bavarian Academy of Fine Arts. Address: Kotelnicheskaya, nab. 1/15, Block W, Apartment 62, Moscow, USSR.

PUBLICATIONS

Verse

Mozaika [Mosaic]. Vladimir, 1960.
Parabola. Moscow, Sovietsky Pisatel', 1960.
Pishetsya kak lyubitsya [I Write as I Love] (in Russian and Italian). Milan, Feltrinelli, 1962.
Treugol'naya grusha [The Triangular Pear]. Moscow, Sovietsky Pisatel', 1962.
Menya pugayut formalizmom [They Frighten Me with Formalism]. London, Flegon Press, 1963.
Selected Poems, translated by Anselm Hollo. New York, Grove Press, 1964.
Antimiry. Moscow, Molodaya Gvardia, 1964; as *Antiworlds,* New York, Basic Books, 1966; augmented edition, as *Antiworlds and the Fifth Ace,* New York, Doubleday, 1967.
Selected Poems, translated by Herbert Marshall. New York, Hill and Wang, and London, Methuen, 1966.
Akhillesovo serdtse [An Achilles Heart]. Moscow, Khudozhestvennaya Literatura, 1966.
Moi lyubovny dnevik [My Diary of Love]. London, Flegon Press, 1966.
Stikhi [Poems]. Moscow, 1967.
Ten' zvuka [The Shadow of Sound]. Moscow, Molodaya Gvardia, 1970.
Vzglyad [The Glance]. Moscow, Sovietsky Pisatel', 1972.
Dogalypse. San Francisco, City Lights, 1972.
Little Woods: Recent Poems. Melbourne, Sun, 1972.
Vypusti ptitsy! [Set the Birds Free]. Moscow, Molodaya Gvardia, 1974.
Dubovy list violonchelny [Violoncello Oak Leaf]. Moscow, Khudozhestvennaya Literatura, 1975.
Vitrazhnykh del master [The Stained-Glass Panel Master]. Moscow, Molodaya Gvardia, 1976.
Izbrannaya lirika [Selected Lyrics]. Moscow, Detskaya Literatura, 1979.

Nostalgia for the Present. New York, Doubleday, 1978; London, Oxford University Press, 1980.
Soblazn [Temptation]. Moscow, Sovietsky Pisatel', 1979.
Bezotchotnoye [The Instinctive]. Moscow, Sovietsky Pistel', 1981.

Plays

Save Your Faces (produced Moscow, 1971-72).

Television Play: *Juno and Avos*, music by Alexei Rybnikov, tanslated by Adrian Mitchell, 1983.

Fiction

Story under Full Sail. New York, Doubleday, 1974.

Other

Sobranie sochineniy [Collected Works]. Moscow, Khudozhestvennaya Literatura, 1983.

*   *   *

Andrei Voznesensky made his debut as a poet in 1957 when Soviet poetry regained its impetus. After the publication of his first two collections of poems, *Mozaika* and *Parabola*, he was recognised as a talent of the first order. Together with Evtushenko and a few other vociferous poets, he participated in mass poetry readings, thus providing the mood and the tonality of the post-Stalin period. Later volumes, such as *Treugol'naya grusha* and *Antiworlds*, bear the mark of Pasternak, although without his majesty and sense of history. Like Pasternak, Voznesensky is carried away by apparently fortuitous associations of ideas, e.g., the name of the Spanish painter Goya linked with the poet's terrifying vision of war. The words of his verse are often forged together by insistent sound. The orchestration of sounds is extraordinarily powerful, and helps to sustain the semantic link between words. The fact that Voznesensky came to poetry from architecture reveals itself in acute visual imagery. Here is how the poet shows man's duel with death:

> And death speaks: Away with you!
> Aren't you all alone?
> Who are you kicking against?
> Against fourmillionfivehundredfortysevenandtwentythreesquaremilesof
> a monster.

Death is shown to overwhelm us by a deluge of numbers, threatening like an immeasurable colossus. And this is mixed with the intrusive language of the streets, the crass argot of commonplace urban existence made larger than life-size. His idiom is often rude, unceremonious, provocative, abounding in cosmic imagery.

Voznesensky's poetic themes are very varied: war, revolution, Lenin, death, love, and the automobile civilisation. He declares himself a partisan of the technical revolution which grows into a spiritual one. For, as he states: "All progress is retrogression if the process breaks man down." Voznesensky has been praised for his bold and startling rhymes and for the dynamism of his rhythms. However, his stylistic originality exceeds his originality of thought and vision. Clive James got it right when he said: "Voznesensky's poetry has the same limitations as most other Soviet literature which has ever been officially published...what ought to be his main subject matter is hardly there." From time to time he attacks "fat-bellied bureaucrats," bad service, and other shortcomings of the Soviet system. But its mechanism of coercion, deceit, and control—all lie outside his field of vision. His critiques and doubts about his country never go beyond the limits of acceptable criticism. Beneath the brilliant surface of Voznesensky's verse is a "lack of grasp of real life" (P. Levi). It is not for nothing that Voznesensky has been made a candidate for the Lenin prize and is allowed frequent visits to the West. If the Western critics consider Voznesensky "profoundly conformist at heart" (M. Bowra), their Soviet colleagues accuse him of formalism, sensational super-modernism, and false complexity. Lately it has become almost fashionable to debunk him, but to no effect. By many he is still treated like a star poet. His rock opera *Juno and Avos* has been recently shown on British television and in December 1983 he brought it to Paris. As far as Russians are concerned, he has never been and is unlikely to become "the conscience of the nation." When evaluating any modern Russian poet, we should remember that this is precisely what the Russian public expects from their great poets.

—Valentina Polukhina

WALSER, Martin. German. Born in Wasserburg, 24 March 1927. Educated at Gymnasium, Lindau, 1938-44; Philosophisch-Theologische Hochschule, Regensburg, 1946-48; University of Tübingen, 1948-51, Ph.D. 1951. Served in the Deutsche Wehrmacht, 1944-45. Married Käthe Jehle in 1950; four daughters. Staff member for Süddeutscher Rundfunk, Stuttgart, 1949-56; visiting professor or fellow, Middlebury College, Vermont, and University of Texas, Austin, 1973, Warwick University, Coventry, 1975, University of West Virginia, Morgantown, 1976, Dartmouth College, Hanover, New Hampshire, 1979, Princeton University, New Jersey, 1981, and University of California, Berkeley, 1983. Recipient: Gruppe 47 Prize, 1955; Hesse Prize, 1957; Free Theatre Hauptmann Prize (Berlin), 1962; Schiller Prize (Baden-Württemberg), 1965; Bodensee Prize, 1967; Schiller Prize (Mannheim), 1980; Heine Medal, 1981; Büchner Prize, 1981. Agent: Suhrkamp Verlag, Postfach 4249, Frankfurt 1. Address: Zum Hecht 36, 777 Überlingen 18, Germany.

PUBLICATIONS

Fiction

Ein Flugzeug über dem Haus und andere Geschichten. Frankfurt, Suhrkamp, 1955.
Ehen in Philippsburg. Frankfurt, Suhrkamp, 1957; as *The Gadarene Club*, London, Longman, 1960; as *Marriage in Philippsburg*, New York, New Directions, 1961.
Lügengeschichten. Frankfurt, Suhrkamp, 1960.
Halbzeit. Frankfurt, Suhrkamp, 1960.
Das Einhorn. Frankfurt, Suhrkamp, 1966; as *The Unicorn*, London, Calder and Boyars, 1971.
Fiction. Frankfurt, Suhrkamp, 1970.

Die Gallistl'sche Krankheit. Frankfurt, Suhrkamp, 1972.
Der Sturz. Frankfurt, Suhrkamp, 1973.
Jenseits der Liebe. Frankfurt, Suhrkamp, 1976; as *Beyond All Love*, New York, Riverrun, 1982; London, Calder, 1983.
Ein fliehendes Pferd. Frankfurt, Suhrkamp, 1978; as *Runaway Horse*, New York, Holt Rinehart, and London, Secker and Warburg, 1980.
Seelenarbeit. Frankfurt, Suhrkamp, 1979.
Das Schwanenhaus. Frankfurt, Suhrkamp, 1980; as *The Swan Villa*, New York, Holt Rinehart, 1982; London, Secker and Warburg, 1983.
Selected Stories. Manchester, Carcanet Press, 1982.
Brief an Lord Liszt. Frankfurt, Suhrkamp, 1982.
Gesammelte Geschichten. Frankfurt, Suhrkamp, 1983.

Plays

Ein grenzenloser Nachmittag, in *Hörspielbuch 1955.* Frankfurt, Europäischer Verlagsanstalt, 1955.
Der Abstecher (produced Munich, 1961). Frankfurt, Suhrkamp, 1961; as *The Detour* (produced Edinburgh, 1964; London, 1967), with *The Rabbit Race*, London, Calder, 1963.
Eiche und Angora: Eine deutsche Chronik (produced Berlin, 1962). Frankfurt, Suhrkamp, 1962; as *The Rabbit Race* (produced Edinburgh, 1963), with *The Detour*, London, Calder, 1963.
Überlebensgross Herr Krott: Requiem für einen Unsterblichen (produced Stuttgart, 1963). Frankfurt, Suhrkamp, 1964.
Der Schwarze Schwan (produced Stuttgart, 1964). Frankfurt, Suhrkamp, 1964.
Die Zimmerschlacht (produced Munich, 1967). Frankfurt, Suhrkamp, 1967; as *Home Front* (produced London, 1971), in *The Contemporary German Theatre*, New York, Avon, 1972.
Wir werden schon noch handeln (as *Der schwarze Flügel*, produced Berlin, 1968). Munich, Hanser, 1968.
Ein Kinderspiel (produced Stuttgart, 1972). Frankfurt, Suhrkamp, 1970.
Aus dem Wortschatz unserer Kämpfe (as *Ein reizender Abend*, produced Luxembourg, 1972). Stierstadt, Eremiten, 1971.
Gesammelte Stücke. Frankfurt, Suhrkamp, 1971.
Der Menschenfreund, from the play *The Philanthropist* by Christopher Hampton (produced Berlin, 1971). Published in *Theater Heute*, February 1971.
Die Wilden, from the play *Savages* by Christopher Hampton (produced Bochum, 1974). Published in *Theater Heute*, February 1974.
Das Sauspiel: Szenen aus dem 16. Jahrhundert (produced Hamburg, 1975). Frankfurt, Suhrkamp, 1975.
In Goethes Hand: Szenen aus dem 19. Jahrhundert (produced Vienna, 1982). Frankfurt, Suhrkamp, 1982.

Verse

Der Grund zur Freude; 99 Sprüche zur Erbauung des Bewusstseins. Dusseldorf, Eremiten, 1978.

Other

Beschreibung einer Form: Versuch über Franz Kafka. Munich, Hanser, 1961.

Erfahrungen und leseerfahrungen. Frankfurt, Suhrkamp, 1965.
Heimatkunde. Frankfurt, Suhrkamp, 1968.
Hölderlin zu entsprechen (address). Biberach an der Riss, Thomae, 1970.
Wie und wovon handelt Literatur: Aufsätze und Reden. Frankfurt, Suhrkamp, 1973.
Wer ist ein Schriftsteller? Aufsätze und Reden. Frankfurt, Suhrkamp, 1978.
Heines Tränen: Essay. Dusseldorf, Eremiten, 1981.
Selbstbewusstsein und Ironie: Frankfurter Vorlesungen. Frankfurt, Suhrkamp, 1981.
Versuch, ein Gefühl zu verstehen, und andere Versuche. Stuttgart, Reclam, 1982.
Liebeserklärungen. Frankfurt, Suhrkamp, 1983.

Editor, *Die Alternative; oder, Brauchen wir eine neue Regierung?* Reinbek, Rowohlt, 1961.
Editor, *Vorzeichen II: Neun neue deutsche Autoren.* Frankfurt, Suhrkamp, 1963.
Editor, *Er: Prosa*, by Kafka. Frankfurt, Suhrkamp, 1963.

*

Bibliography: *Walser: Bibliographie 1952-1970* by Heinz Saueressig and Thomas Beckermann, Biberach an der Riss, Wege und Gestalten, 1970.

Critical Studies: *Über Walser* edited by Thomas Beckermann, Frankfurt, Suhrkamp, 1970; *Walser* edited by Heinz Ludwig Arnold, Munich, Text & Kritik, 1974, revised edition, 1983; *Wife and Mistress: Women in Walser's Anselm Kristlein Trilogy* by Kathryn Rooney, Coventry, University of Warwick Department of German Studies, 1975; *Walser: The Development as Dramatist 1950-1970*, Bonn, Bouvier, 1978, and *Walser*, Munich, Beck, 1980, both by Anthony Waine; *Walser* edited by Klaus Siblewski, Frankfurt, Suhrkamp, 1981.

*   *   *

To judge by the subject-matter of his two most successful works, the play *Home Front* and the novella *Runaway Horse*, Martin Walser might well be described as the marriage guidance counsellor to West German society. In both works the terrain of marriage is reconnoitred and found to be a minefield of biological, psychological, and social conflicts. Common to both the play and the novella (and indeed to several other works by the author) are the themes of sexuality, ageing, role-playing, ritual, and socially determined pressures. Not only do these works portray the male attracted to and repulsed by the female, but also the male in competition with other males. The male is exposed to an awesome combination of threats to his identity, both from within himself and from external forces, but these works end with a guardedly optimistic view that the husband can best overcome his identity crisis by truthfully communicating his problems to his wife.

The issue of identity has in fact preoccupied Walser since his first novel was published in 1957, again symptomatically entitled *Marriage in Philippsburg*. It is not only the domestic sphere in which an individual's self-image is constantly put under strain; his professional work exerts perhaps even more pressure on the individual's sense of self. Invariably this sphere of his life compels him to adopt values which run counter to his own nature and involve him in relationships which compromise his independence. Not surprisingly, therefore, one relationship which recurs frequently in both dramas and novels is that of the master and his servant, usually clothed in some modern guise such as a company director and his chauffeur, as in *The Detour* and *Seelenarbeit*. In those works written before approximately 1970 the relationship is static, but after 1970 Walser begins to demonstrate how the affected individual can and does gain insights into the mechanisms which from childhood to adulthood have conditioned him into a subservient state of mind and how through self-awareness the "inferior" human being can begin to emancipate himself. It is important to note that this process of emancipation is not brought about from outside, i.e., through changed political conditions, for Walser is too much of a realist to posit such a utopian ideal. Instead, it begins within the individual.

Such a positive development happened just a fraction too late for Walser's most illustrious protagonist, Anselm Kristlein, the central figure of the trilogy, *Halbzeit*, *The Unicorn*, and *Der Sturz*. Anselm's social rise and fall against the backdrop of West Germany's "economic miracle" contains a trenchant critique of many false and negative traits of post-war German society: the competition ethic, greed, egotism, opportunism, sexual permissiveness. Anselm helps to promote all these "values" until he is finally destroyed by them. Walser, however, manages to depict Anselm's fate both humorously and critically, and it is one of his great strengths as a writer that we can also laugh at and learn from the tragedies which befall his impressive assortment of anti-heroes.

—Anthony Waine

WEÖRES, Sándor. Hungarian. Born in Szombathely, 22 June 1913. Educated at schools in Szombathely, Győr, and Sopron; University of Pécs, Ph.D. in philosophy 1935. Married to the writer Amy Károlyi. Librarian in Pécs, Székesfehérvár, and Budapest, 1941-50; free-lance writer from 1950. Co-Editor, *Sorsunk*. Recipient: Baumgarten Prize, 1935, 1936; Kossuth Prize, 1970; Austrian State Prize for European Literature, 1974. Address: Muraközi, ut 10/a, Budapest, Hungary.

PUBLICATIONS

Verse

Hideg van [It Is Cold]. Pécs, Kultúra, 1934.
A kő és az ember [The Stone and the Man]. Budapest, Nyugat, 1935.
A teremtés dícsérete [In Praise of Creation]. Pécs, Janus Pannonius Társaság, 1938.
Theomachia. Pécs, Dunántúl, 1941.
Medúza [Medusa]. Budapest, Egyetemi Nyomda, 1943.
Elysium. Budapest, Móricz Zsigmond, 1946.
Gyümölcskosár [A Basket of Fruit]. Budapest, Singerés Wolfner, 1946.
A szerelem ábécéje [The Alphabet of Love]. Budapest, Új idők, 1946.
A fogak tornáca [The Colonnade of Teeth]. Budapest, Egyetemi Nyomda, 1947.
A hallgatás tornya [The Tower of Silence]. Budapest, Szépirodalmi, 1956.
A lélek idézése [Evocation of the Spirit]. Budapest, Európa, 1958.
Tarka forgó [Many-Colored Pinwheel]. Budapest, Magvető, 1958.
Tűzkút [Well of Flames]. Budapest, Magvető, 1964.
Gyermekjátékok [Children's Games]. Budapest, Móra, 1965.
Merülő Saturnus [Saturn Sinking]. Budapest, Magvető, 1968.
Selected Poems, with Ferenc Juhász, translated by Edwin Morgan and David Wevill. London, Penguin, 1970; Magnolia, Massachusetts, Peter Smith, n.d.
Psyché: Egy hajdani költőnő írásai [Psyche: Writings of a Poetess of Yore]. Budapest, Magvető, 1972.
III vers [30 Poems]. Budapest, Szépirodalmi, 1974.
Harmincöt vers [35 Poems]. Budapest, Magvető, 1978.

WEÖRES

Egysoros versek [One-Line Poems]. Budapest, Helikon-Szépirodalmi, 1979.
Ének a határtalanról [Song about the Infinite]. Budapest, Magvető, 1980.

Plays

Hold és Sárkány [The Moon and the Dragon]. Budapest, Magvető, 1967.
A kétfejű fenevad [The Double-Headed Beast], in *Eletünk*, October 1982.

Other

A vers születése [The Birth of the Poem]. Pécs, Dunántúl, 1939.
Bolond Istók [Stevie Crackpot] (miscellany). Budapest, Egyetemi Nyomda, 1943.
A Teljesseg; Gondolatok [Toward Completeness; Thoughts]. Budapest, Móricz Zsigmond, 1945.
Bóbita [Tuft] (verse for children). Budapest, Ifjúsági, 1955.
Zimzizim (verse for children). Budapest, Móra, 1969.
Egybegyűjtött írások [Collected Writings]. Budapest, Magvető, 2 vols., 1970; revised edition, 3 vols., 1975; 4 vols., 1981.
Tizenegy szimfónia [Eleven Symphonies]. Budapest, Szépirodalmi, 1973.
Ha a vilag rigó lenne [If the World Were a Blackbird] (verse for children). Budapest, Móra, 1973.
Áthallások [Subconscious Influences]. Budapest, Szépirodalmi, 1973.
Abc (verse for children). Budapest, Helikon, 1974.
Egybegyűjtött műforditások [Collected Translations]. Budapest, Magvető, 1976.

Editor, *Három veréb hat szemmel* (verse anthology). Budapest, Magvető, 1977.

Translator, *Po Csü Ji versei* [Poems of Po Tsu Yi]. Budapest, Szépirodalmi, 1952.
Translator, *Csü Juan versei* [Poems of Tsu Yuan]. Budapest, Szépirodalmi, 1954.
Translator, *A tigrisbörös lovag* [Knight Dressed in a Tiger Skin], by S. Rustaveli. Budapest, Új Magyar, 1954.
Translator, *Az út és az Erény Konyve* [Tao Te Kings], by Lao Tse. Budapest, Európa, 1958.
Translator, *A lélek idézése* [Evocation of the Spirit]. Budapest, Európa, 1958.
Translator, *A Megszebaditott Prometheus* [Prometheus Unbound], by P.B. Shelley. Budapest, Móra, 1961.
Translator, *Stéphane Mallarmé költeményei* [Poems]. Budapest, Helikon, 1964.
Translator, *Ostromlott derű* [Besieged Cheerfulness], by Vasko Popa. Budapest, Európa, 1968.
Translator, *Fehér hajnalok* [White Dawns], by Kocsa Racin. Budapest, Európa, 1978.
Translator, *Te titok-virág: Válogatott versek* [You: Flower of Mystery: Selected Poems], by Oton Zupačič. Budapest, Európa, 1978.
Translator, *Gita Govinda*. Budapest, Magvető, 1982.

*

Critical Studies: "Weöres Issue" of *Magyar Mühely 2,* 1964; "Conversation with Weöres" by László Cs. Szabó, in *Tri-Quarterly*, Spring 1967; "Weöres: Unity in Diversity" by George Gömöri, in *Books Abroad 43*, 1969.

*   *   *

370

WOLF

Sándor Weöres is probably the greatest living Hungarian poet. His "Mozartian" qualities became apparent already in his early youth—he was still in his teens when his poems were first printed in the leading Hungarian literary review *Nyugat*. His poetry is one of great diversity: his unusual mimetic talents enable him to absorb different cultural influences and speak with many voices, yet his style is unmistakeably original.

In the 1930's he discovered Eastern philosophy and studied ancient civilizations and mythologies, interests which were reflected in many of the longer poems of *A kő és az ember* and *A teremtés dicsérete*. The Greek myth of Kronos, ending with this god's castration and downfall, is the subject of the poetic oratory *Theomachia*. Weöres's interest in the great myths of mankind is an enduring one, much more profound than his involvement in the social and political questions of his times; creation, death, and resurrection are more real to him than mass culture or the party programmes. This explains the numerous gnomic utterances in his "anthropological" poems such as "De Profundis," "Háromrészes ének" (Tryptych), and "A fogak tornáca" (The Colonnade of Teeth), and his deep scepticism towards all salvationist political ideologies (as in "XX. századi freskó", "Mural of the 20th century"). Because of this he was much attacked after the Second World War and it took a long time before Marxist critics stopped censuring his alleged "nihilism." At any rate, Weöres sees himself as an educator who, through widening the scope of poetic investigation into the unknown, helps contemporary man "to rearrange...his closed, finite, existential Ego into an open, social, cosmic, infinite one" (Introduction to *Egybegyűjtött írások*, 1970).

Another aspect of Weöres's poetic talent is his amazing capacity to write in almost any rhythmic pattern. Among his earliest poems there are songs and nursery rhymes, and this trend culminates in the "Rongyszőnyeg" (Patchwork Rug) cycle in 1940 which includes invented Hungarian and foreign folk-songs, humorous epigrams, and unusual metric experiments. Beginning with the collection *Bóbita*, these poems have been published many times over for young readers and have often been set to music; in the main these account for Weöres's popularity. Quite a few of Weöres's nursery rhymes hide sexual symbolism, yet when he first wrote an outspoken poetic tale of physical love (in the charming "Fairy Spring" cycle) it created an uproar. Another pioneering work in a similar vein is *Psyché: Egy hajdani költőnő írásai*, the fake "poetic autobiography" of a 19th-century woman poet whose wild sexual exploits and passionate relationships Weöres relates with obvious glee.

For a poet given to so much play-acting it would be strange not to write plays, and, indeed, Weöres tried his hand at this genre—with varying success. *Hold és Sárkány* comprises two plays with mythical and make-believe characters, whereas his latest play, *A kétfejű fenevad*, published so far only in the Szombathely review *Életünk*, is a blistering parody of politics situated in 17th-century Hungary occupied by the Turks. Weöres is an accomplished translator from practically all languages, Chinese and Georgian included; his collected poetic translations were published in *Egybegyűjtött műfordítások*.

—George Gömöri

WOLF, Christa. German. Born in Landsberg an der Warthe, Germany (now Gorzow, Poland), 18 March 1929. Educated at the universities of Jena and Leipzig, 1949-53, diploma 1953. Married Gerhard Wolf in 1951; two daughters. Editor, *Neue Deutsche Literatur* magazine; reader for Mitteldeutscher Verlag, Halle, and Verlag Neues Lebe, Berlin; worked in a freight car manufacturing company, 1959-62. Recipient: Heinrich Mann Prize, 1963; National Prize, 1964; Raabe Prize, 1972; Fontane Prize (Potsdam), 1972; Bremen Prize, 1978; Büchner Prize, 1980; Schiller Prize (Baden-Württemberg), 1983. Member, German Academy of Arts. Address: Friedrichstrasse 133, DDR-1040 Berlin, Germany.

PUBLICATIONS

Fiction

Moskauer Novelle. Halle, Mitteldeutscher Verlag, 1961.
Der geteilte Himmel. Halle, Mitteldeutscher Verlag, 1963; as *Divided Heaven*, Berlin, Seven Seas, 1965; New York, Adler, 1976.
Nachdenken über Christa T. Halle, Mitteldeutscher Verlag, 1968; as *The Quest for Christa T.*, New York, Farrar Straus, 1970; London, Hutchinson, 1971.
Till Eulenspiegel: Erzählung für den Film. Berlin, Aufbau, 1972.
Unter den Linden: Drei unwahrscheinliche Geschichten. Berlin, Aufbau, 1974.
Kindheitsmuster. Berlin, Aufbau, 1976; as *A Model Childhood*, New York, Farrar Straus, and London, Virago, 1982.
Kein Ort, Nirgends. Berlin, Aufbau, 1979; as *No Place on Earth*, New York, Farrar Straus, 1982; London, Virago, 1983.
Gesammelte Erzählungen. Neuwied, Luchterhand, 1980.
Kassandra. Neuwied, Luchterhand, 1983.
Voraussetzungen einer Erzählung: Kassandra. Neuwied, Luchterhand, 1983.

Other

Lesen und Schreiben: Aufsätze und Prosastücke. Berlin, Aufbau, 1972; revised edition, 1981; as *The Reader and the Writer*, Berlin, Seven Seas, 1977; New York International, 1978.
Fortgesetzter Versuch: Aufsätze, Gespräche, Essays. Leipzig, Reclam, 1979.

Editor, with Gerhard Wolf, *Wir, unsere Zeit*. Berlin, Aufbau, 1959.
Editor, *In diesen Jahren: Deutsche Erzähler der Gegenwart*. Leipzig, Reclam, 1959.
Editor, *Proben junger Erzähler: Ausgewählte deutsch Prosa*. Leipzig, Reclam, 1959.
Editor, *Glauben an Irdisches*, by Anna Seghers. Leipzig, Reclam, 1969.
Editor, *Der Schatten deines Traumes*, by Karoline von Günderrode. Darmstadt, Luchterhand, 1979.
Editor, *Die Günderode*, by Bettina von Arnim. Leipzig, Insel, 1981.

*

Critical Studies: *Wolf* by Alexander Stephan, Munich, Beck, 1976; *Wolf: Materialienbuch* edited by Klaus Sauer, Darmstadt, Luchterhand, 1979.

*   *   *

From unexceptional beginnings as a critic and author in the 1950's Christa Wolf has developed into one of East Germany's foremost writers. Just as her short stories and novels have played an important role in widening the bounds of what the Party regards as permissible in East German literature, so her theoretical essays on writing have contributed significantly to the literary debate in the GDR.

Wolf gained recognition in 1963 with her novel *Divided Heaven*. In recounting the separation of two lovers after the defection of one to the West, it broached the problem of Germany's division. Wolf's unorthodox approach to this sensitive topic, barely a year after the erection of the Berlin Wall, provoked heated controversy. But her commitment to socialism, reflected in the heroine's decision to remain in the GDR, overcame objections, and the novel became one of the first books by a young East German writer to be read widely in both parts of Germany.

Her first really major work, however, came in 1968 with *The Quest for Christa T.* This novella's unvarnished portrayal of hypocrisy and conformism in the GDR was as unparalleled as its formal innovation was startling. The gradual disillusionment and death of the heroine is related in retrospect by a first-person narrator who consciously shifts back and forth in time between events to blur the distinction between "authentic" memories of Christa T. and episodes she admits to inventing. The novella represented Wolf's first attempt to apply her theory of "subjective authenticity," which she elaborated in the collection of essays *The Reader and the Writer*. The essays challenged the Party's insistence on its own version of "objectivity" in literature, and instead emphasized the validity of the writer's relying on his own, subjective, experience of reality and encouraging the reader to do likewise.

Neither this assertion of literary independence, nor the view of reality it led Wolf to portray were acceptable to the Party, and *The Quest for Christa T.* was vehemently denounced. The episode marks a turning-point in Wolf's career as a writer. Although her books have been grudgingly tolerated since the early 1970's, Wolf has continued to write in a style and elaborate ideas which are at odds with the expectations of the GDR establishment. In 1976 she published *A Model Childhood*, a semi-autobiographical novel which probes Germany's Nazi past and speculates on how far the older generation's childhood experience of fascism still influences society in East, as well as West, Germany. And in 1979 *No Place on Earth* appeared, a novella which deals with the isolation of the writer from society in early 19th-century Germany—with implicit reference to Wolf's own situation in the modern GDR. In both works Wolf further develops a highly reflective form of narration; both offer an unorthodox analysis of the GDR's historical roots—and both were given a cool reception by East German critics.

Wolf's most recent works are characterized on the one hand by a note of disappointment at developments in the GDR. At the same time their style has moved increasingly towards a sophisticated synthesis of essay and novel techniques which continually reflects upon the material under consideration.

—Neil Jackson

WOLKERS, Jan (Hendrik). Dutch. Born in Oegstgeest, 26 October 1925. Studied painting and sculpture in Amsterdam and Salzburg, and in Paris under Ossip Zadkine. Married twice. Recipient: Amsterdam Literature Prize, 1962. Address: Huize "Pomona," Rozendijk 23, Westermiend, 1791 PD Den Burg (Texel), Netherlands.

PUBLICATIONS

Fiction

Serpentina's Petticoat. Amsterdam, Meulenhoff, 1961.

Kort Amerikaans [Crew Cut].   Amsterdam, Meulenhoff, 1962.
Gesponnen suiker [Cotton Candy].   Amsterdam, Meulenhoff, 1963.
Een roos van vlees.   Amsterdam, Meulenhoff, 1963; as *A Rose of Flesh*, London, Secker and Warburg, 1967.
De hond met de blauwe tong [The Dog with the Blue Tongue].   Amsterdam, Meulenhoff, 1964.
Terug naar Oegstgeest [Back to Oegstgeest].   Amsterdam, Meulenhoff, 1965.
Horrible tango.   Amsterdam, Meulenhoff, 1967; translated as *Horrible Tango*, London, Secker and Warburg, 1970.
Turks fruit.   Amsterdam, Meulenhoff, 1969; as *Turkish Delight*, London, Calder and Boyars, 1974.
De valgvogel [The Dodo].   Amsterdam, Meulenhoff, 1974.
De kus [The Kiss].   Amsterdam, Meulenhoff, 1977.
De doodshoofdvlinder [The Death's-Head Moth].   Amsterdam, Bezige Bij, 1979.
De perzik van onsterfelijkheid [The Peach of Immortality].   Amsterdam, Bezige Bij, 1980.
Brandende Liefde [Burning Love].   Amsterdam, Bezige Bij, 1981.
Alle verhalen [All the Stories].   Amsterdam, Meulenhoff, 1981.
De junival [Windfalls].   Amsterdam, Bezige Bij, 1982.
Gifsla [Poison Ivy].   Amsterdam, Bezige Bij, 1983.

Plays

Wegens sterfgeval gesloten [Closed on Account of Death].   Amsterdam, Meulenhoff, 1963.
De Babel.   Amsterdam, Bezige Bij, 1963.

Other

18 composities.   1966.
Het afschuwelijkste uit Jan Wolkers [The Most Gruesome Bits of Wolkers].   Amsterdam, Meulenhoff, 1969.
Zwarte advent [Black Advent].   Utrecht, Motion, 1969.
Groeten van Rottumerplaat [Greetings from Rottumerplaat].   Amsterdam, Elsevier, 1971.
Werkkleding [Working Clothes].   Amsterdam, Elsevier, 1971.

*

Critical Studies: *Wolkers* by J.H. Caspers, M.J.C.M. Krekels, and J.G.M. Weck, Amsterdam, Versluys, 1971; *Wolkers* by Ed Popelier, Bruges, Orion, 1977.

*   *   *

Since his comparatively late debut (a decade or more after those of his most famous contemporaries, Hermans, Reve, and Mulisch), Jan Wolkers has established himself as one of the Netherlands' most widely read authors; two novels, *Turkish Delight* and *Kort Amerikaans*, have been filmed and he has been, for a Dutch writer, much translated.

Wolkers's popular appeal derives from a number of interrelated sources. His powerful depiction of a severely orthodox Calvinist upbringing and the hedonistic but guilt-laden rebellion against it, tapped a rich fund of common experience in his home country for the first time in postwar fiction; Wolkers has since been emulated, though not surpassed, by a number of younger talents. Story-telling skill combines with a vigorous plasticity of style, worthy of a painter and sculptor-turned-writer, to produce indelible images, full of Bosch-like distortions and Biblical echoes.

The "shock effect" of his penchant for grotesque and horrific detail and his sexual explicitness, which caused a moral outcry in some quarters when his first books appeared, can be seen with hindsight as both a contribution to and a symptom of the "liberated" Dutch 1960's.

Many of the themes that were to dominate his later work (including his two stylised plays), were already present in concentrated form in the story-collections *Serpentina's Petticoat* and *Gesponnen suiker*, which remain peaks in his career so far. In them, a young, isolated, impressionable and (over-)imaginative protagonist (often a first-person narrator) confronts various forms of death "in the midst of life," as the Bible has it, though death is here, emphatically not in the gateway to eternity, but final and frequently messy extinction. Sexuality is sometimes an assertion of life over death, but in Wolkers's vision remains essentially akin to it. Conflict with authority and consuming guilt are both commonly associated with an elder brother figure, mentor and rival, who does not survive. A deep love of nature exists alongside gruesome cruelty to animals, which make ritualistic atonement for the larger cruelties inflicted by man, that "degenerate ape" as Wolkers sees him, on his fellow-men. *Kort Amerikaans* expands on the theme of despairing and ultimately impotent sexuality, while *Horrible Tango* explores betrayal and guilt in the relationship between two men.

Charges of literary machismo were levelled at Wolkers from the time of the appearance of *A Rose of Flesh* onwards; the latter novel's presentation of woman as part sex-object, part predator was found widely offensive. The best-selling *Turkish Delight*, in which a tumultuous love affair terminates in the heroine's death of a brain tumour, smacked of formula pulp fiction and provoked comparisons with the sentimentality of, for example, Segal's *Love Story*. While there is no doubt that virility looms large in much later fiction and non-fiction, as in the case of the scrap-book *Werkkleding*, and is even flaunted, Mailer-style, the core of his preoccupation is the essential vulnerability of his macho figures.

What began as a political undercurrent in the work of a writer among whose formative experiences had been the Depression of the 1930's, paternalistic denominational government, war and occupation, and the ignominious loss of empire, became explicit anti-colonialism in *De kus* and anti-capitalism in *De perzik van onsterfelijkheid*, and led to such gestures as the much-publicised return of a literary award on political grounds.

Two of Wolkers's artistically most successful books were written in a more sober vein: *Terug naar Oegstgeest* switches back constantly from present to past and attempts (hopelessly) to come to terms with childhood traumas, while *De doodshoofdvlinder* is a moving treatment of bereavement. Some recent work is uneven and repetitive, and occasionally, as with *De junival*, both contrived and maudlin, but throughout his work Wolkers shows himself, for better or worse, a passionate, intemperate writer who can sometimes be undisciplined, vulgar, and overblown, but who is almost always a compellingly readable original.

—Paul Vincent

YEVTUSHENKO, Yevgeny. *See* **EVTUSHENKO, Evgeny.**

YOSHIOKA Minoru. Japanese. Born in Tokyo, in 1919. Served in the military forces in China, 1941-45. Worked for publishing house before World War II; editor after the war until 1978. Recipient: Mr. H. Prize, 1958.

PUBLICATIONS

Verse

Ekitai [Liquid]. Tokyo, Sozensha, 1941.
Seibutsu [Still Life]. Privately printed, 1955.
Soryo [The Monks]. Tokyo, Eureka, 1958.
Bosuikei [The Spindle-Shape]. Tokyo, Sozensha, 1962.
Shizukana Ie [The Quiet House]. Tokyo, Shichosha, 1968.
Shinpitekina Jidai no Shi [Poetry in a Mystical Age]. Tokyo, Yukawa Shobo, 1974.
Safuran Tsumi [Saffron-Gathering]. Tokyo, Seidosha, 1976.
Lilac Garden, translated by Hiroaki Sato. Chicago, Chicago Review Press, 1976.
Natsu no Utage [Summer Banquet]. Tokyo, Seidosha, 1979.
Kusudama [Scent Bag]. Tokyo, Shoshi Tamada, 1983.

*   *   *

Reading *Still Life*, Yoshioka's second collection of poems, one is tempted to baptize him a "poet of the egg," so obsessively recurrent is the image. With a consummate skill of imagistic juxtaposition, the poet creates a world of strange silence and slow disintegration where "the bones/temporarily placed in the fish/now extricate themselves out of the starry sea/and secretly dissolve/on the plate...." It is amid this world of "putrefying time" that he places a lonely egg, which, admirably refusing to be sentimentalized or mythologized, becomes a symbol of profound unrest as well as of autistic peace. The seeming stability of sculpturesque surface is such that a hasty reader might get a deceptive impression of "classicism," though it should be impossible not to sense something underneath that "tilts" (the poet's favorite word) towards uncanniness.

In the next volume, *The Monks*, uncanniness shifts with a jerk into mercilessness, the static into the dynamic, as if the painter in Yoshioka had developed into a curious dramatist. The title poem reads almost like a scenario of the theatre of the absurd, depicting as it does, in a hitherto unprecedented spare style, the life of four monks—their obscene grotesqueries, their works and meals, their writings, and their suicide ("their bones just as thick as winter trees/hand dead till some day the ropes snap"). "The Coolie," a poem generated out of a memory of wartime experience in China, physically vibrates with powerful motions of a horse, incorporating at the same time an acute insight into Japan's recent history of political follies. Another important poem is an attempt at defining this world of ours as a system of dealing with "Dead Children" (the poem's title); its savage indignation is riveting, and yet there is an incandescent beauty of an autonomous poetic form.

The Monks, winning the coveted Mr. H. Prize for Poetry of the year, publicly announced the advent of a poet whose dislocation of poetic grammar was more radical than any experiments by other post-war poets while it maintained a fierce tension with his innate sense of form. The degree to which he rejected humanistic lyricism and exposed himself to the anxiety of identity was also unique.

It cost Yoshioka years of trials and errors to break himself free from the yoke imposed by the perfected style of *The Monks*: only three slim volumes of verses in fifteen years and two years of complete silence. He finally emerged triumphantly in 1976 with a volume entitled *Saffron-Gathering* as a poet who has acquired a new mobility, an agility which thrives on appropriation of the vocabulary external to the poet's own, such as proper nouns, foreign words, and quotations. Interestingly it was Lewis Carroll's photographed girls who triggered off this new mode by inspiring him to write a poem on them. Though he remains as impredictable and disconcerting as ever, Yoshioka's renewed productivity would seem to confirm our belief that he is probably the best successor to the recently deceased master poet, Junzaburo Nishiwaki.

—Yasunari Takahashi

YOURCENAR, Marguerite. Born Marguerite Antoinette Jeanne Marie Ghislaine de Crayencour, in Brussels, 8 June 1903; moved to the United States, 1939: has dual French-American nationality. Educated privately in France. Part-time lecturer in comparative literature, Sarah Lawrence College, Bronxsville, New York, 1939-49. Recipient: Fémina-Vacaresco Prize, 1952; Newspaper Guild of New York award, 1955; Combat Prize, 1963; Fémina Prize, 1968; Monaco Grand Prize, 1972; National Grand Prize for Letters (France), 1974; French Academy Grand Prize, 1977; Erasmus Prize (Amsterdam), 1983. Honorary degrees: Smith College, Northampton, Massachusetts, 1961; Bowdoin College, Brunswick, Maine, 1968; Colby College, Waterville, Maine, 1972; Harvard University, Cambridge, Massachusetts, 1981. Foreign Member, Royal Belgian Academy, 1971; Member, American Academy; Member, French Academy, 1980 (first woman elected). Officer, Legion of Honor. Lives in Northeast Harbor, Maine. Address: c/o Farrar Straus, 19 Union Square West, New York, New York, 10003, U.S.A.

PUBLICATIONS

Fiction

Alexis: ou, Le Traité du vain combat. Paris, Au Sans Pareil, 1929; revised edition, Paris, Plon, 1952.
La Nouvelle Eurydice. Paris, Grasset, 1931.
Denier du rêve. Paris, Grasset, 1934; revised edition, Paris, Plon, 1959; as *A Coin in Nine Hands*, New York, Farrar Straus, 1982; Henley-on-Thames, Oxfordshire, Ellis, 1983.
La Mort conduit l'attelage. Paris, Grasset, 1935.
Nouvelles orientales. Paris, Gallimard, 1938; revised edition, 1963.
Le Coup de grâce. Paris, Gallimard, 1939; revised edition, 1953; as *Coup de Grace*, New York, Farrar Straus, and London, Secker and Warburg, 1957.
Mémoires d'Hadrien. Paris, Plon, 1951; as *Memoirs of Hadrian*, New York, Farrar Straus, 1954; London, Secker and Warburg, 1955.
L'Oeuvre au noir. Paris, Gallimard, 1968; as *The Abyss*, New York, Farrar Straus, and London, Weidenfeld and Nicolson, 1976.
Anna, soror. Paris, Gallimard, 1981.
Comme l'eau qui coule. Paris, Gallimard, 1982.
Oeuvres romanesques. Paris, Gallimard, 1982.

Plays

Électre; ou, La Chute des masques. Paris, Plon, 1954.

Le Mystère d'Alceste, suivi de Qui n'a pas son Minotaure? Paris, Plon, 1963.
Théâtre:
  1. *Rendre à César, La Petite Sirène, Le Dialogue dans le Marécage.* Paris, Gallimard, 1971.
  2. *Électre, Le Mystère d'Alceste, Qui n'a pas son Minotaure?* Paris, Gallimard, 1971.

Verse

Le Jardin des chimères. Paris, Perrin, 1921.
Les Dieux ne sont pas morts. Paris, Chiberre, 1922.
Feux (prose poems). Paris, Grasset, 1936; as *Fires*, New York, Farrar Straus, 1981; Henley-on-Thames, Oxfordshire, Ellis, 1982.
Les Charités d'Alcippe et autres poèmes. Liège, La Flûte Enchantée, 1956; as *The Alms of Alcippe*, New York, Targ, 1982.
La Couronne et la lyre: Poèmes traduits du grec. Paris, Gallimard, 1979.

Other

Pindare. Paris, Grasset, 1932.
Les Songes et les sorts. Paris, Grasset, 1938.
Préface à la Gita-Govinda. Paris, Émile-Paul, 1958.
Sous bénéfice d'inventaire. Paris, Gallimard, 1962.
Le Labyrinthe du monde:
  1. *Souvenirs pieux.* Paris, Gallimard, 1974.
  2. *Archives du nord.* Paris, Gallimard, 1977.
Comment Wang-Fô fut sauvé (juvenile). Paris, Gallimard, 1979.
Les Yeux ouverts (interview), with Matthieu Galey. Paris, Centurion, 1980.
Mishima; ou, La Vision du vide. Paris, Gallimard, 1981.
Notre Dame des Hirondelles (juvenile). Paris, Gallimard, 1982.
Le Temps, ce grand sculpteur: Essais. Paris, Gallimard, 1983.

Editor and Translator, *Fleuve profond, sombre rivière: Les "Negro spirituals."* Paris, Gallimard, 1964.

Translator, *Les Vagues*, by Virginia Woolf. Paris, Stock, 1937.
Translator, *Ce que savait Maisie*, by Henry James. Paris, Laffont, 1947.
Translator, with Constantin Dimaras, *Présentation critique de Constantin Cavafy 1863-1933.* Paris, Gallimard, 1958.
Translator, *Présentation critique d'Hortense Flexner.* Paris, Gallimard, 1969.

*

Critical Study: *Yourcenar* by Jean Blot, Paris, Seghers, 1971.

*   *   *

For a woman who made history and broke a seemingly unbreakable French tradition—which decreed that the highest literary body in the land, the French Academy, should remain a exclusively male preserve—Marguerite Yourcenar is a conservative artist and woman. But then, if she had been an experimental novelist or a prominent feminist, she would not have been elected to the Academy. Her most characteristic novel, *Le Coup de grâce*, is a slight, slender, elegantly written story close in style, manner, and tone to Drieu la Rochelle, a writer so typical of his age and country that he has had little impact outside it. This until recently was the case with Yourcenar also: she is very much a French phenomenon, a writer in a particular classical tradition which she develops rather than subverts.

And yet there are paradoxes. Born the daughter of a minor French nobleman, she has spent most of her life abroad—indeed for many years she held United States citizenship—and took for her life-partner another woman, Grace Frick, an American who died in 1979 and who translated most of her books into English. Yourcenar had to be reinstated in her original French citizenship by special decree in order to take up her seat in the Academy, which is another indication of her unusualness.

Otherwise she is solidly French. Given a solid grounding in classical studies by her father (she was educated privately), she drew on the poets and historians of Greece and Rome for her inspiration in a way that Racine would have understood. In her younger days she wrote passionate love poetry, particularly *Fires*, strongly reminiscent of Sappho and Ovid, in which, as both in the writers of antiquity and in Racine, love is treated as "a form of transcendence." Her most famous novel, *Memoirs of Hadrian*, became a best-seller because it brought vividly to life the great Roman emperor and in particular his tragic love affair with the young man Antinous, who committed suicide to escape the jealousy of the emperor's unloved wife and the enmity of the imperial court. The implication of this story—that even an autocrat cannot control destiny or ensure himself happiness—is one that emerges from much French neoclassical writing, such as Racine's tragedy *Berenice*. Like *Berenice*, too, *Memoirs of Hadrian* was solidly researched, based on many years' familiarity with the primary sources, and on a close study of the Mediterranean background.

In addition to writing poetry and fiction of great power and elegance, Yourcenar has shown herself to be an expert translator, not only from ancient and modern Greek (Cavafy) but also from English (in works as diverse as Henry James and Negro spirituals). She is also a playwright who, like Cocteau, has adapted and up-dated Greek dramatists for the modern stage. This fascination with ancient themes is entirely consistent with her achievement as a novelist who, even when treating contemporary subjects, does so with classical restraint and aloofness.

The same air of fastidious detachment characterises her more recent volumes of autobiography, in which she reveals next to nothing about herself but concentrates on her recollections of others, especially of her colourful father, and on reflections, which to the foreign reader are typically French, about life, death, and destiny, expressed in a prose of old-fashioned elegance and elaboration. As with Gide, this can lead to a rather lofty tone and to a feeling of bloodless polish and smoothness about the writing, but when the chasteness of the utterance perfectly matches the passionate nature of the subject-matter, as it frequently does in Hadrian's laconic confidences as imagined by Yourcenar, the effect has the universality and sempiternality which French classicism has always aspired to.

—John Fletcher

TITLE
INDEX

The following list of titles cites all works included in the fiction, play, and verse sections of the individual entries in the book, and uncategorized titles for some entrants. The name(s) in parenthesis is meant to direct the reader to the appropriate entry, and not necessarily to give complete information about the work. The date given is that of first publication (or production of a play, if earlier). The following abbreviations are used:

f   fiction

p   play

v   verse

These should refer the reader to the appropriate sections of the entry. The lack of one of the three abbreviations indicates that the publications of the entrant are not divided into categories. Revised and translated titles, if different from the original title, are listed with their appropriate dates.

A B C de Castro Alves (f Amado), 1941
A.B.C. de notre vie (p Tardieu), 1969
A cena col commendatore (f Soldati), 1950
A ciascuno il suo (f Sciascia), 1966
À coeur joual (f Blais), 1974
A Educação pela Pedra (v Melo Neto), 1966
A la altura de las circunstancias (v Guillén), 1957
A la mitad del camino (f Matute), 1961
A la orilla del mundo y primer día (v Paz), 1942
A la pata de palo (f Cela), 1965
A la pintura (v Alberti), 1945
À la santé du serpent (v Char), 1954
À une sérénité crispée (v Char), 1951
Aan de evenaar (f Claus), 1973
Aanslag (f Mulisch), 1982
Abahn Sabana David (f Duras), 1970
Abath al aqdar (f Mahfouz), 1939
Abel (f Matute), 1948
Abel et Bela (p Pinget), 1971
Abendstunde in Spätherbst (p Dürrenmatt), 1959
Abismo (v Torga), 1932
Abierto a todas horas (v Alberti), 1964
Abito nuovo (p De Filippo), 1937
Abominable Homme des neiges (p Char), 1967
About Face (p Fo), 1983
About Mortin (p Pinget), 1967
Above the Sky Monster (f Oe), 1977
Absence (f Johnson), 1969
Absent Without Leave (f Böll), 1965
Abstecher (p Walser), 1961
Abtötungsverfahren (v Kunert), 1980
Abyss (f Yourcenar), 1976
Accents (v Tardieu), 1939
Accidental Death of an Anarchist (p Fo), 1979
Accomplices (f Simenon), 1964
Account Unsettled (f Simenon), 1962
Achilles a želva (v Holub), 1960
Achterloo (p Dürrenmatt), 1983
Ačkoli (v Holub), 1969
Acqainted with the Night (f Böll), 1954
Acrobat (f Reve), 1956
Across the Street (f Simenon), 1954
Act of Passion (f Simenon), 1952
Action de la justice est éteinte (v Char), 1931
'Adala wa Fann (f Tawfiq), 1953
Adam, One Afternoon (f Calvino), 1957
Adam und Eva (p Hacks), 1973
Adam, Where Art Thou? (f Böll), 1955
'Adame Miroir (p Genet), 1948

Addio diletta Amelia (f Soldati), 1979
Ad-Dunya Riwaya Hazaliya (p Tawfiq), 1974
Adefesio (p Alberti), 1944
Adioses (f Onetti), 1954
Adrienne Mesurat (f Green), 1927
Advertisement (p Ginzburg), 1968
Afanismos tis Milos (v Ritsos), 1974
Affair in Capri (f Soldati), 1957
Affaire Saint-Fiacre (f Simenon), 1932
Affairs of Destiny (f Simenon), 1942
Affirmation (v Guillén), 1967
Afternoon of Monsieur Andemas (f Duras), 1964
Agadir (v Lundkvist), 1961
Agatha (p Duras), 1981
Âge cassant (v Char), 1965
Âge de craie (v Pieyre de Mandiargues), 1961
Âge de discrétion (f Beauvoir), 1968
Age of Discretion (f Beauvoir), 1969
Agnes Bernauer (p Kroetz), 1976
Agonía confutans (p Benet), 1970
Agonia da noite (f Amado), 1954
Agostino (f Moravia), 1944
Agrandissement (f Mauriac), 1963
Ağridaği Efsanesi (f Kemal), 1970
Agrypnia (v Ritsos), 1954
Agua quemada (f Fuentes), 1981
Agua y viento (v Paz), 1959
Ah! Ernesto (f Duras), 1971
Ah...Law Arifa ash-Shabab (p Tawfiq), 1981
Ahasver (f Heym), 1981
'Ahd ash-Shaytan (f Tawfiq), 1938
Ahl al-Fann (f Tawfiq), 1934
Ahl al-Kahf (p Tawfiq), 1933
Ahola no es de leil (p Sastre), 1979
Ai no megane wa irogarasu (p Abe), 1973
Ailleurs (v Michaux), 1948
Ainé des ferchaux (f Simenon), 1945
Airborn (v Paz), 1981
Aire de un crimen (f Benet), 1980
Aire nuestro (v Guillén), 1968
Airone (f Bassani), 1968
Airs (v Jaccottet), 1967
Akçasazin Ağalari (f Kemal), 1974
Akhillesovo serdtse (v Voznesensky), 1966
Akhshav uba-yamin na aherim (v Amichai), 1955
'Akshav ba-ra'nsh (v Amichai), 1968
Akt przerywany (p Różewicz), 1966
Al fuoco della controversia (v Luzi), 1978
Al Gözüm Seyreyle Salih (f Kemal), 1976

383

Al-'Alam al-Majhul (p Tawfiq), 1973
Al-Amira al-Bayda aw Bayad an-Nahar (f Tawfiq), 1978
Al-Aydi an-Na'ima (p Tawfiq), 1954
Alba ai vetri (v Bassani), 1963
Alba del alheli (v Alberti), 1927
Aleph (f Borges), 1949
Alexis (f Yourcenar), 1929
Alfabel (v Lucebert), 1955
Algunos muchachos (f Matute), 1968
Al-Hamir (p Tawfiq), 1975
Al-Hubb (p Tawfiq), 1973
Al-Hubb fawqa Hadabat al-Haram (f Mahfouz), 1979
Al-Hubb Tahta al-Matar (f Mahfouz), 1973
Alibi (v Morante), 1958
Al-Jarima (f Mahfouz), 1973
Al-Karnak (f Mahfouz), 1974
All Fires the Fire (f Cortázar), 1973
All Men Are Mortal (f Beauvoir), 1956
All Women Are Fatal (f Mauriac), 1964
Alla periferia (f Cassola), 1941
Allegoria e derisione (f Pratolini), 1966
Allegra (f Mallet-Joris), 1976
Allégresse (v Char), 1960
Al-Liss wa-l-Kilab (f Mahfouz), 1961
Al-Malik Udib (p Tawfiq), 1949
Al-Maraya (f Mahfouz), 1972
Alms of Alcippe (v Yourcenar), 1982
Alouette (p Anouilh), 1953
Al-qahira al-jadida (f Mahfouz), 1946
Al-Qasr al-Mashur (f Tawfiq), 1936
Als der Krieg ausbrach, Als der Krieg zu Ende war (f Böll), 1962
Als der Krieg zu Ende war (p Frisch), 1948
Al-Sarab (f Mahfouz), 1949
Al-Shahhadh (f Mahfouz), 1965
Al-Shaytan ya'iz (f Mahfouz), 1979
Al-Sukkariva (f Mahfouz), 1957
Al-Summan wa-l-Kharif (f Mahfouz), 1962
Al-Tariq (f Mahfouz), 1964
Although (v Holub), 1971
Al-Thulathiya (f Mahfouz)
Altra Libertà (v Bassani), 1951
Altra vita (f Moravia), 1973
Al-Warta (p Tawfiq), 1966
Am Ziel (p Bernhard), 1981
Amagerdigte (v Rifbjerg), 1965
Amant complaisant (p Anouilh), 1962
Amante (v Alberti), 1926
Amante anglaise (f Duras), 1967
Amante infelice (f Moravia), 1943
Amants du métro (p Tardieu), 1952
Ámbito (v Aleixandre), 1928

Ambizioni sbagliate (f Moravia), 1935
Amédée (p Ionesco), 1954
Amen (v Amichai), 1978
American Bride (f Soldati), 1979
Amiche (f Pratolini) 1943
Amicizia (p De Filippo), 1952
Amico gesuita (f Soldati), 1943
Amor de Castro Alves (f Amado), 1947
Amor do soldado (f Amado), 1958
Amore coniugale (f Moravia), 1949
Amori difficuli (f Calvino), 1970
Amour (f Duras), 1971
Amours impossibles (p Arrabal), 1966
Amphitryon (p Hacks), 1968
Amras (f Bernhard), 1964
Amsterdamse school (v Lucebert), 1955
Amulet (v Lucebert), 1957
An der Baumgrenze (f Bernhard), 1969
An 1964 (v Char), 1964
Ana Kleiber (p Sastre), 1957
Ana wa'l-Qanun wal-Fann (f Tawfiq), 1973
Anabaptists (p Dürrenmatt), 1976
Analfabeten (f Lo-Johansson)
Análisis espectral de un Comando al servicio de la Revolución Proletaria (p Sastre), 1979
Anamneza (v Holub), 1964
Anastas (p Benet), 1970
Anatolian Tales (f Kemal), 1968
And Never Said a Word (f Böll), 1978
And Quiet Flows the Don (f Sholokhov), 1934
And They Put Handcuffs on the Flowers (p Arrabal), 1971
And Where Were You, Adam? (f Böll), 1974
Anděl strážný (p Havel), 1969
Anderer K (p Kunert), 1977
Andorra (p Frisch), 1961
Âne rouge (f Simenon), 1933
Angel Comes to Babylon (p Dürrenmatt), 1962
Anger (p Ionesco), 1969
Anglais décrit dans le château fermé (f Pieyre de Mandiargues), 1953
Angst des Tormanns beim Elfmeter (f Handke), 1970
Aniki Bobó (v Melo Neto), 1958
Anita und das Existenzminimum (p Böll), 1955
Anna (I) Anna (f Rifbjerg), 1982
Anna (jeg) Anna (f Rifbjerg), 1969
Anna Karenina (p Anouilh), 1948
Anna Kleiber (p Sastre), 1962
Anna, soror (f Yourcenar), 1981

Anna's World (f Blais), 1984
Anneaux de Bicetre (f Simenon), 1963
Année dernière à Marienbad (f Robbe-Grillet), 1961
Anniversaries (f Johnson), 1975
Anisichten eines Clowns (f Böll), 1963
Ansiedade (v Torga), 1928
Antagonista (f Cassola), 1976
Anthropos me to garyfallo (v Ritsos), 1952
Antica moneta (v Volponi), 1955
Antigone (p Anouilh), 1944
Antigone (p Carmi), 1969
Antigua casa madrileña (v Aleixandre), 1961
Antimiry (v Voznesensky), 1964
Anti-Platon (v Bonnefoy), 1962
Anti-Poems (v Parra), 1960
Antiworlds (v Voznesensky), 1966
Antoine et Julie (f Simenon), 1953
Antwort aus der Stille (f Frisch), 1937
Any potachti Politeia (v Ritsos), 1958
Apocalypse (v Cardenal), 1977
Apocrief (v Lucebert), 1952
Apocryphe (f Pinget), 1980
Apoheretismos (v Ritsos), 1957
Apollo Society (p Tardieu), 1968
Apparences (f Blais), 1970
Apparitions (v Michaux), 1946
Apprendre à marcher (p Ionesco), 1960
Apprenti psychiâtre (f Green), 1976
Apprentice Psychiatrist (f Green), 1920
Après-midi de Monsieur Andesmas (f Duras), 1962
Apuntes carpetovetónicos (f Cela), 1965
Aquila o sol? (v Paz), 1951
År (p Rifbjerg), 1970
Aracoeli (f Morante), 1982
Araignée (v Ponge), 1952
Arbetares liv (f Lo-Johansson), 1977
Arcangeli non giocano a flipper (p Fo), 1966
Archibald Strohalm (f Mulisch), 1952
Archipel Lenoir (p Salacrou), 1947
Architect and the Emperor of Assyria (p Arrabal), 1967
Architecte et l'empereur d'Assyrie (p Arrabal), 1967
Architectoniki ton dentron (v Ritsos), 1958
Architruc (p Pinget), 1961
Arctis (v Heinesen), 1980
Ardèle (p Anouilh), 1948
Arid Heart (f Cassola), 1964
Arini Allah (f Tawfiq), 1953
Aristokraten (p Müller), 1968
Arkivet (f Rifbjerg), 1967

Arktiske Elegier (v Heinesen), 1921
Ärliga bedragaren (f Jansson), 1982
Armas secretas (f Cortázar), 1959
Armer Ritter (p Hacks), 1978
Armes miraculeuses (v Césaire), 1946
Aromates chasseurs (v Char), 1975
Arrepentido (f Matute), 1961
Arrest (p Anouilh), 1974
Arrestation (p Anouilh), 1975
Ar-Ribat al-Muqaddas (f Tawfiq), 1944
Ars Amandi (p Arrabal), 1970
Arsenal (v Char), 1929
Arsène et Cléopâtre (p Pieyre de Mandiargues), 1981
Art bref (v Char), 1950
Arte della commedia (p De Filippo), 1965
Artefactos (v Parra), 1972
Artine (v Char), 1930
Arturo's Island (f Morante), 1959
Arzt wider Willen (p Müller), 1970
Ärztinnen (p Hochhuth), 1980
Asalto nocturno (p Sastre), 1964
Ash'ab, Amir at-Tufayliyin (f Tawfiq), 1963
Ashab as-Sa'ada az-Zawjiya (p Tawfiq), 1981
Ashwak as-Salam (p Tawfiq), 1957
Así en la paz como en la guerra (f Cabrera Infante), 1960
Askatasuna! (p Sastre), 1974
Asno (p Ruibal), 1970
Asperos tempos (f Amado), 1954
As-Safqa (p Tawfiq), 1956
Assassin (f Simenon), 1937
Assignment (p Müller), 1984
As-Sultan al-Ha'ir (p Tawfiq), 1960
Astronauci (f Lem), 1951
Astronomens hus (f Lo-Johansson), 1966
Astillero (f Onetti), 1961
Astyanax (v Pieyre de Mandiargues), 1956
At the Gai-Moulin (f Simenon), 1940
At the Stone of Losses (v Carmi), 1983
Atlas-Hôtel (p Salacrou), 1931
Atom Station (f Laxness), 1961
Atómstödin (f Laxness), 1948
At-Ta'am Li-Kull Fam (p Tawfiq), 1963
Attenzione (f Moravia), 1965
Attore (f Soldati), 1970
Au bout du rouleau (f Simenon), 1947
Au Château d'Argol (f Gracq), 1938
Au pays de la magie (v Michaux), 1941
Au rendez-vous des Terre-Neuvas (f Simenon), 1931
Audience (p Havel), 1976
Auf der Erde und in der Hölle (v Bernhard),

1957
Auftrag (p Müller), 1980
Augen der Vernunft (f Heym), 1955
August 1914 (f Solzhenitsyn), 1972
Aún es de día (f Delibes), 1949
Aunt Jeanne (f Simenon), 1953
Aunt Julia and the Scriptwriter (f Vargas Llosa), 1982
Aura (f Fuentes), 1962
Aurélia Steiner (p Duras), 1979
Aurore rouge et noire (p Arrabal), 1969
Aus dem Tagebuch einer Schnecke (f Grass), 1972
Aus dem Wortschatz unserer Kämpfe (p Walser), 1971
Ausgefragt (v Grass), 1967
Aussatz (p Böll), 1969
Aussi Longue Absence (p Duras), 1961
Auto-da-Fé (f Canetti), 1946
Automa (f Moravia), 1963
Automat svět (f Hrabal), 1966
Automobile Graveyard (p Arrabal), 1960
Autostop (p Havel), 1961
Autour de Mortin (p Pinget), 1965
Autre (f Green), 1971
Autre sommeil (f Green), 1931
Autres (f Simenon), 1962
Autumn of the Patriarch (f García Márquez), 1976
Avarice House (f Green), 1927
Ave Vergil (v Bernhard), 1981
Avenir est dans les oeufs (p Ionesco), 1957
Aventura en lo gris (p Buero Vallejo), 1955
Aveva due pistole con gli occhi bianchi e neri (p Fo), 1966
Avgust chetyrnadtsatovo (f Solzhenitsyn), 1971
Avonden (f Reve), 1947
Avvento notturno (v Luzi), 1940
Avventure di Mandrin (p Soldati), 1952
Awakening (f Matute), 1963
Awdat al-Ruh (f Tawfiq), 1933
Awlad Haratina (f Mahfouz), 1967
Axel (p Mulisch), 1977
Axion esti (v Elytis), 1959

Baal Babylon (f Arrabal), 1961
Baal Babylone (f Arrabal), 1959
Babel (p Wolkers), 1963
Babylon—gudarnas sköka (f Lundkvist), 1981
Babylónsky příběh (f Skvorecky), 1967
Bacalao (p Ruibal), 1971
Baga (f Pinget), 1958

Ba-ginah ha-tsiburit (v Amichai), 1959
Bahnof von Zimpren (f Böll), 1959
Bajka (f Ćosić), 1966
Bajki robotów (f Lem), 1964
Bajo tu clara sombra (v Paz), 1937
Baker, The Baker's Wife, and the Baker's Boy (p Anouilh), 1972
Bal des voleurs (p Anouilh), 1938
Balada de Carbanchel (v Sastre), 1976
Balada y canciones del Paraná (v Alberti), 1954
Balcon (p Genet), 1956
Balcon en forêt (f Gracq), 1958
Balcony (p Genet), 1957
Balcony in the Forest (f Gracq), 1959
Bald Soprano (p Ionesco), 1956
Baltics (v Tranströmer), 1975
Banana Tourist (f Simenon), 1946
Bank al-Qalaq (p Tawfiq), 1966
Banlieue de l'aube à l'aurore (v Butor), 1968
Bara en mor (f Lo-Johansson), 1939
Baraja de invenciones (f Cela), 1953
Barby (p Hacks), 1983
Barca (v Luzi), 1935
Barn Náttúrunnar (f Laxness), 1919
Baron in the Trees (f Calvino), 1959
Barone rampante (f Calvino), 1957
Barrage contre le Pacifique (f Duras), 1950
Basement Window (p Buero Vallejo), 1981
Bass Saxophone (f Skvorecky), 1977
Bassaxofon (f Skvorecky), 1967
Bašta, pepeo (f Kiš), 1965
Bataille de Pharsale (f Simon), 1969
Bateau d'Émile (f Simenon), 1954
Battle of Nerves (f Simenon), 1951
Battle of Pharsalus (f Simon), 1971
Bau (p Müller), 1974
Baueren (p Müller), 1975
Baxter—Vera Baxter (p Duras), 1977
Bayn al-Qasrayn (f Mahfouz), 1956
Bayt sayyi al-suma (f Mahfouz), 1965
Bazar de la providencia (p Alberti), 1934
Beatrice Cenci (p Moravia), 1958
Beau Ténébreux (f Gracq), 1945
Beauté du diable (p Salacrou), 1950
Beaux' Stratagem (p Carmi)
Bébo's Girl (f Cassola), 1962
Becket (p Anouilh), 1959
Beelden in het heden (v Lucebert), 1977
Beerdigung findet in aller Stille Statt (f Kunert), 1968
Befehl (p Hochwälder), 1967
Befristeten (p Canetti), 1964
Beggars (p Ruibal), 1968

Begging Machine (p Ruibal), 1975
Begrüssung des Aufsichtsrats (f Handke), 1967
Behind the Door (f Bassani), 1972
Behouden huis (f Hermans), 1952
Bel paese (v Erba), 1956
Bella Ciao (p Arrabal), 1972
Bella vita (f Moravia), 1935
Belle (f Simenon), 1954
Belle Bête (f Blais), 1959
Belle Captive (p Robbe-Grillet), 1983
Belle Vie (p Anouilh), 1980
Belles Images (f Beauvoir), 1966
Bells and Trains (p Amichai), 1966
Bells in Winter (v Milosz), 1978
Bells of Bicetre (f Simenon), 1964
Be-merhak shete tikrot (v Amichai), 1958
Bene mio e core mio (p De Filippo), 1955
Berättelser för vilsekomna (f Lundkvist), 1961
Berg (p Bernhard), 1970
Bergelon (f Simenon), 1941
Berget och svalorna (f Lundkvist), 1957
Berichte zur Gesinnungslage der Nation (f Böll), 1975
Berliner Antigone (f Hochhuth), 1964
Berretto a Sonagli (p De Filippo), 1936
Be-ruah ha-nora'ah ha-zot (f Amichai), 1961
Berühmten (p Bernhard), 1976
Beskedne (f Rifbjerg), 1976
Best House in Naples (p De Filippo), 1956
Bestialité érotique (p Arrabal), 1969
Bestiario (f Cortázar), 1951
Besuch der alten Dame (p Dürrenmatt), 1956
Besvärjelser till tröst (v Lundkvist), 1969
Bête dans la jungle (p Duras), 1962
Beton (f Bernhard), 1982
Beton (v Holub), 1970
Betty (p Fo), 1980
Betty (f Simenon), 1961
Between Fantoine and Agapa (f Pinget), 1982
Between Life and Death (f Sarraute), 1969
Beyond All Love (f Walser), 1982
Bezoekuur (p Mulisch), 1974
Bezotchotnoye (v Voznesensky), 1981
Bezsenność (f Lem), 1971
Biale malzeństwo (p Rósewicz), 1975
Bibliothèque est en feu (v Char), 1956
Bichos (f Torga), 1940
Bicyclette du condamné (p Arrabal), 1961
Bidaya wa-nihaya (f Mahfouz), 1949
Biedermann und die Brandstifter (p Frisch), 1953
Bifnim (v Carmi), 1981
Big Bob (f Simenon), 1969
Big Mama's Funeral (f García Márquez), 1971
Bilan maletras (f Simenon), 1948
Bilanz (p Böll), 1957
Bilanz (p Kroetz), 1972
Billard um Halbzehn (f Böll), 1959
Billiards at Half Past Nine (f Böll), 1961
Billigesser (f Bernhard), 1980
Bin (f Frisch), 1945
Binboğalar Efsanesi (f Kemal), 1971
Biografie (p Frisch), 1967
Biography (p Frisch), 1969
Bird of Paper (v Aleixandre), 1982
Bird of the East (f Tawfiq), 1966
Bitter Honeymoon (f Moravia), 1954
Bittere Lorbeer (f Heym), 1950
Black Rain (f Simenon), 1947
Blacks (p Genet), 1960
Blaesende Gry (f Heinesen), 1934
Blanc à lunettes (f Simenon), 1937
Blanco (v Paz), 1967
Blaubart (f Frisch), 1982
Blauw blauw (p Claus), 1973
Blaze of Embers (f Pieyre de Mandiargues), 1971
Blechtrommel (f Grass), 1959
Blendung (f Canetti), 1936
Blijde en onvoorziene week (v Claus), 1950
Blind Alley (f Simenon), 1946
Blinde (p Dürrenmatt), 1948
Blindenschrift (v Enzensberger), 1964
Blood of Others (f Beauvoir), 1948
Blow-Up (f Cortázar), 1968
Blue Room (f Simenon), 1964
Bluebeard (f Frisch), 1983
Bo ni natta otoko (p Abe), 1969
Bobette et ses satyres (f Simenon), 1928
Bodies of Love (f Lo-Johansson), 1971
Boh (f Moravia), 1976
Bonito crimen del carabinero (f Cela), 1947
Bonnes (p Genet), 1946
Book of Flights (f Le Clézio), 1971
Book of Laughter and Forgetting (f Kundera), 1980
Book of Sand (f Borges), 1977
Boring Afternoon (p Hrabal), 1965
Borrowed Time (f Rasputin), 1981
Bösen Köche (p Grass), 1961
Bosuikei (v Yoshioka), 1962
Botta e resposta (p Soldati), 1950
Bottom of the Bottle (f Simenon), 1954

Bouches inutiles (p Beauvoir), 1945
Bouddha s'est mis à trembler (f Mauriac), 1979
Bought and Sold (f Moravia), 1973
Boulanger, la boulangère, et le petit mitron (p Anouilh), 1968
Boule de verre (p Salacrou), 1958
Boule noire (f Simenon), 1955
Boulevard Durand (p Salacrou), 1960
Bourgmestre de Furnes (f Simenon), 1939
Bourgomaster of Furnes (f Simenon), 1952
Box Man (f Abe), 1975
Brandende Liefde (f Wolkers), 1981
Brass Serpent (v Carmi), 1964
Bratsk Station (v Evtushenko), 1966
Bratskaya GES (v Evtushenko), 1965
Bread of Our Early Years (f Böll), 1957
Bread of Those Early Years (f Böll), 1976
Breathings (v Jaccottet), 1974
Brekkukotsannáll (f Laxness), 1957
Breton Sisters (f Simenon), 1943
Brevet til Gerda (f Rifbjerg), 1972
Bride in the Morning (p Claus), 1960
Brief an Lord Liszt (f Walser), 1982
Brief Life (f Onetti), 1976
Brindisi (v Luzi), 1946
Brot der frühen Jahre (f Böll), 1955
Brothers Rico (f Simenon), 1954
Brücke von Berczaba (p Böll), 1952
Bruid in de morgen (p Claus)
Bruno Santini (f Pratolini), 1965
Buenas conciencias (f Fuentes), 1959
Buenos Aires en tinta china (v Alberti), 1951
Bugie con le gambe tunghe (p De Filippo), 1948
Buh do domu (p Skvorecky), 1980
Burial of Monsieur Bouvet (f Simenon), 1955
Burial of the Sardine (f Arrabal), 1965
Burning Plain (f Rulfo), 1967
Burnt Water (f Fuentes), 1981
Busta orancione (f Soldati), 1966
Bütün Hikâyeler (f Kemal), 1967
Butt (f Grass), 1977

Cabeza de la hidra (f Fuentes), 1978
Cacáu (f Amado), 1934
Cacciatore (f Cassola), 1964
Cachorros (f Vargas Llosa), 1967
Cadastre (v Césaire), 1961
Cadaveri si spediscono e le donne si spon-
gliano (p Fo), 1962
Café Céleste (f Mallet-Joris), 1959

Cafe de artistas (f Cela), 1953
Cage de verre (f Simenon), 1971
Cahier d'un retour au pays natal (v Césaire), 1947
Caifanes (p Fuentes), 1967
Caimán (p Buero Vallejo), 1981
Cajón de sastre (f Cela), 1957
Çakircale efe (f Kemal), 1972
Cal y canto (v Alberti), 1929
Calendario del '67 (v Pratolini), 1978
Calling for Help (p Handke), 1972
Câmara ardente (v Torga), 1962
Camarada oscuro (p Sastre), 1979
Camino (f Delibes), 1950
Camion (p Duras), 1977
Camouflage (v Rifbjerg), 1961
Cancer Ward (f Solzhenitsyn), 1968
Cancionero sin nombre (v Parra), 1937
Canciones del alto valle del Aniene (v Alberti), 1972
Canciones rusas (v Parra), 1967
Candido (f Sciascia), 1977
Candle in the Wind (p Solzhenitsyn), 1973
Cani e gatti (p De Filippo), 1970
Canne à pêche (p Hébert), 1959
Cannibals (f Heym), 1958
Can't Pay, Won't Pay (p Fo), 1981
Cantar de ciegos (f Fuentes), 1964
Cantata dei giorni dispari (p De Filippo), 1951
Cantata dei giorni pari (p De Filippo), 1959
Cantatrice chauve (p Ionesco), 1950
Cántico (v Guillén), 1928
Cántico do homen (v Torga), 1950
Canto de siempre (v Alberti), 1980
Canto nacional (v Cardenal), 1973
Ção sem Plumas (v Melo Neto), 1950
Capitães de Areia (f Amado), 1937
Capolavori (p De Filippo), 1973
Capri Letters (f Soldati), 1955
Captain Pantoja and the Special Service (f Vargas Llosa), 1978
Car Cemetery (p Arrabal), 1962
Cara de la desgracia (f Onetti), 1960
Card Index (p Rósewicz), 1967
Cargamento de sueños (p Sastre), 1948
Carnet du bois de pins (v Ponge), 1947
Caro Michele (f Ginzburg), 1973
Caroline chérie (p Anouilh), 1951
Carta del cielo (f Soldati), 1980
Cartas boca abajo (p Buero Vallejo), 1957
Cartolines et dédicaces (v Pieyre de Man-
diargues), 1960
Casa de campo (f Donoso), 1978

Casa del perché (f Soldati), 1982
Casa di via Valadier (f Cassola), 1956
Casa verde (f Vargas Llosa), 1966
Casi un cuento de hadas (p Buero Vallejo), 1953
Casilla de los Morelli (f Cortázar), 1973
Caso Marini (p Fo), 1974
Casseur d'assiettes (p Salacrou), 1924
Castello dei destini incrociati (f Calvino) 1973
Castilla, esta es mi tierra (p Delibes), 1983
Castle of Argol (f Gracq), 1951
Castle of Crossed Destinies (f Calvino), 1977
Cat (f Simenon), 1967
Cat and Mouse (f Grass), 1963
Catch as Catch Can (p Anouilh), 1967
Catira (f Cela), 1955
Cavalcade d'amour (p Anouilh), 1939
Cavaliere inesistente (f Calvino), 1959
Cave of Night (v Aleixandre), 1976
Cavern (p Anouilh), 1966
Ce formidable bordel (p Ionesco), 1973
Ce que parler veut dire (p Tardieu), 1951
Ce que savait Morgan (p Duras), 1974
Cécile (p Anouilh), 1951
C'est beau (p Sarraute), 1975
Cement (p Müller), 1979
Ceñidor de Venus desceñido (v Alberti), 1948
Centana (v Paz), 1969
Cerchio aperto (v Erba), 1983
Cercle des Mahé (f Simenon), 1946
Ceremonias (f Cortázar), 1968
Cérémonie pour un noir assassiné (p Arrabal), 1965
Ceremony for a Murdered Black (p Arrabal), 1972
Certain Plume (v Michaux), 1930
Césarée (p Duras), 1979
Cette voix (f Pinget), 1975
Ceux de la soif (f Simenon), 1938
Chac Mool (f Fuentes), 1973
Chagrin d'amour et d'ailleurs (f Mallet-Joris), 1981
Chain of Chance (f Lem), 1978
Chaîne dans le parc (f Langevin), 1974
Chairs (p Ionesco), 1957
Chaises (p Ionesco), 1952
Chambre (p Simenon), 1955
Chambre bleue (f Simenon), 1964
Chambre rouge (f Mallet-Joris), 1955
Chambre-Antichambre (v Lucebert), 1978
Chambres de bois (f Hébert), 1958

Change of Heart (f Butor), 1959
Change of Light (f Cortázar), 1980
Chanson des étages (v Char), 1955
Chant d'amour (p Genet), 1950
Chantage op het leven (f Mulisch), 1953
Chants de la Balandrame (v Char), 1977
Chants d'en bras (v Jaccottet), 1974
Chants d'ombre (v Senghor), 1945
Chants pour Naëtt (v Senghor), 1949
Chants secrets (v Genet), 1947
Chapeaugaga (v Pieyre de Mandiargues), 1968
Chaque homme dans sa nuit (f Green), 1960
Charités d'Alcippe (v Yourcenar), 1956
Charleston (f Donoso), 1960
Charlie (p Mrozek), 1964
Charlotte (p Hacks), 1980
Chartina (v Ritsos), 1974
Charretier de "La Providence" (f Simenon), 1931
Chast rechi (v Brodsky), 1976
Chat (f Simenon), 1967
Cheimerine diavgeia (v Ritsos), 1957
Cheironomies (v Ritsos), 1972
Chemin sans issue (f Simenon), 1938
Cher Antoine (p Anouilh), 1969
Chéri de Tantine (f Simenon), 1925
Chers Zoizeaux (p Anouilh), 1976
Cheval blanc (f Simenon), 1938
Chevalier de la nuit (p Anouilh), 1953
Chèvre sur un nuage (p Arrabal), 1967
Chez Krull (f Simenon), 1939
Chez les Flamands (f Simenon), 1932
Chi è cchiù felice 'e me! (p De Filippo), 1932
Chi ruba un piede è fortunato in amore (p Fo) 1966
Chein de coeur (v Char), 1969
Chien jaune (f Simenon), 1931
Children Are Civilians Too (f Böll), 1970
Children of Chaos (f Goytisolo), 1958
Children of Gebelawi (f Mahfouz), 1981
Children of the Black Sabbath (f Hébert), 1977
Chinese Wall (p Frisch), 1961
Chinesische Mauer (p Frisch), 1946
Chit of a Girl (f Simenon), 1949
Choriko ton sfougarhadon (v Ritsos), 1983
Christianity at the Glacier (f Laxness), 1972
Christine (f Green), 1930
Chronicle of a Death Foretold (f García Márquez), 1982
Chronicle of Exile (v Ritsos), 1977
Chronicles of Bustos Domecq (f Borges), 1979

Chroniko (v Ritsos), 1957
Chrysothemis (v Ritsos), 1972
Chyba (p Havel), 1983
Ci ragione e canto (p Fo), 1972
Ciegos (f Cela), 1958
Ciel et la merde (p Arrabal), 1972
Cieli della sera (f Prisco), 1970
Cien años de soledad (f García Márquez), 1967
Ciencia de birlibirloque (p Ruibal), 1970
Cilindro (p De Filippo), 1966
Cimarron (p Enzensberger), 1970
Cimetière des voitures (p Arrabal), 1958
Cinco horas con Mario (f Delibes), 1966
Cinq poésies en hommage à Georges Braque (v Char), 1958
Cinque storie ferraresi (f Bassani), 1956
Cintas magneticas (p Sastre), 1973
Ciociara (f Moravia), 1957
Cipreses creen en Dios (f Gironella), 1953
Circle of Love (p Anouilh), 1964
Circo (f Goytisolo), 1957
Circulito de tiza (p Sastre), 1967
Circusjongen (f Reve), 1975
Cirque (p Mauriac), 1968
Cita en el cementerio (f Gironella), 1983
Citoyens (v Tranströmer), 1974
Città ha i miei trent'anni (v Pratolini), 1967
Città di pianura (f Bassani), 1940
Città invisibili (f Calvino), 1972
City of Yes and the City of No (v Evtushenko), 1966
Ciudad deshabitada (v Cardenal), 1946
Ciudad y los perros (f Vargas Llosa), 1963
Ciudadano Iscariote Reclús (f Cela), 1965
Clacson, trombette e pernacchi (p Fo)
Claire (p Char), 1967
Clamor (v Guillén), 1957
Clan des Ostendais (f Simenon), 1947
Claustrum (v Claus), 1980
Clavier un autre (p Tardieu), 1975
Clear Ponds (p Akhmadulina), 1965
Clefs de la mort (f Green), 1928
Clients d'Avrenos (f Simenon), 1935
Clin d'oeil de l'ange (f Mallet-Joris), 1983
Cloches sur le coeur (v Char), 1928
Clope au dossier (p Pinget), 1961
Close Watch on the Trains (f Hrabal), 1968
Closed Garden (f Green), 1928
Closely Observed Trains (p Hrabal), 1967
Closely Watched Trains (f Hrabal), 1968
Clověk zahrada šírá (v Kundera), 1953
Cloven Viscount (f Calvino), 1962
Clown (f Böll), 1965

Club Archimède (p Tardieu), 1975
Codfish (p Ruibal), 1972
Coeur tout neuf (f Mauriac), 1980
Coi capelli bianchi (p De Filippo), 1938
Coin in Nine Hands (f Yourcenar), 1982
Colère (p Ionesco), 1963
Collin (f Heym), 1979
Colmena (f Cela), 1951
Colombe (p Anouilh), 1951
Colonel's Photograph (f Ionesco), 1967
Colore del cristallo (f Prisco), 1977
Colpa è sempre del diavolo (p Fo), 1966
Colpo di pistola (p Moravia), 1941
Columbus (p Hacks), 1972
Comedia sonámbula (p Sastre), 1949
Comedy of Vanities (p Canetti), 1982
Command and I Will Obey You (f Moravia), 1969
Commander Comes to Dine (f Soldati), 1952
Comme ceci, comme cela (v Tardieu), 1979
Comme l'eau qui coule (f Yourcenar), 1982
Comme les chardons (p Salacrou), 1964
Comme Shirley (v Butor), 1966
Commissaris Fennedy (p Reve), 1962
Commune présence (v Char), 1964
Communion solennelle (p Arrabal), 1964
Compagnons dans le jardin (v Char), 1956
Compañías convenientes (f Cela), 1963
Complices (f Simenon), 1956
Concerning the Angels (v Alberti), 1967
Concert at Saint Ovide (p Buero Vallejo), 1970
Concert dans un oeuf (p Arrabal), 1965
Concierto de San Ovidio (p Buero Vallejo), 1962
Condemned Man's Bicycle (p Arrabal), 1967
Condenados a vivir (f Gironella), 1971
Conducting Bodies (f Simon), 1974
Confession (f Soldati), 1958
Confessional (f Simenon), 1967
Confessione (f Soldati), 1955
Confessionnal (f Simenon), 1966
Configurations (v Paz), 1971
Conformer (p Dürrenmatt), 1975
Conformist (f Moravia), 1951
Conformista (f Moravia), 1951
Congreso (f Borges), 1970
Congress (f Borges), 1974
Conjugal Love (f Moravia), 1951
Conjuration (p Char), 1967
Conserve (f Hermans), 1947
Consiglio d'Egitto (f Sciascia), 1963

Dama duende (p Alberti), 1944
Dame de Pique (p Green), 1965
Danger Ahead (f Simenon), 1955
Danger at Sea (f Simenon), 1954
Dangerous Game (f Dürrenmatt), 1960
Daniele Cortis (p Soldati), 1947
Dans la pluie giboyeuse (v Char), 1968
Dabs le labyrinthe (f Robbe-Grillet), 1959
Dans le leurre du seuil (v Bonnefoy), 1975
Dans les années sordides (v Pieyre de Man-
diargues), 1943
Dans van de reiger (p Claus), 1962
Danseuse de Gai-Moulin (f Simenon), 1931
Dantons dood (p Claus), 1958
Dark Journey (f Green), 1929
Dark Room of Damocles (f Hermans), 1962
Dark Stranger (f Gracq), 1951
Darunga (f Lundkvist), 1964
Dauphins (p Moravia), 1960
Davar Aher (v Carmi), 1970
David Sterne (f Blais), 1967
Davor (p Grass), 1969
Dawn: Red and Black (p Arrabal), 1971
Day He Himself Shall Wipe My Tears
Away (f Oe), 1977
Day Is Dark (f Blais), 1967
Days in the Trees (p Duras), 1966
De la main à la main (v Char), 1930
De moment en moment (v Char), 1957
De Pretore Vincenzo (p De Filippo), 1957
De un momento a otro (p Alberti), 1937
Dead Letter (p Pinget), 1961
Dead Yesterdays (f Ginzburg), 1956
Deadly Game (p Dürrenmatt), 1963
Deaf to the City (f Blais), 1981
Dear Antoine (p Anouilh), 1971
Dear Michael (f Ginzburg), 1975
Death of a Harbor Master (f Simenon),
1941
Death of Artemio Cruz (f Fuentes), 1964
Death of Mr. Baltisberger (f Hrabal), 1975
Death of Monsieur Gallet (f Simenon), 1932
Death of the Inquisitor (f Sciascia), 1967
Death Thrust (p Sastre), 1967
Deathwatch (p Genet), 1954
Decorated Man (f Mulisch), 1984
Déficient mental (p Hébert), 1960
Dégourdis de la onzième (p Anouilh), 1936
Degrees (f Butor), 1961
Degrés (f Butor), 1960
Dehors la nuit est gouvernée (v Char), 1938
Dejemos Hablar al viento (f Onetti), 1980
Dekaochto lianotragouda tes pikres patri-
das (v Ritsos), 1973

Delfini (p Moravia), 1960
Délire à deux (p Ionesco), 1962
Déluge (f Le Clézio), 1966
Déménagement (f Simenon), 1967
Demirciler Çarsisi Cinayeti (f Kemal), 1974
Demoiselles de Concarneau (f Simenon),
1936
Demoiselles de la nuit (p Anouilh), 1948
Démon de l'irréalité (v Tardieu), 1946
Den'gi dlya Marii (f Rasputin), 1968
Denier du rêve (f Yourcenar), 1934
Deniz Küstü (f Kemal), 1978
Denní služba (v Holub), 1958
Dentelles de Montmirail (v Char), 1960
Dentro tis fylakis kai he gynaikes (v Rit-
sos), 1963
Deobe (f Ćosić), 1961
Dépendance de l'adieu (v Char), 1936
Deputy (p Hochhuth), 1964
Dertien manieren om een fragment van
Alechinsky te zien (v Claus), 1980
Des Arbres et des hommes (p Tardieu), 1969
Des Cobras à Paris (f Pieyre de Mandi-
argues), 1982
Des Deux Maîtresses (f Simenon), 1929
Des journées entières dans les arbres
(f Duras), 1954
Désert (f Le Clézio), 1980
Destin des Malou (f Simenon), 1948
Destinations (f Simenon), 1955
Destroy, She Said (f Duras), 1970
Destruccíon o el amor (v Aleixandre), 1935
Deszcz (f Mrozek), 1962
Detonación (p Buero Vallejo), 1977
Detour (p Walser), 1963
Détruire, dit-elle (f Duras), 1969
Deu de braise (f Pieyre de Mandiargues),
1959
Deuil des nevons (v Char), 1954
Deuil des roses (f Pieyre de Mandiargues),
1983
Deutsche Geschichte (v Handke), 1969
Deux Bourreaux (p Arrabal), 1958
Deux Destins (p Blais), 1974
Deux sous de violettes (p Anouilh), 1951
Developments (p Rifbjerg), 1974
Diablo vuelve a casa (f Matute), 1980
Diadromos kai skala (v Ritsos), 1973
Diafaneia (v Ritsos), 1980
Dialogo (p Ginzburg), 1973
Diálogos del cococimiento (v Aleixandre),
1974
Dialogue dans le Marécage (p Yourcenar),
1971

Dream Weaver (p Buero Vallejo), 1967
Dreambook for Our Time (f Konwicki), 1969
Dreamer (f Green), 1934
Dreamtigers (v Borges), 1963
Drei Berliner Geschichten (f Kunert), 1979
Drengene (f Rifbjerg), 1977
Drie lagen diep (v Lucebert), 1969
Dritte Buch über Achim (f Johnson), 1961
Drôle de mic-mac (p Hébert), 1954
Drömmar i ovädrens tid (f Lundkvist), 1963
Drømmen on København (f Rifbjerg), 1967
Drugi pokój (p Herbert), 1970
Drugie danie (p Mrozek), 1973
Drveni sanduk Tomasa Vulfa (p Kiš), 1983
Dry Heart (f Ginzburg), 1949
Du fährst zu oft nach Heidelberg (f Böll), 1979
Du mouvement et de l'immobilité de Douve (v Bonnefoy), 1953
Duas Águas (v Melo Neto), 1956
Dubovy list violonshelny (v Voznesensky), 1975
Duck Hunt (f Claus), 1965
Ducking Out (p De Filippo), 1982
Due città (f Soldati), 1964
Due cortigiane (f Moravia), 1945
Due milioni per un sorriso (p Soldati), 1939
Duel (p Ionesco), 1979
Duelo en el paraíso (f Goytisolo), 1955
Dúfnaveislan (p Laxness), 1966
Dunkle Sol (v Heinesen), 1936
Dunya Allah (f Mahfouz), 1963
Durer's Angel (f Blais), 1976
Dust over the City (f Langevin), 1954
Dve pary lyzh (v Evtushenko), 1982
Dvě usi dvě svatby (p Kundera), 1968
Dvukhmuzhnyaya (f Sholokhov), 1925
Dwa listy (f Mrozek), 1970
Dzienniki gwiazdowe (f Lem), 1957
Dziura w niebie (f Konwicki), 1959

E l'amor che mi rovina (p Soldati), 1951
È stato così (f Ginzburg), 1947
Each in His Darkness (f Green), 1961
Eagle or Sun? (v Paz), 1970
Earini Symfonia (v Ritsos), 1938
Earth Erect (v Popa), 1973
Eaux et forêts (p Duras), 1965
Ecluse no. 1 (f Simenon), 1933
Eden Cinéma (p Duras), 1977
Eden et après (p Robbe-Grillet), 1970
Effraie (v Jaccottet), 1953
Effroi la joie (v Char), 1971

Efterkrig (v Rifbjerg), 1957
Egysoros vers (v Weöres), 1979
Ehe des Herrn Mississippi (p Dürrenmatt), 1952
Ehen in Philippsburg (f Walser), 1957
Ehrenhändel (p Kunert)
Eiche und Angora (p Walser), 1962
8 nombres de Picasso (v Alberti), 1970
Eighteen Short Songs of the Bitter Motherland (v Ritsos), 1974
Einhorn (f Walser), 1966
Ejercicios de terror (p Sastre), 1973
Ekitai (v Yoshioka), 1941
El Erets Aheret (v Carmi), 1977
Élan d'Amérique (f Langevin), 1972
Eldtema (v Lundkvist), 1939
Eldur í Kaupinhafn (f Laxness), 1946
Électre (p Yourcenar), 1954
Elégie pour Alizés (v Senghor), 1969
Elegio de la sombra (v Borges), 1969
Elegy (v Tranströmer), 1973
Elegy to John Donne (v Brodsky), 1967
Elektra (p Kiš), 1969
Elektra, kvinna år 2070 (f Lo-Johansson), 1967
Eleonor (p Blais), 1962
Elephant (f Mrozek), 1962
Elisabeth, petite fille (v Char), 1958
Elle est là (p Sarraute), 1978
Elseneur (p Butor), 1979
Elysium (v Weöres), 1946
Emerald (f Soldati), 1977
Emergency Poems (v Parra), 1972
Emigranci (p Mrozek), 1975
Emigrés (p Mrozek), 1976
Emöke (f Skvorecky), 1977
Empire Céleste (f Mallet-Joris), 1958
Emploi du temps (f Butor), 1956
Empty Canvas (f Moravia), 1961
Emvatirio tou okeanou (v Ritsos), 1940
En case de malheur (f Simenon), 1956
En el estade (f Benet), 1977
En esta tierra (f Matute), 1955
En gång i Nineve (f Lundkvist), 1978
En la ardiente oscuridad (p Buero Vallejo), 1950
En la red (p Sastre), 1961
En trente-trois morceaux (v Char), 1956
En un vasto dominio (v Aleixandre), 1962
Enchanted Night (p Mrozek), 1964
Enciklopedija mrtvih (f Kiš), 1983
End of a Mission (f Böll), 1967
End of the Game (f Cortázar), 1967
Ende des Flanierens (v Handke), 1976

Flood (p Grass), 1967
Flood (f Le Clézio), 1968
Flores rojas para Miguel Servet (f Sastre), 1967
Flounder (f Grass), 1978
Flowers and Bullets (v Evtushenko), 1970
Flüchtling (p Hochwälder), 1945
Flugzeug über dem Haus (f Walser), 1955
Flux de l'aimant (v Char), 1965
Flykten och överlevandet (f Lundkvist), 1977
Fogak tornáca (v Weöres), 1947
Foire d'empoigne (p Anouilh), 1960
Folket och herrarna (f Lo-Johansson), 1973
Folle de Chaillot (p Carmi), 1979
Fond de la bouteille (f Simenon), 1949
Food for the Millions (p Tawfiq), 1981
Fools Are Passing Through (p Dürrenmatt), 1958
fools say (f Sarraute), 1977
Foot of the Wall (p Ionesco), 1971
For the Good of the Cause (f Solzhenitsyn), 1964
Force of Habit (p Bernhard), 1976
Författaren (f Lo-Johansson)
Formeries (v Tardieu), 1976
Formica argentina (f Calvino), 1965
Formy (v Rósewicz), 1958
Formynderfortaellinger (f Sørensen), 1964
Fortabte Spillemaend (f Heinesen), 1950
Fortress Besieged (f Ch'ien Chung-shu), 1979
Fortryllede Lys (f Heinesen), 1957
Fortuna con l'effe maiuscola (p De Filippo), 1942
45° à l'ombre (f Simenon), 1936
44 novelle per l'estate (f Soldati), 1979
Fótatak manna (f Laxness), 1933
Fotograpfías al minuto (f Cela), 1972
Fotohendro ke i tetarti omorfia (v Elytis), 1971
Fotospår i vattnet (v Lundkvist), 1949
Fou de Bergerac (f Simenon), 1932
Four Days in a Lifetime (f Simenon), 1953
Four Wise Men (f Tournier), 1982
Foursome (p Ionesco), 1963
Fourth Dimension (v Ritsos), 1976
Fourth Wall (p Fo), 1983
Fous de bassan (f Hébert), 1982
Fragole e panna (p Ginzburg), 1967
Françoise (f Erba), 1982
Frank V (p Dürrenmatt), 1959
Freedom to Kill (v Evtushenko), 1970
Frénétiques (p Salacrou), 1934

Frenzy for Two (p Ionesco), 1965
Frères Rico (f Simenon), 1952
Friday (p Claus), 1972
Friday (f Tournier), 1969
Frieden (p Hacks), 1962
Friends (p Abe), 1969
Friends, You Drank Some Darkness (v Tranströmer), 1975
Frist (p Dürrenmatt), 1977
From a Roman Balcony (p Moravia), 1960
From Desire to Desire (v Evtushenko), 1976
From the Diary of a Snail (f Grass), 1973
Frost (f Bernhard), 1963
Fruits d'or (f Sarraute), 1963
Fuga in Francia (p Soldati), 1948
Fugative (f Blais), 1978
Fugitive (f Simenon), 1955
Fuite de M. Monde (f Simenon), 1945
Fundación (p Buero Vallejo), 1974
Funeral de um Lavrador (v Melo Neto), 1967
Funeral Rites (f Genet), 1969
Funerale del padrone (p Fo), 1970
Funerales de la mamá grande (f García Márquez), 1962
Funny Old Man (p Rósewicz), 1970
Fuochi a mare (f Pratolini), 1961
Fuori (f Soldati), 1968
Fureur et mystère (v Char), 1948
Furie des Verschwindens (v Enzensberger), 1980
Fürsorgliche Belagerung (f Böll), 1979
Furstarna (f Lo-Johansson), 1974
Fustigada luz (v Alberti), 1980
Future Is in Eggs (p Ionesco), 1960
Futurological Congress (f Lem), 1974

Gabriela, Clove and Cinnamon (f Amado), 1962
Gabriela, cravo e canela (f Amado), 1958
Gadarene Club (f Walser), 1960
Galère (v Genet), 1947
Gallarda (p Alberti), 1959
Gallego y su cuadrilla (f Cela), 1951
Gallistl'sche Krankheit (f Walser), 1972
Gallo de oro (f Rulfo), 1980
Glasenapp Case (f Heym), 1962
Gamaliels Besaettelse (f Heinesen), 1960
Gantenbein (f Frisch), 1982
Garden, Ashes (f Kiš), 1976
Garden of Delights (p Arrabal), 1974
Garden of the Finzi-Continis (f Bassani), 1965
Garden Party (p Havel), 1969

Gårdfarihandlaren (f Lo-Johansson)
Gargoyles (f Bernhard), 1970
Garito de hospicianos (f Cela), 1963
Gaspard, Melchior et Balthazar (f Tournier), 1980
Gast aus England (f Kunert), 1973
Gato malhado e a andorinha sinha (f Amado), 1976
Gavilla de fábulas sin amor (f Cela), 1962
Gdzie wschodzi slonce i kedy zapada (v Milosz), 1974
Géants (f Le Clézio), 1973
Gebroken rietlijn (v Lucebert), 1959
Gefyra (v Ritsos), 1960
Gehen (f Bernhard), 1971
Geisterbahn (p Kroetz), 1972
Geitonies tou Kosmou (v Ritsos), 1957
Gemini (f Tournier), 1981
Gendarme's Report (f Simenon), 1951
Geniet (f Lo-Johansson), 1947
Gennariniello (p De Filippo), 1932
Gens d'en face (f Simenon), 1933
Georgiques (f Simon), 1981
German Love Story (f Hochhuth), 1980
Germania Tod in Berlin (p Müller), 1977
Gerontisses k'he thalassa (v Ritsos), 1959
Gerpla (f Laxness), 1952
Gerska aefintýrid (f Laxness), 1938
Geschichte eines alten Wittibers in Jahre 1637 (p Hacks), 1957
Gesponnen suiker (f Wolkers), 1963
Gespräch im Haus Stein über den abwesenden Herrn von Goethe (p Hacks), 1976
Geste pour un autre (p Tardieu), 1951
Gestoblene Ton (p Hacks), 1953
Gestures (v Ritsos), 1971
Geteilte Himmel (f Wolf), 1963
Gethsemani, Ky. (v Cardenal), 1960
Getuigen (p Claus), 1955
Geverfde ruiter (v Claus), 1961
Geyerstein's dynamik (f Hermans), 1982
Gezicht op Kerstmis (v Reves), 1965
Gezochte spiegel (f Mulisch), 1983
Ghost at Noon (f Moravia), 1955
Giants (f Le Clézio), 1975
Giardino dei Finzi-Contini (f Bassani), 1962
Gifsla (f Wolkers), 1983
Gigante cieco (f Cassola), 1976
Gignesthai (v Ritsos), 1977
Gigolo (p Mallet-Joris), 1962
Gilles et Jeanne (f Tournier), 1983
Gioco segreto (f Morante), 1941
Giornata balorda (p Moravia), 1960

Giornata d'uno scrutatore (f Calvino), 1963
Giorno della civetta (f Sciascia), 1961
Girigbukarna (f Lo-Johansson), 1969
Girl Beneath the Lion (f Pieyre de Mandiargues), 1958
Girl in His Past (f Simenon), 1952
Girl in Waiting (f Simenon), 1957
Girl on the Motorcycle (f Pieyre de Mandiargues), 1966
Girl with a Squint (f Simenon), 1978
Gisella (f Cassola), 1974
Giullarata (p Fo), 1975
Giusto della vita (v Luzi), 1960
Glass Cage (f Simenon), 1973
Gleisdreieck (v Grass), 1960
Gli esami non finiscono mai (p De Filippo), 1973
Gli uomini, che mascalzoni! (p Soldati), 1932
Glissements profressifs du plaisir (f Robbe-Grillet), 1974
Globales Interesse (p Kroetz), 1972
Glöd (v Lundkvist), 1928
Gloire en images (p Arrabal), 1976
Glos anonima (v Rósewicz), 1961
Glos Pana (f Lem), 1968
Goalie's Anxiety at the Penalty Kick (f Handke), 1972
God Denkbaar, Denkbaar de god (f Hermans), 1956
Gode Håb (f Heinesen), 1964
Godnatt, jord (f Lo-Johansson), 1933
God's World (f Mahfouz), 1973
Godzina smutku (f Konwicki), 1954
Golden Fruits (f Sarraute), 1964
Gold-Rimmed Spectacles (f Bassani), 1960
Goldsborough (f Heym), 1953
Golem XIV (f Lem), 1981
Gommes (f Robbe-Grillet), 1953
Gone Out (p Rósewicz), 1969
Good Conscience (f Fuentes), 1961
Goubbiah (p Genet), 1955
Goudland (p Claus), 1966
Gout de miel (p Mallet-Joris), 1960
Graal Flibuste (f Pinget), 1956
Grand Bob (f Simenon), 1954
Grand Guignol (p Arrabal), 1969
Grand Magic (p De Filippo), 1976
Grande magia (p De Filippo), 1949
Grande pantomima con bandiere e papuzzi piccoli e medi (p Fo), 1975
Grande Revue du XXe siècle (p Arrabal), 1972
Grandes Chaleurs (p Ionesco), 1953

Graf Öderland (p Frisch), 1951
Grafe tyflou (v Ritsos), 1979
Graganda (v Ritsos), 1973
Grass (f Simon), 1960
Great Fury of Philipp Hotz (p Frisch), 1963
Great Tranquility (v Amichai), 1983
Green House (f Vargas Llosa), 1968
Green Rose (v Rósewicz), 1982
Green Thermos (f Simenon), 1944
Grens (f Mulisch), 1975
Grenzenloser Nachmittag (p Walser), 1955
Grieche sucht Griechin (f Dürrenmatt), 1955
Grobnica za Borisa Davidoviča (f Kiš), 1976
Groene ridder en de paladijnen (f Claus), 1973
Grosse Wut des Philipp Hotz (p Frisch), 1958
Grotte (p Anouilh), 1961
Group Portrait with Lady (f Böll), 1973
Groupuscule of My Heart (p Arrabal), 1969
Grund zur Freude (v Walser), 1978
Grupa Laokoona (p Rósewicz), 1962
Gruppenbild mit Dame (f Böll), 1971
Gucio zaczarowany (v Milosz), 1965
Gudsgjafathula (f Laxness), 1972
Guêpe (v Ponge), 1946
Guerillas (p Hochhuth), 1970
Guernica (p Arrabal), 1961
Guerra del fin del mundo (f Vargas Llosa), 1981
Guerra di popolo in Cile (p Fo), 1973
Guerras de nuestras antepasados (f Delibes), 1975
Guerre (f Le Clézio), 1970
Guerre du mille ans (p Arrabal), 1975
Guichet (p Tardieu), 1955
Guillermo Tell tiene los ojos tristes (p Sastre), 1960
Guinguette à deux sous (f Simenon), 1932
Guinguette by the Seine (f Simenon), 1940
Guirnalda civil (v Guillén), 1970
Gulliver (f Simon), 1952
Gute Besserung (p Kroetz), 1972
Gutter in the Sky (f Genet), 1956
Gyermekjatekok (v Weöres), 1965
Gyümölcskosár (v Weöres), 1946

Ha estallado la paz (f Gironella), 1966
Ha llegado el invierno y tú no estas aquí (v Gironella), 1945
Ha sonado la muerte (p Sastre), 1946
Haar van de hond (p Claus), 1982
Habana para un infante difunto (f Cabrera

Infante), 1979
Hacedor (v Borges), 1960
Hadrat al-Muhtaram (f Mahfouz), 1975
Hakootoko (f Abe), 1973
Halbzeit (f Walser), 1960
Hallgatás tornya (v Weöres), 1956
Halvfärdiga himlen (v Tranströmer), 1962
Hamlet (p Buero Vallejo), 1961
Hamlet (p Carmi), 1981
Hamlet (p Müller), 1977
Hamletmaschine (p Müller), 1978
Hams al-junun (f Mahfouz), 1939
Happy Warriors (f Laxness), 1958
Hard-Boiled Egg (p Ionesco), 1976
Harlekýnovy milióny (f Hrabal), 1981
Harnäckig (p Kroetz), 1971
Harvest on the Don (f Sholokhov), 1960
Hate (f Sholokhov), 1942
Hatter's Ghost (f Simenon), 1956
Hatter's Phantom (f Simenon), 1976
Ha' unicorn Mistakel Banar'ah (v Carmi), 1967
Haus ohne Hüter (f Böll), 1954
Hausfriedensbruch (p Böll), 1969
Hausierer (f Handke), 1967
Haut mal (f Simenon), 1933
Haute surveillance (p Genet), 1949
Havana Inquiry (p Enzensberger), 1973
Havoc by Accident (f Simenon), 1943
Hayam Ha'aharon (v Carmi), 1958
Headbirths (f Grass), 1982
Heart of a Man (f Simenon), 1951
Hebamme (p Hochhuth), 1971
Hedera (v Pieyre de Mandiargues), 1945
Hedge (f Delibes), 1983
Heer Everzwijn (v Claus), 1970
Heilige Experiment (p Hochwälder), 1943
Heilige und der Räuber (p Böll), 1953
Heimarbeit (p Kroetz), 1971
Heimsljós (f Laxness), 1955
Heirs to the Wind (f Prisco), 1953
Helas (f Simenon), 1929
Held der westlichen Welt (p Hacks), 1956
Helene (v Ritsos), 1972
Hell Hath No Limits (f Donoso), 1972
Hell of a Mess (p Ionesco), 1975
Hellige aber (f Rifbjerg), 1981
Héloïse (f Hébert), 1980
Hemerologhia exorias (v Ritsos), 1975
Hemligheter på vägen (v Tranströmer), 1958
Her skal danses (f Heinesen), 1980
Herakles 5 (p Müller), 1966
Herbe (f Simon), 1958
Herbege (p Hochwälder), 1956

Hercules and the Augean Stables (p Dürrenmatt), 1966
Here Comes a Chopper (p Ionesco), 1971
Herinneringen van een engelbewaarden (f Hermans), 1971
Herkules und der Stall des Augias (p Dürrenmatt), 1960
Hermans is hier geweest (f Hermans), 1957
Hermes, pies i gwiazda (v Herbert), 1957
Hermine (p Anouilh), 1932
Hermit (f Ionesco), 1974
Hero of Our Time (f Pratolini), 1951
Hero of Today (f Pratolini), 1951
Heron (f Bassani), 1970
Herr Puntila und sein Knecht Matti (p Carmi), 1962
Herrumbrosas lanzas (f Benet), 1983
Herzliche Grüsse aus Grado (p Kroetz), 1972
Hid ljósa man (f Laxness), 1944
Hideg van (v Weöres), 1934
Hier régnant désert (v Bonnefoy), 1958
Hija de Rappaccini (p Paz), 1956
Hijo único de Guillermo Tell (p Sastre), 1983
Hijos del aire (v Paz), 1981
Hijos muertos (f Matute), 1958
Hikaya bila bidaya wala nihaya (f Mahfouz), 1971
Hikayat Haratina (f Mahfouz), 1975
Hilferufe (p Handke), 1967
Himbeerpflücker (p Hochwälder), 1965
Himlens vilja (f Lundkvist), 1970
Himmelsfärd (f Lundkvist), 1935
Hiroshima mon amour (p Duras), 1959
His Young Wife (p Soldati), 1945
Histoire (f Simon), 1967
Histoire de rire (p Salacrou), 1939
Histoires de vertige (f Green), 1984
Histoires obscures (v Tardieu), 1961
Historia de una escalera (p Buero Vallejo), 1949
Historia del corazón (v Aleixandre), 1940
Historia universal de la infamia (v Borges), 1935
Historias de cronopios y de famas (f Cortázar), 1962
Historias de España (f Cela), 1958
Historias de la Artámila (f Matute), 1961
Historier mellan åsarna (f Lundkvist), 1969
History (f Morante), 1977
Hitchhiker (f Simenon), 1955
Hitnatslut Hamehaber (v Carmi), 1974
Hive (f Cela), 1953

Høbjergning ved Havet (v Heinesen), 1924
Hochwasser (p Grass), 1957
Hochzeit (p Canetti), 1932
Hoja roja (f Delibes), 1959
Hojarasca (f García Márquez), 1955
Hold és Sárkány (p Weöres), 1967
Hóll sumarlandsins (f Laxness), 1938
Holy Places (f Fuentes), 1972
Homage to the American Indians (v Cardenal), 1973
Homage to the Lame Wolf (v Popa), 1979
Hombre (f Gironella), 1946
Hombre deshabitado (p Alberti), 1930
Hombre y la mosca (p Ruibal), 1977
Home (p Duras), 1973
Home Front (p Walser), 1971
Home Is the Sailor (f Amado), 1964
Home Town (f Simenon), 1944
Homenaje (v Guillén), 1967
Homenaje a los indios americanos (v Cardenal), 1969
Homenaje al Bosco (p Cela), 1969
Homeworker (p Kroetz), 1974
Homme assis dans le couloir (p Duras), 1980
Homme Atlantique (p Duras), 1982
Homme au petit chien (f Simenon), 1964
Homme aux valises (p Ionesco), 1975
Homme comme les autres (p Salacrou), 1936
Homme de la Tour Eiffel (f Simenon), 1950
Homme de Londres (f Simenon), 1934
Homme est venu me voir (p Duras), 1968
Homme que regardait passer les trains (f Simenon), 1938
Homme qui marchait dans un rayon de soleil (p Char), 1967
Homme qui ment (p Robbe-Grillet), 1968
Homo Faber (f Frisch), 1957
Hond met de blauwe tong (f Wolkers), 1964
Hondsdagen (f Claus), 1952
Hopscotch (f Cortázar), 1966
Hora 0 (v Cardenal), 1960
Hora cero (v Cardenal), 1971
Horatians (p Müller), 1976
Horatier (p Müller), 1972
Horizonte (p Müller), 1969
Hořkej svět (f Skvorecky), 1969
Horloger d'Everton (f Simenon), 1954
Hornissen (f Handke), 1966
Horrible Tango (f Wolkers), 1967
Horror coeli (v Hermans), 1946
Horský hotel (p Havel), 1977
Hostage (p Carmi)

Jackass (p Ruibal), 1970
Jacques (p Ionesco), 1954
Jacques et son maître (p Kundera), 1981
J'adore ce qui me brûle (f Frisch), 1943
Jagdgesellschaft (p Bernhard), 1974
Jahrestage (f Johnson), 1970
Jahrmarktsfest zu Plundersweilern (p Hacks), 1975
Jak daleko stad, jak blisko (p Konwicki), 1971
Jak jsem obsluhoval anglického kralé (f Hrabal), 1980
Jalousie (f Robbe-Grillet), 1957
Jan de Lichte (v Claus), 1981
Jansenisme (v Claus), 1977
Januari (v Lucebert), 1964
Jardin de al lado (f Donoso), 1981
Jardín de senderos que se bifurcan (v Borges), 1942
Jardin des chimères (v Yourcenar), 1921
Jardin des délices (p Arrabal), 1969
Jaskinia filozofów (p Herbert), 1970
Jaune le soleil (p Duras), 1971
Jdi a otevři dveře (v Holub), 1962
Je est un autre (p Green), 1954
Jealousy (f Robbe-Grillet), 1959
Jeanne qu'on brûla verte (v Char), 1956
Jeannette (p Anouilh), 1960
Jefes (f Vargas Llosa), 1959
Jehr (p Hochwälder), 1933
Jen, Shou, Kuei (f Ch'ien Chung-shu), 1946
Jenzeits der Liebe (f Walser), 1976
Jessica! (p Claus), 1977
Jeu avec le feu (p Robbe-Grillet), 1975
Jeu du souterrain (f Mallet-Joris), 1973
Jeune Fille à marier (p Ionesco), 1953
Jeune Homme à marier (p Ionesco), 1966
Jeune Homme et le lion (p Anouilh), 1976
Jeunes barbares d'aujourd'hui (p Arrabal), 1975
Jeunesse illustrée (p Arrabal), 1967
Jeux de massacre (p Ionesco), 1970
J'irai comme un cheval fou (p Arrabal), 1973
Joan of the Angels? (p Konwicki), 1961
Joke (f Kundera), 1969
Joker (f Rifbjerg), 1979
Jolanda (p Soldati), 1952
Jomfruin goda og husid (f Laxness), 1959
Jordisk prosa (f Lundkvist), 1930
Jordproletärerna (f Lo-Johansson), 1941
Joualonais, sa joualonie (f Blais), 1973
Journey among the Dead (p Ionesco), 1983
Jour (f Le Clézio), 1964

Jour est noir (f Blais), 1962
Journalisten (f Lo-Johansson)
Jours pétrifiés (v Tardieu), 1948
Jovita (p Konwicki), 1967
Jowita (p Konwicki), 1967
Joyeux retour (p Tardieu), 1975
Juan sin tierra (f Goytisolo), 1975
Juan the Landless (f Goytisolo), 1977
Jubiabá (f Amado), 1935
Judge and His Hangman (f Dürrenmatt), 1954
Judge and the Hatter (f Simenon), 1956
Jueces en la noche (p Buero Vallejo), 1979
Juegos de manos (f Goytisolo), 1954
Jumbo-Track (p Kroetz), 1981
Jument perdue (f Simenon), 1948
Junival (f Wolkers), 1982
Juno and Avos (p Voznesensky), 1983
Juntacadáveres (f Onetti), 1964
Jürg Reinhart (f Frisch), 1934
Juristen (p Hochhuth), 1979
Justice (f Simenon), 1949

Kaiser von Hondu (p Kunert), 1959
Kalendarz i klepsydra (f Konwicki), 1976
Kalkwerk (f Bernhard), 1970
Kam teče krev (v Holub), 1963
Kamouraska (f Hébert), 1970
Kannibalen (f Heym), 1953
Kapnismeno tsoukali (v Ritsos), 1974
Karol (p Mrozek), 1963
Karriäristerna (f Lo-Johansson), 1969
Karsch (f Johnson), 1964
Kartoteka (p Rósewicz), 1961
Kaspar (p Handke), 1968
Kassandra (f Wolf), 1983
Kater svyazi (v Evtushenko), 1966
Katar (f Lem), 1976
Kato ap 'ton iskio tou vounou (v Ritsos), 1962
Katz und Maus (f Grass), 1961
Kazan University (v Evtushenko), 1973
Kazansky universitet (v Evtushenko), 1971
Kein Ort. Nirgends (f Wolf), 1979
Kemonotachi wa kokyo o mezasu (f Abe), 1957
Keruzfahre von heute (f Heym), 1950
Kétfeju fenevad (p Weöres), 1982
Keyhole (p Tardieu), 1962
Khammarat al-qitt al-aswad (f Mahfouz), 1968
Khan al-Khalili (f Mahfouz), 1945
Kifah Tiba (f Mahfouz), 1944
Kiga domei (f Abe), 1954

Kiks (f Rifbjerg), 1976
Killer (p Ionesco), 1960
Killing Game (p Ionesco), 1974
Kimsecik (f Kemal), 1980
Kind en kraai (v Mulisch), 1975
Kinder (p Hacks), 1984
Kindergarten (p Evtushenko), 1983
Kindergeschichte (f Handke), 1981
Kindermöderin (p Hacks), 1959
Kindheitsmuster (f Wolf), 1976
King David Report (f Heym), 1973
King Kong (p Hermans), 1972
King Oedipus (p Tawfiq), 1981
Kingdom of the Earth (f Heinesen), 1974
Kinobesuch (f Kunert), 1977
Klanger och spår (v Tranströmer), 1966
Kleine Aber (v Kunert), 1976
Kleine reeks (v Claus), 1947
Klopfzeichen (p Böll), 1960
Kluby poezie (f Hrabal), 1981
Klyvnadens tid (v Lo-Johansson), 1958
Kniha smichu a zapomnění (f Kundera), 1981
Knop (p Mulisch), 1961
Ko és az ember (v Weöres), 1935
Kodoku na seinen no kyuka (f Oe), 1960
Kodonostasio (v Ritsos), 1974
Koele minnaar (f Claus), 1956
Kojinteki na taiken (f Oe), 1964
Komedi i hägerskog (f Lundkvist), 1959
Komödie der Eitelkeit (p Canetti), 1950
Kompleks polski (f Konwicki), 1977
Konec nylonového věku (f Skvorecky), 1967
Konets prekrasnoy epokhi (v Brodsky), 1977
Konfrontation (v Rifbjerg), 1960
König Johann (p Dürrenmatt), 1968
König-David-Bericht (f Heym), 1972
Kontynenty (v Milosz), 1958
Konzert für vier Stimmen (p Böll), 1964
Kopfgeburten (f Grass), 1980
Kora (v Popa), 1953
Koreni (f Ćosić), 1954
Korrektur (f Bernhard), 1975
Korrektur (p Müller), 1958
Korsväg (v Lundkvist), 1942
Kort Amerikaans (f Wolkers), 1962
Korte ad det lange (f Rifbjerg), 1976
Kozo wa Shinda (f Abe), 1979
Kozui wa waga tamashii ni oyobi (f Oe), 1973
Kramen in Fächern (f Kunert), 1969
Krasnoe koleso (f Solzhenitsyn), 1983

Krasnogvardeitsy (f Sholokhov), 1925
Krasosmutnění (f Hrabal), 1977
Kray vozle samovo neba (f Rasputin), 1966
Kreuzbrave Liederbuch (v Kunert), 1961
Kristnihald undir Jökli (f Laxness), 1968
Król Popiel (v Milosz), 1962
Kroniske uskyld (f Rifbjerg), 1958
Kronika wypadków milosnych (f Konwicki), 1974
Ksiegz robotów (f Lem), 1961
Kuća nasred druma (v Popa), 1975
Kungsgatan (f Lo-Johansson), 1935
Kur mod onde Ånder (f Heinesen), 1967
Kurze Brief zum langen Abschied (f Handke), 1972
Kus (f Wolkers), 1977
Kuslar da Gitti (f Kemal), 1978
Kussen door een rag van woorden (v Hermans), 1944
Kusudama (v Yoshioka), 1983
Kvaedakver (v Laxness), 1930
Kvartett (v Tranströmer), 1967
Kynolog w Rozterce (p Mrozek), 1963
Kyra ton Ambelion (v Ritsos), 1975

La'bat al-Mawt (p Tawfiq), 1957
Labyrinth (p Arrabal), 1967
Labyrinthe (p Arrabal), 1961
Lacune (p Ionesco), 1965
Ladera este (v Paz), 1969
Ladron de niños (p Alberti), 1943
Lady Godiva (f Moravia), 1975
Lady of the Vineyards (v Ritsos), 1981
Lai de Barabbas (p Arrabal), 1969
Lalek (p Herbert), 1970
Lamentação (v Torga), 1942
Lanciatore del giavellotto (f Volponi), 1981
Landessprache (v Enzensberger), 1960
Landet Atlantis (v Rifbjerg), 1981
Landingspoging op Newfoundland (f Hermans), 1957
Langsame Heimkehr (f Handke), 1979
Långt borta, mycket nära (f Lundkvist), 1970
Lark (p Anouilh), 1955
Lassalle (f Heym), 1969
Last Year at Marienbad (f Robbe-Grillet), 1962
Lastbara berättelser (f Lo-Johansson), 1974
Laughable Loves (f Kundera), 1974
Laylat az-Zifat (f Tawfiq), 1966
Lazaretti (p Hochwälder), 1975
Lazorevaya step (f Sholokhov), 1926
Le connaissez-vous? (p Ionesco), 1953

Lost Moorings (f Simenon), 1946
Lost Musicians (f Heinesen), 1971
Loup (p Anouilh), 1953
Loup (f Blais), 1972
Love on the Riviera (p Moravia), 1958
Love Poems (v Amichai), 1981
Love Poems (v Evtushenko), 1977
Love Song (v Claus), 1963
Love-Girl and the Innocent (p Solzhenitsyn), 1969
Lovers in the Metro (p Tardieu), 1962
Lovers of Viorne (p Duras), 1971
Lubie (p Pinget), 1981
Lugar del crimen—Unheimlich (f Sastre), 1982
Lugar sin límites (f Donoso), 1966
Lügengeschichten (f Walser), 1960
Luk i lira (v Evtushenko), 1959
Lumpen, marginación, y jerigonca (f Sastre), 1980
Luna de enfrente (v Borges), 1925
Luna silvestre (v Paz), 1933
Lungo viaggio di Natale (p Pratolini), 1954
Lustgårdens demoni (f Lundkvist), 1973
Luz no tunel (f Amado), 1954
Lvíče (f Skvorecky), 1969
Lyckan (f Lo-Johansson), 1962
Lysistrate und die Nato (p Hochhuth), 1973
Lyssnerskan (f Jansson), 1971

M.S.V. (p Sastre), 1976
Ma'a az-Zaman (p Tawfiq), 1973
Maascheroen (p Claus), 1967
Macbeth (p Müller), 1972
Macbett (p Ionesco), 1972
Macchina mondiale (f Volponi), 1965
Macht der Gewohnheit (p Bernhard), 1974
Mad Shadows (f Blais), 1960
Madame de... (p Anouilh), 1959
Mademoiselle (p Genet), 1966
Madman of Bergerac (f Simenon), 1940
Madrasa al-Mughaddalin (f Tawfiq), 1953
Madrasa ash-Shaytan (f Tawfiq), 1955
Madre (f Ginzburg), 1957
Madre Coraje y sus hijos (p Buero Vallejo), 1966
Madrugada (p Buero Vallejo), 1953
Mafia Vendetta (f Sciascia), 1963
Mafiosi (p Sciascia), 1976
Magician (f Simenon), 1955
Magnet of Doom (f Simenon), 1948
Mahu (f Pinget), 1952
Maid to Marry (p Ionesco), 1960
Maids (p Genet), 1954

Maigret series (f Simenon)
Main (f Simenon), 1968
Mains négatives (p Duras), 1979
Maison de rendez-vous (f Robbe-Grillet), 1965
Maison des sept jeunes filles (f Simenon), 1941
Maison du canal (f Simenon), 1933
Maître (p Ionesco), 1953
Majitelé kliču (p Kundera), 1962
Majlis al-'Adl (p Tawfiq), 1972
Makbara (f Goytisolo), 1980
Makrino (v Ritsos), 1977
Mala apokalipsa (f Konwicki), 1979
Mala hora (f García Márquez), 1962
Malacca Cane (f Soldati), 1973
Maladie de la mort (p Duras), 1983
Male minore (v Erba), 1960
Maledictions d'une Furie (p Tardieu), 1969
Malempin (f Simenon), 1940
Malenkie lato (f Mrozek), 1956
Malfaiteur (f Green), 1955
Malik at-Tufayliyin (f Tawfiq), 1946
Malombra (p Soldati), 1942
Mama, kijk, zonder Handen (p Claus), 1959
Man, a Dictionary (p Kroetz), 1976
Man and the Fly (p Ruibal), 1970
Man from Everywhere (f Simenon), 1941
Man in the Holocene (f Frisch), 1980
Man on the Bench in the Barn (f Simenon), 1970
Man Who Lies (p Robbe-Grillet), 1968
Man Who Turned into a Stick (p Abe), 1975
Man Who Watched the Trains Go By (f Simenon), 1942
Man with Bags (p Ionesco), 1977
Man with the Little Dog (f Simenon), 1965
Man with the Luggage (p Ionesco), 1979
Måna är död (f Lo-Johansson), 1932
Mandarine (p Anouilh), 1933
Mandarins (f Beauvoir), 1954
Man'en gannen no futtoboru (f Oe), 1967
Manivelle (p Pinget), 1960
Mann, ein Wörterbuch (p Kroetz), 1977
Mann mit den Messern (f Böll), 1958
Männersache (p Kroetz), 1972
Mano dello straniero (p Soldati), 1953
Man's Blessing (f Sciascia), 1968
Mansarda (f Kiš), 1962
Mantatoforos (v Ritsos), 1975
Manuscrits de Pauline Archange (f Blais), 1968
Manuscripts of Pauline Archange (f Blais), 1970

Maquina de pedir (p Ruibal), 1970
Mar (p Torga), 1941
Mar morto (f Amado), 1936
Marbre (f Pieyre de Maniargues), 1953
Marche royale (p Arrabal), 1973
Marcolfa (p Fo), 1962
Marcovaldo (f Calvino), 1963
Mare colore del vino (f Sciascia), 1973
Marea (f Gironella), 1949
Maremágnum (v Guillén), 1957
Margarete in Aix (p Hacks), 1969
Marge (f Pieyre de Mandiargues), 1967
Margin (f Pieyre de Mandiargues), 1969
Marguerite (p Salacrou), 1941
María Carmen Portela (v Alberti), 1956
Maria Magdalena (p Kroetz), 1973
Maria Nefeli (v Elytis), 1978
María Sabina (v Cela), 1967
Mariage Blanc (p Rósewicz), 1983
Mariazuehren (v Grass), 1971
Marie du port (f Simenon), 1938
Marie qui louche (f Simenon), 1952
Marie-Jeanne (p Anouilh), 1940
Marilyn Monroe (v Cardenal), 1975
Marin de Gibraltar (f Duras), 1952
Marinero en tierra (v Alberti), 1925
Marion und die Marionotten (f Frisch), 1946
Marjuana della mamma è la più bella (p Fo), 1976
Marks of Identity (f Goytisolo), 1969
Marquise sortit a cinq heures (f Mauriac), 1961
Marquise Went Out at Five (f Mauriac), 1962
Marriage in Philippsburg (f Walser), 1961
Marriage Italian Style (p De Filippo), 1964
Marriage of Mr. Mississippi (p Dürrenmatt), 1959
Marronnier (f Pieyre de Mandiargues), 1968
Marteau sans maître (v Char), 1934
Martereau (f Sarraute), 1953
Marts 1970 (f Rifbjerg), 1970
Martyrdom of Piotr Ohey (p Mrozek), 1967
Martyrerna (f Lo-Johansson), 1968
Martyries (v Ritsos), 1963
Masa' le-Ninveh (p Amichai), 1962
Mascarets (f Pieyre de Mandiargues), 1971
Mascherata (f Moravia), 1941
Masir Sarsar (p Tawfiq), 1966
Maska (f Lem), 1976
Masscheroen (p Claus), 1967
Matador (v Alberti), 1979
Matière de rêves (f Butor), 1975

Matinaux (v Char), 1950
Matka Joanna od Aniolów (p Konwicki), 1961
Matrimonio all'italiana (p De Filippo), 1964
Matrimonio del dopoguerra (f Cassola), 1957
Matryona's House (f Solzhenitsyn), 1975
Matryonin dvor (f Solzhenitsyn), 1963
Matura (p Konwicki), 1965
Mauser (p Müller), 1975
Mausoleum (v Enzensberger), 1975
Mauvais Lieu (f Green), 1977
Mavros Hagios (v Ritsos), 1961
Max (p Grass), 1972
Mayapán (v Cardenal), 1968
Maze of Justice (f Tawfiq), 1947
Mazurca para dos muertos (f Cela), 1983
Me scusa, quello non è il padrone? (p Fo), 1972
Me-ahore kol zeh mistater osher gadol (v Amichai), 1974
Measure for Measure (p Carmi), 1979
Meczenstwo Piotra O'Heya (p Mrozek), 1963
Medea (p Anouilh), 1956
Medea (p Sastre), 1958
Médecin du nord (p Hébert), 1954
Médée (p Anouilh), 1953
Medico dei pazzi (p De Filippo), 1957
Meditación (f Benet), 1969
Medúza (v Weöres), 1943
Meeting at Telgte (f Grass), 1981
Meier Helmbrecht (p Hochwälder), 1947
Mein Name sei Gantenbein (f Frisch), 1964
Mehanički Lavovi (p Kiš), 1983
Memed, My Hawk (f Kemal), 1961
Mémoires d'Hadrien (f Yourcenar), 1951
Memoirs Found in a Bathtub (f Lem), 1973
Memoirs of a Space Traveller (f Lem), 1982
Memoirs of Hadrian (f Yourcenar), 1954
Memorandum (p Havel), 1968
Memorandum (f Volponi), 1967
Memorandum on My Martinique (v Césaire), 1947
Memoriale (f Volponi), 1962
Memories of the Golden Triangle (f Robbe-Grillet), 1984
Memushiri kouchi (f Oe), 1958
Men of Darkness (p Salacrou), 1948
Medigos (p Ruibal), 1969
Meninas (p Beuro Vallejo), 1960
Mensch Adam Deigl und die Obrigkeit (p Kroetz), 1974
Mensch erscheint im Holozän (f Frisch),

Mono piadoso (p Ruibal), 1969
Monochroda (v Ritsos), 1980
Monogramma (v Elytis), 1972
Monologue (f Beauvoir), 1968
Monology (v Kundera), 1957
M. Gallet décédé (f Simenon), 1931
Monsieur La Souris (f Simenon), 1938
Monsieur Levert (f Pinget), 1961
Monsieur Moi (p Tardieu), 1966
Monsieur Monde Vanishes (f Simenon), 1967
Monsieur monsieur (v Tardieu), 1951
Monsieur Songe (f Pinget), 1982
Monsieur Tête (p Ionesco), 1970
Monsieur Vincent (p Anouilh), 1947
Monstres (p Arrabal), 1971
Montanha (f Torga), 1941
Montauk (f Frisch), 1975
Mont-Cinère (f Green), 1926
Monte Mario (f Cassola), 1973
Montée de la nuit (v Char), 1961
Monumento (p De Filippo), 1970
Mooi uitzicht en andere kurioziteiten (v Lucebert), 1980
Moonlight Sonata (v Ritsos), 1975
Morala del branco (f Cassola), 1980
Morecambe (p Kroetz), 1975
Mordaza (p Sastre), 1954
Morituri (p Claus), 1968
Moritz Tassow (p Hacks), 1965
Mörkerseende (v Tranströmer), 1970
Mörkskogen (f Lundkvist), 1967
Mort conduit l'attelage (f Yourcenar), 1935
Mort de belle (p Anouilh) 1961
Mort de Belle (f Simenon), 1952
Mort d'Auguste (f Simenon), 1966
Mort d'Ivan Ilytch (p Green), 1965
Mortaja (f Delibes), 1969
Mortal Engines (f Lem), 1977
Mort accidentale di un anarchico (p Fo), 1970
Morte dell'inquisitore (f Sciascia), 1964
Morte e a morte de Quincas Berro Dágua (f Amado), 1962
Morte e resurrezione di un pupazzo (p Fo), 1971
Morte e Vida Severina (v Melo Neto), 1965
Morti non fanno paura (p De Filippo), 1952
Morto da vendere (p Fo), 1962
Morytáty a legendy (f Hrabal), 1968
Moskauer Novelle (f Wolf), 1961
Mot pour un autre (p Tardieu), 1950
Motet (p Claus), 1969
Mother and Son (f Freyre), 1967

Motorcyclette (f Pieyre de Mandiargues), 1963
Motor Show (p Ionesco), 1963
Motorcycle (p Pieyre de Mandiargues), 1966
Motýl na antene (p Haval)
Mournful Demeanour of Lieutenant Boruvka (f Skvorecky), 1973
Mouse (f Simenon), 1966
Mouvements (v Michaux), 1952
Move (f Simenon), 1968
Moyovassia (v Ritsos), 1982
Mozaika (v Voznesensky), 1960
Much Ado about Nothing (p Carmi), 1982
Muerte de Artemio Cruz (f Fuentes), 1962
Muerte en el barrio (p Sastre), 1959
Muerte y la brújala (f Borges), 1951
Muerte y la niña (f Onetti), 1973
Muhammad (p Tawfiq), 1936
Mujer, levántate y anda (f Gironella), 1962
Müller von Sanssouci (p Hacks), 1958
Mum Vahalom (v Carmi), 1951
Mumei shishu (v Abe), 1948
Münchner Kindl (p Kroetz), 1973
Mündel will Vormund sein (p Handke), 1969
Mundo a solas (v Aleixandre), 1950
Murder in the Ironsmiths Market (f Kemal), 1979
Murderer (f Simenon), 1949
Murmures (p Blais), 1976
Musée noir (f Pieyre de Mandiargues), 1946
Musen (p Hacks), 1981
Museu de tudo (v Melo Neto), 1975
Music (p Duras), 1966
Musica (p Duras), 1965
Mutantes (p Ruibal), 1969
Mutmassungen über Jakob (f Johnson), 1959
My Foot My Tutor (p Handke), 1971
My Troubles Began (f Volponi), 1964
Mystère d'Alceste (p Yourcenar), 1963
Mystère de la parole (v Hébert), 1960
Mystery of the Polarlys (f Simenon), 1942
Mytologier (v Rifbjerg), 1970

Na czworakach (p Rósewicz), 1971
Na pelnym morzu (p Mrozek), 1963
'Na santarella (p De Filippo), 1972
Nachdenken über Christa T. (f Wolf), 1968
Nächtliches Gespräch mit einem Menschen (p Dürrenmatt), 1957
Nacimiento último (v Aleixandre), 1953
Nader tot u (f Reve), 1966

Nahr al-Junun (p Tawfiq), 1937
Naked Streets (f Pratolini), 1952
Naket liv (v Lundkvist), 1929
Naopal (v Holub), 1982
Napis (v Herbert), 1969
Napoli milionaria! (p De Filippo), 1945
Narrene (p Rifbjerg), 1971
Nashid al-Anshad (p Tawfiq), 1940
Nasledniki Stalina (v Evtushenko), 1963
Nastro di Moebius (v Erba), 1980
Natale in casa Cupiello (p De Filippo), 1931
Nathalie Granger (p Duras), 1972
Nattens broar (v Lundkvist), 1936
Natsu no Utage (v Yoshioka), 1979
Natuurgetrouw (f Claus), 1954
Nauka nenavisti (f Sholokhov), 1971
Navire Night (p Duras), 1978
Ne réveillez pas Madame (p Anouilh), 1970
Nef des sorcières (p Blais), 1976
Nègre (f Simenon), 1957
Nègres (p Genet), 1958
Negro qui hizo esperar a los ángeles (f García Márquez), 1972
Nehash Hanehoshet (v Carmi), 1961
Neige était sale (f Simenon), 1948
Neighbours (f Simenon), 1968
Nejlepší rocky pani Hermanové (p Havel), 1962
Nekro spiti (v Ritsos), 1962
Nel magma (v Luzi), 1963
Nepočin-polje (v Popa), 1956
Nesnesitelná lehkost bytí (f Kundera)
Nest (p Kroetz), 1975
Never Say Die (p Salacrou), 1966
New Lease on Life (f Simenon), 1963
New Men and Women (p Skvorecky), 1977
New Tenant (p Ionesco), 1956
New York d'Arrabal (v Arrabal), 1973
Newhaven-Dieppe (f Simenon), 1942
Nezhost' (v Evtushenko), 1962
Nezoufejte (v Skvorecky), 1980
Niagara (p Butor), 1969
Nic albo nic (f Konwicki), 1971
Nic w plaszczu Prospera (v Rósewicz), 1962
Nichijo seikatsu no boken (f Oe), 1971
Nicht Fisch nicht Fleisch (p Kroetz), 1981
Nicht nur zur Weihnachtszeit (f Böll), 1952
Nièce-Épouse (p Ionesco), 1953
Niece-Wife (p Ionesco), 1971
Niels Peter (f Heinesen), 1939
Niepokój (v Rósewicz), 1947
Niezwyciezony (f Lem), 1964
Night Vision (v Tranströmer), 1971
Night-Club (f Simenon), 1979

Nights in the Underground (f Blais), 1982
Nihil Sibi (v Torga), 1948
Nihilist (f Dürrenmatt), 1950
1934 (f Moravia), 1982
Niños tontos (f Matute), 1956
No Answer (f Pinget), 1961
No digo más que lo que no digo (v Alberti), 1970
No Laughing Matter (p Salacrou), 1957
No One Writes to the Colonel (f García Márquez), 1971
No pasarán! (v Paz), 1937
No Place on Earth (f Wolf), 1982
No Way (f Ginzburg), 1974
Noatun (f Heinesen), 1938
Nóc i magia (p Kiš), 1983
Noc ksiezycowa (f Lem), 1963
Noces de Poitiers (f Simenon), 1946
Noch einen Löffel Gift, Liebling? (p Hacks), 1972
Noch zehn Minuten bis Buffalo (p Grass), 1954
Noche de guerra en el Museo del Prado (p Alberti), 1956
Noches Lúgubres (f Sastre), 1964
Nocturnes (v Senghor), 1961
Noé (p Carmi)
Noia (f Moravia), 1960
Nokkrar sógur (f Laxness), 1923
Nombril (p Anouilh), 1981
Non approfondire (p Moravia), 1957
Non si paga, non si paga (p Fo), 1974
Non ti pago! (p De Filippo), 1940
Non tutti i ladri vengono per nuocere (p Fo), 1962
Non-Existent Knight (f Calvino), 1962
Nooit meer slapen (f Hermans), 1966
Nordanstulkan (p Laxness), 1972
Nostalgia for the Present (v Voznesensky), 1978
Nostri antenati (f Calvino), 1960
Not a Thing Out of Place (p Tawfiq), 1981
Not of This Time, Not of This Place (f Amichai), 1968
Notebook of a Return to My Native Land (v Césaire), 1979
Notes of a Clay Pigeon (v Holub), 1977
Notizen in Kreide (v Kunert), 1970
Notre-Dame des Fleurs (f Genet), 1944
Notte del '43 (f Bassani), 1960
Nous avons (v Char), 1959
Nouveau dans la ville (f Simenon), 1951
Nouveau Locataire (p Ionesco), 1955
Nouvelle Eurydice (f Yourcenar), 1931

One Autumn Evening (p Dürrenmatt), 1968
One Day in the Life of Ivan Denisovich (f Solzhenitsyn), 1963
One Hundred Years of Solitude (f García Márquez), 1970
1003 (p Hochwälder), 1964
One Way or Another (f Sciascia), 1977
One Way Out (f Simenon), 1943
'Oneiro kalokerinou messimeriou (v Ritsos), 1980
Oni srazhalis' za rodinu (f Sholokhov), 1971
Onkel, Onkel (p Grass), 1958
Only Ten Minutes to Buffalo (p Grass), 1967
Onore del vero (v Luzi), 1957
Onorevole (p Sciascia), 1965
Onze vrienden (f Reve), 1972
Oog om oog (v Claus), 1964
Oogsten in de dwaaltuin (v Lucebert), 1981
Oostakkerse gedichten (v Claus), 1955
Op weg naar het einde (f Reve), 1963
Opadly líscie z drzew (f Rósewicz), 1955
Operaelskeren (f Rifbjerg), 1966
Operaio conosce 300 parole il padrone 1000 per questo lui e il padrone (p Fo), 1970
Opowiadania traumatyczne (f Rósewicz), 1979
Opowieści o Pilocie Pirxie (f Lem), 1968
Opus gran (v Mulisch), 1982
Ora marítima (v Alberti), 1953
Oración por Marilyn Monroe (v Cardenal), 1965
Oráculo sobre Managua (v Cardenal), 1973
Orgasmo Adulto (p Fo), 1983
Oraison (p Arrabal), 1958
Orange Envelope (f Soldati), 1969
Orchestra (p Anouilh), 1967
Orchestre (p Anouilh), 1962
Ordalie (p Anouilh), 1966
Order (p Hochwälder), 1970
Ordets makt (f Lo-Johansson), 1973
Ordine! (p Fo), 1972
Ore nude (p Moravia), 1964
Orestes (p Claus), 1976
Orestes (v Ritsos), 1966
Orfeu rebelde (v Torga), 1958
Orians upplevelser (f Lundkvist), 1960
Orilleros (f Borges), 1955
Orison (p Arrabal), 1962
Ornifle (p Anouilh), 1955
Oro de los tigres (v Borges), 1972
Orphan Street (f Langevin), 1976
Ortadirek (f Kemal), 1960
Ortlich betäubt (f Grass), 1969

Ostanovka v pustyne (v Brodsky), 1970
Ostatni dzień lata (p Konwicki), 1958
Ostenders (f Simenon), 1952
Ostersjöar (v Tranströmer), 1974
Ostrava (v Ritsos), 1967
Ostře sledované vlaky (f Hrabal), 1965
Oswald et Zénaïde (p Tardieu), 1951
Otages (p Anouilh), 1939
Otan erchetai ho xenos (v Ritsos), 1958
Other One (f Green), 1973
Other Shore (v Alberti), 1981
Others (f Simenon), 1975
Otoño del patriarca (f García Márquez), 1975
Otoño, otra vez (v Alberti), 1960
Otra casa de Mazón (f Benet), 1973
Otra, el mismo (v Borges), 1969
Ottsovsky slukh (v Evtushenko), 1975
Oubli (f Mauriac), 1966
Oud en eenzaam (f Reve), 1978
Oude lucht (f Mulisch), 1977
Our Ancestors (f Calvino), 1980
Our Lady of the Flowers (f Genet), 1949
Ours en peluche (f Simenon), 1960
Out at Sea (p Mrozek), 1962
Outlaw (f Simenon), 1941
Outro amor do Dr. Paula (f Freyre), 1977
Outro livro de job (v Torga), 1936
Overgebleven gedichten (v Hermans), 1968
Oversight (p Ionesco), 1971
Owarishi michino shirubeni (f Abe), 1948
Owl's Insomnia (v Alberti), 1973
Oznob (v Akhmadulina), 1968

Pa 'amonim ve-rakavot (p Amichai), 1968
Paal en perk (v Claus), 1955
Pabellón de reposo (f Cela), 1943
Pábitelé (f Hrabal), 1964
Padre (p Ruibal), 1969
Paese di mare (p Ginzburg), 1973
Paese di Pulcinella (v De Filippo), 1951
Paichnidia t'ouranou kai tou nerou (v Ritsos), 1964
País do carnaval (f Amado), 1932
Paisajes después de la batalla (f Goytisolo), 1982
Paix dans les brisements (v Michaux), 1959
Pajára pinta (p Alberti), 1931
Palabras en la arena (p Buero Vallejo), 1949
Palace (f Simon), 1962
Palia Mazurka se sythmo vrohis (v Ritsos), 1943
Palomar (f Calvino), 1983
Pamietnik znaleziony w wannie (f Lem),

Porta sbagliata (p Ginzburg), 1973
Porte (f Simenon), 1962
Porte dell'Appennino (v Volponi), 1960
Porte dévergondée (f Pieyre de Mandiargues), 1965
Portraet (f Rifbjerg), 1963
Portrait de l'artiste en jeune singe (f Butor), 1967
Portrait d'un inconnu (f Sarraute), 1948
Portrait of a Man Unknown (f Sarraute), 1958
Portrait of a Planet (p Dürrenmatt), 1973
Portrait of Helena (f Cassola), 1975
Porträt eines Planeten (p Dürrenmatt), 1970
Poručika Boruvky series (f Skvorecky)
Posle Stalina (v Evtushenko), 1962
Poslední máj (v Kundera), 1955
Posledny srok (f Rasputin), 1976
Postepoweic (f Mrozek), 1960
Postřižiny (f Hrabal), 1976
Pour nous, Rimbaud (v Char), 1956
Pour preparer un oeuf dur (p Ionesco), 1966
Pourquoi la journée vole (v Char), 1960
Pourquoi pas moi? (p Salacrou), 1948
Poussière sur la ville (f Langevin), 1953
Power of Language (v Ponge), 1979
Powrót (f Lem), 1957
Powrot z gwiazd (f Lem), 1961
Powtórka (f Lem), 1979
Poyushchaya damba (v Evtushenko), 1972
Pozo (f Onetti), 1939
Präsident (p Bernhard), 1975
Prato più verde (v Erba), 1977
Prazagora (p Tawfiq), 1939
Pregão Turístico (v Melo Neto), 1955
Premier (f Simenon), 1961
Premières allivions (v Char), 1950
Premios (f Cortázar), 1960
Presencia (v Cortázar), 1938
Presencias (v Aleixandre), 1965
President (p Bernhard), 1982
Président (f Simenon), 1958
Presqu'île (f Gracq), 1970
Prete di Ratmaná (v Erba), 1959
Prexaspes (p Hacks), 1975
Příběh inženýra lidských duší (f Skvorecky), 1977
Příliš hlucná samota (f Hrabal), 1980
Prima sezóna (f Skvorecky), 1975
Primera memoria (f Matute), 1959
Primizie del deserto (v Luzi), 1952
Princess Sunshine (p Tawfiq), 1981
Princesse (p Arrabal), 1966
Príncipe destronado (f Delibes), 1973

Principessa Tarakanova (p Soldati), 1938
Printemps 1981 (f Blais), 1984
Prinzessin von Chimay (p Hochwälder), 1982
Prison (f Simenon), 1968
Prison Song (f Reve), 1968
Prisoners (p Solzhenitsyn), 1983
Private View (p Havel), 1984
Privatlivets fred (p Rifbjerg), 1974
Prize Stock (f Oe), 1977
Prjónastofan Sólin (p Laxness), 1962
Procès-Verbal (f Le Clézio), 1963
Proclama del conquistador (v Cardenal), 1947
Proêmes (v Ponge), 1948
Professeur Froeppel (p Tardieu), 1978
Profesores (v Parra), 1971
Proino astro (v Ritsos), 1955
Project for a Revolution in New York (f Robbe-Grillet), 1972
Projet pour une révolution à New York (f Robbe-Grillet), 1970
Proletärförtfattaren (f Lo-Johansson)
Prologo patético (p Sastre), 1964
Prometheus (p Müller), 1969
Prophecy (p Handke), 1972
Prophets (p Mrozek), 1970
Prosanatolismoi (v Elytis), 1939
Prospect of Ferrara (f Bassani), 1962
Protest (p Havel), 1978
Provence, point Omega (v Char), 1965
Provincia addormentata (f Prisco), 1949
Provinciale (p Moravia), 1952
Provinciale (p Soldati), 1953
Provino (p Moravia), 1955
Prozess um des Esels Schatten (p Dürrenmatt), 1959
Prussian Night (v Solzhenitsyn), 1977
Prusskiye nochi (v Solzhenitsyn), 1974
Przerwany egzamin (f Rósewicz), 1960
Przy budowie (f Konwicki), 1950
Psalam 44 (f Kiš), 1962
Psalms of Struggle and Liberation (v Cardenal), 1971
Psicologia da composição (v Melo Neto), 1947
Psyché (v Weöres), 1972
Ptákovina (p Kundera), 1969
Public Prosecutor (p Hochwälder), 1957
Public Prosecutor Is Sick of It All (p Frisch), 1973
Publikumsbeschimpfung (p Handke), 1966
Pum pum! chi è? La polizia! (p Fo), 1972
Punk et punk et Colégram (p Arrabal), 1978

Punto franco (f Prisco), 1965
Puppet Caravan (p Blais), 1967
Putyom vzaimnoy perepiski (f Voinovich), 1979
Pyle (v Ritsos), 1978
Pygmalion (p Tawfiq), 1942
Pyramides (v Ritsos), 1935

Qalb al-Layl (f Mahfouz), 1975
Qasr al-Shawq (f Mahfouz), 1957
Quaderna (v Melo Neto), 1960
Quand prime le spirituel (f Beauvoir), 1979
Quand tombent les toits (p Michaux), 1973
Quanderno gotico (v Luzi), 1947
Quarry (f Dürrenmatt), 1961
Quartet (p Müller), 1983
Quartett (p Müller), 1981
Quartier Nègre (f Simenon), 1935
Quartiere (f Pratolini), 1944
Quartieri alti (p Soldati), 1943
Quatre fascinants (v Char), 1951
Quatre Jours du pauvre homme (f Simenon), 1949
Quatres Cubes (p Arrabal), 1967
Quauhquauhtinchan in den vreemde (f Mulisch), 1962
...que van a dar en la mar (v Guillén), 1957
Queen Against Defoe (f Heym), 1974
Quei figuri di trent'anni fa (p De Filippo), 1932
Quel bandito sono io! (p Soldati), 1949
Quelqu'un (f Pinget), 1965
Querelle de Brest (f Genet), 1947
Querelle of Brest (f Genet), 1966
Queremos tanto a Glenda (f Cortázar), 1981
Quest for Christa T. (f Wolf), 1970
Questi fantasmi! (p De Filippo), 1946
Qui est là (p Tardieu), 1949
Qui je fus (v Michaux), 1927
Qui n'a pas son Minotaure? (p Yourcenar), 1963
Quinto piano, ti saluto! (p De Filippo)), 1936
Quire of Seven (f Laxness), 1974
Quodlibet (p Handke), 1970

R.R. (f Rifbjerg), 1972
Rabbit Race (p Walser), 1963
Rabo (p Ruibal), 1969
Racconti del Maresciallo (f Soldati), 1967
Racconti d'estate (p Moravia), 1958
Racconti romani (f Moravia), 1954
Radio nuit (f Mauriac), 1982
Radubis (f Mahfouz), 1943

Ragazza di Bube (f Cassola), 1960
Ragazza di Passaggio (p Duras), 1973
Ragazze di Sanfrediano (f Pratolini), 1953
Rage de l'expression (v Ponge), 1952
Ragnarok (f Sørensen), 1982
Rain (v Ponge), 1969
Raíz del hombre (v Paz), 1937
Rakovy korpus (f Solzhenitsyn), 1968
Ralentir travaux (v Char), 1930
Ramarro (v Volponi), 1948
Rampa (v Torga), 1930
Ranafelli (p Heinesen), 1929
Rani jadi (f Kiš), 1970
Raport z oblezonego miasta (v Herbert), 1983
Rapport du gendarme (f Simenon), 1944
Rapture of Lol V. Stein (f Duras), 1967
Raqisa al-Ma'bad (f Tawfiq), 1939
Raspberry Picker (p Hochwälder), 1967
Ratas (f Delibes), 1962
Ratujmy Kosmos (f Lem), 1966
Ravishing of Lol Stein (f Duras), 1967
Ravissement de Lol V. Stein (f Duras), 1964
Rayuela (f Cortázar), 1963
Razvedchiki grydushchevo (v Evtushenko), 1952
Reach to Eternity (f Ćosić), 1978
Real Silvestri (f Soldati), 1961
Rebanque (v Char), 1960
Rebounding Stone (v Melo Neto), 1967
Recitazione della controversia liparitana (p Sciascia), 1976
Reconstructie (p Claus, Mulisch), 1969
Recurrent Melody (f Pinget), 1975
Red Cats (v Evtushenko), 1961
Red Lights (f Simenon), 1955
Red Room (f Mallet-Joris), 1956
Régicide (f Robbe-Grillet), 1978
Regio (v Rósewicz), 1969
Región más transparente (f Fuentes), 1958
Registreren (v Claus), 1948
Rehearsal (p Anouilh), 1957
Reigen (p Hochwälder)
Reinos originarios (p Fuentes), 1971
Reise ins Glück (p Kroetz), 1975
Reivindicación del Conde don Julián (f Goytisolo), 1970
Reizender Abend (p Walser), 1972
Rejsende (f Rifbjerg), 1969
Rekonstrukcja poety (p Herbert), 1970
Relais d'Alsace (f Simenon) 1931
Relato de un náufrago (f García Márquez), 1970
Relazione (f Cassola), 1969

Relikwie (v Claus), 1967
Rempart de brindilles (v Char), 1952
Rempart des Béguines (f Mallet-Joris), 1951
Renard et la boussole (f Pinget), 1953
Rendez-vous de Senlis (p Anouilh), 1941
Rendre à César (p Yourcenar), 1971
Renga (v Paz), 1971
Repeat Performance (p Mrozek), 1972
Répétition (p Anouilh), 1950
Representative (p Hochhuth), 1963
Request Concert (p Kroetz), 1976
Request Programme (p Kroetz), 1974
Requie all'anima soia (p De Filippo), 1932
Requiem (v Jaccottet), 1947
Resaca (f Goytisolo), 1958
Rescapés du Télémaque (f Simenon), 1938
Reseau aerien (p Butor), 1962
Respublika truda (p Solzhenitsyn), 1981
Rest Home (f Cela), 1961
Restless Heart (p Anouilh), 1957
Retornos de lo vivo lejano (v Alberti), 1952
Retour amont (v Char), 1966
Retratos con nombre (v Aleixandre), 1965
Return from the Stars (f Lem), 1980
Return to My Native Land (v Césaire), 1968
Return to Region (f Benet), 1984
Rêve d'Irénée (f Butor), 1979
Révolution-Imagination (p Arrabal), 1969
Reyes (p Cortázar), 1949
Rez (v Popa), 1981
Rhinocéros (p Ionesco), 1959
Rhume onirique (p Ionesco), 1953
Rich Man (f Simenon), 1971
Richard III (p Anouilh), 1964
Riche Homme (f Simenon), 1970
Richter und sein Henker (f Dürrenmatt), 1952
Richtige Einstellung (f Heym), 1976
Ride Across Lake Constance (p Handke), 1972
Rideau rouge (p Anouilh), 1952
Rideaux blancs (p Duras), 1966
Rietsuiker (f Reve), 1974
Rihla al-Ghad (p Tawfiq), 1957
Rihla ar-Rabi' wa-l-Kharif (p Tawfiq), 1964
Rimskiye elegii (v Brodsky), 1982
Ring round the Moon (p Anouilh), 1950
Río (f Matute), 1963
Rio (v Melo Neto), 1954
Rip van Winkle (p Frisch), 1953
Ritt über den Bodensee (p Handke), 1971
Rivage des Syrtes (f Gracq), 1951
River of Madness (p Tawfiq), 1963
Rivers and Forests (f Duras), 1964

Ro tou erota (v Elytis), 1972
Road to the City (f Ginzburg), 1949
Robinsoe Crusoe (p Erba), 1977
Roi de Sodome (p Arrabal), 1979
Roi des Aulnes (f Tournier), 1970
Roi pêcheur (p Gracq), 1948
Roi se meurt (p Ionesco), 1962
Rojsty (f Konwicki), 1956
Roman Tales (f Moravia), 1956
Romana (f Moravia), 1947
Romanzo di Ferrara (f Bassani), 1974
Romeo and Jeannette (p Anouilh), 1958
Roméo et Jeannette (p Anouilh), 1946
Romiossini (v Ritsos), 1969
Romulus der Grosse (p Dürrenmatt), 1949
Ronde (p Anouilh), 1964
Ronde (f Le Clézio), 1982
Roos van vlees (f Wolkers), 1963
Roptro (v Ritsos), 1978
Rosales (p Luzi), 1983
Rose of Flesh (f Wolkers), 1967
Rosen der Einöde (p Bernhard), 1959
Rosencrantz and Guildenstern Are Dead (p Carmi)
Rosie träumt (p Hacks), 1975
Rostros del amor (f Onetti), 1968
Roulotte aux poupées (p Blais), 1962
Route des Flandres (f Simon), 1960
Równina (v Rósewicz), 1954
Rozmowa z ksieciem (v Rósewicz), 1960
Rua (f Torga), 1942
Rue aux trois poussins (f Simenon), 1963
Rue noire (p Salacrou), 1967
Ruined Map (f Abe), 1969
Ruisseau des solitudes (v Pieyre de Mandiagrues), 1968
Runaway Horse (f Walser), 1980
Rythme à trois temps (p Tardieu), 1959
Rzeznia (p Mrozek), 1975

Sabato, domenica e lunedi (p De Filippo), 1959
Sabine (f Pieyes de Mandiargues), 1963
Sacre de la nuit (p Tardieu), 1966
Sacre du printemps (f Simon), 1954
Sacred Families (f Donoso), 1977
Sacrifice (f Simenon), 1958
Sad Are the Eyes of William Tell (p Sastre), 1970
Saere historier (f Sørensen), 1953
Safety Net (f Böll), 1982
Safuran Tsumi (v Yoshioka), 1976
Saga of a Seagull (f Kemal), 1981
Sagittal Section (v Holub), 1980

Sagittario (f Ginzburg), 1957
Sailor from Gibraltar (f Duras), 1966
Sailor's Rendezvous (f Simenon), 1940
St. Lawrence Blues (f Blais), 1974
Saint-Denys-Garneau (p Hébert), 1960
Saint-Fiacre Affair (f Simenon), 1940
Saison au Congo (p Césaire), 1966
Saison dans la vie d'Emmanuel (f Blais),
    1965
Sakebigoe (f Oe), 1962
Salamandra (v Paz), 1962
Salka Valka (f Laxness), 1931
Sällskap för natten (f Lundkvist), 1965
Salmace (v Soldati), 1929
Salmos (v Cardenal), 1967
Salon de l'automobile (p Ionesco), 1953
Salt in the Wound (f Sciascia), 1969
Salto (p Konwicki), 1965
Salutations (p Ionesco), 1963
Salzburger Stücke (p Bernhard), 1975
Samira wa Hamdi (p Tawfiq), 1973
San Camilo, 1936 (f Cela), 1970
Sands of Torremolinos (f Goytisolo), 1962
Sang des autres (f Beauvoir), 1945
Sange mod Vaardybet (v Heinesen), 1927
Sangre de Dios (p Sastre), 1955
Sanningsbarriären (v Tranströmer), 1978
Sans merveille (p Duras), 1964
Santa Balbina 37, gas en cada piso (f Cela),
    1952
Santa Cruz (p Frisch), 1946
Santos inocentes (f Delibes), 1981
São Jorge dos Ilhéus (f Amado), 1944
Sari Sicak (f Kemal), 1952
Satan's Children (f Simenon), 1953
Saturday, Sunday, Monday (p De Filippo),
    1973
Saúl ante Samuel (f Benet), 1980
Sauspiel (p Walser), 1975
Sauvage (p Anouilh), 1938
Savannah Bay (p Duras), 1983
Save Your Faces (p Voznesensky), 1971
Scénario (p Anouilh), 1976
Scène à quatre (p Ionesco), 1959
Scener fra det daglige liv (v Rifbjerg), 1973
Schaamte (f Claus), 1972
Schatten und Licht (f Heym), 1960
Scherzo capriccioso (f Skvorecky), 1984
Schlacht (p Müller), 1975
Schlacht bei lobositz (p Hacks), 1956
Schluck Erde (p Böll), 1961
Schmähschrift (f Heym), 1970
Schöne Helena (p Hacks), 1964
School of the Sun (f Matute), 1963

Schuhu und die fliegende Prinzessin
    (f Hacks), 1966
Schwanenhaus (f Walser), 1980
Schwarze Flügel (p Walser), 1968
Schwarze Schwan (p Walser), 1964
Schwarzen Schafe (f Böll), 1951
Schwarzenberg (f Heym), 1984
Scialle andaluso (f Morante), 1963
Science of Hatred (f Sholokhov), 1943
Scorzetta di limone (p De Filippo), 1933
Screens (p Genet), 1962
Scripture of the Blind (v Ritsos), 1979
Se una notte d'inverno un viaggiatore
    (f Calvino), 1979
Sea of Troubles (f Duras), 1953
Sea Wall (f Duras), 1952
Seagull (f Kemal), 1981
Seara vermelha (f Amado), 1946
Season in the Congo (p Césaire), 1969
Season in the Life of Emmanuel (f Blais),
    1966
Second Thoughts (f Butor), 1958
Secret Rendezvous (v Abe), 1979
Secretaria (p Ruibal), 1969
Sedmiramenný svícen (f Skvorecky), 1964
Seeds of Tomorrow (f Sholokhov), 1935
Seelenarbeit (f Walser), 1979
Segretaria (p Ginzburg), 1967
Seibutsu (v Yoshioka), 1955
Seifuku (p Abe), 1955
Seine (v Ponge), 1950
Seinen no omei (f Oe), 1974
Seis problemas para don Isidro Parodi
    (v Borges), 1942
Seiseijú, mikil ósköp (f Laxness), 1977
Seiteki ningen (f Oe), 1963
Seizoen (v Lucebert), 1968
Seizure of Power (f Milosz), 1955
Selbstbezichtigung (p Handke), 1966
Self-Accusation (p Handke), 1969
Semillas para un himno (v Paz), 1954
Señal que se espera (p Buero Vallejo), 1952
Señas de identidad (f Goytisolo), 1966
Senecas Tod (p Hacks), 1978
Senhor Ventura (f Torga), 1943
Sennik wspolczesny (f Konwicki), 1963
Señorita de Tacna (p Vargas Llosa), 1981
Senorita from Tacna (p Vargas Llosa), 1983
Sens interdit (p Salacrou), 1953
Sense of Guilt (f Simenon), 1955
Sensualità (p Moravia), 1951
Sentiero dei nidi di ragno (f Calvino), 1947
Separate Notebook (v Milosz), 1984
Séparation (p Simon), 1963

Tatala (f Simenon), 1943

Te lucis ante (v Bassini), 1947

Teach Us to Outgrow Our Madness (f Oe), 1977

Teddy Bear (f Simenon), 1971

Tegenlicht (v Mulisch), 1975

Teiresias (v Ritsos), 1983

Tejedora de sueños (p Buero Vallejo), 1952

Teken van de hamster (v Claus), 1979

Teleftea pro Anthropou hekatontaetia (v Ritsos), 1975

Témoin invisible (v Tardieu), 1943

Témoins (f Simenon), 1955

Tempête (p Césaire), 1969

Tempi memorabili (f Cassola), 1966

Tempi nostri (p Moravia), 1952

Temps d'Anaïs (f Simenon), 1951

Temps des hommes (f Langevin), 1956

Temps du verbe (p Tardieu), 1956

Temps sauvage (p Hébert), 1967

Ten' zvuka (v Voznesensky), 1970

Tenda dos milagres (f Amado), 1969

Tender Hands (p Tawfiq), 1981

Teneke (f Kemal), 1955

Tent of Miracles (f Amado), 1971

Ten-Thirty on a Summer Night (f Duras), 1962

Teratodes aristourghima (v Ritsos), 1978

Terceira feira (v Melo Neto), 1961

Teremtés dícsérete (v Weöres), 1938

Tereza Batista, cansada de guerra (f Amado), 1972

Tereza Batista, Home from the Wars (f Amado), 1975

Terme epars (v Char), 1966

Terra amata (f Le Clézio), 1968

Terra firme (p Torga), 1941

Terra nostra (f Fuentes), 1975

Terras do sem fin (f Amado), 1942

Terre est ronde (p Salacrou), 1938

Territorios (f Cortázar), 1978

Terror inmóvil (p Buero Vallejo), 1954

Terug naar Oegstgeest (f Wolkers), 1965

Testament Donadieu (f Simenon), 1937

Testarium (p Mrozek), 1973

Tetarte diastase (v Ritsos), 1972

Tête blanche (f Blais), 1960

Tête d'un homme (f Simenon), 1931

Tevi'ah (v Carmi), 1967

Texter i snön (v Lundkvist), 1964

Thanatos ke anastasis tou Konstandinou Paleologhou (v Elytis), 1971

Tharthara fawq al-Nil (f Mahfouz), 1966

That Voice (f Pinget), 1982

Théâtre (p Anouilh), 1970

Théâtre bouffe (p Arrabal), 1978

Théâtre de guérilla (p Arrabal), 1969

Théâtre en marge (p Arrabal), 1970

Théâtre panique (p Arrabal), 1965

Theatrical Orchestrations (p Arrabal), 1960

Then Shall the Dust Return (f Green), 1941

Theomachia (v Weöres), 1941

Thérèse (p Mauriac), 1963

They Alone Knew (p Tardieu), 1968

They Are Dying Out (p Handke), 1975

They Burn the Thistles (f Kemal), 1973

Thieves' Carnival (p Anouilh), 1952

Things (v Ponge), 1971

Third Book about Achim (f Johnson), 1967

13 bandas y 48 estrellas (v Alberti), 1936

This Land, This Time (f Ćosić), 1983

This Sunday (f Donoso), 1967

Thordur gamli halti (f Laxness), 1935

Three Beds in Manhattan (f Simenon), 1964

Three Trapped Tigers (f Cabrera Infante), 1971

Three Travelers (f Blais), 1967

Thuis (p Claus), 1975

Thyestes (p Claus), 1966

Thyroreio (v Ritsos), 1976

Ti con zero (f Calvino), 1967

Ti ho sposato per allegria (p Ginzburg), 1966

Tía Julia y el escribidor (f Vargas Llosa), 1977

Ticket of Leave (f Simenon), 1954

Tidal Wave (f Simenon), 1954

Tiempo (f Matute), 1957

Tiempo de abrazar (f Onetti), 1974

Tiempo de morir (p Fuentes), 1966

Tien vrolijke verhalen (f Reve), 1961

Teirra de nadie (f Onetti), 1941

Tierra roja (p Sastre), 1960

Tierras de Valladolid (p Delibes), 1966

Tieta do Agreste (f Amado), 1977

Tieta the Goat Girl (f Amado), 1979

Tiger in the Kitchen (f Sørensen), 1957

Tikhos mesa ston kathrefti (v Ritsos), 1974

Tikhy Don (f Sholokhov), 1928

Till Eulenspiegel (f Wolf), 1972

Time (v Amichai), 1979

Time and the Hunter (f Calvino), 1970

Time for Loving (p Anouilh), 1971

Time of Death (f Ćosić), 1978

Time of Desecration (f Moravia), 1980

Time of Indifference (f Moravia), 1953

Time of the Hero (f Vargas Llosa), 1966

Time Remembered (p Anouilh), 1954

Timoteo el incomprendido (f Cela), 1952

Tin Drum (f Grass), 1962

Tired Lovers They Are Machines (v Lucebert), 1974

Titus Andronicus (p Dürrenmatt), 1970

To Any Lengths (f Simenon), 1958

Tobogán de hambrientos (f Cela), 1962

Tocar el cielo (v Cardenal), 1981

Tod eines Jägers (p Hochhuth), 1976

Todo modo (f Sciascia), 1974

Todos los fuegos el fuego (f Cortázar), 1966

Todos los gatos son pardos (p Fuentes), 1970

Toichokolletes (v Ritsos), 1978

Tom Sawyers grosses Abenteuer (p Heym), 1952

Tomb for Boris Davidovich (f Kiš), 1978

Tomb of the Kings (v Hébert), 1967

Tombeau des rois (v Hébert), 1953

Tombeau des secrets (v Char), 1930

Tommaso D'Amalfi (p De Filippo), 1966

Tomadachi, Enemoto Takeako (p Abe), 1967

Tomorrow and Yesterday (f Böll), 1957

Tonnere sans orage (p Tardieu), 1969

Tontos (f Cela), 1958

Too Many Ghosts (p De Filippo), 1958

Topologie d'une cité fantôme (f Robbe-Grillet), 1976

Topology of a Phantom City (f Robbe-Grillet), 1977

Toreo de salón (f Cela), 1963

Torre herida por el rayo (f Arrabal), 1983

Torre vigía (f Matute), 1971

Torrent (f Hébert), 1950

Tortue nommée Dostoïevsky (p Arrabal), 1969

Tote Mann und der Philosoph (p Enzensberger), 1978

Tour à terre (p Salacrou), 1925

Tour de Babel (p Arrabal), 1976

Tour prends garde (f Arrabal), 1983

Touriste de bananes (f Simenon), 1938

Tourmente (v Butor), 1968

Tous les hommes sont mortels (f Beauvoir), 1946

Toutes les femmes sont fatales (f Mauriac), 1951

Tower at the End of the World (f Heinesen), 1980

Tower of Babel (f Canetti), 1947

Tragaluz (p Buero Vallejo), 1967

Tragedia fantástica de la gitana Celestina (p Sastre), 1979

Tragédie du roi Christophe (p Césaire), 1963

Tragedy of King Christophe (p Césaire), 1970

Tragic Moon (f Simenon), 1942

Tragica notte (p Soldati), 1941

Tragoudi tes adelfis mou (v Ritsos), 1937

Train (f Simenon), 1961

Train de Venise (f Simenon), 1965

Train Was on Time (f Böll), 1956

Trakter (v Ritsos), 1934

Traktat poetycki (v Milosz), 1957

Traktor (p Müller), 1974

Traktorn (f Lo-Johansson), 1943

Trampa (f Matute), 1969

Tranen der acacia's (f Hermans), 1950

Trans-Europ-Express (p Robbe-Grillet), 1967

Transgressor (f Green), 1957

Transparents (v Char), 1967

Traps (f Dürrenmatt), 1960

Travaux d'approche (v Butor), 1972

Traveller, If You Come to Spa (f Böll), 1956

Traveller Without Luggage (p Anouilh), 1959

Traversée inutile (f Green), 1927

Tre cazune furtunate (p De Filippo), 1958

Tre corsari (p Soldati), 1952

Tre mesi dopo (p De Filippo), 1934

Treasures of the Night (v Genet), 1981

Trébol florido (p Alberti), 1959

Tree Climber (p Tawfiq), 1966

Treffen in Telgte (f Grass), 1979

Tres novelitas burguesas (f Donoso), 1973

Tres tristes tigres (f Cabrera Infante), 1965

Tres y un sueño (f Matute), 1961

Trety sneg (v Evtushenko), 1955

Treugol'naya grusha (v Voznesensky), 1962

Tria poiemata me simaia evkairias (v Elytis), 1982

Trial of Bebe Donge (f Simenon), 1952

Triangel in de jungle (v Lucebert), 1951

Tributo (v Torga), 1931

Tricheur (f Simon), 1945

Tricycle (p Arrabal), 1958

Triptych (p Frisch), 1981

Triptych (f Simon), 1976

Triptychon (p Frisch), 1978

Triptyque (f Simon), 1973

Triumph of Death (p Ionesco), 1971

Trochonomos (v Ritsos), 1978

Trois âges de la nuit (f Mallet-Joris), 1968

Trois Chambres à Manhattan (f Simenon), 1947

Trois coups sous les arbres (p Char), 1967
Trois personnes entrées dans des tableaux (p Tardieu), 1969
Trop belle pour elle (f Simenon), 1929
Tropismes (f Sarraute), 1939
Tropisms (f Sarraute), 1963
Troppo tardi (f Cassola), 1975
Troun (v Reve), 1973
Truth Barriers (v Tranströmer), 1980
Trzy zimy (v Milosz), 1936
Tu étais si gentil quand tu étais petit (p Anouilh), 1971
Tuerto es rey (p Fuentes), 1970
Tueur sans gages (p Ionesco), 1958
Tumba (f Benet), 1982
Tumba sin nombre (f Onetti), 1959
Turkish Delight (f Wolkers), 1974
Turks fruit (f Wolkers), 1969
Tussen hamer en aambeeld (f Mulisch), 1952
Tutta casa, letto, e chiesa (p Fo), 1978
Tutti i nostri ieri (f Ginzburg), 1952
Tutti uniti! Tutti insieme! (p Fo), 1971
Tutto per la donna (p Soldati), 1940
Tüzkút (v Weöres), 1964
Tvivla, korsfarare! (f Lundkvist), 1972
Twarz (v Rósewicz), 1964
Twarz trzecia (v Rósewicz), 1968
Twee vrouwen (f Mulisch), 1975
25 desperate digte (v Rifbjerg), 1974
Twist (f Rifbjerg), 1976
Two (f Moravia), 1972
Two Adolescents (f Moravia), 1950
Two Brothers (f Pratolini), 1962
Two Deaths of Quincas Wateryell (f Amado), 1965
Two Executioners (p Arrabal), 1960
Two of Us (f Moravia), 1972
Two Views (f Johnson), 1966
Two Women (f Moravia), 1958
Two Women (f Mulisch), 1980

Úa (p Laxness), 1970
Über allen Gipfeln ist Ruh (p Bernhard), 1981
Über die Dörfer (p Handke), 1981
Überlebensgross Herr Krott (p Walser), 1963
Üç Anadolu Efsanesi (f Kemal), 1967
Ucieczka na poludnie (f Mrozek), 1961
Události (v Holub), 1971
Udviklinger (p Rifbjerg), 1965
Ue (p Abe), 1975
Ufarlige (f Sørensen), 1955

Ugupu Bird (f Mrozek), 1968
Uilenspiegel (p Claus), 1965
Uit talloos veel miljoenen (f Hermans), 1981
Ultima frontiera (f Cassola), 1976
Ultimi anni di Clelia Trotti (f Bassani), 1955
Ultimo bottone (p De Filippo), 1932
Ultimo incontro (p Moravia), 1951
Ultimo viaje del buque fantasma (f García Márquez), 1976
Ultimo viene il corvo (f Calvino), 1949
Umsiedlerin (p Müller), 1961
Unadlige Gräfin (p Hacks), 1957
Unbearable Lightness of Being (f Kundera), 1984
Unberechenbare Gäste (f Böll), 1956
Uncertain Friend (f Heym), 1969
Und sagte kein einziges Wort (f Böll), 1953
Under the Skin of the Statue of Liberty (p Evtushenko), 1972
Under vejr med mig selv (v Rifbjerg), 1956
Underground Game (f Mallet-Joris), 1974
Underground Lovers (p Tardieu), 1968
Undir Helgahnúk (f Laxness), 1924
Undying Grass (f Kemal), 1977
Une et l'autre (v Char), 1957
Ungdomsnoveller (f Lo-Johansson), 1948
Ungebetene Gast (v Kunert), 1965
Ungenach (f Bernhard), 1968
Unguarded House (f Böll), 1957
Unicorn (f Walser), 1971
Universal History of Infamy (v Borges), 1971
Unknown Woman of Arras (p Salacrou), 1948
Unruhiger Schlaf (v Kunert), 1979
Unschuld der Natur (v Kunert), 1966
Unschuldige (p Hochwälder), 1949
Unter dem Eisen des Mondes (v Bernhard), 1958
Unter den Linden (f Wolf), 1974
Unter diesem Himmel (v Kunert), 1955
Untergang der Titanic (v Enzensberger), 1978
Untergeher (f Bernhard), 1983
Unternehmen der Wega (p Dürrenmatt), 1958
Unterwegs nach Utopia (v Kunert), 1977
Unvernünftigen sterben aus (p Handke), 1973
Uomo e galantuomo (p De Filippo), 1933
Uomo e il cane (f Cassola), 1977
Uomo nudo i l'uomo in frak (p Fo), 1962
Uomo solo (f Cassola), 1978

Uptight (p Grass), 1970
Ur en befolkad ensamhet (f Lundkvist), 1958
Uraniia (v Brodsky), 1984
Uranio 235 (p Sastre), 1946
Urfaust (p Dürrenmatt), 1970
Uroki muzyki (v Akhmadulina), 1969
Usage de la parole (f Sarraute), 1980
Use of Speech (f Sarraute), 1980
'Usfur min ash-Sharq (f Tawfiq), 1938
Uśmiechy (v Rósewicz), 1955
Uspravna zemlja (v Popa), 1972
Usurpers (f Milosz), 1955
Utrenny narod (v Evtushenko), 1978
Utvandring till paradiset (f Lundkvist), 1979

V Anglii (v Brodsky), 1977
V kruge pervom (f Solzhenitsyn), 1968
V polny rost (v Evtushenko), 1977
Vagabundos (f Matute), 1956
Val voor vliegengod (v Lucebert), 1959
Valčik na rozloučenou (f Kundera), 1979
Valentino (f Ginzburg), 1957
Valgvogel (f Wolkers), 1974
Valle del Po al tempo dei Galli e dei Romani (p Erba), 1983
Vällustingarna (f Lo-Johansson), 1970
Valse des toréadors (p Anouilh), 1952
Vampiros nultinacionales (f Cortázar), 1975
Van de afground en de luchtmens (v Lucebert), 1953
Van de koude grond (v Claus), 1978
Van horen zeggen (v Claus), 1970
Vandrarens träd (f Lundkvist), 1941
Vanishing Point (p Cabrera Infante), 1970
Vanité (f Butor), 1980
Var engang en krig (p Rifbjerg), 1966
Världens härlighet (v Lundkvist), 1975
Varouna (f Green), 1940
Vase (p Ionesco), 1974
Vatzlaw (p Mrozek), 1970
Vecchi compagni (f Cassola), 1953
Vefarinn mikli frá Kasmír (f Laxness), 1927
Vejen ad hvilken (f Rifbjerg), 1975
Vejrdage (f Sørensen), 1980
Velhos marinheiros (f Amado), 1961
Ve-lo 'al menat lizkor (v Amichai), 1971
Vendredi (f Tournier), 1967
Venice Train (f Simenon), 1974
Vent (f Simon), 1957
Vera Baxter (p Duras), 1980
Veraneo (f Donoso), 1955
Verdacht (f Dürrenmatt), 1953
Verdriet van België (f Claus), 1983

Verfassungsfeinde (p Kroetz), 1981
Verhör von Habana (p Enzensberger), 1970
Verità sul casa Motta (f Soldati), 1941
Vérité sur Bébé Donge (f Simenon), 1942
Verkommenes Ufer Medeamaterial Landschaft mit Argonauten (p Müller), 1983
Verkündigung des Wetters (v Kunert), 1966
Verlangen (f Claus), 1978
Verlangen nach Bomarzo (V Kunert), 1978
Verlorene Ehre der Katharina Blum (f Böll), 1974
Vernisáž (p Havel), 1976
Vero Silvestri (f Soldati), 1957
Vers la complétude (v Michaux), 1967
Verses on the Winter Campaign 1980 (v Brodsky), 1982
Versierde mens (f Mulisch), 1957
Versos de salón (v Parra), 1962
Versos sueltos de cada dia (v Alberti), 1982
Versprechen (f Dürrenmatt), 1958
Verte y no verte (v Alberti), 1935
Verteidigung der Wölfe (v Enzensberger), 1957
Verteller (f Mulisch), 1970
Verwondering (f Claus), 1963
Verzoeking (f Claus), 1980
Vestörung (f Bernhard), 1967
Veuf (f Simenon), 1960
Veuve Couderc (f Simenon), 1942
Viaducs de la Seine-et-Oise (p. Duras), 1960
Viaducts of Seine-et-Oise (p Duras), 1967
Viaje a U.S.A. (f Cela), 1965
Viaje de invierno (f Benet), 1972
Vice-Consul (f Duras), 1966
Victimes du devoir (p Ionesco), 1953
Victims of Duty (p Ionesco), 1958
Victor (p Anouilh), 1962
Victory Celebrations (p Solzhenitsyn), 1983
Vida breve (f Onetti), 1950
Vida de Luis Carlos Prestes (f Amado), 1942
Via comme neuve (f Simenon), 1951
Vie dans les plis (v Michaux), 1949
Via de' Magazzini (f Pratolini), 1942
Vie en rose (p Salacrou), 1931
Vie tranquille (f Duras), 1944
Vieille (f Simenon), 1959
Viejos amigos (f Cela), 1960
Viejos olivos (v Alberti), 1960
Viento entero (v Paz), 1965
Vier wintervertellingen (f Reve), 1963
Vierde man (f Reve), 1981
View of Dawn in the Tropics (f Cabrera Infante), 1978

Yesterday, Today, and Tomorrow (p Moravia), 1963
Yilani Öldürseler (f Kemal), 1976
You Were So Sweet (p Anouilh), 1974
Young Assassins (f Goytisolo), 1959
Young Cardinaud (f Simenon), 1956
Yume no tobo (f Abe), 1968
Yurei wa kokoniiru (p Abe), 1959
Yusufçuk Yüsuf (f Kemal), 1975

Z oblczonego miasta (f Konwicki), 1956
Zabawa (p Mrozek), 1963
Zadnudzki (p Konwicki), 1961
Zahradní slavnost (p Havel), 1963
Zazà (p Moravia), 1942
Zbabělci (f Skvorecky), 1958
Zcela nesoustavná zoologie (v Holub), 1963
Zdobycie wladzy (f Milosz), 1955
Ze wspomnień Ijona Tichego (f Lem), 1971
Ze života lepší společnosti (f Skvorecky), 1965
Zebrácká opera (p Havel), 1976
Zehn Tage, die die Welt Erschütterten (p Müller), 1957
Zement (p Müller), 1973
Zero Hour (v Cardenal), 1980
Zert (f Kundera), 1967
Zhivi i pomni (f Rasputin), 1975
Zielona róza (v Rósewicz), 1961
Zii di Sicilia (f Sciascia), 1958
Zimmerschlacht (p Walser), 1967
Zimowy zmlerzch (p Konwicki), 1957
Zingend hart (v Reve), 1973
Zivo meso (v Popa), 1975
Zivot de jinde (f Kundera), 1979
Zločin v dívči škole (p Skvorecky), 1966
Zločin v šantánu (p Skvorecky), 1968
Zona sagrada (f Fuentes), 1967
Zonder vorm van process (v Claus), 1950
Zoo Story (p Carmi)
Zug war pünktlich (f Böll), 1949
Zum Tee bei Dr. Borsig (p Böll), 1955
Zurich Transit (p Frisch), 1966
Ztížená možnost soustředění (p Havel), 1968
Zuqaq al-Midaqq (f Mahfouz), 1947
Zwarte keizer (f Claus), 1958
Zwarte licht (f Mulisch), 1956
Zwei Ansichten (f Johnson), 1965
Zwischenspiel in Baden-Baden (f Hochhuth), 1959

NOTES
ON
ADVISERS
AND
CONTRIBUTORS

ADAMS, M. Ian. Associate Professor, University of Wyoming, Laramie. Author of *Three Authors of Alienation: Bombal, Onetti, Carpentier*, 1975. **Essays:** Juan Carlos Onetti; Juan Rulfo.

ANDERSEN, Hans Christian. Lector in Danish, University of Newcastle upon Tyne. **Essay:** Klaus Rifbjerg.

ARNOLD, A. James. Professor of French, University of Virginia, Charlottesville. Author of *Paul Valéry and His Critics: A Bibliography*, 1970, *"Les Mots" de Sartre*, 1973, *Modernism and Negritude: The Poetry and Poetics of Aimé Césaire*, 1981, and the entry on Valéry in *A Critical Bibliography of French Literature*, vi, 2, 1980. Editor of *Caligula (1941)* by Camus, 1984. **Essays:** Aimé Césaire; Philippe Jaccottet.

BARFOOT, Gabrielle. Lecturer in Italian, Queen's University, Belfast. Author of "Dante in T.S. Eliot's Criticism" in *English Miscellany*, 1973, and "The Theme of Usury in Dante and Pound" in *Rivista di Letterature Moderne e Comparate*, 1977. **Essay:** Carlo Cassola.

BEATON, Roderick. Lecturer in Modern Greek Language and Literature, King's College, University of London. Author of *Folk Poetry of Modern Greece*, 1980, and articles on modern and medieval Greek literature, oral poetry, and traditional music. **Essays:** Odysseus Elytis; Yannis Ritsos.

BECKER, Lucille Frackman. Professor of French, Drew University, Madison, New Jersey. Author of *Henry de Montherlant*, 1970, *Louis Aragon*, 1971, and *Georges Simenon*, 1977. **Essays:** Françoise Mallet-Joris; Georges Simenon.

BERGIN, Thomas G. Sterling Professor of Romance Languages Emeritus, Yale University, New Haven, Connecticut. Author of many books, including *Giovanni Verga*, 1931, *Dante*, 1965 (as *An Approach to Dante*, 1965), *A Diversity of Dante*, 1969, *Petrarch*, 1970, and *Boccaccio*, 1981. Editor or translator of works by Dante, Petrarch, Vico, Shakespeare, William of Poitou, Quasimodo, and editor of collections of Italian and French literature.

BOND, David J. Professor of French and Head of the Department of French and Spanish, University of Saskatchewan, Saskatoon. Author of *The Fiction of André Pieyre de Mandiargues*, 1982, *The Temptation of Despair: A Study of the Quebec Novelist André Langevin*, 1982, and articles in *Canadian Literature, Esprit Créateur, Mosaic, Romanic Review*, and other journals. **Essay:** André Pieyre de Mandiargues.

BOSCHETTO, Sandra María. Assistant Professor of Romance Languages and Literatures, Michigan Technological University, Houghton. Author of articles on Claude Mauriac, Pirandello, Unamuno, Giorgio Saviane, Azorín, and Donoso, in *International Fiction Review, Selecta, Hispania*, and other journals. **Essay:** Claude Mauriac.

BRASS, Denis. Professor Extraordinary in the University of Coimbra, Portugal. Author of *Portugal*, 1960, *António Vieira: O Nosso Contemporâneo*, 1973, and *The Rounding of Cape Bojador*, 1974, and many critical articles on Miguel Torga and other writers. Translator of *Farrusco the Blackbird*, 1950, and other works by Torga. Formerly Senior Lecturer in Spanish and Portuguese, University of Bristol. **Essay:** Miguel Torga.

BROOME, Peter. Reader in French, Queen's University, Belfast. Co-Author of *The Appreciation of Modern French Poetry 1850-1950*, 1976, and author of *Henri Michaux*, 1977. Co-Editor of *An Anthology of Modern French Poetry 1850-1950*, 1976, and editor of *Au pays de la magie* by Michaux, 1977. **Essay:** Henri Michaux.

BROTHERSTON, Gordon. Professor of Literature, University of Essex, Wivenhoe. Author of *Manuel Machado: A Revaluation*, 1968, *Latin American Poetry: Origins and Presence*, 1975, *The Emergence of the Latin American Novel*, 1977, and *Image of the New World*, 1979. Editor or co-editor of *Selected Poems* by César Vallejo, 1976, *Ficciones* by Borges, 1976, and collections of Spanish American fiction and poetry.

BURNE, Glenn S. Professor of English, University of North Carolina, Charlotte. Author of *Rémy de Gourmont: His Ideas and Influence in England and America*, 1963, *Julian Green*, 1972, and *Richard F. Burton* (forthcoming). Translator of *Selected Writings of Rémy de Gourmont*, 1966. **Essay:** Julien Green.

CASE, Sue-Ellen. Assistant Professor of Drama, University of Washington, Seattle. Author of articles on Heiner Müller, theatre in the GDR, Karl Valentin, and Hrotsvit, in *Performing Arts Journal*, *Theater Heute*, *Yale Theater*, and *Theatre Journal*. **Essay:** Heiner Müller.

CAWS, Mary Ann. Distinguished Professor of French and Comparative Literature, City University of New York Graduate Center. Author of many books, including *Surrealism and the Literary Imagination*, 1966, *The Poetry of Dada and Surrealism*, 1970, *The Inner Theatre of Recent French Poetry*, 1972, *The Eye in the Text*, 1981, *A Metapoetics of the Passage*, 1981, *Yves Bonnefoy*, 1984, two books on André Breton, two books on René Char, and books on Robert Desnos and Pierre Reverdy. Editor or translator of works by Tristan Tzara, Char, Reverdy, Mallarmé, Breton, and Saint-John Perse, and editor of critical collections on French writing. **Essay:** Yves Bonnefoy.

COHN, Ruby. Professor of Comparative Drama, University of California, Davis. Author of *Samuel Beckett: The Comic Gamut*, 1962, *Currents in Contemporary Drama*, 1969, *Edward Albee*, 1969, *Dialogue in American Drama*, 1971, *Back to Beckett*, 1974, *Modern Shakespeare Offshoots*, 1976, *Just Play: Beckett's Theatre*, 1980, and *New American Dramatists 1960-1980*, 1982.

COWAN, Suzanne. Graphic Artist, World Affairs Council of Northern California. Author of "Theatre, Politics, and Social Change in Italy since the Second World War," in *Theatre Quarterly*, Autumn 1977, "Counter-culture, Revolt, and Repression in the Heart of Italy's 'Red Belt,'" in *Radical America*, November-December 1977, "Political Terrorism and the Dilemma of the Italian Left," in *Democracy and Power*, 1978, and "Dario Fo: Bibliography, Playography," in *Theatre Quarterly*, 1978. Translator of *Accidental Death of an Anarchist* by Fo, in *Yale Theater*, Winter 1979. **Essay:** Dario Fo.

COWARD, David. Senior Lecturer in French, University of Leeds, Yorkshire. Author of *Duras: Moderato Cantabile*, 1981, *Marivaux: La Vie de Marianne and Le Paysan parvenu*, 1982, and articles in *Sunday Times*, *Guardian*, *Times Literary Supplement*, and other periodicals. **Essay:** Marguerite Duras.

(CROFT), Sally McMullen. Ph.D. student, Cambridge University. **Essay:** Francis Ponge.

DAYDI-TOLSON, Santiago. Assistant Professor of Spanish, University of Virginia, Charlottesville. Author of *The Post-Civil War Spanish Social Poets*, 1983, and articles on Gabriel Mistral, José Angel Valente, and other writers. Editor of *Vicente Aleixandre: A Critical Appraisal*, 1981, and *Five Poets of Aztlán* (forthcoming). **Essays:** Vincente Aleixandre; Ernesto Cardenal.

DONAHUE, Thomas J. Associate Professor of Modern Languages, St. Joseph's University, Philadelphia. Author of *The Theatre of Arrabal: A Garden of Earthly Delights*, 1980, and an article on Arrabal in *Journal of Spanish Studies*, Fall 1975. **Essay:** Fernando Arrabal.

ERMOLAEV, Herman. Professor of Russian Literature, Princeton University, New Jersey. Author of *Soviet Literary Theories 1917-1934: The Genesis of Socialist Realism*, 1963, and *Mikhail Sholokhov and His Art*, 1982. Editor and translator of *Untimely Thoughts* by Gorky, 1968. **Essays:** Mikhail Sholokov; Alexander Solzhenitsyn.

FLETCHER, John. Professor of Comparative Literature, University of East Anglia, Norwich. Author of *The Novels of Samuel Beckett*, 1964, *Samuel Beckett's Art*, 1967, *New Directions in Literature*, 1968, *Claude Simon and Fiction Now*, 1975, *Novel and Reader*, 1980, and *Alain Robbe-Grillet*, 1983. **Essays:** Eugène Ionesco; Alain Robbe-Grillet; Claude Simon; Marguerite Yourcenar.

FOWLIE, Wallace. Professor Emeritus of French, Duke University Durham, North Carolina. Author of many books, including poetry, a novel, studies of Villon, Mallarmé, Rimbaud, Claudel, Proust, Gide, Cocteau, Stendhal, and Lautréamont, general books on French literature, and autobiographical works. Editor or translator of works by Maurice Scève, Balzac, Saint-John Perse, Cocteau, Claudel, Baudelaire, Molière, François Mauriac, Rimbaud, and of several anthologies. **Essays:** René Char; Jean Genet.

FREEMAN, Michael. Lecturer in French, University of Leicester. Author of articles on Pierre de Larivey, Guillaume Coquillart, and the *sottie*. Editor of *Oeuvres* by Coquillart, 1975, and *Les Esprits* by Larivey, 1979.

GARTON, Janet. Lecturer in Scandinavian Studies, University of East Anglia, Norwich; Assistant Editor, *Scandinavica*. Author of *Writers and Politics in Modern Scandinavia*, 1978, and several articles on modern Scandinavian literature.

GOETZ-STANKIEWICZ, Marketa. Professor of Comparative Literature and Head of the Department of Germanic Studies, University of British Columbia, Vancouver. Author of *The Silenced Theatre: Czech Playwrights Without a Stage*, 1979. Editor of *New Plays: Czechoslovakia*, 1984. **Essay:** Václav Havel.

GÖMÖRI, George. Lecturer in Slavonic Studies, Cambridge University. Author of *Polish and Hungarian Poetry 1945 to 1956*, 1966, and *Cyprian Norwid*, 1974. Editor, with others, of *Love of the Scorching Wind* by László Nagy, 1973, and *Forced March* by Miklós Radnóti, 1979. **Essays:** Zbigniew Herbert; Czeslaw Milosz; Tadeusz Rózewicz; Sándor Weöres.

GRAVES, Peter. Lecturer in Scandinavian Studies, University of Aberdeen. Author of *Jan Fridegård: Lars Hård*, 1977, and "The Collective Novel in Sweden," in *Scandinavica 12*, 1973. **Essay:** Artur Lundkvist.

GROSSMAN, Edith. Associate Professor of Spanish, Dominican College, Orangeburg, New York. Author of *The Antipoetry of Nicanor Parra*, 1975, "Myth and Madness in Carlos Fuentes' *A Change of Skin*," in *Latin American Literary Review*, Fall-Winter 1975, and other articles and reviews. Translator of *Missing* by Ariel Dorfman, 1981, "Sermons and Preaching of the Christ at Elqui" by Parra, in *New Directions 41*, 1980, and "Inquest in the Andes" by Mario Vargas Llosa, in *New York Times Magazine*, 31 July 1983. **Essays:** Carlos Fuentes; Nicanor Parra.

HABERLY, David T. Associate Professor of Portuguese, University of Virginia, Charlottesville. Author of *Three Sad Races: Racial Identity and National Consciousness in Brazilian Literature*, 1983, and numerous articles on Brazilian, Portuguese, Spanish American, and comparative literature. **Essays:** Gilberto Freyre; João Cabral de Melo Neto.

HÁJEK, Igor. Lecturer in Slavonic Languages and Literatures, University of Glasgow. Co-Editor and contributor, *Modern Slavic Literatures 2*, 1976, and *Dictionary of Czech*

Writers 1948-1979, 1982; author of numerous articles and reviews. **Essays:** Miroslav Holub; Bohumil Hrabal; Josef Skvorecký.

HALMAN, Talat S. Formerly, Turkey's Minister of Culture and Ambassador for Cultural Affairs; Professor of Turkish Studies, Princeton University, New Jersey. Author of *I Am Listening to Istanbul: Poetry of Orhan Veli Kanik*, 1971, *The Humanist Poetry of Yunus Emre*, 1972, *Modern Turkish Drama*, 1976, *Shadows of Love* (poetry), 1979, *Contemporary Turkish Literature*, 1982, *Mevlana Celaleddin Rumi and the Whirling Dervishes*, 1983, and many books in Turkish. Editor of *The Republic of Poetry: An Anthology of Modern Turkish Verse*, 1984, and works by Yunus Emre and Sait Faik. **Essay:** Yashar Kemal.

HAWKESWORTH, E.C. Lecturer in Serbo-Croat, University of London. Author of *Ivo Andrić: A Bridge Between East and West*, 1984. **Essay:** Dobrica Ćosić.

HENKELS, Robert M., Jr. Professor, Department of Foreign Languages, Auburn University, Alabama. Author of *Robert Pinget: The Novel as Quest*, 1979, and many articles on modern French literature in *The Review of Contemporary Fiction*, *The French American Review*, *Présence Francophone*, and other journals. **Essay:** Robert Pinget.

HODGSON, Richard G. Assistant Professor of French, University of British Columbia, Vancouver. Author of "Un roman à métamorphoses: Éléments baroques dans *Neige noire* d'Hubert Aquin," in *Présence Francophone*, Autumn 1981, and "Time and Space in André Langevin's *L'Élan d'Amérique*," in *Canadian Literature*, Spring 1981. **Essay:** André Langevin.

HUTCHINS, William M. Associate Professor, Philosophy-Religion Department, Appalachian State University, Boone, North Carolina. Translator of *Plays, Prefaces, and Postscripts*, 2 vols., 1981-83, and *Awakening Egypt* (forthcoming), both by Tawfiq al-Hakim, and *Al-Mazini's Egypt*, 1984. **Essays:** Naguib Mahfouz; Tawfiq al-Hakim.

HUTCHINSON, Peter. Fellow of Selwyn College, Cambridge. Author of *Literary Presentations of Divided Germany*, 1977, and *Games Author Play*, 1983. **Essay:** Stefan Heym.

JACKSON, Neil. Lector for English, University of Munich. Author, with Barbara Saunders, of "Christa Wolf's *Kindheitsmuster*: An East German Experiment in Political autobiography," in *German Life and Letters*, July 1980. **Essays:** Günter Kunert; Christa Wolf.

JANES, Regina. Associate Professor of English, Skidmore College, Saratoga Springs, New York. Author of *Gabriel García Marquez: Revolutions in Wonderland*, 1981, articles on Carlos Fuentes, Mary Wollstonecraft in *Journal of the History of Ideas*, 1978, and Edmund Burke in *Bulletin of Research in the Humanities*, 1979, and interviews with Guillermo Cabrera Infante and Carlos Fuentes in *Salmagundi*, 1978 and 1981. **Essays:** Gabriel García Márquez; Mario Vargas Llosa.

JONES, W. Glyn. Professor of Scandinavian Studies, University of Newcastle upon Tyne. Author of *Johannes Jörgensen*, 1969, *Denmark*, 1970, *William Heinesen*, 1974, *Danish: A Grammar* (with K. Gade), 1981, *Tove Jansson*, 1984, and two books in Danish. Translator of *Seneca: The Humanist at the Court of Nero* by Villy Sørensen, 1984. **Essays:** William Heinesen; Tove Jansson; Halldór Laxness; Villy Sørensen.

KIBLER, Louis. Associate Professor of Italian, Wayne State University, Detroit. Author of "Imagery as Expression: Moravia's *Gli indifferenti*," in *Italica 49*, 1972, "The Reality and Realism of Alberto Moravia," in *Italian Quarterly 17*, 1973, and "Moravia and Guttuso," in *Italica 56*, 1979. **Essay:** Alberto Moravia.

KIRSNER, Robert. Professor of Spanish, University of Miami, Coral Gables, Florida. Author of *The Novels and Travels of Camilo José Cela*, 1964, and several articles on Benito Pérez Galdós and Cela. **Essays:** Camilo José Cela; José María Gironella.

KLINE, George L. Milton C. Nahm Professor of Philosophy, Bryn Mawr College, Pennsylvania. Author of *Spinoza in Soviet Philosophy*, 1952, and *Religious and Anti-Religious Thought in Russia*, 1969. Editor or translator of *Russian Philosophy* (with others), 3 vols., 1965, *Seven Poems* by Boris Pasternak, 1969, and *Selected Poems*, 1973, and *A Part of Speech*, 1980, both by Joseph Brodsky. **Essay:** Joseph Brodsky.

KLOPP, Charles. Associate Professor of Romance Languages, Ohio State University, Columbus. Author of " 'Peregrino' and 'Errante' in the *Gerusalemme liberata*," in *Modern Language Notes*, 1979, the entry on Giosuè Carducci in *European Writers: The Romantic Century* (forthcoming), and articles on Italian literature. **Essay:** Giorgio Bassani.

LEVIN, Harry. Irving Babbitt Professor of Comparative Literature, Harvard University, Cambridge, Massachusetts. Author of many critical books, the most recent being *The Myth of the Golden Age in the Renaissance*, *Grounds for Comparison*, *Shakespeare and the Revolution of the Times*, and *Memories of the Moderns*. Editor of works by Jonson, Rochester, Joyce, Shakespeare, and Hawthorne, and of anthologies.

LICASTRO, Emanuele. Professor of Italian, State University of New York, Buffalo. Author of *Luigi Pirandello, dalle novelle alle commedie*, 1974, and *Ugo Betti: A Reading of His Plays*, 1984. **Essay:** Eduardo De Filippo.

LUCENTE, Gregory L. Associate Professor of Romance Languages, Johns Hopkins University, Baltimore. Author of *The Narrative of Realism and Myth: Verga, Lawrence, Faulkner, Pavese*, 1981, and of articles on D'Annunzio, Joyce, Silone, and *verismo*. **Essay:** Elsa Morante.

McMAHON, Keith. Member of the Faculty, Princeton University, New Jersey. **Essay:** Ch'ien Chung-shu.

MINER, Earl. Townsend Martin Professor of English and Comparative Literature, Princeton University, New Jersey. Author of *Dryden's Poetry*, 1967, *An Introduction to Japanese Court Poetry*, 1968, *The Metaphysical Mode from Donne to Cowley*, 1969, *The Cavalier Mode from Jonson to Cotton*, 1971, *Seventeenth-Century Imagery*, 1971, *The Restoration Mode from Milton to Dryden*, 1974, *Literary Uses of Typology*, 1977, and *Japanese Linked Poetry*, 1979. Editor of *A History of Japanese Literature* by Jin'ichi Konishi, from 1984. Translator, with Hiroko Odagiri, of *The Monkey's Straw Raincoat and Other Poetry of the Basho School*, 1981.

MINOGUE, Valerie. Professor of French and Head of the Romance Studies Department, University College, Swansea; Co-Editor of *Romance Studies*. Author of *Proust: Du côté de chez Swann*, 1973, *Nathalie Sarraute and the War of the Words*, 1981, and many articles on the *nouveau roman*. **Essay:** Nathalie Sarraute.

MITCHELL, Michael. Lecturer in German, University of Stirling. Author of an essay on Peter Hacks in *The Writer and Society in the GDR*, 1983. **Essay:** Peter Hacks.

PALLOTTA, Augustus. Associate Professor of Italian, Syracuse University, New York. Author of articles on modern and contemporary Italian writers in *Forum Italicum, Italica, Italian Quarterly*, and other journals; regular contributor to the annual *The Romantic Movement: A Selective and Critical Bibliography*. **Essays:** Luciano Erba; Michele Prisco; Paolo Volponi.

435

PÉREZ, Janet. Professor of Spanish, Texas Tech University, Lubbock; Editor for Spanish for the Twayne World Authors Series. Author of *The Major Themes of Existentialism in the Works of José Ortega y Gasset*, 1970, *Ana María Matute*, 1971, *Miguel Delibes*, 1971, *Gonzalo Torrente Ballester*, 1984, and many articles on contemporary Spanish literature. Editor of *Novelistas femeninas de la postguerra española*, 1983. **Essay:** Juan Benet.

PIKE, Christopher R. Lecturer in Russian Studies, University of Keele, Staffordshire; Editor of the journal *Essays in Poetics*. Author of "Formalist and Structuralist Approaches to Dostoevsky," in *New Essays on Dostoevsky* edited by Malcolm V. Jones and Garth M. Terry, 1983. Editor of *The Futurists, The Formalists and the Marxist Critique*, 1980.

PIRIE, Donald Peter Alexander. Writer and teacher. **Essay:** Slawomir Mrozek.

POLUKHINA, Valentina. Lecturer in Russian, University of Keele, Staffordshire. Author of an article and a forthcoming monograph on Joseph Brodsky's poetry, and of entries on Russian and Soviet writers for *The Fontana Biographical Companion to Modern Thought*, 1983. **Essays:** Evgeny Evtushenko; Andrei Voznesensky.

PORTER, Robert. Lecturer in Russian Studies, University of Bristol. Author of *Milan Kundera: A Voice from Central Europe*, 1981, and *Understanding Soviet Politics Through Literature*, 1984. **Essays:** Milan Kundera; Vladimir Voinovich.

PUVAČIĆ, Dušan. Lecturer in Yugoslav Studies, University of Lancaster. Contributor to Yugoslav literary journals. Editor of *Kritički radovi Branka Lazarevića*, 1975, and translator into Serbo-Croat of many works of English and American literature. **Essays:** Danilo Kiš; Vasko Popa.

RAGUSA, Olga. Da Ponte Professor and Chairman of the Department of Italian, Columbia University, New York; Editor of the journal *Italica*. Author of *Mallarmé in Italy: A Study in Literary Influence and Critical Response*, 1957, *Verga's Milanese Tales*, 1964, *Narrative and Drama: Essays in Modern Italian Literature from Verga to Pasolini*, 1976, *Luigi Pirandello: An Approach to His Theatre*, 1980, and an essay in *"Romantic" and Its Cognates: The European History of a Word* edited by H. Eichner, 1972.

RAWSON, Judy. Senior Lecturer and Chairman of the Department of Italian, University of Warwick, Coventry. Editor of *Fontamara* by Ignazio Silone, 1972. **Essays:** Italo Calvino; Natalia Ginzburg; Leonardo Sciascia.

REID, J.H. Senior Lecturer in German, University of Nottingham. Author of *Critical Strategies: German Fiction in the Twentieth Century* (with E. Boa), 1972, *Heinrich Böll: Withdrawal and Re-Emergence*, 1973, and articles in *Modern Language Review*, *German Life and Letters*, *Renaissance and Modern Studies*, *Forum for Modern Language Studies*, and other periodicals. **Essay:** Heinrich Böll.

ROBINSON, Michael. Lecturer in the Department of English and Drama, Loughborough University, Leicestershire. Author of *The Long Sonata of the Dead: A Study of Samuel Beckett*, 1969, *Sven Delblanc: Åminne*, 1981, and essays on Ibsen, Strindberg, and Beckett. **Essay:** Ivar Lo-Johansson.

RORRISON, Hugh. Lecturer in the Department of German, University of Leeds, Yorkshire. Author of essays in the collections *Modern Austrian Writing*, 1980, and *Brecht in Perspective*, 1982, and of "Kroetz Checklist" in *Theatrefacts 3*, 1976. Editor of *Erwin Piscator: The Political Theatre* (also translator), 1978, and *Mother Courage* by Brecht, 1983; adviser on German theatre for *Oxford Companion to the Theatre*, 1983. **Essays:** Peter Handke; Franz Xaver Kroetz.

ROSENGARTEN, Frank. Professor of Italian, Queens College, City University of New York. Author of *Vasco Pratolini: The Development of a Social Novelist*, 1965, *The Italian Anti-Fascist Press 1919-1945*, 1968, and *Silvio Trentin dall'interventismo alla Resistenza*, 1980. **Essay:** Vasco Pratolini.

ROTHFORK, John. Associate Professor of Humanities, New Mexico Institute of Mining and Technology, Socorro. Author of "Cybernetics and a Humanistic Fiction," in *Research Studies*, September 1977, and articles on Stanislaw Lem in *Southwest Review*, Summer 1981, *Über Stanislaw Lem*, 1981, and *Stanislaw Lem in the Eyes of World Literary Criticism*, 1984. **Essay:** Stanislaw Lem.

RYDEL, Christine A. Associate Professor of Russian, Chairman of the Department of Foreign Languages and Literatures, and Director of the Honors Program, Grand Valley State College, Allendale, Michigan; Associate Editor of *Russian Literature Triquarterly*. Author of *A Nabokov Who's Who*, 1984. Editor of *The Ardis Anthology of Russian Romanticism*, 1983. **Essays:** Bella Akhmadulina; Natalya Gorbanevskaya.

SAUNDERS, Barbara. Social worker. Author of *Contemporary German Autobiography: Literary Approaches to the Problem of Identity* (forthcoming), "Christa Wolf's *Kindheitsmuster*: An East German Experiment in Political Autobiography" (with Neil Jackson), in *German Life and Letters*, July 1980, and an article on Max Frisch in *Modern Language Studies 18*, 1982. **Essays:** Thomas Bernhard; Elias Canetti.

SCHERR, Barry P. Associate Professor of Russian, Dartmouth College, Hanover, New Hampshire. Author of "Notes on Literary Life in Petrograd, 1918-1922: A Tale of Three Houses," 1977, "Gor'kij's *Childhood*: The Autobiography as Fiction," 1979, and "Russian and English Versification: Similarities, Differences, Analysis," 1980; co-author of "Russian Verse Theory since 1974: A Commentary and Bibliography," 1980. **Essay:** Valentin Rasputin.

SCHULMAN, Grace. Poetry Editor of *The Nation*, New York; Professor at Baruch College, City University of New York. Author of two books of poetry—*Burn Down the Icons*, 1976, and *Hemispheres*, 1984—and poems, essays, and translations in *New Yorker, Hudson Review, Poetry, Antaeus*, and several anthologies. Editor of *Ezra Pound: A Collection of Criticism*, 1974. Co-Translator of *Songs of Cifar* by Pablo Antonio Cuadra, 1979, and translator of *At the Stone of Losses* by T. Carmi, 1983. **Essays:** Yehuda Amichai; T. Carmi.

SCHWARTZ, Kessel. Professor of Modern Languages and Literatures, University of Miami, Coral Gables. Author of *A New History of Spanish Literature* (with R. Chandler), 1961, *Introduction to Modern Spanish Literature*, 1968, *Vincente Aleixandre*, 1970, *The Meaning of Existence in Contemporary Hispanic Literature*, 1970, *Juan Goytisolo*, 1970, *A New History of Spanish American Fiction*, 1972, and *Studies on Twentieth-Century Spanish and Spanish American Literature*, 1983. **Essays:** Rafael Alberti; Miguel Delibes; Juan Goytisolo; Ana María Matute.

SCOBBIE, Irene. Reader in Scandinavian Studies, University of Aberdeen. Author of *Pär Lagerkvist: An Introduction*, 1963, *Sweden: Nation of the Modern World*, 1972, *Pär Lagerkvist's Gäst hos verkligheten*, 1974, and articles on Lagerkvist, Strindberg, P.O. Sundman, Stig Claesson, and other writers. Editor and contributor, *Essays on Swedish Literature from 1880 to the Present Day*, 1978. **Essay:** Tomas Tranströmer.

SINGH, G. Professor of Italian, Queen's University, Belfast. Author of *Leopardi and the Theory of Poetry*, 1964, *Leopardi e l'Inghilterra*, 1968, *Montale: A Critical Study of His Poetry, Prose and Criticism*, 1973, and *Ezra Pound*, 1979. Editor of *It Depends: A Poet's Notebook* by Montale, 1980, and *Collected Essays of Q.D. Leavis*, vol. 1, 1983. Translator of *New Poems* by Montale, 1976. **Essay:** Mario Luzi.

SMITH, C.N. Senior Lecturer, School of Modern Languages and European History, University of East Anglia, Norwich; Editor of *Seventeenth-Century French Studies*. Author of many articles and of reviews of the performing arts. Editor of works by Antoine de Montchrestien, Jacques de la Taille, and Pierre Matthieu. **Essays:** Julien Gracq; Armand Salacrou; Léopold Senghor.

SOUZA, Raymond D. Professor of Spanish, University of Kansas, Lawrence; Assistant Editor, *Latin American Theatre Review*. Author of *Major Cuban Novelists: Innovation and Tradition*, 1976, *Lino Novás Calvo*, 1981, and *The Poetic Fiction of José Lezama Lima*, 1983. **Essay:** Guillermo Cabrera Infante.

STAMM, James Russell. Associate Professor of Spanish and Portuguese, New York University. Author of *A Short History of Spanish Literature*, 1966 (revised edition, 1979), and numerous articles on the early Spanish novel and theatre. Editor, with Herbert E. Isar, of *Dos novelas cortas: Miguel de Unamuno*, 1967. **Essays:** Antonio Buero Vallejo; Alfonso Sastre.

STEWART, Mary E. Fellow and Lecturer in German, Robinson College, Cambridge. Author of numerous articles on the German novel since 1880 in *Modern Language Review*, *German Life and Letters, Journal of European Studies*, and other periodicals. **Essays:** Max Frisch; Uwe Johnson.

SUBIOTTO, Arrigo V. Professor and Head of the Department of German, University of Birmingham. Author of *Bertolt Brecht's Adaptations for the Berliner Ensemble*, 1975, and of many articles on Brecht, Grass, Hochhuth, Dürrenmatt, Frisch, Müller, and other writers. **Essays:** Günter Grass; Rolf Hochhuth.

YASUNARI TAKAHASHI. Professor of English, University of Tokyo. Author of *The Genealogy of Ecstasy: From Donne to Beckett*, 1966, *Samuel Beckett*, 1971, *Summa Nonsensologica*, 1977, and "Beckett and the Noh," in *Encounter*, April 1982. **Essay:** Yoshioka Minoru.

THODY, Philip. Professor of French Literature, University of Leeds, Yorkshire. Author of two books on Camus and two books on Sartre, books on Genet, Anouilh, Laclos, Aldous Huxley, and Barthes, and a novel, *Dog Days in Babel*, 1979. Editor of works by Camus and Sartre. **Essays:** Jean Anouilh; Simone de Beauvoir; Michel Tournier.

VERANI, Hugo J. Professor of Spanish-American Literature, University of California, Davis. Author of *Narrativa contemporánea*, 1979, *Onetti: El ritual de la impostura*, 1981, and *Octavio Paz: Bibliografía crítica*, 1983. **Essays:** Jorge Luis Borges; Julio Cortázar; Octavio Paz.

VERTHUY, Maïr. Associate Professor of French, and Fellow of the Simone de Beauvoir Institute, Concordia University, Montreal; Editor of *Canadian Women's Studies*. Author of articles on Hélène Parmelin, Christiane Rochefort, Roger Vailland, Michèle Mailhot, and other writers. Editor of *Femme*, 1984. **Essays:** Marie-Claire Blais; Anne Hébert.

VINCENT, Paul. Lecturer in Dutch, University College, London; Editor of *Dutch Crossing: A Journal for Students of Dutch*. Co-Editor, *European Context: Studies in the History and Literature of the Netherlands*, 1971. **Essays:** Hugo Claus; Willem Frederik Hermans; Lucebert; Harry Mulisch; Gerard Reve; Jan Wolkers.

WAELTI-WALTERS, Jennifer. Professor and Chairperson of the Department of French, University of Victoria, British Columbia. Author of *Alchimie et littérature*, 1975, *J.-M.G. Le Clézio*, 1977, *Michel Butor*, 1977, *Icare ou l'évasion impossible: Étude psycho-mythique de J.-M.G. Le Clézio*, 1981, and *Fairytales and the Female Imagination*, 1982. **Essays:** Michel

Butor; J.-M.G. Le Clézio.

WAINE, Anthony. Lecturer in German Studies, University of Lancaster. Author of *Martin Walser: The Development as Dramatist 1950-1970*, 1978, and *Martin Walser*, 1980. Editor, with Graham Bartram, *Brecht in Perspective*, 1982, and *Culture and Society in the GDR*, 1984. **Essays:** Hans Magnus Enzensberger; Martin Walser.

WALSH, George. Publisher and free-lance writer. **Essays:** Jorge Amado; José Donoso; Mario Soldati.

WEISSBORT, Daniel. Professor of Comparative Literature, and Director of the Translation Workshop, University of Iowa, Iowa City; Co-Founding Editor, with Ted Hughes, *Modern Poetry in Translation*. Author of three books of poetry, *The Leaseholder*, 1971, *In an Emergency*, 1972, and *Soundings*, 1977. Editor and translator of many books, including works by Gorbanevskaya, Vinokurov, Evtushenko, and Claude Simon, and of collections of Russian poetry.

WELLWARTH, George E. Professor of Theatre and Comparative Literature, State University of New York, Binghamton; Co-Editor of *Modern International Drama*. Author of *The Theater of Protest and Paradox*, 1964 (new edition, 1974), and *Spanish Underground Drama*, 1972. Editor or translator of *Concise Encyclopaedia of the Modern Drama*, 1964, *Modern French Theatre*, 1964, *Postwar German Theatre*, 1967, *Modern Spanish Theatre*, 1968, *The New Wave Spanish Drama*, 1970, *German Drama Between the Wars*, 1972, *Themes of Drama*, 1972, *New Generation Spanish Drama*, 1976, and *Three Catalan Dramatists*, 1976. **Essays:** Fritz Hochwälder; José Ruibal; Jean Tardieu.

WELSH, David. Professor Emeritus, University of Michigan, Ann Arbor. Author of *Russian Comedy*, 1966, *Adam Mickiewicz*, 1966, *Ignacy Krasicki*, 1969, and *Jan Kochanwoski*, 1974. **Essay:** Tadeusz Konwicki.

WHITTON, Kenneth S. Chairman of the School of European Studies, University of Bradford, Yorkshire. Author of *Theatre of Friedrich Dürrenmatt: A Study in the Possibility of Freedom*, 1980, *Dietrich Fischer-Dieskau: Mastersinger*, 1981, *Lieder for the Layman: An Introduction to German Song*, 1984, several textbooks, and *Wir waren vier*, a series for British television. Translator of *Schubert's Songs* by Fischer-Dieskau, 1977. **Essay:** Friedrich Dürrenmatt.

HISAAKI YAMANOUCHI. Associate Professor of English, University of Tokyo. Author of *The Search for Authenticity in Modern Japanese Literature*, 1978. **Essays:** Abe Kobo; Oe Kenzaburo.

YUDIN, Florence L. Professor of Spanish, Florida International University, Miami. Author of *The Vibrant Silence in Jorge Guillén's "Aire nuestro,"* 1974, and of articles on the *novela corta*, the *novela comediesca*, García Lorca, and Lawrence Durrell. **Essay:** Jorge Guillén.